Desire, Love, & Identity

Philosophy of Sex and Love | Edited by Gary Foster

OXFORD
UNIVERSITY PRESS

OXFORD
UNIVERSITY PRESS

Oxford University Press is a department of the University of Oxford.
It furthers the University's objective of excellence in research, scholarship,
and education by publishing worldwide. Oxford is a registered trade mark of
Oxford University Press in the UK and in certain other countries.

Published in Canada by
Oxford University Press
8 Sampson Mews, Suite 204,
Don Mills, Ontario M3C 0H5 Canada

www.oupcanada.com

Library and Archives Canada Cataloguing in Publication

Desire, love, and identity : philosophy of sex and love / edited by
Gary Foster.

Includes bibliographical references.
ISBN 978-0-19-901520-7 (paperback)

1. Sex--Philosophy. 2. Love--Philosophy. 3. Desire (Philosophy).
4. Identity (Philosophical concept). I. Foster, Gary, 1964-, editor

BD436.D48 2016   128'.46   C2016-902884-4

Cover image: © iStock/Stephen Moore

Oxford University Press is committed to our environment.
Wherever possible, our books are printed on paper which comes from
responsible sources.

Printed by Integrated Books International, United States of America

5 6 7 — 24 23 22

Contents

Part 1 Sex

Section I Sexual Desire

Section II Objectification and Sexual Identity

Chapter Five ~ Sexual Objectification

Chapter Six ~ Derivatization and Degenitalization

Section III Ethics and Sexual Issues

Chapter Seven ~ The Ethics of Sex Work

Chapter Eight ~ Other Ethical Issues

Part 2 Love

Introduction to the Philosophy of Love   169

Section IV The Nature of Love

Section V Romantic Love

Chapter Eighteen ~ Friendship and Love Online

Bibliography   378

Credits   379

Contributors

Lauren Bialystok is assistant professor in the Department of Humanities, Social Science and Social Justice, Ontario Institute for Studies in Education, University of Toronto.

Elizabeth Brake is associate professor of philosophy in the School of History, Philosophy, and Religious Studies at Barrett Honors College, Arizona State University.

Yolanda Estes is an independent scholar and artist living in Quito, Ecuador.

Réal Fillion is associate professor in the Department of Philosophy, Université de Sudbury.

Michael Gilbert is professor of philosophy in the Department of Philosophy, York University.

Ada S. Jaarsma is associate professor in the Department of Humanities, Mount Royal University.

Rockney Jacobsen is associate professor in the Department of Philosophy, Wilfrid Laurier University.

Tony Milligan is teaching fellow in ethics and the philosophy of religion in the Department of Theology and Religious Studies, King's College London.

Rekha Navneet is associate professor in the Department of Philosophy, Gargi College, University of Delhi.

Emily Ann Parker is assistant professor of philosophy in the Department of Philosophy and Religious Studies, Towson University.

Glenn Parsons is associate professor in the Department of Philosophy, Ryerson University.

Jill Rusin is associate professor in the Department of Philosophy, Wilfrid Laurier University.

John Russon is professor of philosophy in the Department of Philosophy, University of Guelph.

Alexis Shotwell is associate professor in the Department of Sociology and Anthropology, Carleton University.

Chloë Taylor is assistant professor in the Department of Women's and Gender Studies, University of Alberta.

Preface

In response to the popularity of a course that I taught for several years at Wilfrid Laurier University called Philosophy of Sex, Love, and Friendship, I once joked to colleagues that we should include the word *sex* in all of our course titles: Sex and Formal Logic, Epistemology and Sex, Business Ethics and Sex, Sexistentialism, and so on. Sex has always been a popular topic among university students and, in this day of Viagra-powered performance, it has retained its allure into middle age and beyond. Of course, one wonders if its popularity among younger generations might be surpassed by video games or epic fantasy series (*Game of Thrones* and so on), but my suspicion is that sex, that hybrid concept that is a product of both nature and culture, will continue to fascinate us in new ways in future generations. I believe that the same is true of love in its various forms, including the form that we call friendship.

Indeed, instead of surpassing our interest in sex and love, new technology has created new ways of exploring both. The Internet offers us the possibility of online friendships, romantic relationships, and online sexual relationships. The online universe even allows us to explore alternative identities, including our sexual identities, through sophisticated sites such as *Second Life*. In this cyberworld setting, a man can take on the persona of a woman or a woman can take on that of a man. A shy person can create an extroverted character, while a physically slight individual can have an online identity of a muscular or athletic person. Moreover, these online *personae* or *persons* can have affairs with each other. This raises certain familiar ethical questions in unfamiliar ways. For instance, if a person is in a relationship in real life and his or her avatar has an affair with another avatar in *Second Life*, has he or she committed an infidelity in *real* life? Or does relationship infidelity in this case rely on the person being in a relationship *in Second Life*? That is, in order to be an adulterer in *Second Life*, must the person be married in *Second Life*? These kinds of scenarios raise not only ethical questions but metaphysical ones as well. If I am having an affair in *Second Life*, does that mean that *I* am having an affair, or is it my avatar or my online *persona* who is having the affair? If it is the latter, do we attribute an identity to my avatar that is in some way independent of my own offline identity? Can this identity or *person* be held morally responsible? Or, do we ultimately ground all responsibility in my offline person—in *real life*, as it were? I think that our natural response is to side with this latter option, but technology allows us to raise legitimate questions about this assumption.

Love and sex have been of interest to philosophy at least since Plato's time. Philosophers have discussed the two phenomena in relation to each other (Plato, Schopenhauer), in relation to morality (Kant), to religion (Augustine, Aquinas) and to politics (Marx, de Beauvoir, Firestone). But the exploration of sex and love emerged as a specialized and recognized area of study in academic philosophy in the twentieth century primarily through the work of Irving Singer and Alan Soble. Singer's three-volume work titled *The Nature of Love* presented an historical look at the development of ideas of love in Western thought. He used the distinction between bestowal—characteristic of *agape*—and appraisal—characteristic of *eros*—to examine the history of the concept love. Soble's *The Structure of Love* examines these two basic approaches to love analytically. He characterizes the structure of agapic love as subject-centred in the sense that the source of love is to be found in the lover. Erosic love, on the other hand, is object-centred as love is motivated by the beloved and her properties. Singer's valuable trilogy gives us an historical look at the philosophy of love in the West, which illuminates how our concepts of love evolved in the context of philosophical, religious, and literary ideas. Soble, on the other hand, in his equally valuable work, explores specific philosophical problems associated with love such as identifying the object of love, questioning the alleged non-fungibility of the beloved as well as the role of exclusivity in love, and more. He explores these issues with great care and impressive analytic skill. Soble, founder of The Society for the Philosophy of Sex and Love, has also written extensively on sex, and his books *The Philosophy of Sex*, *The Philosophy of Sex and Love*, and *Sexual Investigations* have contributed greatly to the rise of the philosophy of sexuality as an area of teaching and research in universities.

In recent times, we have seen a plethora of books and articles on the philosophy of sex and love that cover a wide range of issues and respond to challenges both new and old. Debates continue over issues such as pornography and prostitution, while new discussions have arisen concerning cybersex and online dating. Some of these debates are ethical ones, exploring how we view and treat other human beings. This certainly applies to issues such as pornography and prostitution as well as to practices such as BDSM. Discussions of sexual objectification encompass a range of attitudes and practices regarding the treatment and characterization of human beings in general and women in particular. Debates about value in the philosophy of sex and love may also take a political form. Marriage and sometimes romantic love itself have been characterized as vehicles of sexual inequality. Other debates in this area are of the metaphysical variety. These debates include questions about the nature of love itself. These are the kinds of questions that Singer and Soble ask in *The Nature of Love* and *The Structure of Love*, respectively. Further questions arise regarding love's object(s), which open the door to discussions of personal identity in the context of romantic or personal love.

This textbook will address these issues and more. What is unique about the approach found here is the emphasis on the issue of identity, which pervades many of the articles. It is my belief that the issue of identity is not peripheral to the study of the philosophy of sex and love; instead, it is central to such study. Alternatively, I could say that love and sex are not merely accessories to one's identity but are rather defining features. This emphasis on identity was not originally a planned feature of the book; as the collection took shape, it emerged as a theme that reflects a contemporary trend in philosophy. Much attention is being paid to the general theme of identity across different areas of philosophy. We see an emphasis on the study of personal identity in that area of philosophy known as metaphysics. What is a person? We see this issue explored today in the work of Derik Parfit, Galen Strawson, Marya Schechtman, and many more. The issue of identity has been a major theme of a lot of work in political philosophy and feminist philosophy. These approaches tend to talk about identity less in metaphysical terms and more through the lens of social and political theories. Thus, considerations of identity in this area tend to explore the social and political conditions that shape who we are and the way that we see the world. The current text includes discussions of love and sex that come from a variety of perspectives and reflect a number of different approaches to the related issue of identity. This volume includes readings from analytic, continental, and feminist perspectives along with a few classic works that predate these distinctions.

Sixteen new articles have been written specifically for this volume. They are: Rockney Jacobsen, "Objects of Desire," John Russon, "Why Sexuality Matters," Réal Fillion, "Challenging Norms: The Co-creative Core of Erotic Life," Ada S. Jaarsma, "The Speaker's Benefit and the Case of Dan Savage," Emily Ann Parker, "Sexual Assault as Derivatization," Michael Gilbert, "Cross-Dressing, Trans, and All Stops In-Between," Chloë Taylor, "Sex Work and Desexualization: Foucauldian Reflections on Sex Work," Yolanda Estes, "BDSM: My Apology," Rekha Navneet, "The Ethical and Mystical Import of *Kama*: Sexual/Erotic Passion in Classical Indian Tradition," Glenn Parsons, "Physical Beauty and Romantic Love," Alexis Shotwell, "Ethical Polyamory and Responsibility," Lauren Bialystok, "Different and Unequal: Rethinking Justice in Intimate Relationships," Jill Rusin, "The Meaning of Marriage," Elizabeth Brake, "Marriage for Everybody: What Is Marriage Equality?," Tony Milligan, "The Politics of Love," and Gary Foster, "Internet Dating: Challenges to Love and Personal Identity."

In addition to the commissioned readings, I have included a number of excerpts from classic texts on this topic by philosophers such as Plato, Aristotle, Immanuel Kant, Jean-Paul Sartre, and Simone de Beauvoir. As well, I have chosen certain articles/excerpts that are relatively recent and either have been important to the evolution of the study of the philosophy of sex and love or, in my judgment, would make an influential contribution. Among these I include work by Irving Singer, Alan Soble, Harry Frankfurt, Martha Nussbaum, Patricia Marino, Robert Sharp, Noël Merino, Thomas Nagel, Michel Foucault, Robert Solomon, Greta Cristina, Julia O'Connell Davidson, Christopher Bartel, and Annette C. Baier.

I would like to thank the Oxford University Press staff, who have been tremendously helpful, professional, and understanding during this process. Stephen Kotowych originally contacted me and asked if I would consider taking on this project. His help and encouragement during the early stages kept me going and believing. Thanks to Meg Patterson, the developmental editor of this volume. Without her suggestions, encouragement, resourcefulness, and patience this book would not have seen the light of day. I would also like to thank Cailen Swain and Eric Sinkins for their valuable contributions. I would especially like to thank the copy editor, Joanne Muzak, whose corrections, editorial suggestions, and overall attention to detail has been invaluable. I would also like to thank the many students who have taken my course, The Philosophy of Sex, Love, and Friendship at Wilfrid Laurier University over the years. Much of this book is inspired by the questions, comments, and discussions that arose in that class. Finally, I would like to thank my colleagues in the philosophy department at Wilfrid Laurier University for their encouragement and support. In particular, I would like to thank Byron Williston and Rockney Jacobsen, both of whom encouraged me to pursue this project and provided me with feedback when I was at the proposal stage. It was Dr. Jacobsen who, in the fall of 1999, asked me if I was interested in teaching the above-mentioned course. My decision to accept that offer changed the direction of my teaching and my research.

Gary Foster
Waterloo, Ontario
March 2016

mirrors. At some point Romeo notices Juliet. He is moved, somehow, by the softness of her hair and the diffidence with which she sips her martini, and this arouses him sexually. Let us say that *X senses Y* whenever *X* regards *Y* with sexual desire. (*Y* need not be a person, and *X*'s apprehension of *Y* can be visual, tactile, olfactory, etc., or purely imaginary; in the present example we shall concentrate on vision.) So Romeo senses Juliet, rather than merely noticing her. At this stage he is aroused by an unaroused object, so he is more in the sexual grip of his body than she of hers.

Let us suppose, however, that Juliet now senses Romeo in another mirror on the opposite wall, though neither of them yet knows that he is seen by the other (the mirror angles provide three-quarter views). Romeo then begins to notice in Juliet the subtle signs of sexual arousal: heavy-lidded stare, dilating pupils, faint flush, et cetera. This of course renders her much more bodily, and he not only notices but senses this as well. His arousal is nevertheless still solitary. But now, cleverly calculating the line of her stare without actually looking her in the eyes, he realizes that it is directed at him through the mirror on the opposite wall. That is, he notices, and moreover senses, Juliet sensing him. This is definitely a new development, for it gives him a sense of embodiment not only through his own reactions but through the eyes and reactions of another. Moreover, it is separable from the initial sensing of Juliet; for sexual arousal might begin with a person's sensing that he is sensed and being assailed by the perception of the other person's desire rather than merely by the perception of the person.

But there is a further step. Let us suppose that Juliet, who is a little slower than Romeo, now senses that he senses her. This puts Romeo

in a position to notice, and be aroused by, her arousal at being sensed by him. He senses that she senses that he senses her. This is still another level of arousal, for he becomes conscious of his sexuality through his awareness of its effect on her and of her awareness that this effect is due to him. Once she takes the same step and senses that he senses her sensing him, it becomes difficult to state, let alone imagine, further iterations, though they may be logically distinct. If both are alone, they will presumably turn to look at each other directly, and the proceedings will continue on another plane. Physical contact and intercourse are perfectly natural extensions of this complicated visual exchange, and mutual touch can involve all the complexities of awareness present in the visual case, but with a far greater range of subtlety and acuteness.

Ordinarily, of course, things happen in a less orderly fashion—sometimes in a great rush—but I believe that some version of this overlapping system of distinct sexual perceptions and interactions is the basic framework of any full-fledged sexual relation and that relations involving only part of the complex are significantly incomplete. The account is only schematic, as it must be to achieve generality. Every real sexual act will be psychologically far more specific and detailed, in ways that depend not only on the physical techniques employed and on anatomical details, but also on countless features of the participants' conceptions of themselves and of each other, which become embodied in the act. (It is a familiar enough fact, for example, that people often take their social roles and the social roles of their partners to bed with them.)

The general schema is important, however, and the proliferation of levels of mutual awareness it involves is an example of a type of complexity that typifies human interactions. Consider aggression, for example. If I am angry with someone, I want to make him feel it, either to produce self-reproach by getting him to see himself through the eyes of my anger, and to dislike what he sees—or else to produce reciprocal anger or fear, by getting him to perceive my anger as a threat or attack. What I want will depend on the details of my anger, but in either case it will involve a desire that the object of that anger be aroused. This accomplishment constitutes the fulfillment of my emotion, through domination of the object's feelings.

Another example of such reflexive mutual recognition is to be found in the phenomenon of meaning, which appears to involve an intention to produce a belief or other effect in another by bringing about his recognition of one's intention to produce that effect. (That result is due to H.P. Grice,[2] whose position I shall not attempt to reproduce in detail.) Sex has a related structure: it involves a desire that one's partner be aroused by the recognition of one's desire that he or she be aroused.

It is not easy to define the basic types of awareness and arousal of which these complexes are composed, and that remains a lacuna in this discussion. I believe that the object of awareness is the same in one's own case as it is in one's sexual awareness of another, although the two awarenesses will not be the same, the difference being as great as that between feeling angry and experiencing the anger of another. All stages of sexual perception are varieties of identification of a person with his body. What is perceived is one's own or another's *subjection* to or *immersion* in his body, a phenomenon which has been recognized with loathing by St. Paul and St. Augustine, both of whom regarded "the law of sin which is in my members" as a grave threat to the dominion of the holy will.[3] In sexual desire and its expression the blending of involuntary response with deliberate control is extremely important. For Augustine, the revolution launched against him by his body is symbolized by erection and the other involuntary physical components of arousal. Sartre too stresses the fact that the penis is not a prehensile organ. But mere involuntariness characterizes other bodily processes as well. In sexual desire the involuntary responses are combined with submission to spontaneous impulses: not only one's pulse and secretions but one's actions are taken over by the body; ideally, deliberate control is needed only to guide the expression of those impulses. This is to some extent also true of an appetite like hunger, but the takeover there is more localized, less pervasive, less extreme. One's whole body does not become saturated with hunger as it can with desire. But the most characteristic feature of a specifically sexual immersion in the body is its ability to fit into the complex of mutual perceptions that we have described. Hunger leads to spontaneous interactions with food; sexual desire leads to spontaneous interactions with other persons, whose bodies are asserting their sovereignty in the same way, producing involuntary reactions and spontaneous impulses in *them*. These reactions are perceived, and the perception of them is perceived, and that perception is in turn perceived; at each step the domination of the person by his body is reinforced, and the sexual partner becomes more possessible by physical contact, penetration, and envelopment.

Desire is therefore not merely the perception of a preexisting embodiment of the other, but ideally a contribution to his further embodiment which in turn enhances the original subject's sense of himself. This explains why it is important that the partner be aroused, and not merely aroused, but aroused by the awareness of one's desire. It also explains the sense in which desire has unity and possession as its object: physical possession must eventuate in creation of the sexual object in the image of one's desire, and not merely in the object's recognition of that desire, or in his or her own private arousal. (This may reveal a male bias: I shall say something about that later.)

To return, finally, to the topic of perversion: I believe that various familiar deviations constitute truncated or incomplete versions of the complete configuration, and may therefore be regarded as perversions of the central impulse.

In particular, narcissistic practices and intercourse with animals, infants, and inanimate objects seem to be stuck at some primitive version of the first stage. If the object is not alive, the experience is reduced entirely to an awareness of one's own sexual embodiment. Small children and animals permit awareness of the embodiment of the other, but present obstacles to reciprocity, to the recognition by the sexual object of the subject's desire as the source of his (the object's) sexual self-awareness.

Sadism concentrates on the evocation of passive self-awareness in others, but the sadist's engagement is itself active and requires a retention of deliberate control which impedes awareness of himself as a bodily subject of passion in the required sense. The victim must recognize him as the source of his own sexual passivity, but only as the active source. De Sade claimed that the object of sexual desire was to evoke involuntary responses from one's partner, especially audible ones. The infliction of pain is no doubt the most efficient way to accomplish this, but it requires a certain abrogation of one's

own exposed spontaneity. All this, incidentally, helps to explain why it is tempting to regard as sadistic an excessive preoccupation with sexual technique, which does not permit one to abandon the role of agent at any stage of the sexual act. Ideally one should be able to surmount one's technique at some point.

A masochist on the other hand imposes the same disability on his partner as the sadist imposes on himself. The masochist cannot find a satisfactory embodiment as the object of another's sexual desire, but only as the object of his control. He is passive not in relation to his partner's passion but in relation to his nonpassive agency. In addition, the subjection to one's body characteristic of pain and physical restraint is of a very different kind from that of sexual excitement: pain causes people to contract rather than dissolve.

Both of these disorders have to do with the second stage, which involves the awareness of oneself as an object of desire. In straightforward sadism and masochism other attentions are substituted for desire as a source of the object's self-awareness. But it is also possible for nothing of that sort to be substituted, as in the case of a masochist who is satisfied with self-inflicted pain or of a sadist who does not insist on playing a role in the suffering that arouses him. Greater difficulties of classification are presented by three other categories of sexual activity: elaborations of the sexual act; intercourse of more than two persons; and homosexuality.

If we apply our model to the various forms that may be taken by two-party heterosexual intercourse, none of them seem clearly to qualify as perversions. Hardly anyone can be found these days to inveigh against oral-genital contact, and the merits of buggery are urged by such respectable figures as D.H. Lawrence and Norman Mailer. There may be something vaguely sadistic about the latter technique (in Mailer's writings it seems to be a method of introducing an element of rape), but it is not obvious that this has to be so. In general, it would appear that any bodily contact between a man and a woman that gives them sexual pleasure, is a possible vehicle for the system of multi-level interpersonal awareness that I have claimed is the basic psychological content of sexual interaction. Thus a liberal platitude about sex is upheld.

About multiple combinations, the least that can be said is that they are bound to be complicated. If one considers how difficult it is to carry on two conversations simultaneously, one may appreciate the problems of multiple simultaneous interpersonal perception that can arise in even a small-scale orgy. It may be inevitable that some of the component relations should degenerate into mutual epidermal stimulation by participants otherwise isolated from each other. There may also be a tendency toward voyeurism and exhibitionism, both of which are incomplete relations. The exhibitionist wishes to display his desire without needing to be desired in return; he may even fear the sexual attentions of others. A voyeur, on the other hand, need not require any recognition by his object at all: certainly not a recognition of the voyeur's arousal.

It is not clear whether homosexuality is a perversion if that is measured by the standard of the described configuration, but it seems unlikely. For such a classification would have to depend on the possibility of extracting from the system a distinction between male and female sexuality; and much that has been said so far applies equally to men and women. Moreover, it would have to be maintained that there was a natural tie between the type of sexuality and the sex of the body, and also that two sexualities of the same type could not interact properly.

Certainly there is much support for an aggressive-passive distinction between male and female sexuality. In our culture the male's arousal tends to initiate the perceptual exchange, he usually makes the sexual approach, largely controls the course of the act, and of course penetrates whereas the woman receives. When two men or two women engage in intercourse they cannot both adhere to these sexual roles. The question is how essential the roles are to an adequate sexual relation. One relevant observation is that a good deal of deviation from these roles occurs in heterosexual intercourse. Women can be sexually aggressive and men passive, and temporary reversals of role are not uncommon in heterosexual exchanges of reasonable length. If such conditions are set aside, it may be urged that there is something irreducibly perverted in attraction to a body anatomically like one's own. But alarming as some people in our culture may find such attraction, it remains psychologically unilluminating to class it as perverted. Certainly if homosexuality is a perversion, it is so in a very different sense from that in which shoe-fetishism is a perversion, for some version of the full range of interpersonal perceptions seems perfectly possible between two persons of the same sex.

In any case, even if the proposed model is correct, it remains implausible to describe as perverted every deviation from it. For example, if the partners in heterosexual intercourse indulge in private heterosexual fantasies, that obscures the recognition of the real partner and so, on the theory, constitutes a defective sexual relation. It is not, however, generally regarded as a perversion. Such examples suggest that a simple dichotomy between perverted and unperverted sex is too crude to organize the phenomena adequately.

I should like to close with some remarks about the relation of perversion to good, bad, and morality. The concept of perversion can hardly fail to be evaluative in some sense, for it appears to involve the notion of an ideal or at least adequate sexuality which the perversions in some way fail to achieve. So, if the concept is viable, the judgment that a person or practice or desire is perverted will constitute a sexual evaluation, implying that better sex, or a better specimen of sex, is possible. This in itself is a very weak claim, since the evaluation might be in a dimension that is of little interest to us. (Though, if my account is correct, that will not be true.)

Whether it is a moral evaluation, however, is another question entirely—one whose answer would require more understanding of both morality and perversion than can be deployed here. Moral evaluation of acts and of persons is a rather special and very complicated matter, and by no means all our evaluations of persons and their activities are moral evaluations. We make judgments about people's beauty or health or intelligence which are evaluative without being moral. Assessments of their sexuality may be similar in that respect.

Furthermore, moral issues aside, it is not clear that unperverted sex is necessarily *preferable* to the perversions. It may be that sex which receives the highest marks for perfection *as sex*

is less enjoyable than certain perversions; and if enjoyment is considered very important, that might outweigh considerations of sexual perfection in determining rational preference.

That raises the question of the relation between the evaluative content of judgments of perversion and the rather common *general* distinction between good and bad sex. The latter distinction is usually confined to sexual acts, and it would seem, within limits, to cut across the other: even someone who believed, for example, that homosexuality was a perversion could admit a distinction between better and worse homosexual sex, and might even allow that good homosexual sex could be better *sex* than not very good unperverted sex. If this is correct, it supports the position that, if judgments of perversion are viable at all, they represent only one aspect of the possible evaluation of sex, even *qua sex*. Moreover it is not the only important aspect: certainly sexual deficiencies that evidently do not constitute perversions can be the object of great concern.

Finally, even if perverted sex is to that extent not so good as it might be, bad sex is generally better than none at all. This should not be controversial: it seems to hold for other important matters, like food, music, literature, and society. In the end, one must choose from among the available alternatives, whether their availability depends on the environment or on one's own constitution. And the alternatives have to be fairly grim before it becomes rational to opt for nothing.

Notes

- My research was supported in part by the National Science Foundation.
1 Translated by Hazel E. Barnes (New York: Philosophical Library: 1956).
2 "Meaning," *Philosophical Review*, LXVI (3 July 1957): 377–388.
3 See Romans, VII, 23; and the *Confessions*, Book 8, v.

Discussion

Why do Sartre and Nagel complicate the matter of sexual desire in the way that they do? Common sense tells us that sexual desire arises from certain facts about our physiology. Both philosophers acknowledge the common sense view but their point is that ordinary accounts of physiology do not capture all that we mean by sexual desire. Sexual desire is not simply the desire for orgasm or indeed for pleasure, but is rather one of our fundamental ways of being with and for others. This way of being with and for others is not limited to the aim of procreation since sexual desire is present in those who are incapable of such (children, the elderly, the sterile, eunuchs). The assumption here is that we, as human beings, are organisms that cannot be adequately understood in reductionist terms. We have evolved to be creatures who are concerned with meaning—which includes the meaning of our relations with others. The American psychologist Rollo May recognized this when he said, "given self-consciousness, sex becomes a new gestalt as is demonstrated in therapy all the time. Sexual impulses are now conditioned by the *person* of the partner."[1]

For Sartre in particular this desire has much to do with our identity. It is through our relation with the Other[2] that we come to have an identity or we come to identify with a certain picture of our self. Through the *caress* I seek an experience with the Other that reveals to me my identity as a sexual being. I am the recipient of the caress of the Other and the Other is the recipient of my caress. Through this experience of touching we both seek a kind of completeness that comes from experiencing ourselves as subjects and objects. The caress aims at a "double reciprocal incarnation." What does this mean? To be incarnate means to have or to be given a body. When we speak of the "incarnation of Christ" we are talking about the idea that God takes on the bodily form of a human being. Of course, we who are born human already have bodies (unlike God), but Sartre uses the term *incarnation* in this context to highlight the experience we have of realizing or becoming aware of our embodied nature through the touch of the Other. To have a double reciprocal incarnation then is to experience myself through the caress of another person as an embodied being and to cause that other person to experience embodiment as well. It is in this sense that sexual desire expresses the desire *to be* in concrete terms. But, like the desire to be God itself, sexual desire ultimately fails in its aim according to Sartre. Either I experience myself as touching the other person or I experience her touch. I can never experience both simultaneously.

Nagel, rather than focusing on the tactile side of our experience, focuses on the visual aspect. Sartre focuses on the visual aspect in *Being and Nothingness* in a section titled "The Look." In his analysis of the look, Sartre tells us that it is through the look of the Other that I come to see myself as an object. I need the Other to reveal to me the object side of my being. Sartre does not explicitly discuss the look in the context of sexual identity, but Nagel takes up that task to a certain extent. It is through the experience of being looked at that Romeo and Juliet experience the various levels of arousal that he describes. Ultimately, Nagel thinks that the experience of Romeo and Juliet in the cocktail lounge full of mirrors shows that the aim of sexual desire as Sartre characterizes it is (in disagreement with Sartre himself) possible. Romeo is able to experience himself as both a subject and object of sexual desire by becoming aroused at Juliet's arousal, which was based, not on simply seeing Romeo, but on the fact that she senses his arousal and is aroused by this. This gives Romeo an embodied experience of his sexuality since not only is he experiencing himself as the *subject* of sexual desire for whom Juliet is the object, but through the fact that he realizes that Juliet's arousal is due to him, he is able to experience himself at the same time as the bodily *object* of sexual desire. The same is true of Juliet, which would seem to imply that a double reciprocal incarnation is possible.

Thus, through both the look and the caress my identity as a sexual being is revealed to me. The Other sees my sexual identity or sees me as a sexual being in many ways before these aspects are revealed to me. He or she sees my mannerisms, my flirtations (conscious or unconscious), my sense of style, and so on. These are expressions of my sexual identity and ultimately of my identity.

In his article titled "Plain Sex," Alan Goldman calls into question the approach to understanding sex and sexual desire that we see in Sartre and Nagel. He characterizes Nagel's account, and by implication Sartre's, as examples of what he calls "means-end analysis." This form of analysis understands the meaning of sexual activity as relying on some kind of external goal or purpose such as procreation, love, and so on. In Sartre's case the external goal or purpose is understood in terms of the desire to be (or to be complete), whereas with Nagel the goal is the complex interpersonal awareness that he describes in the Romeo and Juliette example.

With his concept of "plain sex," Goldman characterizes sexual desire as a "desire for contact with another person's body and for the pleasure that such contact produces."[3] Goldman suggests that the idea that we need to attach an external goal or purpose to sexual desire or sexual activity is derived from our Platonic-Christian heritage. Both Platonism and Christianity diminish or degrade sexual desire in favour of more spiritual or intellectual goals. Platonism sees sexuality as a means towards experiencing true beauty, whereas Christianity, historically speaking at least, viewed the only legitimate purpose of sexuality to be procreation (within marriage, I might add). All other aims of sexuality (including self-pleasure) were deemed sinful. Goldman thinks that means-ends analyses of sexual desire ignore the intrinsic value of sex and sexual pleasure. For Goldman, we need not look beyond sexual activity itself in order to find the purpose or the object of such desire. The pleasure that accompanies sex is enough to make it meaningful. Of course we might argue that, in Goldman's view, "pleasure" is an external goal that sexual desire aims at. We rarely, if ever, truly have sex for its own sake, but for the sake of the pleasure it provides. But, for Goldman, sexual pleasure is not a goal "external" to sex or sexual desire. It is intrinsic to the nature of sexual desire and sexual activity in the way that thirst quenching is intrinsic to the desire for drink.

But is he right about this? Is sexual desire and the pleasure of sex primarily an end in itself, or does it play a more significant role in our interpersonal relations? Is the fact that I learn something about myself and my identity simply a by-product of sexual activity and sexual relations, or does it help us in defining or understanding those activities and relations? I suppose one possible way of addressing this is to suggest that the notion of *primary* is out of place here, or to ask the question "primary in what sense?" Goldman is concerned that sex is degraded when it is seen as subordinated to other higher or loftier purposes for which it is a means. Historically speaking, he does have a point. But at the same time, sex need not be degraded by understanding sexual desire as part of some larger purpose or desire. To say that sexual desire expresses the desire to be (Sartre) or multi-level awareness of oneself and the other person (Nagel) need not degrade sex for its own sake. Nagel's own account admittedly does suggest that sex for its own sake is a perversion, but he does not regard perversions as immoral simply by virtue of being perversions. Sartre makes no suggestion that incomplete sex, as Nagel calls it, is a perversion, but suggests that whether we know it or not this desire is highly interpersonal. It is the interpersonal nature of sexuality that John Russon will discuss in Chapter 2.

Notes

1   Rollo May, "Existential Basis of Psychotherapy," *American Journal of Orthopsychiatry* 30, no. 4 (1960): 692.
2   When Sartre speaks of the Other (capital O) he is not referring to other specific people but rather something like the influence or effect that the existence of others in general has on my own life.
3   Alan Goldman, "Plain Sex," *Philosophy and Public Affairs* 6, no 3 (1977): 268.

Suggestions for Further Reading

Alan Goldman, "Plain Sex," *Philosophy and Public Affairs* 6, no. 3 (Spring 1977): 267–87.
Janice Moulton, "Sexual Behaviour: Another Position," *The Journal of Philosophy* 73, no. 16 (1976): 537–46.
Igor Primoratz, "Sexual Perversion," *American Philosophical Quarterly* 34, no. 2 (April 1997): 245–58.
Sara Ruddick, "Better Sex," in *Philosophy and Sex*, edited by Robert Baker and Frederick Elliston (Buffalo, NY: Prometheus Books, 1995), 280–99.
Robert C. Solomon, "Sexual Paradigms," *The Journal of Philosophy* 1, no. 11 (June 13, 1974): 336–45.

Chapter Two
The Object(s) of Sexual Desire

Introduction

In Chapter 1, we discussed issues concerning the nature and structure of sexual desire. Chapter 2 furthers this discussion by drawing our attention to the objects of sexual desire and the significance of sexual experience in our lives.

Rockney Jacobsen gives us several examples of activities for which different people have experienced sexual desire and asks what it is that these activities have in common that makes the desire for them *sexual*. In attempting to answer this question, he presents us with two different strategies: an object-based strategy, which attempts to define sexual desire in terms of the kinds of things that are desired, and a feature-based strategy, which characterizes sexual desire in terms of certain features of the objects that make them desirable. As you will see, Jacobsen argues that the feature-based approach offers a more promising account of what makes desires specifically sexual.

As you are reading Jacobsen's article, ask yourself what it is about objects of sexual desire that makes them sexual. That is, what features or characteristics make something sexual? Are the kinds of features that make another person an object of sexual desire different from the kinds of features that make an inanimate object—for instance, a shoe or piece of fine leather—sexual? Both Nagel and Sartre, you will recall, thought that non-perverted sexual desire has as its object a particular kind of experience with another person.

ROCKNEY JACOBSEN

Objects of Desire

1.

Sexual desire blossoms in endless variety, ranging from the blasé to the bizarre. One person desires intercourse with a loving partner; a second person desires intercourse with the warm exhaust pipe of an automobile; still others desire to wear furs, or inflict pain, to be drenched in urine, peek through keyholes, or to sodomize sheep. The apparently endless variety threatens our grip on the very idea of sexual desire. What could these dissimilar activities share that makes a desire for them *sexual*? A desire for a common sexual activity can sometimes be a nonsexual desire—consider a sex worker's desire to make a living. But a desire for a common nonsexual activity (playing with dolls, or dressing in furs) can also be sexual. How well do we understand what distinguishes sexual from nonsexual desire?

In what follows, I recommend a simple, intuitive account of how sexual desire differs from other kinds of desire. I identify a common feature shared by all sexual desires, but that still allows for the endless proliferation of paraphilia. I begin, in the next section, with some general observations about the nature of desire, and locate two distinct strategies for clarifying the nature of sexual desire—an object-based strategy and a feature-based strategy. The following section then raises several objections to the first strategy, and a final section sketches a feature-based account of sexual desire and describes some of its advantages.

2.

Two characteristics of desire will play a prominent role in the discussion to follow. First, desires are always desires *for something*—to desire nothing is not to have a desire at all. Desires are always *directed at*, or *toward*, some activity, state of affairs, or entity. Whether we want a glass of water, a glimpse of the moon, or a better life, those things all count as the objects of our desire—they are the objectives for which we aim when we set out to satisfy our desires.

This characteristic of desires suggests one broad strategy for distinguishing among kinds of desires and, so, for saying why some desires are sexual. Perhaps sexual desires are distinguished from other desires by their distinctive class of objects. If the many diverse forms of sexual desire share a common object or kind of object, then having an object of that kind is what constitutes any desire as sexual. We will call an *object-based strategy* any strategy that attempts to define sexual desire by locating a distinctive object capable of constituting a desire for it as sexual.

A second characteristic of desires is that they tend to focus on what we think is desirable and, thus, to reflect our preferences or values. There is invariably something about the objects of our desire—some feature we judge them to have—that makes them desirable to us and, so, explains our desiring them. For example, I desire food *because of* the nourishment it provides; I want to listen to music *in virtue of* the pleasure it gives me, and I desire to make love to Esmeralda *because of* her ravishing beauty.

In these examples, the phrases "because of" or "in virtue of" suggest that nourishment, pleasure, and ravishing beauty each plays a role in explaining or rationalizing my desire. When I think the object of my desire has something about it that—in light of my preferences and values—makes it desirable, that feature of the object helps to make sense of my desire for it.

This second characteristic of desires allows another strategy for defining sexual desire. Perhaps a desire is constituted as sexual not by the distinctive kind of object it has, but by the feature (or features) in virtue of which it is found to be desirable. According to this *feature-based strategy* for defining sexual desire, it is not *what I desire* but *what makes that thing desirable to me* that qualifies my desire for it as sexual.

Philosophers have not always found a stable distinction between (i) the objects of our desire and (ii) the features in virtue of which we desire those things. It will be worth our trouble to secure the distinction from one kind of criticism. Plato held that as we acquire wisdom we eventually come to realize that our love for one, or many, beautiful bodies is really only love for Beauty, and not for the body that we find so beautiful—before wisdom settles into our souls we are simply mistaken about the objects of our desire.[1] So what at first seems to be the object of our desire (the beautiful body) is only a means to the real object (Beauty itself). Generalizing, we can put Plato's point in the form of a simple principle: To desire an object, X, in virtue of its having some feature, F, is to desire F, not X.[2] Plato's principle has two dramatic implications. First, it invites skepticism about our desires and their objects—our sincere declarations of desire notwithstanding, we seldom know what our own desires are, or are for. In our blind pursuit of all those beautiful bodies we don't know that what we really want is something else. Second, Plato's principle threatens to erase any distinction between the *objects* of desire and the *features* of those objects that make them desirable—what we mistake for "features" are really the objects of our desire. Our concern now is with this second and—as we shall see—problematic idea.

What our second characteristic of desire tells us is that there is normally some answer—whether we know it or not—to the question why we desire one thing rather than another. There is something about the object of our desire that contributes to its being desirable to us—something that explains, or rationalizes, our desiring it. But if Plato is right, *no* object of desire can have *any* features that make it desirable to us. In his view, if there were something about an object of desire that made it desirable, then it—that feature of the object—would be what we really desired. And if that feature is itself the object of our desire, then it, in turn, cannot be desired for any further feature that it has, for any such further feature would then be the real object of our desire. Consequently, our desires can *never* be explained or rationalized, even in part, by features of the things we desire, or by features that we take them to have. But there is surely *something* about Esmeralda the gypsy dancer that explains—indeed, even rationalizes—my desiring her rather than, say, a saucer of mud.[3] The point of the second characteristic of desire is that it is not always irrational to find something desirable. To preserve this natural thought, we must reject Plato's principle. To do so is to accept that the objects of our desire normally do have features in virtue of which we desire them—features that make them desirable to us in light of our preferences and values—even though those features are not themselves further objects of desire.

The purpose of this brief diversion has been to secure the distinction between our two characteristics of desires—that they have objects, and that their objects are normally desirable to us in virtue of features that we take them to have. By retaining the distinction, we make possible two quite different strategies for understanding what makes a desire sexual.

3.

According to the object-based strategy for defining sexual desires, kinds of desire differ because they are desires for different kinds of things. Thus sexual desires differ from other kinds of desires because they have different kinds of objects. Robert Solomon describes just this strategy when he says, "Sexual desire is distinguished, like all desires, by its aims and objects" (1974, 337). Advocates of the strategy have made numerous proposals about the distinctive, constitutive object of sexual desire.

Thomas Nagel (1969), adapting a suggestion from Jean-Paul Sartre (1943), proposes that a sexual desire is a desire for sensings of other's sensings of our sensings of them. Robert Solomon (1974) argues that all sexual desire is a desire for interpersonal communication in body language. Alan Goldman (1977) and Alan Soble (1996) claim that sexual desire is simply desire for sexual pleasure. Each proposal attempts to say what makes a desire sexual by specifying a distinctive object that is shared by all and only sexual desires. All such views share the skepticism about our avowed desires that we already saw in Plato—if my taste for peeking through keyholes, and your wish to be handcuffed to the bedpost both express

desires for the same thing, then there is no reason to suppose that either of us knows what we really want. There are significant problems for the object-based strategy, most of which can be traced to the polymorphous perversity of sexual desire. Consider two initially plausible efforts to deploy the strategy.

A first natural suggestion is that *a sexual desire is a desire for sex* (for sexual activity). The problem, greatly exacerbated by the existence of sexual paraphilia, is that we don't know which activities are sexual (or why). The astonishing variety of sexual tastes and temperaments strongly suggests that, in principle, anything whatsoever might be desired as the object of a sexual desire. If any activity can be the object of someone's sexual desire, then every activity qualifies as a sexual activity. A second problem is that the object of one person's sexual desire can also be the object of another person's nonsexual desires. Perhaps your peeking though keyholes expresses only your intellectual curiosity, while for me it is a source of sexual excitement and satisfaction. But if the same activity can be the object of both sexual and nonsexual desires, then the difference between the two kinds of desires cannot be explained by a difference between the kinds of activities desired. This second problem hints that the object-based strategy might be putting the cart before the horse. Rather than explaining sexual desire in terms of sexual activity, we might be better off trying to define sexual activity in terms of sexual desire. For example, an activity like peeking through keyholes might qualify as sexual only when it expresses, or is motivated by, a sexual desire. But if so, we can't use the idea of sexual activity to explain sexual desire.

A second, and equally natural suggestion, is that *a sexual desire is a desire for sexual pleasure.* This accords well with common motives for sexual encounters—sex can be a source of immense pleasure, and is understandably pursued for just that reason. On the proposed definition, the wide variety of desired activities—from the most mundane masturbation to the most peculiar perversions—are sexually desired when they are desired as a means to sexual pleasure. This also explains how we can desire the same activity, while only one of us has a sexual desire. You peek through keyholes for knowledge, but I peek for sexual pleasure, so only my voyeuristic desire is sexual.

The current proposal has several serious problems. First, we get pleasure from a dear friend's hug, or from a toddler's goodnight kiss, but the pleasure we receive is not sexual pleasure. So in order to define sexual desire as desire for *sexual pleasure*, we will first need to say what constitutes certain pleasures as sexual. This is a more challenging problem than it might seem, but we will not pause for it here—other and more serious problems lie ahead.[4]

Second, however natural or common it is to have sexual encounters for pleasure, it is difficult to see why pleasure must *always* be the object of our sexual desires. A couple who desire intercourse in order to have a baby might take pleasure in the activity, but it can distort matters to say that the pleasure they received was the object of their desire. We can easily imagine scenarios (the appropriate religious upbringing) in which they are embarrassed or made uncomfortable by any pleasure they receive, and so they take care to reduce or eliminate it. Their desire for intercourse is still plausibly a sexual desire, but it would misrepresent the case to say that what they desire is sexual pleasure, even if some pleasure results.

An additional problem for this view of sexual desire arises from the fact that it reduces our lovers to mere instruments for our pleasure—we use them to assist in the production of pleasurable sensations, but they are otherwise dispensable. Although there are moral issues raised by this instrumental view of others, my present concern is that it misrepresents the role that others play in our desires. Masturbation is less complicated and more readily available; it does not require the co-operation of others, and it is a highly reliable source of pleasant sexual sensations (if that is what we really seek). Perhaps other people can provide us with a marginally greater quantity or intensity of pleasant sensations than we can produce for ourselves, but even that can be remedied by relatively simple technology. So according to this view of sexual desire, if we are sufficiently skilful self-lovers, or if we have the aid of the right technology, other people are sexually dispensable. But this distorts matters—others are not instruments to compensate for our own autoerotic inadequacies. In the normal case, we sexually fantasize about something—some person, or some activity— because it is what we desire. When sexual fantasies are deployed in aide of masturbation, they better reveal the objects of our desires than does our autoerotic practice. But the objects of desire that figure in our masturbatory fantasies are not the pleasant sensations we would get from the scenarios we fantasize about. And that tells us that the objects of our desires are those scenarios, with those partners and practices, and not the sensations they might produce. There is all the difference in the world between desiring the pleasurable sensations (which, as it happens, Esmeralda causes me to have) and desiring that Esmeralda cause me to have pleasurable sensations. Since she, and not those sensations, stars in my sexual fantasies, then Esmeralda, and not those sensations, is the object of my desire.

Our discussion has so far assumed that sexual pleasure would consist in a distinctive class of pleasant bodily sensations. But this may be an unfair caricature. Some philosophers have suggested that we need a more robust understanding of what sexual pleasure is, and of the many forms it can take.[5] We can acquire a more robust conception by distinguishing the pleasant bodily sensations that *result from* an activity and the pleasure (enjoyment) we *take in* the activity. To illustrate—suppose I inject a powerfully euphoric drug into my bloodstream, with a resulting rush of pleasant sensations throughout my body. The pleasant sensations are the *result* of my activity of preparing the syringe and then injecting myself. But I do not enjoy either of these activities—I take no pleasure at all in injecting myself. So pleasant sensations can be the consequence of an activity in which we take no pleasure. Which kind of pleasure is sexual pleasure—is it the pleasant sensations that *result from* our preferred sexual activities, or is it the pleasure that we *take in* those activities?

On the one hand, if sexual pleasure reduces to bodily sensations that result from sexual activities, then we can in principle always get the same pleasure from a pill, or from skilful unassisted masturbation. As we have just seen, this would make sexual pleasure—viewed as bodily sensation, however produced—an implausible candidate for the constitutive object of our sexual desires. On the other hand, if sexual pleasure is pleasure taken in an activity—if it is enjoyment of sex—then we can acquire sexual pleasure only by engaging in sexual activity, and our understanding of sexual pleasure depends on our prior grasp of which activities are sexual. But we have already encountered reason to suspect that the idea of sexual activity presupposes the idea of sexual desire and, so, cannot be used to explain it. It therefore seems unlikely that any notion of sexual pleasure—whether simple or more robust—can be used to define sexual desire.

4.

The source of our trouble is, I suggest, the object-based strategy we are employing to provide an account of sexual desire. The alternative, feature-based strategy offers immediate gains. Simply contrast the respective roles that might be assigned to sexual pleasure under the different strategies. The object-based strategy counts a desire as sexual if (and only if) sexual pleasure is its object—if, that is, sexual pleasure is what we aim at when we strive to satisfy our sexual desires. A feature-based strategy that makes use of the notion of sexual pleasure would characterize a desire as sexual if it has an object—which could be *any* person, or *any* practice—that is desired *in virtue of* the pleasure it brings. The account leaves entirely open what the object of the desire might be. There are several gains to be had from simply shifting the location of sexual pleasure from the position of the object of desire to the position of a feature in virtue of which an object is found desirable.

First, the strategy no longer places limits on the possible *objects* of sexual desire—in principle, anything can be the object of a sexual desire, if we desire it in virtue of the pleasure it brings. Second, sexual and nonsexual desire can have the same object—what you desire in virtue of the pleasure it gives I might desire for another reason. The object-based strategy for defining sexual desire attempts to finesse similar results by denying that we generally know what we want—our desires can only *appear* to have wildly different objects, sexual and non-sexual desires can only *appear* to close in on the same objects. But in so far as our desires are sexual, they must have the same (constitutive) objects. So the third gain from the feature-based strategy is that it no longer has any need for such skepticism—it can allow that, for the most part, we want just what we think we want.

We have already seen how problematic the notion of sexual pleasure can be, and I will not attempt to make pleasure any part of the explanation of why a desire qualifies as sexual. *Of course* we sexually desire many activities for, among other things, the pleasure they bring. But that does not mean that what constitutes our desires for those activities as sexual is the pleasure we desire to get from them. To ground a feature-based account of sexual desire, the concept of sexual arousal is a much more promising candidate than the concept of sexual pleasure.

Sexual arousal is not the same thing as sexual desire, even though there are important relationships between them. Indeed, the key to understanding sexual desire is found in those relationships. Keeping in mind that analogies have their limits, we can initially understand states of sexual arousal on analogy with itches. Itches are objectless bodily states and, for that reason alone, they are very unlike desires. But they generally give rise to desires to scratch—where scratching is behaviour designed to relieve the itch. The object of the relevant desire—what we want—is to scratch, and scratching is an activity we desire in virtue of the effect it has on our itch. In the analogy, sexual arousal is, like an itch, an objectless bodily state that naturally gives rise to a desire to do something about it—for example, to do something that will assuage it. The analogy helps us to keep track of the crucial contrast between the state of sexual arousal (the itch), which is not itself a desire, and the particular desire (to scratch) to which it gives rise. The value of the analogy is that it portrays sexual arousal as an

objectless state, distinct from any desire, but nonetheless deeply implicated in some of the desires we do have.

We need to insist on the limitations of any analogy, and ours is no exception. Unlike having an itch, being sexually aroused—being turned on—is not always an unpleasant state. Furthermore, the activities that assuage or "relieve" our sexual arousal can also be far more enjoyable than scratching. As a result, we sometimes form desires to *produce* states of sexual arousal, desires to *sustain or continue* a state of sexual arousal, and desires to *heighten* states of arousal. If itches were pleasant states, and if scratching were more enjoyable—and perhaps more sociable—then we would surely find ways to generate itches, to heighten their intensity, and to make them last longer. Our analogy erodes further when we note that itches are a relatively uniform phenomenon, varying primarily in location, duration, and intensity. But sexual arousal is a multiform phenomenon, varying between the sexes and among individuals. Sexual arousal is, in the primary case, arousal of the sexual (i.e., reproductive) organs—an erection, or swelling and lubrication of the vagina. But flushed faces, tingling earlobes, or a quickening pulse can also count as forms of sexual arousal when they are part of a cluster of symptoms that, if allowed to progress, would include the familiar changes in the reproductive organs. In effect, numerous secondary symptoms of arousal qualify as sexual because of the company they are known to keep.

With the distinction between arousal and desire in hand, we are now in a position to identify a special class of desires that can be defined by reference to our states of sexual arousal. Just as some activities are desired precisely because of the effect they have on our itches (scratching is desired because it relieves itches, and moisturizing is desired because it prevents them), so some activities are desired precisely because of the effects they have on our states of sexual arousal—they are desired because they arouse us, because they heighten our arousal, or because they assuage our arousal. A sexual desire can be defined as a subject's desire for something—some activity, person, or object—in virtue of the effect that it is expected to have on the subject's own states of sexual arousal. The object of a sexual desire is the activity (person, etc.) that has those effects on our states of arousal—those persons or activities, whatever they might be, that turn us on. That they have those effects on our arousal—that they turn us on—is the very feature of those persons or activities that makes them sexually desirable to us. On this account, whatever we desire—whatever the object of our desire—it can also be desired nonsexually. But whenever we desire it in virtue of its anticipated effects on our states of sexual arousal, then our desire for it becomes sexual. Once again: we desire some activities in virtue of their effects on our

states of arousal—those effects can be pleasurable, and that is sometimes why we desire the activities that have such effects. But it is because they are effects on our states of arousal, not because they are pleasurable, that our desire for them is sexual.

The account of sexual desire just sketched is a feature-based account. It does not require sexual desires to have specific sorts of objects, so the diversity and occasional perversity of human sexual tastes can easily be accommodated, and the same objects can be desired either sexually or nonsexually. It only requires that the objects of our sexual desires, whatever they might be, are found desirable for specific sorts of reasons—because they turn us on. It's not what we desire, but why we find it desirable—the special kind of interest we take in it—that constitutes our desire as sexual. It is, then, not inconceivable—and let us hope, not unusual—for two lovers to find each other's sexual arousal to be sexually arousing. In such cases, the line between sexual self-interest and sexual altruism dissolves, and we have chemistry, not philosophy.[6]

Notes

1   See Plato, *Symposium*.
2   The principle can also be formulated in terms of a contrast between means and the ends to which they are subordinated—the beautiful body is desired only as a means to a more remote end (Beauty). Whichever formulation we use, the objection is the same: by Plato's principle, the true objects of desire, or the remote ends, can never be desired because *there is something about them* that makes then desirable to us.
3   Writing about a man who requests a saucer of mud, G.E.M. Anscombe says that if "he does not want it for anything, he just wants it," then he is

only a "dull babbling loon" (Anscombe 1957, 70). Plato's principle requires us to view all desire in just this way, and so makes babbling loons of us all.
4   For discussion of the many challenges that will be encountered along this route, see the discussions of sexual pleasure in Alan Goldman (1977) and Alan Soble (1996).
5   See Gareth Moore (1995) and Seiriol Morgan (2003) for more sophisticated views about sexual pleasure.
6   The feature-based account sketched in the final section is developed in more detail in Jacobsen (1993).

Bibliography

Anscombe, Elizabeth. 1957. *Intention*. Cambridge, MA: Harvard University Press.

Goldman, Alan. 1977. "Plain Sex." *Philosophy and Public Affairs* 6 (3): 267–87.

Jacobsen, Rockney. 1993. "Arousal and the Ends of Desire." *Philosophy and Phenomenological Research* 53 (3): 617–32.

Moore, Gareth. 1995. "Sexual Needs and Sexual Pleasures." *International Philosophical Quarterly* 35 (2): 193–204.

Morgan, Seiriol. 2003. "Sex in the Head." *Journal of Applied Philosophy* 20 (1): 1–16.

Nagel, Thomas. 1969. "Sexual Perversion." *Journal of Philosophy* 66 (1): 5–17.

Plato. 1920. *Symposium*. translated by Benjamin J Oxford University Press.

Sartre, Jean-Paul. (1943) 1956. *Be ness: A Phenomenological Essay on On* lated by Hazel Barnes. New York: W Square Press.

Shaffer, Jerome A. 1978. "Sexual Desire." *Journal Philosophy* 75 (4): 175–89.

Soble, Alan. 1996. *Sexual Investigations*. New York: New York University Press.

Solomon, Robert. 1974. "Sexual Paradigms." *Journal of Philosophy* 71 (11): 336–45.

JOHN RUSSON

Why is sex so important in most of our lives? One common answer is that it arises from a biological need. Another answer might be that it is highly pleasurable. Both of these points factor into Goldman's view, which I discussed in the previous chapter. In addition to these factors, we might argue that advertising and mass media have attributed to sex an exaggerated importance. Our lives are inundated with messages and images about sex and sexuality.

John Russon takes us through an exercise that is meant to help us answer the question of why sex is important by first having us answer the question of what we, as individuals, desire from sex. Russon's writing shares certain features with Sartre's, but Russon challenges us to develop a self-reflexive approach to understanding sexuality. He invites us to ask ourselves what we personally want in our sexual life. This is something that only we can answer, and it may not be a question that we have previously considered. In challenging us to answer this question for ourselves, Russon reminds us of the nineteenth-century Danish philosopher Søren Kierkegaard whose *indirect communication* was meant to free the reader from the authority of the author so that the reader could come to experience truth *subjectively*. Russon wants us to see the truth about our own sexuality and about what we desire in a way that is not determined by the dominant narratives about sex that pervade our society.

In *The Dialogues of Plato*,
...wett, 503–55. Oxford:

...*ng and Nothing-*
...ology*. Trans-
...shington

...*of*

; sexual desire as inherently interpersonal. It is not
...pleasures inherent in it. The real object of sexual
...y an occasion for experiencing one's own sexual
...e discovers things about herself and about the
...es the interpersonal nature of sexuality, including
...Nagel's account. He also puts importance on the
...us of Robert Solomon's view in his essay "Sexual
...tic experience extend beyond our personal pleas-
...ble in ethical experience. Sexuality represents one
...ters with another person, and it is the recognition
...ering, hardships, joys, hopes, ambitions, and so

Why Sexuality Matters

We use the word *sex* easily, but how well do we really understand what it means? I propose to take up the question of what sex is, and thereby to show how and why it is one of the most important things in our lives—but also one that we often misunderstand. To carry out this investigation, I will first set things up through three short reflections on familiar aspects of our lives. I will then use the results of this discussion to think about the experience of growing up, especially focusing on the experience of "losing one's virginity." I will conclude by reflecting on how we most effectively fulfill our erotic desires.

1. Three Short Reflections

Though my goal is to understand something about the importance of sexuality in our lives, I want to begin with a short reflection on something seemingly unrelated. I want to begin by thinking about public speaking, and, in particular, I want to consider the emotional dimensions—both the ones that make it difficult and the ones that make it desirable—that we encounter when we are called to speak in front of a group. I do not intend to give a scientific study of this experience, but simply to acknowledge familiar features that any of us should easily recognize.

First, there are some well-known ways in which that experience can be difficult. It is quite a common experience to feel nervous in front of a group:[1] we "feel butterflies" in our stomachs, we get dry-mouthed and choked up as we begin to speak. Perhaps we blush, shake, or perspire. Why does this happen? I think most people would agree that we feel these things and react this way because we notice that we are being looked at by others: we experience ourselves as being evaluated by them—judged—and, most basically, we fear that we will not perform well.[2] Typically, we embark on the project of speaking because we have something we want to share, but we become nervous because we fear that we will not speak well enough to be engaging, or that we will not communicate ourselves clearly, or that others will not be receptive to what we have to offer.

Of course, public speaking can also be exhilarating. This very experience of being under the gaze of others can be energizing and enlivening. It can spur us to creativity—to think or to speak or to act in unanticipated ways that we would otherwise be unable or unwilling to do. We can relish the "spotlight," enjoying the fact that we can command others' attention—that we are being recognized. And we can be gratified personally or morally because we are succeeding in getting an important message across and having an impact.

Surely there are many more things that we could say about the experience of public speaking—or, really, any performing in public—but I trust that these few remarks sketch out clearly enough some feelings with which we are all familiar. We have something we want to share with those others, and the experience of having the others' attention directed towards us is both exhilarating and challenging. We desire to have an impact on those others and to win their approval, but we also risk the possible humiliation of having them judge us to be failures.

Holding those thoughts about public speaking in the background, let us now reflect upon a second topic, this time a thought more obviously connected with our theme of sexuality. I would like now to think about the familiar stories we learn in our culture about what sexuality is.[3] I am not proposing here that we think about the learned and insightful theories we may have developed, but instead about the familiar cultural narratives we grow up hearing.

Of course we hear many stories, and I do not intend to canvas them in any thorough or detailed way, but I think there are some stories that we should all easily recognize as being part of our familiar cultural heritage. We hear, typically, that sex is about genitals—about vaginas, penises, semen, orgasms. We hear that sex is something that properly involves two people, and that it can be engaged in either with fidelity or as cheating. We hear that it is exciting—perhaps the most exciting thing of all—but also something that should be kept private, perhaps even secret, as there is a significant degree of shame attached to it as well. Though same-sex practices are widely recognized as legitimate, they are still commonly challenged and, indeed, most of the images we see of sexuality are heterosexual images—images of provocatively clad young women with shapely legs, thin waists, and round breasts, connecting with usually slightly older self-controlled men whose tall bodies are surely crafted through time at the gym . . ., men with perhaps a rough edge, or a "nerdy" but adorable edge, or a look of reliable professionalism and confidence.[4] As we are growing up, and still when we are older, our familiar cultural stories—on television, in the movies, in pop songs, in advertisements—communicate that "sex" is what grown-ups do, and that "getting it"—finding yourself in this story, doing these things with a person like that—is success. Obviously, this story could be told with much greater detail and complexity, but I imagine that anyone in our contemporary society will quickly recognize the familiarity and pervasiveness of this general portrayal of sex.

We have now reflected briefly first on the experience of public speaking and then on the common way in which sex is portrayed. Now, I propose a third and final short reflection, after which I will turn to my own claims about why sexuality matters. For this final reflection, I would like to think about our own most intimate sexual desires—what is it that we really want, that we really would hope for in our sexual life. This third thought is not one I can write about, however, because I am asking about what is, for each of us, most personal. I could articulate my own most intimate and private desires (or at least I could try), but I cannot say what yours are. This third reflection, then, each reader must perform for her- or himself, and so I ask you now, in reading this, to pause for a moment and think honestly and truly about what you really want sex to be.

2. Why Sexuality Matters

Losing Your Virginity

What I want to do now is to bring the results of the above three reflections together into my own account of why sexuality matters. I brought out these three thoughts in particular—about public speaking, about common cultural portrayals of sex, and about our most intimate desires—because I think each of them takes us into a distinct and an essential aspect of our sexuality. In order to see this, I want us to think about the experience of children as they grow up into the world of sexuality. Let us consider, then, what it is like to be a child.

Children grow up hearing about "sex."[5] They hear how exciting it is, but they also hear about it as something they are not part of. Sex is something for older people—the bigger kids at school in the higher grades, older brothers and sisters, the grown-ups on television—but not something they can yet have or understand. For children, sex is presented as a question, as something to which they are destined, but something into which they currently have no insight. Children wonder what sex is, and they anticipate it, having only its popular "reputation"—the very reputation we just described—to go on. With this in mind, let us now think about what happens when

children grow up and do in fact enter into the world of sexual experience.

Of course, entry into sexual experience takes all kinds of different forms—some brutal and unfair, to be sure, others no doubt thrilling and satisfying—and I will not try to catalogue them all.[6] I will simply point to what are some central features of this experience as it typically occurs. Typically, it will be as adolescents—teenagers—that this issue becomes a burning one, and commonly an adolescent will have a first sexual experience in private with another young person.[7] For the sake of simplicity, let us imagine this to be a reasonably happy experience, (though this is by no means always the case), and let us think about what is involved in the experience.[8]

An obvious dimension of this experience will be the pleasure in the nice bodily sensations produced by being touched. Our familiar cultural stories often focus on this dimension of pleasure. We see images of the woman writhing and moaning with pleasure under the touch of the man, or of the man expressing in his tightened face his submission to the transporting pleasure of orgasm, no doubt coupled with the pleasure of forceful and energetic bodily engagement. Presumably, such bodily pleasure is typically a significant dimension of the first sexual experience. This bodily pleasure, however, is not the only pleasure that is going on here, nor even the most prominent. To make this first point, let us note two other significant dimensions to the pleasure of this experience.

Prior to this first sexual experience, sex was a provocative mystery, and not having entered the world of being "sexually active" counted as evidence of one's immaturity. For that reason, one of the most powerful dimensions of the first sexual experience is the sense that *our question is being answered*, our sense that "I've made it" and crossed the threshold into the world of people who have "done it." Indeed, much of the reason one pursues this initial sexual experience is "to find out," to become initiated. Once we have participated in sexual experience with someone else, we say, "*Now* I know what it is," or "So *that's* what it's like," and we have a sense of accomplishment or maturity, seeing ourselves as doing the "grown-up" thing, or perhaps a sense of relief, feeling that we have now been able to leave behind the stigma of immaturity and failure that can come with being "a virgin," (or, indeed, a sense of shame at not having waited for the proper time and the proper person, or for being interested in "wrong" practices).⁹

Here, then, we begin to see the significance of our earlier thoughts about the public "reputation" of sex: the cultural stories we have heard about sex set sexual initiation up for us as a goal, and our sexual experience is thus wrapped up with a sense of our succeeding according to the imperatives of our culture. This experience of cultural success, then, of having "made it," is the second pleasure involved in that first sexual experience. I will return to this point a bit later, but before doing that let us focus a bit more on the specifics of the last point I made about the experience of relief in "losing one's virginity" in order to identify a third dimension to the pleasure involved in that first experience.

Why might it be "relief" in particular that one experiences in losing one's virginity? As we noted above, it is no doubt in part simply a matter of arriving at a destination one has been anticipating, but there is also more to it than just that. To see what else is involved, let us consider again the experience of the person growing up. When each of us is growing up, though we hope and expect to enter the promised world of

grown-up sexual life, we are not sure we will in fact get to have sex, we are not sure we will "lose our virginity." Why are we not sure? Because losing one's virginity is not something one can do on one's own: to do it, one must be chosen as a partner by someone else. This observation reveals the third dimension of the pleasure of the sexual experience, which is the pleasure of being chosen, the pleasure of having been attractive to another, of having appeared in the other's eyes as someone desirable. The pleasure in that first experience, then, in addition to being the pleasure of bodily stimulation and the pleasure of social success, is the pleasure of being desired, the pleasure of mattering to another person.

And, again, I was presuming this first experience to be pleasant, but it is important to remember that the experience can also be unpleasant. Thus, to correspond to the thrill of bodily stimulation, social success, and interpersonal recognition, we can also understand why anticipation of "losing one's virginity" can equally be a matter of fear of bodily pain, fear of negative social judgement, and fear of personal rejection. But whether the experience is positive or negative, the main point I want to make is that the pleasure or pain involved in sexual experience involves much more than bodily stimulation. In fact, it seems to me that, despite what we are told in our cultural narratives, these latter two dimensions that I have identified—the pleasure or pain of cultural success or failure and the pleasure or pain of being desired or rejected by another—do much more to shape our sexuality than the pleasure or pain of bodily sensation does. I want now to explore a bit more fully these other dimensions of our sexuality. Let us look first at the distinct issues that arise from the fact that what we seek is the pleasure of being desired by another person.¹⁰

Desire

Typically, the person whose desire we seek is a person whom we ourselves find desirable. Winning that person's desire is what we want, and knowing about ourselves that we are pleasing that person is what will exhilarate us and satisfy our desire.[11] Ideally, we should thus experience a situation of two people happily enjoying their shared experience of mutual desire. But because that other person has the power to give or withhold his or her desire for us, we can also feel captive to that desire and thus treat the other person's desire as a "prize" to be won or a challenge to be overpowered. We may thus live out our sexual life as a practice of seduction, trying to turn ourselves into a desirable object that captivates the other. In an extreme form, this can lead us to enter into sexual life not focusing on our own pleasures but instead entering into sexual experiences for the sake of "winning" the other's desire, affirming to ourselves our own desirability by being able to command the desire of the other. Indeed, even in a more reciprocal situation in which we do not reduce our own desire to the attempt to be attractive to another, the essential dimension of our pleasure can still be the sense of success in actually being able to make the other happy; this can be true to such a degree that not being able to satisfy the other's desires can make all the experiences of our own pleasure turn into pain, as we feel incompetent, guilty, selfish, or impotent in our inability to reciprocate. These ways in which the possible pleasure of the other can also be a site of pain can point to other sorts of sexual behaviour.

In order to minimize the threat to our own self-esteem that might come from opening ourselves up to the other and failing to satisfy them or, worse, being rejected by them, we can become cold with our partners, closing off our emotional attachment so as to avoid the situations that could be sites of possible pain. Or again, we may become possessive or controlling, trying to use force to contain the constant threat that the other person's desire might turn elsewhere. Or perhaps we deal with our own insecurity by turning our moral condemnation on our partners to make them feel guilty for having the desires that leave us feeling vulnerable. Or, more extremely, we become intentionally cruel to the other so as to demonstrate to ourselves our ability to have an emotional impact on that other, or to prove to ourselves that we are not dependent upon them.[12] In other words, though what we initially seek is the pleasure of being desired by someone we find desirable, our fear of failing can lead us to become cold, controlling, or hurtful in our treatment of that other person.

What we are seeing in these examples is the way that our sexuality—*because it is a domain of experience that can only be unfolded through the help of another*—is always a domain charged with issues of emotional vulnerability and that it will therefore always be shaped by the practices and strategies we adopt for dealing with that vulnerability—practices that can be healthy or unhealthy. Sexual life is the domain in which we navigate interpersonal issues of care, self-esteem, and power, and, more basically than being a domain defined by the experience of pleasing bodily sensations, sex is an activity in and through which we establish—both to ourselves and to others (either our sexual partner or others through whose eyes we evaluate ourselves)—a sense of our own desirability to other persons. Through our seductive posturing or our cool indifference, through our skills in touching or our responses to being touched, through our dramatic demonstrations of ecstatic abandonment or our subtle expressions of disappointed detachment, we position ourselves with respect to the "dialogue" of desire: we communicate through our behaviour—at a level "beneath" our explicit words—our affirmation of disapproval of the other and our openness or closedness to our own vulnerability. In so doing, we hope to demonstrate or to discover our desirability, our strength—indeed, our very worth as persons. Sexuality, in other words, is by its nature a phenomenon of interpersonal vulnerability and communication and it is this that provides the context that will determine the significance of whatever pleasant (or unpleasant) bodily sensations we encounter.[13]

We can now see the significance of our earlier thoughts about public speaking. The example of public speaking allows us to bring into focus what sorts of issues are at stake in encountering other people—experiencing oneself as an object being judged and evaluated, experiencing exhilaration at the thought of being recognized and appreciated, having unknown strengths drawn forth from us or feeling ourselves shut down without ever having adequately expressed ourselves. Those earlier reflections allow us to bring into focus precisely the issues we are actually grappling with in sexual experience, because sex, like public speaking, is first and foremost a matter of our desire to be desired by another—a matter of being evaluated by the perspective of another. What we see from our reflection on public speaking, though, is that the issues at stake in that encounter are quite different from matters of bodily pleasure. We will understand what "sex" is much better if we take public speaking, rather than the writhings of naked porn stars, as our image of what is going on in our sexual experiences.

Intimacy

When we look at what is really happening psychologically in our sexual experiences, we can see that what we desire in sexuality is not primarily bodily pleasure; what we desire is another *person*. We desire the other's desire: we desire that our desires be desirable to that other, and we ourselves desire to fulfill the desires of the other. Let us think a little bit further about what this implies. Inasmuch as I desire to satisfy that other person, *what that other person really wants* is what I want to answer to. Inasmuch as I desire that *I myself* be desirable to the other, what I really want is that that other person want to satisfy *me*; that is, I want that other person to desire to offer me *what I really want*. What is ultimately at issue here, then, is *intimacy*. It is my most intimate desires and your most intimate desires that are called into play in our sexual engagement with each other, our deepest, most vulnerable core of desire and aspiration. This brings us back to the third thought with which we began. For each of us, our sexuality is about the unique, and uniquely intimate, personal desires we—and our partners—have. What is really at stake, then, in our sexuality is our shared embrace of that within us that is most personal and intimate. The real pleasure in sexuality is the pleasure of accomplishing a shared intimacy.[14]

Notice what this means, though. Because, for each of us, our most intimate desires are unique, there is no way to know, outside of our communication, what form our sexual satisfaction will take. There is no way to say, in other words, what specifically we want in sexuality, what specifically gives us pleasure, without learning that from each other singly. There is, in short, no "general" answer to this question, no answer that is true for all. The answer, rather, could only be found uniquely by us in our joint accomplishing of a shared intimacy, an accomplishment only realized through communication and mutual learning. What form our sexuality should take cannot be defined outside us; we must, rather, create it jointly through a process of learning from each other who and how we want to be. We must approach each other, then, not knowing what it will mean for us to be sexual with each other, without knowing what we want or how we should behave, for those things will all have to be learned through our unique and intimate interpersonal dialogue.

But now we can see more pointedly the real significance of our cultural narratives about sexuality. Our cultural narratives precisely present themselves as an answer to the question "What is sex and how should you do it?" We have already seen that these familiar stories are misguided because they misrepresent the inherent dimension of interpersonal desire as a simple dimension of bodily pleasure. But more than this these stories are wrong in principle, precisely because they present sex as a settled meaning, a settled pattern and formula. These stories present themselves as the *answer* to the question about sex, whereas we are seeing that what is most essential about sex is *that it be a question for us.* What our sexuality calls for, then, is, in effect, that we return to the attitude of the child, and acknowledge our ignorance about sexuality, rather than substituting cultural clichés for the satisfying of our deepest needs for interpersonal intimacy.

Conclusion: Erotic Life

But if sexuality is not, in fact, a young man and a young woman who look like porn stars writhing and grimacing in their pursuit of orgasm, then what is it? Where, if not here, do we find an image of sex? Once we get past equating sex with the activities portrayed in advertising, we can appreciate the much broader and richer range of activities that constitute erotic life.

I will point to three of our most important human practices that should, I believe, be understood as, at root, erotic experiences.

Sexuality is where the experience of our own singular importance comes together with the experience of the importance of being responsive to others. It is also the site of experiencing this coming together as calling for our singular action and initiative, and, further, the experience of the need to be creative in a situation in which there is nowhere else to turn for "the right answer." We can thus see in sexuality, in this call to creatively realizing a joint care for you and me, the original *ethical* experience. Indeed, in its validating of the essentiality of one's own intimate needs and desires, our sexuality lays a foundation for one's independent pursuit of mental health, self-development, and happiness, and in its validating of the inherent worth of the other, it lays the foundation for a broader sense of the value of persons in general, offering the foundation for a sense of political responsibility. And, inasmuch as our sexuality is the embrace of the "question" that characterizes our identity, it points, in all these domains—to the personal, the interpersonal, and the political—to the need for creativity, rather than to the following of established rules and patterns. Thus, such behaviours as conscientious disobedience and political insurrection can at root be understood as profound developments of our erotic experience. In contrast, then, to familiar portrayals of sex as something dirty or base, we can see that, in fact, it is from our sexuality that our deepest concerns with goodness and value can grow.

Further, inasmuch as these challenges of shaping our personal, interpersonal, and political identities are all enacted within the arena of human sharing—of communication—they also point to the creative embrace of the sphere of human expression itself: art. In our artistic practices, we creatively redefine our capacities for self-expression and self-definition, and thereby deepen our ability to engage with and share the most intimate dimensions of our lives. In this way, we can see that artistic practice is itself a response—a profound response—to the erotic impulse within us.

Finally, inasmuch as the creative embrace of our shared nature involves understanding and insight, we can see that our sexuality cannot be fulfilled without learning, and without an enthusiasm for the ways in which our intellectual powers open us up to an appreciation of the realities and the possibilities of our human world. In our creative thought we hold ourselves answerable to the deepest desire to

let wha
which tc
how we s
namely, the
to appreciat
human worl
phy is itself a
it is the erotic
erotic nature in
formation and de

In sum, then, ...ıd better images of sex, if, instead of looking at advertising, we look instead to our practices of ethics, art, and philosophy, for these practices shows us more profoundly what is germinating in that original erotic impulse, that question that is sexuality.[15]

Notes

1   The fear of public speaking is regularly reported and there are innumerable articles, websites, groups, and counselling services devoted to addressing it. A survey by the World Health Organization investigating the presence of different forms of social anxiety around the world found that about one out of eight adults has a fear of public speaking; see Stein et al., "Subtyping Social Anxiety Disorder." For an introduction to the scholarly discussion of glossophobia or speech anxiety, see Ayres and Hopf, *Coping with Speech Anxiety.*

2   For a classic study of the experience of "the look" of the other person, see Sartre, *Being and Nothingness*, 301–3, 340–62.

3   On the portrayal of sexuality in entertainment media and the impact of this on attitudes about sexuality, see Brown, "Mass Media Influences on Sexuality"; Ward, "Understanding the Role of Entertainment Media in the Sexual Socialization of American Youth"; and Carpenter, "From

Girls into Women." See also Galician, *Sex, Love, and Romance in the Mass Media.*

4   On the portrayal of women, see Dittmar and Howard, "Professional Hazards?"; Lin and Kulik, "Social Comparison and Women's Body Satisfaction"; and Sands and Wardle, "Internalization of Ideal Body Shapes in 9–12-Year-Old Girls." In *The Beauty Myth*, Wolf investigates the social and political consequences of these portrayals of women. On the portrayal of men, see Agliata and Tantleff-Dunn, "The Impact of Media Exposure on Males' Body Image"; Pope et al., "Evolving Ideals of Male Body Image as Seen through Action Toys"; and Pope, Phillips, and Olivardia, *The Adonis Complex.*

5   See Wallis and VanEvery, "Sexuality in the Primary School"; Robinson, "'Difficult Citizenship'"; Bay-Cheng, "The Trouble of Teen Sex"; Reis and Wright, "Knowledge of Sex-Role Stereotypes in Children Aged 3 to 5"; and Carter and Patterson, "Sex Roles as Social

...cess by which children
...nd the salience of this for the
... of personality is central to Freud's
...nalysis; see especially *Three Essays on
...Theory of Sexuality.*

On this topic, see Sprecher, Barbee, and Schwartz, "'Was It Good for You Too?'" According to this research, men report both more pleasure and more anxiety than women, and men also report less guilt. Both genders report more pleasure, less anxiety, and less guilt when sex occurs in a close rather than a casual relationship.

7 See Bozon and Kontula, "Sexual Initiation and Gender in Europe." See also Bozon, "Reaching Adult Sexuality," and Kontula, Rimpelä, and Ojanlatva, "Sexual Knowledge, Attitudes, Fears and Behaviours of Adolescents in Finland." For a comprehensive study, see Laumann, Gagnon, Michael, and Michaels, *The Social Organization of Sexuality.*

8 On the theme of coercion in first experiences of genital intercourse, see Dickson, Paul, Herbison, and Silva, "First Sexual Intercourse." See also Wang and Ho, "'Female Virginity Complex' Untied."

9 On these themes, see Carpenter, "The Ambiguity of 'Having Sex.'"

10 For a parallel discussion of these different forms in which we can shape our sexual relationships in order to deal with the distinctive challenges posed by the fact that we desire the other's desire, see Sartre's discussion of "Concrete Relations with Others" in *Being and Nothingness*, 471–558.

11 This is Hegel's point in his study of "The Dependence and Independence of Self-Consciousness," in *Phenomenology of Spirit*, paragraphs 178–96.

12 For a rich discussion of the manipulative strategies we use to negotiate these power relations, see Berne, *Games People Play.*

13 I have taken up this approach to the study of sexuality in Russon, *Bearing Witness to Epiphany*, 71–94.

14 On this theme, see also Russon, *Human Experience*, 105–21.

15 This idea that *eros* is the driving force behind our "highest" human activities is famously expressed in Diotima's speech from Plato's *Symposium*, 208e–212c.

Bibliography

Agliata, Daniel, and Stacey Tantleff-Dunn. 2004. "The Impact of Media Exposure on Males' Body Image." *Journal of Social and Clinical Psychology* 23 (1): 7–22.

Ayres, Joe, and Tim Hopf. 1993. *Coping with Speech Anxiety.* Norwood, NJ: Greenwood Publishing

Bay-Cheng, Laina Y. 2003. "The Trouble of Teen Sex: The Construction of Adolescent Sexuality through School-Based Sexuality Education." *Sex Education: Sexuality, Society and Learning* 3 (1): 61–74.

Berne, Eric. 1996. *Games People Play: The Basic Handbook of Transactional Analysis.* New York: Ballantine Books.

Bozon, Michel. 1996. "Reaching Adult Sexuality: First Intercourse and Its Implications." In *Sexuality and the Social Sciences: A French Survey on Sexual Behaviour*, edited by Michel Bozon and Henri Léridon. Aldershot, UK: Dartmouth.

Bozon, Michel, and Osmo Kontula. 1998. "Sexual Initiation and Gender in Europe: A Cross-Cultural Analysis of Trends in the Twentieth Century." In *Sexual Behaviour and HIV/AIDS in*

Europe: Comparisons of National Surveys, edited by Michel Hubert, Nathalie Bajos, and Theo Sandfort. London: Routledge.

Brown, Jane D. 2002. "Mass Media Influences on Sexuality." *Journal of Sex Research* 39 (1): 42–45.

Carpenter, Laura M. 1998. "From Girls into Women: Scripts for Sexuality and Romance in *Seventeen* Magazine, 1974–1994." *Journal of Sex Research* 35:158–68.

———. 2001. "The Ambiguity of 'Having Sex': The Subjective Experience of Virginity Loss in the United States." *Journal of Sex Research* 38:127–39.

Carter, D. Bruce, and Charlotte J. Patterson. 1982. "Sex Roles as Social Conventions: The Development of Children's Conceptions of Sex-Role Stereotypes." *Developmental Psychology* 18 (6): 812–24.

Dickson, Nigel, Charlotte Paul, Peter Herbison, and Phil Silva. 1998. "First Sexual Intercourse: Age, Coercion and Later Regrets Reported by a Birth Cohort." *British Medical Journal* 316:29–33.

Dittmar, H., and S. Howard. 2004. "Professional Hazards? The Impact of Models' Body Size on Advertising Effectiveness and Women's Body-Focused Anxiety in Professions That Do and Do Not Emphasize the Cultural Ideal of Thinness." *British Journal of Social Psychology* 43 (4): 477–97.

Freud, Sigmund. 1975. *Three Essays on the Theory of Sexuality*. New York: Basic Books.

Galician, Mary-Lou. 2002. *Sex, Love, and Romance in the Mass Media: Analysis and Criticism of Unrealistic Portrayals and their Influence*. Mahwah, NJ: Erlbaum.

Hegel, G.W.F. 1977. *Phenomenology of Spirit*. Translated by A.V. Miller. Oxford: Oxford University Press.

Kontula, Osmo, M. Rimpelä, and A. Ojanlatva. 1992. "Sexual Knowledge, Attitudes, Fears and Behaviours of Adolescents in Finland (the Kiss Study)." *Health Education Research* 7 (1): 69–77.

Laumann, E., J.H. Gagnon, R.T. Michael, and S. Michaels. 1994. *The Social Organization of Sexuality: Sexual Practices in the United States*. Chicago: University of Chicago Press.

Lin, L.F., and J.A. Kulik. 2002. "Social Comparison and Women's Body Satisfaction." *Basic and Applied Social Psychology* 24 (2): 115–23.

Plato. 1989. *Symposium*. Translated by Alexander Nehamas and Paul Woodruff. Indianapolis: Hackett.

Pope, H.G. Jr., Katharine A. Phillips, and Roberto Olivardia. 2000. *The Adonis Complex: The Secret Crisis of Male Body Obsession*. New York: Simon and Schuster.

Pope, H.G. Jr., R. Olivardia, A.J Gruber, J.J. Borowiecki. 1999. "Evolving Ideals of Male Body Image as Seen through Action Toys." *International Journal of Eating Disorders* 26:65–72.

Reis, Henry T., and Stephanie Wright. 1982. "Knowledge of Sex-Role Stereotypes in Children Aged 3 to 5." *Sex Roles* 8:1049–56.

Robinson, Kerry H. 2012. "'Difficult Citizenship': The Precarious Relationship between Childhood, Sexuality and Access to Knowledge." *Sexualities* 15 (3/4): 257–76.

Russon, John. 2003. *Human Experience: Philosophy, Neurosis, and the Elements of Everyday Life*. Albany: State University of New York Press.

———. 2009. *Bearing Witness to Epiphany: Persons, Things, and the Nature of Erotic Life*. Albany: State University of New York Press.

Sands, E.R., and J. Wardle. 2003. "Internalization of Ideal Body Shapes in 9–12-Year-Old Girls." *International Journal of Eating Disorders* 33 (2): 193–204.

Sartre, Jean-Paul. 1984. *Being and Nothingness*. Translated by Hazel E. Barnes. New York: Washington Square Press.

Sprecher, Susan, Anita Barbee, and Pepper Schwartz. 1995. "'Was It Good for You Too?': Gender Differences in First Sexual Intercourse Experiences." *Journal of Sex Research* 32 (1): 3–15.

Stein, Dan J., et al. 2010. "Subtyping Social Anxiety Disorder in Developed and Developing Countries." *Depression and Anxiety* 27 (4): 390–403.

Wallis, Amy, and Jo VanEvery. 2000. "Sexuality in the Primary School" *Sexualities* 3 (4): 409–23.

Wang, Xiying, and Sik Ying Ho. 2011. "'Female Virginity Complex' Untied: Young Chinese Women's Experience of Virginity Loss and Sexual Coercion." *Smith College Studies in Social Work* 81 (2/3): 184–200.

Ward, L. Monique. 2003. "Understanding the Role of Entertainment Media in the Sexual Socialization of American Youth: A Review of Empirical Research." *Developmental Review* 23 (3): 347–88.

Wolf, Naomi. 2002. *The Beauty Myth: How Images of Beauty Are Used against Women.* New York: HarperPerennial.

Discussion

Is it true that anything (or just about anything) can be the object of a sexual desire? What makes a desire sexual? Is the feature-based strategy an improvement over the object-based one when it comes to helping us understand what it is that makes a desire sexual? Can you think of an object for which it is not possible to have a sexual desire? If so, does this mean that the object in question cannot possibly have any of the features that sexual desire entails? Jacobsen's account suggests that trying to understand sexual desire in terms of a specific aim or object of this aim will be problematic. How might a feature-based strategy challenge the general view put forth by Sartre and Nagel?

Nagel, and presumably Sartre, would view sexual desire for something other than another human being as a form of perversion, even if neither of them would necessarily condemn perversions. Even certain kinds of desires for incomplete sexual experiences with human beings constitute perversions in this view. This suggests that sexual desire cannot be understood entirely in terms of its object or its features when these are taken in isolation from the relationship between the subject and object of desire. In this view, sexual desire for inanimate objects or the desire for certain incomplete sex acts with another person are really desires for complete sex acts with another person that, through choice or circumstances, have fallen short of their true aim. This falling short may be viewed as failure in one sense—if one accepts Sartre and Nagel's picture of sexual desire—or it may be viewed as a creative, innovative, or personal expression of this desire. The assumption that informs this picture of sexual desire is that it is inherently interpersonal. It is the interpersonal nature of sexuality that John Russon explored in his article in this chapter.

The picture of sexuality in general and sexual desire specifically that Russon presents in his article does not allow an easy answer to the question of what the object of sexual desire is, because desire's object can only be understood in the interpersonal context. It is true that he, like Sartre, says that what we desire is a person, but it is not some feature of the person that we desire at least in the ordinary sense in which we use the term *feature*. What we desire rather, on Russon's account, is *intimacy*, and intimacy is not so much a feature of a person but rather a relational quality, state, or—perhaps better—a relational *experience*. The experience of intimacy that Russon has in mind takes on the structure that we saw in Sartre's account, a structure that Russon attributes to Hegel, whose master-slave story greatly influenced Sartre. The desire for intimacy, rather than expressing the desire for an object or for features of an object, indicates a desire for the subjective recognition or desire of the other person. This desire cannot be satisfied in a one-sided way without being illusory. One must come to know the other person so that she can know when her own desire for having the other person desire her is being fulfilled.

What is the significance of losing one's virginity? Russon compares it to the anxiety one experiences before engaging in public speaking. Is this a good analogy? How is the issue of losing one's virginity affected by the sense of *mystery* that surrounds this experience prior to our initiation? Russon claims that the familiar cultural stories about sex are misguided in their representation of the significance of sex. The meaning of sex is not something that we are given, but it is something that is worked out interpersonally in the intimate relationship between two people. This meaning is not to be found in the images portrayed in popular culture or through the porn industry. Our own attitude toward exploring our sexuality should be like the child for whom sex is a mystery in that we should not view its meaning as settled for us in advance. This allows us to explore sexuality in a way that reflects both our own desires and creativity as well as the desires and creativity of our partner. Do you agree with this? Are there some concrete alternative meanings that you can think of that might be open to intimate couples?

Suggestions for Further Reading

Laina Y. Bay-Cheng, "The Trouble of Teen Sex: The Construction of Adolescent Sexuality through School-Based Sexuality Education," *Sex Education: Sexuality, Society and Learning 3*, no. 1 (2003): 61–74.

Michel Bozon, "Reaching Adult Sexuality: First Intercourse and Its Implications," in *Sexuality and the Social Sciences: A French Survey on Sexual Behaviour*, edited by M. Bozon and H. Leridon (Aldershot, UK: Dartmouth, 1996).

Jane D. Brown, "Mass Media Influences on Sexuality," *The Journal of Sex Research* 39, no. 1 (2002): 42–45.

Jerome A. Shaffer, "Sexual Desire," *Journal of Philosophy* 75, no. 4 (1978): 175–89.

Alan Soble, *Sexual Investigations* (New York: New York University Press, 1996).

Chapter Three
Sex: Art or Science?

Introduction

In Volume 1 of *The History of Sexuality*, Michel Foucault contrasts "two great procedures for producing the truth of sex."[1] The procedures that he refers to are called *ars erotica* and *scientia sexualis*. *Ars erotica* treats sexuality, or more specifically, the erotic, as a form of art. Just as in art, a certain kind of non-conceptual truth or profound experience is revealed through a painting or a piece of music, so in sexuality the truth is revealed through pleasure and erotic experience. *Scientia sexualis*, on the other hand, treats sexuality more as a science. Foucault hypothesizes that the Christian confession, which emerged in Europe during the Middle Ages, has evolved and transformed into a scientific form of analysis about sexuality. Whereas once one laid bare his soul to the priest and confessed in detail his erotic transgressions (actions and thoughts), now discourse about sexuality takes the form of a kind of confession to a therapist or some other authority figure. The truth about sexuality is no longer revealed through the art of the erotic but is taken as an object to be studied, analyzed, and broken down into its constituents. One's conception of sexuality, viewed as an art or a science, will have a profound impact on one's sexual experience and on one's sexual identity.

Note

1 Michel Foucault, *The History of Sexuality, Volume 1: An Introduction* (New York: Vintage Books), 57.

MICHEL FOUCAULT

Scientia Sexualis

Historically, there have been two great procedures for producing the truth of sex.

On the one hand; the societies—and they
are numerous: China, Japan, India, Rome, the
Arabo-Moslem societies—which endowed
themselves with an *ars erotica*. In the erotic art,
truth is drawn from pleasure itself, understood
as a practice and accumulated as experience;
pleasure is not considered in relation to an
absolute law of the permitted and the forbidden, nor by reference to a criterion of utility,
but first and foremost in relation to itself; it is
experienced as pleasure, evaluated in terms of
its intensity, its specific quality, its duration, its
reverberations in the body and the soul. Moreover, this knowledge must be deflected back
into the sexual practice itself, in order to shape
it as though from within and amplify its effects.
In this way, there is formed a knowledge that
must remain secret, not because of an element
of infamy that might attach to its object, but
because of the need to hold it in the greatest
reserve, since, according to tradition, it would
lose its effectiveness and its virtue by being di-
vulged. Consequently, the relationship to the
master who holds the secrets is of paramount
importance; only he, working alone, can trans-
mit this art in an esoteric manner and as the
culmination of an initiation in which he guides
the disciple's progress with unfailing skill
and severity. The effects of this masterful art,
which are considerably more generous than
the spareness of its prescriptions would lead
one to imagine, are said to transfigure the one
fortunate enough to receive its privileges: an
absolute mastery of the body, a singular bliss,

obliviousness to time and
life, the exile of death and its threats.

On the face of it at least, our civilization
possesses no *ars erotica*. In return, it is undoubtedly the only civilization to practice a *scientia sexualis*; or rather, the only civilization to
have developed over the centuries procedures
for telling the truth of sex which are geared to
a form of knowledge-power strictly opposed to
the art of initiations and the masterful secret: I
have in mind the confession.

Since the Middle Ages at least, Western
societies have established the confession as
one of the main rituals we rely on for the production of truth: the codification of the sac-
rament of penance by the Lateran Council in
1215, with the resulting development of confessional techniques, the declining importance
of accusatory procedures in criminal justice,
the abandonment of tests of guilt (sworn statements, duels, judgments of God), and the development of methods of interrogation and
inquest, the increased participation of the royal administration in the prosecution of infrac-
tions, at the expense of proceedings leading to
private settlements, the setting up of tribunals
of Inquisition: all this helped to give the confession a central role in the order of civil and
religious powers. The evolution of the word
avowal and of the legal function it designated is itself emblematic of this development:
from being a guarantee of the status, identity,
and value granted to one person by another,
it came to signify someone's acknowledgment
of his own actions and thoughts. For a long
time, the individual was vouched for by the
reference of others and the demonstration of
his ties to the commonweal (family, allegiance,

_tion); then he was authenticated by the discourse of truth he was able or obliged to pronounce concerning himself. The truthful confession was inscribed at the heart of the procedures of individualization by power.

In any case, next to the testing rituals, next to the testimony of witnesses, and the learned methods of observation and demonstration, the confession became one of the West's most highly valued techniques for producing truth. We have since become a singularly confessing society. The confession has spread its effects far and wide. It plays a part in justice, medicine, education, family relationships, and love relations, in the most ordinary affairs of everyday life, and in the most solemn rites; one confesses one's crimes, one's sins, one's thoughts and desires, one's illnesses and troubles; one goes about telling, with the greatest precision, whatever is most difficult to tell. One confesses in public and in private, to one's parents, one's educators, one's doctor, to those one loves; one admits to oneself, in pleasure and in pain, things it would be impossible to tell to anyone else, the things people write books about. One confesses—or is forced to confess. When it is not spontaneous or dictated by some internal imperative, the confession is wrung from a person by violence or threat; it is driven from its hiding place in the soul, or extracted from the body. Since the Middle Ages, torture has accompanied it like a shadow, and supported it when it could go no further: the dark twins.[1] The most defenseless tenderness and the bloodiest of powers have a similar need of confession. Western man has become a confessing animal.

Whence a metamorphosis in literature: we have passed from a pleasure to be recounted and heard, centering on the heroic or marvelous narration of "trials" of bravery or sainthood, to a literature ordered according to the infinite task of extracting from the depths of oneself, in between the words, a truth which the very form of the confession holds out like a shimmering mirage. Whence too this new way of philosophizing: seeking the fundamental relation to the true, not simply in oneself—in some forgotten knowledge, or in a certain primal trace— but in the self-examination that yields, through a multitude of fleeting impressions, the basic certainties of consciousness. The obligation to confess is now relayed through so many different points, is so deeply ingrained in us, that we no longer perceive it as the effect of a power that constrains us; on the contrary, it seems to us that truth, lodged in our most secret nature, "demands" only to surface; that if it fails to do so, this is because a constraint holds it in place, the violence of a power weighs it down, and it can finally be articulated only at the price of a kind of liberation. Confession frees, but power reduces one to silence; truth does not belong to the order of power, but shares an original affinity with freedom: traditional themes in philosophy, which a "political history of truth" would have to overturn by showing that truth is not by nature free—nor error servile—but that its production is thoroughly imbued, with relations of power. The confession is an example of this.

One has to be completely taken in by this internal ruse of confession in order to attribute a fundamental role to censorship, to taboos regarding speaking and thinking; one has to have an inverted image of power in order to believe that all these voices which have spoken so long in our civilization—repeating the formidable injunction to tell what one is and what one does, what one recollects and what one has forgotten, what one is thinking and what one thinks he is not thinking—are speaking to us of freedom. An immense labour to which the West has submitted generations in order to produce—while other forms of work ensured the accumulation of capital—men's subjection: their constitution as subjects in both senses of the word. Imagine how exorbitant must have seemed the order given to all Christians at the beginning of the thirteenth century, to kneel at least once a year and confess to all their transgressions, without omitting a single one. And think of that obscure partisan, seven centuries later, who had come to rejoin the Serbian resistance deep in the mountains; his superiors asked him to write his life story; and when he brought them a few miserable pages scribbled in the night, they did not look at them but only said to him, "Start over, and tell the truth." Should those much-discussed language taboos make us forget this millennial yoke of confession?

From the Christian penance to the present day, sex was a privileged theme of confession. A thing that was hidden, we are told. But what if, on the contrary, it was what, in a quite particular way, one confessed? Suppose the obligation to conceal it was but another aspect of the duty to admit to it (concealing it all the more and with greater care as the confession of it was more important, requiring a stricter ritual and promising more decisive effects)? What if sex in our society, on a scale of several centuries, was something that was placed within an unrelenting system of confession? The transformation of sex into discourse, which I spoke of earlier, the dissemination and reinforcement of heterogeneous sexualities, are perhaps two elements of the same deployment: they are linked together with the help of the central element of a confession that compels individuals to articulate their sexual peculiarity—no matter how extreme. In Greece, truth and sex were linked, in the form of pedagogy, by the transmission of a precious knowledge from one body to another; sex served as a medium for initiations into learning. For us, it is in the confession that truth and sex are joined, through the obligatory and exhaustive expression of an individual secret. But this time it is truth that serves as a medium for sex and its manifestations.

The confession is a ritual of discourse in which the speaking subject is also the subject of the statement; it is also a ritual that unfolds within a power relationship, for one does not confess without the presence (or virtual presence) of a partner who is not simply the interlocutor but the authority who requires the confession, prescribes and appreciates it, and intervenes in order to judge, punish, forgive, console, and reconcile; a ritual in which the truth is corroborated by the obstacles and resistances it has had to surmount in order to be formulated; and finally, a ritual in which the expression alone independently of its external consequences, produces intrinsic modifications in the person who articulates it: it exonerates, redeems, and purifies him; it unburdens him of his wrongs, liberates him, and promises him salvation. For centuries, the truth of sex was, at least for the most part, caught up in this discursive form. Moreover, this form was not the same as that of education (sexual education confined itself to general principles and rules of prudence); nor was it that of initiation (which remained essentially a silent practice, which the act of sexual enlightenment or deflowering merely rendered laughable or violent). As we have seen, it is a form that is far removed from the one governing the "erotic art." By virtue of the power structure immanent in it, the confessional discourse cannot come from above, as in the *ars erotica*, through the sovereign will of a master, but rather from below, as an obligatory act of speech which, under some imperious compulsion, breaks the bonds of discretion or forgetfulness. What secrecy it presupposes is not owing to the high price of what it has to say and the small number of those who are worthy of its benefits, but to its obscure familiarity and its general baseness. Its veracity is not guaranteed by the lofty authority of the magistery, nor by the tradition it transmits, but by the bond, the basic intimacy in discourse between the one who speaks and what he is speaking about. On the other hand, the agency of domination does not reside in the one who speaks (for it is he who is constrained), but in the one who listens and says nothing; not in the one who knows and answers, but in the one who questions and is not supposed to know. And this discourse of truth finally takes effect, not in the one who receives it, but in the one from whom it is wrested. With these confessed truths, we are a long way from the learned initiation into pleasure, with their technique and their mystery. On the other hand, we belong to a society which has ordered sex's difficult knowledge, not according to the transmission of secrets, but around the slow surfacing of confidential statements.

The confession was, and still remains, the general standard governing the production of the true discourse on sex. It has undergone a considerable transformation, however. For a long time, it remained firmly entrenched in the practice of penance. But with the rise of Protestantism, the Counter Reformation, eighteenth-century pedagogy, and nineteenth-century medicine, it gradually lost its ritualistic and exclusive localization; it spread; it has been employed in a whole series of relationships: children and parents, students and educators, patients and psychiatrists, delinquents and experts. The motivations and effects it is expected to produce have varied, as have the forms it has taken: interrogations, consultations, autobiographical narratives, letters; they have been recorded, transcribed, assembled into dossiers, published, and commented on. But more important, the confession lends itself, if not to other domains, at least to new ways of exploring the existing ones. It is no longer a question simply of saying what was done—the sexual act—and how it was done; but of reconstructing, in and around the act, the thoughts that recapitulated it, the obsessions that accompanied it, the images, desires, modulations, and quality of the pleasure that animated it. For the first time no doubt, a society has taken upon itself to solicit and hear the imparting of individual pleasures.

A dissemination, then, of procedures of confession, a multiple localization of their constraint, a widening of their domain: a great archive of the pleasures of sex was gradually constituted. For a long time this archive dematerialized as it was formed. It regularly disappeared without a trace (thus suiting the purposes of the Christian pastoral) until medicine, psychiatry, and pedagogy began to solidify it: Campe, Salzmann, and especially Kaan, Krafft-Ebing, Tardieu, Molle and Havelock Ellis carefully assembled this whole pitiful, lyrical outpouring from the sexual mosaic. Western societies thus began to keep an indefinite record of these people's pleasures. They made up a herbal of them and established a system of classification. They described their everyday deficiencies as well as their oddities or exasperations. This was an important time. It is easy to make light of these nineteenth-century psychiatrists, who made a point of apologizing for the horrors they were about to let speak, evoking "immoral behavior" or "aberrations of the genetic senses," but I am more inclined to applaud their seriousness: they had a feeling for momentous events. It was a time when the most singular pleasures were called upon to pronounce a discourse of truth concerning themselves, a discourse which had to model itself after that which spoke, not of sin and salvation, but of bodies and life processes—the discourse of science. It was enough to make one's voice tremble, for an improbable thing was then taking shape: a confessional science, a science which relied on a many-sided extortion, and took for its object what was unmentionable but admitted to nonetheless. The scientific discourse was scandalized, or in any case repelled, when it had to take charge of this whole discourse from below. It was also faced with a theoretical and methodological paradox: the long discussions concerning the possibility of constituting a science of the subject, the validity of introspection, lived experience as evidence, or the presence of consciousness to itself were responses to this problem that is inherent in the functioning of truth in our society: can one articulate the production of truth according to the old juridico-religious model of confession, and the extortion of confidential evidence according to the rules of scientific discourse? Those who believe that sex was more rigorously elided in the nineteenth century than ever before, through a formidable mechanism of blockage and a deficiency of discourse, can say what they please. There was no deficiency, but rather an excess, a redoubling, too much rather than not enough discourse, in any case an interference between two modes of production of truth: procedures of confession, and scientific discursivity.

And instead of adding up the errors, naïvetés, and moralisms that plagued the nineteenth-century discourse of truth concerning sex, we would do better to locate the procedures by which that will to knowledge regarding sex, which characterizes the modern Occident, caused the rituals of confession to function within the norms of scientific regularity: how did this immense and traditional extortion of the sexual confession come to be constituted in scientific terms? . . .

Scienda sexualis versus *ars erotica*, no doubt. But it should be noted that the *ars erotica* did not disappear altogether from Western civilization; nor has it always been absent from the movement by which one sought to produce a science of sexuality. In the Christian confession, but especially in the direction and examination of conscience, in the search for spiritual union and the love of God, there was a whole series of methods that had much in common with an erotic art: guidance by the master along a path of initiation, the intensification of experiences extending down to their physical components, the optimization of effects by the discourse that accompanied them. The phenomena of possession and ecstasy, which were quite frequent in the Catholicism of the Counter Reformation, were undoubtedly effects that had got outside the control of the erotic technique immanent in this subtle science of the flesh. And we must ask whether, since the nineteenth century, the *scientia sexualis*—under the guise of its decent positivism—has not functioned, at least to a certain extent, as an *ars erotica*. Perhaps this production of truth, intimidated though it was by the scientific model, multiplied, intensified, and even created its own intrinsic pleasures. It is often said that we have been incapable of imagining any new pleasures. We have at least invented a different kind of pleasure: pleasure in the truth of pleasure, the pleasure of knowing that truth, of discovering and exposing it, the fascination of seeing it and telling it, of captivating and capturing others by it, of confiding it in secret, of luring it out in the open—the specific pleasure of the true discourse on pleasure.

The most important elements of an erotic art linked to our knowledge about sexuality are not to be sought in the ideal, promised to us by medicine, of a healthy sexuality, nor in the humanist dream of a complete and flourishing sexuality, and certainly not in the lyricism of orgasm and the good feelings of bio-energy (these are but aspects of its normalizing utilization), but in this multiplication and intensification of pleasures connected to the production of the truth about sex. The learned volumes, written and read; the consultations and examinations; the anguish of answering questions and the delights of having one's words interpreted; all the stories told to oneself and to others, so much curiosity, so many confidences offered in the face of scandal, sustained—but not without trembling a little—by the obligation of truth; the profusion of secret fantasies and the dearly paid right to whisper them to whoever is able to hear them; in short, the formidable "pleasure of analysis" (in the widest sense of the latter term) which the West has cleverly been fostering for several centuries: all this constitutes something like the errant fragments of an erotic art that is secretly transmitted by confession and the science of sex. Must we conclude that our *scientia sexualis* is but an extraordinarily subtle form of *ars erotica*, and that it is the Western, sublimated version of that seemingly lost tradition? Or must we suppose that all these pleasures are only the by-products of a sexual science, a bonus that compensates for its many stresses and strains?

In any case, the hypothesis of a power of repression exerted by our society on sex for economic reasons appears to me quite inadequate if we are to explain this whole series of reinforcements and intensifications that our preliminary inquiry has discovered: a proliferation of discourses, carefully tailored to the requirements of power; the solidification of the sexual mosaic and the construction of devices capable not only of isolating it but of stimulating and provoking it, of forming it into focuses of attention, discourse, and pleasure; the mandatory production of confessions and the subsequent establishment of a system of legitimate knowledge and of an economy of manifold pleasures. We are dealing not nearly so much with a negative mechanism of exclusion as with the operation of a subtle network of discourses, special knowledges, pleasures, and powers. At issue is not a movement bent on pushing rude sex back into some obscure and inaccessible region, but on the contrary, a process that spreads it over the surface of things and bodies, arouses it, draws it out and bids it speak, implants it in reality and enjoins it to tell the truth: an entire glittering sexual array, reflected in a myriad of discourses, the obstination of powers, and the interplay of knowledge and pleasure.

All this is an illusion, it will be said, a hasty impression behind which a more discerning gaze will surely discover the same great machinery of repression. Beyond these few phosphorescences, are we not sure to find once more the somber law that always says no? The answer will have to come out of a historical inquiry. An inquiry concerning the manner in which a knowledge of sex has been forming over the last three centuries; the manner in which the discourses that take it as their object have multiplied, and the reasons for which we have come to attach a nearly fabulous price to the truth they claimed to produce. Perhaps these historical analyses will end by dissipating what this cursory survey seems to suggest. But the postulate I started out with, and would like to hold to as long as possible, is that these deployments of power and knowledge, of truth and pleasures, so unlike those of repression, are not necessarily secondary and derivative; and further, that repression is not in any case fundamental and overriding. We need to take these mechanisms seriously, therefore, and reverse the direction of our analysis: rather than assuming a generally acknowledged repression, and an ignorance measured against what we are supposed to know, we must begin with these positive mechanisms, insofar as they p knowledge, multiply discourse, induce p ure, and generate power; we must investiga the conditions of their emergence and operation, and try to discover how the related facts of interdiction or concealment are distributed with respect to them. In short, we must define the strategies of power that are immanent in this will to knowledge. As far as sexuality is concerned, we shall attempt to constitute the "political economy" of a will to knowledge.

Note

1   Greek law had already coupled torture and confession, at least where slaves were concerned, and Imperial Roman law had widened the practice.

RÉAL FILLION

In his paper "Challenging Norms: The Co-creative Core of Erotic Life," Réal Fillion picks up on one of Foucault's themes. According to Foucault, the discourse around sexuality itself displays a certain kind of power by normalizing certain sexual practices and classifying others as forms of deviance. In particular, *scientia sexualis* has caused us to understand or interpret our sexual practices in a certain way. We come to understand ourselves as heterosexual, homosexual, or bisexual, or we understand ourselves as deviant, normal, sexually confused, and so on. Fillion explores the possibility or the challenge of creating the norms that govern our erotic lives and sexual identities through our sexual engagements with other people. Instead of having the realm of the sexual defined for us, we become active players in creating the governing norms.

In talking about creating or co-creating the norms which govern our sexual life, Fillion reminds us of Russon's essay where we were encouraged to approach sexuality with the attitude of one who is on the verge of losing his or her virginity where the unknown territory we are exploring invites us with excitement, fear, curiosity, and, most importantly, a question about our own identity and the role of sex in revealing that identity. Indeed, Fillion draws from the work of Russon as well as Foucault in developing his own approach, which encourages us not to let our sexuality and sexual identity be defined for us by society or by other people but rather in that intimate context that constitutes our relationship. In that context, we are told, the conversations that we have, the truth that we discover together, is every bit as important to our sexual intimacy as the bodily experiences that we share.

orms:
Core of Erotic Life

in her book *Bodies and
! the Politics of Sexual Nor-
now* as an adolescent, in the face of pressure to identify herself as homosexual, she asked herself, "Why do I have to be judged as a sexual being at all? Why does *that* have to be the most important thing about me?" (1999, 9). A good question: What is the relative importance of recognizing each other as sexual beings?

If, following Michel Foucault and Ladelle McWhorter, we see in the discourse of sexuality various forms of normalization (where what is normal is constituted through the identification and classification of differences as deviances), it is surely because our sexual awareness of each other inherently challenges that which is familiar. Appealing to Foucault's distinction between a *scientia sexualis* and an *ars erotica*, this essay will discuss how examining the dynamics of our erotic lives shows them to be animated by the challenge of co-creating the norms that will govern them.

Admit it: as exciting as the kissing, caressing, and fondling are, what is really beginning to blow your mind are the *conversations*. You can talk about *anything* with her. There are no restrictions. No judgments. She listens. And you listen to her. At first, you talked about yourself—your family, where you are from, why you are here at this university. Your "story." And she told you hers, but soon enough, perhaps because the sudden seriousness seemed incongruous and ended up making you both laugh, the conversations veered off into all kinds of different directions, punctuated with expressions of something you can best identify as your "thoughts," kinds of observations you have made, views you have been forming

that attempt to make sense of things, stuff you don't usually say to anyone. You feel exhilarated when she says that she thinks the same way, or something like it, only adding things you hadn't considered, which make even more sense. But as you pursue the line of thought opened up, sometimes in thrilling agreement, sometimes surprised by what each of you says next, laughter again overtakes you, and you collapse against each other, push each other away, grasp each other again, and now in each other's arms you continue to talk, and touch each other, and talk. And you have never felt more alive. And yourself. And free.

What I want to emphasize here in this common experience is how your sense of being yourself and being free can be connected to engaging your self *with another as mediated by bodily pleasure*, opening a new perspective on what it means to be the self you otherwise take yourself to be, and by extension, presenting a challenge to the sense of who we are outside of such engagements. As John Russon suggests,

> As the site where our reality is not ready-made but awaits creation, sexuality can be experienced as deeply liberating, joyful, or playful, but equally as intimidating, frightening, or destructive. It is here that we encounter the co-creative character that is definitive of our humanity, and our sexual behaviour will be our gesture of affirming or denying this nature. (Russon 2003, 108)

Rather than refer to our humanity and nature, though, I would like to insist on how this co-creative space at the core of our erotic lives can be a challenge to our subjection to the norms that govern something we are made to understand as "sexuality," this latter term understood as the transformation or putting into "discourse" of sex that Foucault traces in his *History of Sexuality: An Introduction*.

In the middle part of that work (whose title in French is "The Will to Know"), Foucault, having previously shown how "sex was constituted as a problem of truth" (Foucault 1980, 56), draws our attention to the contrast between "two great procedures for producing the truth of sex" (57): an ancient *ars erotica* and the *scientia sexualis*, which structure and inform the deployment of our discourse of sexuality today. According to Foucault, what distinguishes the former is that

> truth is drawn from pleasure itself, understood as a practice, and accumulated as experience; pleasure is not considered in relation to an absolute law of the permitted and the forbidden, nor by reference to a criterion of utility, but first and foremost in relation to itself; it is experienced as pleasure, evaluated in terms of its intensity, its specific quality, its duration, its reverberations in the body and the soul. (57)

By way of contrast, tracing its roots in the practices of confession of Christian penance, Foucault argues that the "slowly developed discursive practice which constitutes the *scientia sexualis*" produced as its correlative what we identify as "sexuality" with a very different relation to truth. Rather than being "drawn from pleasure itself," sexuality reconfigures the relation to truth by being defined, in its very "nature" as "a domain susceptible to pathological processes, and hence calling for therapeutic or normalizing interventions; a field of meanings to decipher; the site of processes concealed by specific mechanisms; a focus of indefinite causal relations; and an obscure speech (*parole*) that had to be ferreted out and listened to" (68).

As an illustration, consider Ladelle Mc-Whorter, who, in her *Bodies and Pleasures: Foucault and the Politics of Sexual Normalization*, recounts how, at twelve years of age, she asked her mother the definition of the word "homosexual" (a term she came upon in a magazine). She "had been erotically and romantically involved with another girl for some time already" (1999, 1), and was taken aback, not by her mother's definition ("It's a kind of person that falls in love with a person of their own sex") but by the revulsion with which she said it and the fact that it, and the discourse it deploys, turned her into a "kind of person" subject to imposed norms and processes of normalization, which she also recounts as she describes her painful adolescence.

While I do not want to overidealize McWhorter's characterization of her erotic and romantic involvement prior to being subjected to a regime identifying her as "a homosexual" (something she, at first, repeatedly declared she did not want to be), there is a sense that the space it created was initially one of exploratory bodily pleasure as opposed to being the site of a specific *kind* of "desire." No doubt, desire was present, but it might be worthwhile to distinguish within that space itself a mutuality fostered by shared pleasure as something other than the dynamics of mutual desire that surely had a role in bringing it into being, without however completely determining it. This might enable us to appreciate better the co-creativity of that space of pleasure and the freedom it makes possible.

Before examining the space as co-creative, let's first look a little more closely at how desire works. When you want or desire something, you are noticing two things: the thing that you want and the fact that you don't have it. That is, in wanting or desiring, you relate both to the thing you want or desire and to yourself as something lacking the thing that you want. This is a different kind of self-relation than the self-relation that expresses itself in your awareness of your own feelings, which can shift and change without any real participation from you, from your developed sense of yourself. Think of moods. You are relating to yourself in your moods. They are your moods. And yet, in a way, they are *not* you, or not the you that you feel directly responsible for. You might be short with someone, and when they point this out to you, you might apologize and say that you didn't mean to answer like that; you are just in a bad mood. But of course, in apologizing, you are recognizing that you did do what you did, and you are claiming responsibility for that; but at the same time you explain that what you did was shaped by something more than what you are able to claim responsibility for; it was shaped by your mood, something that shapes the way you relate to the world pre-consciously, as it were, simply in a feeling way. We are always in some mood or another, because we are always relating to ourselves and to our place in the world at this basic feeling level (Russon 2003, 44).

Wanting or desiring something presents a different relation to oneself and the world. (Indeed, in certain moods, we don't know what we want at all; in others, we feel ourselves open to *everything*!) In wanting or desiring, you demonstrate a conscious awareness of specific things in the world and your relation to them in the specific form of lacking them. In other words, you are noticing something *specific* about yourself, as much as you are noticing something about the world as distinct from yourself. This, too, is a distinct form of relating to yourself and to the world. You can be aware of things around you and yourself as something distinct from them without experiencing any want or desire. Note that what is being emphasized in wanting or desiring is not merely that you are relating to yourself and to the world in terms of the awareness that you are lacking something, but that that felt lack sparks your awareness of *your own self* as so lacking.

This might be illustrated by considering the difference between a more generalized sense of wanting and the specific characteristics of *desire*. Let us say that we are all sitting around watching television, but more or less indifferently—that is, we are not really engaged in the show. Indeed, some of you might be surfing on your phone or laptop, somebody else leafing through a magazine. Suddenly, you notice something about yourself, something about how you are feeling, which you identify as being hungry. You mention this to the others. The others consult their own feelings and report on them: I just ate; no, I'm good; I could eat; yeah, me too. So you get up and go into the kitchen to see if there is anything to eat. You open the cupboards and the fridge and report on what is available. One of your friends replies: yeah, whatever. Another says: never mind. You bring some of what is available into the living room. Your friends (surprisingly, all of them!) take some of the food and eat it, but without much expression. You, on the other hand, are dissatisfied. Nothing that is available appeals to you. Your awareness of your own hunger and of the food available to you does not lead you to eat. The lack you became aware of when you noticed how you were feeling sharpens into the keener sense of wanting, which we call desire. This signals a different relation to your feeling in that it distinguishes itself from your conscious self. (Contrast it to your friend who, despite having said he didn't want anything, is now nevertheless eating, strictly out of a kind of habitual reaction to food placed between him and a television!) The lack that you are now aware of throws up a sharper sense of your own self in relation to yourself and to what you do not have. You are now not merely conscious of the world around you, and picking from it what is available to you out of habit; you are distinctly *self*-conscious as a *desiring* (self).

This desiring (self) is manifest to you so long as you are desiring and not satisfied by what is available to you to take and consume.

The basic idea here is that a more developed sense of your self, as distinct from the cycle of satisfying the wants that arise out of your habitual engagement with the world, engages a self-consciousness that underscores a sense of self that is lacking and incomplete *on its own*. One of the most direct ways to illustrate the developing and dynamic quality of this self-consciousness is of course through sexual desire, the erotic desire for someone else. The first thing to note about sexual or erotic desire is that it is the desiring of another *person*, or individual. I am fully aware that the expression of sexual or erotic desires can take on all kinds of forms, but I will agree with Thomas Nagel (1969) in calling forms that are not directed to other persons as specific individuals' perversions (understood in the etymological sense of a "turning away," or perhaps as a truncated form of desiring) of the basic character of erotic desire as desiring another person's desire. Put another way, whatever you might be sexually aroused by, given your habituated forms of dealing with the world (which includes myriad images about what is meant to be arousing), understanding the *desire* at the heart of it involves an appreciation of your sense of relating to another person.

When, through sexual attraction, we become conscious of sexual desire, then, we become conscious of ourselves and of what we are lacking, but now what we are lacking is something *like* our own self in being another person. This engages a process of attempting to satisfy our desire with very different results than the satisfaction of other desires, as in our example of hunger. If food is readily available and consumed, then the self-consciousness that arises with and accompanies desire is quickly extinguished and we fall back into habitual modes of dealing with

the world. Attempting to satisfy your (sexual) desire for another person means encountering another desire, the desire of that other person, which can include a rejection of your attempt to satisfy your desire. Such rejection will of course throw you back onto your own sense of a self that is lacking something (and indeed this can become acute). But insofar as your desire is *not* rejected by the desire of the other person, but instead is *reciprocated* in some way, then your desire and the self it manifests are engaged in a new and potentially transformative manner, one that can sustain the cycle of desire and satisfaction in a way that does not, through increasing *self-consciousness*, involve extinguishing the sense of self that manifests itself in and accompanies desire. Such reciprocation might not go beyond the narrative of a particular sexual encounter, of course. But the point is that the sexual encounter is itself *defined* in terms of the reciprocation of desire—that is, of a desire desiring another's desire whose desire desires your desire.[1]

The key feature of such erotic exchanges is that it opens us to our own selves through others in a way that is distinctively different from the relation to the familial and familiar others that have gone into shaping our personalities as we grew up. With it comes an increased sense of being one's own self. And we must understand this self-consciousness not only in the specific technical sense of a self born out of the self-relating feeling of lack we have been following, but also the kind of "self-consciousness" we *feel* beneath the gaze and the touch of others. In our self-conscious desire engaging another person's desire, we of course continue to be the persons we have grown up to be, psychically invested and habituated to doing things in the familiarly "appropriate" ways in terms of the values and norms that have shaped us so far. However, in our erotic engagements and in the self-consciousness (and vulnerability) that accompanies them, we open that familiar self to another in a way that in effect challenges our sense of familiarity as we become responsive to the other's desire through our own desire. Russon puts this quite well:

> It is precisely through our dependence upon—our immersion within—the strange and autonomous power of the other that we are offered a route out of our familiar places, out of our familiar temporality, and into a new order, a new world. The other offers a route into a different setting of the terms of our lives. The erotic other is, in many ways, both the means and the end, both the goal and the resources we draw upon, in our process of self-transformation. The erotic other is essentially interwoven in our inhabiting a new way of perceiving. (2009, 120)

It is in this sense that such erotic engagements can open up a space for *challenging* the norms that have up to now served as guides to our behaviour and sense of self. In its reciprocation, a new form of mutuality begins to take shape, one that goes beyond the relative immediacy of established familiar and familial bonds (immediate in the sense that the established patterns of recognition within them go largely unquestioned) and opens up the possibility of a reshaping of our selves in more explicitly self-conscious ways. In attending to the other's desire and in their attending to our own, the mutuality thereby established is, in Russon's terms, effectively *co-creative* in that who we are manifests itself through the mutual engagement with each other,[2] and this therefore becomes an important site of our sense of ourselves as *free*.

But of course our coming together in mutual desire can also carry with it the more mundane sense of self-consciousness, one which brings to the sexual encounter a self-consciousness about one's body, implying and sometimes enacting a certain sense of distance, a lack of confidence, a concern with performance and various inhibitions (Klein 2012, 33–4), as any number of professional sex therapists will remind us. However, such observations about sexuality and sexual desire do not arise principally from the site of our erotic engagement per se, but in the confessional space of therapy where their dynamics are brought under the scrutinizing concern of the *scientia sexualis* (as well-meaning as those therapists might be) discursively reshaping one's relation to what one *feels* in specifically normalizing ways.

By contrast, I still want to emphasize this other mundane experience of becoming self-conscious, but this time born of the sheer mutual pleasure of bodily contact in a co-creative space of unfolding self-expression, as described in my opening paragraph. While far from the more elaborate *ars erotica* of ancient times, we can nevertheless see in such a space a relation to truth "drawn from pleasure itself." It is not a question of confessing things to one another, but of expressing oneself *before* the other in a free space. It is not so much a question of *revealing* a self under the scrutiny of another, as *exploring* a communicative space that feels less tied down to familiar normative expectations, without of course leaving them completely behind. As Judith Butler puts it, "The fact that I am other to myself precisely at the place where I expect to be myself follows from the fact that the sociality of norms exceeds my inception and my demise, sustaining a temporal and spatial field of operation that exceeds my self-understanding" (2004, 15). But when that temporal and spatial field is one of intimate self-exploratory communication through pleasure, then the sociality of norms loosens its hold on our self-consciousness, and we can let go of the weight of the normalized world we struggle with daily for a moment and reconstitute it in our shared emerging thoughts and gestures.

But further, what such experiences suggest is that to be yourself is in effect to move beyond yourself through expressing your *thoughts* and having them reflected (which includes allowing them to be challenged) in the thoughts of another. It is in this way that the self-expressive mutuality experienced in erotic engagement opens up self-consciousness to the universality of reasoned thoughtful expression. And this, I want to suggest—not *only* because I am a philosophy professor, but certainly *because* I am a philosophy professor—is part of the thrill of it: through your erotic engagement and the co-creative expressiveness it allows, you see how there is more to your being who you are than what you have so far understood, and that understanding what that "more" is involves a further engagement with the expressiveness fostered by the pleasure shared with the other person, both in terms of the way you respond to what she tries to express about herself and in terms of how she responds to what you are expressing. Thus, in opening ourselves up to each other, we in effect become mutually *answerable* to each other,[3] and it is this mutual answerability that is at the heart of the sustained self-and-other consciousness that we might still call *reason* or the kind of intelligently engaged thoughtfulness we find ourselves capable of exercising in concert. It is within this context of explicit mutuality and receptivity that we are afforded the opportunity to ponder what we are actually saying, to actually stop and consider whether or not what we are saying is something we mean and hold to be truthful, and not merely words we use and repeat thoughtlessly. In the thrill

of conversation, the speaking to each other involved in this intimate context is as much about itself as it is about each of the speakers. The words, and more importantly, the *thoughts* being expressed are actually taking shape, as it were, for the first time, or rather, out of the conversation itself, initiated but not determined by the desire to recognize each other's desire (perhaps because, for the moment, the physical thirst had been slaked) and now guided by the sheer pleasure of a bodily co-presence. Inchoate thoughts, perhaps, about what it feels like to be alive and therefore destined to die; thoughts about what matters most, about what it means to be a good person, what it means to do wrong; thoughts about how important beauty is in drawing us out of ourselves, out of the familiar and into the strangeness of the world. That is, your thoughts, in being expressed in this way and at this time, are coming *from* you but in order precisely to be *shared*, and in a sense surrendered to another, not in the spirit of communicating something already established, as somehow already formed within you, not as something that the other is meant to confirm or to contradict, or even to assess or evaluate as fully formed, but rather to receive through a similar sharing of her own nascent thoughts.

Thus the co-creative space we create for ourselves through shared bodily pleasure is, I want to say, a privileged initiatory space of *truthfulness*, understood as an expressive effort to articulate what one is thinking both in the light of what the body next to yours is thinking and as a challenge to those views unthinkingly held, including one's own up to this point. It offers us the possibility of confronting the norms that have shaped us and are made to govern us in our everyday lives with a sense of those exploratory norms born of the artful bodily pleasure of being together.

Notes

1 Of course, this way of describing mutual desire is in an important sense ideally conceived. For the different ways this ideal can be distorted, consider John Russon's discussion of desire in his "Why Sexuality Matters" in this volume.

2 In *Human Experience: Philosophy, Neurosis, and the Elements of Everyday Life*, Russon tells us, "Sex is the epiphany of the other, and the substance of our sexual life is how we bear witness (or fail to) to this epiphany. The erotic experience of another is the experience of the freedom of mutual creativity, of codefinition. In our sexual encounter, it is 'up to us' to shape what will be. Here, with this other person, we are actually enacting our identity, and we need not be constrained by established norms, by others' familiar perceptions of ourselves, and so on. Sexuality is the sphere in which our initiative, our freedom, is decisive" (Russon 2003, 108).

3 In a later work titled *Bearing Witness to Epiphany: Persons, Things, and the Nature of Erotic Life* Russon says, "In sexuality, I, as a body, experience the call to be *with you*, as a body, and thus, in erotic life, we experience our bodies as the locus of the communication between us, and the site of our answerability to each other's perspective. In erotic experience, my experience of my body is of this dialectic of mutual answerability. Indeed, this is why our sexual life is so intimately intertwined with issues of shame, pride, and self-image, and equally with questions of 'right and wrong' and 'good and bad.' Erotic experience is fundamentally the experience that *who I am for you* matters to me, and our erotic life is our negotiating with this experience" (Russon 2009, 78).

Bibliography

Butler, Judith. 2004. *Undoing Gender.* New York: Routledge.

Foucault, Michel. 1980. *The History of Sexuality, Volume I: An Introduction.* Translated by Robert Hurley. New York: Vintage Books.

Klein, Marty. 2012. *Sexual Intelligence: What We Really Want from Sex and How to Get It.* New York: HarperCollins.

McWhorter, Ladelle. 1999. *Bodies and Pleasures: Foucault and the Politics of Sexual Normalization.* Bloomington: Indiana University Press.

Nagel, Thomas. 1969. "Sexual Perversion." *The Journal of Philosophy* 66 (1): 5–17.

Russon, John. 2003. *Human Experience: Philosophy, Neurosis, and the Elements of Everyday Life.* Albany: State University of New York Press.

———. 2009. *Bearing Witness to Epiphany: Persons, Things, and the Nature of Erotic Life.* Albany: State University of New York Press.

Discussion

What is it that most profoundly shapes our sense of our self as a sexual being? In other words, what is it that shapes our sexual identity or our sexual persona? How do we view our sexual activities and ourselves as sexual beings? There is a tendency to view ourselves as being a certain kind of person. We are gay, straight, sexually conservative, sexually adventurous, monogamous, promiscuous, and so on. What are the effects of these classifications or identifications? Is it possible to understand our erotic lives independent of the public norms and concepts that define them? Is it possible to define them through our sexual relations or with our sexual partners? How differently would we experience sexuality if we were to view it in terms of *ars erotica* rather than, as Foucault claims we do, through the procedure of *scientia sexualis*?

To view our sexuality in the manner of *scientia sexualis* is to view it in accordance with a system of classification modelled after that of the sciences. Instead of understanding our sexuality or our sexual identity as emerging through our confession to a priest, we now understand it through the lens of psychology. We may not literally describe our sexuality to a therapist, but our own sexual identity is one that has been interpreted for us by the clinical categories and classifications that we learn at school, through the media, from our families, and so on. We speak a therapeutic language often when we describe our experiences. We live in a scientific and therapeutic age in which much of our self-understanding has been drawn from a deep reservoir of sexual categories. We are heterosexual, homosexual, bisexual, transgendered, sexually repressed, sexually liberated, frigid, conflicted, and so on. Is it possible to escape such sexual classifications and to explore sexuality, sexual identity, and intimacy in an individual and intimate way with another person? Are there advantages to treating sexuality as something more akin to artistic creativity? What might this entail? In what sense is sexual intimacy itself a kind of dialogue or conversation between two people, as Fillion suggests?

Think for a minute of your own sexual identity or sexual persona. How do you express yourself sexually? How do you perceive other people's sexual personae? We sometimes hear it said of a person that she exudes sexuality. Have you met a person about whom you would make this claim? If so, what is it about him or her that you find sexual? The people that we find sexy do not always fit the ideals of physical perfection put forth by our society. Often we find a certain attitude (confidence, indifference, playfulness) sexy, or we find someone's sense of taste or his or her intelligence sexy. What is it that makes these things sexual? What is it that makes these things attractive? Even though there are certain people who many people find sexy, think about someone who (to your knowledge) only *you* find sexy. What is it about that person that you are attracted to?

Suggestions for Further Reading

Marty Klein, *Sexual Intelligence: What We Really Want from Sex and How to Get It* (New York: HarperCollins, 2012).

Ladelle McWhorter, *Bodies and Pleasures: Foucault and the Politics of Sexual Normalization* (Bloomington: Indiana University Press, 1999).

John Russon, *Bearing Witness to Epiphany: Persons, Things, and the Nature of Erotic Life* (Albany: State University of New York Press, 2009).

Chapter Four
Talking about Sex

Introduction

We live in a day when sex is talked about. Indeed, sex is talked about a lot. But why is this so? Why is it so important for us to talk about sex? Michel Foucault introduces the idea of a "repressive hypothesis" and the "speaker's benefit" as potential explanations.

According to the repressive hypothesis, we believe that we have been in, or are coming out of, an age of sexual repression. According to this story, our more recent tendency to talk about sex is a sign of liberation. We see ourselves as no longer under the domination of conservative sexual mores. We have embraced our newfound sexual freedom and are able to talk about it. We may even see ourselves as subversive, ignoring these repressive norms and the power they represent. Foucault, however, offers a different take on this situation. He thinks that the repressive hypothesis itself represents a kind of power. It licenses us to speak about sex or to "preach" about sex in the context of opposing repression. Instead of asking the question "Why are we repressed?" Foucault asks, "Why do we say . . . that we are repressed?" The one who speaks out about this repression is afforded what Foucault calls the "speaker's benefit." One incurs this benefit by appearing as subversive in light of the hypothesis that says we have been repressed. Foucault believed that the speaker herself in this case speaks from a position of power in the discourse about sex.

MICHEL FOUCAULT

We "Other Victorians"

For a long time, the story goes, we supported a Victorian regime, and we continue to be dominated by it even today. Thus the image of the imperial prude is emblazoned on our restrained, mute, and hypocritical sexuality.

At the beginning of the seventeenth century a certain frankness was still common, it would seem. Sexual practices had little need of secrecy; words were said without undue reticence, and things were done without too much concealment; one had a tolerant familiarity with the illicit. Codes regulating the coarse, the obscene, and the indecent were quite lax compared to those of the nineteenth century. It was a time of direct gestures, shameless discourse, and open transgressions, when anatomies were shown and intermingled at will, and knowing children hung about amid the laughter of adults: it was a period when bodies "made a display of themselves."

But twilight soon fell upon this bright day, followed by the monotonous nights of the Victorian bourgeoisie. Sexuality was carefully confined; it moved into the home. The conjugal family took custody of it and absorbed it into the serious function of reproduction. On the subject of sex, silence became the rule. The legitimate and procreative couple laid down the law. The couple imposed itself as model, enforced the norm, safeguarded the truth, and reserved the right to speak while retaining the principle of secrecy. A single locus of sexuality was acknowledged in social space as well as at the heart of every household, but it was a utilitarian and fertile one: the parents' bedroom. The rest had only to remain vague; proper demeanour avoided contact with other bodies, and verbal decency sanitized one's speech. And sterile behaviour carried the taint of abnormality; if it insisted on making itself too visible, it would be designated accordingly and would have to pay the penalty.

Nothing that was not ordered in terms of generation or transfigured by it could expect sanction or protection. Nor did it merit a hearing. It would be driven out, denied, and reduced to silence. Not only did it not exist, it had no right to exist and would be made to disappear upon its least manifestation—whether in acts or in words. Everyone knew, for example, that children had no sex, which was why they were forbidden to talk about it, why one closed one's eyes and stopped one's ears whenever they came to show evidence to the contrary, and why a general and studied silence was imposed. These are the characteristic features attributed to repression, which serve to distinguish it from the prohibitions maintained by penal law: repression operated as a sentence to disappear, but also as an injunction to silence, an affirmation of nonexistence, and, by implication, an admission that there was nothing to say about such things, nothing to see, and nothing to know. Such was the hypocrisy of our bourgeois societies with its halting logic. It was forced to make a few concessions, however. If it was truly necessary to make room for illegitimate sexualities, it was reasoned, let them take their infernal mischief elsewhere: to a place where they could be reintegrated if not in the circuits of production, at least in those of profit. The brothel and the mental hospital would be those places of tolerance: the prostitute, the client, and the pimp, together with the psychiatrist and his hysteric—those "other Victorians," as Steven Marcus would say—seem to have surreptitiously transferred the pleasures that are unspoken into the order of things that are counted. Words and gestures, quietly authorized, could be exchanged there at the going rate. Only in those places would untrammeled sex have a right to (safely insularized) forms of reality, and only to clandestine, circumscribed, and coded types of discourse. Everywhere else, modem puritanism imposed its triple edict of taboo, nonexistence, and silence.

But have we not liberated ourselves from those two long centuries in which the history of sexuality must be seen first of all as the chronicle of an increasing repression? Only to a slight extent, we are told. Perhaps some progress was made by Freud; but with such circumspection, such medical prudence, a scientific guarantee of innocuousness, and so many precautions in order, to contain everything, with no fear of "overflow," in that safest and most discrete of spaces, between the couch and discourse: yet another round of whispering on a bed. And could things have been otherwise? We are informed that if repression has indeed been the fundamental link between power, knowledge, and sexuality since the Classical age, it stands to reason that we will not be able to free ourselves from it except at a considerable cost: nothing less than a transgression of laws, a lifting of prohibitions, an irruption of speech, a reinstating of pleasure within reality, and a whole new economy in the mechanisms of power will be required. For the least glimmer of truth is conditioned by politics. Hence, one cannot hope to obtain the desired results simply from a medical practice, nor from a theoretical discourse, however rigorously pursued. Thus, one denounces Freud's conformism, the normalizing functions of psychoanalysis, the obvious timidity underlying Reich's vehemence and all the effects of integration ensured by the "science" of sex and the barely equivocal practices of sexology.

This discourse on modern sexual repression holds up well, owing no doubt to how easy it is to uphold. A solemn historical and political guarantee protects it. By placing the advent of the age of repression in the seventeenth century, after hundreds of years of open spaces and free expression, one adjusts it to coincide with the development of capitalism:

it becomes an integral part of the bourgeois order. The minor chronicle of sex and its trials is transposed into the ceremonious history of the modes of production; its trifling aspect fades from view. A principle of explanation emerges after the fact: if sex is so rigorously repressed, this is because it is compatible with a general and intensive work imperative. At a time when labour capacity was being systematically exploited, how could this capacity be allowed to dissipate itself in pleasurable pursuits, except in those—reduced to a minimum—that enabled it to reproduce itself? Sex and its effects are perhaps not so easily deciphered; on the other hand, their repression, thus reconstructed, is easily analyzed. And the sexual cause—the demand for sexual freedom, but also for the knowledge to be gained from sex and the right to speak about it—becomes legitimately associated with the honour of a political cause: sex too is placed on the agenda for the future. A suspicious mind might wonder if taking so many precautions in order to give the history of sex such an impressive filiation does not bear traces of the same old prudishness: as if those valorizing correlations were necessary before such a discourse could be formulated or accepted.

But there may be another reason that makes it so gratifying for us to define the relationship between sex and power in terms of repression: something that one might call the speaker's benefit. If sex is repressed, that is, condemned to prohibition, nonexistence, and silence, then the mere fact that one is speaking about it has the appearance of a deliberate transgression. A person who holds forth in such language places himself to a certain extent outside the reach of power; he upsets established law; he somehow anticipates the coming freedom. This explains the solemnity with which one speaks of sex nowadays. When they had to allude to it, the first demographers and psychiatrists of the nineteenth century thought it advisable to excuse themselves for asking their readers to dwell on matters so trivial and base. But for decades now, we have found it difficult to speak on the subject without striking a different pose: we are conscious of defying established power, our tone of voice shows that we know we are being subversive, and we ardently conjure away the present and appeal to the future, whose day will be hastened by the contribution we believe we are making. Something that smacks of revolt, of promised freedom, of the coming age of a different law, slips easily into this discourse on sexual oppression. Some of the ancient functions of prophecy are reactivated therein. Tomorrow sex will be good again. Because this repression is affirmed, one can discreetly bring into coexistence concepts which the fear of ridicule or the bitterness of history prevents most of us from putting side by side: revolution and happiness; or revolution and a different body, one that is newer and more beautiful; or indeed, revolution and pleasure. What sustains our eagerness to speak of sex in terms of repression is doubtless this opportunity to speak out against the powers that be, to utter truths and promise bliss, to link together enlightenment, liberation, and manifold pleasures; to pronounce a discourse that combines the fervour of knowledge, the determination to change the laws, and the longing for the garden of earthly delights. This is perhaps what also explains the market value attributed not only to what is said about sexual repression but also to the mere fact of lending an ear to those who would eliminate the effects of repression. Ours is, after all, the only civilization in which officials are paid to listen to all and sundry impart the secrets of their sex:

as if the urge to talk about it, and the interest one hopes to arouse by doing so, have far surpassed the possibilities of being heard, so that some individuals have even offered their ears for hire.

But it appears to me that the essential thing is not this economic factor, but rather the existence in our era of a discourse in which sex, the revelation of truth, the overturning of global laws, the proclamation of a new day to come, and the promise of a certain felicity are linked together. Today it is sex that serves as a support for the ancient form—so familiar and important in the West—of preaching. A great sexual sermon—which has had its subtle theologians and its popular voices—has swept through our societies over the last decades; it has chastised the old order, denounced hypocrisy, and praised the rights of the immediate and the real; it has made people dream of a New City. The Franciscans are called to mind. And we might wonder how it is possible that the lyricism and religiosity that long accompanied the revolutionary project have, in Western industrial societies, been largely carried over to sex.

The notion of repressed sex is not, therefore, only a theoretical matter. The affirmation of a sexuality that has never been more rigorously subjugated than during the age of the hypocritical, bustling, and responsible bourgeoisie is coupled with the grandiloquence of a discourse purporting to reveal the truth about sex, modify its economy within reality, subvert the law that governs it, and change its future. The statement of oppression and the form of the sermon refer back to one another; they are mutually reinforcing. To say that sex is not repressed, or rather that the relationship between sex and power is not characterized by repression, is to risk falling into a sterile paradox. It not only runs counter to a well-accepted argument, it goes against the whole economy and all the discursive "interests" that underlie this argument.

This is the point at which I would like to situate the series of historical analyses that will follow, the present volume being at the same time an introduction and a first attempt at an overview: it surveys a few historically significant points and outlines certain theoretical problems. Briefly, my aim is to examine the case of a society which has been loudly castigating itself for its hypocrisy for more than a century, which speaks verbosely of its own silence, takes great pains to relate in detail the things it does not say, denounces the powers it exercises, and promises to liberate itself from the very laws that have made it function. I would like to explore not only these discourses but also the will that sustains them and the strategic intention that supports them. The question I would like to pose is not, Why are we repressed? but rather, Why do we say, with so much passion and so much resentment against our most recent past, against our present, and against ourselves, that we are repressed? By what spiral did we come to affirm that sex is negated? What led us to show, ostentatiously, that sex is something we hide, to say it is something we silence? And we do all this by formulating the matter in the most explicit terms, by trying to reveal it in its most naked reality, by affirming it in the positivity of its power and its effects. It is certainly legitimate to ask why sex was associated with sin for such a long time—although it would remain to be discovered how this association was formed and one would have to be careful not to state in a summary and hasty fashion that sex was "condemned"—but we must also ask why we burden ourselves today with so much guilt for having once made sex a sin. What paths have brought us to the point where we are "at fault" with respect to our own sex? And how have we come to be a civilization so peculiar as to tell itself that, through an abuse of power which has not ended, it has long "sinned" against sex? How does one account for the displacement which, while claiming to free us from the sinful nature of sex, taxes us with a great historical wrong which consists precisely in imagining that nature to be blameworthy and in drawing disastrous consequences from that belief?

ADA S. JAARSMA

Ada S. Jaarsma sees this speaker's benefit exemplified in the work of contemporary *sexpert* Dan Savage. Savage is highly influential and uses multiple media platforms to convey his liberatory messages about sex. Following Foucault, Jaarsma sees in modern-day sex talk in general, and Dan Savage's work in particular, a participation in a structure of power that has risen from the repressive hypothesis. And while power itself is not the problem, the repressive hypothesis gives the sexpert, or the advocate of progressive attitudes towards sex, the false impression that they are rebels fighting against the repression that has arisen from the conservative sexual regime. The speaker's benefit in this context enables the person with the message of liberation to speak from a position of relative power.

In Chapter 3, Réal Fillion discussed the distinction between *scientia sexualis* and *ars erotica* as contrasted by Foucault in *The History of Sexuality*, Volume 1. It is in that same work that Foucault introduces us to the notions of "the speaker's benefit" and "the repressive hypothesis." In his essay, Fillion advocates the creation of norms and experiences that do not necessarily conform to the structure of what is "normal" or "expected" in the sexual realm. Jaarsma suggests, instead of helping liberate us from cultural norms, the modern sexpert, such as Dan Savage, may be making use of the modern confessional that Foucault characterizes as part of *scientia sexualis*, which causes us to understand our sexuality in therapeutic terms. By understanding sex in terms of the repressive hypothesis and by participating in the larger discourse on sex, which is influenced by this view, we fail to experience our sexuality and sexual pleasure individually or creatively. This realm is shaped for us by the message of liberation and the norms that have emerged out of this narrative.

The Speaker's Benefit and the Case of Dan Savage

What about *your* sexual pleasure? What about *your* orgasms?
— Dan Savage, *Savage Lovecast,*
episode 17

Tomorrow, sex will be good again.
— Michel Foucault, *The History of Sexuality, Volume 1*[1]

Dan Savage: Modern Sexpert

"How weird am I?" (episode 52), someone asks. Another person muses, "If I watch lesbian porn, does that make me a lesbian?" (episode 101). Someone else says, "If you could give me some moral guidance, that would be great" (episode 273). These are messages left by anonymous individuals on the *Savage Lovecast*, Dan Savage's weekly advice show. "I like people to be direct and realistic," Dan explains in one of his podcasts (episode 12), and, indeed, people share with Dan intimate details about a range of sexual predicaments.

Is it wrong, for example, for a woman who's a feminist to have rape fantasies? What about enjoying porno fantasies that you would never want to have happen in real life? "You've said before," a caller reminds Dan, "that people can't change their fantasies. So what should I do?" (episode 7). In response to questions like these, Dan supplies his own brand of direct and realistic instructions. "If you have an unrealizable fantasy," he tells someone, "you shouldn't obsess about it. You can explore it through fantasy play, but you need to have a real life too" (episode 318).

As you can tell from these opening questions, people reach out to Dan Savage as a contemporary sex sage. He has reached thousands of people through various media, including his ongoing podcast, a 2012 MTV show called *Savage U*, the It Gets Better campaign, and numerous publications. As he broadcasts his advice, he coins terms and invents rules that equip people with tools for navigating modern sexual lives. While Dan has many acolytes (and is producing a new television sitcom called *The Real O'Neals*, which premiered in 2016), his advice prompts others to challenge his terms and rules, and these challenges, in turn, inform the vocabulary of Dan's sex talk.[2]

In this essay, we will consider how Dan Savage—and his followers and critics—exemplify what Michel Foucault calls "the speaker's benefit." According to Foucault, there is something about the ways in which we speak about sex that provides us with motivating and reassuring benefits. As we consider the nature of these benefits, we might find ourselves identifying closely with the speakers themselves: with those who turn to Dan for advice, with Dan himself, or with Dan's critics. As we do so, we are implicated in Foucault's critical take on sex talk and its promises.

In sex talk, Foucault points out, sex becomes the explanation for everything (78). As the explanation for everything, sex promises liberation and progress in the fervent conviction that "it gets better." This promise hinges on two assumptions in particular: that sex reveals essential truths, especially truths about ourselves, and that sex emancipates us. As the speakers of sex talk lay claim to these promises of truth and freedom, Foucault prompts us to situate the speaker's benefit in its modern historical context, and in this way, we will scrutinize Dan Savage and sex talk as a phenomenon—a phenomenon in which, according to Foucault, *sexuality* is produced and deployed. Although the speaker's benefit lays claim to a certain natural, pre-given status to sexuality, as you can see, Foucault's critique takes aim at this claim directly.

The Repressive Hypothesis

At the beginning of *The History of Sexuality*, Volume 1, Foucault coins the phrase "the speaker's benefit" to describe the self-satisfied feelings that result from modern sex talk (6). Put simply,

the speaker feels a great sense of benefit from talking about sex. One of the most palpable aspects of this sense emerges out of what Foucault calls "the repressive hypothesis": the hypothesis that sex was repressed in the past and, all too often, continues to be repressed today.

Foucault calls this claim (that sex used to be repressed) a hypothesis because he wants to foreground its conditional status. We moderns, he explains, like to tell this story in part because it grants us as speakers a direct benefit: "If sex is repressed, that is, condemned to prohibition, nonexistence, and silence, then the mere fact that one is speaking about it has the appearance of a deliberate transgression" (6). If the puritans, the Victorians, and other non-progressive people undermine sex through taboos, censorship, and denial, then the very act of calling out such repression is an act of emancipation. And so, when we tell the story of the repressive hypothesis and say "no" to the naysayers, we are saying "yes" to sex.

Foucault is stressing the "if" of this story in order to draw out the hypothetical nature of sex's repression. The hypothesis does not stand up to historical scrutiny. Despite its historical inaccuracies, however, it is the consistent story that we tell about sex in part because of the benefits granted to us as its storytellers. By saying "yes," we are laying claim to our ability to resist repressions like the Victorian bedroom (in which sex is only permitted in the context of legal and married heterosexual reproduction). By saying "yes," in other words, we are asserting our own political prowess. After all, how else could we defy the still pervasive negativity of repression if not for our own ability to overturn established laws and conventions?

The speaker's benefit, Foucault explains, includes these kinds of self-righteous tones of revolt. As we participate in the repressive hypothesis, "we are conscious of defying an established power, our tone of voice shows that we know we are being subversive, and we ardently conjure away the present and appeal to the future, whose day will be hastened by the contribution we believe we are making" (6). Sex positivity, in this way, sets itself up as an effective way to link the revolutionary emancipation from the past with our own pleasures. This is in part why Foucault describes modern sex talk in terms of one prophecy or sermon in particular: "Tomorrow, sex will be good again" (7). Sex will be good again, according to this sermon, because speaking about sex is essentially liberatory. When Dan tells a listener, "You have a right to the direct kind of intense feeling that it takes to get you off" (episode 4), he is professing this aspect of the speaker's benefit.

Such liberatory claims, however, are made possible by the repressive hypothesis itself, which is "part of the same historical network as the thing it denounces" (Foucault 1978, 10). Modern sex talk affirms itself as liberatory because it sets itself against what it identifies as power—a very specific understanding of power, according to Foucault. The repressive hypothesis sees power as legalistic, prohibitive, and demanding (88). "Where sex and pleasure are concerned," according to the repressive hypothesis, "power can 'do' nothing but say no to them" (83).

Foucault's question is not the question that Dan Savage might ask ("why are we repressed?") but rather, "Why do we say . . . that we are repressed" (8)? The issue is not whether one says yes or no to sex, in other words, but "to account for the fact that it is spoken about, to discover who does the speaking, the positions and viewpoints from which they speak, the institutions which prompt people to speak

about it and which store and distribute the things that are said" (11).

It Gets Better

Disputing the hypothesis that power represses, Foucault points out that power actually incites and multiplies, rather than inhibits. Consider the contrast that Dan Savage frequently makes between sex positivity and the repression that he finds exemplified by religious communities. Referring to a scandal in which evangelical leader Ted Haggard is found out to be paying male prostitutes for sex, Dan declares, "I think we should make a joyful noise unto something or other. We should always be happy when a hypocrite is exposed. *Closeted* people are the ones who do damaging desperate pathetic risky horseshit to get their needs met: expressions of self-loathing" (episode 4; see also Savage 2006).

The sex talking speaker receives benefits on the assumption that, whereas power rejects, excludes, refuses, blocks, conceals, and masks (what Dan is indicting in this example as closeted desperation), sex talk liberates us from such negativity. When Dan invites his listeners to "make a joyful noise to something or other" because a hypocrite is facing public shaming, he is positioning religious adherents squarely within the repressive effects of juridical power. We should be happy when bigots are exposed, he explains, because we, the yaysayers, are advancing the causes of liberation.

In another example, he tells a twenty-three-year-old Mormon man who is unsure about leaving his religious community in order to come out as gay, "The longer you wait, the longer you're going to be living this lie that you're living now, and the harder it's going to be to live with a little integrity and be who you are and tell your family and friends the truth" (episode 54). Dan's advice to this young Mormon man is to embrace the speaker's benefit. His advice exemplifies a broader message about what it means to be modern and self-liberating. As Dan puts it to another young man, "You will be able to move to a bigger city when you are older; in the meantime, masturbate and work out" (episode 13). Moving to the city, in this message, marks a shift away from closeted intolerance to a tolerant, better life for everyone.

"It Gets Better," the phrase for which Dan is perhaps most famous, is the name of a media empire that began in September 2010 when Dan and his husband, Terry Miller, uploaded a video to YouTube. Responding to what they perceived as a crisis of youth suicides, the It Gets Better campaign combines testimonies by thousands of people about their own progress towards happiness with directives (like "move to a bigger city") about how queer youth can attain such happiness (Grzanka and Mann 2014, 378). If we situate this message—that it gets better for individuals and for all of us when the religious turn secular, when the closeted come out, and when repression yields to sex talk—in terms of Foucault's critique of the repressive hypothesis, we confront the productivity of sex talk itself. According to Foucault, power is exercised rather than held (94), produced from one moment to the next. And so, in contrast to the repressive hypothesis, Foucault concludes, "We must not think that by saying yes to sex, one says no to power" (157) because power is immanent in every relation (93).

This is a key claim. If we understand power as positive, rather than solely negative or prohibitive, we can begin to recognize the concrete and historical frameworks within which power operates. This is one way to understand Foucault's claim that power is *immanent*. There is no way to stand outside of history:

our practices, techniques, relations, and even subjectivities are immanent to the situations in which they emerge and interact. They are contingent, rather than universal or inevitable. In this way, the link that Dan draws between "self-loathing" and "religious" in that earlier example is part of a modern secularization of tolerance. To be progressive, on these terms, is to move out of the closet and beyond religious bigotry.

This progress narrative cannot acknowledge the provisional nature of its own categories ("religious" and "secular"), however, because to do so would undermine the basis of "It Gets Better"—namely, that whereas religious or closeted people remain somehow caught in backwards-looking repression, the lives of sexually liberated people participate in ongoing social bettering. In contrast to this religious/secular divide, when we draw out the immanence of power relations, we can see how the religious right actually approaches sex talk in precisely the same ways as Dan Savage— by enabling sex to be explanatory, scientific, and manageable through the expert insights of specialists (Jordan 2011).[3]

Truth and the Knowledge of Sexperts

The very identification of someone as closeted, as ex-gay, or as even as "not gay," depends upon authorized discourse.[4] Rather than uncovering sexuality or "freedom" as some kind of undiscovered territory or natural given, sex talk *produces* sexuality and gives rise to a proliferation of sexualities (Foucault 1978, 105, 34). Sex talk, in other words, has effects that we can track; it is part of what Foucault calls a "regime of power-knowledge" (11). The "homosexual," for example, became a species in the nineteenth century—a person with an identity, a past, and a body entirely determined by sexuality: "Nothing that went into his total composition was unaffected by his sexuality. It was everywhere present in him" (43).

If something becomes a "species," it can be diagnosed as such by experts. It can also start to self-identify and lay claim to emancipation. Exactly in this way, Foucault explains, "homosexuality began to speak in its own behalf" (101), often using the very same vocabulary by which it was rendered deviant by medical experts. In terms of more recent proliferations, Dan Savage's listeners adopt his terms in order to lay claim to the explanatory powers of sex: "I'm a GGG straight woman," someone declares in a message, for example: good, giving, and game. If sex talk produces new forms of regulation or subjugation, it also produces new schemas of knowledge (like being "GGG"). As another example, Dan coins the acronym NALT ("not all like that") so that religious people who renounce repression can self-identify in alliance with sex positivity.[5]

Above all, "sex" itself is produced as an ideal: as something desirable that we need to know and discover. And so, whether we are talking about the religious right or followers of Dan Savage, "it is this desirability that makes us think we are affirming the rights of our sex against all power, when in fact we are fastened to the deployment of sexuality that has lifted up from deep within us a sort of mirage in which we think we see ourselves reflected—the dark shimmer of sex" (Foucault 1978, 157). Sex becomes the key to unlocking who we really are (78)—*because* sex is transformed into discourse (21). We endeavour to tell the truth of sex, Foucault explains, because sex has become a problem that requires truth-seeking (56).

It may well be that we talk about sex more than anything else because we never run out of more truths to confess or more truths to pursue (33). As Dan puts it, you need to be able to say who you are by naming what you are looking for. "It really falls to you," he explains to one caller, "to say that's what you are" (episode 7). Sex is understood to be *the* access point for our own intelligibility (even if this point is actually imaginary), and therefore sex is something to say—to say exhaustively and to say compellingly (Foucault 1978, 155–6, 32). Sex must be put into words so that it can yield its revelatory insights: you discover who you are by reconstructing your desires or illuminating your obsessions. Dan exclaims in one episode, "You have to find out the way that your erotic imagination works!" (episode 54). And in turn, your obsessions will reveal the truth about who you are.

At the same time, sex becomes scientifically fraught through such confession, since its discoveries lead to predicaments that require expert help. ("You are the common denominator in these fucked-up relationships," Dan tells a caller in episode 105). This is why sex talk requires specialists, people who are paid to listen to everyone share the secrets of their sex and help eliminate the effects of repression (Foucault 1978, 7).[6] According to Foucault, the issue is *not* whether sex talk leads to truth about sex or even false statements that conceal the truth about sex. Rather, in scrutinizing this discourse and its effects, we need to draw out the "will to knowledge" that supports sex talk and also serves as its instrument (12).

One example of such will to knowledge is the medicalization of sexuality (41): sex is able to serve as the explanation for everything because its causation is understood in the empirical terms of science. Statistical research into the norms of sexual behaviour enables us to manage our erotic proclivities, as we learn what is normal and abnormal, effective and doomed to misfire. Dan often invokes the statistic, for example, that 75 per cent of women require external stimulation in order to have orgasms (episode 4). What Foucault wants us to notice about the "truth" that sex talk elicits is that it reflects a desire to manage and regulate sex (24). Experts supply us with a set of practices by which to make sex function as optimally as possible (practices by which to liberate ourselves so that we can be the best moderns we can be). Rather than presuming that vaginal penetration will yield orgasm, science tells women in this case to acquire the means for external stimulation: buying sex toys (the *Savage Lovecast* often advertises progressive sex toy stores) and never ever faking orgasms. Chastising women who do "fake" when they have sex with men, Dan explains, "A lot of boys are bad in bed because the women they've been sleeping with allow them to get away with it" (1998, 123).

As sex becomes an object of management, it becomes part of a whole machinery for "speechifying, analyzing, and investigating" (Foucault 1978, 32). You are not entitled to anything, Dan tells a listener sternly in episode 1. While this might seem to contradict the earlier claim that we all have the right to good sex, Dan is invoking a broader regime of modern knowledge that Foucault links, at the very end of *The History of Sexuality*, Volume 1, to bio-power (140–3). "Are you revolting?" Dan asks the caller. "What are you doing wrong?" You must be willing, he explains, to make some changes and make yourself attractive: do some sit ups, move out of your mom's house, and put down the video games. Through mechanisms

like the *Savage Lovecast*, power penetrates and controls everyday pleasures, permeating discourses "in order to reach the most tenuous and individual modes of behaviour" (11), including what we eat, how we exercise, and how we see ourselves.

The Resistance of Pleasure

And so there is another reason for subjecting sex talk to critique, besides the falsity of its repressive hypothesis and its wrongly universalizing claims that we noted above. If we examine the "immense verbosity" of sex talk (33), Dan Savage is emblematic of the techniques through which bio-power manages life. Such power, Foucault explains, "is situated at the level of life, the species, the race, and the large-scale phenomena of population" (137). When Dan invokes ideals of hygiene and underlines the importance of public health, he is participating in a modern form of eugenics. Like nineteenth- and twentieth-century eugenics, "biology" is invoked as a way to justify the policing and purification of bodies (54). Eugenics reflects pernicious assumptions about which lives should thrive and which should die out, often cutting this boundary along racist lines.[7] The kinds of policies that advance eugenics make horrifying interventions in the everyday lives and futures of those deemed less valuable by the state. It only "gets better," therefore, as Jasbir Puar points out, for those who participate in the liberal eugenics of upward mobility, gentrification, and other forms of lifestyle programming: on these terms, gay emancipation intensifies white supremacy (2011).

Resistance to such violence, however, can be *neither* a matter of saying say yes to sex (since this would reinforce the hypothesis that sex talk liberates us from repression) *nor a matter* of saying no to power (since this would reinforce the hypothesis that power is always repressive). Remember that "liberation" itself is an ideal produced by the relations of power in which sexuality is an especially dense transfer point (102). There is no "good sex" outside of power, in other words.

Are there practices of freedom that do not reinforce the "liberatory" progress narratives of sex talk? Foucault points out that there is in fact a plurality of resistances within the power network. If power is immanent, so too is resistance (95). Whereas we need to break away from the agency and revelatory effects of sex, he proposes that we look to bodies and pleasures as transformative resources of resistance (157). While the ramifications of this proposition are contested among Foucault scholars, Colin Koopman puts it like this: rather than looking to rebels (who are likely partaking of some form of the repressive hypothesis), let's think of "silent inventors

and steady experimentalists" (2012, 174), people who resist the deployment of sexuality through humble, hesitant, and exploratory practices. In other words, instead of looking to sex sages to provide us with examples that we can seek to emulate, let's discover pleasures that surprise us: pleasures that are playful, that expand our capacities for even more pleasure. "Pleasure, like power," Ladelle McWhorter explains, "is creative" (1999, 177).

We cannot remove ourselves from our own historical contexts. But we can seek ways to live differently, taking care of ourselves in ways that cultivate bodily pleasures and subvert the sexpert authority of sex talk. Instead of legitimating what is already known, Foucault explains, let us explore "how and to what extent it might be possible to think differently"—an exploration that begins by contextualizing knowledge-practices as historical and therefore contingent and mutable (Foucault 1990, 9) and that finds ways to cultivate power relations that are creative and pleasure-inducing.

Notes

1 Many of the quotations in this essay come from the *Savage Lovecast* podcast. I indicate the episode number in parentheses. While the quotations are verbatim, I have not included the ellipses that would indicate pauses in speech or asides, in the interest of readability. The other text that I cite frequently is Foucault's *History of Sexuality, Volume 1: An Introduction*, translated by Robert Hurley (New York: Vintage Books, 1978). I indicate it solely by page numbers.

2 At several public forums in fall 2011, trans activists glitter bombed Dan Savage in protest of

his use of transphobic language (Hill-Meyer 2011). In response to the glitter protests, Dan has shifted his vocabulary in ways that accommodate the critique. The following claim from one of his books, however, expresses a certain defensiveness at the heart of his discourse: "I'm all for direct questions and open debate—so long as those who claim to want it so badly don't invoke the 'politically correct' bogeyman every goddamned time you lose a round" (1998, 134).

3 See Robert Nichols (2012) for an incisive look at how queer liberation movements often

participate in the secularization of freedom and the resurrection of the repressive hypothesis.

4 As Jordan points out, "There is no ex-gay without gay" (2011, 151). The somewhat defunct ex-gay movement has recently shifted into the language of "not gay," as seen in the TLC reality show *My Husband's Not Gay*. In this show, Mormon husbands acknowledge same-sex attractions while rejecting the identity of "gay." Dan Savage, among organizations like GLAAD, calls the show dangerous and irresponsible (episode 430).

5 The NALT moniker has given rise to the NALT Christians Project, inspired by the It Gets Better campaign (notalllikethat.org).

6 According to Foucault, while confessional practices emerged out of monastic Catholicism, the rituals of confession began to function in the nineteenth century within the norms of science (65). In this way, sex became the *rational* and *scientific* explanation for everything because of the scientific experts (psychiatrists, sexologists, criminologists) who had the skills to decipher and draw out the healing powers of truth (67).

7 We recognize such lines today as racist, but Ladelle McWhorter explains that the very term *racist* emerged in the mid-twentieth century as a way to distance American eugenics practices from Nazi practices. In fact, these practices participated in the same regimes of bio-power (2009, 203).

Bibliography

Foucault, Michel. 1978. *The History of Sexuality, Volume 1: An Introduction*. Translated by Robert Hurley. New York: Vintage Books.

———. 1990. *The History of Sexuality, Volume 2: The Use of Pleasure*. Translated by Robert Hurley. New York: Vintage Books.

Grzanka, Patrick R., and Emily S. Mann. 2014. "Queer Youth Suicide and the Psychopolitics of 'It Gets Better.'" *Sexualities* 17 (4): 369–93.

Hill-Meyer, Tobi. 2011. "Dan Savage Glittered Again, Student Arrested." *The Bilerico Project*, November 14. www.bilerico.com/2011/11/dan_savage_glittered_again_student_arrested.php.

Jordan, Mark D. 2011. *Recruiting Young Love: How Christians Talk about Homosexuality*. Chicago: University of Chicago Press.

Koopman, Colin. 2012. *Genealogy as Critique: Foucault and the Problems of Modernity*. Bloomington: Indiana University Press.

McWhorter, Ladelle. 1999. *Bodies and Pleasures: Foucault and the Politics of Sexual Normalization*. Bloomington: Indiana University Press.

———. 2009. *Racism and Sexual Oppression in Anglo-America: A Geneaology*. Bloomington: Indiana University Press.

Nichols, James. 2015. "Dan Savage's Life to Serve as Basis for New ABC Sitcom." *Huffington Post*, January 27. www.huffingtonpost.com/2015/01/27/dan-savage-abc-sitcom_n_6555860.html.

Nichols, Robert. 2012. "Empire and the Dispositif of Queerness." *Foucault Studies* 14:41–60.

Puar, Jasbir K. 2011. "Coda: The Cost of Getting Better: Suicide, Sensation, Switchpoints." GLQ 18 (1): 149–58.

Savage, Dan. 1998. *Savage Love: Straight Answers from America's Most Popular Sex Columnist*. New York: Penguin Putnam.

———. 2006. "The Code of the Callboy" (Op-Ed.). *New York Times*, November 8. www.nytimes.com/2006/11/08/opinion/08savage.html?_r=0.

Savage, Dan, and Terry Miller, eds. *It Gets Better: Coming Out, Overcoming Bullying, and Creating a Life Worth Living*. New York: Dutton, 2011.

GRETA CRISTINA

How do we know when we are having sex? The answer to this question seems so obvious to most of us that it is hardly worth asking. In her article, Greta Cristina shows us that the answer is not quite as simple as we might have assumed. She does so by taking us through some of her own experiences that raised real questions for her about what actually constitutes sex. Must sex involve intercourse? Does mutual masturbation count as sex? Does solitary masturbation count as sex? Has sex taken place between two people when one or both of them do not have orgasm? Cristina's fun and funny article explores these questions. As you are reading her essay, think about your own view of what constitutes sex. Does her article challenge that view?

Are We Having Sex Now or What?

When I first started having sex with other people, I used to like to count them. I wanted to keep track of how many there had been. It was a source of some kind of pride, or identity anyway, to know how many people I'd had sex with in my lifetime. So, in my mind, Len was number one, Chris was number two, that slimy awful little heavy metal barbiturate addict whose name I can't remember was number three, Alan was number four, and so on. It got to the point where, when I'd start having sex with a new person for the first time, when he first entered my body (I was only having sex with men at the time), what would flash through my head wouldn't be "Oh baby baby your cock feels so good inside me," or "What the hell am I doing with this creep?" or "This is boring I wonder what's on TV." What flashed through my head was: "Seven!"

Doing this had some interesting results. I'd look for patterns in the numbers. I had a theory for a while that every fourth lover turned out to be really great in bed, and would ponder what the cosmic significance of this phenomenon might be. Sometimes I'd try to

determine what kind of person I was by how many people I'd had sex with. At 18, I'd had sex with ten different people; did that make me normal, repressed, a total slut, a free-spirited bohemian, or what? Not that I compared my numbers with anyone else's—I didn't. It was my own exclusive structure, a game I played in the privacy of my own head.

Then the numbers started getting a little larger, as numbers tend to do, and keeping track became more difficult. I'd remember that the last one was Seventeen and so this one must be Eighteen, but then I'd start having doubts about whether I'd been keeping score accurately or not. I'd lie awake at night thinking to myself, well, there was Brad, and there was that guy on my birthday, and there was David, and . . . no, wait, I forgot that guy I got drunk with at the social my first week at college . . . so that's seven, eight, nine . . . and by two in the morning I'd finally have it figured out. But there was always a nagging suspicion that maybe I'd missed someone, some dreadful tacky little scumball that I was trying to forget about having invited inside my body. And, as much as I maybe wanted to forget about the sleazy little scumball, I wanted more to get that number right.

It kept getting harder, though. I began to question what counted as sex and what didn't. There was that time with Gene, for instance. I was pissed off at my boyfriend David for cheating on me. It was a major crisis, and Gene and I were friends and he'd been trying to get at me for weeks and I hadn't exactly been discouraging him. So I went to see him that night to gripe about David. He was very sympathetic of course, and he gave me a backrub, and we talked and touched and confided and hugged, and then we started kissing, and then we snuggled up a little closer, and then we started fondling each other, you know, and then all heck broke loose, and we rolled around on the bed groping and rubbing and grabbing and smooching and pushing and pressing and squeezing. He never did actually get it in. He wanted to, and I wanted to too, but I had this thing about being faithful to my boyfriend, so I kept saying, "No you can't do that," "Yes that feels so good," "No wait that's too much," "Yes yes don't stop," "No stop that's enough." We never even got our clothes off. Jesus Christ, though, it was some night. One of the best, really. But for a long time I didn't count it as one of the times I'd had sex. He never got inside, so it didn't count.

Later, months and years later, when I lay awake at night putting my list together, I'd start to wonder: Why doesn't Gene count? Does he not count because he never got inside? Or does he not count because I had to preserve my moral edge over David, my status as the patient, ever-faithful, cheated-on, martyred girlfriend, and if what I did with Gene counts, then I don't get to feel wounded and superior?

Years later, I did end up fucking Gene and I felt a profound relief because, at last, he definitely had a number, and I knew for sure that he did in fact count.

Then I started having sex with women, and boy howdy, did *that* ever shoot holes in the system. I'd always made my list of sex partners by defining sex as penile-vaginal intercourse. You know, fucking. It's a pretty simple distinction, a straightforward binary system. Did it go in or didn't it? Yes or no? One or zero? On or off? Granted, it's a pretty arbitrary definition; but it's the customary one, with an ancient and respected tradition behind it, and when I was just screwing men, there was no really compelling reason to question it.

But with women . . . Well, first of all there's no penis, so right from the start the tracking system is defective. And then, there are so many ways women can have sex with each other, touching and licking and grinding and fingering and fisting—with dildos or vibrators or vegetables or whatever happens to be lying around the house, or with nothing at all except human bodies. Of course, that's true with sex between women and men as well. But between women, no one method has a centuries-old tradition of being the one that counts. Even when we do fuck each other there's no dick, so you don't get that feeling of This Is What's Important We Are Now Having Sex, objectively speaking, and all that other stuff is just foreplay or afterplay. So when I started having sex with women, the binary system had to go, in favour of a more inclusive definition.

Which meant, of course, that my list of how many people I'd had sex with was completely trashed. In order to maintain it I'd have had to go back and reconstruct the whole thing and include all those people I'd necked with and gone down on and dry-humped and played touchy-feely games with. Even the question of who filled the all-important Number One slot, something I'd never had any doubts about before, would have to be re-evaluated. By this time I'd kind of lost interest in the list any-way. Reconstructing it would be more trouble than it was worth. But the crucial question remained: What counts as having sex with someone?

It was important for me to know. I mean, you have to know what qualifies as sex, be-cause when you have sex with someone your relationship changes. Right? Right? It's not that sex itself has to change things all that much. But knowing you've had sex, being conscious of a sexual connection, standing around making polite conversation with someone thinking to yourself, "I've had sex with this person," that's what always changes things. Or so I believed. And if having sex with a friend can confuse or change the friendship, think of how bizarre things can get when you're not sure whether you've had sex with them or not.

The problem was, as I kept doing more dif-ferent kinds of sexual things, the line between Sex and Not-Sex kept getting more hazy and indistinct. As I brought more into my sex-ual experience, things were showing up on the dividing line demanding my attention. It wasn't just that the territory I labelled "sex" was expanding. The line itself had swollen, di-lated, been transformed into a vast grey region. It had become less like a border and more like a demilitarized zone.

Which is a strange place to live. Not a bad place, you understand, just strange. It feels like juggling, or watchmaking, or playing the piano—anything that demands complete con-centrated awareness and attention. It feels like cognitive dissonance, only pleasant. It feels like waking up from a very compelling and realistic bad dream. It feels the way you feel when you realize that everything you know is wrong, and a bloody good thing too, 'cuz it was painful and stupid and really fucked you up.

But for me, living in a question naturally leads to searching for an answer. I can't simply shrug, throw up my hands, and say, "Damned if I know." I have to explore the unknown fron-tiers, even if I don't bring back any secret treas-ure. So even if it's incomplete or provisional, I do want to find some sort of definition of what is and isn't sex.

I know when I'm feeling sexual. I'm feeling sexual if my pussy's wet, my nipples are hard, my palms are clammy, my brain is fogged, my skin is tingly and super-sensitive, my butt mus-cles clench, my heartbeat speeds up, I have an orgasm (that's the real giveaway), and so on. But feeling sexual with someone isn't the same as having sex with them. Good Lord, if I called it sex every time I was attracted to someone who returned the favour I'd be even more bewil-dered than I am now. Even being sexual with someone isn't the same as having sex with them. I've danced and flirted with too many people, given and received too many sexy would-be-seductive backrubs, to believe otherwise.

I have friends who say if you thought of it as sex when you were doing it, then it was. That's an interesting idea. It's certainly helped me construct a coherent sexual history with-out being a revisionist swine and redefining my past according to current definitions. But it really just begs the question. It's fine to say that sex is whatever I think it is; but then what do I think it is? What if, when I was doing it, I was wondering whether it counted?

Perhaps having sex with someone is the conscious, consenting, mutually acknow-ledged pursuit of shared sexual pleasure. Not a bad definition. If you are turning each other on and you say so and you keep doing it, then it's sex. It's broad enough to encompass a lot of sexual behaviour beyond genital contact/ orgasm; it's distinct enough to not include every instance of sexual awareness or arousal; and it contains the elements I feel are vital—acknowledgement, consent, reciprocity, and the pursuit of pleasure. But what about the situation where one person consents to sex without really enjoying it? Lots of people (myself included) have had sexual interactions that we didn't find satisfying or didn't really want, and unless they were actually forced on us against our will, I think most of us would still classify them as sex.

Maybe if both of you (or all of you) think of it as sex, then it's sex whether you're having fun or not. That clears up the problem of sex that's consented to but not wished for or enjoyed. Unfortunately, it begs the question again, only worse: now you have to mesh different people's vague and inarticulate notions of what is and isn't sex and find the place where they overlap. Too messy.

How about sex as the conscious, consenting, mutually acknowledged pursuit of sexual pleasure of at least one of the people involved. That's better. It has all the key components, and it includes the situation where one of the people involved is doing it for a reason other than sexual pleasure—status, reassurance, money, the satisfaction and pleasure of someone they love, etc. But what if neither of you is enjoying it, if you're both doing it because you think the other one wants to? Ugh.

I'm having a bit of trouble here. Even the conventional standby—sex equals intercourse—has a serious flaw; it includes rape, which is something I emphatically refuse to accept. As far as I'm concerned, if there's no consent, it ain't sex. But I feel that's about the only place in this whole quagmire where I have a grip. The longer I think about the subject, the more questions I come up with. At what point in an encounter does it become sexual?

If an interaction that begins nonsexually turns into sex, was it sex all along? What about sex with someone who's asleep? Can you have a situation where one person is having sex and the other isn't? It seems that no matter what definition I come up with, I can think of some real-life experience that calls it into question.

For instance: A couple of years ago, I attended (well, hosted) an all-girl sex party. Out of the twelve other women there, there were only a few with whom I got seriously physically nasty. The rest I kissed or hugged or talked dirty with or just smiled at, or watched while they did seriously physically nasty things with each other. If we'd been alone, I'd probably say that what I'd done with most of the women there didn't count as having sex. But the experience, which was hot and sweet and silly and very special, had been created by all of us, and although I only really got down with a few, I felt that I'd been sexual with all of the women there. Now, whenever I meet one of the women from that party, I always ask myself: Have we had sex?

For instance: When I was first experimenting with sadomasochism, I got together with a really hot woman. We were negotiating about what we were going to do, what would and wouldn't be ok, and she said she wasn't sure she wanted to have sex. Now we'd been explicitly planning all kinds of fun and games—spanking, bondage, obedience—which I strongly identified as sexual activity. In her mind, though, "sex" meant direct genital contact, and she didn't necessarily want to do that with me. Playing with her turned out to be a tremendously erotic experience, arousing and stimulating and almost unbearably satisfying. But we spent the whole night without even touching each other's genitals. And the fact that our definitions were so different made me wonder: Was it sex?

For instance: I worked for a few months as a nude dancer at a peep show. In case you've never been to a peep show, it works like this: the customer goes into this tiny dingy black box, kind of like a phone booth, and they put in quarters, and a metal plate goes up, and they look through a window at a little room/stage where naked women are dancing. One time, a guy came into one of the booths and started watching me and masturbating. I came over and squatted in front of him and started masturbating as well, and we grinned at each other and watched each other and masturbated, and we both had a fabulous time.

(I couldn't believe I was being paid to masturbate—tough job, but somebody has to do it . . .). After he left, I thought to myself: Did we just have sex?

I mean, if it had been someone I knew, and if there had been no glass and no quarters, there'd be no question in my mind. Sitting two feet apart from someone, watching each other masturbate? Yup, I'd call that sex all right. But this was different, because it was a stranger, and because of the glass, and because of the quarters. Was it sex?

I still don't have an answer.

Discussion

Why do we talk about sex as much as we do? How does talk about sex affect our views of sex? Foucault thinks that our discourse about sex, framed as it is as a response to repression, is itself a form of power. The power of this discourse is seen in the way that it shapes our attitudes towards sex. In past times, the penitent confessed his sexual deeds or his impure thoughts. Today, we confess our sins against sex itself, over and over in the form of saying that it has been repressed. But does sex talk need to take this confessional form?

How is talk about sex related to our sexual identity? Our sexual identity is shaped to a great extent by the way that we talk about our sexual lives just as our personal identity is shaped to a great extent by the way that we talk about our lives in general. The stories that we tell about ourselves and our relations to others, as well as the stories that they tell about us, provide the content for our identity. Our identity is also shaped by the larger stories that are active in our culture, such as the idea that the individual is the primary category for understanding society or the story that arises from the repressive hypothesis. Our sexual identity then emerges and evolves through a kind of dialogue with others and an engagement with the sexual concepts at our disposal in a given society. We learn about this identity through our interactions with others as they see a side of our sexuality that we do not. We learn about ourselves through our flirtations at the dance club, our romantic dates, or our late night conversations with our roommates, and even through our interactions and reactions in classroom discussions. Sometimes we discover that we are attracted to a person who expresses him or herself with conviction or with irony in one of our classes. But we are shaped, not only by interactions with other specific people, but also by the discourse in which we participate. It is this discourse that provides us with the concepts by which we understand ourselves. It is this discourse that has the power to shape our sexual identity by providing us with a language to characterize that identity (sexually liberated, prudish, stylish, etc.).

Do modern sexperts such as Dan Savage provide us with liberation from repressive attitudes about sex? Does talk about sex itself actually liberate us in any way? Is it possible that all of our talk about sex, including the emphasis on sexual openness in mainstream television shows and movies, is itself part of our participation in the speaker's benefit, a participation that re-enforces a certain conformist view of sexuality? Is Foucault's calling into question of the idea that we have emerged out of a sexually repressive period in the West exaggerated? Is it not true that institutions such as the Church have had a repressive influence on our sexuality that has been quite influential at least until quite recently? Seen in this light, isn't the kind of liberation of sexual attitudes advocated by Dan Savage a healthy thing?

Greta Cristina talks about sex in a way that is not primarily concerned with the issue of liberation but that rather *assumes* it. Her quest for a satisfactory definition of sex emerges out of an attitude that might be characterized as post-Foucauldian in the sense that she creatively explores it as a question for herself rather than as one that is set against the background of the repressive hypothesis. "But for me, living in a question naturally leads to searching for an answer," she tells us. This "living in a question" has been the impetus for philosophy from Socrates to Camus and beyond. The most important philosophical questions arise, not from idle speculation or from solitary contemplation, but from living our lives and confronting life's real problems. Cristina's moment of existential crisis took place in the context of the seemingly banal practice of keeping count of her sexual experiences. How many people had she had sex with? This had become her primary way of experiencing sex. When questions arose about the soundness or legitimacy of her criterion for what counted as sex, she could no longer continue in this way. It is difficult to count sexual experiences when you are not sure whether or not an experience *counts* as sex.

Think about your own experiences. Do you think of having sex as only being limited to experiences of intercourse? Wouldn't this mean that sexual experiences between two women wouldn't count as instances of "having sex"? Sometimes religious individuals concerned with maintaining their virginity will engage in sexual activity that stops short of vaginal penetration. Are such individuals fooling themselves by adhering to the letter of the law concerning sexual abstinence? What about masturbation? Does this count as sex? Or does sex require physical contact with another person? If the latter, does this mean that two people who are mutually masturbating in each other's presence are not having sex? If they are having sex, do we want to say that two people who are mutually masturbating over Skype, for instance, are having sex?

Cristina gives us some good reasons to consider certain acts that do not involve heterosexual intercourse as acts of sex. It is only by holding this traditional view of sex as the paradigm and by considering it as that which is important that we come to deny other experiences the status of "having sex." Of course, Cristina, in true philosophical fashion, leave us with as many questions as answers when it comes sex, but she uncovers a number of our common assumptions about sex, and by clearing up some of the issues, she points us in the direction of answering these questions for ourselves. Many of these questions can only be tackled once we have drawn a line between what it means to have *sexual experiences* and what it means to have *sex*. What do you think constitutes having sex? Do you have your own criterion or set of criteria? After reading Greta Cristina's article, have you revised your own view of what constitutes having sex?

Suggestions for Further Reading

Michel Foucault, *The History of Sexuality, Volume 2: The Use of Pleasure*. Translated by Robert Hurley (New York: Vintage Books, 1990).

Patrick R. Grzanka and Emily S. Mann, "Queer Youth Suicide and the Psychopolitics of 'It Gets Better,'" *Sexualities* 17, no. 4 (2014): 369–93.

Dan Savage, *Savage Love: Straight Answers from America's Most Popular Sex Columnist* (New York: Penguin Putnam, 1998).

Dan Savage and Terry Miller, eds. *It Gets Better: Coming Out, Overcoming Bullying, and Creating a Life Worth Living* (New York: Dutton, 2011).

Section II Objectification and Sexual Identity

Chapter Five
Sexual Objectification

Introduction

Given the fact that we exist as creatures whose embodied nature means that we are objects in the world, some sort of objectification seems unavoidable. But what sort and in what context? The famous modern philosopher Immanuel Kant (1724–1804) argues that, outside of the context of marriage, sex itself is wrong because one turns the person into an *object* or a *thing* by making him or her a mere means to an end—namely, the satisfaction of one's own sexual inclination. "As soon as the person is possessed [sexually], and the appetite sated, they are thrown away, as one throws away a lemon after sucking the juice from it." Indeed! Kant's restriction applies not only to sex for pay, as in the case of prostitution, but also to cases where two people agree to have sex for the sake of mutual pleasure. Even in the latter cases, two people are using each other as mere means and not as ends. In marriage alone is there a mutual giving of the right to each other's bodies: "*Matrimonium* signifies a contract between two persons, in which they mutually accord equal rights to one another, and submit to the condition that each transfers his whole person entirely to the other, so that each has a complete right to the other's whole person."

IMMANUEL KANT

Of Duties to the Body in Regard to the Sexual Impulse

Man has an impulse directed to others, not so that he may enjoy their works and circumstances, but immediately to others as objects of his enjoyment. He has, indeed, no inclination to enjoy the flesh of another, and where that occurs, it is more a manner of warlike vengeance than an inclination; but there remains in him an inclination that may be called appetite, and is directed to enjoyment of the other. This is the sexual impulse. Man can certainly enjoy the other as an instrument for his service; he can utilize the others' hands or feet to serve him, though by the latter's free choice. But we never find that a human being can be the object of another's enjoyment, save through the sexual impulse. There is a sort of sense underlying this, which may be called the sixth sense, whereby one human being is pleasing to the appetite of another. We say that somebody loves a person, insofar as he is inclined to them. If we consider this love as human affection, if he loves this person from true human affection, he must make no distinction in regard to them. This person may be young or old, yet he may still love them from true human affection. But if he loves them merely from sexual inclination, it cannot be love; it is appetite. Love, as human affection, is the love that wishes well, is amicably disposed, promotes the happiness of others and rejoices in it. But now it is plain that those who merely have sexual inclination love the person from none of the foregoing motives of true human affection, are quite unconcerned for their happiness, and will even plunge them into the greatest unhappiness, simply to satisfy their own inclination and appetite. In loving from sexual inclination, they make the person into an object of their appetite. As soon as the person is possessed, and the appetite sated, they are thrown away, as one throws away a lemon after sucking the juice from it. The sexual impulse can admittedly be combined with human affection, and then it also carries with it the aims of the latter, but if it is taken in and by itself, it is nothing more than appetite. But, so considered, there lies in this inclination a degradation of man; for as soon as anyone becomes an object of another's appetite, all motives of moral relationship fall away; as object of the other's appetite, that person is

in fact a thing, whereby the other's appetite is sated, and can be misused as such a thing by anybody. There is no case where a human being would already be determined by nature to be the object of another's enjoyment, save this, of which sexual inclination is the basis. This is the reason why we are ashamed of possessing such an impulse, and why all strict moralists, and those who wish to be taken for saints, have sought to repress and dispense with it. To be sure, a person who did not have this impulse would be an imperfect individual, in that one would have to believe that he lacked the necessary organs, which would thus be an imperfection on his part, as a human being; yet such has been the pretension, and people have sought to refrain from this inclination, because it debases man. Since the sexual impulse is not an inclination that one human has for another, *qua* human, but an inclination for their sex, it is therefore a *principium* of the debasement of humanity, a source for the preference of one sex over the other, and the dishonouring of that sex by satisfying the inclination. The desire of a man for a woman is not directed to her as a human being; on the contrary, the woman's humanity is of no concern to him, and the only object of his desire is her sex.

So humanity here is set aside. The consequence is, that any man or woman will endeavour to lend attraction, not to their humanity, but to their sex, and to direct all actions and desires entirely towards it. If this is the case, humanity will be sacrificed to sex. So if a man wishes to satisfy his inclination, and a woman hers, they each attract the other's inclination to themselves, and both urges impinge on one another, and are directed, not to humanity at all, but to sex, and each partner dishonours the humanity of the other. Thus humanity becomes an instrument for satisfying desires and inclinations; but by this it is dishonoured and put on a par with animal nature. So the sexual impulse puts humanity in peril of being equated with animality.

Now since man, after all, possesses this impulse by nature, the question arises: To what extent is anyone entitled to make use of their sexual impulse, without impairing their humanity? How far can a person allow another person of the opposite sex to satisfy his or her inclination upon them? Can people sell or hire themselves out, or by any kind of contract allow use to be made of their *facultales sexuales?*[1] All philosophers censure this inclination only for its pernicious effects, and the ruin it brings, partly to the body, and partly to the general welfare, and see nothing reprehensible in the act as such; but if this were so, if there were no inner abhorrency and damage to morality in employing the inclination, then anyone who could simply obviate these ill-effects might make use of his impulse in any way conceivable; for what is forbidden only by the rule of prudence is forbidden only in a conditional sense, and in that case the act is good in itself, and harmful only under particular circumstances. Yet here there is something contemptible in the act itself, which runs counter to morality. Hence conditions must be possible, under which alone the use of the *facultales sexuales* is compatible with morality. There must be a ground that restricts our freedom in regard to the use of our inclination, so that it conforms to morality. We shall be looking for these conditions, and this ground. Man cannot dispose over himself, because he is not a thing. He is not his own property—that would be a contradiction; for so far as he is a person, he is a subject, who can have ownership of other things. But now were he something owned by himself, he would be

a thing over which he can have ownership. He is, however, a person, who is not property, so he cannot be a thing such as he might own; for it is impossible, of course, to be at once a thing and a person, a proprietor and a property at the same time.

Hence a man cannot dispose over himself; he is not entitled to sell a tooth, or any of his members. But now if a person allows himself to be used, for profit, as an object to satisfy the sexual impulse of another, if he makes himself the object of another's desire, then he is disposing over himself, as if over a thing, and thereby makes himself into a thing by which the other satisfies his appetite, just as his hunger is satisfied on a roast of pork. Now since the other's impulse is directed to sex and not to humanity, it is obvious that the person is in part surrendering his humanity, and is thereby at risk in regard to the ends of morality.

Human beings have no right, therefore, to hand themselves over for profit, as things for another's use in satisfying the sexual impulse; for in that case their humanity is in danger of being used by anyone as a thing, an instrument for the satisfaction of inclination. This method of satisfying the sexual urge is *vaga libido,*[2] in which the other's impulse is satisfied for profit; it can be carried on by both sexes. Nothing is more vile than to take money for yielding to another so that his inclination may be satisfied and to let one's own person out for hire. The moral ground for so holding is that man is not his own property, and cannot do as he pleases with his body; for since the body belongs to the self, it constitutes, in conjunction with that, a person; but now one cannot make one's person a thing, though this is what happens in *vaga libido.* Hence this method of satisfying the sexual impulse is not sanctioned by morality.

Is it not permitted, though, to satisfy one's impulse by the second method, namely, *concubinatus*?[3] Where the persons mutually satisfy their desires, and have no thought of monetary gain, the one merely serving to gratify the inclination of the other? There seems to be nothing at all repugnant in this; yet one condition makes even this case impermissible. Concubinage occurs when a person surrenders to the other merely to satisfy inclination, but retains freedom and rights in regard to other circumstances affecting their person, viz., the concern for happiness and future well-being. But those who give themselves to another person, merely to satisfy inclination, still continue to let their person be used as a thing; for the impulse is still always directed to sex merely, and not to humanity. Now it is evident that if someone concedes a part of himself to the other, he concedes himself entirely. It is not possible to dispose over a part of oneself, for such a part belongs to the whole. Yet by concubinage I have no right to the whole person, but only to one part of it, namely the *organa sexualia*.[4] Concubinage presupposes a *pactum*, but this *pactum sexuale*[5] relates only to enjoyment of one part of the person, not to the total state thereof. It is a contract, to be sure, but an unequal one, in which the rights of the two parts are not the same. Yet if, in concubinage, I enjoy one part of the other, I thereby enjoy the whole person. Now since, under the terms of concubinage, I have no right to that whole, but only to a part of it, it follows that I am treating the whole person as a thing; hence this method of satisfying one's inclination is likewise impermissible on moral grounds.

The sole condition, under which there is freedom to make use of one's sexual impulse, is based upon the right to dispose over the whole person. This right to dispose over the other's whole person relates to the total state of happiness, and to all circumstances bearing upon that person. But this right that I have, so to dispose, and thus also to employ the *organa sexualia* to satisfy the sexual impulse—how do I obtain it? In that I give the other person precisely such a right over the whole person, and this happens only in marriage. *Matrimonium* signifies a contract between two persons, in which they mutually accord equal rights to one another, and submit to the condition that each transfers his whole person entirely to the other, so that each has a complete right to the other's whole person. It is now discernible through reason, how a *commercium sexuale*[6] may be possible without debasement of humanity or violation of morality. Marriage is thus the sole condition for making use of one's sexual impulse. If a person now dedicates himself to the other, he dedicates not only his sex, but his whole person; the two things are inseparable. If only one partner yields to the other his person, his good or ill fortune, and all his circumstances, to have right over them, and does not receive in turn a corresponding identical right over the person of the other, then there is an inequality here. But if I hand over my whole person to the other, and thereby obtain the person of the other in place of it, I get myself back again, and have thereby regained possession of myself; for I have given myself to be the other's property, but am in turn taking the other as my property, and thereby regain myself, for I gain the person to whom I gave myself as property. The two persons thus constitute a unity of will. Neither will be subject to happiness or misfortune, joy or displeasure, without the other taking a share in it. So the sexual impulse creates a union among persons, and only within this union is the use of it possible. This condition upon utilizing the sexual impulse, which is possible only in marriage, is a moral one. Were this to be worked out further, and in a more systematic way, it would also have to follow that nobody, even in *matrimonium*, can have two wives; for otherwise each wife would have half a husband, since she has given herself totally to him, and thus has a total right to his person as well. There are therefore moral grounds that tell against *vagae libidines*; grounds that tell against concubinage; and grounds that tell against polygamy in *matrimonium*; so in the latter we only have monogamy. Under this condition alone may I employ the *facultas sexualis*. We can say no more on the subject at present.

Notes

1 sexual capacities
2 indiscriminate lust
3 concubinage

4 sexual organs
5 sexual contract
6 sexual intercourse

MARTHA C. NUSSBAUM

What Kant found morally objectionable about sex outside of marriage was that it served only to satisfy the sexual impulse and in so doing, it turned one's sexual partner into an object or a thing rather than a human being. Much of the feminist discussion of objectification in the second half of the twentieth century focused specifically on the problem of the objectification of women in a male-dominated society. As with Kant, many feminist thinkers found the objectification of persons to be morally objectionable, but, unlike Kant, these thinkers noted that the tendency to do so was divided disproportionately between men and women. There was a greater tendency to sexually objectify women. This sexual objectification was (and still is) pervasive in Western culture, having been greatly enabled by our constantly evolving means of mass media.

In her article, Martha Nussbaum presents a nuanced exploration of the different forms that objectification takes and examines the moral ramifications of these differences. In certain circumstances, she tells us, objectification is morally problematic, but in others, certain types of objectification may be a necessary part of good sex. She lists seven different aspects of objectification and argues that context is the crucial factor in determining whether or not a particular instance of objectification is morally justified. Treating people instrumentally outside of a context of regard for their humanity is always morally problematic. But objectifying someone in certain limited ways within the context of a relationship of relative social equality or within the framework of a loving equal relationship may sometimes be appropriate.

Objectification

Sexual objectification is a familiar concept. Once a relatively technical term in feminist theory, associated in particular with the work of Catharine MacKinnon and Andrea Dworkin, the word *objectification* has by now passed into many people's daily lives. It is common to hear it used to criticize advertisements, films, and other representations, and also to express skepticism about the attitudes and intentions of one person to another, or of oneself to someone else. Generally it is used as a pejorative term, connoting a way of speaking, thinking, and acting that the speaker finds morally or socially objectionable, usually, though not always, in the sexual realm . . . .

But the term *objectification* can also be used, somewhat confusingly, in a more positive spirit. Indeed, one can find both of these apparently conflicting uses in the writings of some feminist authors: for example, legal theorist Cass Sunstein, who has been generally supportive of MacKinnon's critique of sexuality. Throughout his earlier writings on pornography, Sunstein speaks of the treatment of women as objects for the use and control of men as the central thing that is bad in pornographic representation.[1] On the other hand, in a mostly negative review of a recent book by Nadine Strossen defending pornography,[2] Sunstein writes the following:

> People's imaginations are unruly . . . It may be possible to argue, as some people do, that objectification and a form of use are substantial parts of sexual life, or wonderful parts of sexual life, or ineradicable parts of sexual life. Within a context of equality, respect, and consent, objectification—not at all an easy concept to define—may not be so troublesome.[3]

To be sure, Sunstein expresses himself very cautiously, speaking only of an argument that might be made and not indicating his own support for such an argument. Nonetheless, to MacKinnon and Dworkin, who have typically represented opposition to objectification as at the heart of feminism, this paragraph might well seem puzzling. They might well wish to ask: What does Sunstein wish to defend? Why should "objectification and a form of use" ever be seen as "wonderful" or even as "ineradicable" parts of sexual life? Wouldn't it always be bad to use a "someone" as a "something"? And why should we suppose that it is at all possible to combine objectification with "equality, respect, and consent"? Isn't this precisely the combination we have shown to be impossible?

My hunch, which I shall pursue, is that such confusions can arise because we have not clarified the concept of objectification to ourselves, and that once we do so we will find out that it is not only a slippery, but also a multiple, concept. Indeed, I shall argue that there are at least seven distinct ways of behaving introduced by the term, none of which implies any of the others, though there are many complex connections among them. Under some specifications, objectification, I shall argue, is always morally problematic. Under other specifications, objectification has features that may be either good or bad, depending upon the overall context. (Sunstein was certainly right to emphasize the importance of context, and I shall dwell on that issue.) Some features of objectification, furthermore, I shall argue, may in fact in some circumstances, as Sunstein suggests, be either necessary or even wonderful features of sexual life. Seeing this will require, among other things, seeing how the allegedly impossible combination between (a form of) objectification and "equality, respect, and consent" might after all be possible. . . .

Now we need to begin the analysis. I suggest that in all cases of objectification what is at issue is a question of treating one thing as another: One is treating *as an object* what is really not an object, what is, in fact, a human being. . . . We need to ask what is involved in the idea of treating *as an object*. I suggest that at least the following seven notions are involved in that idea:

1. *Instrumentality*: The objectifier treats the object as a tool of his or her purposes.
2. *Denial of autonomy*: The objectifier treats the object as lacking in autonomy and self-determination.
3. *Inertness*: The objectifier treats the object as lacking in agency, and perhaps also in activity.
4. *Fungibility*: The objectifier treats the object as interchangeable (a) with other objects of the same type, and/or (b) with objects of other types.
5. *Violability*: The objectifier treats the object as lacking in boundary-integrity, as something that it is permissible to break up, smash, break into.
6. *Ownership*: The objectifier treats the object as something that is owned by another, can be bought or sold, etc.
7. *Denial of subjectivity*: The objectifier treats the object as something whose experience and feelings (if any) need not be taken into account.

. . . Thinking for a bit about our familiar ways of treating things will help us to see that these seven features are commonly present, and distinct from one another. Most inanimate objects are standardly regarded as tools of our purposes, though some are regarded as worthy of respect for their beauty, or age, or naturalness. Most inanimate objects are treated as lacking autonomy, though at times we do regard some objects in nature, or even some machines, as having a life of their own. Many objects are inert and/or passive, though not by any means all. Many are fungible with other objects of a similar sort (one ballpoint pen with another), and also, at times, with objects of a different sort (a pen with a word processor), though many, of course, are not. Some objects are viewed as "violable"[4] or lacking in boundary-integrity, though certainly not all: we will allow a child to break and destroy relatively few things in the house. Many objects are owned, and are treated as such, though many again are not. (It is interesting that the unowned among the inanimate objects—parts of nature for the most part—are also likely to be the ones to which we especially often attribute a kind of autonomy and an intrinsic worth.) Finally, most objects are treated as entities whose experiences and feelings need not be taken into account, though at times we are urged to think differently about parts of the natural environment, whether with illicit anthropomorphizing or not I shall not determine here. In any case, we can see on the list a cluster of familiar attitudes to things, all of which seem to play a role in the feminist account of the objectification of persons. What objectification is, is to treat a human being in one or more of these ways.

Should we say that each is a sufficient condition for the objectification of persons? Or do we need some cluster of the features, in order to have a sufficient condition? I prefer not to answer this question, since I believe that use is too unclear. On the whole, it seems to me that "objectification" is a relatively loose cluster-term, for whose application we sometimes treat any one of these features as sufficient, though more often a plurality of features is present when the term is applied.

How are the features connected? It will be helpful to turn, first, to two examples from the thing-world: a ballpoint pen, and a Monet painting. The way in which a ballpoint pen is an object involves, it would seem, all the items on this list, with the possible exception of violability. That is, it might be thought inappropriate or at least wasteful to break up ballpoint pens, but I don't think that worry would rise to great moral heights. Certainly it seems that to treat the pen as a tool, as non-autonomous, as inert, as fungible (with other pens and at times with other instruments or machines), as owned, and as lacking in subjectivity—all this is exactly the standard and appropriate way to treat it. The painting, on the other hand, is certainly non-autonomous, owned, inert (though not passive), and lacking in subjectivity; it is definitely not fungible, either with other paintings or, except in the limited sense of being bought and sold, which doesn't imply thoroughgoing fungibility, with anything else either; its boundaries are precious, and there is a real question whether it is simply a tool for the purposes of those who use and enjoy it. . . .

We see from the case of the painting that lack of autonomy does not necessarily imply instrumentality, though treating as instrumental may well imply treating as non-autonomous; the fact that most objects are inert should not conceal from us, for our later purposes, the fact that inertness is not a necessary condition of either lack of autonomy or instrumentality. . . .

In fact, what we are discovering is that autonomy is in a certain sense the most exigent of the notions on our list. It seems difficult if

not impossible to imagine a case in which an inanimate object is treated as autonomous, though we can certainly imagine exceptions to all the others. . . .

On the other hand, there is one way in which *instrumentality* seems to be the most morally exigent notion. We can think of many cases in which it is permissible to treat a person or thing as non-autonomous (the Monet painting, one's pets, one's small children), and yet inappropriate to treat the object merely or primarily as a tool of our own purposes. . . .

Notice, however, that instrumentalization does not seem to be problematic in all contexts. If I am lying around with my lover on the bed, and use his stomach as a pillow[5] there seems to be nothing at all baneful about this, provided that I do so with his consent (or, if he is asleep, with a reasonable belief that he would not mind), and without causing him pain, provided, as well, that I do so in the context of a relationship in which he is generally treated as more than a pillow.[6] This suggests that what is problematic is not instrumentalization per se, but treating someone primarily or merely as an instrument. The overall context of the relationship thus becomes fundamental, and I shall return to it.

. . . We must observe one fundamental point: In the matter of objectification, context is everything. . . .

This can easily be seen if we consider a simple example. W, a woman, is going out of town for an important interview. M, an acquaintance, says to her, "You don't really need to go. You can just send them some pictures." If M is not a close friend of W, this is almost certain to be an offensively objectifying remark. It reduces W to her bodily (and facial) parts, suggesting, in the process, that her professional accomplishments and other personal attributes do not count.

The remark certainly seems to slight W's autonomy; it treats her as an inert object, appropriately represented by a photograph; it may suggest some limited sort of fungibility. It may also, depending on the context, suggest instrumentalization: W is being treated as an object for the enjoyment of the male gaze. Suppose, now, M is W's lover, and he says this to her in bed. This changes things, but we really don't know how, because we don't know enough. We don't know what the interview is for (a modelling job? a professorship?). And we don't know enough about the people. If M standardly belittles her accomplishments, the remark is a good deal worse than the same remark made by a stranger, and more deeply suggestive of instrumentalization. If, on the other hand, there is a deeply understood mutual respect between them, and he is simply finding a way of telling her how attractive she is, and perhaps of telling her that he doesn't want her to leave town, then things become rather different. It may still be a risky thing to say, far more risky than the very same thing said by W to M, given the social history that colours all such relationships. Still, there is the sense that the remark is not reductive—that instead of taking away from W, the compliment to her appearance may have added something. (Much depends on tone of voice, gesture, sense of humour.) Consider, finally, the same remark made to W by a close friend. W knows that this friend respects her accomplishments, and has great confidence in his attitude toward her in all respects pertinent to friendship; but she wishes he would notice her body once in a while. In this case, the objectifying remark may come as a pleasant surprise to W, a joke embodying a welcome compliment. Though we still need to know more about what the interview is all about, and how it is related to W's capacities

(and though we still should reflect about the fact that it is extremely unlikely, given the way our society currently is, that such a remark will ever be made by W to M), it may well seem to her as if the remark has added something without taking anything away. . . .

It is worth noting that Lawrentian objectification is frequently connected with a certain type of reduction of persons to their bodily parts, and the attribution of a certain sort of independent agency to the bodily parts. Consider this scene from *Lady Chatterley*:

"Let me see you!"

He dropped the shirt and stood still, looking towards her. The sun through the low window sent a beam that lit up his thighs and slim belly, and the erect phallus rising darkish and hot-looking from the little cloud of vivid gold-red hair. She was startled and afraid.

"How strange!" she said slowly. "How strange he stands there! So big! and so dark and cocksure! Is he like that?"

The man looked down the front of his slender white body, and laughed. Between the slim breasts the hair was dark, almost black. But at the root of the belly, where the phallus rose thick and arching, it was gold-red, vivid in a little cloud.

"So proud!" she murmured, uneasy. "And so lordly! Now I know why men are so overbearing. But he's lovely, really, like another being! A bit terrifying! But lovely really! And he comes to me—" She caught her lower lip between her teeth, in fear and excitement.

The man looked down in silence at his tense phallus, that did not change. . . . "Cunt, that's what tha'rt after. Tell lady Jane tha' wants cunt. John Thomas, an' th' cunt o' lady Jane!—"

"Oh, don't tease him," said Connie, crawling on her knees on the bed towards him and putting her arms round his white slender loins, and drawing him to her so that her hanging swinging breasts touched the top of the stirring erect phallus, and caught the drop of moisture. She held the man fast. . . .

The intense focusing of attention on the bodily parts seems an addition, rather than a subtraction, and the scene of passion, which is fraught for Constance with a sense of terror, and the fear of being overborne by male power, is rendered benign and loving, is rendered in fact liberating, by this very objectification, in the manner in which Mellor undertakes it, combining humour with passion.

Why is Lawrentian objectification benign, if it is? We must point, above all, to the complete absence of instrumentalization, and to the closely connected fact that the objectification is symmetrical and mutual— and in both cases undertaken in a context of mutual respect and rough social equality.[7] The surrender of autonomy and even of agency and subjectivity are joyous, a kind of victorious achievement in the prison-house of English respectability. Such a surrender constitutes an escape from the prison of self-consciousness that, in Lawrence's quite plausible view, seals us off from one another and prevents true communication and true receptivity. In the willingness to permit another person to be this close, in a position where the dangers of being dominated and overborne are, as Constance knows, omnipresent, one sees, furthermore, enormous trust, trust that might be thought to be impossible in a relationship that did not include at least some sort of mutual respect and concern—although in Lawrence's depictions of a variety of more or less tortured male/female relationships we discover that this is complex. Where there is loss of autonomy in sex, the

context is, or at least can be, one in which, on the whole, autonomy is respected and promoted; the success of the sexual relationship can have, as in Constance's case, wide implications for flourishing and freedom more generally. We do not need to find every single idea of Lawrence's about sexuality appealing in order to see in the scene something that is of genuine value. Again, where there is a loss in subjectivity in the moment of lovemaking, this can be and frequently is accompanied by an intense concern for the subjectivity of the partner at other moments, since the lover is intensely focused on the moods and wishes of that one person, whose states mean so much for his or her own. Brangwen's obsession with his wife's fluctuating moods shows this very clearly. . . .

The objectification in *Playboy* is in fact a profound betrayal of the Lawrientian ideal. For *Playboy* depicts a thoroughgoing fungibility and commodification of sex partners, and, in the process, severs sex from any deep connection with self-expression or emotion . . . In *Playboy* sex is a commodity, and women become very like cars, or suits, namely, expensive possessions that mark one's status in the world of men.

Who is objectified in *Playboy*? In the immediate context, it is the represented woman who is being objectified and, derivatively, the actress whose photograph appears. But the characteristic *Playboy* generalizing approach ("why we love tennis," or "women of the Ivy League")—assisted in no small measure by the magazine's focus on photographs of real women, rather than on paintings or fictions—strongly suggests that real-life women relevantly similar to the tennis player can easily be cast in the roles in which *Playboy* casts its chosen few. In that way it constructs for the reader a fantasy objectification of a class of real women. Used as a masturbatory aid, it encourages the idea that an easy satisfaction can be had in this uncomplicated way, without the difficulties attendant on recognizing women's subjectivity and autonomy in a more full-blooded way.[8] . . .

To conclude, let me return to the seven forms of objectification and summarize the argument. It would appear that Kant, MacKinnon, and Dworkin are correct in one central insight: that the instrumental treatment of human beings, the treatment of human beings as tools of the purposes of another, is always morally problematic; if it does not take place in a larger context of regard for humanity, it is a central form of the morally objectionable. It is also a common feature of sexual life, especially, though not only, in connection with male treatment of women. As such, it is closely bound up with other forms of objectification, in particular with denial of autonomy, denial of subjectivity, and various forms of boundary-violation. In some forms, it is connected with fungibility and ownership or quasi-ownership: the notion of "commodification."

On the other hand, there seems to be no other item on the list that is always morally objectionable. Denial of autonomy and denial of subjectivity are objectionable if they persist throughout an adult relationship, but as phases in a relationship characterized by mutual regard they can be all right, or even quite wonderful in the way that Lawrence suggests. In a closely related way, it may at times be splendid to treat the other person as passive, or even inert. Emotional penetration of boundaries seems potentially a very valuable part of sexual life, and some forms of physical boundary-penetration also, though it is less clear which ones these are. Treating-as-fungible is suspect when the person so treated is from a group that has frequently been commodified and used as a tool, or a prize; between social equals these problems disappear, though it is not clear that others do not arise.

Notes

1   Cass Sunstein, *The Partial Constitution* (Cambridge, MA: Harvard University Press, 1993) pp. 257–90; also "Neutrality in Constitutional Law (with Special Reference to Pornography, Abortion, and Surrogacy," *Columbia Law Review* 92 (1992): 1–52.

2   *Defending Pornography: Free Speech, Sex, and the Fight for Women's Rights* (New York: Scribner, 1995).

3   Sunstein, review of Strossen, *The New Republic*, 9 January 1995.

4   I put this in quotes because I am conscious that the word is not ideal; it is too anthropomorphic for things like ballpoint pens.

5   I owe this example to Lawrence Lessig.

6   One way of cashing this out further would be to ask to what extent my use of him as a pillow prevented him from either attaining or acting on important capacities with which he identifies his well-being. Am I preventing him from getting up to eat? From sleeping? From walking around? From reading a book? And so forth.

7   I mean here to say that a working-class man in England of that time is roughly comparable in social power to an upper-class woman. As for Brangwen and his wife, her higher-class origins and her property give her a rough parity with him.

8   See Assiter, "Autonomy and Pornography," p. 66–69. One may accept this criticism of *Playboy* even if one is not convinced that its portrayal of women is sufficiently depersonalizing to count as objectification.

PATRICIA MARINO

In her article, Patricia Marino characterizes Nussbaum's account in terms of what she calls the "standard view." The standard view of objectification says that use of persons need not be morally problematic. It only becomes so when the objectification lacks "ameliorating conditions such as intimacy, symmetry, and mutuality." It is the "context" that matters when judging instances of sexual objectification. Marino argues against the standard view claiming that what is most important when considering the ethics of objectification is not context but rather "respect for a person's autonomy." She grants that context is important, but it is the background social and political context, rather than the specific relations between people, that is the crucial determinant in judgments about the morality of objectifying sexual practices. This is so because genuine autonomous consent is only possible in the context of social and political equality. This history of inequality between men and women has created a situation where it is often difficult to determine whether or not genuine consent to objectification is present.

The Ethics of Sexual Objectification: Autonomy and Consent

It is now a platitude that sexual objectification is wrong. As is often pointed out, however, the situation is complex: much sexual activity seems to involve some kind of objectification or use of another, sometimes in ways that seem morally permissible and even quite appealing—as when lovers are so inflamed by passion that they temporarily fail to attend to the complexity and humanity of their partners. But the platitude figures in many discussions about the wrongs of pornography, prostitution, and some kinds of casual sex; in these interactions, the thinking goes, a person is "objectified," used as a mere means for sexual pleasure, treated as an object in a way that is morally wrong. This raises the question, just when is sexual objectification benign, and when isn't it?

Reflecting on this question in a 1995 book review, Cass Sunstein suggests a possible intuitive answer: "Within a context of equality, respect, and consent, objectification—not at

all an easy concept to define—may not be so troublesome."[1] This raises obvious questions: What context is relevant and how? How should we evaluate equality and respect?

With respect to questions about context, there are two ways of thinking: on the one hand, we might focus on the context of the participants and their relationship, and even on the particular mode of interaction at hand, and on the other, we might look to the background social and political context against which the action takes place. Taking the former approach is one way to establish what I think of as the standard view: that while objectification can be morally permissible as a part of intimate, loving sex between those who care about one another, it is generally otherwise morally wrong, and this is why pornography, prostitution, and some kinds of casual sex are inherently morally suspect.

I'll argue here that the standard view is false. The crux of the matter with respect to the ethics of objectification, I claim, has to do with respect for a person's autonomy, and not with other qualities of a relationship or a particular interaction. Therefore, proper context is indeed crucial, but it is the background social and political context that matters most, because background equality is necessary for genuine consent. The qualities of the relationship matter only insofar as they, too, render meaningful consent possible.

1. Martha Nussbaum on context: Intimacy, symmetry, and mutuality

In an attempt to flesh out Sunstein's intuition in a plausible way, Martha Nussbaum's elegant paper[2] focuses on the fact that there are lots of ways to treat someone as an object. Instrumentality: the objectifier treats the object as a tool of his or her purposes; Denial of autonomy: the objectifier treats the object as lacking in autonomy and self-determination; Inertness: the objectifier treats the object as lacking in agency, and perhaps also in activity; Fungibility: the objectifier treats the object as (a) interchangeable with other objects of the same type, and/or (b) with objects of other types; Violability: the objectifier treats the object as lacking in bodily integrity, as something that it is permissible to break up, smash, or break into; Ownership: the objectifier treats the object as something that is owned by another, can be bought or sold, etc., and Denial of Subjectivity: the objectifier treats the object as something whose experience and feelings (if any) need not be taken into account.[3]

Nussbaum argues that the various modes of objectification come with greatly varying moral aspects. In some cases, she says, objectification can be a wonderful part of sexual life, and nothing to be feared or shunned. In *Lady Chatterley's Lover*, Nussbaum finds characters who become sexually inflamed by one another

partly through a process of objectification: they reduce one another to body parts; they stop seeing one another fully as individuals; they surrender—and ask others to surrender—autonomy, agency, subjectivity in their being overcome with sexual passion. Nussbaum finds this passion enlivening, and particularly wholesome and admirable. But what makes it morally acceptable? "Why," Nussbaum asks, "is Lawrentian objectification benign, if it is?"

> We must point to the absence of instrumentalization, and to the closely connected fact that the objectification is symmetrical and mutual—and in both cases, undertaken in a context of mutual respect and rough social equality. The surrender of autonomy and even of agency and subjectivity are joyous, a kind of victorious achievement in the prison-house of English respectability.[4]

But just to be used for another's purposes is not like this. It is when objectification involves instrumental use and the denial of the autonomy of the other that it involves a moral wrong; these are the most pressing forms of objectification and often lead to the others. But even using a person as a means to satisfy one's sexual urges need not be bad, as long as it is done in the right context and in the right way: if I use my lover's stomach as a pillow, she says, this is morally acceptable as long as our relationship is one in which he is treated as fully human the rest of the time, and he doesn't mind what I am doing. What this shows, she explains, is that "what is problematic is not instrumentalization per se, but treating someone *primarily* or *merely* as an instrument."[5]

To have the kind of relationship in which objectification is benign, Nussbaum suggests, one needs a certain kind of intimacy or at least what she calls a "narrative history." "For in the absence of any narrative history with the person," she asks, "how can desire attend to anything else but the incidental, and how can one do more than use the body of the other as a tool of one's own states?"[6] From the Lawrence discussion, it seems that symmetry and mutuality are also important. I am not sure what the difference is, exactly, between these, but one thing she suggests is this: that while symmetry involves each person using the other in a roughly comparable way, mutuality requires that each person's use of the other be linked together.

Interpreting Nussbaum this way leads to the "standard view": use can be morally benign in certain contexts, but because pornography, prostitution, and some kinds of casual sex involve sexual objectification that is one-sided, or anonymous, they are morally wrong; this wrongness is inherent in the acts themselves, because they involve using a person—primarily, merely—as an instrument in the absence of ameliorating conditions such as intimacy, symmetry, and mutuality.

2. Two kinds of instrumental use, and the irrelevance of intimacy, symmetry, and mutuality

But as I see it, this way of arguing for the standard view fails. Even the best sexual objectification involves a weak kind of instrumental use, while intimacy, symmetry, and mutuality cannot play a vindicating role for instrumental use of any kind. For what kind of instrumental use of another is generally morally problematic, but rendered morally permissible by these elements?

First, consider the specific claim that using someone instrumentally can be moral if done in an otherwise respectful relationship. As Alan Soble has pointed out, there is something immediately odd about this. For how could the fact that A usually treats B with respect on most occasions make it permissible to treat B as a mere means on other occasions?[7] Usually when we say that one mustn't treat someone "merely" as a means, we mean not that it is permissible to treat them only as a means at some times in some ways as long as they are treated as ends at other times in other ways, but rather that one mustn't treat a person as a means without treating them as, at the same time, an end in themselves.

In fact, contexts of intimacy, symmetry, and mutuality can make instrumental use more morally troubling rather than less. Consider again the story of using one's lover as a pillow. Nussbaum's sense of what makes this benign is that the lover is (tacitly) consenting, and is, in the context of the relationship, a full human participant. But considerations about the relationship become less obviously salient when we start considering permutations. Strange as it would be, there seems to be nothing wrong with putting an ad up on Craigslist, offering hourly wages for work as a pillow for a hardworking philosopher. And of course, one is often used by employers in this way, in the absence of intimacy, symmetry, and mutuality, and this is morally benign.

Conversely, instrumental use of various kinds in otherwise respectful relationships can be quite morally troubling. Consider, for example, a wife whose husband is affectionate and helpful, and who explains to her, in the most loving way, that what he needs in life is a helpmate, a partner in life, and what he really needs help with in life is typing: he needs someone to type his manuscript. Imagine this wife is a great typist, but feels the work is beneath her talents—a poor use of her time. If this happens in the context of a happy relationship, it is easy to imagine that it would feel cold and unloving to say "No,"—that one would be almost unable not to say "Yes" to such a request. And yet it is easy to imagine that the request might feel manipulative, and that the wife would feel herself instrumentally used in a way she did not enjoy or want. Being in relationships puts complicated demands on the participants, demands that are sometimes welcome and sometimes not. It would be easier to refuse such a request in almost any other context.

The fact that someone can choose to be used—as a pillow, or a worker, or a typist—suggests that there is some unclarity in the idea of "using a person as a mere means." Let me distinguish two versions of this. In the strong sense, this might involve utter disregard for the autonomy of the other person: A uses B as a genuine tool of A's purposes, really as a thing, when A fails to consider B's decisions, when A coerces B, or deceives B or simply forces B to do what A wants. Such use is always morally problematic; and intimacy, symmetry, and mutuality do not seem to help, nor do they create special conditions under which such use may be benign. Let's call this "strong instrumental use."

The second kind of instrumental use does not involve violations of autonomy: it is the way we treat a person when we do not care about their ends, or take their general wishes and desires into account. This seems to be the relevant kind of use in the pillow story: I do ask my lover "May I put my head here?" But I do not worry about whether he has some unexpressed desire to go into the kitchen or check his email. I figure if he decides he wants to get up he'll protest.

This "weak" kind of instrumental use is, I claim, one of central importance in thinking about sexual morality, and is usefully distinguished from violations of autonomy. If A has sex with B in a way that is non-consensual, this is one kind of moral situation; this is generally morally wrong. If A has sex with B and fails to take all of B's ends and desires into account, while respecting B's autonomy and self-determination, this is a quite different moral situation. This kind of behaviour on the part of A is highly characteristic of "sexual use" as we ordinarily think of it. It covers cases in which A is so lost in passion that A temporarily ignores B's desires and wishes, using B to satisfy or increase A's own pleasure; it covers cases in which B wants to be dominated in sex, and asks to have his or her wishes ignored; and it covers cases in which A is self-centred and self-absorbed and just doesn't bother to take B's desires and wishes into consideration. It covers actions such as A using B's body to stimulate or excite his penis, A allowing his or her thigh, or hands, or whatever, to be used to stimulate or excite B's clitoris, and A's being sexually stimulated by B's appearance.

Understood this way, it is not at all clear that Lawrentian sex is, as Nussbaum says, free from instrumentalization; the process of becoming sexually inflamed by another person often involves a temporarily self-absorbed focus on one's own pleasure, and this self-absorption is often taken as a sign of satisfying passion in one's partner. Indeed, it is because this sort of instrumental use in this latter kind of context seems so appealing that sexual use is puzzling in the first place. It is not only appealing to the user, it is appealing to the usee: a partner who is moved by intense desire and sexual excitement to become momentarily focused on his or her self is often taken to be part of the ideal sexual encounter. This seems, indeed, part of what Nussbaum finds admirable in Lawrentian sex.

Again, this kind of instrumental use may be—may even typically be—more morally troubling in contexts of intimacy than otherwise. We tend to have an intuition that cases of being "lost in passion" provide good reasons to use another instrumentally, and that being selfish is a bad reason to use another instrumentally, but notice that having a sexually selfish partner when one wants attention is probably more upsetting in cases of intimacy than in cases involving strangers.

And symmetry and mutuality do not seem to matter in the right way here either. If partners each ignore one another's desires and wishes symmetrically, how could this improve use that is otherwise problematic? It doesn't seem to help to think that A's ignoring B's desires is prompted by B's ignoring of A's. Even if the relationship of the participants is caring and respectful in all domains but one, and then they use one another only in this domain—ignoring one another's desires and wishes—this doesn't seem to make such use any better. Unless, of course, they want and agree to do so. Presumably the idea that symmetry and mutuality matter comes from an intuition that pleasure in sex should be spread around equally. But there is no moral rule that this must be so if the participants do not want it to be so, and certainly there are sex acts in which A may forego A's own pleasure to focus on B, purely out of excitement or the desire to make B happy. And this shows it is the choices of the participants that matter, not symmetry or mutuality.

3. Consent to sexual use and sexual objectification

I take it that strong sexual instrumental use—acting in ways that violate consent—is generally morally wrong; I won't discuss this further. If I am right about the distinction, however, our next question is, when, if ever, is it appropriate to sexually instrumentally use people in other ways? The answer I am going to pursue is, whenever they consent to, or ask for, or want, to be used in this way—whenever, that is, autonomy is not being violated. I share the intuition suggested above that equality and respect are essential for morally acceptable objectification, but I will argue that what matters is largely background social and political equality, and that the reason these matter is that only in their presence is consent genuine; the context of the relationship is significant only in the minimal sense that the relationship must not be used to coercive ends, as it is, say, when an employer demands sex for promotion. If this is right, the crux of the moral matter when it comes to sexual objectification is simply respect for autonomy.

It is sometimes argued that if an interaction is consensual, no one has "used" anyone, since the relevant kind of "use" is only when autonomy is violated.[8] But I claim that one *can* consent to being used. I said above that the weaker kind of instrumental use, in which consent is respected but one's desires and wishes are ignored, is a highly significant one in the sexual realm, and the examples I mentioned show that there is an important moral question as to when it is morally benign. But consent here is not to any particular activity, it is rather to a certain mode of interaction. Typically, in the kind of example mentioned above, in which passion causes A to temporarily pursue A's own pleasure and ignore B's desires and wishes, B won't mind, because B wants A to have this experience; it's often part of what one hopes for in having sex with another person.

Notice: consenting to be used frequently goes beyond consent to a particular interaction. Imagine I dress up in a micro-mini skirt and high heels, intending to give sexual pleasure to those who see me, and unconcerned about both the nature of that pleasure and whether it is reciprocated; it seems I have consented not just to being looked at, but to being looked at in a certain range of ways, unspecified in advance, and also to a certain mode of interaction. If I put sexually suggestive pictures up on the Internet (as many people of both sexes do), intending for others to see them and sexually enjoy them, it doesn't seem quite right to say that I am consenting to an interaction; what I'm consenting to is being used for sexual pleasure. This suggests that it makes more sense to say that one can consent to being used than to say that consensual activities are ones in which a person is not used after all; it is in this sense that we have more than a mere verbal quibble.

So how does one consent to such a mode of interaction? It may seem that there is a sort of paradox here, since respecting autonomy requires paying attention to personhood, whereas agreeing to be weakly instrumentally used involves having one's personhood ignored. But in fact A can respect B's autonomy while using B sexually as a means in this weaker way. To see how the mechanics of this work, consider the case of consensual role-playing involving sexual dominance and submissiveness. In such role-playing, respect for consent is necessary and deeply felt; nonetheless, to be

instrumentally used—and objectified—in the sense I am describing can in some cases be an important part of the interaction. Those who engage in such role-playing have practices set up that will allow them to signal to one another whether B's consent is ongoing—special words, gestures, etc.—even while B is being treated as an object, having his or her wishes and desires in a certain sense ignored.

I propose that we can understand the combination of consent and weak instrumental use in the ordinary sexual domain similarly. A uses B in the weakly instrumental way when A generally ignores B's particular desires and wishes, and uses B to pursue his own ends, but is attentive to whether B's consent—both to particular practices and to the use itself—is ongoing.

Now we're in a position to discuss other kinds of objectification, since the choice to participate is relevant in the same way and informs us about the morality of choosing to be objectified across the board. Notice that other kinds of objectification are generally taken to be benign in nonsexual contexts when they are consistent with respect for autonomy: workers are appropriately treated as fungible, and their feelings need not be taken into account at all times. We can choose to have our physical bodies "violated"—as we do in, say, consenting to cosmetic surgery. We can choose to be treated as inert, however strange that would be. Ownership, however, does seem to be generally morally wrong, because it violates autonomy.

If I am right about consent and objectification, respect for autonomy and consent are what matter, and it is the background context that is important, since it is crucial to ensuring that consent is possible and genuine. Insofar as society is so organized that some persons must allow themselves to be used or otherwise objectified—because they are poor, because they are regarded as non-autonomous, because they are simply regarded as sexual objects and therefore always used—there isn't morally acceptable sexual use. Thus sexism and inequality of various kinds can make sexual use morally problematic because they make consent impossible. One possibility along these lines might be that because of sexist cultural pressures, our "desires" or "choices" to be used in these ways can never really be autonomous ones—they are always "adaptive preferences."

It follows that as long as background conditions are right, there is nothing wrong with one-sided, anonymous, or just-for-sexual-pleasure objectification. And then there is no general argument that because they objectify persons, pornography, prostitution, and one-sided, anonymous, or just-for-sexual-pleasure casual sex are wrong. So the standard view is false; it is wrong to say that while objectification can be morally permissible as a part of intimate, loving sex between those who care about one another, it is otherwise morally wrong; it is wrong to say that this is why pornography, prostitution, and one-sided, anonymous, or just-for-sexual-pleasure casual sex are inherently morally

suspect. They are suspect, if at all, because of sexism and inequality, including the power inequalities of the participants, if these are used to coerce. This is the way in which "context" matters.

Conclusion

My conclusions about consent lead to a prima facie argument for the morality of pornography, prostitution, and one-sided, anonymous, or just-for-sexual-pleasure casual sex, under the right background conditions. These, if consensual, involve weak instrumental use, which is benign. I say "prima facie" here advisedly, since there are many other arguments for moral concern over these practices, and I cannot consider them all here. I hope to have at least established that it is not enough to say, "These practices objectify persons and for this reason they are inherently wrong," and to have shown why, when one says, with Nussbaum, unless instrumental use takes place "in a larger context of regard for humanity," it is "a central form of the morally objectionable," what matters is not the context of the nature of the relationship but rather the ways in which background context—especially background social and political context—allow for genuine consent and for respect for autonomy.[9]

Notes

1   Sunstein, 1995.

2   Nussbaum, 1995.

3   Ibid., 257.

4   Ibid., 275.

5   Ibid,. 265.

6   Ibid., 287.

7   Soble, 2001, 241.

8   See, e.g., Mappes 1987, 249–50.

9   Thanks to Emma Dewald, Jonathan Dewald, Lisa Schwartzman, Alan Soble, Helga Varden, and three anonymous referees for this journal. An early version of this paper was presented at the Twenty-Third International Social Philosophy Conference in August 2006; thanks also to all the participants.

References

Mappes, Thomas. (1987). "Sexual Morality and the Concept of Using Another Person." In Thomas Mappes and Jane Zembaty (Eds.), *Social Ethics: Morality and Social Policy*, 3rd ed., pp. 248–62 (New York: McGraw-Hill).

Nussbaum, Martha. (1995). "Objectification." *Philosophy and Public Affairs*, 24, pp. 249–91.

Soble, A. [2001] (2002). "Sexual Use and What to Do about It." In A. Soble (Ed.), *Philosophy of Sex*, 4th ed., pp. 225–258 (Lanham, MD: Rowman and Littlefield). An earlier version was first published in *Essays in Philosophy*.

Sunstein, C. (1995). "Review of *Defending Pornography*." *The New Republic*, January 9, 1995, pp. 42–45.

Discussion

Can we avoid *objectifying* other people? Assuming that we always objectify other people at least sometimes, what is it that makes certain cases of objectification wrong? Is *sexual* objectification sometimes justified? In Chapter 1 we saw that Sartre thought that we were equally both subjects and objects. In his view, the object side of our identity is something that we actively want to discover. We want to know how others see us, and in trying to capture the perspective of the *Other*, we are trying to capture our *object-identity*. This is specifically true of our sexual identity since as *embodied* beings we express our subjectivity in a bodily form. Our personality shows through in our expressions, movements, seductive actions, and so on. If we want to have the *objective* side of our sexual identity revealed to us through others, then can we avoid sexual objectification by others? Likewise, what we are attracted to about others is not some abstract "subject" residing within them, but rather that subject as expressed in bodily form—that is, as an object in the world. Arguably, an important part of this bodily expression takes a sexual form (sexual in the broad sense of the term).

Martha Nussbaum argues that context is the all-important feature when it comes to judging the appropriateness or the morality of objectification. Do you agree with her? Can the individual context (a relationship between lovers who are more or less equal, for instance) mitigate or overrule the problems associated with objectification in a society where there is a history of sexual inequality? How do we know when a context is a morally appropriate or morally problematic one for sexual objectification to take place in? How does the asymmetry between the first-person and third-person perspective on objectification figure into this question? In other words, is there a tendency to see objectification as benign when one is doing the objectifying but as problematic when one is being objectified?

Patricia Marino's article is a response to Nussbaum's article and focuses on the issue of autonomy or, to be more precise, autonomous consent. In order for sexual objectification to qualify as moral, it requires *real* consent on the part of the person being objectified. Real consent requires that it take place against the background of social and political equality, a background that has often not existed in relations between men and women. As Marino tells us, her own view leads to a *possible* moral defence of practices such as "pornography, prostitution, and one-sided, anonymous, or just-for-sexual-pleasure casual sex." Do you think that it is possible to ever attain the right background conditions required to morally justify prostitution or pornography according to Marino's criterion of genuine autonomous consent? What specific kinds of conditions might make the objectification involved in various types of casual sex morally benign? Or do you think that the objectification involved in casual sex is morally benign to begin with? How do Nussbaum's and Marino's concerns about objectification differ from Kant's?

Suggestions for Further Reading

Catharine MacKinnon, *Feminism Unmodified: Discourses on Life and Law* (Cambridge, MA: Harvard University Press, 1987).

Thomas Mappes, "Sexual Morality and the Concept of Using Another Person," in *Social Ethics: Morality and Social Policy*, 3rd ed., edited by Thomas Mappes and Jane Zembaty (New York: McGraw-Hill, 1987), 248–62.

Alan Soble, "Sexual Use," in *Philosophy of Sex*, 5th ed., edited by Alan Soble, 259–88 (Lanham, MD: Rowman and Littlefield, 2008). An earlier version was first published in *Essays in Philosophy*.

Cass R. Sunstein, *The Partial Constitution* (Cambridge, MA: Harvard University Press, 1993).

Cass R. Sunstein, "Review of *Defending Pornography*" by Nadine Strossen, *The New Republic*, January 9, 1995, 42–4.

Chapter Six
Derivatization and Degenitalization

EMILY ANN PARKER

As we have seen, Martha Nussbaum and Patricia Marino identify different ways which we can objectify another person. In her paper Emily Parker examines the issue of sexual violence through Nussbaum's discussion of objectification as well as Ann Cahill's notion of derivitization. Through the use of stories told by Daisy Hernández, Parker shows us that sexual violence is a concept that is broader than both sexual harassment and sexual assault, even though these are the two most common forms. Sexual violence is also implied in coercive attempts to make someone else fit one's own conception of gender identity. This is illustrated in the case of Gwen Araujo, who was sexually assaulted and then killed by Michael Magidson and José Merel. Gwen, who had previously been known as Eddie, posed a problem for these boys and for their own conception of gender identity. Gwen did not fit their ideas or expectations of what a girl should be. Because of this, they suspected that she was not a girl at all, but rather an imposter. Their suspicions about Gwen and their categorization of Gwen cannot be adequately characterized as "objectification" since what is at issue is not limited to treating her non-autonomously or instrumentally. What is at issue is that the boys treated Gwen according to their own conception of what it is to be a boy or a girl, a conception that has been taught and reinforced by the society they were raised in. It is for this reason that Parker thinks that perhaps Cahill's notion of derivatization better characterizes what is taking place here. To derivatize a person is to treat them in a way that reflects one's own reality without letting the reality of the other person penetrate the meaning of one's experience.

Sexual Assault as Derivatization

Objectification continues to offer one way of distinguishing sexual violence from the inarticulable magic of world-expanding, gut-tingling sexual encounters. Martha Nussbaum has attempted to clarify objectification, which she defines as the instrumental treatment of a human being as a tool for one's own purposes (Nussbaum 1999, 218, 233). Without the larger context of a person's autonomous and individual character, it is always morally problematic to treat her as a thing. Ann Cahill has suggested an alternative definition of sexual violence, however, which she names "derivatization." If to objectify is to turn someone into a something, then to derivatize, Cahill offers, is to turn someone into a someone who reflects me back to myself (2011, 32). In other words, to derivatize is to look at another person and see, not another person whose life and body might be quite different from my own, whose sense of self might challenge what I'd previously thought to be true about all of human life, but instead to see someone who must reinforce my own desire, my own sense of self, and therefore my own definitions of others' lives.

In this essay I aim to explore these two distinct ways of understanding sexual violence, not in the hope of defining the complexity out of sexuality or asexuality, both of which I take to be so close to what it means to be the animal that I am that words vaporize in my every attempt, but rather to provide a focus for reflection on the regularity with which the ridiculous desire to compel or coerce intervenes on a chance to witness another's world. Why is sexual violence so common? I think of college campuses, military sites, prisons, private businesses, cooperative enterprises, detention centers, homes, sports camps, fraternity parties, and places where religion is practiced. And yet to pose this question, to indict these spaces where so much else goes on, is to presuppose the meaning of "sexual violence." I want, not to analyze sexual violence, as if it's clear what this phrase means, but rather to explore two fundamentally different ways of identifying instances of sexual involvement as violent. It might be understood as either objectification or derivatization, so I will explore both. Ultimately, I will suggest that derivatization allows me to articulate what might in fact make the difference between a thrilling, exhilarating objectification and a compelling, coercive objectification; however, I leave it to you, the reader, to decide which understanding of sexual violence is less compelling and which articulates better the vividness of your own life, precisely that which cannot be observed by someone else.

In her 2014 memoir, *A Cup of Water under My Bed*, Daisy Hernández recounts what it was like to grow up in New Jersey, the child of immigrants from Cuba (her father) and Colombia (her mother and aunts, or *tías*). She offers an image of sexual violence by weaving together many stories. One of these stories is about Michael Magidson, José Merel, and Gwen Araujo. In 2002, in Newark, California, a teenager named Gwen Araujo was sexually assaulted and then killed at a party to which she'd been invited by friends (Bettcher 2007, 43–45; Hernández 2014, 89–103). At the time, Gwen was seventeen and planning to be a makeup artist. According to Hernández, the most basic sexual violence committed at this party by Magidson and Merel was to demand that Gwen prove her girlhood to them. You have to understand that for most of Gwen's life her family and friends knew her as Eddie, having been designated "male" by her community long before she had any choice or even awareness of the matter. But in her teens, she told her mother, Sylvia Guerrero, to call her Gwen (Bettcher 2007, 44).

Gwen had refused to give in to Michael and José's pleas to see more for a while now, which prompted another boy to suggest that she might not be a girl at all. So, at the party, Michael and José demand that Gwen prove she's a girl. Michael forces himself into the bathroom where Gwen is hiding because she's being prevented from simply leaving the party by its guests. One of the other women at the party, Nicole, José's brother Paul's girlfriend, says she will go into the bathroom; she will touch Gwen. Nicole does, and then runs back out, yelling, frantic over what everyone takes to be Gwen's strangeness, not their own. Except for Gwen, no partygoer senses that this is in fact sexual assault, an assault on Gwen's life. Only for what comes next will Michael and José receive second-degree murder convictions—but not hate-crime convictions. It must be remembered that Gwen Araujo was beaten, murdered, and then buried almost 250 kilometres from the party by Michael and José and others, and for this reason many rightly focus on the injustice of such irreversible violence. But neither should the interrogation and sexual assault leading up to Gwen's death be forgotten. In the most salient moral language that North American society recognizes, Nicole will not be considered guilty of anything, neither will Jaron Nabors or Jay Casares or Paul Merel, even though all of them together constituted this party, this cage in which Gwen was trapped (Hernández 2014, 101). In the months before these events, Gwen had difficulty finding work because her driver's licence simply read "male," although she was *Gwen* to those she encountered (Bettcher 2007,

44). She has also experienced harassment at school. Prior to the party, Michael, José, and untold others had discussed and disputed whether Gwen was correct about her own sense of self.

Another story—perhaps a different sort of story—that Daisy Hernández weaves is about a conversation with her Tía Chuchi. To recall this conversation, Hernández flashes back to a moment from her college days—not the first but an utterly uncinematic and yet paradigm-shifting moment—in which she registers that she, a girl, could kiss a girl (Hernández 2014, 81). In this moment she feels revealed and exposed, yet curious and awake. It feels like discovering a new limb, she says (93). Because of this moment, which was invisible to the rest of the people in the same room with her at this college event, she begins to try to meet a girl who will share a kiss with her. She is uninitiated and cautious at first, but years later she finds herself responding to her incredulous Aunt Chuchi who insists "you need a man for the equipment": "Tía," she says, "you can buy the equipment" (85). Her Catholic aunt furiously folds into a Hail Mary, spiritually washing herself.

In telling these stories Hernández gives her reader a picture of sexual violence, the sort that prepares the way for sexual harassment and sexual assault, the sorts of sexual violence to which generally more attention is given. In my view it is mostly appropriate that more attention goes to more intensely violent moments. But if those are the only moments upon which we reflect, we will miss the more subtle moments that create the circumstances that enable them. Hernández's stories accentuate the importance of attention to ubiquitous sexual violence. Which meaning of this phrase "sexual violence"— objectification or derivatization—more completely illuminates the harms that Hernández articulates?

According to Martha Nussbaum's understanding of sexual violence, Michael and José have instrumentalized Gwen, denying her autonomy and individuality. Instrumentalization, Nussbaum argues, is one distinct mode of objectification. Objectification can mean treating someone as a tool, but also denying her autonomy, treating her as interchangeable, breakable, or buyable (Nussbaum 1999, 218). It can also mean literally treating a person as an object, denying that she has any experiences at all. Except for one, all seven of these modes of objectification might be quite wonderful, if they characterize interactions between socially equal adults (238). After all, parents and other caretakers in their very caretaking lovingly call into question the autonomy of the one for whom they cook or clean or run to the bank (221–22). In energizing sexual experiences, it seems welcome to forget momentarily the subjectivity, the world of another person. A social equal can enter into commercial exchanges without being ethically harmed. And what's more, to vanish together into a vital, mutual attraction does not require moment by moment a conscious recognition of how the other person is experiencing the moment. There are generally no words, or there are only exuberant, out of the ordinary words, to express such an absence of self. You can't even try to communicate, clearly, directly, with precision, what is happening. We are not one in moments like this. And we do not necessarily in such moments have need of linguistic communication. We are communicating already.

Sexual violence occurs, according to Nussbaum, when the objectification is instrumentalization by another (Nussbaum 1999, 238). Instrumentalization alone—this one mode of objectification—is always inappropriate. This is when the other's body—the body of the other, the other who is not simply her body—is for me a tool to extend my own autonomous interests. Michael and José demand to confirm that Gwen is a girl, as they understand "girl," and in doing so they deny Gwen autonomous individuality because they need to confirm that they have not been tricked into lusting after a boy, as they understand "boy." They need to set the world straight, to make themselves feel safe. They are afraid of what it might mean to admit that they, boys, had wanted a boy. And so they demand at a party that Gwen lift her shirt. Another time they demand that she let them feel her body wherever they want to. These demands are what lead up to the party on October 3, 2002. It's impossible to know now exactly how Gwen experienced these unfair demands, but perhaps she was caught in a situation many will find familiar: What do you do when someone seems to want you, and though you want very much to be wanted, the demands are unfair or bullying or cruel? For Nussbaum, the problem is the very making of the demand to another that she allow you to explore sexually, without taking into consideration what this exploration might mean for her whole life, in a world where girls end their lives rather than endure the public cautionary role of sexual object, the passive role that they are in fact expected to be. What is going wrong is that Michael and José are enticing and then coercing Gwen, actively ignoring her myriad expressions of resistance. They are treating her as a thing, which, by definition, has no say in what happens.

But there is another layer of concern here. It is not only the case that Michael and José are treating Gwen as a tool, which would be on Nussbaum's account morally suspect enough. Additionally, there is the concern that Michael and José are in fact trying to confirm that Gwen is the sort of tool that they think she is. Gwen could clearly neither simply "be herself" around them nor risk seeming to be actively deceiving them (Bettcher 2007, 50). Talia Bettcher articulates this as a double bind: Gwen as a fundamentally non-normative girl was caught between two impossible options of either being "honest" about her genitalia or "hiding" her genitalia, this supposed proof about who she is. No amount of bravery—though Gwen clearly had lots—could untie the knot. Extending Nussbaum's account, we might say that Michael and José cruelly overlook Gwen's inner sense of self, her character. They inappropriately reduce her to her body, which is not who Gwen is.

I would like to suggest that something is not adding up here. Is the problem really that they are treating Gwen as a thing? Yes, they want her to be the sort of body that will confirm their sense of the truth of human bodies—namely, that they come in two sorts: male, female. These biological sorts grow into two styles: man, woman. The magnetic metaphor of opposition offers the only clear sense of order. Men want women, and women passively accept this wanting by men. Two norths repel each other; they don't attract. This magnetic metaphor has its own ubiquitous magnetism. But there's still more going on in Michael and José's story. Women have vulvas, and men have penises. The bodies of women are this; the bodies of men are that. In this way of thinking about human life, there is no room for ambiguity. How many exceptions does it take to break a rule? Perhaps for Michael and José and Nicole and Paul and Jaron and Jay it's not so much that there is a rule, but a world of real people, outside of which live people who are

not real (Bettcher 2007, 49). Such an unsettled and partitioned world requires vigilance. You must militantly verify and protect yourself against the fakes. So while, yes, they want her to be the sort of body that will confirm their own belief that she is wrong about herself, in doing so they also want to know whether she is warranted in believing herself to be a girl. They want to be able to confirm or deny that she is a certain sort of life.

What will Nussbaum's account say about the story of Daisy and her Tía Chuchi, her mother's sister, the *tía* who had lived with Daisy and her family since Daisy was fourteen? It was Tía Chuchi who patiently responded with complex and imaginative stories to Daisy's first-generation-in-the-States-kid questions about her father's religion, helping Daisy to put her growing world together. For Nussbaum, she is being treated as a device that confirms the finality of Chuchi's own experiences. But does Tía Chuchi instrumentalize Daisy? Does she treat her as an object, a tool to exert her own autonomy and deny Daisy's? For what purpose is Daisy being used by her aunt? In what way is Daisy an object or tool here for her aunt's purposes? In other words, what is the nature of this violence? Isn't Chuchi, as much as she is trying to ignore Daisy, to wash Daisy's words out of her life, demanding that Daisy be a different sort of person, have a different sort of life?

According to this sense of sexual violence as instrumental objectification, you are a character who animates a body. My body can only appropriately be my own instrument. The relationship between my character, my autonomous self, and my body is perhaps more complex than can be conveyed, but certainly to reduce me to my body, to consider me as a body alone, is an insult. It is constitutive of cases of social inequity. In encounters devoid of sexual violence, characters provide the context for the simultaneous, exuberant collision of bodies. Thus, to be invested in another as a character of any sort is on this account a sign of admiration. It is ethical. Insofar as the actions of Michael and José are inspired by their suffusion in the person of Gwen, Nussbaum's account suggests that there is nothing wrong here. Likewise, insofar as the reaction of Tía Chuchi to Daisy is a reaction to Daisy's person, there is nothing wrong.

Ann Cahill offers a distinct meaning of sexual violence, one that I think clears up the conundrums to which Nussbaum's account leads and harmonizes with the complexities of Hernández's articulations. For Cahill, there is no violence in treating someone as a something, because according to Cahill, we are things. You are a thing, a body, a vital material life (Cahill 2011, 26). You are a "body-as-subject" (35). On this account, it is necessary to face the fact that we value very poorly "embodiment" and bodies. Even this word *embodiment* bears the evidence of millennia of meanings in which something immaterial animates a body, giving it a life that it itself does not have (Massumi 2014, 28–29). The prefix *em-* means "to bring into the condition of": an immaterial life is brought into the condition of material life. Nussbaum's account, I fear, continues this priority of the immaterial in its insistence on the autonomy of character as the locus of human dignity. Cahill argues that one of the results of the pre-eminence of immateriality in North American culture is the hatred of bodies. They are ugly, messy, sweaty, burdensome. They prevent us from soaring above the earth, beyond sickness, old age, exhaustion. We forget that our ability to think is a function of psycho-physiological stress; we forget that stress is a function of one's larger social and ecological world. We crudely

partition these as if they aren't a tapestry of variable materialities. Instead, we focus on the imagined purity of minds, souls, consciousness, character: these have a life that doesn't age.

But perhaps what is most problematic about bodies, what we fear most about being bodies, is that our own bodies are objects for others, necessarily. I am a body-as-subject only for myself. No one else experiences this world as the life, the body, that I am. To others, this body conveys meaning, not inherently, but always in a social world in which nothing goes uninterpreted. We interpret clouds and birth dates. We find meaning in accidents. We avoid adopting black kittens. This is no less true in the case of human bodies. In many communities, skin colour or tone has immense meaning; it cannot be seen without its interpretation. In many communities, two girls kissing has intense meaning; this cannot be seen without its interpretation. In many communities, someone with one arm is seen as someone with "only one arm." Someone with one arm might even be tempted to describe his, her, its, or their body as having "only one arm." Interpretations do change, morph, expand, contract. We share these meanings. But we do not "have" the same bodies. Because we don't have, or rather because we aren't the same bodies, and because bodies regularly defy our fundamentally imaginative typologies for them, we don't experience the world of meanings that we share in the same way. For example, we might share this gut sense that Michael and José have, and perhaps even Gwen feared, that only men have penises. But Gwen's own transgendered body called this into question. She lived the violence and died by the violence of the biology textbook truth that women have vulvas. That every body clearly and always instantiates the presumed distinction between penis and vulva.

Cahill suggests that what Michael and José have done is not instrumentally objectify Gwen, but rather they have derivatized her. To derivatize is to treat someone as a someone whose life, whose body, reflects and reinforces my sense of my own life. It conveys back to me what I already know about the world. They have made her an imitation of themselves, or rather they've demanded that she be a body-as-subject in imitation of what reinforces their senses of self. Men are tautologically masculine, have penises and desire tautologically feminine women. In a social world where men of colour must both demonstrate that they are in fact men and yet are not so masculine as to teeter off into the abyss of violence that humans frequently attribute to other animals' animality, I want to argue that it is not necessary to insist on the personal responsibility of either Michael or José. Instead, they, too, navigated the intricate web of social meanings according to which, to this day, Gwen is called Eddie in news reports of the violence of Michael and José. To derivatize is to act in accordance with such socially shared senses of what counts as human, as either girl or boy but never both and never neither. Not to derivatize requires encountering a person, even a person one might want to have sex with, without asking what this encounter says about me. Of course I should ask what this encounter says about me in the sense that I should reflect on my interactions. But that I surprise myself in my attractions, my excitements, my curiosities— on these I cannot ever fully, completely reflect. Not to derivatize another person means not confusing my encounter with her for a horrifying portrait of myself, an event that is entirely about me. This would have been for Michael and José a countercultural gesture.

To say that there is derivatization in Tía Chuchi's rejection of Daisy's revelation will not be to suggest that this aunt instrumentalized her niece-object Daisy, but instead that she expected Daisy to be someone that Daisy writes she is not. To say that there is derivatization in Tía Chuchi's reaction to Daisy would be to say that Chuchi is demanding that Daisy be someone whom Tía Chuchi thinks she needs Daisy to be in order for Tía Chuchi to be who she is. She is demanding that Daisy be autonomous, but also identical to her. But a vital body-as-subject will be its own incomparable and unpredictable life. This is what Chuchi's irritation reacts to: the life that is the body of the other person. Near the end of Daisy's memoir, she tells her reader that Tía Chuchi has begun to write her own memoir, one that means that she will have to "make phone calls to Colombia and inquire about details, because memories are like thread. They can be tugged and loosened and stitched in different directions" (Hernández 2014, 180). These are threads that Daisy the narrator wants very much to read.

On Nussbaum's account one must resist reducing the character of the other to her body. One must resist a flattening account in which a body is just a body. In this way, Nussbaum suggests that even though attention to the specificity of body parts can be an important ethical gesture, it is in the name of the character of the other, distinguishable from her body, that such a gesture is required. What if what is necessary for denouncing sexual violence is interruption of the intuition that there is something insulting or demeaning about appreciating you just as a body, an unpredictable materiality? What if what is necessary is admitting that I can never be your body, and you can never be mine? There is magic in this simple claim that sexual violence characteristically denies. To try to compel you according to my own desires isn't to use you as a tool so much as to try to get you to be a body you are not. What makes the difference between an electrifying objectification and a coercive objectification is whether or not I mistake your life for a derivatization of my own.

Note

Many thanks to Ann Cahill and Ada Jaarsma who generously read and commented on drafts of this essay.

Bibliography

Bettcher, Talia Mae. 2007. "Evil Deceivers and Make-Believers: On Transphobic Violence and the Politics of Illusion." *Hypatia* 22 (3): 43–65.

Cahill, Ann J. 2011. *Overcoming Objectification: A Carnal Ethics.* New York: Routledge.

Hernández, Daisy. 2014. *A Cup of Water under My Bed: A Memoir.* Boston: Beacon Press.

Massumi, Brian. 2014. *What Animals Teach Us about Politics.* Durham, NC: Duke University Press.

Nussbaum, Martha C. 1999. *Sex and Social Justice.* New York: Oxford University Press.

MICHAEL GILBERT (A.K.A. MIQQI ALICIA GILBERT)

I introduced the notion of gender identity in Chapter 4 in contrast to both senses of the term *sexual identity*. In this chapter, Michael Gilbert discusses transgender identity specifically in contrast to the predominant categories of male and female. As Gilbert tells us, attitudes towards trans identities are slowly changing, but with the changes come new challenges. One recent issue has to do with public washrooms. Do transwomen use the women's washroom? Do transmen use the men's washroom? Or should we make more non-gendered or unisex washrooms available?

Gilbert, like Parker, points to the problems and dangers that arise from society's constructs of gender identity. We assume, largely based on appearance, that someone is male or female. Once we have determined this, we expect certain kinds of corresponding behaviours. When we cannot determine someone's gender, or when the gender we assign to a person does not match their behaviours, we are often confused. This confusion gives rise to a variety of responses, some of which are negative. Gilbert suggests that, to overcome the negative effects of our categorization and expectations of gender, what we need is *degenitalization*. Degenitalization requires that we no longer base our conception of gender on the type of genitals a person has.

Cross-Dressing, Trans, and All Stops In-Between

Introduction: An Experiment

Before you begin this essay, I'm going to ask you to do something. First, I assume that you are part of the 95 percent of the population that is content with your gender assignment. You were born a girl or a boy, have the typical matching genitals and, by and large, you have not doubted what you are. If this is the case, then you are what's called *cisgendered*: you are a cis-man or cis-woman, someone whose sex and gender match and who is content with that. What I want you to do may sound strange because you may never have done it before. I want you to think about how you know you are a girl or you are a boy, and how clear and certain that is to you. This can be hard because the knowledge of your sexual identity and category is so thoroughly embedded in who you are. Questions such as the following make no sense to you: When did you first know you were a girl? How long have you thought you were a boy? Now please keep this thought experiment in mind as you will be asked to reflect on it later on.

In what follows I am going to rely on the traditional distinction between sex and gender. While we have come to realize that the distinction is far more subtle and can easily get wobbly, it will serve us here, but be aware that I am tightening the cover on a can of worms (Cowan 2005).[1] By *sex* I refer strictly to physical biological facts: genitals, wombs, testes, hormones, breasts, and the like.[2] By *gender* I refer to the multitude of social behaviours and expectations that are socially, politically, and institutionally mandated and expected. So wearing skirts, hose and heels, using jewellery, nail polish, and cosmetics are feminine

behaviours, and are expected of women, and prohibited of men. Today, the limitations on women are much less rigid than in earlier times and than for men. Being a "tomboy" is—within limits—quite acceptable, but being a "sissy" leads to bullying and torment. Nonetheless, the way we dress, walk, talk, eat, lounge, play, and work are all governed by gender rules. So, while I want to remind you that the distinction between sex and gender is much more complicated and subtle than the way in which I am using it, I will nonetheless do so.

There are numerous definitions of what it means to be transgendered. Some have been created by the medical or academic establishment, some by trans communities, and still others by various political and social groups. Each of these definitions, like every definition, has as its purpose the delineation of a set of people who are entitled or mandated to apply the term to themselves. So, for example, if you define a homosexual as someone who has ever thought erotically about a member of the same sex, you get a much larger group than if you say it is someone who has had actual sexual relations with a same sex member. The definition to be used here will be very broad, because there will be a number of subsets introduced to help clarify individual groups. So, to begin with:

> A person will be considered *trans* or *transgendered* if that person sometimes or all the time demonstrates or experiences a dissatisfaction with their birth-designated gender.

There are several things to note about this definition. First, it excludes people who perform cross gender activities simply for fun, sex, or recreation. You are not trans if you dress up as the opposite gender for Halloween; nor are you trans if you and your partner indulge in a bit of role-playing during sex. Moreover, many if not most people have, at one time or another, questioned whether they live up to the "standards" of their gender: Jill might wonder if she's "woman enough," and Jack if he's "really a man." These questions have little to do with being trans, and much to do with the difficulty we all sometimes have of living up to the ideals of our gender.

The people who are covered by this definition include cross-dressers, transsexuals, transgenderists, gender queers, and a very large number of subgroups that appear under each of those categories, as well as a host of groups between these categories. Since it's always better to begin simple, we'll take that approach.

- *Gender* is the social role associated with one of the two standard biological sexes. Woman is associated with female, and man with male. The societal expectation is that a female will identify as a woman and behave, to one degree or another, following feminine rules, and that a male will identify as a man and follow masculine rules.[3]
- Traditionally, a *transsexual* is a female who identifies as a man and behaves in a masculine way, or a male who identifies as a female and behaves in a feminine way.
- A *cross-dresser* is a male who identifies as a man but sometimes adopts the feminine gender, or a female who identifies as a woman but sometimes adopts the masculine gender.[4]

What we have above is a major oversimplification of some very complex categories and identities. I have, for example, met transsexuals who do not at all behave in the manner of

their self-identified gender, and who appear to be, say, perfectly average males, but who know with certainty that they are women. There are also females who eschew feminine clothes and styles but completely identify as women. So what we need to do now is to take these simple ideas and begin to complicate them. That will be the task of the remainder of this essay. It is also worth noting that many in trans communities use the term *transgender* rather than *transsexual*. However, in this chapter because we want to make certain distinctions important to the discussion, I will use *transsexual*.

Transsexuality

Return for a moment to the opening experiment, called a *gedanken* experiment or thought experiment. If you are like most people, you realized you were very sure of your sex and your gender. You're so certain about your gender that it's not something you question, and doubting it just makes no sense. Now imagine that everyone is insisting that you are wrong. They all are telling you that you are a girl, not a boy, so stop being ridiculous; or everyone insists that you are a boy and must not wear dresses and play with dolls. You're a boy! Get over it! All these people are denying your reality: imagine how it must feel to be as clear about something as you can possibly be, as clear as knowing that you are alive and are a person, and yet have that denied. You have a Cartesian clarity about your sex, and denying it seems to require an outright contradiction.

Transsexuals can be divided into a wide variety of groups depending on the divider's interests and purposes. One such division has to do with the age that transsexuality presents itself. Some writers use "primary transsexuality" and "secondary transsexuality," but we will use "early onset" transsexuality and "late onset" or "adult onset" transsexuality on the grounds that "primary" and "secondary" have implicit value connotations. Interestingly, small children barely out of toddlerhood can demonstrate very strong cross-gender feelings. Our culture is so strict with regard to behaviour and appearance when it comes to gender that children learn very early just what belongs to which gender. So if little Jack believes he is really a girl, then he knows his hair should be long and he should wear dresses.

These days there is a lot of discussion both academically and in the popular media concerning how much support parents should offer transgender children, and how much intervention should be sought from the medical establishment. These are not easy decisions. For many years, the approach was to treat the tendency as a phase and even use aversion therapy to discourage the inclination (Zucker and Bradley 1995). Indeed, in Ontario, Canada, as in other jurisdictions, aversion therapy has been outlawed, and the clinic that was using it has been closed. Parents now can find support for their gender diverse children, and can themselves be more supportive. The decision to support is certainly not an easy one. For parents, the change can be wrenching when the child you raised as a daughter for ten years transitions to a son. There is always a fear that just maybe it is a stage, and that Jill will just grow up to be a masculine woman, or maybe even a butch lesbian. But to change sexes? To completely leave one's birth gender and join the other?

Most parents who end up supporting their children will tell you that in the end they felt they had no choice; their child was so depressed and so miserable that they feared for her or his life. And rightly so. The suicide attempt rate among unsupported trans youth is over 90 percent, while the rate for those who are supported is the same as for cisgendered children. It is far too soon to know if the early interventions currently favoured will bring reliably positive results, but it looks good so far (Bernstein 2008). One point, however, is clear: young people, whether four years old, twelve, or sixteen, seem very clear and are very emphatic about their internal gender identity.

In older individuals there are more ways and varieties of being trans. Late onset transsexuality is frequently, though not necessarily, preceded by cross-dressing. As a result, I would like to take a detour into cross-dressing before moving ahead. First, I reiterate that keeping things simple, as must be done here, means not covering all the bases and sometimes stating things in a way that misses significant facts, ideas, or subtleties. Please keep this in mind, and prepare for further study if those issues interest you.

Cross-Dressers

The problem with describing cross-dressers is that there are numerous varieties, and a given cross-dresser (CD) will morph over time. Typically, a CD, often a male, begins an attraction to women's clothing before or at puberty. The initial stage is most often erotic and involves masturbation. The young boy will be attracted to items of lingerie left around or in the laundry hamper, try them on, become aroused, masturbate, and quickly hide the garments. He knows this is wrong, even shameful, and is embarrassed, and he knows not to tell anyone. This highly eroticized stage can continue for a long time, but at some point other clothes—bras, skirts, blouses, dresses, and so on—are added. This marks a turning point because while there is still a strong erotic flavour, there is a growing sense of a woman-self identification. In other words, rather than only feeling an erotic rush, the boy or young man now wants to spend time in women's clothes feeling feminine. The clothes more and more become a means to acquiring a feeling of relaxation and femininity that the CD identifies as womanly. Of course, this is how he imagines a woman feels, and is not, so far as he can know, really how a woman feels—that surety is not possible (Gilbert 2001). At this point, the episodes of cross-dressing still almost always end in sexual release. As the CD matures, there tends to be a divergence onto one of two tracks. The one remains more or less static, and never really moves from this position; this might be called the fetishistic cross-dresser. This CD remains invisible and is impossible to count as there is never a step out of the closet. As such, we are going to suppose that our CD is of the other type, one who continues progressing and changing.

As this type of CD matures, say in his twenties and thirties, the erotic aspect recedes in favour of spending more time feeling his feminine aspect, feeling, as I put it, his woman-self (Gilbert 2000). It is at this point that he may make contact with other CDs and join a local club and/or attend conferences or events held in hotels or resorts. In the "olden days"—that is, before the advent of ubiquitous home computers—finding a group was not easy. He might see a small ad in an alternative newspaper, or notice a posting in an LGBTQ*+ bookstore. Timorously, he might attend a meeting and suddenly have a whole world open up to him. Now there are people to talk to and compare notes with—people who are happy to help in the improvement of his feminine image. They will encourage him to go out with them to a restaurant or the club's weekend away. He may begin reading books and articles

about cross-dressing and learn that there is a worldwide community, not to mention theory and politics. If he really matures as a committed cross-dresser (Gilbert 2000), then he will begin to think about what it means to really be a woman, to have that place in society, to have those responsibilities, to communicate and live in a woman's world. With luck he will embrace feminism.

This more or less continuum runs from a secret panty-wanker at one end to a mature person who has and works at having a real understanding of his woman-self, and what it is to really be a woman (Gilbert 2006). This CD gets beyond "grass is greener" thinking and jealousy of the sensual nature and variety of women's clothing into an awareness that being a women is as hard as being a man, just different. But so long as the CD identifies as a man, and knows he is a man even though he sometimes feels like a woman, he is a cross-dresser.

Late Onset Transsexual

We can now return to our discussion of transsexuality, and in particular those individuals who decide that they need to live full time as the "other" gender when they are adults. Failure to do so, can frequently end in suicide or other forms of self-harm; that is the sense of "need" referenced here. Do remember that not everyone who transitions later in life is a late onset transsexual. Someone may have felt their transsexuality all their lives, but not acted upon it for any number of reasons (Samons 2008). But for many, they were first cross-dressers, and came to realize that, in fact, they were not "just" cross-dressers, but women. This awareness can dawn slowly or come as an epiphany as it did to Deirdre McCloskey. Deirdre, née Donald, was a life long cross-dresser, mature and committed, when in her fifties she had the sudden awareness that she was, indeed, a woman (Mc-Closkey 1999). No one does this lightly. It can't be because it turns you on sexually, since taking female hormones, an essential step for any male-to-female (MTF) transsexual, eliminates your sex drive. And the idea that you might do it so you can win a medal at women's sports makes no sense. First, the entire process is far too arduous, expensive, and takes too long to make it worthwhile, and, moreover, you end up producing less testosterone, the male hormone, than an average woman. No, the truth is that unless a person has mental issues, transitioning from one gender to another is something one is compelled to do for survival, not on a whim.

While cross-dressing is often a predecessor to late onset transsexuality, this is not, strictly speaking, the case with female-to-male (FTM) transsexuals. Most, though not all, FTMs begin as lesbians, and usually are butch—that is, masculine to one degree or another. They don't have to wear men's clothing because the range of women's clothing available to them that is not overly feminine is quite wide (and fits better). Women do not *have* to wear dresses, skirts, frills, pink, heels, or the host of other sartorial items specifically assigned to females. Of course, as they come to identify more as men, they may prefer to shop in the men's department, wear male underclothing, and eschew any woman identifiers. Eventually, such a lesbian comes to the awareness that she is not a butch lesbian, but that he is a man. The road then becomes much more difficult.

No Easy Time

Return for a moment to the opening *gedanken* experiment. Your certainty that you're a woman or a man has not really diminished. You may have had it all your life, or it may have come to you as an adult. Regardless, you have suppressed it for as long as you can, and now you know you must be true to yourself or die. This means you must transition from one gender to another.[5] There's nothing else for it.

All transsexuals have a very difficult time in their transition. For FTMs, the first step is usually male hormones—namely, testosterone, usually just called T. This and breast binding just begins the journey. As time goes on, he will want to remove his breasts with a double mastectomy, have a hysterectomy, and possibly have a penis surgically constructed. An MTF almost always begins with facial hair removal, usually by electrolysis, the only permanent and reliable method. This can take months and cost thousands of dollars, but facial hair is an absolute signification of maleness. It is for this reason that adult FTMs who are taking T tend to pass more easily: the testosterone produces facial hair or a beard.

The second step for an MTF is hormones, which produce breasts and redistribute body fat to the hips and buttocks. Converting a penis to a vagina is often, though far from always, a final step, and will cost a minimum of $6,000 in the United States. Some provinces in Canada cover sex reassignment surgery (SRS), but it is often difficult to obtain and guarded by many professional gatekeepers. The total cost can range anywhere from $10,000 to $30,000 depending on many factors.[6]

The cost is only one of the many difficulties facing the trans person. One of the greatest costs concerns family and friends, many of whom find the change difficult to accept. A woman who married a man who transitions to a woman finds herself in a lesbian relationship, though she still identifies as heterosexual. Many spouses cannot handle this change, and divorce is common, though not universal. Parents, too, have difficulties and hesitations.

Imagine raising a daughter for twenty years who you now need to refer to as your son and call "he" rather than "her." This "pronominal dysphoria," as Bornstein calls it, plagues those who have known trans folk in their previous identities (Bornstein 1994). In current times, these transitions are becoming easier. The widespread discussion of trans in the media has made it less startling to many people, and more and more people even know a trans person. Still, the last hurdle, workplace discrimination, is only slowly beginning to change. Most jurisdictions do not protect trans people from being fired or from other kinds of discrimination in the workplace, or, for that matter, in housing. Only 18 states in the United States provide protection from discrimination to trans people.

Socio-Political Identity

There are a number of major issues facing the trans community, both from without and within. While most feminists are accepting of transwomen, some are not and insist that they are really males, cis-men, and nothing can change that. In other words, the biological issues cannot be overcome. This is ironic since feminism has forever been insisting that biology is not destiny, and that females cannot and must not be categorized simply because they have breasts and a uterus. Such women are called TERFs: trans-exclusionary radical feminists. The *Urban Dictionary* puts the definition nicely: "TERF: Acronym for *Trans-Exclusionary Radical Feminist*. That group of feminists that claims that transwomen aren't really women, as biological determinism is only a fallacy when used against them, not when they use it against others."[7] The corollary for transmen is that they are often rejected by the lesbian community in which they thrived

for years. They are even considered traitors by some, which can mean the loss of a major support system and many friends.

The moment of gender sign change is also contentious. At what point can a person born a female claim that he is a man? And, vice versa, when can a person born a male declare he is a woman? Obviously, TERFs say never; whatever you were born is what you remain (Califia 1997). Fortunately, many governments do this and permit sex change on identity papers after undergoing certain procedures. But what procedures? For a very long time surgery was required—vaginoplasty for males and phalloplasty for females, both expensive and potentially dangerous surgeries. More recently, hormones have been deemed sufficient, and in some places, such as Britain, a simple declaration is all that is required.

This same issue raises its head within the trans community. Some transwomen who have had surgery, who are called "post-op," claim that anyone who has not had it are not women at all.[8] Yet many transwomen (and transmen) are non-op, that is, they do not feel the need for surgery to live the life they want as a woman (or man). Moreover, the status of surgery for FTMs is still fairly unsatisfactory with the end result being aesthetically and socially valuable but not functionally, which lessens the attraction of phalloplasty. There is another awkwardness: we all assume that women have been women forever and were girls before that, and grown men were once boys. This is one great advantage held by early onset transsexuals who can talk about their favourite dolls and their first menstruation, or playing Little League, Minor Hockey, or joining Cub or Beaver Scouts, while late onset transsexuals have to make up their history.[9]

One major issue that arises regularly when discussing trans people and their rights is the bathroom problem. Anti-trans activists and Christian fundamentalists often run fear-mongering ads claiming that perverts will put on a dress and attack women and girls in public bathrooms. The thing is, according to the Transgender Legal Defence and Education Fund, there has *never* been such an attack. There has never been a complaint of this type and certainly never an arrest. On the other hand, transwomen have been attacked by cis-women in a women's washroom, and a horribly large number of trans people have been beaten, brutalized, and murdered for being trans. You can see a filmed episode of a transwoman being attacked. You can search this on YouTube: "Trans Woman Attacked McDonalds," but be aware it is very disturbing. In reality, all a trans person wants to do in a bathroom is just what you do—have a pee. They even learn the rules: transmen learn quickly that a visit to the washroom is not, as it used to be when they were women, a social experience. Men don't talk to anyone unless it's to make a joke about beer. Also, transwomen are often too intimidated to socialize the way cis-women do and tend to do their business and depart. Bathrooms are not about sex; they are about human necessities.

Degenitalization

The most basic thing we know about someone, Freud said the first thing, is their sex. But, in point of fact, that's not true. What we know about them is their gender, and from that we deduce or assume their sex, but we do this on the basis of their appearance and not our knowledge of what's going on around or in their bodies. If you sit on a bench at a mall and have a coffee for an hour, you will likely see more people in that time than you will see naked in your life (Kessler and McKenna 1978). Yet in virtually every case you categorized that person into one of the two sex categories (West and Zimmerman 1987). The underlying assumption to all this is that gender entails sex: *gender → sex* is the foundational axiom of our sexual relations, and placing someone in the male box or female box indicates how you will relate to them, socialize with them, communicate with them, form expectations of them, identify with them, sexualize them, and on and on. All of this is based on *assumptions* about genitals. We genitalize people so that we know how to relate to them—and perhaps that is not awful. But when we have difficulty doing that, or we realize we were wrong, then the *gender → sex* axiom puts the onus on *them*, they who deceived us (Bettcher 2007). As a result, they can be abused or punished, humiliated, excluded, and even murdered.

What the world needs now, to steal from a song, is *degenitalization*: a separation of gender from genitals, enabling one to assume a gender without implicitly declaring the possession of a vagina or a penis (Gilbert 2009). This would lessen the need for trans people to pass, to have "proper" histories, to be afraid of entering the "wrong" bathroom, to be inappropriate for a job and a host of other social factors. It would also mean that a cross-dresser would not live in terror of his neighbours or employer finding out about his gender diversity. It could even make life better for masculine women and feminine men. This goal is a long way off, but I do believe we are on the path to degenitalization insofar as laws are changing and more and more people are becoming familiar with the idea that our biology is not always our destiny.

Notes

1. The issue is often one of identity politics. Some people insist, for example, they are not just women, but females, and what they have changed is their sex, not their gender. For them, the idea of gender is not deep enough.

2. Here I am completely ignoring the intersexed who are born or turn out to be biologically diverse.

3. I include females in this definition, but a true female cross-dresser is relatively rare.

4. LGBTQ* is short for LGBTTIQQ2SA, which stands for Lesbian, Gay, Bisexual, Transsexual, Transgender, Intersex, Queer/Questioning, Two-Spirited, Asexual, which no one can remember.

5. Just a reminder that some trans people insist they are changing sex, not gender, and I am not taking a stand on that issue.

6. The costs vary so widely because the high end includes facial feminization surgery, which decreases the male brow ridge, and the shape of the chin, among other things.

7. *Urban Dictionary*, s.v., "TERF," last modified March 15, 2011, http://www.urbandictionary.com/define.php?term=TERF&defid=5671188.

8. Most of this discussion occurs in online chat rooms, though "screed" rooms might be a more apt name.

9. Bornstein says that transsexuality is the only "disease" where the cure is to lie.

Bibliography

Bernstein, Susan David. 2008. "Transparent." *Women's Studies Quarterly* 36 (3/4): 271–78.

Bettcher, Talia. 2007. "Evil Deceivers and Make-Believers: On Transphobic Violence and the Politics of Illusion." *Hypatia* 22 (3): 43–65.

Bornstein, Kate. 1994. *Gender Outlaw: On Men, Women, and the Rest of Us.* New York: Vintage Books.

Califia, Patrick. 1997. *Sex Changes: The Politics of Transgenderism.* San Francisco, CA: Cleis Press.

Cowan, Sharon. 2005. "'Gender Is No Substitute for Sex': A Comparative Human Rights Analysis of the Legal Regulation of Sexual Identity." *Feminist Legal Studies* 13:67–96.

Gilbert, Michael A. 2000. "The Transgendered Philosopher." *International Journal of Transgenderism* 4 (3): 1–16.

———. 2001. "A Sometime Woman: Gender Choice and Cross-Socialization." In *Unseen Genders: Beyond the Binaries*, edited by F. Haynes and T. McKenna, 41–50. New York: Peter Lang.

———. 2006. "The Feminist Crossdresser." In *Trans/Forming Feminisms*, edited by K. Scott-Dixon. Toronto: Sumach Press.

Gilbert, Miqqi Alicia. 2009. "Defeating Bigenderism: Changing Gender Assumptions in the 21st Century." *Hypatia* 24 (3): 93–112.

Kessler, Suzanne J., and Wendy McKenna. 1978. *Gender: An Ethnomethodological Approach.* Chicago: University of Chicago Press.

McCloskey, Deirdre N. 1999. *Crossing: A Memoir.* Chicago: University of Chicago Press.

Samons, Sandra L. 2008. *When the Opposite Sex Isn't: Sexual Orientation in Male-to-Female Transgender People.* New York: Brunner-Routledge.

West, Candace, and Don H. Zimmerman. 1987. "Doing Gender." *Gender and Society* 1 (2): 125–51.

Zucker, Kenneth J., and S.J. Bradley. 1995. *Gender Identity Disorder and Psychosexual Problems in Children and Adolescents.* New York: Guilford Press.

Discussion

Think about how we typically experience the identity of another person. How much of our experience of another person's identity is influenced by our perception of that person's gender? Why is it important to people to know the gender of another person? Why is it important for people to know their own gender? How might a lack of clarification about one's own gender affect one's sense of identity? Is this lack of clarity a bigger problem for other people who want to know the gender of the person they are interacting with? Where does the urgency to know one's own gender come from? Can a person be comfortable with an ambiguous gender identity? If not, is this due to societal attitudes or to the nature of identity (or gender identification) itself? If the former, then are there ways that these attitudes can change that will make a difference to a person without a clearly defined gender identity? Michael Gilbert suggests that we need to degenitalize gender identity. Since we do not actually see the genitals of the vast majority of people we meet, this sounds like a reasonable proposal. Some people have bodies that are anatomically male and yet identify themselves fundamentally as female. Likewise, some people have female bodies but regard themselves as male. Would degenitalization help those whose bodies and gender identity do not match? Could it be a way of helping others to be more accepting of various types of transgendered identities?

How is derivatization distinct from objectification? What is the significance of this distinction? How does derivitization affect our experience of another person? How does the notion of derivitization help us understand the stories of Daisy Hernández, according to Parker? Can you think of other stories that have happened to someone you know or that you have heard about in the news that provide examples of derivatization?

What does it mean to say that we are *embodied* beings? How would you describe your relationship to your own body? How do you experience the bodies of others? How are sexual identity and gender identity related to each other (if at all)? Do you tend to experience the sexual identity of another person before you have identified their gender identity, or is it important to you that you are clear about the latter before you consider the former?

Suggestions for Further Reading

Ann J. Cahill, *Overcoming Objectification: A Carnal Ethics* (New York: Routledge, 2011).

Patrick Califia, *Sex Changes: The Politics of Transgenderism* (San Francisco: Cleis Press, 1997).

Michael Gilbert, "The Transgendered Philosopher." *International Journal of Transgenderism* 4, no. 3 (2000): 1–16.

Michael Gilbert, "A Sometime Woman: Gender Choice and Cross-Socialization," in *Unseen Genders: Beyond the Binaries*, edited by F. Haynes and T. McKenna (New York: Peter Lang, 2001), 41–50.

Daisy Hernández, *A Cup of Water under My Bed: A Memoir* (Boston: Beacon Press, 2014).

Section III   Ethics and Sexual Issues

Chapter Seven
The Ethics of Sex Work

Introduction

The ethics of sex work, or "prostitution" as it has been traditionally called, is an issue that has divided philosophers for some time. Many feminist philosophers, for instance, have regarded sex work as one of the most obvious forms of patriarchal exploitation, whereas other philosophers, some of whom are also feminists, have argued that sex workers provide a valuable service akin to that of health care workers. According to the latter view, what is wrong is not sex work itself but the societal labels and attitudes towards it.

CHLOË TAYLOR

In her discussion of sex work, Chloë Taylor raises some important questions about the relation between sex and personal identity, which arise from her consideration of the work of Michel Foucault. Following Foucault, Taylor asks whether we have tied our identity too closely to our sexuality. The result of doing so suggests that who we are is closely related to our sexual practices or preferences. Hence, a sex worker is seen as a certain kind of person because of her profession in a way that, say, a waiter or a carpenter is not. Employing a distinction found in Foucault's work, Taylor suggests that a shift in our thinking about sexuality away from *scientia sexualis*—by which we view our identity as a kind of thing—and toward *ars erotica*—where our sexuality is understood as more of an art and not as an identity—may remove the stigma surrounding sex work. As you are reading Taylor's article, ask yourself whether or not the close relation that we often experience between our identity and our sexuality is a good thing.

Sex Work and Desexualization: Foucauldian Reflections on Sex Work

The ethical and political debates around sex work can be approached from Foucauldian perspectives in at least five ways. In what follows, I will briefly sketch each of these five perspectives, and then elaborate on the last of them.

First, Foucault's theories of disciplinary power, biopower, and governmentality are useful for analyzing the shifting legal and social measures that have been used to manage the sex worker populations given social concerns with venereal diseases, immigration (or illegal migrant sex workers), and sexual morality. Unsurprisingly, there is thus a considerable historical and sociological literature on sex work that—although it does not always draw on Foucault explicitly or in any depth—speaks of the management of the sex worker population using key Foucauldian terms such as "disciplining" and "regulation" (see, for example, Bernstein and Schaffner 2005).

Second, Foucault's genealogical method may be used to show the contingency of our current intuitions about sex work, and thus the malleability of the phenomenon. Indeed, it is notable that philosophers, who rarely historicize the subjects of their work, when writing about prostitution very often point to the diverse ways that sex work has been experienced and perceived historically, and in particular to the fact that prostitution has not always been seen as degrading labour that permanently marks or constitutes an individual's sexuality. Genealogies of sex work allow us to consider the significance of thinking historically about the ethical issue of sex work. In particular, genealogies of prostitution show

that sex work has been constructed very differently in various times and places, and thus that the future of sex work can also be different from how we perceive, imagine, and experience it today.

Third, one can take up Foucault's suggestion in *The History of Sexuality* that we might approach sex not in terms of science, but rather as an art, and consider what this would mean for sex work. In Volume 1 of *The History of Sexuality* Foucault contrasts the Western *scientia sexualis* with Eastern *ars erotica*, while in Volumes 2 and 3 of *The History of Sexuality* he considers an ethics of sexual acts as one part of an aesthetics of existence. Whether looking to the East or to the distant past in Western history for an alternative to our own scientific approach to sexuality, Foucault considers the possibility of sex as an art form. This idea resonates with arguments of feminist sexologists such as Leonore Tiefer, who have wondered why we approach sex in terms of functional norms rather than as a forum for creative self-expression (Tiefer 2004, 2–3). If we were to take up this idea of sex as art rather than as an object of scientific inquiry, then our sexual experts would no longer be scientists or doctors but people who technically excel at sex, or who have a talent and skill for producing sexual pleasure. In this context, we might consider Janice Irvine's (2005) examination of the role of sex workers as experts in William Masters's and Virginia Johnson's sexological research and Ann Cahill's discussion of prostitution in *Overcoming Objectification*, in which she imagines prostitution being valorized for the sexual expertise that it provides (2010, 106–26).

Fourth, we can draw on Foucault's analysis, in Volume 1 of *The History of Sexuality*, of the ways that modern, Western (scientific and disciplinary) approaches to sexuality produce sexual identities in order to consider the clients of sex workers. As clients rather than sex workers have increasingly become the sites of problematization, pathologization, and police intervention (we may think, for instance, of the phenomenon of "john schools"), purchasing sex is increasingly being understood by psychiatrists and clients alike as a sexual identity. Teela Sanders's sociological research on men who buy sex shows that clients now have websites on which they converse with one another, and some now meet socially for non-sex-related activities. Such men express a need to have opportunities to meet others like themselves and to speak openly about who they are (Sanders 2008, 64). This, I argue, illustrates Foucault's argument that pathologization implants "perversions" as identities in an age that identifies sex with sexuality and sexuality with who we are.

Finally, we can also draw on Foucault's analysis of the ways that sexual identities are produced in the modern West to consider the identities of sex workers. It is this topic that I will now examine in more depth.

A number of theorists have defended the legalization and destigmatization of sex work by arguing that sex work is analogous to other kinds of socially accepted, non-stigmatized, and even valorized labour. Lars Ericsson compares the work of a prostitute to that of a "nurse, whose job it is to take care of the intimate hygiene of disabled patients. Both help to satisfy important human needs, and both get paid for doing so" (1979, 342). Similarly, Igor Primoratz compares the work of prostitutes to that of waiters and hairdressers, since in each case the employee must stifle the expression of her true feelings in order to serve and please customers (2002, 465). Former

sex worker Annie Sprinkle has compared sex workers to sex therapists, educators, and entertainers (Shrage 2006, 245), while Martha Nussbaum compares prostitution to being a masseuse, housekeeper, assembly line worker, philosophy professor, and colonoscopy artist (2006, 175–208). In each of these cases, workers must "sell their bodies," or do things with parts of their bodies to accomplish tasks for which they are paid, often providing comfort, satisfaction, relief, or pleasure to clients in the process. According to Nussbaum, the fact that sex work is stigmatized while these other professions are not is the result of current sexual and class prejudices rather than anything intrinsic to sex work. In another era, she observes, opera singers, dancers, actors, and professional athletes were stigmatized for the kind of work they did, while today these are respectable and even venerated professions. In contrast, prostitution has not always been stigmatized: Nussbaum mentions the *hetairai* of ancient Greece, while Laurie Shrage discusses ancient Babylonian temple prostitution and medieval French prostitution, as examples of cultures in which sex work was respected or at least not stigmatized (2002, 435–50). For these reasons, Nussbaum argues, we can destigmatize sex work in the way that opera singing has been destigmatized. Indeed, we can imagine a day when it will strike people as odd to know that sex work was ever stigmatized, just as it strikes us as odd today to know that opera singing and ballet dancing were once stigmatized professions.

In contrast to such a view, one reason that anti-sex work feminist theorists have rejected the analogy between prostitution and other potentially exploitative and dangerous jobs is that sex is tied up with personal identity and integrity in a way that other activities are not. This makes the selling of one's body or the use of parts of one's body for sexual services psychosexually harmful in a way that distinguishes it from other forms of labour involving the sale or use of one's body parts. For instance, feminist political theorist Carole Pateman writes, "identity is inseparable from the sexual construction of the self. In modern patriarchy, sale of women's bodies in the capitalist market involves sale of a self in a different manner, and in a more profound sense, than sale of the body of a male baseball player or sale of command over the use of the labour (body) of a wage slave" (2006, 69). For Pateman, there is a certain truth to the expression that a prostitute "sells herself." She does not just sell her service or even her body; she sells—or at least tampers with—her soul. Not only is a woman selling herself rather than her services in the "prostitution contract," according to Pateman, but men are buying women—not just something that the women do. Pateman writes, "When a man enters into the prostitution contract, he is not interested in sexually indifferent, disembodied services; he contracts to buy sexual use of a *woman* for a given period. Why else are men willing to enter the market and pay for 'hand relief'?" (60). Pateman's point is that if clients were only buying a service, as opposed to a woman, they would never buy manual sex since this is a service that they can provide for themselves. Moreover, were clients of sex workers merely buying a service, they would be as indifferent to whether one sex worker or another provided them with hand relief as they are to whether they pass through one cashier's cash register or another's at the grocery store—and this is not the case. Pateman thus rejects arguments for the legalization of sex work that are based on analogies between prostitution and other

kinds of employment that also involve the use of one's body for the pleasure, entertainment, or servicing of others. This view is also apparent in the title of an anti-sex work feminist anthology, *Not for Sale: Feminists Resisting Prostitution and Pornography* (Stark and Whisnant 2004). The cover of this volume features the face of a woman, with the words "Not for Sale" written across her eyes and forehead, suggesting that it is women themselves and not just sexual services that get sold in the practices of prostitution and pornography.

Pateman is probably right that for many (but not all) women sex work would be and is experienced as personally harmful or psychosexually traumatic in a way that other low-paying and exploitative jobs are not. Even pro-prostitution philosopher Igor Primoratz is willing to "grant the empirical claim that a life of prostitution is liable to wreck one's sex life," although he deems it paternalistic to forbid sex workers from opting for this occupational hazard (2002, 455). Books for and against the legalization of sex work frequently include testimonials and articles by former and current sex workers. Some of these women testify to the harm they have suffered as sex workers, and are venomous towards middle-class, white, academic feminists who argue for the legalization of prostitution. Vednita Carter and Evelina Giobbe, for instance, accuse such feminists of being racist and complicit in the rape and degradation of working-class and often non-white women in the sex trades (2006, 17–39). Black feminist theorist Audre Lorde criticizes white feminists who argue that sex work is no different from marriage: "Poor women and women of Color know there is a difference between the daily manifestations of marital slavery and prostitution because it is our daughters who line 42nd Street" (1984, 112).

Other feminist writings, however, including writing by sex workers, defend sex work and are equally dismissive of anti-sex work academic feminists whom they see as sexually conservative or "sex-negative," bourgeois, and maternalistic. In "Thinking Sex," Gayle Rubin, for instance, describes the contemporary Western "sexual value system" as distinguishing between "'good,' 'normal,' and 'natural'" sexuality that "should ideally be heterosexual, marital, monogamous, reproductive, and non-commercial. It should be coupled, relational, within the same generation, and occur at home. It should not involve pornography, fetish objects, sex toys of any sort, or roles other than male and female. Any sex that violates these rules is 'bad,' 'abnormal,' or 'unnatural.'" In contrast, "Bad sex may be homosexual, unmarried, promiscuous, non-procreative, or commercial. It may be masturbatory or take place at orgies, may be casual, may cross generational lines, and may take place in 'public,' or at least in the bushes or the baths. It may involve the use of pornography, fetish objects, sex toys, or unusual roles" (Rubin [1984] 2006, 152). She writes of the "Charmed Circle" of "Good, Normal, Natural, Blessed Sexuality," which is, among other things, "free," in contrast to "The Outer Limits" of "Bad, Abnormal, Unnatural, Damned Sexuality," which includes sex "for money" (153). Thus, Rubin associates aversion to commercial sex with homophobia and conservative sexual mores that condemn extramarital and non-procreative sex as well as sex with children. Rubin argues that feminist criticism of sex work "resonates with conservative, anti-sexual discourse," and that "sex-negative" feminists have condemned not just sex work but

> virtually every variant of sexual expression as anti-feminist. Within this framework, monogamous lesbianism that occurs within long-term, intimate relationships, and that does not involve playing with polarized roles, has replaced married, procreative heterosexuality at the top of the value hierarchy. Heterosexuality has been demoted to somewhere in the middle. Apart from this change, everything else looks more or less similar. The lower depths are occupied by the usual groups and behaviours: prostitution, transsexuality, sadomasochism, and cross-generational activities. Most gay male conduct, all casual sex, promiscuity, and lesbian behaviour that does involve roles or kin or non-monogamy are also censured. (165–66)

Although highly critical of "sex-negative" feminists like Pateman, Rubin agrees that in the modern West sex work has become a kind of identity, albeit in a different sense than sexual identities that are also "preferences" or "orientations." She writes,

> Prostitution began to change from a temporary job to a more permanent occupation as a result of nineteenth-century agitation, legal reform, and police persecution. Prostitutes, who had been part of the general working-class population, became increasingly isolated as members of an outcast group. Prostitutes and other sex workers differ from homosexuals and other sexual minorities. Sex work is an occupation, while sexual deviation is an erotic preference. Nevertheless, they share some common features of social organization. Like homosexuals, prostitutes are a criminal sexual population stigmatized on the basis of sexual activity. Prostitutes and male homosexuals are the primary prey of vice police everywhere. Like gay men, prostitutes occupy well-demarcated urban territories and battle with police to defend and maintain those territories. The legal persecution of both

populations is justified by an elaborate ideology which classifies them as dangerous and inferior undesirables who are not entitled to be left in peace. (156)

Sex work has thus become an identity, for Rubin, not because it reflects an innate sexual orientation, but because it is an occupation that, unlike most other occupations, *permanently* marks a worker as a member of a stigmatized and criminalized outcaste group. Sex work is thus damaging to a worker's identity, for Rubin, but not because of anything intrinsic to this kind of labour; rather, sex work is damaging to a worker's identity because of the kinds of social consequences that it has in a sexually conservative or "sex-negative" society.

Things have changed since Rubin wrote "Thinking Sex" in 1984: most sex work is now negotiated online rather than in "well-demarcated urban territories," and arguably the phenomenon of middle-class, white women paying their way through college by engaging in sex work before moving on to white-collar careers has, to some degree, shifted perceptions of the practice (Bernstein 2007). While we cannot, therefore, generalize, it seems true that many but not all women today feel (or think that they would feel) personally and sexually damaged by engaging in sex work in a more fundamental way than were they to engage in exploitative jobs that do not involve the sale of sex. There thus seems to be some truth to Pateman's point, and yet Nussbaum and Rubin are convincing when they characterize this state of affairs as historical and thus contingent. Shrage writes that "we assume that a person's sexual practice renders her or him a particular 'kind' of person, for example, 'a homosexual,' 'a bisexual,' 'a whore,' 'a virgin,' 'a pervert,' and so on" (2002, 440). Pat Califia, similarly, notes

that "the prostitute's identity is currently rather rigid, partly because once you have been 'soiled' by that work you are never supposed to be able to escape the stigma" (2002, 479). For both Shrage and Califia, as for Nussbaum, Rubin, and Sprinkle, however, it is precisely this culturally specific belief that sex work is soiling that needs to change if sex work is to become a less oppressive practice. Pateman herself qualifies her argument with the words "in modern patriarchy," suggesting that in an earlier time or in a non-patriarchal society sex might not be so tied up with personal identity, and thus sex work would not be as harmful as it is today.

From a Foucauldian perspective we can bring together what seems right about Pateman's, Nussbaum's, Califia's, Rubin's, and Shrage's arguments. That is, we can explain the fact that sex is perceived, constructed, and experienced as intrinsic to identity in the modern West, as well as lend support to the view that this is a contingent and undesirable state of affairs. In the first volume of *The History of Sexuality*, Foucault (1978) argues that sexuality is conceived of and thus produced to be central to personal identity in the modern West, in contrast to earlier periods in which blood and alliance (or biological kin and marriage ties) were more significant to self-definition than sexual experiences or desires. Foucault would thus agree with Pateman's argument that engaging in sexual labour today will have a different impact on one's sense of self, and how that self is perceived by others, than non-sexual forms of labour, even while, like Nussbaum, he would historicize this predicament. Because, for Foucault, identity is caught up with sexuality today, what we do or have done with our sexual bodies will likely have great significance for all aspects of our lives and our sense of who we are. From this it would follow that sex work is indeed significant to identity in a way that other kinds of work are not, but it is crucial for Foucault that this need not be the case.

Foucault not only thinks that the current manner of seeing sexuality as the key to personal identity is contingent, but also that it is problematic; in the second and third volumes of *The History of Sexuality* (1990b, 1988), he explores alternatives to the modern view of sex as individuating identity. In ancient Greece and Rome, Foucault shows, sex was approached as a category of actions with respect to which one could cultivate and demonstrate one's self-mastery through exercising moderation. What was important for ancient Greek and Roman sexual ethics was not what one desired, what one fantasized about, what type of person one desired or the gender of the people to whom one was attracted. Rather, what mattered was that one demonstrated autonomy through the sexual restraint that one practiced, regardless of whether this meant resisting the temptations of women or boys. According to Foucault, other cultures, particularly Eastern cultures, have approached sex as an art of pleasures or *ars erotica*. In such cultures, knowledge about sex meant knowledge of how to produce intense pleasures, or the skill to bring such pleasures about. Foucault suggests that the sexual sciences of medicine, sexology, psychiatry, and psychoanalysis that characterize sexual culture in the modern West have led us to approach sexuality as something individual and inherent in us, rather than as a body of external and de-individuated knowledge about practices and pleasures. Today we tend to believe that each of us has a personal sexuality that is either hardwired at birth or acquired by a fairly early age. We believe that it is desirable to acquire information about our individual sexual identities because knowing the truth of our sexuality is necessary for self-understanding, authenticity, and happiness. Because sexuality is thought to be inherent in individual psyches, it is not simply deduced from the sexual activities in which an individual engages, but rather from an analysis of her desires, of which her acts may or may not be an authentic reflection. Understanding an individual's sexual desires will, in the modern West, be crucial to understanding her entire life and not merely her sex life, potentially enabling her to become her authentic self. The sexual sciences thus midwife our sexual confessions, introspections, self-revelations, comings-out-of-closets, and declarations of who we are.

Importantly, for Foucault these sexual selves to which we confess are not pre-given or prior to the discursive acts in question. In another age, with other discourses of identity, selfhood was grounded otherwise. Sexual confessions do not liberate us to become our true selves; rather, they construct those selves, fixing them to a particular sexual identity, and in so doing constrain them. In this process, we become constructed as some *thing*, an object of scientific knowledge, an instance of a taxonomical category of the sexual sciences. Consequently, rather than experimenting with or exploring new sexual pleasures and new possibilities of our bodies or ways of being, we now concentrate on being the kind of sexual being with which we have identified or been identified. In the end, one unfortunate consequence of the current sexualization of identity is that our confessional discourses make us less free, even though we engage in them because we think they are liberating. Meanwhile, those who identify with a stigmatized kind of sexuality find their entire beings stigmatized, and not just one aspect of their lives.

Foucault therefore proposes desexualization, or the disentanglement of sexuality from truth and identity. What would be some of the consequences of desexualization, or the dissolution of sexual identities? Most importantly, while the sexual liberation movement of the 1960s and 1970s misled people to believe that they would be liberated if they confessed to their sexualities and desires—often to a sexual scientist—for Foucault, there is no "sexual liberation" or sexuality prior to and outside of power relations. We would do better to actively explore bodily pleasures than to engage in the sexual discourses of psychological and scientific truth. As he famously wrote, "The rallying point for the counterattack against the deployment of sexuality ought not to be sex-desire, but bodies and pleasures" (1978, 158).

To take up some specific consequences and strategies of desexualization, Foucault would suggest that if we could distance sex from identity then rape might be experienced as no different from any other kind of assault: "there is no difference, in principle, between sticking one's fist into someone's face or one's penis into their sex" (Foucault 1990a, 200). Rape would still be a traumatic, an illegal assault to be taken seriously, but it would not be traumatic to a *sexual* self or productive of a *sexual* identity. Foucault tentatively considers whether we should treat rape like sexual assault precisely in order to bring about desexualization, or to cease privileging sex as different from everything else that the body does or undergoes. In an equally controversial example, Foucault argues against age of consent or statutory rape laws, suggesting that non-coerced and non-violent child–adult sex would cease to be traumatic in a desexualized society because it would no longer result in categories of sexual identity such as "child abuse survivor" and "child molester" (1990c, 271–85). In other words, in cases where it is consensual—and Foucault assumes that minors *can* consent to sex—much of the trauma that frequently follows child–adult sex today is discursively constructed, and not inherent to the acts in question. Along similar lines—and far less controversially—we can argue that with the desexualization of identity, sex work would no longer be perceived and experienced as different from other kinds of work, and would cease to be inherently traumatic, damaging, or stigmatized, thus removing one—but not all—of the occupational hazards associated with sex work.

Bibliography

Bernstein, Elizabeth. 2007. *Temporarily Yours: Intimacy, Authenticity, and the Commerce of Sex*. Chicago and London: University of Chicago Press.

Bernstein, Elizabeth, and Laurie Schaffner, eds. *Regulating Sex: The Politics of Intimacy and Identity*. New York: Routledge, 2005.

Cahill, Ann. 2010. *Overcoming Objectification: A Carnal Ethics*. London and New York: Routledge.

Califia, Pat. 2002. "Whoring in Utopia." In *The Philosophy of Sex: Contemporary Readings*, edited by Alan Soble, 475–81. Lanham, MD: Rowman and Littlefield.

Carter, Vednita, and Evelina Giobbe. 2006. "Duet: Prostitution, Racism and Feminist Discourse." In *Prostitution and Pornography: Philosophical Debate about the Sex Industry*, edited by Jessica Spector, 17–39. Stanford: Stanford University Press.

Ericsson, Lars. 1980. "Charges against Prostitution: An Attempt at a Philosophical Assessment." *Ethics* 90 (3): 335–66.

Foucault, Michel. 1978. *The History of Sexuality, Volume 1: An Introduction*. Translated by Robert Hurley. New York: Vintage.

———. 1988. *The History of Sexuality, Volume 3: The Care of the Self*. Translated by Robert Hurley. New York: Vintage.

———. 1990a. "Confinement, Psychiatry, Prison." In *Michel Foucault: Politics, Philosophy, Culture. Interviews and Other Writings, 1977–1984*, revised ed., edited by Lawrence. D. Kritzman, 178–210. New York: Routledge.

———. 1990b. *The History of Sexuality, Volume 2: The Use of Pleasure*. Translated by Robert Hurley. New York.

———. 1990c. "Sexual Morality and the Law." In *Michel Foucault: Politics, Philosophy, Culture. Interviews and Other Writings, 1977–1984*, edited by Lawrence D. Kritzman, 271–85. New York: Routledge.

Irvine, Janice. 2005. *Disorders of Desire: Sexuality and Gender in Modern American Sexology*. Rev. ed. Philadelphia: Temple University Press.

Lorde, Audre. 1984. "The Master's Tools Will Never Dismantle the Master's House." In *Sister Outsider: Essays and Speeches by Audre Lorde*, 110–13. Freedom, CA: The Crossing Press.

Nussbaum, Martha. 2006. "'Whether from Reason or Prejudice': Taking Money for Bodily Services." In *Prostitution and Pornography: Philosophical Debate about the Sex Industry*, edited by Jessica Spector, 175–208. Stanford: Stanford University Press.

Pateman, Carole. 2006. "What's Wrong with Prostitution?" In *Prostitution and Pornography: Philosophical Debate about the Sex Industry*, edited by Jessica Spector, 50–79. Stanford: Stanford University Press.

Primoratz, Igor. 2002. "What's Wrong with Prostitution?" In *The Philosophy of Sex: Contemporary Readings*, edited by Alan Soble, 451–74. Lanham, MD: Rowman and Littlefield.

Rubin, Gayle. (1984). 2006. *Culture, Society, and Sexuality: A Reader*, edited by Peter Aggleton and Richard Parker, 143–78. New York: Routledge.

Sanders, Teela. 2008. *Paying for Pleasure: Men Who Buy Sex*. Cullompton: Willan.

Shrage, Laurie. 2002. "Should Feminists Oppose Prostitution?" In *The Philosophy of Sex: Contemporary Readings*, edited by Alan Soble, 435–50. Lanham, MD: Rowman and Littlefield.

———. 2006. "Prostitution and the Case for Decriminalization." In *Prostitution and Pornography: Philosophical Debate about the Sex Industry*, edited by Jessica Spector, 240–46. Stanford: Stanford University Press.

Stark, Christine, and Rebecca Whisnant, eds. 2004. *Not for Sale: Feminists Resisting Prostitution and Pornography*. Melbourne: Spinifex.

Tiefer, Leonore. 2004. *Sex Is Not a Natural Act and Other Essays*. 2nd ed. New York: Basic Books.

JULIA O'CONNELL DAVIDSON

Julia O'Connell Davidson looks at both sides of the issue of prostitution and argues that there is something wrong with the debate itself in its current form. She suggests that both sides have legitimate concerns: on the one hand, prostitution as it currently exists in the world reflects social and sometimes political inequalities between men and women. On the other hand, given that prostitution does exist and does not appear to be going away soon, the rights of those who are employed as sex workers need to be protected.

The Rights and Wrongs of Prostitution

Feminists are deeply divided on the issue of prostitution, and debate between what might loosely be termed the "sex work" and the "abolitionist" lobbies is often both heated and bitter. This can be disconcerting for those like me who find themselves in sympathy with elements of both "sides" of the debate and yet also feel it is the wrong debate to be having about prostitution. My own research on prostitution over the past eight years has involved ethnographic and interview work with prostitutes, third-party organizers of prostitution, and clients in both affluent and poor countries (O'Connell Davidson 1998). In all the countries where I have conducted research, female prostitutes are legally and socially constructed as a separate class of persons, and as such are subjected (to varying degrees) to a range of civil and human rights abuses. I am in complete sympathy with "sex work" feminists' calls for prostitutes to be accorded the same legal and political rights and protections as their fellow citizens. I also agree that the vast majority of those who enter prostitution without being coerced into it by a third party do so for economic reasons, and that prostitution therefore represents a form of

work. At the same time, however, none of the data from my research have made me want to celebrate the existence of a market for commoditized sex; rather, the reverse (see O'Connell Davidson 2001; O'Connell Davidson and Sanchez Taylor 1999). In this sense, I am in sympathy with the feminist abolitionist case. This essay argues that what is wrong with much contemporary Euro-American feminist debate on prostitution is that it disallows the possibility of supporting the rights of those who work in prostitution as workers, but remains critical of the social and political inequalities that underpin market relations in general, and prostitution in particular.

Prostitution and Property in the Person

There is a longstanding tension within liberal political thought regarding the relationship between the body, property, and labour. John Locke is famous for this dictum: "Everyman has a property in his own person. This nobody has any right to but himself. The labour of his body, and the work of his hands, we many say, are properly his" (1993, 274). This dictum allows for the commodification of a person's bodily capacity to labour. Yet, as Bridget

Anderson notes, because he viewed the body as God-given and sacred, Locke also considered that "a man does not stand in the same relation to his body as he does to any other type of property. . . So a man does not have the right to kill himself, or put himself into slavery, because he is the work of God" (2000, 3).

The liberal concept of property in the person thus leaves open certain questions about what can, and cannot, properly be commodified and contractually exchanged across a market. In this sense, it appears to have set the agenda for much contemporary Euro-American feminist debate on prostitution. For instance, do the body's sexual capacities constitute property in the person, or is it impossible to detach sex from personhood without moral harm? Does prostitution law violate the prostitute's natural right to engage in voluntary transfers of her rightful property, or does the prostitution contract itself violate her natural right to dignity? (See, for example, Pateman 1988; Barry 1995; Jeffreys 1997; Chapkis 1997.)

Marxist thinkers view liberal discourse on property, labour, contractual consent, and freedom as a series of fictions that serve to conceal or naturalize huge asymmetries of economic, social, and political power. Their arguments suggest that a person's labour (whether sexual, emotional, mental, or manual) is, in Braverman's words, "like all life processes and bodily functions . . . an inalienable property of the human individual." Because it cannot be separated from the person of the labourer, it is not labour that is exchanged, sold, or surrendered across a market. What workers sell, and what employers buy "is not an agreed amount of labor, but the power to labor over an agreed period of time" (1974, 54). Since property in the person cannot be separated from the person, the wage labour contract actually involves a transfer of powers of command over the person. In exchange for x amount of money, the employer gets the right to direct the worker to perform particular tasks, or to think about particular problems, or provide particular forms of service to customers.

Likewise, sex or sexual labour is not exchanged in the prostitution contract. Rather, the client parts with money and/or other material benefits in order to secure powers over the prostitute's person that he (or more rarely she) could not otherwise exercise. He pays in order that he may direct the prostitute to make body orifices available to him, to smile, dance, or dress up for him, to whip, spank, urinate upon, massage, or masturbate him, to submit to being urinated upon, shackled, or beaten by him, or otherwise act to meet his desires (O'Connell Davidson 1998). It is not that the prostitution contract allows the client to buy the person of the prostitute while the employment contract merely allows the employer to buy the worker's fully alienable labour power. Both contracts transfer powers of command from seller to buyer (the extent of those powers and the terms of the transfer being the subject of the contract), and so require the seller to temporarily surrender or suspend aspects of her will.

Liberal theorists generally regard the invasion of an individual's will to be a heinous violation of fundamental human rights, and take a dim view of pre-capitalist and "traditional" social formations within which dominant groups exercised personalistic power to force their subordinates to do their bidding. But because market relations are imagined to involve the exercise of power over commodities rather than persons, and because employers do not usually use personalistic power to force workers to surrender their "property," the wage labour contract can be presented as an equivalent, mutual, and voluntary exchange. Money, the universal medium for the expression of the exchange values of commodities, is exchanged for the "commodity" of labour power. In capitalist liberal democracies, formal rights of equal participation in the process of commodity exchange are interpreted as a form of freedom for capitalist and worker alike, even though it is through this very process of exchange that the political and economic dominance of the capitalist class is maintained and reproduced. The beauty of the concept of property in the person, then, is that it conceals the relations of power and dependence that exist between those who pay others to do their will, and those who get paid to surrender their own will and do someone else's bidding.

For anyone who is remotely swayed by this critique, questions about whether or not sex can be commercialized in the same way as labour are the wrong questions to ask about rights. To paraphrase Anatole France, granting rich and poor, men and women, white and black, "First World" and "Third World," an equal right to engage in prostitution under the bridges of Paris is hardly to strike a blow for human equality or freedom. And yet feminists who discuss prostitutes' rights to freely alienate their sexual labour certainly wish to promote greater equality and freedom. Indeed, they arrive at their position out of a concern to challenge the very serious civil and human rights violations that have historically been and still are routinely faced by women prostitutes all over the world (documented in, for example, Walkowitz 1980; Alexander 1997; Cabezas 1999; Uddin et al. 2001).

"Sex work" feminists note that these violations are linked to the legal and social construction of women prostitutes as sexual deviants, rather than as workers, and to counter this, they emphasize the continuities between prostitution and other forms of wage labour. From here, it would seem a straightforward matter to move to a critical analysis of the class, gender, race, and global power relations that underpin the contemporary sex industry. But instead, "sex work" feminists often take a rather different turn, and one that is rarely made by those concerned with the rights of workers in other sectors. Having discussed ways in which the market for commodified sex is shaped by global and/or gender inequalities, some analysts move to talk about the selling of sexual labour as though it can represent a form of resistance to those inequalities (see, for example, Bell 1994; Kempadoo and Doezema 1998; Nagel 1997). This is not a leap that directly follows from the proposition that prostitution is a form of labour. Few would, for example, describe the sweatshop worker as "challenging" poverty by stitching garments, the airline flight attendant as "defying" sexism by smilingly serving drinks, or the black child selling shoeshine service in the Caribbean as "resisting" racism by polishing the shoes of white tourists. What makes prostitution different? The answer, I think, has to do with the vexed relationship between sex and selfhood.

Sex and Selfhood Revisited

"What is wrong with prostitution?" Carole Pateman asks, and answers that for the client to buy mastery of an objectified female body, the prostitute must sell herself in a very different and much more real sense than that which is required by any other occupation (1988, 207). This damages the prostitute. To contract out sexual use of the body requires the woman to sever the integrity of body and self, something that carries grave psychological consequences (see, for example, Jeffreys 1997 and Barry 1995). Critiquing such analyses, many "sex work" feminists point to similarities between prostitution and other personal service occupations, arguing that prostitution is better understood as involving a form of emotional labour. Such labour is not always or necessarily harmful to the worker. Wendy Chapkis (1997), for example, notes that while the flight attendants in Arlie Hochschild's 1983 classic study of emotional labour often believed that performing emotion work had changed them in some way, they "most often described that transformation as a positive one, of gaining greater control." In the same way, Chapkis argues, sex workers can experience "the ability to summon and contain emotion within the commercial transaction . . . as a useful tool in boundary maintenance rather than as a loss of self" (1997, 75). If sex and emotion are "stripped of their presumed unique relationship to nature and the self, it no longer automatically follows that their alienation or commodification is simply and necessarily destructive" (Chapkis 1997, 76).

Chapkis then moves on to observe that in some settings, emotion work is "socially rewarded and personally gratifying," and yet, "the respect given to emotional labor in the theatre, a psychotherapists' office, or a day care center rarely extends to the brothel" (1997, 79). Picking up on Hochschild's argument that a lack of control over the terms and conditions of employment intensifies the human costs of performing emotional labour, Chapkis concludes that it is not the commodification of emotion per se that is problematic in sex work; rather "mundane concerns like status differences between worker and client, employee/employer relations and negative cultural attitudes toward the work performed, may be at the root of the distress and damage experienced by some workers. This is less grand, less poetic, than the image of a soul in necessary and mortal danger through the commodification of its most intimate aspects. Such a formulation, however, has the advantage of pointing critics in the direction of practical interventions such as workplace organizing and broader political campaigns to increase the status and respect accorded to those performing the labor" (1997, 82).

It strikes me that this formulation also has advantages for anyone who wants to pay for sexual experience but still retain their feminist credentials (it provides a blueprint for how to be a "good" and "responsible" client, prostitution's equivalent of a "green consumer"), and that this is surely significant for Chapkis, who opens the final chapter of her book by saying, "After years of researching the subject of sex for money, I decided to finally have some" (1997, 215).[1] Chapkis's identification with the wish to consume commercial sex helps to explain why, unlike Hochschild, she pays little attention to "the human cost of becoming an 'instrument of labor'" (Hochschild 1983, 3), or to questions about the exploitative and alienating nature of the capitalist labour process, and does not really develop a critique of commercialism in relation to prostitution. Nor does Chapkis's analysis of prostitution refer to broader debates on class or labour movements, despite the mention of employment relations and workplace organizing in the passage quoted above.

So whilst Chapkis's *Live Sex Acts* provides a detailed and well-crafted case for women prostitutes' full civil and political inclusion, it does not question orthodox liberal narratives about property in the person, market relations, and human rights. Meanwhile, the emphasis on increasing "the status and respect" accorded to sex workers, alongside the inclusion of a chapter "sharing" the details of her own "commercial sexual experience," suggests that Chapkis believes that the sexual-emotional labour involved in prostitution, like the emotion work involved in psychotherapy, acting, or the provision of day care, has some intrinsic social value. The implication is that sex work should be respected and socially honoured because it expresses (or at least can, under the right circumstances express) a form of care or creativity.

This view is more explicitly elaborated in the work of "sex radical" feminists. Sex radical theory holds that the legal and social binaries of normal/abnormal, healthy/unhealthy, pleasurable/dangerous sex, as well as of gender itself, are profoundly oppressive. Thus, sex radicals celebrate consensual sexual practices that can be read as subverting such binaries (Vance 1984; Rubin 1999; Califia 1994). Through this lens, both the buying and selling of commercial sex appear as legitimate features of "erotic diversity." Pat Califia, for example, holds that prostitution serves valuable social functions and would not disappear even in a society that had achieved full gender, race, and class equality: "There will always be people who don't have the charm or social skill to woo a partner. In a society where mutual attraction and sexual reciprocity are the normal bases for bonding, what would happen to the unattractive people, those without the ability or interest to give as good as they get? Disabled people, folks with chronic or terminal illnesses, the elderly, and the sexually dysfunctional would continue to benefit (as they do now) from the ministrations

of skilled sex workers who do not discriminate against these populations" (1994, 245).

Fetishists would also continue to provide demand for commercial sex, Califia goes on, since "many fetishist scripts are simply elaborate forms of sublimated and displaced masturbation that do not offer anything other than vicarious pleasure to the fetishist's partner" (1994, 245). Prostitution obviates the need for anyone to, in Califia's words, "play the martyr" in a relationship by selflessly indulging a partner's fetish. And in her utopia, sex workers "would be teachers, healers, adventurous souls—tolerant and compassionate. Prostitutes are all of these things today, but they perform their acts of kindness and virtue in a milieu of ingratitude" (1994, 247).

In Chapkis's and Califia's writings, then, arguments about prostitution as a form of labour get conflated with claims about the social value of sex work and the client's rights to access the services of prostitutes (see also Perkins and Bennett 1985; Queen 1997). Prostitutes should be socially honoured because they facilitate the gratification of erotic needs that would otherwise go unmet, just as health care professionals and teachers should be honoured because they meet the population's health and educational needs. And because it meets human needs, prostitution, like medicine and education, would persist in a society that had achieved full gender, race, and class equality.

This takes us a long way from the idea of prostitution as mere service work, for if the comparison were made with, say, jobs in the hotel industry or domestic work, the same arguments would be rather less convincing. (There will always be people who are too busy or important, or who simply cannot be bothered, to open the door for themselves, make their own beds, wash their own clothes, clean the lavatory after they have used it, and come the revolution, these people would continue to benefit, as they do now, from the ministrations of skilled and professional doorpersons, chamber maids, and domestic workers.) Indeed, the fact that these writers compare sex work to healing or psychotherapy and think in terms of some kind of transcendental human need for prostitution suggests that they are quite as reluctant as "radical" feminists to strip sex of its "unique relationship to the self," albeit for very different reasons. Where "radical feminists" think prostitution is fundamentally wrong because it commodifies something that cannot be detached from the self, the "sex work" feminists considered here think it is fundamentally right because it provides clients with access to something they require to fulfill their human needs and express their true selves. This latter belief is certainly shared by the clients I have interviewed, who invariably explain their own prostitute use through reference to the idea of sexual "need" (O'Connell Davidson 1998). But what does it mean to speak of erotic "needs?"

From Erotic "Needs" to Despotic Subjects

Deprived of sexual gratification, people do not suffer in the same way they do when other basic bodily needs are denied or when medical attention is refused.[2] There is no biological imperative to orgasm any set number of times a day, week, or year, and though people may find it unpleasant or even uncomfortable to go without sexual release (assuming they are unable or find it undesirable to masturbate), the absence of a sexual partner to bring them to orgasm does not actually threaten their physical survival. Human sexual desire is grounded in emotional

and cognitive, as much as physiological, processes. If the urge to reach orgasm were a simple biological function, such as the impulse to evacuate the bowels, it would hardly matter whether the person with whom you had sex was old or young, or man or woman. Equally, if a lack of sexual contact posed a threat to health, such that one needed the "ministrations" of a sex worker in the same way one needs those of a doctor or a nurse when suffering from other ailments, then the physical appearance, age, gender, and race of the prostitute would be unimportant. But sex is not a mere bodily function or physical need. Our erotic life is grounded in the ideas we use to categorize, interpret, and give meaning to human experience and sociality, and specific sexual desires do not, therefore, directly express some fundamental, timeless, or general human need for sex. To treat them as if they do is hugely problematic.

What follows from the assertion that every individual is entitled to satisfy their exact erotic "requirements?" Califia asks us to accept that wanting "to be kicked with white patent-leather pumps with thirteen straps and eight-inch heels" (1994, 245) is an erotic need. But what if someone felt s/he could only be sexually gratified if it was Princess Anne or Queen Latifa wearing the patent leather pumps? Would that also be a "need?" And what of, say, a white racist's specific and narrowly focused desire to anally penetrate black women, or an adult male's "need" to be fellated by eleven-year-old children? Since non-masturbatory sex by definition involves another person or persons, to grant one the right to control the if, when, with whom, and how of having sex would very often be to deny those same rights to another.

Gayle Rubin has argued, "In Western culture, sex is taken all too seriously. A person is not considered immoral, is not sent to prison, and is not expelled from her or his family for enjoying spicy cuisine. But an individual may go through all this and more for enjoying shoe leather. Ultimately, of what possible social significance is it if a person likes to masturbate over a shoe? . . . If sex is taken too seriously, sexual persecution is not taken seriously enough. There is systematic mistreatment of individuals and communities on the basis of erotic taste or behavior" (1999, 171). But it seems to me that sex radicals also take certain aspects of sexual life far too seriously. Certainly it is ridiculous that a person's shoe fetish can provoke community revulsion and expulsion. But it is equally ridiculous to elevate that person's ability to indulge this fetish to the status of human right. If we are to say "so what?" about the fact someone likes to masturbate over a shoe, surely we can equally say "so what?" about the fact that s/he might have to make do with fantasizing about a shoe while masturbating, rather than thinking it imperative to set in place a social institution that will guarantee her/him access to a shoe whenever the urge to masturbate over one should arise.

At the same time, sex radical theory does not pay sufficient attention to the fact that "talk about sex is about a great deal else than organs, bodies and pleasures" (Laqueur 1995, 155). In using the example of a masturbatory fetish, Rubin evades the difficult issues that arise from the fact that non-masturbatory sex is, by definition, relational. To be sure, it is an intolerant and illiberal society that condemns a person for masturbating over a shoe. But since Rubin stresses that sex must be consensual, her own tolerance probably would not extend to an unknown man who happened to feel the "need" to masturbate over her shoe as they sat

together in Starbucks, for example. Like Califia, she reserves for everyone both the right to gratify themselves as they wish, and the right not to "play the martyr" by indulging other people when it will bring them no personal gratification. Everyone, that is, except prostitutes, who are instead awarded the right to give up their right to personal pleasure from sex in exchange for payment.

The essence of the prostitution contract is that the prostitute agrees, in exchange for money or another benefit, not to use her personal desire or erotic interests as the determining criteria for her sexual interaction.[3] What this means is that the prostitute must, at least during working hours, assume her or himself as the Other, fix her or himself as an object, in order that everyone else may always be able satisfy their erotic "needs" on demand. In other words, the existence of a market for commodified sex leaves room for every non-prostitute to become, in Simone de Beauvoir's (1953) terms, a "despotic subject" should she or he so choose.

For feminist abolitionists, this subject/object distinction in prostitution necessarily corresponds to a patriarchal order within which men achieve self-sovereignty through the political subordination of women. This is to essentialize gender, and also implies an over-optimistic view of women, who are perfectly capable of pursuing "masculine" self-sovereignty through the objectification of racialized and/or classed Others, as demonstrated by the research of Jacqueline Sanchez Taylor (2001) on female sex tourism and that of Bridget Anderson (2000) on employers of migrant domestic workers. Feminist abolitionists further imagine that in requiring a woman to temporarily fix herself as an object, prostitution permanently, completely, and literally extinguishes her as a subject. This glosses over the important (and sometimes hugely painful) fact that people do not either literally become, or come to see themselves as, objects even when they are treated as such. It also ignores the immense political dangers that go along with refusing any group of people full subjectivity, even when one's aim is to help or "save" that group. But the sex radical position on prostitution, which embraces despotic subjecthood as a delightful and ideal condition, is surely every bit as politically dangerous.

The Politics of Rights and Respect

Noting that the early feminist movement called for the labour involved in mothering and caring for the old, the sick, or the disabled to be recognized as work, Mary McIntosh argues that the term "sex worker" both means that prostitutes "are women who are paid for what they do" and that "as with other women, what they do should be respected as a skilled and effortful activity and not considered simply as a natural capacity of every woman" (1994, 13). But feminist calls for the labour involved in social reproduction to be recognized and rewarded have generally been advanced on the basis that this labour has intrinsic social worth, not simply because it is skilled and effortful. Indeed, this is partly why domestic and caring labour remains a difficult issue for feminists, for as Anderson's work shows, socially reproductive labour does not simply fulfill physical needs but "is bound up with the reproduction of life-style and, crucially, of status" (2000, 14). So, for example, the tasks performed by paid domestic workers often serve to demonstrate or raise their employer's status rather than having an inherent social value. There are even employers who demand that their domestic

worker wash the anus of the family pet after it has defecated (Anderson 2000, 26), something which requires skill and effort, but is hardly necessary either to any individual or to our collective survival.

Given the enormity of the stigma that attaches to female prostitution and its consequences for women's lives, it is easy to understand sex workers' rights activists' impulse to try to reconstruct prostitution as an intrinsically honourable profession that serves socially valuable ends. But without insisting that human beings have sexual "needs," rather than socially constructed desires, this position is difficult to sustain. It is fairly easy to make the case that we should attach social honour to the task of changing a baby's diaper, but hard to see how one would argue that social honour should be attached to the task of cleaning the anus of a perfectly healthy dog, or to the tasks performed by prostitutes in order to satisfy their clients' sexual whims.

To attempt to destigmatize prostitution by insisting on its social value also carries risks as a political strategy. There is a danger of simply creating new hierarchies and fresh divisions. If prostitutes are to be respected because they undertake socially valuable work, surely those who specialize in working with severely disabled clients will be deemed somehow more respectable than those who give blow jobs to able-bodied men out on their stag night, for example? This division already exists in the Netherlands where "sex surrogates" who work with disabled people are legally and socially constructed as different from prostitutes who work with able-bodied clients. And does this argument not construct the prostitute who meets a client's erotic needs as somehow more worthy of respect than the domestic worker who acquiesces to an employer's demands?

In an unequal world, opportunities to de-vote one's life to socially honoured goals are classed, gendered, and raced. The fact that an individual engages in a form of labour not considered socially valuable thus says noth-ing about her personal integrity or honour, and vice versa. Becoming a heart surgeon is not proof of the nobility of spirit of a white, middle-class man, and becoming a university professor does not demonstrate the personal integrity of a white, middle-class woman. A person's human, civil, and labour rights, and their right to respect and social value as a hu-man being, cannot be contingent upon whether or not they perform labour that is socially val-ued. The university teacher, the heart surgeon, the prostitute, and the domestic worker are all equally entitled to rights and protection as eco-nomic actors. Those who work in prostitution have rights and deserve respect not because or despite the fact they work as prostitutes, but because they are human beings. Likewise, our claim to legal recognition, rights, dignity, and respect lies in the fact that we are human be-ings, not that we are able-bodied or disabled, black or white, straight or gay, shoe fetishist or vanilla sex fetishist.

Behind and Beyond the Market

It is tempting to conclude that what is wrong with contemporary Euro-American feminist de-bate on prostitution is simply, as Delia Aguilar suggests, its lack of reference to "the basic con-cepts of class and social relations of produc-tion" (2000, 2). Certainly, the questions about prostitution that preoccupy many Euro-Amer-ican feminists can seem irrelevant to a world in which vast numbers of people live in poverty, and the gulf between rich and poor continues to widen. Consider, for example, the fact that

in India, a country with a per capita GDP of US$383, some 2.3 million females are esti-mated to be in prostitution, a quarter of whom are minors; or that Burma, a country with a per capita GDP of just US$69, exports an estimated 20,000 to 30,000 women and girls to work in prostitution in Thailand, while several thou-sand more cross the border into China to sell sex (Lim 1998; AMC 2000). Though some of these women and children have been forced into prostitution by a third party, it is dull economic compulsion that drives many of them into sex work, just as in America (a country with a per capita GDP of US$21,558), many women and girls "elect" to prostitute themselves rather than join the 35 percent of the female workforce earning poverty-level wages (Castells 1998). To describe such individuals as exercising rights of self-sovereignty seems as spurious as stating that their prostitution represents a violation of their right to dignity. There is no dignity in poverty, which denies the person full powers of agency. Yet the right to sell one's labour (sexual or otherwise) does not guarantee the restitution of dignity or moral agency.

But can simple appeal to basic concepts of class and social relations of production move forward the feminist debates on prostitution? Marxian analysts have rarely engaged with questions about the myriad historical and contemporary forms of sexual and gender oppression. Indeed, class theorists have often failed to critique liberal fictions about "public" and "private" as two distinct and clearly sep-arated realms of human experience, instead focusing almost exclusively upon the injus-tices affecting (straight, white, male, skilled) workers in the supposedly "public" sphere of productive labour. Though they have very effectively critiqued liberal discourse on property, labour, and contractual consent as fictions concealing class power, Marxists have traditionally paid little attention to the ways in which liberal discourse shrouds and naturalizes power relations that are gendered, sexualized, and raced.

The concepts of class and social relations of production, as found in the conceptual toolbox of orthodox class theorists, may thus prove to be unwieldy instruments with which to explore the specificity of prostitution as a form of exploitation. To conceptualize prostitution without reference to questions about the relationship between sexuality, gender, selfhood, and community would be as unsatisfactory as to conceptualize prostitution without reference to class. We need to return to the fact that sex occupies a special and privileged place in both abolitionist and "sex work" feminist accounts of the rights and wrongs of prostitution. In this, both "sides" of the prostitution debate recognize and take seriously aspects of human existence and forms of oppression that are typically overlooked or trivialized in Marxian theory. What happens if we take such concerns seriously but simultaneously remain critical of liberal discourse?

Thomas Laqueur has observed that for centuries masturbation and prostitution have been condemned with almost equal vigour in Judeo-Christian thought. Both have been constructed as fundamentally asocial, degenerative sexual practices, the antithesis of the "socially constructive act of heterosexual intercourse" (1995, 157). Both therefore represent a threat to the heterosexual family unit: "While masturbation threatened to take sexual desire and pleasure inward, away from the family, prostitution took it outward . . . The problem with masturbation and prostitution is essentially quantitative: doing it alone and doing it with lots of people rather than

doing it in pairs" (Laqueur 1995, 159–60; see also Agustin 2000).

The fact that, in Euro-American societies, people who do not choose to embrace reproductive heterosexual coupledom have historically been, and still often are, viewed with such loathing, fear, and repugnance tells us something about how little we have actually managed to realize ourselves as the "abstract individuals" or "sovereign selves" of liberalism. Marx may have been correct (at least insofar as white, middle-class, male experience was concerned) to say that capitalism "is the realized principle of individualism; the individual existence is the final goal; activity, work, content, etc., are mere means" (qtd. in Sayer 1991, 58), but the idea of the solitary individual, as a subject, was and is conceivable primarily in relation to economic life. As sexual and engendered beings, we remain largely tied to our social context, our identities given by our position within a sexual community and gender hierarchy.

Marx observed that, in the act of commodity exchange, "the individual, each of them, is reflected in himself as the exclusive and dominant (determining) subject of the exchange. With that the complete freedom of the individual is posited" (qtd. in Sayer 1991, 59). Sex radicals apply this bourgeois fiction to prostitution, imagining that by exchanging money for commodified sex, the individual is liberated from her or his fixed relationship to the sexual community, recognized as a sexual subject and set completely free. But any such "freedom" is contingent upon the existence of a particular, and highly unequal, set of political, economic, and social relations, since in general, people "choose" neither wage labour nor prostitution unless denied access to alternative means of subsistence. It is merely the "freedom" to picture the self in radical abstraction from social relations of power and to become a "despotic subject." We need an alternative vision of the self. As Laura Brace observes, we need to "move beyond the liberal conception of the abstracted individual, without drowning the sovereign subject in the ocean of nondifferentiation" (1997, 137).

Masturbation may offer a useful starting point for any re-visioning of the sovereign sexual subject. Prostitute use can largely be understood as a response to the social de-valuation of masturbation and sexual fantasy, the construction of masturbation as a form of sexual expression and experience that simply "does not count." But as Paula Bennett and Vernon Rosario argue, "Beyond the constraints of orthodox reproductive practices, solitary pleasure is a fundamentally generative form of sexual behavior, deeply implicated in the creative process and therefore basic to much that is good and enriching in human life" (1995, 15). To recognize masturbation as such would carry enormous equalizing potential.

We would not be debating whether disabled people need "sex surrogates," but rather emphasizing the need to develop and make available technologies that would allow the disabled to enjoy the same access to solitary pleasure that is currently enjoyed by the able bodied. It would no longer be assumed that within a couple, it was each partner's absolute responsibility to fulfill the other's sexual "needs" or that love and emotional intimacy implied a sexual claim over our partner's person. No one would "need" to sublimate and displace masturbation by paying a prostitute to temporarily surrender aspects of her will.

I am not proposing that we attempt to sidestep the relational nature of sexuality by simply replacing sexual interaction with masturbation, nor am I arguing that fantasies and fetishes should never be enacted. I would not even claim that masturbation and fantasy are necessarily as pleasurable or satisfying as sex with other people and/or the enactment of fantasies. But if masturbation was socially valued in the same way that heterosexual coupling now is, we would all be in a position to recognize and realize ourselves as sexual subjects, without turning anyone else into an object. And on those occasions that we happened to be lucky enough to find mutual and reciprocal desire with another or others, whether partner, friend, or stranger, it might then be possible to appreciate, value, and choose non-masturbatory sex for its relational qualities and connective potential.

As well as being right to call for prostitutes to be accorded the same legal and political rights and protections as their fellow citizens, it seems to me that "sex work" feminists are right to (implicitly) argue that we should refuse traditional demands to subordinate our sexual selves to socially "productive" goals through heterosexual coupling. But if they wish to represent or advance the interests of more than just a privileged minority of "First World" women, they need to look beyond the market for an alternative to the yoke of tradition, and beyond liberal discourse on property, contractual consent, and freedom for ways of conceptualizing the rights and wrongs of prostitution as a form of work.

Notes

I am grateful to Bridget Anderson, Jacqueline Sanchez Taylor, Laura Agustin, the individuals who refereed this paper, and above all to Laura Brace, for extremely helpful comments on the ideas in this paper.

1 The chapter provides an account of how Chapkis and twenty other women paid a "sacred prostitute" and her "consort" to provide a milieu within which they could have group sex with each other. Nobody had any form of sexual contact with the women who organized and charged for the event. It seems unlikely that many prostitutes' clients would part with money for this, and Chapkis does not explicitly stake out her position on the rights or wrongs of more conventional forms of prostitute use. However, it seems reasonable to conclude that she does not find anything problematic in the demand for commercial sex per se.

2 It is true that people can be profoundly harmed when they are socially, politically, and legally excluded or marginalized on grounds of their supposed sexual "Otherness," but the psychological and emotional distress they may suffer is linked to something rather more complex than the inability to instantly gratify a wish for a particular kind of sex at a particular moment in time.

3 Skilled and professional prostitutes who work independently and who are not economically desperate certainly impose limits on the contact (refusing clients who are drunk or threatening, turning down requests for unprotected sex, or for sexual acts that they find particularly intrusive or unpleasant, for example). But few prostitutes would be able to make a living if they only ever agreed to sex with clients they found attractive or to perform acts they personally found sexually or psychologically gratifying.

References

Aguilar, Delia. 2000. "Questionable Claims: Colonialism Redux, Feminist Style." *Race & Class* 41 (3): 1–12.

Agustin, Laura. 2000. "Those Who Leave Home for Sex—and Those Who Are Opposed to It." Paper presented to International Institute for the Sociology of Law "Sexuality and the State" workshop, Onati, Spain, June 14–16.

Alexander, Priscilla. 1997. "Feminism, Sex Workers' Rights and Human Rights." In *Whores and Other Feminists*, ed. Jill Nagle, 83–97. London: Routledge.

AMC. 2000. *Asian Migrant Yearbook*. Hong Kong: Asian Migrant Center.

Anderson, Bridget. 2000. *Doing the Dirty Work? The Global Politics of Domestic Labour*. London: Zed.

Barry, Kathleen. 1995. *The Prostitution of Sexuality*. New York: New York University Press.

Bell, Shannon. 1994. *Reading, Writing and Rewriting the Prostitute Body*. Bloomington: Indiana University Press.

Bennett, Paula, and Vernon Rosario. 1995. "The Politics of Solitary Pleasures." In *Solitary Pleasures*, ed. Paula Bennett and Vernon Rosario. New York: Routledge.

Brace, Laura. 1997. "Imagining the Boundaries of a Sovereign Self." In *Reclaiming Sovereignty*, ed. Laura Brace and John Hoffman. London: Pinter.

Braverman, Harry. 1974. *Labor and Monopoly Capital*. New York: Monthly Review Press.

Cabezas, Amalia 1999. "Women's Work Is Never Done: Sex Tourism in Sosúa, the Dominican Republic." In *Sun, Sex and Gold: Tourism and Sex Work in the Caribbean*, ed. Kamala Kempadoo. Lanham, MD: Rowman & Littlefield.

Califia, Pat. 1994. *Public Sex: The Culture of Radical Sex*. Pittsburgh: Cleis Press.

Castells, Manuel. 1998. *End of Millennium*. Oxford: Blackwell.

Chapkis, Wendy. 1997. *Live Sex Acts: Women Performing Erotic Labour*. London: Cassell.

De Beauvoir, Simone. 1953. *The Second Sex*. London: Penguin.

Hochschild, Arlie. 1983. *The Managed Heart: Commercialization of Human Feeling*. Berkeley: University of California Press.

Jeffreys, Sheila. 1997. *The Idea of Prostitution*. Melbourne: Spinifex.

Kempadoo, Kamala, and Jo Doezema, eds. 1998. *Global Sex Workers: Rights, Resistance and Redefinition*. New York: Routledge.

Laqueur, Thomas. 1995. "The Social Evil, the Solitary Vice, and Pouring Tea." In *Solitary Pleasures*, ed. Paula Bennett and Vernon Rosario. New York: Routledge.

Lim, Lin Leam. 1998. *The Sex Sector: The Economic and Social Bases of Prostitution in Southeast Asia*. Geneva: ILO.

Locke, John. 1993. "The Second Treatise on Civil Government (1689)." In *Locke's Political Writings*, ed. David Wootton. London: Penguin.

McIntosh, Mary. 1994. "The Feminist Debate on Prostitution." Paper presented to BSA Annual Conference, Sexualities in Context, Preston, UK, March 28–31.

Nagel, Jill, ed. 1997. *Whores and Other Feminists*. London: Routledge.

O'Connell Davidson, Julia. 1998. *Prostitution, Power and Freedom*. Cambridge: Polity.

———. 2001. "The Sex Tourist, the Expatriate, His Ex-Wife and Her 'Other': The Politics of Loss, Difference and Desire." *Sexualities* 4 (1): 5–24.

O'Connell Davidson, Julia, and Jacqueline Sanchez Taylor. 1999. "Fantasy Islands: Exploring the Demand for Sex Tourism." In *Sun, Sex and Gold: Tourism and Sex Work in the Caribbean*, ed. Kamala Kempadoo. Lanham, MD: Rowman & Littlefield.

Pateman, Carole. 1988. *The Sexual Contract*. Cambridge: Polity.

Perkins, Roberta, and Gary Bennett. 1985. *Being a Prostitute*. St Leonards, New South Wales: Allen and Unwin.

Queen, Carol. 1997. "Sex Radical Politics, Sex-Positive Feminist Thought, and Whore Stigma." In *Whores and Other Feminists*, ed. Jill Nagle. London: Routledge.

Rubin, Gayle. 1999. "Thinking Sex: Notes for a Radical Theory of the Politics of Sexuality." In *Culture, Society and Sexuality: A Reader*, ed. Richard Parker and Peter Aggleton. London: UCL.

Sanchez Taylor, Jacqueline. 2001. "Dollars Are a Girl's Best Friend? Female Tourists' Sexual Behavior in the Caribbean." *Sociology* 35 (3): 749–64.

Sayer, Derek. 1991. *Capitalism and Modernity: An Excursus on Marx and Weber*. London: Routledge.

Uddin, Farin, Monira Sultana, and Sultan Mahmud. 2001. *Childhood in the Red Light Zone: Growing up in the Daulatdia and Kandapara Brothel Communities of Bangladesh*. Report for Save the Children Australia.

Vance, Carol. 1984. *Pleasure and Danger: Exploring Female Sexuality*. Boston: Routledge & Kegan Paul.

Walkowitz, Judith. 1980. *Prostitution and Victorian Society: Women, Class and the State*. Cambridge: Cambridge University Press.

Discussion

Is there something inherently problematic about sex work? When a person (most often a woman), accepts money for engaging in sex acts, is it true to say that she is selling herself? What is implied when we say that she "sells herself"? We seem to have no problem separating the work of other labourers from their identity. Why should this be a problem in the case of sex work? What assumptions must exist in order for us to make this identification?

In earlier chapters, we looked at the sense in which our sexual identity is not just something added on to our sense of personal identity but rather an integral part of it. But Chloë Taylor, referring to the work of Foucault, calls this identification into question. The suggestion here is that perhaps the close identification that we make between sexuality and identity is partly to blame for the harmful effects of certain attitudes. This identification is what causes us to see someone as being a certain kind of person: virgin, whore, pervert, and so on. It also, arguably, adds to the trauma of sexual assault by making it more than a case of assault (which is already bad enough) but by making it something that violates who we are in a more fundamental sense. Would loosening the connection between sex and our identity be a good thing in this case? Does this close identification increase the psychological harm done to the victim of sexual assault by making her or him a certain kind of victim—one which has a specific kind of stigma attached to it?

Desexualization separates sexuality from identity. What would be the effect of Foucauldian desexualization? Would it allow us to think of sex workers more in terms of *sex therapists* or *sex specialists* rather than as *prostitutes* or *whores*? In other words, could such a shift in orientation or identification in this case bring about a shift in how we view sex in our culture? Could this be positive? Would it free us to pursue sexuality more in terms of *ars erotica* rather than *scientia sexualis*? In a later chapter, we will see Rekha Navneet discuss the ancient Indian text known as the *Kama Sutra*. This will give us a sense of what Foucault means by the characterization of sex as *ars erotica*.

Alternatively, is there something positive to be said about the identification that we make between sex and identity? Does it serve an important purpose? Would the severing of the bond between the two signal a return to the attitude associated with Platonism and Christianity whereby sexuality is viewed as a necessary yet unimportant aspect of our lives? Of course, Foucault recognized that sexuality was much more important to Christianity than it admitted. His discussion of the repressive hypothesis calls into doubt claims to the contrary.

Julia O'Connell Davidson discusses the writings of "sex work feminists" such as Pat Califia and Wendy Chapkis, both of whom cast sex work, or at least its potential, in a positive light. In such a view, a sex worker can be seen as a specialist who provides a service to those who desire or "need" it. (Of course, the issue of whether ordinary sexual desires are also needs and, if so, in what sense, is a matter of debate, as O'Connell Davidson notes in her article.) Those who need it may be "disabled people, folks with chronic or terminal illnesses, the elderly, and the sexually dysfunctional." Of course, those who desire/need such services may fall into none of these categories and may simply have failed to attract another person with whom to have a sexual relationship. Life is unfair in many ways and the distribution of opportunities for sexual experience is one example. Societies deal with other instances of unfairness through various means, whether this be through making affordable housing available, making buildings accessible, redistributing wealth to various degrees, and so on, which can be done through private or public agencies. Does the idea that sex too can be redistributed make sense? Is it a plausible idea? Is paying for sex fundamentally different from paying for a massage or for extensive homecare in the case of someone who is elderly or whose mobility has been greatly reduced? In each of these cases, the worker is often exposed to the naked or mostly naked body of the patient or client. Does the involvement of sex make a fundamental difference?

O'Connell Davidson calls into question the idea of sexual or erotic *needs*. Being denied sex, while perhaps resulting in frustration, discomfort, and disappointment, is not a case of being denied something necessary to physical survival. If this is so, then does it make sense to claim that people are *entitled* to sexual fulfillment? What considerations must be taken into account when considering the person desiring sex? What considerations must be taken into account when considering the person who is willing to sell her or his sexual services?

Suggestions for Further Reading

Pat Califia, *Public Sex: The Culture of Radical Sex* (Pittsburgh: Cleis Press, 1994).

Wendy Chapkis, *Live Sex Acts: Women Performing Erotic Labour* (London: Cassell, 1997).

Carole Pateman, "What's Wrong with Prostitution?" *Women's Studies Quarterly* 27, no. 1/2 (1999): 53–64.

Laurie Shrage, "Should Feminists Oppose Prostitution?" in *The Philosophy of Sex: Contemporary Readings*, edited by Alan Soble (Lanham, MD: Rowman and Littlefield, 2002), 435–50.

Chapter Eight
Other Ethical Issues

CHRISTOPHER BARTEL

The virtual world that characterizes the realm of gaming presents new moral challenges. One of the main concerns or questions can be expressed as follows: Do the moral rules that apply to real life apply as well to the virtual worlds in which we participate? Of course this question in its current formulation is ambiguous or incomplete. When we ask whether the rules that apply to real life should apply to the virtual world, are we asking whether they apply to the real person playing the game, or do they apply to the person's game character? Assuming we can clarify this issue, we can return to the main question and ask whether the rules that apply in real life and that concern real people—both as actors and patients or as perpetrators and victims—should apply to the interactions of virtual people. Most gamers (and most people, I assume) would say "no." Games explore the realm of fantasy. They allow us to "explore" dimensions that we cannot or would not want to explore in real life. But are there ethical limitations to this exploration? In his article "The Gamer's Dilemma," Morgan Luck presents a problem that connects the morality of real life with that of the virtual world of gaming. The dilemma Luck poses has to do with the fact that certain defences of virtual murder in video games would also seem to defend virtual paedophilia. In the following article, Christopher Bartel tries to solve the problem raised by Luck's argument by alerting us to a feature of virtual paedophilia that Luck overlooks.

Resolving the Gamer's Dilemma

In his essay "The Gamer's Dilemma," Morgan Luck raises a potentially troubling problem for gamers who enjoy video games that allow the player to commit acts of virtual murder. The problem simply is that the arguments typically advanced to defend virtual murder in video games would appear to also support video games that allowed gamers to commit acts of virtual paedophilia. The basic argument to defend virtual murder in video games goes: murder is wrong, but committing an act of murder in a video game does not cause any actual harm, so it is morally permissible to commit virtual acts of murder in a video game. This argument seems intuitively plausible, and indeed is an argument commonly offered by gamers and game developers in defence of virtual murder. Luck's worry, however, is that the same argument could apply to virtual paedophilia with equal force: paedophilia is wrong, but committing an act of paedophilia in a video game does not cause any actual harm, so it is morally permissible to commit virtual acts of paedophilia in video games. Though this argument appears analogous to the defence of virtual murder, it seems to go against intuition—intuitively, we feel that paedophilia, whether actual or virtual, must be morally wrong. But, Luck argues that there is no relevant moral distinction forthcoming—he offers five possible arguments that seek to identify the relevant distinction between virtual murder and 'virtual paedophilia, and he argues that each argument is insufficient. If this is correct, then the gamer seems to be left with two undesirable choices: "Either they acknowledge that acts of virtual murder and virtual paedophilia are morally prohibited, or they acknowledge that both are morally permissible."[1] What is needed, according to Luck's dilemma, is some morally relevant distinction between virtual murder and virtual paedophilia that justifies the gamer's disparate treatment of these two.

Luck's arguments are persuasive, however, there is one line of argument that he does not consider, which may provide the relevant distinction: as virtual paedophilia involves the depiction of sexual acts involving children, it is therefore an instance of child pornography.

So virtual murder is morally permissible while virtual paedophilia is not because the latter is an instance of child pornography. The central purpose of my essay is to point out an avenue that the gamer could explore in order to defend the claim that virtual murder is morally permissible while virtual paedophilia is not. Whether my claim—that virtual paedophilia is morally impermissible because it is child pornography—is able to resolve the dilemma will depend on the resolution of many wider issues, which I cannot hope to fully examine here. While I will attempt to offer a route through these issues, my examination of these will be unfortunately brief. However, I hope to show that there is a route available that may offer the gamer a resolution to Luck's dilemma, which is deserving of further consideration. In what follows, I will briefly canvas the five arguments that Luck offers, and will then examine the distinction offered above.

Luck's Five Arguments

Most gamers who commit acts of virtual murder do not feel like they have done anything wrong. However, Luck's dilemma, if sustainable, would be deeply worrying to the gamer—my students exhibit wide-eyed terror when they realize the implications of the dilemma! Moreover, Luck demonstrates that some seemingly intuitive solutions to the dilemma would be unhelpful. As I have no criticism regarding Luck's analysis of these arguments, I will examine these only briefly.

First, some might argue that virtual murder is morally permissible while virtual paedophilia is not simply because the former has become a socially acceptable norm while the latter is still deeply taboo. The appeal of this argument is understandable as such social forces are deeply engrained. For evidence of this, consider that, throughout the history of fiction, murder has long been a plot point at the centre of many enjoyable works of fiction; alternatively, paedophilia rarely is. However, Luck rightly points out that this merely offers an explanation of our intuitions; it does not offer a justification for why our intuitions ought to be correct on this matter. If we ought to hold that virtual murder is morally permissible while virtual paedophilia is not, then we need some justification for this normative claim.

Second, Luck considers the argument that virtual murder is acceptable because the likelihood that gamers will go on to commit actual murder is low, but the likelihood that gamers will go on to commit actual paedophilia is much higher. Luck rejects this argument on the grounds that there is little empirical evidence in support of its premises, and some empirical evidence to suggest that the opposite of these premises is actually true—it is not clear that virtual paedophilia would lead to an increase in actual paedophilia, and there have been many studies to show that violence in video games may lead to an increase in actual violence. Thus, the truth of this argument's premises is questionable.

Third, some might seek to advance an Aristotelian argument to the effect that virtual paedophilia causes self-harm to one's moral character whereas virtual murder does not. The argument would hold that virtual murder is enjoyed by gamers for instrumental reasons—that is, gamers do not commit virtual murder for its own sake, but rather for the sake of competition or to complete the game. Alternatively, the argument goes, if some gamers commit acts of virtual paedophilia, then they do so because such acts are enjoyed for their own sake. Thus, virtual paedophilia may be

a source of self-harm to the gamer: "were you to enjoy virtual paedophilia, presumably you find something pleasurable about the notion of actual paedophilia. If this were the case, by fostering a pleasure for actual paedophilia you are harming yourself; on the grounds that such a trait injures your character."[2] Luck rejects this argument for two reasons: this argument holds that there is nothing intrinsically wrong with virtual paedophilia as it would be possible to develop a game where the player is given the choice to commit an act of paedophilia in order to complete the game, in which case the argument advanced in defence of virtual murder could equally be applied to defend some instances of virtual paedophilia; and some instances of virtual murder are committed for their own sake, which would seem to force us to acknowledge that such instances are morally impermissible. In both cases, Luck's argument is that there can be no moral distinction between virtual murder and virtual paedophilia such that the former is morally permissible while the latter is not—either both are morally permissible or both are not. In addition, Luck notes that gamers often go out of their way to commit acts of virtual murder, suggesting that there is something intrinsic to such acts that gamers actually like. Such acts are voluntary—meaning that participating in the act is not instrumental to completing the game—and so the enjoyment of these acts for gamers appears intrinsic to the act.

Fourth, some might hold that virtual paedophilia is morally impermissible because one group—i.e., children—is being unfairly singled out for harm. As Luck notes, there is some intuitive appeal to this solution: a video game in which the player only murdered Jews or homosexuals would likely not be tolerated, so it seems that "unfairly singling out a group for harm is, in itself, additionally harmful."[3] Against this, Luck objects that "this argument seems to suggest that if a computer game allowed players to molest people of all different age groups, including children, it would be morally permissible to play such a game," which seems absurd.[4]

Finally, one might hold that harming children, even virtually, is morally impermissible because of the special status of children. This argument holds that harming a child is worse than harming an adult, and so the virtual murder of an adult would be morally permissible while virtual paedophilia is not. Luck claims that, while we might accept that child molestation is a worse offence than adult molestation, or that child murder is a worse offence than adult murder, it is not clear that child molestation is a worse offence than adult murder. Such comparisons seem intuitively impossible to justify because all things are not equal.

To remind the reader, I have no objection to any of Luck's five arguments. I am willing to accept each. However, there is one further argument that Luck overlooks—namely, that virtual murder is morally permissible while virtual paedophilia is not because the latter, and not the former, constitutes an instance of child pornography. This is the argument that I will pursue in the next section.

However, before continuing, I should note one skeptical worry regarding Luck's assumptions, which I will not pursue further. Luck seems to suppose that gamer's treat all instances of virtual murder as morally permissible; but it is not clear to me that gamer's actually paint all virtual murders with the same brush. First, some video games allow for virtual murders that are truly heinous and malicious, while others do not. Imagine a video game in which the player is able to commit virtual murder by shooting at random victims from a distance, and compare that to a game in which the player is able to commit virtual murder by slowly and painfully torturing to death a helpless victim. While both acts would result in a virtual death, there is a more disturbing psychological aspect to the latter, which may push such cases over the threshold of impermissibility. Second, while many video games allow for virtual murder, there is often a great difference in the attitude that seems to be promoted by the game towards such violence. Compare *Grand Theft Auto* and *Red Dead Redemption*, both of which allow the player to commit virtual murder (and there is a comparable degree to which those murders can be gruesome or sadistic in each game). In *Grand Theft Auto*, there are often pragmatic reasons within the game to avoid violence—such as avoiding the attention of the police. However, the game does not offer any further deterrence against violence. If the player is particularly adept at avoiding the police, then the game allows the player to commit whatever act she can get away with. Alternatively, in *Red Dead Redemption*, players lose points towards their Honor rating whether they are caught or not.[5] Additionally, while violence and cruelty are certainly allowed within *Red Dead Redemption*, such acts go against the central storyline of the game, which is about a man seeking redemption for his wicked past. Given the two points raised above, it is not clear to me that all instances of virtual murder are morally equivalent and equally justifiable, or that hard-core gamers would themselves treat all instances of virtual murder as morally equivalent. While some gamers might feel that some virtual murders are morally permissible—reasoning that it is simply harmless fun—it is not clear that all virtual murders are. Even hard-core gamers might balk at virtual sadism. One may be tempted here to question this assumption of Luck's. Perhaps a more nuanced distinction between various acts of virtual murder could offer another avenue to resist Luck's dilemma. I am unsure that such an argument is possible, and I will not pursue this line here. This skeptical concern aside, we can now turn to the argument I wish to defend.

Virtual Paedophilia Is Child Pornography

In the cases of virtual murder that Luck is concerned with—cases like *Grand Theft Auto*—the gamer voluntarily chooses to commit the virtual murder and the murders are graphically depicted. So, analogously, imagine a video game in which the gamer is allowed to voluntarily commit an act of virtual paedophilia and the act is graphically depicted. In such a case, the graphic depiction of a character—who is clearly depicted as an adult—engaging in sexual acts with another character—who is clearly depicted as a child—would count as an instance of child pornography. While these may be virtual instances of paedophilia, they are still actual instances of child pornography.[6] On the other hand, the graphic depiction of virtual murder, however, disturbing it might be, is not thereby pornographic. While the participation in an act of virtual paedophilia involves the indulgence in an actual instance of child pornography, there is no obvious parallel that we can recognize in the case of virtual murder.[7] The distinction that the gamer needs in order to avoid Luck's dilemma is this: insofar as the depiction of adults engaging in sexual acts with children is itself morally reprehensible, then to

that extent virtual paedophilia is also morally reprehensible because the latter necessarily involves the former.

My claim can be divided into three parts: (a) that virtual paedophilia amounts to child pornography as it necessarily involves the depiction of sexual acts involving children; (b) that virtual paedophilia is morally objectionable insofar as child pornography is morally objectionable; and (c) that virtual murder is distinct from virtual paedophilia as the latter necessarily involves child pornography while the former does not. This argument, if successful, would offer the gamer the distinction needed to resolve the dilemma. In what follows, I will concentrate on offering some justification for premises (a) and (b) and will consider some possible objections.

Is Virtual Paedophilia a Genuine Case of Pornography?

What counts as pornography is a thorny issue, and many proposals have been offered. Still, I take it that this much is not in dispute: a video game that depicts virtual paedophilia is one that thereby depicts sexual acts involving children. Still, not all depictions of sexual acts are pornographic. While the question of whether virtual paedophilia should count as child pornography will depend on how we are to define pornography, there is strong reason to suspect that this should be successful. These two claims will be central to my argument: that virtual paedophilia necessarily involves the depiction of sexual acts involving children, and that gamers who voluntarily commit these acts do so for some reason that they find intrinsically enjoyable. If these two claims are correct, then at least we can say that there is much that virtual paedophilia shares in common with canonical examples of pornography.

In seeking to define pornography, a common starting point is to presume that pornography is distinguished by an intention to produce objects of a particular kind. This could be called the intention-model, an example of which is Levinson's (2005). The intention-model defines pornography as "images intended to sexually arouse in the interest of sexual release."[8] This definition focuses on the production of pornography and offers a neat way to distinguish between pornography and, say, sexually explicit works of art, some of which presumably are not intended to sexually arouse in the interest of sexual release. If we were to adopt this model, then the question of whether virtual paedophilia should count as child pornography would depend on whether the scenes depicting virtual paedophilia are intended to sexually arouse the gamer in the interest of sexual release. Surely, this model then makes it contingent on the intentions of the video game producers whether the game is pornographic or not.

However, there is good reason not to adopt this model. The main problem is that there would appear to be many objects that serve the function of pornography—that is, objects that sexually arouse some consumers and are used for sexual satisfaction—that were not produced with that intention, at least not explicitly. For example, one might think of *Sports Illustrated*'s Swimsuit Issue, or a Victoria's Secret lingerie catalogue.[9] Other more extreme cases push further against this model—consider the case of a foot fetishist who finds shoe catalogues to be highly sexually arousing. Intuition here would suggest that objects can be put to "pornographic use" regardless of what the object's producers may have intended—thus, the focus shifts from the production of pornography to its consumption. This could

be called the usage-model, of which Rea's (2001) account is an example. On Rea's definition, objects can be described as "pornography" in two senses: if the object is put to pornographic use, or if "it is reasonable to believe that the object will be used as pornography by most of the audience for which it was produced."[10]

So, is it reasonable to believe that gamers who commit acts of virtual paedophilia treat those games as pornography? At least we could say this much: in the hypothetical game we are considering, the gamer's choice to commit an act of virtual paedophilia is voluntary. Luck makes the point that gamers often commit voluntary acts of virtual murder presumably because there is something about it that they like intrinsically. If we grant Luck this presumption, which seems reasonable, then we can say the same: if gamers commit voluntary acts of virtual paedophilia, then presumably they do so because there is something about it that they like intrinsically. While it is not clear what it means to "treat something pornographically," taking enjoyment in the depiction of sexual acts involving children for its own sake intuitively sounds like it should count as treating such depictions pornographically. Thus, it is reasonable to believe that virtual paedophilia is child pornography.

The Graphicness of the Image
One might hold that the belief that virtual paedophilia is pornographic depends on the graphic or explicit depiction of sexual acts. But, what if the video game does not depict the sexual act explicitly? I think it is a mistake to think that sexual explicitness is a necessary condition for thinking that some depiction is pornographic, which is a claim that seems to have much evidence in its favour. There are many works

that are considered to be pornographic that fail to be sexually explicit—consider the classic cheesecake pin-ups by Elvgren, or much of the work of Bettie Page. Additionally, being sexually explicit is not sufficient for something to be pornographic—the work of artists like Jenny Saville and Lucian Freud are often quite explicit, but are generally not taken therefore to be works of pornography. So, being sexually explicit is neither necessary nor sufficient for something to be pornographic. What matters for my purposes is that virtual paedophilia would be analogous to virtual murder if the act of virtual paedophilia is enjoyed for its own sake. If that is the case, then the enjoyment of virtual paedophilia (which necessarily involves the depiction of sexual acts involving children) for its own sake would offer sufficient reason for thinking of those depictions as pornographic, and it would matter not at all whether those depictions where sexually explicit or not. Finally, if a video game does not depict the sexual act at all—that is, if the act occurs "off camera"—then such cases would be disanalogous to the acts of virtual murder that Luck is concerned with; so these cases can be set aside.

The Moral Status of Virtual Pornography

Finally, the strength of my argument depends on our accepting, along with premise (b), that child pornography is morally impermissible. Should we accept this claim? Common intuition holds that child pornography is obviously morally reprehensible. Unfortunately, philosophers have not spent much time defending this intuition. King (2008) offers a utilitarian defence of this claim, and I suspect that it would not be terribly difficult to construct other defences using the main ethical theories currently on offer. (One could perhaps go further and suggest that any ethical theory that fails to count child

pornography as morally impermissible ought to be rejected for that reason as a poor ethical theory.) Despite this widespread intuition, there remains one potential worry regarding my argument. The worry is that if virtual paedophilia is to count as child pornography, then we must admit that it is virtual child pornography—that is, it is not the depiction of actual children engaging in sexual acts, rather it is the depiction of computer-generated virtual children. One might think that, as no actual child is involved in virtual child pornography, then at least the immoral status of such pornography is diminished, and perhaps may even be morally permissible.

Levy (2002) draws attention to a United States Supreme Court case in which the Child Pornography Prevention Act was struck down as unconstitutional. If successful, the act would have prohibited the production and consumption of virtual child pornography, among other things. However, the court ruled that, as no actual child is involved in the production of such images, then those images could be protected under free speech. This objection threatens to support Luck's dilemma—if virtual murder is morally permissible because no actual person is harmed, then virtual child pornography, and virtual paedophilia, should also be permissible as no actual child is harmed by either. To avoid this objection, it needs to be shown that virtual child pornography is morally impermissible. Levy offers an effective, if surprising, argument to that effect. Levy argues that, though it seems to go against intuition, the court's reasoning is justified—there is no reason to think that virtual child pornography harms actual children. However, Levy goes on to argue that child pornography is still morally impermissible, though for reasons other than one would expect. Mainstream pornography, it is argued, harms all women by reinforcing the unequal status of women through its depiction of women as being sexually submissive objects for the enjoyment of men. This sexual inequality has the knock-on effect of reinforcing the inequality and subordination of women's position in society generally by encouraging "both men and women to think of women as naturally inferior."[11] Levy argues that, while these arguments might show that pornography is harmful to women, an analogous argument cannot be made to show that child pornography is harmful to children simply because children do occupy an unequal position within society. Instead, Levy argues that child pornography is harmful to women. Child pornography eroticizes inequality—as children cannot be depicted as sexual equals, then "sexualizing children for adult viewers is necessarily sexualizing inequality."[12] This eroticization of inequality inherent within child pornography is harmful to women because it undermines the promotion of sexual equality for women; and it matters not whether child pornography is actual or virtual to negatively impact the equality of women. So, the surprising result is that virtual child pornography is morally objectionable, not because it harms children, but rather because it harms women.

One Final Objection

Perhaps one might seek to undermine my distinction by arguing that the enjoyment of violent imagery for its own sake should be regarded as its own kind of pornography— perhaps we need some new category, like "murder porn." As an example, one might think of the *Saw* series of films, fans of which appear to take gruesome pleasure in these films' depiction of torture and death despite their lacking

any further aesthetic or artistic value. If these should count as murder porn, then violent video games should too—if gamers commit virtual murder because they find it intrinsically enjoyable, then they seem to be treating the video game as murder porn.[13] In response to this objection, I would admit that there does seem to be something rather disturbing about taking pleasure in the depiction of murder and torture; however, I think this argument should be resisted for two reasons. First, it is not clear to me that we should regard this as an instance of pornography as to do so would seem to trivialize the concept pornography. If taking pleasure in the depiction of violence for its own sake should count as pornography, then pornography seems simply to be a concept denoting "things people may take pleasure in that they ought not to." In that case, the enjoyment of junk food and schadenfreude should also count as instances of pornography. Second, it is not obvious to me that the ethical analysis offered by Levy (above) could equally be applied in the case of "murder porn." If pornography is immoral because it is the eroticization of inequality, then could the same be said of murder porn? It is difficult to see how this could work. If taking pleasure in the depiction of violence is morally impermissible, then it would likely be for some other reason.

Conclusion

Luck challenges the gamer to find some relevant moral distinction between virtual murder and virtual paedophilia that justifies the intuition that these acts are morally unequal. The relevant moral distinction between virtual murder and virtual paedophilia that the gamer needs is simply that the latter is an instance of child pornography while the former is not.

It has been argued by Levy that child pornography, whether actual or virtual, is morally objectionable because, through the eroticization of inequality, it undermines women's efforts to achieve genuine equality. Alternatively, depictions of virtual murder are not guilty of an eroticization of inequality, and so are not morally objectionable for this reason.[14] Given this distinction, virtual murder and virtual paedophilia are not on equal footing. While this is not to say that all instances of virtual murder are morally permissible, some are; alternatively, all instances of virtual paedophilia

are morally impermissible. Finally, to reject my account and maintain that the gamer's dilemma is unresolved, one would need to demonstrate either (a) that virtual paedophilia does not count as child pornography despite the fact that it necessarily involves the depiction of sexual acts involving children; (b) that child pornography is not morally objectionable; or (c) that there is no relevant moral distinction between virtual murder and child pornography. If none of these arguments are forthcoming, then we can take the gamer's dilemma to have been resolved.

Notes

1   Luck (2009, p. 35).

2   Ibid., p. 33.

3   Ibid., p. 34.

4   Ibid., p. 35.

5   A similar rating system is featured in various versions of *Grand Theft Auto*—such as the Respect rating system in *Grand Theft Auto: San Andreas*—however, it is important to note that these rating systems are often measures of gang loyalty. While the Honor rating in *Red Dead Redemption* carries an inherent moral aspect as honour is a moral concept, the Respect rating in *Grand Theft Auto* does not.

6   In making this claim, I do not mean to suggest that virtual paedophilia involves an actual child. Rather, I mean to point out that, whether the depicted child is virtual or not, the depiction of sexual acts involving a child constitutes child pornography of a kind. Given this, it may be more accurate to say that each instance of virtual paedophilia is an actual instance of virtual child pornography.

7   I am grateful to an anonymous reader for this journal for this suggestion.

8   Levinson (2005, p. 230).

9   Certainly, one might think that these publications are produced with the intention to be sexually interesting, but Levinson (2005) argues that this is insufficient to count these publications as pornographic. Levinson defends a three-part distinction between pornography, which is produced with the intention to be sexually arousing in the interest of sexual release, erotic art, which is intended to sexually stimulate while also rewarding some artistic interest, and erotica, which is intended to sexually stimulate without rewarding any artistic interest. So, on Levinson's account, a Victoria's Secret catalogue might fall into the category of erotica, not pornography.

10 Rea (2001, p. 120).

11 Levy (2002, p. 322).

12 Ibid.

13 I am grateful to an anonymous reader for this journal for posing this problem.

14 I leave it open whether some depictions of virtual murder are morally objectionable for other reasons. I trust that those cases which are morally objectionable for some other reason fall outside of the scope of Luck's dilemma.

References

King, P. (2008). No plaything: Ethical issues concerning child pornography. *Ethical Theory and Moral Practice, 11*(3), 327–345.

Levinson, J. (2005). Erotic art and pornographic pictures. *Philosophy and Literature, 29,* 228–240.

Levy, N. (2002). Virtual child pornography: The eroticization of inequality. *Ethics and Information Technology, 4*(4), 319–323.

Luck, M. (2009). The gamer's dilemma: An analysis of the arguments for the moral distinction between virtual murder and virtual paedophilia. *Ethics and Information Technology, 11*(1), 31–36.

Rea, M. (2001). What is pornography? *Nous, 35*(1), 118–145.

YOLANDA ESTES

Yolanda Estes introduces the term *erotic identity*, which seems to combine the two senses of the term *sexual identity* as we have explored it so far. On the one hand, it seems to capture the idea of a sexual orientation—in this case BDSM as opposed to homosexual, heterosexual, and so on. On the other hand, she ties her erotic identity in with other aspects of her personhood. "I believe that BDSM activity is integral to my personal and human welfare," she tells us. In her article below, Estes attempts to give an apology for BDSM. The term *apology* used here means a defence or justification for something. Given the importance of BDSM activity to her own identity and welfare, as well as the identity and welfare of many others who adhere to this lifestyle, Estes attempts to clear up some of the misconceptions surrounding BDSM practices and to explore some of the ethical issues related to BDSM.

BDSM: My Apology

Morally problematic, socially divisive, and legally suspect: devotees of BDSM (Bondage-Discipline, Domination-Submission, or Sadism-Masochism) are often treated as the problem children of sexual ethics. This essay is my apology, or defence, for BDSM, which I shall argue can satisfy criteria for mutually respectful erotic interaction but also provokes legitimate ethical concerns within a diverse, complex world. I do not presume to offer a comprehensive discussion of BDSM, to address every ethical issue related to its practice, or to speak for the experience or position of every BDSM identity. Several aspects of my intellectual, social, and personal background—including my transcendental idealism, my feminism, and my BDSM orientation—inform and motivate my account.

As a transcendental idealist, whose philosophy is influenced by J.G. Fichte, I claim that mutually respectful erotic interactions provide a natural milieu—wherein human beings cultivate their ability for reciprocal influence by expressing desires guided by both feeling and reason—that facilitates social, and ultimately moral, consciousness.[1] As a socially and politically conscious woman, whose ethics is coloured by the second and third waves of feminism, I think that social and political justice entails advocating women's efforts to determine, improve, and value their gendered existence, including their diverse, unique sexual experiences.[2] As an individual, whose erotic identity is inseparable from BDSM, I believe that BDSM activity is integral to my personal and human welfare.

Conceptions and Misconceptions of BDSM

I would like to offer a rudimentary conception—and counter some basic misconceptions—of BDSM. BDSM encompasses a multiplicity of erotic inclinations, interests, and behaviours, which may include corporal or behavioural *restraints* (e.g., bondage and discipline); bodily or emotional *control* (e.g., domination and submission); physical or mental *pain* (e.g., sadism and masochism). Erotic partners may engage in *topping* (relatively giving, active) roles or in *bottoming* (relatively receiving, passive) roles within particular erotic interactions. These interactions may be fantastical, theatrical, visual, or aural, or they may be concrete, actual, tactile, or corporeal, but in either case, they elicit a gamut of diverse feelings that vary widely in intensity.

BDSM interactions do not typically entail males harming females, adults molesting youngsters, or culturally central, socially powerful individuals exploiting culturally marginal, socially powerless individuals. Participants are generally consenting adults of similar cultural and social background. Tops and bottoms may be heterosexual men, heterosexual women, gays, lesbians, bisexuals, or transsexuals. Tops are not usually socially domineering, psychologically sadistic personalities and bottoms are not usually socially submissive, psychologically masochistic personalities. Outside of specific erotic contexts, few BDSM participants enjoy inflicting or enduring restraint, control, or pain. Relative to the range of actual sexual practice, participants rarely experience extraordinary sexually related emotional distress, psychosocial dysfunction, or ethical conflict.[3]

Reciprocal Consent, Concern, and Desire

Reciprocal consent, concern, and desire are criteria for *mutually respectful sexual interaction*, which BDSM can meet.[4] Mutual respect requires that sexual partners give explicit, or at least implicit, expression of their voluntary participation in a particular interaction. Additionally, it demands that each exhibits concern for the other's human and personal interests within that interaction. Finally, it compels that both show erotic desire for the other within that interaction.

Within a particular sexual interaction, *reciprocal consent* means that each partner offers compelling evidence of their uncompromised, unforced choice to engage in those activities with the other in a specific context. It is necessary for mutual respect because, without indication that both are willing participants, there is evidence for believing either is an unwilling victim. *Reciprocal concern* means that each partner demonstrates adequate regard for the other as a whole person within that interaction and context. It is essential because the partners' sexualities are inseparable from their unique personalities and overall humanity; and thus, without deference to each person's individual interests and human needs within a sexual interaction, there is ground for thinking that interaction would undermine one or the other's welfare. *Reciprocal desire* means that both partners express complementary erotic expectations and goals for their interaction and that both promote the satisfaction of those expectations and goals within that interaction. It is necessary because without attuned erotic aspirations, there is reason to suspect their interaction would produce sensual or emotional displeasure at best and physical or psychological suffering at worst.

There is no fail-safe, trouble-free method for obtaining reasonable, conscientious belief that reciprocal consent, concern, and desire exist between sexual partners. People are sometimes uncertain about their own volition, interests, and desires, so they can never be certain about their partners'. Esteem, affection, or even love between partners fails to guarantee their mutually respectful interaction. There are only indicators, more or less precise, and signs, more or less ambiguous, to guide sexual activities, which ultimately, everyone must judge before the tribunal of their own conscience. Despite these difficulties, sexual partners are morally obliged to make a *strong effort* to properly solicit, recognize, and interpret *compelling evidence* of analogous volitions, interests, and desires. Moreover, certain precautions increase the probability of mutual respect. Prior to sexual interaction, potential partners can test their compatibility by discussing desires and interests. In the initial stages of interaction, partners can facilitate communication by proceeding cautiously and inquisitively. Before, during, and after sex, each can monitor the other's behaviour, encourage the other's reactions and then, reflect diligently on their observations.

It would be difficult for supporters of BDSM to show that any sexual interaction, including a BDSM interaction, certainly or completely includes mutual respect; but it would be equally difficult for opponents of BDSM to show that any sexual interaction, including a BDSM interaction, certainly and completely precludes mutual respect. Some BDSM partners and some non-BDSM partners adopt precautions that increase the probability of mutual respect whereas other BDSM partners and other non-BDSM partners forgo those precautions. It seems plausible that both BDSM and non-BDSM interactions might involve mutual respect, and thus that some BDSM interactions are morally acceptable, so I shall focus on some common ethical concerns about BDSM.

Inappropriate and Appropriate Concerns about BDSM

I want to dismiss some inappropriate ethical concerns—and reveal some appropriate ethical concerns—associated with BDSM. Although adherents argue that BDSM usually involves consensual erotic interactions, some outsiders regard it as coercive and abusive for a top to inflict seemingly unpleasant, probably dangerous, or potentially injurious actions on a bottom despite explicit protests and pleas for mercy. Had top and bottom not previously negotiated the nature and limits of their interaction (including the protests and pleas), it would be coercive and abusive, but usually they did, so most likely it is not. Nonetheless, some detractors would complain that rational subjects can never morally or legally consent to participate in unpleasant, dangerous, or injurious activities.

Many of these concerns about consent are misguided and disturbingly presumptuous or inconsistent. Some BDSM activities might seem disagreeable, but it is presumptuous to deny participants' perceptions simply because they have unusual sensible tastes. Moreover, apparently rational people willingly (and morally) engage in unpleasant activities, such as child-bearing, civil disobedience, and fasting or other body mortifications. Some BDSM activities are risky, but most are not especially perilous or harmful, and it is inconsistent to deny participants' rationality simply because they make different pragmatic judgments. Moreover, purportedly rational people voluntarily (and legally) participate in dangerous or injurious activities, such as unprotected casual sex, "extreme" sports, and optional surgeries or other body modifications.

There are some legitimate concerns about consent in BDSM particularly, and in sex generally. Consent constitutes an indefinite, limited, and insufficient justification for sexual interaction. It can always be compromised, and can never eliminate the obligation of considering whether it ought to be given and thus, whether it ought to be accepted. Consent implies preliminary permission for one partner to initiate a particular activity and then, to continue or cease according to the other's response. Nonetheless, preliminary consent neither includes immediate permission to initiate any possible activity nor precludes eventual withdrawal of permission to sustain any actual activity. Erotic partners must be attentive and responsive enough to address subtle signs of pleasure, satiation, fear, or distress because initial delighted enthusiasm may become dismayed reluctance or agonized loathing and thus, a consensual interaction may become non-consensual.

These reflections apply to any sexual activity that might compromise consent, but they apply especially to certain BDSM activities. Without some proficiency, otherwise pleasurable, safe activities can turn miserable and hazardous, so each participant must comprehend techniques and risks. The contradictory messages, strained boundaries, and impulsive assaults favoured by some participants might be overplayed or misinterpreted. Responsibly subtle, spontaneous interactions require some intimate familiarity between partners. The psycho-physical intensity of some activities could impair a bottom's self-control, judgment, or communication. When this occurs, a conscientious top assumes responsibility for safely limiting the interaction. Since most BDSM participants are aware of these issues, they tend to be punctilious about consent. Nonetheless, predetermined limits, contracts, scripts, and safe words offer no immunity from error.

Although supporters claim BDSM interactions generally involve adults from similar social classes and include representatives of diverse racial, cultural, and gendered perspectives, some opponents fear that these interactions mimic, exalt, and thereby reinforce, patterns of oppression. Some feminist critics believe that BDSM participants, including gays and lesbians, eroticize misogyny, which they claim is the radical root of all injustice.[5] Clearly, some BDSM participants indulge in role-playing games, such as mistress/servant, teacher/student, or guardian/child, wherein they imitate traditional relationships of domination and submission. Other common scenarios that fete subjugation include possession (treating people like slaves or property), feminization (treating men like women), dehumanization (treating people like pets or livestock), or infantilization (treating adults like babies or children). In these interactions, some participants borrow racial, sexual, or cultural epithets as well as costumes, props, or scripts that evoke objectionable mores and values.

Many concerns about BDSM buttressing oppression are inappropriate and fairly naïve or hypocritical. Contrary to popular representations, BDSM need not entail fantasy, theatre, or even domination and submission. If interactions sometimes imitate, and possibly reinforce, the actual subordination of women, they sometimes initiate, and possibly promote, the potential elevation of women. Participants are as likely to undermine as to support other oppressive patterns insofar as they often subvert conventional models of power and authority.[6] It remains unclear what the assertion that the mechanisms of oppression are embedded within BDSM implies, because those mechanisms are embedded within every social group, and possibly within every human interaction, including the sexual. Is BDSM an erotically cathartic parody of ubiquitous injustice or is ubiquitous injustice an erotically constipated parody of BDSM? In either case, the questionable mores and values expressed by some BDSM participants might simply reveal that many people are woefully conservative and unimaginative regardless of their sexual orientations.

The marks of oppression cannot be erased from sexual or any other human interactions, but they can often be redrawn within human interactions, including the sexual. The human capacity for viciousness sours the sweetness and dulls the colours of existence. This malignant power transforms quotidian pleasures—work, family, bodies, affection, sex—into mordant, shaded tokens of shame and anguish. Usually, this perpetuates a cycle of cruelty, but occasionally someone usurps the machines of tyranny, reclaims the delights of existence, and amends the past on his or her own terms. Such redemption is not achieved by eschewing the tainted aspects of life but by seizing them and then redefining them within a joyful context. BDSM can be an imaginative milieu wherein new meanings are created.

There are appropriate concerns about the relation between socio-political oppression and private erotic activities, including BDSM activities.[7] Individually gratifying, intimate interactions have social and political implications. The interests of upper class, white participants have been overrepresented in many organized, communal BDSM activities. Justice requires participants to consider how their personal relations influence society and state, vulnerable individuals and groups, as well as impressionable youths with BDSM orientations. Nonetheless, the admonition to reflect on the connection between the personal and the political applies to everyone regardless of their sexual orientation.

Although nothing indicates BDSM is more hazardous than myriad other occupations and recreations, some doubters fear it is unduly dangerous. Indeed, some representatives of medicine, law, and government believe the risk of harm to participants warrants regulating or criminalizing BDSM.[8] A common rationale for juridical control is the legal difficulty of distinguishing between authentic consensual and disingenuous non-consensual activities. Another justification appeals to the social need to preserve public health and safety by investigating likely cases of abuse, negligence, or incompetence. The social and legal obligation to prevent indecent, obscene, and offensive behaviour has also been used as a validation.

These concerns about the social or legal rights (and responsibilities) of BDSM participants are mistaken and alarmingly discriminatory. Although practical legal distinction between consent and non-consent always raises thorny problems in cases involving private, informal agreements, compromised consent in private relations does not become inevitable in sex generally, or in BDSM particularly. Many fears that BDSM obfuscates legal consent derive from ignorance of sexual practices, speculation about exceptional possibilities, or overreaction to sensationalized incidents rather than from observation of mundane events.

Health care, social service, and law enforcement professionals should investigate suspicious injury, psychosocial dysfunction, and other indications of abuse and negligence or of mental and physical disability. Nonetheless, demeaning, censorious, or punitive intrusions on the privacy of evidently consenting, competent sexual partners promotes non-compliance, secrecy, and fear rather than medically safe, socially responsible behaviour. Even relatively reckless, uninformed, or incompetent partners would usually benefit more from a referral to a counsellor, who is educated about sexuality, than from a criminal report or charge.

Competent adults are allowed to participate in sundry activities entailing physical risks that range from mild to severe injury, minor to serious illness, temporary to permanent disfigurement, and even to death. They are also permitted to pursue activities that undermine their emotional or social welfare. Some harmful activities are censured within the society or state, but it is inconsistent to prohibit BDSM activities that involve physical, psychological, or social dangers commensurate with permitted occupational, recreational, or sexual activities. Likewise, the legal conundrums that arise from private consensual interactions resulting in manslaughter or suicide are hardly restricted to BDSM-related crimes. Moreover, a just state has some limited obligation to prevent unduly offensive (or otherwise obscene and indecent) public behaviour, but it has no unlimited authority to proscribe obscene and indecent (or otherwise offensive) private behaviour.

There are justified concerns about the physical and psychological dangers of BDSM. Even light play can result in harm, but some heavy play involves risks of critical or life-threatening injury. Intrinsically perilous activities include forceful insertion of large objects in bodily orifices; many forms of electro-stimulation; most strangulation and asphyxiation techniques; heavy or extensive beating, cutting, or burning; and some bondage practices. Psychological damage in BDSM should not be treated as less common or significant than physical harm. Sexually inexperienced or confused, mentally or emotionally fragile, and socially disadvantaged or impaired participants are especially susceptible to injury within callous, unsupportive interactions.

Although any erotic activity involves risk, conscientious participants take appropriate precautions against physical and psychological hazards. Worse than erotically odious, ignorance is morally suspect, and recklessness is unconscionable in BDSM. The need for painstaking forethought increases with the inherent risks of the activities and the particular vulnerabilities of the participants. Sensible, considerate interaction demands accessible information and candid discussion about safety issues pertinent to BDSM. Most activities can be performed safely, but many dictate vigilance and expertise, and some preclude sound, responsible practice.

Conclusion: BDSM in a Diverse, Complex, and Imperfect World

In conclusion, I would like to suggest some lingering ethical issues related to BDSM. BDSM can be consistent with mutually respectful sexual interaction. It is potentially liberating and respectful rather than essentially oppressive and denigrating. It poses moral, socio-political, and legal problems that are mostly ordinary and soluble rather than extraordinary and insoluble. BDSM participants tend toward reflective and cautious behaviour rather than thoughtless or reckless behaviour. Nonetheless, BDSM participants are diverse, complex, and imperfect individuals living in a diverse, complex, and imperfect world.

Abusive relationships, coercive encounters, and sexist, racist, or other oppressive attitudes exist among BDSM participants. Many participants disagree about abuse, coercion, and oppression. Some tolerate or overlook these problems. As a result, many victims avoid seeking help because they feel ashamed and isolated or because they fear condemnation and retaliation. These difficulties increase when society generally misconstrues BDSM as harmful and perverse or censures it as immoral and criminal. BDSM participants should scrutinize their own interactions and relationships, educate and support other participants, and promote comprehension and tolerance of sexual diversity.

Although many health care professionals provide informed, sympathetic service, some regard BDSM as a physically or mentally harmful practice that indicates either a psychosocial disorder or an ethical deficiency. Anxiety about vilifying treatment, social exposure, or legal repercussions discourages some BDSM participants from soliciting medical consultation. Inadequate medical counsel is especially problematic for participants lacking access to the information and support provided by many BDSM communities. Without knowledge of the pertinent health and safety issues, uninformed BDSM participants and medical workers may engage in dicey, inept behaviour. When crises occur, participants may postpone urgent care or receive desultory treatment.

Adequate mental health care also eludes participants, who cannot be entirely forthright or compliant if some psychiatrists, psychologists, or therapists still pressure them to disown their sexual identities. The tendency to conflate sexually related problems and sexual disorders impedes healthy recognition, acceptance, and development of a BDSM orientation. Worry about insinuations of abuse and incompetence deters some participants from receiving couple or family therapy.

Informed, insightful health care helps sustain physically safe, mentally sound, and ethically responsible sexual practice.[9] Members of the health care professions should provide diligent, sound, and courteous care to clients regardless of their sexual orientations. Most health care professionals realize that reproaching clients' sexuality compromises their welfare. Although many professionals have good intentions, some need additional training about sexuality in general and BDSM in particular.

Social and legal censure shrouds BDSM in mysteries that hinder public discussion, rational inquiry, and ethical reflection. Shame or fear dissuades many people from talking about BDSM. Wrangles between more vociferous factions, or dialogues within unique sexual communities, cannot substitute for open conversations incorporating many different voices. The dearth of public discussion perpetuates secrecy and ignorance. Misinformation and obscurity impede intelligent investigation. Most research focuses on exceptional individuals whose behaviour runs them afoul of the law, unfortunate personalities whose difficulties bring them to the attention of social and health services, and privileged minorities

whose activities are supported by BDSM organizations or communities. Little is known about the diverse experiences of most other people with BDSM orientations. The paucity of rational inquiry spawns moral dogmatism and social chauvinism. Ethical reflection about BDSM cannot flourish within an environment that scorns honest discussion, inquiry, and contemplation.

Notes

1 I address this position in more detail in "J.G. Fichte's Account of Human Sexuality: Gender Difference as the Basis for Equality in a Just Society," *Social Philosophy Today* 25 (2009): 63–73.

2 I have considered the connection between sexuality and personal identity and welfare in "Prostitution: A Subjective Position" in *The Philosophy of Sex*, ed. Alan Soble (New York: Rowan and Littlefield, 2007), 353–65 and in "The Myth of the Happy Hooker" in *Violence against Women: Philosophical Perspectives*, eds. Wanda Teays, Laura Purdy, and Stanley French (New York: Cornell, 1998), 152–58.

3 To be sure, there is inadequate demographic information about BDSM for two main reasons. First, BDSM has been a neglected topic in most fields. Second, most demographic information has been obtained through the study of members of organized BDSM communities. One can imagine that some new demographic information will emerge as studies become more frequent and more representative. Nonetheless, recent studies suggest that the BDSM community is diverse and that its members do not differ significantly from members of the general population except for their practice of BDSM. See J. Richter, R.O. De Visser, C.E. Rissel, A.E. Grulich, and A.M. Smith, "Demographic and

Psychosocial Features of Participants in Bondage and Discipline, 'Sadomasochism' or Dominance and Submission (BDSM): Data from a National Survey," *Journal of Sexual Medicine* 5 (2008): 1660–68; Pamela H. Connolly, "Psychological Functioning of Bondage/Domination/ Sadomasochism (BDSM) Practitioners," *Journal of Psychology and Human Sexuality* 18, no. 1 (2006): 79–120; Herbert Weaver, "An Examination of Personality Characteristics Associated with BDSM Orientations," *Canadian Journal of Human Sexuality* 23, no. 2 (2014): 106–15; Thomas S. Weinberg, ed., *S&M: Studies in Dominance and Submission* (New York: Prometheus, 1995).

4 For a detailed discussion of mutual consent, concern, and desire as criteria for mutually respectful and morally acceptable sex, see my "Mutual Respect and Sexual Morality: How to Have College Sex Well" in *College Sex: Philosophy for Everyone*, eds. Michael Bruce and Robert M. Stewart (Singapore: Wiley-Blackwell, 2010), 209–19.

5 For example, see Robin Ruth Linden ed., *Against Sadomasochism: A Radical Feminist Analysis* (Palo Alto, CA: Frog in the Well, 1982). For a differing claim, see Patrick Hopkins, "Rethinking Sadomasochism: Feminism, Interpretation, and Simulation" *Hypatia* 19, no. 1 (1994): 116–41.

During the Sex Wars of the late 1970s and early 1980s, anti-BDSM feminists, such as Andrea Dworkin, and pro-BDSM feminists, such as Gayle Rubin, argued bitterly over whether feminism and BDSM were compatible. During this time, the anti-BDSM cause was represented by the feminist group Women Against Violence in Pornography and Media, and the pro-BDSM cause was represented by the feminist group Samois.

6   For discussions of these issues, see Robin Bauer, "Transgressive and Transformative Gendered Sexual Practices and White Privileges: The Case of the Dyke/Trans in BDSM Communities," *Women's Studies Quarterly* 36, no. 3/4 (2008): 233–53; and Laura Zambelli, "BDSM in Italy: Analyzing Stereotypes about Gender, Sexuality, and the Body" in *Gender, Sexuality, and the Body*, eds. Sofia Aboim and Pedro Vasconelos (Lisbon: Estudos e Relatórios, 2014), 90–100.

7   For a discussion of some of these issues, see Jenna Basiliere, "Political is Personal: Scholarly manifestations of the Sex Wars," *Michigan Feminist Studies* 22, no. 1 (2008/09): 1–25.

8   For discussions of the legal status and implications of BDSM, see Maneesha Deckha, "Pain, Pleasure, and Consenting Women: Exploring Feminist Responses to S/M and Its Legal Regulation in Canada through Jelinek's *The Piano Teacher*," *Harvard Journal of Law and Gender* 2, no. 30 (2007): 425–59; Theodore Bennett, "A Polyvocal (Re)Modeling of the Jurisprudence of Sadomasochism," *Australian Law Review* 199 (2012/13): 199–221; Chris White, "The Spanner Trials and the Changing Law on Sadomasochism in the UK," *Journal of Homosexuality* 50, no. 2/3 (2006): 167–87; Annette Houlihan, "When 'No' means 'Yes' and 'Yes' means Harm: Gender, Sexuality, and Sadomasochism Criminality," *Law and Sexuality* 20, no. 31 (2011): 31–60.

9   For discussions of medical care for BDSM participants, see Keely Kolmes, Wendy Stock, and Charles Moser, "Investigating Bias in Psychotherapy with BDSM Clients," *Journal of Homosexuality* 50, no. 2/3 (2006): 301–24; Gabriele Hoff and Richard A. Sprott, "Therapy Experiences of Clients with BDSM Sexualities: Listening to a Stigmatized Sexuality," *Electronic Journal of Human Sexuality* 12 (2009), http://www.ejhs.org/Volume12/bdsm.htm; Charles Moser, "Demystifying Alternative Sexual Behaviors," *Sexuality, Reproduction, and Menopause* 4, no. 2 (2006): 86–90.

Discussion

Are there problems inherent in the practice of BDSM? In Chapter 1 Thomas Nagel characterized BDSM as a perversion. Does this make it morally problematic? Nagel did not think so, but he did think that BDSM practices were incomplete sex practices. Do you agree with him? Do you think that Yolanda Estes, whose sexual identity is tied up with BDSM, would agree with Nagel's characterization? How might she respond to Nagel?

Estes notes that critics of BDSM are concerned about the fact that many of its practices mimic the inequality, oppression, and abuse that we have been trying to rid society of. The worry here is that such practices might reinforce the very attitudes that we have been fighting against. While acknowledging that there are legitimate ethical concerns with BDSM practices, Estes notes that these practices have also subverted traditional power structures. Often participants who are dominant in "real" life play a submissive role in BDSM and those who are generally submissive take on a role of dominance. Could this reversal of roles prove cathartic, as Estes suggests? If, as she claims, the mechanisms of oppression are embedded not only in BDSM but also "within every social group, and possibly within every human interaction, including the sexual," then could BDSM practices present a challenge to these very structures?

While there are many differences between the world of BDSM and the virtual world of video games, they do give rise to a common ethical concern. The activities associated with both practices raise the question of whether the same ethical rules that apply *outside* of a given practice or activity are the same rules that apply *within* that activity. We have already raised this issue in the context of gaming where the *victims* are not real people but are rather virtual characters. In the context of BDSM, the participants are real flesh and blood people whose bodies can be injured. Outside of the context of this practice, the activities engaged in would be considered immoral if not illegal. Do the context and the voluntary nature of these practices affect the ethical considerations involved? Can the normal moral rules be suspended in this case?

One might also bring in a specific type of ethical consideration when considering both of these activities. The ethics of the ancient Greek philosopher Aristotle emphasized the idea of virtue and the ideal of a virtuous character. To be virtuous one must engage in practices that express or help one to acquire courage, temperance, or other virtues. Can violence in video games or violence in BDSM practices have a negative effect on one's character? Do such practices affect who we are outside of the specific realm in which they are indulged? If, as Estes claims, her sexual identity is intimately tied to BDSM practices, does this mean that she cannot be virtuous in the Aristotelian sense? Or, can one engage in virtuous BDSM practice? Given that the practice requires a high degree of judgment in order to be ethical and safe as Estes tells us, the possibility would seem to exist of developing something like a concept of a virtuous BDSM ideal. Likewise, can participation in video games in the right way help develop a virtuous character? Bartel suggests this might be possible when he notes that *Red Dead Redemption* in contrast to *Grand Theft Auto* has an "Honor rating" whereby one loses points for committing certain kinds of violent acts. This suggests that either individual gamers can develop virtuous practices within games or the game designers themselves can incorporate a possible structure for virtuous activity or choices into their games. Alternatively, it might be healthy or good to work out in fantasy or role-playing what one would not want to explore in real life. Perhaps the benefit lies not in trying to make these activities themselves virtuous, but in providing an avenue for catharsis for certain negative desires or emotions. Is there perhaps something healthy about this given one's sexual desires?

Suggestions for Further Reading

Pamela H. Connolly, "Psychological Functioning of Bondage/Domination/Sadomasochism (BDSM) Practitioners," *Journal of Psychology and Human Sexuality* 18, no. 1 (2006): 79–120.

Maneesha Deckha, "Pain, Pleasure, and Consenting Women: Exploring Feminist Responses to S/M and Its Legal Regulation in Canada through Jelinek's *The Piano Teacher*," *Harvard Journal of Law and Gender* 2, no. 30 (2007): 425–459.

Morgan Luck, "The Gamer's Dilemma: An Analysis of the Arguments for the Moral Distinction Between Virtual Murder and Virtual Paedophilia," *Ethics and Information Technology* 11 (2009): 31–36.

Morgan Luck and Nathan Ellerby, "Has Bartel Resolved the Gamer's Dilemma?" *Ethics and Information Technology* 15 (2013): 229–33.

Part 2 Love

Introduction to the Philosophy of Love

As mentioned in the Preface, Irving Singer and Alan Soble have contributed greatly to the establishment of the philosophy of love as a field of study in academic philosophy. Both Singer and Soble focus on two forms of love that are prominent in Western thinking: *eros* and *agape*. The consideration of these two concepts raises a number of important questions about the nature of love.

Agape and Eros: Two Types of Love

In his monumental work *Agape and Eros*, the Swedish theologian Anders Nygren elaborated the differences between these two kinds of love. Nygren characterized them as representing two distinct attitudes towards life or two distinct systems of value. He characterized agape in terms of four main features: it is (1) spontaneous and unmotivated, (2) indifferent to value, (3) creative, and (4) it is the initiator to fellowship with God. By contrast, Nygren characterized eros as (1) acquisitive love, (2) the human way to the divine, and (3) as egocentric love.[1] In short, agape has its source in God and is given to humankind as a gift. Eros, on the other hand, originates with humankind and expresses the human desire to reach the divine (the Good or Beauty in Plato's version of eros). According to Nygren, the two different systems of value expressed by these concepts of love are incommensurable. To live inside of one system requires rejecting the terms of the other.

Now agape, strictly speaking, is God's love. Presumably only God can love in a purely agapic way. But some theologians believed that humans could love agapically by way of God's grace. This means that either God enables human beings to love in this manner by helping them remove the egoistic aspect of their love or God loves *through* them. Søren Kierkegaard's neighbour love would seem to be an example of this.[2] An alternative form of the agapic view is presented to us by Harry Frankfurt. Although Frankfurt does not call his view of love agapic, this form of love is clearly agapically structured. The main difference between his view and the traditional view of agape is that he characterizes it in naturalistic terms with humans rather than God as the source.[3]

This distinction between agape and eros, as I mentioned in the Preface, played an important role in Irving Singer's characterization of love. Singer contrasts *bestowal*, characteristic of agape, with *appraisal*, characteristic of eros. Indeed, Singer's three-volume work is an attempt to show how these two concepts can be reconciled in a notion of love. For Singer, love cannot be mere appraisal, since then we could not distinguish it from other forms of desire-based evaluations. On the other hand, love cannot be merely bestowal, for "unless we appraised we could not bestow a value that goes beyond appraisal."[4] Singer discusses historical attempts to reconcile the two notions of love such as the medieval synthesis contained in the idea of *caritas*.[5] His own work can be seen as a continuation of this historical quest to reconcile these two loves.

In his work *The Structure of Love*, Alan Soble argues that Singer fails to bring about a true reconciliation of these two concepts in his notion of love. As mentioned in the Preface, Soble distinguishes between erosic and agapic love according to how these forms of love are structured. Erosic love is object-centred while agapic love is subject-centred. This means that, in the erosic view of love, it is the beloved and/or his properties that give rise to the love of the lover, while in the agapic view, the lover herself is the source of that love. The opposition between these two views, Soble notes, gives rise to a *Euthyphro* problem concerning love. Do I love someone because they are loveable (i.e., have loveable or attractive properties), or are they loveable (attractive, valuable) because I love them? Soble ultimately thinks that the agapic view is irrational. To love someone for no prior reasons or without consideration for the properties that constitute him makes no sense. Love relies on reasons or properties of the beloved in order to be discriminant; otherwise, why would we love one person more than another? Soble admits that a bestowal takes place at some point in love, but it is a bestowal on the properties of the person and it is these properties that ultimately ground love.[6] This bestowal plays a part in love that is subordinate to the appraisive or erosic aspect, but, according to Soble, the role that it plays is misrepresented by characterizing it in terms of a reconciliation with appraisal.

Love and Identity

As was the case with sexual desire, love plays an important role in our identity. Who we love, who we are loved by, how we love, and how we conceive of love are all important aspects of who we are. Just as he analyzed sexual desire in terms of the more fundamental desire *to be*, so Sartre also analyzes love. Sartre associates love with a general attitude toward other people that is, among other things, masochistic. Now this sounds like an odd characterization of love, but in order to understand what he means, it is important to keep in mind Sartre's ontology. The desire to be, remember, involves striving to experience oneself as both subject and object. In the project of love, according to Sartre, I make myself an object in order to seduce the Other. To seduce is to make oneself a fascinating object for the

Other's subjectivity. One does this to capture the freedom of the Other. Once again, the aim of this is so that I can experience my object side through the look of my beloved. As was the case with sexual desire and indeed the general desire to be, the game is fixed. Love is destined to fail. Either I make myself into a fascinating object for the Other (the masochistic attitude) to seduce her, and in so doing lose sight of my own subjectivity, or I experience my own subjectivity while viewing the Other as an object (the sadistic attitude).[7] I cannot experience both simultaneously. Sartre's account of love is *romantic* in the true sense of having been shaped by ideas that emerged from the artistic and philosophic movement called Romanticism. The most common theme of romantic love is the idea that two separate individuals come together to form some kind of union or a new *shared* identity. The romantic idea of love of course had its predecessor in the view put forth by Aristophanes in Plato's *Symposium*, which is included in this volume. If we take Aristophanes' story in a non-literal way (and since he was a comic, then why wouldn't we?), what we have is an account that is very much like modern romantic love.

Sartre's long-time partner, Simone de Beauvoir, would characterize love—romantic love in particular—as something that men and women experience quite differently. In her major work, *The Second Sex*, which was very influential in the feminist movement of the twentieth century, de Beauvoir tells us that traditionally women have lost their identity in the love relationship. The *shared identity* that was the goal of romantic love turned out to be shared in an unequal manner. The woman, de Beauvoir tells us, found her identity within this union or shared identity, whereas the man kept his identity separate or made the relationship only one aspect of that identity. For the woman in love, her *self* was to be found in the relationship, whereas, for the man, this *self* was independent. Is this inequality a product of romantic love itself or is it, as Robert Solomon has argued, the effect of experiencing romantic love under the conditions of sexual inequality?[8]

Friendship

In addition to agape and eros, the ancient Greeks also possessed a form of love called *philia*, which is normally defined as friendship love. In his *Nicomachean Ethics*, Aristotle presents an important discussion of friendship. In Chapter VIII he describes three different types of friendships: (1) friendship based on usefulness, (2) friendship based on pleasure, and (3) perfect friendship. The first two forms of friendship, Aristotle tells us, rely on an attribute of the friend (usefulness or pleasure), which, if it disappears, implies the dissolving of the friendship. The third, however, is a friendship not for the sake of some attribute but for the sake of the friend himself. We might say that in the first two types of friendship, the friend is valued *extrinsically* or for the sake of something he can provide; whereas in the third type of friendship, the friend is valued *intrinsically* or for his own sake.[9]

Although Aristotle would seem to hold the view that we may need all three types of friendship, he argues that we particularly need the third kind to live a good life. I think that even today we would agree with Aristotle on this point, or at least we would agree that we need something approximating his highest form of friendship. Friends play an important role in our lives. Not only do friends help us in tough times and celebrate with us in good times, they provide a kind of mirror to ourselves so that we can see aspects of ourselves that we could not see on our own. They also help us to think and act, according to Aristotle. As we discuss our ideas or thoughts with friends they give us valuable responses and help keep us from making serious mistakes. They also help add new words, ideas, or concepts to our vocabulary and thinking so that we get an expanded understanding of the world, of others, and of our self. Likewise, by allowing us to play a similar role in their lives (celebrating their victories or comforting them through loss), friends allow us to be compassionate, to do good works, and to experience the wide range of emotions and practices that make us human. In an important way, our experience with close friends, like our experience with a romantic partner or spouse, helps us to understand ourselves and opens the door for us to become a better version of our *self.*

Friendship, as with other forms of love, plays a role in shaping and maintaining our identity. Friends see aspects of us that need our attention both positively and negatively. A friend may see some bad attitude that we express or a bad habit that we possess and to which we are oblivious. On the other hand, a friend may see some strength or talent of which we might not be fully aware and they may encourage us to develop it. In this sense, a friend plays the role of Sartre's Other in helping us to understand that side of our self that is normally hidden from our view. Of course, we need not accept Sartre's characterization of friendship or love as expressing the desire *to be* in order to see the value of this point. Friends, whether they help complete us or not, make us become more aware of ourselves or encourage us to gain self-knowledge. They also help us better understand others and the world around us, and in this sense assist us in developing ethical virtues.

Notes

1   Anders Nygren, *Eros and Agape* (Chicago: University of Chicago Press, 1982).

2   See Søren Kierkegaard, *Works of Love*, ed. and trans. Howard V. Hong and Edna H. Hong (Princeton: Princeton University Press), 1995.

3   Harry G. Frankfurt, *The Reasons of Love* (Princeton: Princeton University Press), 40.

4   Irving Singer, *The Nature of Love 1: Plato to Luther*, 2nd ed. (Chicago: University of Chicago Press, 1984), 9.

5   Ibid., 312–42.

6   Alan Soble, *The Structure of Love* (New Haven, CT: Yale University Press, 1990), 23–28.

7   I should mention that Sartre expresses a more optimistic view of love later in life in his notes for a work on ethics that was never completed but that has since been published in its incomplete form. See Jean-Paul Sartre, *Notebooks for an Ethics*, trans. David Pellauer (Chicago: University of Chicago Press, 1992).

8   Robert Solomon, *Love: Emotion, Myth and Metaphor* (Garden City, NY: Doubleday, 1981).

9   Aristotle, *Aristotle: Selected Works*, trans. Hippocrates G. Apostle and Lloyd P. Gerson (Grinnell, IA: Peripatetic Press, 1983), 503–8.

Section IV   The Nature of Love

Chapter Nine
Traditions of Love

Introduction

Love and philosophy have a very long-term relationship. Over 2,500 years ago, Plato wrote two dialogues about love: the "Phaedrus" and the "Symposium." Part of the latter has been included in this chapter. The Symposium takes place at the home of Agathon. It is an odd sort of banquet where many of the guests were terribly hungover from partying too much the night before. Eryximachus, the physician, proposes that those present give speeches to honour Love. The group agrees to this and seven separate speeches follow. Although each of the speeches presents us with interesting and colourful accounts of love, we will look at only two very influential ones. Aristophanes' speech about the origins of love has been seen as a precursor to our modern notion of romantic love. The writer of comedies tells us the humorous story of how the primeval being who had two heads, four arms, four legs, and two privy members was split in two by the gods. Love, according to Aristophanes, is expressed in that desire to be reunited with one's other half. Now you know where that idea comes from. Socrates' speech is a report of what he learned from Diotima—his instructress in the art of love. According to Diotima, love arises out of a desire for the Good or the Beautiful. The life of the lover (or the philosopher in this case) consists in the pursuit of true Beauty. We begin by learning to love one beautiful body but move on to loving many. We must not become too attached to one body because true Beauty consists in that which the many particular beautiful things have in common. From the beauty of bodies we move on to see the beauty of souls and then the beauty inherent in laws and institutions. In other words, love moves us towards things whose beauty is more and more universal since true Beauty is that which makes all particular things beautiful. Thus, love in Plato's view involves an *ascent* from lower forms where beauty is seen or understood imperfectly towards higher forms that are closer to true Beauty. The ultimate end of love's pursuit is true and perfect beauty, which cannot be experienced through the body but only by way of the intellect. In his view of love, then, Plato, somewhat paradoxically, encourages a form of promiscuity on the one hand (we must not become attached to one form of beauty as expressed in a particular body but must explore beauty in all its forms), and, on the other, a faithfulness to love's one true object—Beauty itself.

PLATO

From *The Symposium*: Aristophanes' Speech and Socrates' Speech

Aristophanes' Speech

Then Aristophanes took over (so Aristodemus said): "The hiccups have stopped all right—but not before I applied the Sneeze Treatment to them. Makes me wonder whether the 'orderly sort of Love' in the body calls for the sounds and itchings that constitute a sneeze, because the hiccups stopped immediately when I applied the Sneeze Treatment."

"You're good, Aristophanes," Eryximachus answered. "But watch what you're doing. You are making jokes before your speech, and you're forcing me to prepare for you to say something funny, and to put up my guard against you, when otherwise you might speak at peace."

Then Aristophanes laughed. "Good point, Eryximachus. So let me 'unsay what I have said.' But don't put up your guard. I'm not worried about saying something funny in my coming oration. That would be pure profit, and it comes with the territory of my Muse. What I'm worried about is that I might say something ridiculous."

"Aristophanes, do you really think you can take a shot at me, and then escape? Use your head! Remember, as you speak, that you will be called upon to give an account. Though perhaps, if I decide to, I'll let you off."

"Eryximachus," Aristophanes said, "indeed I do have in mind a different approach to speaking than the one the two of you used, you and Pausanias. You see, I think people have entirely missed the power of Love, because, if they had grasped it, they'd have built the greatest temples and altars to him and made the greatest sacrifices. But as it is, none of this is done for him, though it should be, more than anything else! For he loves the human race more than any other god, he stands by us in our troubles, and he cures those ills we humans are most happy to have mended. I shall, therefore, try to explain his power to you; and you, please pass my teaching on to everyone else."

First you must learn what Human Nature was in the beginning and what has happened to it since, because long ago our nature was not what it is now, but very different. There were three kinds of human beings, that's my first point—not two as there are now, male and female. In addition to these, there was a third, a combination of those two; its name survives, though the kind itself has vanished. At that time, you see, the word "androgynous" really meant something: a form made up of male and female elements, though now there's nothing but the word, and that's used as an insult. My second point is that the shape of each human being was completely round, with back and sides in a circle; they had four hands each, as many legs as hands, and two faces, exactly alike, on a rounded neck. Between the two faces, which were on opposite sides, was one head with four ears. There were two sets of sexual organs, and everything else was the way you'd imagine it from what I've told you. They walked upright, as we do now, whatever direction they wanted. And whenever they set out to run fast, they thrust out all their eight limbs, the ones they had then, and spun rapidly, the way gymnasts do cartwheels, by bringing their legs around straight.

Now here is why there were three kinds, and why they were as I described them: The male kind was originally an offspring of the sun, the female of the earth, and the one that combined both genders was an offspring of the moon, because the moon shares in both. They were spherical, and so was their motion, because they were like their parents in the sky.

In strength and power, therefore, they were terrible, and they had great ambitions. They made an attempt on the gods, and Homer's story about Ephialtes and Otus was originally about them: how they tried to make an ascent to heaven so as to attack the gods.[1] Then Zeus and the other gods met in council to discuss what to do, and they were sore perplexed. They couldn't wipe out the human race with thunderbolts and kill them all off, as they had the giants, because that would wipe out the worship they receive, along with the sacrifices we humans give them. On the other hand, they couldn't let them run riot. At last, after great effort, Zeus had an idea.

"I think I have a plan," he said, "that would allow human beings to exist and stop their misbehaving: they will give up being wicked when they lose their strength. So I shall now cut each of them in two. At one stroke they will lose their strength and also become more profitable to us, owing to the increase in their number. They shall walk upright on two legs. But if I find they still run riot and do not keep the peace," he said, "I will cut them in two again, and they'll have to make their way on one leg, hopping."

So saying, he cut those human beings in two, the way people cut sorb-apples before they dry them or the way they cut eggs with hairs. As he cut each one, he commanded Apollo to turn its face and half its neck towards the wound, so that each person would see that he'd been cut and keep better order. Then Zeus commanded Apollo to heal the rest of the wound, and Apollo did turn the face around, and he drew skin from all sides over what is now called the stomach, and there he made one mouth, as in a pouch with a drawstring, and fastened it at the center of the stomach. This is now called the navel. Then he smoothed out the other wrinkles, of which there were many, and he shaped the breasts, using some such tool as shoemakers have for smoothing wrinkles out of leather on the form. But he left a few wrinkles around the stomach and the navel, to be a reminder of what happened long ago.

Now, since their natural form had been cut in two, each one longed for its own other half, and so they would throw their arms about each other, weaving themselves together, wanting to grow together. In that condition they would die from hunger and general idleness, because they would not do anything apart from each other. Whenever one of the halves died and one was left, the one that was left still sought another and wove itself together with that. Sometimes the half he met came from a woman, as we'd call her now, sometimes it came from a man; either way, they kept on dying.

Then, however, Zeus took pity on them, and came up with another plan: he moved their genitals around to the front! Before then, you see, they used to have their genitals outside, like their faces, and they cast seed and made children, not in one another, but in the ground, like cicadas. So Zeus brought about this relocation of genitals, and in doing so he invented interior reproduction, *by the man in* the woman. The purpose of this was so that, when a man embraced a woman, he would cast his seed and they would have children; but when male embraced male, they would at least have the satisfaction of intercourse, after which they could stop embracing, return to their jobs, and look after their other needs in life. This, then, is the source of our desire to love each other. Love is born into every human being; it calls back the halves of our original nature together; it tries to make one out of two and heal the wound of human nature.

Each of us, then, is a "matching half" of a human whole, because each was sliced like a flatfish, two out of one, and each of us is always seeking the half that matches him. That's why a man who is split from the double sort (which used to be called "androgynous") runs after women. Many lecherous men have come from this class, and so do the lecherous women who run after men. Women who are split from a woman, however, pay no attention at all to men; they are oriented more towards women, and lesbians come from this class. People who are split from a male are male-oriented. While they are boys, because they are chips off the male block, they love men and enjoy lying with men and being embraced by men; those are the best of boys and lads, because they are the most manly in their nature. Of course, some say such boys are shameless, but they're lying. It's not because they have no shame that such boys do this, you see, but because they are bold and brave and masculine, and they

tend to cherish what is like themselves. Do you want me to prove it? Look, these are the only kind of boys who grow up to be real men in politics. When they're grown men, they are lovers of young men, and they naturally pay no attention to marriage or to making babies, except insofar as they are required by local custom. They, however, are quite satisfied to live their lives with one another unmarried. In every way, then, this sort of man grows up as a lover of young men and a lover of Love, always rejoicing in his own kind.

And so, when a person meets the half that is his very own, whatever his orientation, whether it's to young men or not, then something wonderful happens: the two are struck from their senses by love, by a sense of belonging to one another, and by desire, and they don't want to be separated from one another, not even for a moment.

These are the people who finish out their lives together and still cannot say what it is they want from one another. No one would think it is the intimacy of sex—that mere sex is the reason each lover takes so great and deep a joy in being with the other. It's obvious that the soul of every lover longs for something else; his soul cannot say what it is, but like an oracle it has a sense of what it wants, and like an oracle it hides behind a riddle. Suppose two lovers are lying together and Hephaestus[2] stands over them with his mending tools, asking, "What is it you human beings really want from each other?" And suppose they're perplexed, and he asks them again: "Is this your heart's desire, then—for the two of you to become parts of the same whole, as near as can be, and never to separate, day or night? Because if that's your desire, I'd like to weld you together and join you into something that is naturally whole, so that the two of you are made into one. Then the two of you would share one life, as long as you lived, because you would be one being, and by the same token, when you died, you would be one and not two in Hades, having died a single death. Look at your love, and see if this is what you desire: wouldn't this be all the good fortune you could want?"

Surely you can see that no one who received such an offer would turn it down; no one would find anything else that he wanted. Instead, everyone would think he'd found out at last what he had always wanted: to come together and melt together with the one he loves, so that one person emerged from two. Why should this be so? It's because, as I said, we used to be complete wholes in our original nature, and now "Love" is the name for our pursuit of wholeness, for our desire to be complete.

Long ago we were united, as I said; but now the god has divided us as punishment for the wrong we did him, just as the Spartans divided the Arcadians.[3] So there's a danger that if we don't keep order before the gods, we'll be split in two again, and then we'll be walking around in the condition of people carved on gravestones in bas-relief, sawn apart between the nostrils, like half dice. We should encourage all men, therefore, to treat the gods with all due reverence, so that we may escape this fate and find wholeness instead. And we will, if Love is our guide and our commander. Let no one work against him. Whoever opposes Love is hateful to the gods, but if we become friends of the god and cease to quarrel with him, then we shall find the young men that are meant for us and win their love, as very few men do nowadays.

Now don't get ideas, Eryximachus, and turn this speech into a comedy. Don't think I'm pointing this at Pausanias and Agathon.

Probably, they both do belong to the group that are entirely masculine in nature. But I am speaking about everyone, men and women alike, and I say there's just one way for the human race to flourish: we must bring love to its perfect conclusion, and each of us must win the favours of his very own young man, so that he can recover his original nature. If that is the ideal, then, of course, the nearest approach to it is best in present circumstances, and that is to win the favour of young men who are naturally sympathetic to us.

If we are to give due praise to the god who can give us this blessing, then, we must praise Love. Love does the best that can be done for the time being: he draws us towards what belongs to us. But for the future, Love promises the greatest hope of all: if we treat the gods with due reverence, he will restore to us our original nature, and by healing us, he will make us blessed and happy.

"That," he said, "is my speech about Love, Eryximachus. It is rather different from yours. As I begged you earlier, don't make a comedy of it. I'd prefer to hear what all the others will say—or, rather, what each of them will say, since Agathon and Socrates are the only ones left."

"I found your speech delightful," said Eryximachus, "so I'll do as you say. Really, we've had such a rich feast of speeches on Love, that if I couldn't vouch for the fact that Socrates and Agathon are masters of the art of love, I'd be afraid that they'd have nothing left to say. But as it is, I have no fears on this score." . . .

Socrates' Speech

Then Aristodemus said that Phaedrus and the others urged him to speak in the way he thought was required, whatever it was.

"'Well then, Phaedrus," said Socrates, "allow me to ask Agathon a few little questions, so that, once I have his agreement, I may speak on that basis."

"You have my permission," said Phaedrus. "Ask away."

After that, said Aristodemus, Socrates began: "Indeed, Agathon, my friend, I thought you led the way beautifully into your speech when you said that one should first show the qualities of Love himself, and only then those of his deeds. I must admire that beginning. Come, then, since you have beautifully and magnificently expounded his qualities in other ways, tell me this, too, about Love. Is Love such as to be a love of something or of nothing? I'm not asking if he is born *of* some mother or father (for the question whether Love is love of mother or of father would really be ridiculous), but it's as if I'm asking this about a father—whether a father is the father *of* something or not. You'd tell me, of course, if you wanted to give me a good answer, that it's *of* a son or a daughter that a father is the father. Wouldn't you?"

"Certainly," said Agathon.

"Then does the same go for the mother?"

He agreed to that also.

"Well, then," said Socrates, "answer a little more fully, and you will understand better what I want. If I should ask, "What about this: a brother, just insofar as he *is* a brother, is he the brother of something or not?"

He said that he was.

"And he's of a brother or a sister, isn't he?"

He agreed.

"Now try to tell me about love," he said. "Is Love the love of nothing or of something?"

"Of something, surely!"

"Then keep this object of love in mind, and remember what it is.[4] But tell me this much: does Love desire that of which it is the love, or not?"

"Certainly," he said.

"At the time he desires and loves something, does he actually have what he desires and loves at that time, or doesn't he?"

"He doesn't. At least, that wouldn't be likely," he said.

"Instead of what's *likely*," said Socrates, "ask yourself whether it's *necessary* that this be so: a thing that desires desires something of which it is in need; otherwise, if it were not in need, it would not desire it. I can't tell you, Agathon, how strongly it strikes me that this is necessary. But how about you?"

"I think so too."

"Good. Now then, would someone who is tall, want to be tall? Or someone who is strong want to be strong?"

"Impossible, on the basis of what we've agreed."

"Presumably because no one is in need of those things he already has."

"True."

"But maybe a strong man could want to be strong," said Socrates, "or a fast one fast, or a healthy one healthy: in cases like these, you might think people really do want to be things they already are and do want to have qualities they already have—I bring them up so they won't deceive us. But in these cases, Agathon, if you stop to think about them, you will see that these people are what they are at the present time, whether they want to be or not, by a logical necessity. And who, may I ask, would ever bother to desire what's necessary in any event? But when someone says 'I am healthy, but that's just what I want to be,' or 'I am rich, but that's just what I want to be,' or 'I desire the very things that I have,' let us say to him: 'You already have riches and health and strength in your possession, my man, what you want is to possess these things in time to come, since in the present, whether you want to or not, you have them. Whenever you say, *I desire what I already have*, ask yourself whether you don't mean this: '*I want the things I have now to be mine in the future as well.*' Wouldn't he agree?"

According to Aristodemus, Agathon said that he would.

So Socrates said, "Then this is what it is to love something which is not at hand, which the lover does not have: it is to desire the preservation of what he now has in time to come, so that he will have it then."

"Quite so," he said.

"So such a man or anyone else who has a desire desires what is not at hand and not present, what he does not have, and what he is not, and that of which he is in need; for such are the objects of desire and love."

"Certainly," he said.

"Come, then," said Socrates. "Let us review the points on which we've agreed. Aren't they, first, that Love is the love of something, and, second, that he loves things of which he has a present need?"

"Yes," he said.

"Now, remember, in addition to these points, what you said in your speech about what it is that Love loves. If you like, I'll remind you. I think you said something like this: that the gods' quarrels were settled by love of beautiful things, for there is no love of ugly ones.[5] Didn't you say something like that?"

"I did," said Agathon.

"And that's a suitable thing to say, my friend," said Socrates. "But if this is so, wouldn't Love have to be a desire for beauty, and never for ugliness?"

He agreed.

"And we also agreed that he loves just what he needs and does not have."

"Yes," he said.

"So Love needs beauty, then, and does not have it."

"Necessarily," he said.

"So! If something needs beauty and has got no beauty at all, would you still say that it is beautiful?"

"Certainly not."

"Then do you still agree that Love is beautiful, if those things are so?"

Then Agathon said, "It turns out, Socrates, I didn't know what I was talking about in that speech."

"It was a beautiful speech, anyway, Agathon," said Socrates. "Now take it a little further. Don't you think that good things are always beautiful as well?"

"I do."

"Then if Love needs beautiful things, and if all good things are beautiful, he will need good things too."

"As for me, Socrates," he said, "I am unable to contradict you. Let it be as you say."

"Then it's the truth, my beloved Agathon, that you are unable to contradict," he said. "It is not hard at all to contradict Socrates."

Now I'll let you go. I shall try to go through for you the speech about Love I once heard from a woman of Mantinea, Diotima—a woman who was wise about many things besides this: once she even put off the plague for ten years by telling the Athenians what sacrifices to make. She is the one who taught me the art of love, and I shall go through her speech as best I can on my own, using what Agathon and I have agreed to as a basis. Following your lead, Agathon, one should first describe who Love is and what he is like, and afterwards describe his works—I think it will be easiest for me to proceed the way Diotima did and tell you how she questioned me.

You see, I had told her almost the same things Agathon told me just now: that Love is a great god and that he belongs to beautiful things.[6] And she used the very same arguments against me that I used against Agathon; she showed how, according to my very own speech, Love is neither beautiful nor good.

So I said, "What do you mean, Diotima? Is Love ugly, then, and bad?"

But she said, "Watch your tongue! Do you really think that, if a thing is not beautiful, it has to be ugly?"

"I certainly do."

"And if a thing's not wise, it's ignorant? Or haven't you found out yet that there's something in between wisdom and ignorance?"

"What's that?"

"It's judging things correctly without being able to give a reason. Surely you see that this is not the same as knowing—for how could knowledge be unreasoning? And it's not ignorance either—for how could what hits the truth be ignorance? Correct judgment, of course, has this character: it is *in between* understanding and ignorance."

"True," said I, "as you say."

"Then don't force whatever is not beautiful to be ugly, or whatever is not good to be bad. It's the same with Love: when you agree he is neither good nor beautiful, you need not think he is ugly and bad; he could be something in between," she said.

"Yet everyone agrees he's a great god," I said.

"Only those who don't know?" she said. "Is that how you mean 'everyone'? Or do you include those who do know?"

"Oh, everyone together."

And she laughed. "Socrates, how could those who say that he's not a god at all agree that he's a great god?"

"Who says that?" I asked.

"You, for one," she said, "and I for another."

"How can you say this!" I exclaimed.

"That's easy," said she. "Tell me, wouldn't you say that all gods are beautiful and happy? Surely you'd never say a god is not beautiful or happy?"

"Zeus! Not I," I said.

"Well, by calling anyone 'happy,' don't you mean they possess good and beautiful things?"

"Certainly."

"What about Love? You agreed he needs good and beautiful things, and that's why he desires them—because he needs them."

"I certainly did."

"Then how could he be a god if he has no share in good and beautiful things?"

"There's no way he could, apparently."

"Now do you see? You don't believe Love is a god either!"

"Then, what could Love be?" I asked. "A mortal?"

"Certainly not."

"Then, what is he?"

"He's like what we mentioned before," she said. "He is in between mortal and immortal."

"What do you mean, Diotima?"

"He's a great spirit, Socrates. Everything spiritual, you see, is in between god and mortal."

"What is their function?" I asked.

"They are messengers who shuttle back and forth between the two, conveying prayer and sacrifice from men to gods, while to men they bring commands from the gods and gifts in return for sacrifices. Being in the middle of the two, they round out the whole and bind fast the all to all. Through them all divination passes, through them the art of priests in sacrifice and ritual, in enchantment, prophecy, and sorcery. Gods do not mix with men; they mingle and converse with us through spirits instead, whether we are awake or asleep. He who is wise in any of these ways is a man of the spirit, but he who is wise in any other way, in a profession or any manual work, is merely a mechanic. These spirits are many and various, then, and one of them is Love."

"Who are his father and mother?" I asked.

"That's rather a long story," she said. "I'll tell it to you, all the same."

"When Aphrodite was born, the gods held a celebration. Poros, the son of Metis, was there among them.[7] When they had feasted, Penia came begging, as poverty does when there's a party, and stayed by the gates. Now Poros got drunk on nectar (there was no wine yet, you see) and, feeling drowsy, went into the garden of Zeus, where he fell asleep. Then Penia schemed up a plan to relieve her lack of resources: she would get a child from Poros. So she lay beside him and got pregnant with Love. That is why Love was born to follow Aphrodite and serve her: because he was conceived on the day of her birth. And that's why he is also by nature a lover of beauty, because Aphrodite herself is especially beautiful.

"As the son of Poros and Penia, his lot in life is set to be like theirs. In the first place, he is always poor, and he's far from being delicate and beautiful (as ordinary people think he is); instead, he is tough and shrivelled and shoeless and homeless, always lying on the dirt without a bed, sleeping at people's doorsteps and in roadsides under the sky, having his mother's nature, always living with Need. But on his father's side he is a schemer after the beautiful and the good; he is brave, impetuous, and intense, an awesome hunter, always weaving snares, resourceful in his pursuit of

intelligence, a lover of wisdom[8] through all his life, a genius with enchantments, potions, and clever pleadings.

"He is by nature neither immortal nor mortal. But now he springs to life when he gets his way; now he dies—all in the very same day. Because he is his father's son, however, he keeps coming back to life, but then anything he finds his way to always slips away, and for this reason Love is never completely without resources, nor is he ever rich.

"He is in between wisdom and ignorance as well. In fact, you see, none of the gods loves wisdom or wants to become wise—for they are wise—and no one else who is wise already loves wisdom; on the other hand, no one who is ignorant will love wisdom either or want to become wise. For what's especially difficult about being ignorant is that you are content with yourself, even though you're neither beautiful and good nor intelligent. If you don't think you need anything, of course you won't want what you don't think you need."

"In that case, Diotima, who *are* the people who love wisdom, if they are neither wise nor ignorant?"

"That's obvious," she said. "A child could tell you. Those who love wisdom fall in between those two extremes. And Love is one of them, because he is in love with what is beautiful, and wisdom is extremely beautiful. It follows that Love *must* be a lover of wisdom and, as such, is in between being wise and being ignorant. This, too, comes to him from his parentage, from a father who is wise and resourceful and a mother who is not wise and lacks resource.

"My dear Socrates, that, then, is the nature of the Spirit called Love. Considering what you thought about Love, it's no surprise that you were led into thinking of Love as you did. On the basis of what you say, I conclude that you thought Love was *being loved*, rather than *being a lover*. I think that's why Love struck you as beautiful in every way: because it is what is really beautiful and graceful that deserves to be loved, and this is perfect and highly blessed; but being a lover takes a different form, which I have just described."

So I said, "All right then, my friend. What you say about Love is beautiful, but if you're right, what use is Love to human beings?"

"I'll try to teach you that, Socrates, after I finish this. So far I've been explaining the character and the parentage of Love. Now, according to you, he is love for beautiful things. But suppose someone asks us, 'Socrates and Diotima, what is the point of loving beautiful things?'

"It's clearer this way: 'The lover of beautiful things has a desire; what does he desire?'"

"That they become his own," I said.

"But that answer calls for still another question, that is, 'What will this man have, when the beautiful things he wants have become his own?'"

I said there was no way I could give a ready answer to that question.

Then she said, "Suppose someone changes the question, putting 'good' in place of 'beautiful,' and asks you this: 'Tell me, Socrates, a lover of good things has a desire; what does he desire?'"

"That they become his own," I said.

"And what will he have, when the good things he wants have become his own?"

"This time it's easier to come up with the answer," I said. "He'll have happiness."[9]

"That's what makes happy people happy, isn't it—possessing good things. There's no need to ask further, 'What's the point of wanting happiness?' The answer you gave seems to be final."

"True," I said.

"Now this desire for happiness, this kind of love—do you think it is common to all human beings and that everyone wants to have good things forever and ever? What would you say?"

"Just that," I said. "It is common to all."

"Then, Socrates, why don't we say that everyone is in love," she asked, "since everyone always loves the same things? Instead, we say some people are in love and others not; why is that?"

"I wonder about that myself," I said.

"It's nothing to wonder about," she said. "It's because we divide out a special kind of love, and we refer to it by the word that means the whole—'love'; and for the other kinds of love we use other words."

"What do you mean?" I asked.

"Well, you know, for example, that 'poetry' has a very wide range.[10] After all, everything that is responsible for creating something out of nothing is a kind of poetry; and so all the creations of every craft and profession are themselves a kind of poetry, and everyone who practices a craft is a poet."

"True."

"Nevertheless," she said, "as you also know, these craftsmen are not called poets. We have other words for them, and out of the whole of poetry we have marked off one part, the part the Muses give us with melody and rhythm, and we refer to this by the word that means the whole. For this alone is called 'poetry,' and those who practice this part of poetry are called poets."

"True."

"That's also how it is with love. The main point is this: every desire for good things or for happiness is 'the supreme and treacherous love' in everyone. But those who pursue this along any of its many other ways—through making money, or through the love of sports, or through philosophy—we don't say that *these* people are in love, and we don't call them lovers. It's only when people are devoted exclusively to one special kind of love that we use these words that really belong to the whole of it: 'love' and 'in love' and 'lovers.'"

"I am beginning to see your point," I said.

"Now there is a certain story," she said, "according to which lovers are those people who seek their other halves. But according to my story, a lover does not seek the half or the whole, unless, my friend, it turns out to be good as well. I say this because people are even willing to cut off their own arms and legs if they think they are diseased. I don't think an individual takes joy in what belongs to him personally unless by 'belonging to me' he means 'good' and by 'belonging to another' he means 'bad.' That's because what everyone loves is really nothing other than the good. Do you disagree?"

"Zeus! Not I," I said.

"Now, then," she said. "Can we simply say that people love the good?"

"Yes," I said.

"But shouldn't we add that, in loving it, they want the good to be theirs?"

"We should."

"And not only that," she said. "They want the good to be theirs forever, don't they?"

"We should add that too."

"In a word, then, love is wanting to possess the good forever."

"That's very true," I said.

"This, then, is the object of love,"[11] she said. "Now, how do lovers pursue it? We'd rightly say that when they are in love they do something with eagerness and zeal. But what is it precisely that they do? Can you say?"

"If I could," I said, "I wouldn't be your student, filled with admiration for your wisdom, and trying to learn these very things."

"Well, I'll tell you," she said. "It is giving birth in beauty,[12] whether in body or in soul."

"It would take divination to figure out what you mean. I can't."

"Well, I'll tell you more clearly," she said. "All of us are pregnant, Socrates, both in body and in soul, and, as soon as we come to a certain age, we naturally desire to give birth. Now no one can possibly give birth in anything ugly; only in something beautiful. That's because when a man and a woman come together in order to give birth, this is a godly affair. Pregnancy, reproduction—this is an immortal thing for a mortal animal to do, and it cannot occur in anything that is out of harmony, but ugliness is out of harmony with all that is godly. Beauty, however, is in harmony with the divine. Therefore the goddess who presides at childbirth—she's called Moira or Eilithuia—is really Beauty.[13] That's why, whenever pregnant animals or persons draw near to beauty, they become gentle and joyfully disposed and give birth and reproduce; but near ugliness they are foul faced and draw back in pain; they turn away and shrink back and do not reproduce, and because they hold on to what they carry inside them, the labour is painful. This is the source of the great excitement about beauty that comes to anyone who is pregnant and already teeming with life: beauty releases them from their great pain. You see, Socrates," she said, "what Love wants is not beauty, as you think it is."

"Well, what is it, then?"

"Reproduction and birth in beauty."

"Maybe," I said.

"Certainly," she said. "Now, why reproduction? It's because reproduction goes on forever; it is what mortals have in place of immortality. A lover must desire immortality along with the good, if what we agreed earlier was right, that Love wants to possess the good forever. It follows from our argument that Love must desire immortality."

All this she taught me, on those occasions when she spoke on the art of love. And once she asked, "What do you think causes love and desire, Socrates? Don't you see what an awful state a wild animal is in when it wants to produce? Footed and winged animals alike, all are plagued by the disease of Love. First they are sick for intercourse with each other, then for nurturing their young—for their sake the weakest animals stand ready to do battle against the strongest and even to die for them, and they may be racked with famine in order to feed their young. They would do anything for their sake. Human beings, you'd think, would do this because they understand the reason for it; but what causes wild animals to be in such a state of love? Can you say?"

And I said again that I didn't know.

So she said, "How do you think you'll ever master the art of love, if you don't know that?"

"But that's why I came to you, Diotima, as I just said. I knew I needed a teacher. So tell me what causes this, and everything else that belongs to the art of love."

"If you really believe that Love by its nature aims at what we have often agreed it does, then don't be surprised at the answer," she said. "For among animals the principle is the same as with us, and mortal nature seeks so far as possible to live forever and be immortal. And this is possible in one way only: by reproduction, because it always leaves behind a new young one in place of the old. Even while each living thing is said to be alive and to be the same—as a person is said to be the

same from childhood till he turns into an old man—even then he never consists of the same things, though he is called the same, but he is always being renewed and in other respects passing away, in his hair and flesh and bones and blood and his entire body. And it's not just in his body, but in his soul, too, for none of his manners, customs, opinions, desires, pleasures, pains, or fears ever remains the same, but some are coming to be in him while others are passing away. And what is still far stranger than that is that not only does one branch of knowledge come to be in us while another passes away and that we are never the same even in respect of our knowledge, but that each single piece of knowledge has the same fate. For what we call *studying* exists because knowledge is leaving us, because forgetting is the departure of knowledge, while studying puts back a fresh memory in place of what went away, thereby preserving a piece of knowledge, so that it seems to be the same. And in that way everything mortal is preserved, not, like the divine, by always being the same in every way, but because what is departing and aging leaves behind something new, something such as it had been. By this device, Socrates," she said, "what is mortal shares in immortality, whether it is a body or anything else, while the immortal has another way. So don't be surprised if everything naturally values its own offspring, because it is for the sake of immortality that everything shows this zeal, which is Love."

Yet when I heard her speech I was amazed, and spoke: "Well," said I, "Most wise Diotima, is this really the way it is?"

And in the manner of a perfect sophist she said, "Be sure of it, Socrates. Look, if you will, at how human beings seek honour. You'd be amazed at their irrationality, if you didn't have in mind what I spoke about and if you hadn't pondered the awful state of love they're in, wanting to become famous and 'to lay up glory immortal forever,' and how they're ready to brave any danger for the sake of this, much more than they are for their children; and they are prepared to spend money, suffer through all sorts of ordeals, and even die for the sake of glory. Do you really think that Alcestis would have died for Admetus," she asked, "or that Achilles would have died after Patroclus, or that your Codrus would have died so as to preserve the throne for his sons,[14] if they hadn't expected the memory of their virtue—which we still hold in honour—to be immortal? Far from it," she said. "I believe that anyone will do anything for the sake of immortal virtue and the glorious fame that follows; and the better the people, the more they will do, for they are all in love with immortality.

"Now, some people are pregnant in body, and for this reason turn more to women and pursue love in that way, providing themselves through childbirth with immortality and remembrance and happiness, as they think, for all time to come; while others are pregnant in soul—because there surely *are* those who are even more pregnant in their souls than in their bodies, and these are pregnant with what is fitting for a soul to bear and bring to birth. And what is fitting? Wisdom and the rest of virtue, which all poets beget, as well as all the craftsmen who are said to be creative. But by far the greatest and most beautiful part of wisdom deals with the proper ordering of cities and households, and that is called moderation and justice. When someone has been pregnant with these in his soul from early youth, while he is still a virgin, and, having arrived at the proper age, desires to beget and give birth, he too will certainly go about seeking the beauty

in which he would beget; for he will never beget in anything ugly. Since he is pregnant, then, he is much more drawn to bodies that are beautiful than to those that are ugly; and if he also has the luck to find a soul that is beautiful and noble and well-formed, he is even more drawn to this combination; such a man makes him instantly teem with ideas and arguments about virtue—the qualities a virtuous man should have and the customary activities in which he should engage; and so he tries to educate him. In my view, you see, when he makes contact with someone beautiful and keeps company with him, he conceives and gives birth to what he has been carrying inside him for ages. And whether they are together or apart, he remembers that beauty. And in common with him he nurtures the newborn; such people, therefore, have much more to share than do the parents of human children, and have a firmer bond of friendship, because the children in whom they have a share are more beautiful and more immortal. Everyone would rather have such children than human ones, and would look up to Homer, Hesiod, and the other good poets with envy and admiration for the offspring they have left behind—offspring, which, because they are immortal themselves, provide their parents with immortal glory and remembrance. "For example," she said, "those are the sort of children Lycurgus[15] left behind in Sparta as the saviours of Sparta and virtually all of Greece. Among you the honour goes to Solon for his creation of your laws. Other men in other places everywhere Greek or barbarian, have brought a host of beautiful deeds into the light and begotten every kind of virtue. Already many shrines have sprung up to honour them for their immortal children, which hasn't happened yet to anyone for human offspring.

"Even you, Socrates, could probably come to be initiated into these rites of love. But as for the purpose of these rites when they are done correctly—that is the final and highest mystery, and I don't know if you are capable of it. I myself will tell you," she said, "and I won't stint any effort. And you must try to follow if you can."

"A lover who goes about this matter correctly must begin in his youth to devote himself to beautiful bodies. First, if the leader[16] leads aright, he should love one body and beget beautiful ideas there; then he should realize that the beauty of any one body is brother to the beauty of any other and that if he is to pursue beauty of form he'd be very foolish not to think that the beauty of all bodies is one and the same. When he grasps this, he must become a lover of all beautiful bodies, and he must think that this wild gaping after just one body is a small thing and despise it.

"After this he must think that the beauty of people's souls is more valuable than the beauty of their bodies, so that if someone is decent in his soul, even though he is scarcely blooming in his body, our lover must be content to love and care for him and to seek to give birth to such ideas as will make young men better. The result is that our lover will be forced to gaze at the beauty of activities and laws and to see that all this is akin to itself, with the result that he will think that the beauty of bodies is a thing of no importance. After customs he must move on to various kinds of knowledge. The result is that he will see the beauty of knowledge and be looking mainly not at beauty in a single example—as a servant would who favoured the beauty of a little boy or a man or a single custom (being a slave, of course, he's low and small-minded)—but the lover is turned to the great sea of beauty, and, gazing upon this, he

gives birth to many gloriously beautiful ideas and theories, in unstinting love of wisdom,[17] until, having grown and been strengthened there, he catches sight of such knowledge, and it is the knowledge of such beauty . . .

"Try to pay attention to me," she said, "as best you can. You see, the man who has been thus far guided in matters of Love, who has beheld beautiful things in the right order and correctly, is coming now to the goal of Loving: all of a sudden he will catch sight of something wonderfully beautiful in its nature; that, Socrates, is the reason for all his earlier labours:

"First, it always *is* and neither comes to be nor passes away, neither waxes nor wanes. Second, it is not beautiful this way and ugly that way, nor beautiful at one time and ugly at another, nor beautiful in relation to one thing and ugly in relation to another; nor is it beautiful here but ugly there, as it would be if it were beautiful for some people and ugly for others. Nor will the beautiful appear to him in the guise of a face or hands or anything else that belongs to the body. It will not appear to him as one idea or one kind of knowledge. It is not anywhere in another thing, as in an animal, or in earth, or in heaven, or in anything else, but itself by itself with itself, it is always one in form; and all the other beautiful things share in that, in such a way that when those others come to be or pass away, this does not become the least bit smaller or greater nor suffer any change. So when someone rises by these stages, through loving boys correctly, and begins to see this beauty, he has almost grasped his goal. This is what it is to go aright, or be led by another, into the mystery of Love: one goes always upwards for the sake of this Beauty, starting out from beautiful things and using them like rising stairs: from one body to two and from two to all beautiful bodies, then from beautiful bodies to beautiful customs, and from customs to learning beautiful things, and from these lessons he arrives[18] in the end at this lesson, which is learning of this very Beauty, so that in the end he comes to know just what it is to be beautiful.

"And there in life, Socrates, my friend," said the woman from Mantinea, "there if anywhere should a person live his life, beholding that Beauty. If you once see that, it won't occur to you to measure beauty by gold or clothing or beautiful boys and youths—who, if you see them now, strike you out of your senses, and make you, you and many others, eager to be with the boys you love and look at them forever, if there were any way to do that, forgetting food and drink, everything but looking at them and being with them. But how would it be, in our view," she said, "if someone got to see the Beautiful itself, absolute, pure, unmixed, not polluted by human flesh or colours or any other great nonsense of mortality, but if he could see the divine Beauty itself in its one form? Do you think it would be a poor life for a human being to look there and to behold

it by that which he ought, and to be with it? Or haven't you remembered," she said, "that in that life alone, when he looks at Beauty in the only way that Beauty can be seen—only then will it become possible for him to give birth not to images of virtue (because he's in touch with no images), but to true virtue (because he is in touch with the true Beauty). The love of the gods belongs to anyone who has given birth to true virtue and nourished it, and if any human being could become immortal, it would be he."

This, Phaedrus and the rest of you, was what Diotima told me. I was persuaded. And once persuaded, I try to persuade others too that human nature can find no better workmate for acquiring this than Love. That's why I say that every man must honour Love, why I honour the rites of Love myself and practice them with special diligence, and why I commend them to others. Now and always I praise the power and courage of Love so far as I am able. Consider this speech, then, Phaedrus, if you wish, a speech in praise of Love. Or if not, call it whatever and however you please to call it.

Notes

1   *Illiad* v.385, *Odyssey* xi.305 ff.
2   Cf. *Odyssey* xi.266 ff.
3   Arcadia included the city of Mantinea, which opposed Sparta, and was rewarded by having its population divided and dispersed in 385 BCE. Aristophanes seems to be referring anachronistically to those events; such anachronisms are not uncommon in Plato.
4   *Cf.* 197b.
5   197b3–5.
6   The Greek is ambiguous between "Love loves beautiful things" and "Love is one of the beautiful things." Agathon had asserted the former

(197b5, 201a5), and this will be a premise in Diotima's argument, but he asserted the latter as well (195a7), and this is what Diotima proceeds to refute.

7   *Poros* means "way," "resource." His mother's name, *Mētis*, means "cunning." *Penia* means "poverty."
8   I.e., a philosopher.
9   *Eudaimonia*: no English word catches the full range of this term, which is used for the whole of well-being and the good, flourishing life.
10 "Poetry" translates *poiēsis*, lit. "making," which can be used for any kind of production or

creation. However, the word *poiētēs*, lit. "maker," was used mainly for poets—writers of metrical verses that were actually set to music.

11 Accepting the emendation *toutou* in b1.

12 The preposition is ambiguous between "within" and "in the presence of." Diotima may mean that the lover causes the newborn (which may be an idea) to come to be within a beautiful person; or she may mean that he is stimulated to give birth to it in the presence of a beautiful person.

13 Moira is known mainly as a Fate, but she was also a birth goddess (*Illiad* xxiv.209), and was identified with the birth-goddess Eilithuia

(Pindar, *Olympian* Odes vi.42, *Nemean Odes* vii.1).

14 Codrus was the legendary last king of Athens. He gave his life to satisfy a prophecy that promised victory to Athens and salvation from the invading Dorians if their king was killed by the enemy.

15 Lycurgus was supposed to have been the founder of the oligarchic laws and stern customs of Sparta.

16 The leader: Love.

17 I.e., philosophy.

18 Reading *teleutēsēi* at c7.

REKHA NAVNEET

Some distance away from Greece another significant philosophical and religious tradition of love and sexuality was evolving. As Rekha Navneet tells us, the *Kamasutra* was written by Vatsyayana in the first century BCE and takes the form of a kind of textbook for sex. The *Gitagovinda*, which was written by Jayadeva in the twelfth century, is a poem that explores erotic love. As Navneet notes in her essay, in both the ancient and Middle Ages, there existed views of sexuality that are more progressive in many ways than in modern-day India and, I would suggest, beyond India as well.

The *Kamasutra* is well known outside of India, but, as Navneet tells us, many people only think of it as a book depicting sexual endeavours or sexual positions. It is that, of course, but the *Kamasutra* is also a text that gives guidance to all areas of one's relationship or married life. Love and sexuality in this tradition go beyond the narrow limits to which we often confine them today and, much like Eros in Plato's *Symposium*, they extend to all aspects of life.

The Ethical and Mystical Import of *Kama*: Sexual/Erotic Passion in Classical Indian Tradition

Compared to modern India's conservative and often oppressive attitudes concerning sexuality, India of the ancient and middle ages had a far more evolved and scholastic attitude and produced literary texts celebrating these facets of life. This article draws on various analyses of how love and sex are presented in two works from the classical Indian tradition, the *Kamasutra* and the *Gitagovinda*. The *Kamasutra*, by Vatsyayana, is well known outside of India and has significantly shaped the world's ideas of sexuality. Less well known but no less significant is the *Gitagovinda*, a twelfth-century poem written by Jayadeva. It depicts the sexual union of Lord

Krishna, an earthly incarnation of the deity Vishnu, and Radha, a human embodiment of the goddess Lakshmi, and examines erotic love in the context of mysticism and religion.

I have endeavoured to contextualize these works in terms of the evolving notion of *kama*, or "desire," while exploring love and erotic union as a divine experience, drawing on a theme that runs throughout the aesthetic philosophical discourse of classical India. In Part I of this paper I present a brief exposition of the most significant portions of the *Kamasutra* and the *Gitagovinda*. In Part II I look at how these two works portray erotic love as an ecstatic experience—a theme that has preoccupied philosophers for centuries.

I. *Kamasutra* and *Gitagovinda*: An Overview

The Kamasutra

Written in Sanskrit, the *Kamasutra*,[1] also popularly known as the *Kamashastra* (*shastra* means "treatise"), is estimated to have been composed by Vatsyayana around the first century BCE. Although we do not know a lot about Vatsyayana, historians believe he was a Hindu religious man and probably belonged to the upper class. He had taken pieces of earlier works from the *Kamashastra* to put together what many in the Western world now consider the paradigmatic textbook on the art of love and sexual technique (Doniger and Kakar 2002, xi). However, Vatsyayana engages the reader in a higher ethical goal: as Doniger and Kakar explain, "He made this work in chastity and in the highest meditation, for the sake of worldly life; he did not compose it for the sake of passion" (2002, vii). Vatsyayana aspired to summarize the texts of the *Kamashastra*, which were not easily accessible. The result, according to Doniger and

Kakar, is an aphoristic summary of the *Kamashastra* that also carries more religious authority than the longer work (2002, xi–xii). In Indian history, *sastras* follow *sutras*, which means "a thread of thoughts and pages put together in such a way to form a string of meaning" (Doniger and Kakar 2002, xvii).

People who believe the *Kamasutra* is only about sexual positions and skilful lovemaking misunderstand what the text really delivers. Indeed, that is only a portion of what the *Kamasutra* has to offer. The Hindu text covers all areas in the art of loving, "from finding a partner, maintaining a marriage, committing adultery, living with courtesans, the use of drugs, and of course, positions of sexual intercourse" (Doniger and Kakar 2002, 4–6). Authors inspired by Vatsyayana composed similar texts: in the eleventh century, Koka Pandit composed the *Ratirahasya*; in the fifteenth century, Kalyanmalla composed the *Ananga Ranga*. All three of these texts are highly regarded for their literary content on love and its pursuit in life (Sinha 1980, 11).

According to lore, the *Kamasutra* originally comprised "thousands of chapters" but was pared down over time to just 36 chapters, divided into 64 sections and 1,250 sutras, all delivered in 7 books, or acts (Doniger and Kakar 2002, 3–7). As Doniger and Kakar explain, the written work of the *Kamasutra* is not composed in such a way as to resemble a rulebook, where each rule is numbered and one must follow from one step to the next. The text is written along the lines of a work of dramatic fiction, and underneath all the sexual content and details of married life it appears to take on the characteristics of classical Indian drama. The *Kamasutra* therefore consists of characters whose sex lives are used to demonstrate the appropriate behaviour to be undertaken by the householders. The man and woman whose lives are illustrated throughout the text are called the hero and the heroine, and the men who assist the hero are termed the libertine, pander, and clown (Doniger and Kakar 2002, 7–13).

Each of the *Kamasutra's* seven acts depicts a different phase of the hero's life (Doniger and Kakar, 2002, 17–20). Act one introduces the idea of love and its role in the lives of men and women. Act two is an in-depth discussion of the beginnings of sexual techniques. Act three describes the process of acquiring a potential wife and engaging in marriage. Act four describes the proper conduct of a wife and her roles in a marriage. Act five depicts how a man goes about seducing other women and other men's wives. Act six is an examination of other women, specifically courtesans. Finally, in Act seven, the hero explores different aphrodisiacs and magic spells as means of attracting others.

The *Kamasutra* is not composed entirely of prose but also includes several *shloka*, or verses, which are cited at the end of each chapter. These *common* verses make up about one-tenth of the total text. The book presents 64 different sexual positions, drawing on a number that is considered sacred within Indian culture. Doniger and Kakar explain that "Vatsyayana believed that there are eight different ways of making love, and within those eight there are eight different positions totalling up to sixty-four forms of the art of love" (2002, 20–21; Sinha 1980, 11).

An example of the text's evolved view of gender roles is the fact the *Kamasutra* prescribes not just how the man should act throughout the householder (non-ascetic) stage but also how the woman should act in the search for *kama*. Of *kama*, or desire, Vatsyayana writes,

Pleasure, in general, consists in engaging the ear, skin, eye, tongue, and nose each in its own appropriate sensation, all under the control of the mind and heart driven by the conscious self. Pleasure in its primary form, however, is a direct experience by the sensual pleasure of erotic arousal that results from the particular sensation of touch. (Sinha 1980, 20)

The 64 forms of art that the woman is encouraged to perform include singing, dancing, cutting leaves into shapes, arranging flowers, playing water sports, making costumes, and the science of strategy, among many others. Vatsyayana actually suggests that women should be encouraged to read the *Kamasutra for themselves, and early in life*—"before she reaches the prime of her youth, and she should continue when she has been given away, if her husband wishes it" (Sinha 1980, 24).

Although many people in Western society today still consider the *Kamasutra* to be concerned solely with depictions of sexual endeavours, only about one-fifth of the text is devoted to the art of lovemaking and sexual pleasure; the rest consists of relationship advice for men and women. Even so, those who understand its nuances will find the *Kamasutra* full of useful insight into the pursuit of love and pleasure, rewarding the reader with an overall experience of happiness or pleasurable delight.

Jayadeva's *Gitagovinda*
Jayadeva's celebrated poem *Gitagovinda* aptly represents the uniqueness of Hinduism by infusing religion with the erotic and portraying sexuality as the most profound and sacred experience.[2] Jayadeva was born either in Bengal or, more likely, in Orissa in the twelfth century. The *Gitagovinda*, also known as *mahakavya*

(a long/epic poem), marks the culmination of classical Sanskrit poetry and heralds the advent of literature and poetry written in India's many regional languages between the thirteenth and nineteenth centuries (Ayengar 2000, 3). The poem's title tells us that the work is about the *gita*, or "song," of Govinda. Govinda is one of the alternative names for Krishna, used primarily when the god is represented in human form as a cowherd. The poem is essentially a love song celebrating a springtime love frolic (*Vasant Rasa*). It recounts the separation and reunion of Radha (a commoner) and Lord Krishna (the divine), and in this way symbolizes the reconciliation of the profane and the sacred, the idealization of an ethereal delight.

The poem is deceptively simple, revolving mainly around Krishna and Radha. A third character, a lady friend or messenger called *Sakhi*, acts as the couple's guide and philosopher. Radha and Krishna pour their hearts out to her, but whether they are expressing love, disappointment, anger, regret, or some other emotion, *Sakhi* has the solution to their problems. She is the thread that binds the lovers together, as well as the vital force that pushes the aspirants towards their divine goal.

Another character who makes his presence felt though he remains invisible is Cupid, addressed in Jayadeva's songs as Kāmā, Kāmadevā, or Manmathā. Cupid's flowery arrows have an intense effect on the emotions of the cowherd maidens, or *gopis*. The song, in explicitly sexual (and specifically heterosexual) language, describes a consuming erotic longing. However, as Radhakrishna observes, "a nuanced and an in-depth understanding of it clearly enunciates a subject matter pertinent to aesthetic and religious experience" (Radhakrishna 2010, 34–35).

The *Gitagovinda* is divided into 12 *sargas* (parts) and 24 *prabandhas* (cantos) of unequal length (Siegel 1976, 41–42). It begins with a simple description of an overcast sky, thick clouds, and dark forests. Against this backdrop, Nanda—foster father of Krishna—instructs Radha to take Krishna home. A benedictory verse—one of several used to open the work—recalls a previous encounter between the poem's main characters. Notable in the poem's opening is the way Jayadeva brings together themes of devotional and sensual acts of love, despite the fact that the sexual arts (known as *vilaskala*) are generally segregated from acts of religious worship. In the poem's introductory lines, Hari is another name for Krishna, and in the colloquial Hindi language also refers to God:

> If remembering Hari[3] gladdens your heart,
>
> If you are curious about the art of erotica
>
> Listen then to Jayadeva, the poet,
>
> Who composes in sweet, tender, lilting rhymes (Ayengar 2000, 69).

Jayadeva goes on to state that he has grasped the physical as the concrete form of the spiritual. Thus the eroticism, as delineated in his *Gitagovinda*, is at once sensual and spiritual (Ayengar 2000, 50).

II. *Kama* and *Rasa* as Representations of Sexual/Erotic and Aesthetic/Religious Delight

In the final part of this reading, I will examine the philosophical evolution of the terms *kama* (as used in the *Kamasutra*) and *rasa* (as used in the *Vasant Rasa*, the "love frolic" central to the *Gitagovinda*). *Kama*, used to mean "desire" in the context of erotic love and relationships, is a key component of the Hindu social ethics delineated in the *Purushartha*, the philosophy of objects of human goals or pursuits. According to this outlook, there are four aims of human life, as defined by Narayanan:

- *dharma*, the discharging of one's duties;
- *artha*, prosperity and power;
- *Kama*, sensual pleasure of many types, including sexual pleasure and the appreciation of beauty; and finally
- *moksa*, or liberation from the cycle of birth and death (2014, 52).

Consider this in the context of the doctrine of *rasa*, which is used to refer to an aesthetic experience. Shyamala Gupta provides an excellent description: Rasa basically means sap or juice or even taste, which more or less refers to the physical side of the delightful experience. Taste is the most intimate of the senses—the taste object is inside the subject and yet still outside; the lover savours the beloved—the beloved is within and yet without. In relation to art/aesthetic experience, rasa has been defined in relation to emotions and feelings. However, the archetype of rasa as an experience has been delineated in terms of a detached-impersonal delight, and hence it has been described as a denotation of a spiritual/divine ecstasy (brahmananda). Rasa resides in every human heart, but only a person with a responsive heart, a refined sensibility, and possessing empathy can experience it (Gupta 1999, 54–56).

. In the Vedic history of Indian philosophy, *Kama* appeared as desire personified, not yet a god of love but a deity who fulfils all desires and the consort of *Rati*. Kama was also chanted in the *Atharva-Veda* in a multi-vocal way, and was regarded as a cosmogenic force. Hence, during the Vedic period, which lasted over many centuries, *kama* was generally used to imply desire, wish, drive, and urge, and was primarily related to the notion of carnality and sensuality (Sinha 1980, 10–11).

By the Epic period *kama* came to mean pleasure as well as desire—both the desire for pleasure and the pleasure itself. In the various *shastras*, it was associated with the concept of the *tri-varga*, or the three ends of life: *kama*, *artha*, and *dharma*. As we have seen, a fourth value, *moksha* (spiritual liberation), was later added. However, in the context of the householders' lifestyle and for the purposes of worldly life, it was considered a worthy aim to reconcile the three values of *kama*, *artha*, and *dharma* (Sinha 1980, 20–22; Gupta 1999, 52–53). In fact, throughout the householder's stage of life, the goals of *kama* and *artha* were considered primary: these goals should be pursued relentlessly by anyone who wished to prosper in society. *Kama* is the vital force: without *kama* there is no desire for *artha*, nor any wish for *dharma*.

Vatsyayana's *Kamasutra* is representative of the Vedic as well as the epic period. It represents the three-value system as it predates the inclusion of *moksha*. This is probably why the *Kamasutra* was not regarded as a *shastra*, since Vatsyayana asserted that the actions of *kama* flowed naturally, whereas *dharma* and *artha* needed to be cultivated and required a learned practice. Due to the predominance of *kama* over the other *purusharthas* in the *Kamasutra*, the dominant feeling and the experience thereof was that of *shringararasa*—that is, erotic delight (Ayengar 2000, 12–13, 70–71).

Sometime around the start of the second millennium and coinciding with the advent of Buddhism and Jainism, the concept of love divested of sensual desire gained prominence in the philosophical and cultural discourse. The emphasis towards spiritual release, or *moksha*, became the focus of social and moral values (Siegel 1976, 21; Ayengar 2000, 42–43). By the middle ages, Hinduism had moved towards finding expressions in poetic literature, dance, and music that reflected the *bhakti* movement towards seeking union with the divine, thus advocating a symbiosis of the erotic longing with the mystical-religious pursuit. This yearning assumed a new terminology: *prema* (Siegel 1976, 41, 181). *Prema* was considered a composite expression of religious devotion and obeisance to the divine order. In the Indian cultural context, *prema* was seen to be more staid than the zealous *kama*, and it has been used, often, in denoting examples of relationships based on authority and respect, such as between parents and children or in terms of friendly ties. However, during the *bhakti* movement, this *prema* epitomized the symbiosis of passion and reason directed towards an impersonalized divine principle. This conception of love was sublimated into a deeply religious sentiment by bringing erotic-religious ideas to bear upon the theme of the Erotic delight (*shringar rasa*).

It was during this time that Jayadeva wrote the *Gitagovinda*, celebrating an experience that combined love, passion, and reason—in other words, an experience in which erotic *rasa* becomes submerged with *bhakti* (the devotional), resulting in divine ecstasy. This experience has been explained, in Indian philosophy, as similar to realizing *moksha*, or spiritual realization (the fourth *purushartha*). In this kind of *rasa* experience, the subject and object merge, and there is no distinction between taster, tasted, and taste (Ayengar 2000, 160). Ascetic meditation is juxtaposed with sensual passion, and

the two—the sacred and the profane—converge in divine *rasa*:

> Oh Lord Hari! Bless the words of Jayadeva
>
> That sing the glory,
>
> And chanting repeatedly the name
>
> Distil the nectar, that can insulate,
>
> Men from the fret and fever of the dark times.
>
> She spoke to Krishna. . . .
>
> Oh Krishna!
>
> Paint a leaf on my breasts,
>
> And decorate my hips with girdle of bells,
>
> And draw on my forehead beautiful marks,
>
> And decorate my hair with flower garlands,
>
> Adorn my hands with bangles,
>
> And with jewelled anklets, my feet.
>
> The yellow robed Krishna did
>
> With delight the behest of Radha.
> (Ayengar 2000, 14)

Inspired by Jayadeva, the medieval poets of the fourteenth and fifteenth centuries, such as Vidypati and Chandidas, would further explore the relationship of Radha and Krishna (Ayengar 2000, 26).

Here I should clarify a point about Radha and, specifically, the union of Radha and Krishna. Most poets saw Radha as a married woman who broke all social norms to be with Krishna. Some folk narratives of this period suggested that she was Krishna's aunt, married to his maternal uncle. Others said she was an older woman while he was a boy. Thus, the *parakiyaa* (the extramarital relation) seems to have been exalted (Ayengar 2000, 41, 69). Even in the *Gitagovinda*, Radha's union with Krishna always takes place in secret. Scholars such as Sudhir Kakar maintain that by making the relationship illicit and clandestine, the poets heightened the emotional quotient of the relationship, portraying it as one of true love that transcended custom and law (Kakar and Ross 1995, 95–97). Devotees came to realize that Radha was the symbol of all those who were "married" to social responsibilities, seeking liberation and union with their true love, God, who is Krishna. The secret meeting of Radha and Krishna, their intriguing encounters, a display of varied emotions, their moods, soft and tender, sometimes angry and jealous, or penitent and frustrated, even pining and lamenting and then the joyous union, are a part of this immortal poem.

Ayengar, however, has challenged this view, drawing on numerous sources to demonstrate that Radha was an inextricable part of the same Supreme Soul—the principle of ecstasy (2000, 26–28, 70–71). He has reiterated the view that Radha simply implied devotion that was beyond the societal and temporal frame. Radha has also been referred to as the chief consort of Krishna—a role that, Ayengar believes, is also covertly implied in the *Gitagovinda*. Metaphysically, Radha came to represent the truth of our soul, the unexpressed, unrequited longings of our heart, suppressed by social realities that cry out to Krishna. Krishna acknowledges this truth of our being, one that society denies, each time he dances with Radha at night, outside the village, in secret. In Ayengar's view, the *Gitagovinda* is like a fairy tale, where the lovers cross several hurdles before finally uniting with each other. Since everything ends happily, the song appeals to the hearts of romantic people.

Conclusion

In this paper, I have endeavoured to emphasize the following points. (a) *Kama*, the name of the Hindu God of love and a derivative of *kamana* (which can be translated as "pleasure" or as a desire or a longing), has been defined in terms of erotic passion. (b) Erotic love is not delineated in terms of romance alone but largely as sexuality. (c) However, this sexuality was not sought only for producing progeny. Neither was this to be seen in abstraction from regulating ethics or religious idealization. There is an insistence on seeking a unity of *dharma* (the ethical value or moral duty). (d) Both of the cited works make it clear that women, presented as freely sexual beings with feelings and love, were viewed as equal participants in erotic love. (e) This sort of union was experienced as an aesthetic/divine *rasa*. (f) Sexual or erotic love was to be idealized in separation from social mores. Hence, love and sexual relations between a man and a woman were not necessarily bound by the conjugal ties or monogamous commitments. (g) While the *Kamasutra* does mention other kinds of union, even hinting at same-sex relationships, it is heterosexual love that forms the main theme, and I have focused on this aspect alone.

Notes

1   I have referred to Wendy Doniger's and Sudhir Kakar's translation of the *Kamasutra* (Doniger and Kakar 2002) and have also referred to *The Essential Sudhir* (Kakar 2011) for the purpose of

citation, analysis, and commentary on it. I have also referred to *The Indians: Portrait of People* (Kakar and Kakar 2007). The *Kamasutra* was first translated into English by Sir Richard Francis Burton in 1893, and the majority of the English world is familiar with the text through this work alone (Doniger and Kakar 2002, ii–iii). I have also alluded to Indra Sinha's translated work *The Love Teachings of Kama Sutra* (Sinha 1980).

2   For an explication of the *Gitagovinda*, I have referred primarily to two commentators and translators, Lee Siegel (1976) and N.S.R. Ayengar (2000). I have used Geeta Radhakrishna's translation (2010) as well.

3   Hari is another name of Krishna, and in colloquial Hindi language, this name also refers to God.

Bibliography

Ayengar, N.S.R., trans. 2000. *Gitagovindam–Sacred Profanation: A Study of Jayadeva's Gitagovinda.* Delhi: Penman Publishers (Oriental Publishers and Booksellers):

Doniger, Wendy, and Sudhir Kakar, trans. 2002. *Vatsyayana's Kamasutra—A New Translation.* Oxford: Oxford University Press.

Gupta, Shyamala. 1999. *Art, Beauty and Creativity: Indian and Western Aesthetics.* New Delhi: D.K. Print World.

Kakar, Sudhir. 2011. *The Essential Sudhir Kakar.* Mumbai: Oxford University Press.

Kakar, Sudhir, and Kathrina Kakar. 2007. *The Indians: Portrait of People.* New Delhi: Penguin/Viking.

Kakar, Sudhir, and John M. Ross. 1986. *Tales of Love, Sex and Danger.* Delhi: Oxford University Press.

Narayanan, Vasudha. 2014. "Hindu Traditions." In *World Religions: Eastern Traditions*, 4th ed., edited by Willard G. Oxtoby, Roy C. Amore, and Amir Hussein, 52. Don Mills, ON: Oxford University Press.

Radhakrishna, Geeta, trans. *Jayadeva's Geetagovinda: A Love Song.* Mumbai: Menon, 2010.

Siegel, Lee. 1976. *Sacred and Profane Dimensions of Love in Indian Traditions As Exemplified in the Gitagovinda of Jayadeva.* Delhi: Oxford University Press.

Sinha, Indra, trans. 1980. *The Love Teachings of Kama Sutra: With Extracts from Kokashastra, Ananga Ranga and Other Famous Indian Works on Love.* New York: Marlowe.

Discussion

In both the Greek and Indian traditions, myths play a powerful role in accounting for love and sexuality. This is true of love in the agapic tradition of Christianity as well where we see God giving his son as a sacrifice for the sins of humankind. Our experiences of love and sexuality are shaped by our cultural stories, which infuse our experiences with specific kinds of meaning. We sometimes think of love as unconditional and as involving sacrifice, as the Christian story teaches us. With regard to erotic or romantic love, we often talk in Aristophanic terms of finding our other half or finding that person who will *complete* us.

As Navneet tells us, on a popular interpretation of the *Gitagovinda*, the illicit nature of the relationship between Krishna and Radha intensifies the emotional aspect and illustrates the fact that true love defies the strictness of the laws. One could argue that these stories, in both the Indian and Greek traditions, heighten our emotions as we come to believe that we are experiencing real love by identifying with a paradigmatic myth.

But what role should these stories play in love? Are the stories of love helpful or harmful? In what ways do they shape our experience or expectations of love? Are our stories of love misrepresentations of the biological phenomenon in question, or are they better understood as expressions of that same reality? Would our experiences of love be impoverished without the accompanying stories that shape the meanings we attach to them? As much as sexuality and indeed love can be understood in biological or physiological terms, so much of what makes these phenomena meaningful to us has to do with the narratives that our cultures have created to characterize them. The characterization of love and sexuality in Hinduism by way of the *Kamasutra* and the *Gitagovinda* brings to mind Foucault's discussion of *ars erotica*, which we saw in Chapter 3. Indeed, lovemaking and the related rituals are portrayed as a kind of art in opposition to the more clinical, reductionist, psychoanalytically inspired approaches that dominate modern Western culture. Western approaches to love and sexuality experience them primarily as phenomena to be *understood* rather than experiences to be created, enjoyed, and perfected.

Suggestions for Further Reading

Wendy Doniger and Sudhir Kakar, *Vatsyayana's Kamasutra: A New Translation* (Oxford: Oxford University Press, 2002).

Sudhir Kakar and Kathrina Kakar, *The Indians: Portrait of People* (New Delhi: Penguin/Viking, 2007).

Lee Siegel, *Sacred and Profane Dimensions of Love in Indian Traditions as Exemplified in The Gitagovinda of Jayaâdeva.* (Delhi: Oxford University Press, 1978).

Chapter Ten
What Is Love?

Introduction

I recently purchased a house that backs onto a large, beautiful old cemetery. When I first stepped onto the back deck and saw the cemetery, the real estate agent remarked that this was the first time she saw me genuinely excited about a house. It was only later, when I told other people about my purchase, that I realized that not everyone is comfortable with the idea of living next door to a cemetery. My house-buying venture helps to illustrate a distinction that Irving Singer makes in the chapter that follows. Singer makes a distinction between objective appraisal and individual appraisal. Objective appraisal is the kind of thing a house appraiser does, for instance. A house appraiser tries to figure out what a house is worth to a community of prospective buyers by considering things such as size, location, proximity to schools, parks, shopping, the price of other houses in the neighbourhood, and so on. By way of contrast with objective appraisal, individual appraisal has to do with what the house is worth to an individual buyer. Individuals value things for specific reasons that may not hold with other prospective buyers. The value that I attached to my view of the cemetery is a case in point.

IRVING SINGER

In the Introduction to the Philosophy of Love, I introduced Irving Singer's distinction between appraisal and bestowal. In this chapter, we see Singer's own characterization of these two terms. These two concepts are central to the two historical forms of love called *eros* and *agape*, but, according to Singer, they have come together to co-constitute our modern notion of love. Appraisal and bestowal are both forms of *valuation*. In the former case, one looks for value in the object of love, whereas, in the latter, one creates value in the beloved.

Bestowal is not quite the same as individual appraisal since the kind of valuation that characterizes it goes beyond any kind of appraising. Bestowal rather involves one's capacity for creativity. Love's imaginative bestowal makes the beloved more valuable to the lover in a way that does not rely on appraisal. For Singer, this does not mean that one imaginatively creates a false image of the beloved, but rather one's *affective* attitude towards the *actual* beloved makes one value her or him more.

Appraisal and Bestowal

I start with the idea that love is a way of valuing something. It is a positive response *toward* the "object of love"—which is to say, anyone or anything that is loved. In a manner quite special to itself, love affirms the goodness of this object. Some philosophers say that love *searches* for what is valuable in the beloved; others say that love *creates* value in the sense that it makes the beloved objectively valuable in some respect. Both assertions are often true, but sometimes false; and, therefore, neither explains the type of valuing which is love.

In studying the relationship between love and valuation, let us avoid merely semantical difficulties. The word "love" sometimes means liking very much, as when a man speaks of loving the food he is eating. It sometimes means desiring obsessively, as when a neurotic reports that he cannot control his feelings about a woman. In these and similar instances the word does not affirm goodness. Liking something very much is not the same as considering it good; and the object of an obsessive desire may attract precisely because it is felt to be bad. These uses of the word are only peripheral to the concept of love as a positive response toward a valued object. As we generally use the term, we imply an act of prizing, cherishing, caring about—all of which constitutes a mode of valuation.

But what is it to value or evaluate? Think of what a man does when he sets a price upon a house. He establishes various facts—the size of the building, its physical condition, the cost of repairs, the proximity to schools. He then weights these facts in accordance with their importance to a hypothetical society of likely buyers. Experts in this activity are called appraisers; the activity itself is appraisal or appraising. It seeks to find an objective value that things have in relation to one or another community of human interests. I call this value "objective" because, although it exists only insofar as there are people who want the house, the estimate is open to public verification. As long as they agree about the circumstances—what the house is like and what a relevant group of buyers prefer—all fair-minded appraisers should reach a similar appraisal, regardless of their own feelings about this particular house. In other words, appraising is a branch of empirical science, specifically directed toward the determining of value.

But now imagine that the man setting the price is not an appraiser, but a prospective buyer. The price that he sets need not agree with the appraiser's. For he does more than estimate objective value: he decides what the house is worth to *him*. To the extent that his preferences differ from other people's, the house will have a different value for him. By introducing such considerations, we relate the object to the particular and possibly idiosyncratic interests of a single person, his likings, his needs, his wants, his desires. Ultimately, all objective value depends upon interests of this sort. The community of buyers whose inclinations the appraiser must gauge is itself just a class of individuals. The appraiser merely predicts what each of them would be likely to pay for the house. At the same time, each buyer must be something of an appraiser himself; for he must have at least a rough idea of the price that other buyers will set. Furthermore, each person has to weigh, and so appraise, the relative importance of his own particular interests; and he must estimate whether the house can satisfy them. In principle these judgments are verifiable. They are also liable to mistake: for instance, when a man thinks that certain desires matter more to him than they really do, or when he expects greater benefits from an object than it can provide. Deciding what something is worth to *oneself* we may call an "individual appraisal." It differs from what the appraiser does; it determines a purely individual value, as opposed to any objective value.

Now, with this in mind, I suggest that love creates a new value, one that is not reducible to the individual or objective value that something may also have. This further type of valuing I call bestowal. Individual and objective value depend upon an object's ability to satisfy prior interests—the needs, the desires, the wants, or whatever it is that motivates us toward one object and not another. Bestowed value is different. It is created by the affirmative relationship *itself*, by the very act of responding favourably, giving an object emotional and pervasive importance regardless of its capacity to satisfy interests. Here it makes no sense to speak of verifiability; and though bestowing may often be injurious, unwise, even immoral, it cannot be erroneous in the way that an appraisal might be. For now it is the valuing alone that *makes* the value.

Think of what happens when a man comes to love the house he has bought. In addition to being something of use, something that gratifies antecedent desires, it takes on special value for him. It is now *his* house, not merely as a possession or a means of shelter but also as something he *cares about*, a part of his affective life. Of course, we also care about objects of mere utility. We need them for the benefits they provide. But in the process of loving, the man establishes another kind of relationship. He gives the house an importance beyond its individual or objective value. It becomes a focus of attention and possibly an object of personal commitment. Merely by engaging himself in this manner, the man bestows a value the house could not have had otherwise.

We might also say that the homeowner acts as if his house were valuable "for its own sake." And in a sense it is. For the value that he bestows does not depend upon the house's capacity to satisfy. Not that love need diminish that capacity. On the contrary, it often increases it by affording opportunities for enjoyment that would have been impossible without the peculiar attachment in which bestowal consists. Caring about the house, the man may find new and more satisfying ways of living in it. At the same time, the object achieves a kind of autonomy. The house assumes a presence and attains a dignity. It makes demands and may even seem to have a personality, to have needs of its own. In yielding to these "needs"—restoring the house to an earlier condition, perhaps, or completing its inherent design—the homeowner may not be guided by any other considerations.

In love between human beings something similar happens. For people, too, may be appraised; and they may be valued beyond one's appraisal. In saying that a woman is beautiful or that a man is handsome, or that a man or woman is good in any other respect, we ascribe objective value. This will always be a function of *some* community of human interests, though we may have difficulty specifying which one. And in all communities people have individual value for one another. We are means to each other's satisfactions, and we constantly evaluate one another on the basis of our individual interests. However subtly, we are always setting prices on other people, and on ourselves. But we also bestow value in the manner of love. We then respond to another as something that cannot be reduced to *any* system of appraisal. The lover takes an interest in the beloved as a *person*, and not merely as a commodity—which she may also be. (The lover may be female, of course, and the beloved may be male; but for the sake of brevity and grammatical simplicity I shall generally retain the old convention of referring to lovers as "he" and beloveds as "she.") He bestows importance upon *her* needs and *her* desires, even when they do not further the satisfaction of his own. Whatever her personality, he gives it a value it would not have apart from his loving attitude. In relation to the lover, the beloved has become valuable for her own sake.

In the love of persons, then, people bestow value upon one another over and above their individual or objective value. The reciprocity of love occurs when each participant receives bestowed value while also bestowing it upon the other. Reciprocity has always been recognized as a desired outcome of love. Since it need not occur, however, I define the lover as one who bestows value, and the beloved as one who receives it. The lover makes the beloved valuable merely by attaching and committing himself to her. Though she may satisfy his needs, he refuses to use her as just an instrument. To love a woman as a person is to desire her for the sake of values that appraisal might discover, and yet to place one's desire within a context that affirms her importance regardless of these values. Eventually the beloved may no longer matter to us as one who is useful. Treating her as an end, we may think only of how we can be useful to *her*. But still it is we who think and act and make this affirmative response. Only in relation to *our* bestowal does another person enjoy the kind of value that love creates.

In saying that love bestows value, I am not referring to the fact that lovers shower good things upon those they love. Gifts may sometimes symbolize love, but they never prove its existence. Loving is not synonymous with giving. We do speak of one person "giving love" to another, but what is given hardly resembles what we usually mean by a gift. Even to say that the lover gives himself is somewhat misleading. Love need not be self-sacrificial. In responding affirmatively to another person, the lover creates something and need lose nothing in himself. To bestow value is to augment one's own being as well as the beloved's. Bestowal generates a new society by the sheer force of emotional attachment, a society that enables the lovers to discard many of the conventions that would ordinarily have separated them. But such intimacy is only one of the criteria by which bestowal may be identified.

The bestowing of value shows itself in many different ways, not all of which need ever occur at the same time or in equal strength: by caring about the needs and interests of the beloved, by wishing to benefit or protect her, by delighting in her achievements, by encouraging her independence while also accepting and sustaining her dependency, by respecting her individuality, by giving her pleasure, by taking pleasures with her, by feeling glad when she is present and sad when she is not, by sharing ideas and emotions with her, by sympathizing with her weaknesses and depending upon her strength, by developing common pursuits, by allowing her to become second nature to him—"her smiles, her frowns, her ups, her downs"—by having a need to increase their society with other human beings upon whom they can jointly bestow value, by wanting children who may perpetuate their love. These are not necessary and sufficient conditions; but their occurrence would give us reason to think that an act of bestowal has taken place.

Through bestowal lovers have "a life" together. The lover accords the beloved the tribute of expressing *his* feelings by responding to *hers*. If he sends her valuable presents, they will signify that he too appreciates what she esteems; if he makes sacrifices on her behalf, he indicates how greatly her welfare matters to him. It is as if he were announcing that what is real for her is real for him also. Upon the sheer personality of the beloved he bestows a framework of value, emanating from himself but focused on her. Lovers linger over attributes that might well have been ignored. Whether sensuous or polite, passionate or serene, brusque or tender, the lover's response is variably fervent but constantly gratuitous. It dignifies the beloved by treating her as *someone*, with all the emphasis the italics imply. Though independent of our needs, she is also the significant object of our attention. We show ourselves receptive to her peculiarities in the sense that we readily respond to them. Response is itself a kind of affirmation, even when it issues into unpleasant emotions such as anger and jealousy. These need not be antithetical to love; they may even be signs of it. Under many circumstances one

cannot respond to another person without the unpleasant emotions, as a parent cannot stay in touch with a wayward child unless he occasionally punishes him. It is when we reject the other person, reducing him to a nothing or expressing our indifference, that love disappears. For then instead of bestowing value, we have withdrawn it.

In general, every emotion or desire contributes to love once it serves as a positive response to an independent being. If a woman is *simply* a means to sexual satisfaction, a man may be said to want her, but not to love her. For his sexual desire to become a part of love, it must function as a way of responding to the character and special properties of this particular woman. Desire wants what it wants for the sake of some private gratification, whereas love demands an interest in that vague complexity we call another person. No wonder lovers sound like metaphysicians, and scientists are more comfortable in the study of desire. For love is an attitude with no clear objective. Through it one human being affirms the significance of another, much as a painter highlights a figure by defining it in a sharpened outline. But the beloved is not a painted figure. She is not static: she is fluid, changing, indefinable—alive. The lover is attending to a *person*. And who can say what that is?

In the history of philosophy, bestowal and appraisal have often been confused with one another, perhaps because they are both types of valuation.[1] Love is related to both; they interweave in it. Unless we appraised we could not bestow a value that goes beyond appraisal; and without bestowal there would be no love. We may speak of lovers accepting one another, or even taking each other as is. But this need not mean a blind submission to some unknown being. In love we *attend* to the beloved, in the sense that we respond to what she is. For the effort to succeed, it must be accompanied by justifiable appraisals, objective as well as individual. The objective beauty and goodness of his beloved will delight the lover, just as her deficiencies will distress him. In her, as in every other human being, these are important properties. How is the lover to know what they are without a system of appraisals? Or how to help her realize her potentialities—assuming that is what she wants? Of course, in bestowing value upon this woman, the lover will "accentuate the positive" and undergo a kind of personal involvement that no disinterested spectator would. He will feel an intimate concern about the continuance of good properties in the beloved and the diminishing of bad ones. But none of this would be possible without objective appraisals.

Even more important is the role of individual appraisal. The person we love is generally one who satisfies our needs and desires. She may do so without either of us realizing the full extent of these satisfactions; and possibly all individual value is somehow based upon unconscious effects. Be this as it may, our experience of another person includes a large network of individual evaluations continually in progress and available to consciousness. At each moment our interests are being gratified or frustrated, fulfilled or thwarted, strengthened or weakened in relation to the other person. Individual value is rarely stable. It changes in accordance with our success or failure in getting what we want. And as this happens, our perception of the beloved also changes. Though the lover bestows value upon the woman as a separate and autonomous person, she will always be a person in *his* experience, a person whom he needs and who may need him, a person whose very nature may

eventually conform to his inclinations, as well as vice versa. The attitude of love probably includes more, not fewer, individual appraisals than any other. How else could a lover, who must respond from his own point of view, really care about the beloved?

Love would not be love unless appraising were accompanied by the bestowing of value. But where this conjunction exists, *every* appraisal may lead on to a further bestowal. By disclosing an excellence in the beloved, appraisal (whether individual or objective) makes it easier for us to appreciate her. By revealing her faults and imperfections, it increases the importance of acting on her behalf. Love may thus encompass all possible appraisals. Once bestowal has occurred, a man may hardly care that his beloved is not deemed desirable by other men. Given a choice, he may prefer her to women who are sexually more attractive. His love is a way of compensating for and even overcoming negative appraisals. If it were a means of repaying the object for value received, love would turn into gratitude; if it were an attempt to give more than the object has provided, it would become generosity or condescension. These are related attitudes, but love differs from them in bestowing value without calculation. It confers importance no matter *what* the object is worth.

When appraisal occurs alone, our attitude develops in the direction of science, ambition, or morality. To do "the right thing" we need not bestow value upon another person; we need only recognize the truth about his character and act appropriately. Admiring a woman's superiority, we may delight in her as an evidence of the good life. We feel toward her what Hume calls "the sense of approbation." We find her socially useful or morally commendable, which is not to say that she excites our love.

If she has faults, they offend our moral sensibility or else elicit our benevolence. In short, we respond to this woman as an abstraction, as a something that may be better or worse, an opportunity for judgment or for action, but not a person whom we love. Appraisal without bestowal may lead us to change other people regardless of what they want. As moralists or legislators, or as dutiful parents, we may even think that this is how we *ought* to behave. The magistrate will then enforce a distance between himself and the criminal, whose welfare he is quite prepared to sacrifice for the greater good of society. The parent will discipline his child in the hope of moulding him "in the most beneficial manner." On this moral attitude great institutions are often built. But it is not a loving attitude. We are not responding affirmatively toward others. We are only doing what is (we hope) in their best interests, or else society's.

When love intervenes, morality becomes more personal but also more erratic. It is almost impossible to imagine someone bestowing value without caring about the other person's welfare. To that extent, love implies benevolence. And yet the lover does not act benevolently for the sake of doing the right thing. In loving another person, we respect *his* desire to improve himself. If we offer to help, we do so because *he* wants to be better than he is, not because *we* think he ought to be. Love and morality need not diverge, but they often do. For love is not *inherently* moral. There is no guarantee that it will bestow value properly, at the right time, in the right way. Through love we enjoy another person as he is, including his moral condition; yet this enjoyment may itself violate the demands of morality. Ethical attitudes must always be governed by appraisal rather than bestowal. They must consider the individual in his relations to other people, as one among many who have equal claims. Faced with the being of a particular person, morality tells us to pick and choose those attributes that are most desirable. It is like a chef who makes an excellent stew by bringing out one flavour and muffling another. The chef does not care about the ingredients as unique or terminal entities, but only as things that are good to eat. In loving another person, however, we enact a nonmoral *loyalty*—like the mother who stands by her criminal son even though she knows he is guilty. Her loyalty need not be immoral; and though she loves her son, she may realize that he must be punished. But what if the value she has bestowed upon her child blinds her to the harm he has done, deters her from handing him over to the police, leads her to encourage him as a criminal? Her love may increase through such devotion, but it will be based on faulty appraisals and will not be a moral love.

Possibly the confusion between appraisal and bestowal results from the way that lovers talk. To love another person is to *treat* him with great regard, to confer a new and personal value upon him. But when lovers describe their beloved, they sometimes sound as if she were perfect just in being herself. In caring about someone, attending to her, affirming the importance of her being what she is, the lover resembles a man who has appraised an object and found it very valuable. Though he is bestowing value, the lover *seems* to be declaring the objective goodness of the beloved. It is *as if* he were predicting the outcome of all possible appraisals and insisting that they would always be favourable.

As a matter of fact, the lover is doing nothing of the sort. His superlatives are expressive and metaphoric. Far from being terms of literal praise, they betoken the magnitude of his at-tachment and say little about the lady's beauty or goodness. They may even be accompanied by remarks that diminish the beloved in some respect—as when a man lovingly describes a woman's funny face or inability to do math-ematics. If he says she is "perfect" that way, he chooses this ambiguous word because it is used for things we refuse to relinquish. As in appraisal we may wish to accept nothing less than perfection, so too the lover calls perfect whatever he accepts despite its appraisal. The lover may borrow appraisive terminology, but he uses it with a special intent. His lan-guage signifies that love alone has bestowed incalculable worth upon this particular per-son. Such newly given value is not a good of the sort that appraisal seeks: it is not an attrib-ute that supplements her other virtues, like a dimple wrought by some magician to make a pretty woman prettier. For it is nothing but the importance that one person assigns to another; and in part at least, it is created by the language. The valuative terms that lovers use—"wonderful," "marvellous," "glorious," "grand," "terrific"—bestow value in them-selves. They are scarcely capable of describing excellence or reporting on appraisals.

If we have any doubts about the lover's use of language, we should listen to the personal appendages he usually adds. He will not say "That woman is perfect," but rather "To me she is perfect" or "I think she is wonderful." In talk-ing this way, he reveals that objective appraisal does not determine his attitude. For objective appraisal puts the object in relation to a com-munity of valuers, whereas love creates its own community. The men in some society may all admire an "official beauty"—as Ortega calls her. Every male may do homage to her excep-tional qualities, as if the lady were a great work of art; and some will want to possess her, as they would want to steal the crown jewels. But this is not the same as love, since that involves a different kind of response, more intimate, more personal, and more creative.

For similar reasons it would be a mistake to think that the lover's language articulates an individual appraisal. If he says that to him the woman is perfect, the lover does not mean that she is perfect *for* him. Unless the beloved satis-fied in some respect, no man might be able to love her. For *she* must find a place in *his* experi-ence; she must come alive for him, stimulate new and expansive interests; and none of this is likely to happen unless she has individual value to him. But though the beloved satisfies the lover, she need not satisfy perfectly. Nor does the lover expect her to. In saying that to him she is perfect, he merely reiterates the fact that he loves this woman. Her perfection is an honorific title which he, and only he, bestows. The lover is like a child who makes a scrib-ble and then announces "This is a tree." The child could just as easily have said "This is a barn." Until he tells us, the scribble represents nothing. Once he tells us, it represents what-ever he says—as long as his attitude remains consistent.

In being primarily bestowal and only sec-ondarily appraisal, love is never elicited by the object in the sense that desire or appro-bation is. We desire things or people for the sake of what will satisfy us. We approve of someone for his commendable properties. But these conditions have only a causal tie to love: as when a man loves a woman *because* she is beautiful, or *because* she satisfies his sexual, domestic, and social needs, or *because* she resembles his childhood memory of mother. Such facts indicate the circumstances under which people love one another; they explain why this particular man loves this particular woman; and if the life sciences were sufficiently developed, the facts could help us to predict who among human beings would be likely to love whom. But explaining the occurrence of love is not the same as explicating the concept. The conditions for love are not the same as love itself. In some circumstances the bestowing of value will happen more easily than in others; but *whenever* it happens, it happens as a new creation of value and exceeds all attributes of the object that might be thought to elicit it. Even if a man loves only a woman who is beautiful and looks like his mother, he does not *love* her for these properties in the same sense in which he might *admire* her for being objectively valuable or *desire* her for satisfying his needs.

For what then does a man love a woman? For being the person she is, for being herself? But that is to say that he loves her for nothing at all. Everyone is himself. Having a beloved who is what she is does not reveal the nature of love. Neither does it help us to understand the saint's desire to love all people. They are what they are. Why should they be loved for it? Why not pitied or despised, ignored or simply put to use? Love supplements the human search for value with a capacity for bestowing it gratuitously. To one who has succeeded in cultivating this attitude, *anything* may become an object of love. The saint is a man whose earthly needs and desires are extraordinarily modest; in principle, every human being can satisfy them. That being so, the saint creates a value system in which all persons fit equally well. This disposition, this freely given response, cannot be elicited from him: it bestows itself and happens to be indiscriminate. To the man of common sense it is very upsetting that love does not limit itself to some prior value in

the object. The idea goes against our purposive ways of thinking. If I wish to drink the best wine, I have reason to prefer French champagne over American. My choice is dictated by an objective goodness in the French champagne. If instead I wish to economize, I act sensibly in choosing a wine I value less highly. We act this way whenever we use purposive means of attaining the good life, which covers a major part of our existence. But love, unlike desire, is not wholly purposive. Within the total structure of a human life it may serve as a lubricant to purposive attitudes, furthering their aims through new interests that promise new satisfactions; but in creating value, bestowing it freely, love introduces an element of risk into the economy. Purposive attitudes are safe, secure, like money in the bank; the loving attitude is speculative and always dangerous. Love is not *practical*, and sometimes borders on madness. We take our life in our hands when we allow love to tamper with our purposive habits. Without love, life might not be worth living; but without purposiveness, there would be no life.

No wonder, then, that the *fear* of love is one of the great facts of human nature. In all men and women there lurks an atavistic dread of insolvency whenever we generate more emotion than something has a right to demand of us. In everyone there is the country bumpkin who giggles nervously at an abstract painting because it looks like nothing on earth. Man finds the mere possibility of invention and spontaneous originality disquieting, even ominous. We are threatened by any new bestowal. Particularly when it means the origination of feelings, we are afraid to run the usual risks of failure and frustration, to expose ourselves in a positive response that can so easily be thwarted. As a character in D.H. Lawrence says of love: "I am almost more afraid of this touch than I was of death. For I am more nakedly exposed to it." Even Pascal, who spoke of the heart's having reasons whereof reason does not know, seemed to think that love adheres to a secret, mysterious quality within the object that only feeling can discern. But Pascal was wrong: Love is sheer gratuity. It issues from the lover like hairs on his head. It can be stimulated and developed, but it cannot be derived from outside.

Love is like awakened genius that chooses its materials in accordance with its own creative requirements. Love does not create its object; it merely responds to it creatively. That is why one can rarely convince a man that his beloved is unworthy of him. For his love is a creative means of *making* her more worthy— in the sense that he invests her with greater value, not in making her a better human being. That may also happen. But more significantly, the lover changes *himself*. By subordinating his purposive attitudes, he transforms himself into a being who enjoys the act of bestowing. There is something magical about this, as we know from legends in which the transformations of love are effected by a philter or a wand. In making another person valuable by developing a certain disposition within oneself, the lover performs in the world of feeling something comparable to what the alchemist does in the world of matter.

Note

1   Though not of "evaluation." That word is usually reserved for appraisal.

GLENN PARSONS

In his article, Glenn Parsons responds to Singer's account of love and in particular his characterization of bestowal. Parsons thinks that the lover's imaginative act of bestowal, which endows the beloved with perfection in the lover's eyes, is problematic as an explanation for love precisely because it creates a false or fictionalized image of the beloved. This means that the object of love does not correspond with the actual person who is loved. Singer, in his own account, denies that the imaginative bestowal implied by love distorts one's picture of the beloved; instead, he suggests, it enhances that picture or presents the beloved in the best possible light.

Parsons offers us an alternative view of the role of imagination in love. He suggests that the lover experiences an "imaginative failure" when in the presence of the beloved. This imaginative failure is caused by the fact that the beloved fills the mind of the lover to the point of pushing out or neutralizing the normal standards of appraisal (perfection, beauty, and so on). In other words, the beloved becomes special not by virtue of imagining him or her as an ideal case of perfection or beauty, but rather by causing the lover to suspend or forget such standards.

Physical Beauty and Romantic Love

The Lover's Paradox

It doesn't take a philosopher to see that physical beauty and romantic love go hand in hand. We fall in love with people for their wonderful and attractive qualities, and physical qualities are among these. Nonetheless, this is not something that we are always comfortable acknowledging. This is, perhaps, due to two facts about physical beauty: first, its close connection with sex, and second the fact that, recently, the very idea of physical beauty has itself attracted much criticism.[1] However, although physical beauty is importantly related to sexual attractiveness, it cannot be understood solely in those terms. We admire and value certain bodily features, for various reasons, and while some of these reasons pertain to sexual attractiveness, not all do. Furthermore, and more importantly, although physical beauty raises many difficulties about how people are treated and how they regard themselves, it is indisputable that, as a matter of fact, lovers are drawn to each other, in part, by physical beauty. To deny this is to reject a central feature of the experience of romantic love as most know and experience it.

In any event, in this essay I will not question the role of physical beauty in romantic love; rather, my goal is to understand it. For upon reflection, there seems something paradoxical about this supposed connection between physical beauty and romantic love. While it seems that physical beauty is, in part, what draws the lover to his beloved, it also appears that the lover is strangely blind to this very quality. For to the lover, the beloved is, apparently, always beautiful, whatever that person actually looks like. The strangeness of this is reinforced by the observation that "beautiful" is, if not a superlative term, something close: we do not naturally talk, for instance, about people being "a little bit beautiful" or "sort of beautiful." To declare someone beautiful is to boldly assert that they realize an ideal—that they achieve a kind of bodily perfection.[2] From the outsider's perspective, these enthusiastic declarations of the lover seem overwrought: the beloved, we see, is imperfect. And yet, from the lover's perspective, the more sober expressions of praise that *we* might think merited—"You are fairly attractive!"—would be laughably inadequate.[3]

Confronted by this odd "beauty blindness," one first doubts that that the lover is sincere, and supposes that his declarations are so much deliberate exaggeration, meant to secure the beloved's affection. But such calculating flatterers are not in love, and the flatterer's clear and cynical perception of reality is far from the lover's perspective. Another possibility is that the lover refers, in his declarations, not to the physical beauty of the beloved, but to his or her "inner beauty," to the wonderful qualities of her character or personality. However, while lovers are certainly drawn to inner beauty as well, "What matters is that you're beautiful on the inside" is the sort of thing we say to friends, not to lovers.

There is, however, an obvious explanation of the lover's patently false declarations that recognizes both their sincerity and the fact that they are directed at physical appearance: the lover is beset by some kind of madness whereby his perception of the beloved's appearance is distorted by feverish feelings of love, sexual attraction, or both. As Shakespeare put it in a *Midsummer Night's Dream*, "the lunatic, the lover and the poet are of imagination all compact" (V.1.7–8). On this view—call it the *delusion explanation* of the lover's declarations of beauty—the beauty the lover sees is a kind of illusion, something akin to the madman's hallucinations.

The delusion explanation is a familiar notion—indeed its central idea of love as benign madness is a cultural trope. Also, the explanation can be filled out, and made more plausible, by viewing the lover's delusion as an adaptive psychological mechanism for strengthening romantic attachments. On this line of thought, lovers who exaggerate qualities such as their lovers' beauty will be more likely to stick with them in the face of obstacles to the relationship, which could be beneficial from a psychological or perhaps even reproductive standpoint.[4] Thus the madness of the lover seems, from the larger psychological perspective, to be an affliction with a kind of purpose.[5]

Nonetheless, I think that the delusion explanation fails to do full justice to the role of beauty in romantic love. While it seems adequate from the third-person perspective, it does little or nothing to illuminate the experience of romantic love "from the inside." I doubt that many of us would be heartened to learn that our lover's praise is merely deluded babbling, even if it is, in some sense, good for the relationship. Moreover, to say that the lover is merely deluded does not shed much light on his experience; from the lovers' point of view, his declarations *seem true*, and we would like some account of how this can be the case. It may be that we can make no sense of this, and we have to ultimately settle for the conclusion that the lover is just irrational, but that should be our last resort. In any case, in this essay I seek an alternative explanation in terms of the imagination. To begin, I examine one such explanation suggested by the writings of Irving Singer.

Singer on Imaginative Love

In his book *The Nature of Love*, Singer attempts to characterize the particular sort of valuing that is involved in romantic love. In doing so, Singer frequently emphasizes its creative and imaginative dimensions. In loving another, Singer writes, "the lover creates something"—"his love is a creative means of *making* [the beloved] more worthy—in the sense that he invests her with greater value" (1966, 15). Picking up on Shakespeare's comparison of the lover with the poet, Singer intriguingly connects this creativity inherent in love with the "imaginative play" that is typical in the arts: just as the artist does not necessarily paint the world as it really is, "the lover recreates another person. By deploying his imagination in the art of bestowing value . . . the lover adds a new dimension to the beloved" (16).

The lover, however, is not only artist, in this scenario, but audience as well, and here too the analogy with art is instructive. In watching a play, one knows that the person on the stage is not in danger, but responds to his situation imaginatively, *as if* he is. That is, one feels fear for him, despite an understanding that, in some sense, this response is not really appropriate or warranted, given that the events being observed are fictional. Just so, Singer's account suggests, the lover feels an admiration in response to the beauty—the perfection—of his beloved, despite understanding that she is not actually perfect.

This last point is made clear in Singer's account by his statement that for the lover, "his superlatives are expressive and metaphoric . . . [and are] far from being terms of literal praise." Such terms, "beauty" among them, are "scarcely capable of describing excellence"; rather, they serve only to express the lover's affection.

"The lover," he writes, "calls perfect whatever he accepts" (1966, 12). Nonetheless, the perfection of the beloved, though "only imaginary," still genuinely moves him.

Singer's account can be nicely applied to explain the puzzling declarations of the lover: they are not the product of mere delusion, nor are they insincere flattery; rather, they are somewhere in between, the more sober but yet genuine products of an imaginative response, in the same way that the tears we shed in the theatre are not expressions of madness, nor insincere fakery, but the sincere product of an imaginative engagement. Let's call this the *imagination explanation* of the lover's declarations.

I think that the imagination explanation is an improvement on the delusion explanation: it provides a richer account of the way in which the lover perceives the beauty of the beloved. However, developed in the particular way that Singer develops it, the imagination explanation suffers from a serious flaw, which is that it does not do justice to the *sincerity* of the lover's declarations. This can be seen in Singer's claim that, in the lover's mouth, words such as "beautiful" and "perfect" do not have their usual meaning: just as the audience member who watches a character "die" onstage and then says "Alas, he is dead!" doesn't *really* assert that anyone has died, so the lover who says "You are beautiful!" doesn't *really* assert that anyone is. However, as we observed earlier on, if it turns out that lovers do not really mean such things, this calls into question the very idea that they are in love.

One way to defend Singer's view here would be to point out that, although the lover does not sincerely *believe* that his lover is beautiful (that is, perfect) it is still the case that he *responds* to her as if she is, and that the sincerity of *this response* is all that matters. This point could again be reinforced by appealing to the analogy of our imaginative experience in the arts. In the theatre, we don't *believe* that the person before us has died, yet we *respond* as if he has, with genuine tears and grief. In the same way, perhaps the lover doesn't believe that his beloved is beautiful, but genuinely responds as if she were. In other words, although the lover's words, in a sense, are not sincere, his feeling is.

However, this defence of Singer's view ultimately fails. To see this, consider the general principle that if a feeling response is to be considered genuine or sincere, it must be directed toward the right kind of object. If someone said that he was feeling sorry for someone who just won the lottery, for example, we would suspect he was being insincere, using the word "sorry" in a deviant way, or, failing these, behaving in a deeply irrational way. This is an application of the principle stated above: you cannot genuinely and rationally feel sorry for someone that is not, in your estimation, a misfortunate person.[6] This principle poses a problem for the genuineness of our responses to the arts, for, as noted, when we watch a play and see a character die, we do not believe that the man on the stage is in peril: we believe that he is just an actor. And yet, we supposedly shed real tears for him. How can this be?[7]

This problem can be resolved by noting that, in the theatre, we respond to the fates of *fictional characters* in fictional situations, and it is the fact that they are the right kind of object that allows our responses to them to be sincere or genuine.[8] So, it is because a character in a fictional narrative suffers ill fortune that we can pity them. In other words, the sincerity of our response is a function of the fiction with which we are engaging, and in particular of the way that fictional narratives create characters of the type appropriate for our emotional responses.

If we carry this line of thought over to the case of the lover, however, we can see that the sincerity and rationality of the lover's response to the beloved would depend upon whether the beloved is the appropriate sort of object for that response. So if the lover's feeling is a sincere and rational response to perfection, rather than something deeply irrational, then it is a response to something perfect. But we know, and the lover himself, on this account, also knows, that the beloved is not perfect. The object of the lover's response, then, cannot be the beloved at all but can only be a fictionalized character, embellished to perfection in the imagination of the lover. Doubtless it is true that some people fall in love, not with real people, but only with a fictionalized character that exists only in their imaginations.[9] But this behaviour seems pathological, rather than typical of romantic love. Lovers do not need to invent imaginary people that are beautiful—to them, *the beloved* is beautiful.[10] The question is, can we understand how this could be?

Imagination Reconsidered

The imagination explanation is as an attempt to show that, through imaginative experience, the lover can have a sincere *response* (an admiration of the beloved's beauty) without the corresponding *belief* about the object (this person is perfect). This would yield an account of the lover's declarations that avoids both insincerity and madness. However, as we have seen, the way that Singer develops the imagination explanation, by way of analogy with our emotional responses to fiction, does not quite succeed in the context of romantic love. It seems that, in order to secure sincerity of feeling *in that context*, the corresponding belief about the object (the actual beloved, in this case) must be

present. But how can we attribute this belief to the lover without slipping once more into the model of delusion or madness? Perhaps what is required here is just a different way of understanding the operation of the imagination.

We can start by examining more closely the belief that, we have determined, we must attribute to the lover. It is simply this: the beloved is physically perfect, or, in other words, she could not be any better than she is. What exactly is involved in believing this? One answer to this question is the following: one has in mind a certain ideal, a set of features or qualities, say, and holds the beloved to measure up to that ideal. This is the straightforward way in which we might believe that, for example, a certain setting of the dinner table is perfect: one has a checklist of features (silverware in certain positions, napkins folded this way, and so on) and inspects the table to make sure that all of these are present. In terms of fulfilling all the features on the list, there is no room for improvement: all the boxes are ticked.

However, there is also another, and perhaps more common, way to find something perfect, or to believe that it could not be better than it is: to simply fail to be capable of imagining anything better, or more ideal. In this case, one does not run through a mental checklist of ideal features and then inspect the object for those features. Indeed, in this sort of case one may not even have any very definite ideal in mind. Rather, one is simply struck by the unimprovability of the object: one cannot imagine any way in which it could be improved. I think that this way of judging things perfect has a particular importance when it comes to judgments of beauty in the context of romantic love.

This account of what it is to believe that the beloved is perfect helps to explain how the lover could have the belief required for his response to be a sincere one, without resorting to madness or delirium. It is not that the lover would see his beloved as ranking higher than others on the various features that make up the ideal of beauty. Rather, it is that the lover experiences a kind of "imaginative failure" when in the presence of the beloved: those ideal features fade from view.

This way of conceiving of the imagination's operation makes for a stark contrast with Singer's conception. The lover is not engaged in a fantasy, embellishing the beloved so that she meets an ideal. The lover's imagination is not running amok; indeed, it is just the opposite. The lover's imagination is stultified as the beloved fills his mind, pushing out whatever ideals or standards of beauty may have dwelled there, and in that cleared space, shines in perfection.

A Dual Role for the Imagination?

Our modified version of the imagination explanation helps us to understand how lovers can believe that the beloved is perfect, for, in their experience, that is how things appear to them. But our explanation as it stands won't quite do. For we must ask, why this peculiar failure of the imagination? Why should this particular person—the beloved—cause the lover's imagination to operate this way? In the case of people other than the beloved, this failure does not occur: we are quite able to hold the appearances of others up against our ideals or standards of physical perfection. Until we have an answer to this question, it might be argued, the declarations of the lover remain mysterious. Of course we could always say that, in the presence of the beloved, the lover suddenly loses his normal capacity to exercise imagination, but

this only takes us back to the model of madness or delusion.

We might try to explain the imaginative failure of the lover in terms of the *intimacy* of the relationship between the lover and the beloved. Lovers spend great amounts of time (as much as they can) in each other's presence, and can come to know each other in deeply personal ways, ways in which they do not know even their best friends. We might suggest, then, that it is this particular closeness to the beloved that results in the lover's failure of imagination. However, this explanation founders on the fact that we spend much time with people other than lovers, and know some of them in deeply personal ways (consider family members, for example). Yet this imaginative failure does not take place with respect to those persons. Moreover, we may be deeply in love with people with whom we have spent little time, and about whom we know almost nothing.

I want to suggest a different explanation: that, perhaps ironically, the failure of the lover's imagination is brought about by an exercise of that very same faculty. What I have in mind is the kind of relentless fantasizing about the beloved in which lovers instinctively engage. This need not be sexual in nature (though some of it typically is): it includes all of those pleasurable imaginings in which the lover visualizes the beloved in his presence, doing all of the wonderful things that, when they are together, will become possible. It is important to note that this exercise of imagination is not the kind of fictionalizing idealization of the beloved that we discussed with respect to Singer's views: it is simply a relentless filling of one's mind with images and thoughts of the beloved. This repeated exposure, I suggest, gives the idea of the beloved a kind of potency that brings about the imaginative failure described above: any standards or ideals against which it could be measured and found wanting are displaced.[11]

This account explains why we experience the imaginative failure we have described for those with whom we are in love, but not for others. For even when other people fill our thoughts, we do not imaginatively project them into pleasurable futures in this same way. For example, we might think a lot about our friends and family members—we may worry about their well-being, or replay images of things they did to us, or fret about how we feel toward them. But we do not spend large stretches of time dreaming about happily being in their presence, as we do with lovers.[12]

Even if this account is accepted, however, it may still be objected that we have failed, ultimately, to avoid the model of delusion or madness. For, it could be argued, the lover's belief in the beauty of the beloved ultimately rests on a kind of idle, unconstrained daydreaming. The lover indulges in airy, baseless dreams of a wonderful future, and has his imagination paralyzed as a result. If this is not quite madness, it certainly looks like some sort of breakdown of rationality.

However, this is too cynical a view of the lover's daydreams. A central part of romantic love is committing yourself to a shared future with another person, a shared future that will ultimately have a great impact upon who you are.[13] From the lover's perspective, then, it makes perfect sense for him to envision his future with the beloved, in all of the minute detail that lovers do. In doing so, the lover weaves the beloved and her excellent qualities into the fabric of his own life and self. When this happens, this positive exercise of the imagination leads to an inhibition of that same faculty, making the beloved—and not merely some fictionalized version of her—beautiful in his eyes.

To conclude, let us return to the paradox with which we began: lovers are drawn to beauty yet seem unable to perceive it rightly, as we do. The standard explanation is that that the lover sees only an illusion of beauty. I have argued, on the contrary, that the lover does see beauty aright, given the particular kind of imaginative relation that he, as a lover, has, and must have, to the beloved. From the outside, what the lover sees may appear only an illusion. But from the inside, the lover merely sees what is truly there for him, as a lover, to see: the beauty of the beloved herself.

Notes

1 This criticism has several dimensions: while feminists have powerfully critiqued the way that women are viewed through the lens of physical attractiveness (Wolfe 1991), others have traced the unfairness of judging people by their physical appearance in the workplace and other parts of social life (Rhode 2010). All of this criticism of beauty has, of course, coexisted with an accelerating emphasis on bodily attractiveness in the media, something that the critics have often identified as a part of the problem. For a more systematic overview of these critiques, see Parsons, "The Merrickites" (forthcoming). For an interesting counterpoint, see Marwick (2004).

2 My claim that "beautiful" is a superlative is at odds with the view, held for example by Roger Scruton that it is "a platitude," that there can be degrees of beauty, or that, as he puts it, "one thing can be more beautiful than another" (2009, 5). I grant that we use "beautiful" in

ways that *suggest* this: we say "She's very beautiful," for example. However, if "beautiful" really was a degree term, we would also say things like "She's a little bit beautiful," which we don't (compare, for example, "It's very warm" and "It's a bit warm"). In the case of "beautiful," words such as "very" function as intensifiers rather than as indications of degree (as in "That's very true," or "The victim is quite dead"). Historically important sources for the idea of beauty as a sort of perfection include Thomas Reid (1785), and the writings of seventeenth- and eighteenth-century German Rationalists, such as Leibniz, Wolff, and Mendelssohn (Guyer 2014).

3   For empirical study of these differences in perceptions of attractiveness between lovers and non-lovers, see Simpson et al. (1990).

4   See Murray et al. (1997).

5   For more philosophical treatments of this theme, see Schopenhauer ([1883] 1969) and Solomon (1999).

6   Of course, one might believe that winning a lot of money is a kind of misfortune, and so pity a person for doing so, but this does not violate the principle stated.

7   This is the philosophical puzzle posed so compellingly by Colin Radford in his well-known essay, "How Can We Be Moved by the Fate of Anna Karenina?" (1975).

8   This solution is offered by Alex Neill (1993). For an overview of the other major responses to Radford's problem, see Neill (2003). It is perhaps worth noting that these other responses are far less promising in terms of application to the case of the lover's response (consider, for example, Kendall Walton's claim that we do not experience real emotions in response to fiction at all, but only "quasi-feelings").

9   This conception of love is captured vividly by Stendhal (1975).

10 Singer might reply to this that romantic love involves not only bestowing value on the beloved, through the imagination, but also appraising the value of the beloved (1966, 9). The latter requires us to see the beloved objectively, rather than imaginatively, and "appraise" him or her as such. If appraisal is also a part of romantic love, then we do not simply fall in love with a fictional persona that our imagination projects onto the beloved: we must also, at some point, engage with the actual person. However, although he insists that romantic love includes a dimension of appraisal, it is unclear how this could be if, as Singer insists, the bestowal of value occurs "without calculation" (Soble 1990, 24). More importantly, insisting that lovers *are* able to objectively "appraise" the appearance of the beloved is tantamount to denying the very phenomenon at issue: the beauty blindness of lovers. The problem is that, pace Singer, the lover seems incapable of fairly appraising the beauty of his beloved.

11 This account might also explain, perhaps, the well-known phenomenon of intellectuals falling in love with their own ideas.

12 The exception to this is the way that parents imaginatively project their own futures with their children. This lines up with the fact that the relationship a parent has to her child (but not vice versa) displays much of the intensity and beauty blindness characteristic of romantic love (on parental perceptions of physical beauty see Parsons 2010). Interestingly, the sociologist Colin Campbell (1987) has identified a similar sort of pleasurable fantasizing about material objects as central to modern consumerism, suggesting that we might now add "shopper" to Shakespeare's list.

13 This often neglected, "future-oriented" aspect of romantic love is nicely emphasized by Keller (2000).

Bibliography

Campbell, Colin. 1987. *The Romantic Ethic and the Spirit of Modern Consumerism*. Oxford: Basil Blackwell.

Guyer, Paul. "18th Century German Aesthetics." *The Stanford Encyclopedia of Philosophy*. Spring 2014 Edition. Last modified March 3, 2014. http://plato.stanford.edu/archives/spr2014/entries/aesthetics-18th-german/.

Keller, Simon. 2000. "How Do I Love Thee? Let Me Count the Properties." *American Philosophical Quarterly* 37 (2): 163–73.

Marwick, Arthur. 2004. *It: A History of Human Beauty*. London: Hambledon and London.

Murray, Sandra L, and John G. Holmes. 1997. "A Leap of Faith? Positive Illusions in Romantic Relationships." *Personality and Social Psychology Bulletin* 23 (6): 586–604.

Neill, Alex. 1993. "Fiction and the Emotions." *American Philosophical Quarterly* 30 (1): 1–13.

———. 2003. "Art and Emotion." In *The Oxford Handbook of Aesthetics*, edited by Jerrold Levinson, 421–35. Oxford: Oxford University Press.

Parsons, Glenn. 2010. "A Face Only a Mother Could Love: On Maternal Assessments of Infant Beauty." In *Motherhood: Philosophy for Everyone: The Birth of Wisdom*, edited by Sheila Lintott, 89–99. Malden, MA: Wiley Blackwell.

———. Forthcoming. "The Merrickites." In *Body Aesthetics*, edited by Sherri Irvin. Oxford and New York: Oxford University Press.

Radford, C. 1975. "How Can we be Moved by the Fate of Anna Karenina?" *Proceedings of the Aristotelian Society*. Supplementary vol. 49:67–80.

Reid, Thomas. 1785. *On the Intellectual Powers of Man*. Edinburgh: John Bell.

Rhode, Deborah. 2010. *The Beauty Bias: The Injustice of Appearance in Life and Law*. Oxford: Oxford University Press.

Schopenhauer, Arthur. (1883) 1969. *The World as Will and Representation*. Translated by E. Payne. New York: Dover.

Scruton, Roger. 2009. *Beauty: A Very Short Introduction*. Oxford: Oxford University Press.

Simpson, Jeffry M., Steven W. Gangestad, and Margaret Lerma. 1990. "Perception of Physical Attractiveness: Mechanisms Involved in the Maintenance of Romantic Relationships." *Journal of Personality and Social Psychology* 59 (6): 1192–201.

Singer, Irving. 1966. *The Nature of Love*. 2nd ed. Chicago: University of Chicago Press.

Soble, Alan. 1990. *The Structure of Love*. New Haven, CT: Yale University Press.

Solomon, Robert. 1999. *The Joy of Philosophy: Thinking Thin versus the Passionate Life*. Oxford: Oxford University Press.

Stendhal. 1975. *Love*. Translated by G. & S. Sale. London: Penguin.

Walton, Kendall. 1990. *Mimesis as Make-Believe*. Cambridge, MA: Harvard University Press.

Wolfe, Naomi. 1991. *The Beauty Myth*. Toronto: Vintage Books.

Discussion

Think of how we experience a person whom we love. Do we love them for their positive qualities or do we find them to have positive qualities because we love them? What role do the two types of valuation that Singer discusses play in love? Is love primarily appraisal or bestowal? When we love someone is it the case that we love them because we judge them to have attractive properties such as beauty, a sense of humour, good taste, musical talent, and so on? This would be a clear case of appraisal love. Or is love more based on bestowal? Is love, as Singer suggests, primarily a bestowal of value by the lover on the beloved that is not based strictly on one's appraisal of the beloved? When we say to our beloved "you are the most beautiful person in the world," are we appraising her beauty, are we deluded, or do we mean that she is the most beautiful person in our eyes?

What role does the imagination play in love? Does imagination play the role that Freud calls "overvaluation" whereby, in romantic love in particular, we bestow an exaggerated value on our beloved? Or, does our imagination play the role that Singer suggests of enhancing the qualities of the beloved by making us experience the beloved's qualities as more valuable than those same qualities in other people? Is this a legitimate role for the imagination? Does this experience of the imagination run the risk of misrepresenting the beloved so that we do not experience who she or he really is?

Do you think that Glenn Parsons correctly identifies a problem in Singer's account of the role of imagination in love when he argues that Singer's object of love "cannot be the beloved at all but can only be a fictionalized character, embellished to perfection in the imagination of the lover"? This sounds like the kind of overvaluation that Freud argued accompanied romantic love. Does Singer's account imply this?

What does Parsons mean when he says that the lover experiences an imaginative failure in the presence of the beloved? Think of your own experience of loving another person. Is your experience described better by Parsons's account whereby thoughts of your beloved fill your mind to the point of not being able to think of someone else being better for you or more beautiful to you? Or does Singer's account better describe your experience? That is, even though you know there are others who might perhaps be considered more beautiful, intelligent, or humorous than your beloved (by the majority of people, let's say), your imagination, affected by your emotions, causes you to see him or her as more humorous, intelligent, beautiful, or handsome than anyone else.

Suggestions for Further Reading

Gary Foster, "Overcoming a *Euthyphro* Problem in Personal Love: Imagination and Personal Identity," *Philosophical Psychology* 24, no. 6 (2011): 825–44.

Simon Keller, "How Do I Love Thee? Let Me Count the Properties," *American Philosophical Quarterly* 37, no. 2 (2000): 163–73.

Roger Scruton, *Beauty: A Very Short Introduction* (Oxford: Oxford University Press, 2009).

Alan Soble, *The Structure of Love* (New Haven, CT: Yale University Press, 1990).

Chapter Eleven
Agape and Eros

ALAN SOBLE

In his exploration of the *structure* of love, Alan Soble presents us with two views: *erosic* love and *agapic* love. Soble characterizes erosically structured love as *property-based*, *reason-dependent*, and *object-centric*. This means that such love is a response to properties or qualities possessed by the beloved and this love can in principle be explained by reasons that the lover has for loving the beloved (many of those reasons will have to do with the properties the beloved possesses). Agapically structured love, on the other hand, is not based on properties (or is not a response to properties), does not depend on reasons (that is, it does not depend on antecedent reasons to make sense of the occurrence of love), and it is subject-centric. In the case of erosic love, the properties of the beloved are the basis or ground of love and in this sense it centres on love's object. Agapic love exists independently of properties of the beloved. Either it has no grounds, or we could say its ground is in the lover and her ability to love. Agapic love is subject-centric in the sense that it emanates from the lover or the subject of love.

Two Views of Love

I. Love Ostensively Defined

More than eight centuries ago, Andreas Capellanus wrote in his treatise on love that "love is a certain inborn suffering derived from the sight of and excessive meditation upon the beauty of the opposite sex."[1] Something not very different was expressed by René Descartes five centuries later: "Love is an emotion of the soul caused by a movement of the spirits, which impels the soul to join itself willingly to objects that appear to be agreeable to it."[2] Today we are inclined to think of Capellanus's "suffering" (inborn or otherwise) as only a contingent symptom or effect of love, not as love itself, and usually present, if at all, only in the early sexual or romantic stages of a love relationship. Nor do we take seriously the idea that love, suffering, or the response to beauty are restricted to heterosexuals. But it is a defensible claim that beauty, or some other attractive or admirable quality of the beloved, has something to do with love. (I wonder, however, whether Capellanus means that the lover is in love with the beauty per se or with a person who is beautiful.) When Descartes writes that love is "caused" by a movement that "impels" the soul, yet the soul joins "willingly" with its beloved object, I worry about his consistency. And today we are not impressed with the idea that the soul is the seat of love, or of anything else. Nevertheless, Descartes's claim that love is an emotion directed at things that are "agreeable" is plausible. His definition also has the merit of alerting us to the *intentionality* of love: the object of love (that which is loved) need not be actually agreeable as long as it at least appears, or is believed, to be agreeable. Moreover, even though Capellanus and Descartes disagree about the details, they are dealing with the same thing; we know what human phenomenon they have in mind, despite the fact that they have so far said very little about it.

I make this point as a mild warning, for I will indicate my object of study only negatively and ostensibly; but if the reader is not confused by Capellanus or Descartes, he or she should not be confused by my procedure. My object of study is love, but that statement is unrevealing, for there are many kinds of love. My object of study is not the love of chocolate or of birds, parental love, filial love, sibling love, or love of country, although the love I am studying may have some of the features of these other loves. The loves that are most relevant to my study

are, on the one hand, those within the *eros* tradition, comprising the eros of Plato's *Symposium*, sexual love, courtly love, and romantic love, and, on the other hand, those within the *agape* tradition, including God's love for humans and Christian neighbour-love. The love I am concerned with is similar to these loves and might be a combination of several either from the same tradition or from both traditions. It is probably a historical development of the loves in the eros tradition, but I do not want to rule out in advance that it displays some features of the loves in the agape tradition. Ostensively defined, my object of study is the love that one person has for another person (usually not a blood relation); that may exist between two people when it is reciprocal (which is often, but not always, the case); that today often leads to or occurs in marriage or cohabitation (but obviously need not); that often has a component of sexual desire (in varying degrees); and that occasionally, for heterosexuals eventuates in procreation.

To clarify this ostensive definition of the love I am concerned with, I could mention examples of love from history and literature—say, the love of John Stuart Mill and Harriet Taylor, or that of Hack and Ray (in Marilyn Hacker's *Love, Death, and the Changing of the Seasons*). Referring to examples from life and literature will be helpful, but relying on them heavily while defining my object of study is dangerous, for I am not doing history, biography, or literary criticism, but philosophy (by which I mean the conceptual and moral analysis of an idea and a practice). If I wanted to study the kind of love for which Mill and Taylor are a paradigm, I would proceed by dissecting that particular relationship (as Phyllis Rose did in *Parallel Lives*). Or if Shakespeare's love life is paradigmatic, I would proceed by rereading the sonnet sequence and doing close textual analysis (say, in the manner of Barthes on Balzac in *S/Z*). However, these historical and literary paradigms are firmly bound in time and place; therefore, what we can learn from them conceptually and morally about our concept and practice of love may be limited in unpredictable ways. And we have too many paradigms; emphasizing some cases from this embarrassment of riches, at the expense of others, would be arbitrary. These examples from life and literature, then, can serve as illustrations rather than as a foundation for a definition or theory of love. In *The Four Loves*, C.S. Lewis half-heartedly apologizes for his habit of referring to *King Lear* and the like: "I am driven to literary examples because you, the reader, and I do not live in the same neighbourhood; if we did, there would . . . be no difficulty about replacing them with examples from real life."[3] But I am able to define my object of study ostensively because my reader and I do live in the same neighbourhood, and because, therefore, our experiences and observations about love are similar. (Lewis, after all, agrees; he can use literary examples only because he and his reader live in the same literary neighbourhood.)

My purpose is served well enough by saying that my concern is the familiar, garden-variety love that we practice in our everyday lives, nothing esoteric; as Anthony Weston puts it, "a somewhat . . . settled condition, though one in which romance may of course play a part."[4] I mean the love that we imagine the couple upstairs has, based on their behaviour in public; the love that in our happier moments we think we have and that we think the upstairs couple, behind closed doors, could never have. I will refer to the love I have in mind as "personal love"—but do not let anything hang on that phrase. (I find the expression "people love" ugly; otherwise, I would prefer it for its neutrality. The problem with the term "personal love" is that it is often a technical term describing "love for the person" rather than love for the properties of a person. It might be true that the love I am studying is "love for the person" in this technical sense; but my use of the term "personal love" does not imply that by definition the love I am concerned with is "love for the person.") I am not going to define love any further; the ostensive definition will have to suffice. I am not even aiming at a general definition of love. I assume that the reader knows what I am talking about. If, when reflecting on my claims, a reader cannot make any sense of my assertions, then my assumption will be proven false. How often this does not happen is the measure of my grasp of our concept and practice of love, of its underlying structure and morality.

One philosophical view of the love I am concerned with characterizes it in terms of a central thesis of the eros tradition; I will call this view "the first view of personal love," "view one," or simply "the eros tradition." In contrast to view one, there is a view of personal love that I will call "the second view," "view two," or "the agape tradition." I define "second view" as any view denying that the central thesis of the first view gives an accurate or complete account of personal love. What logical coherence there is in the second view is provided by a central thesis of the agape tradition. In working out the details of these two different characterizations of personal love, I am interested in several questions: What are the advantages and limits of these views in understanding the love I am concerned with? What would personal love look like if the first view, or the second, happened to be true? What do these two views presuppose about human nature and our ability to love? In particular, there are certain philosophical tangles that purportedly show that the eros tradition is inadequate and that personal love is poorly understood if analyzed by that tradition. Personal love, some have argued, can succeed (or be genuine) only if it is "agapized," that is, transformed by agape into a second view ("agapic") loves.[5] Much of the book defends the eros tradition (or "erosic" love) and argues that the agape tradition may succumb to similar tangles or objections when it is employed to characterize personal love. Does personal love need a dose of agape? Or at the theoretical level: Does conceiving of personal love in terms foreign to the eros tradition provide a better understanding of it? My eventual conclusion is "no."

2. Property-Based and Reason-Dependent Love

In the first view of personal love (that derived from the eros tradition), love is in principle and often in practice comprehensible. In particular, love is what I will call "property-based": When x loves y, this can be explained as the result of y's having, or x's perceiving that y has, some set S of attractive, admirable, or valuable properties; x loves y *because* y has S or because x perceives or believes that y has S. These properties of y are the basis or ground of x's love and hence, in the first view, something about the object of one's personal love is a crucial part of the explanatory source of love; love is "object-centric."[6] In principle, x and y (and outsiders) are capable of knowing why x loves y—that is, of knowing which attractive properties of y, the object, have brought it about that x loves y. Further, personal love is "reason-dependent": when

x loves y, x (given enough self-investigation) will be able to answer "Why do you love y?" by supplying reasons for loving y in terms of y's having S. Because the attractive properties of y figure both in the explanation of x's love and in the reasons x will give for loving y, I will use "property-based" and "reason-dependent" interchangeably. The central claim of the first view is that something about y is central in accounting for x's love for y; the emphasis is on the perceived merit of the object as the ground of love. Such is the structure of erosic personal love.

Several corollaries follow about personal love from the claim that it is property-based and reason-dependent. First, personal love, though susceptible to various kinds of irrationality, is not inherently irrational. If love is intentional—that is, if x loves y in virtue of x's believing or perceiving that y has S—then love is vulnerable to cognitive or psychological mistakes. X, for example, may be deluded in thinking that y has S; x might still love y in this case, even though the foundation of x's love is suspicious. But if personal love is in principle explainable in terms of y's having S, then love is not irrational at its core; it is not unpatterned, unprincipled, or unpredictable. Personal love is not one of the great mysteries of the universe. Second, the object's possessing properties that are unattractive ("defects") must play some role in determining the duration or intensity of personal love. Defects are not theoretically dispensable or ignorable; love exists, and is expected to exist, only up to a point. Third, that y loves x cannot ever suffice as a reason for why x loves y; that y loves x may contribute to the reasons in virtue of which x loves y, but it cannot be the original or the full reason. If y's loving x is allowed as the full reason that x loves y, and this particular reason can operate generally, then x might love y because y loves x—in turn because x loves y. This love is inexplicable.

The distinction between the first and the second view of personal love is not the same as that between "vulgar" love of the body and "heavenly" love of the mind, as described by Pausanias in Plato's *Symposium*. This is a distinction within the eros tradition itself, which in principle places little or no limit on what x may consider a valuable property of y; this is not what differentiates erosic love and agapic personal love. The second view of personal love (remember that the second view is not equivalent to agape but asserts the central thesis of that tradition) denies that personal love is property-based: the love of x for y is not grounded in y's attractive properties S or in x's belief or perception that y has S. If anything, the opposite is true: that is, x finds the properties that y has attractive, or x considers y to be attractive, because x loves y. The ground of personal love is not the perceived merit of the object but something about x, something in the nature of the lover; thus, personal love is subject-centric rather than object-centric. "It is not that the woman loved is the origin of the emotions apparently aroused by her; they are merely set behind her like a light."[7] Since x values y's properties in virtue of loving y, y's valuable properties cannot explain why x loves y. Love, then, is incomprehensible, insofar as the best candidate for the explanation of x's loving y (namely, that y has S) has been eliminated. If personal love is comprehensible at all, the explanation for x's loving y might be that y already loves x. (George Sand wrote in a letter, "If you want me to love you, you must begin by loving me . . . Then . . . anything you tell me will seem divine."[8] So x might find S in y to be valuable because x loves y, where x loves y because y loves x.) Alternatively, the explanation

for x's loving y might be the nature of x (x is filled with love) or x's desire or capacity to love regardless of the object's merit. Further, personal love is not reason-dependent: x should not be called upon to explain or justify loving y by giving reasons in terms of y's attractive properties, or any reasons at all. Love is its own reason and love is taken as a metaphysical primitive.[9] Such is the structure of agapic personal love.

The intentionality of personal love, in the second view, is not an important feature. Since love is not a response of the subject to the attractive properties of its object, love is much less dependent on what x believes about, or perceives in, y; hence, cognitive mistakes play no role in this picture of personal love. (One exception is x's loving y because y loves x, which must be understood as x's loving y because x *believes* that y loves x.) Similarly, defects play no role in personal love. Because x's love for y is not grounded in y's attractive properties, y's having unattractive properties carries no weight; a personal love that does not arise as a response to attractive properties is not a love that is extinguished or prevented by unattractive properties. That x finds S in y valuable because x loves y even implies that there is no distinction between y's attractive and unattractive properties until x develops a loving attitude toward y. (Analogously, x's hating y would explain, instead of being explained by, the fact that x finds properties of y to be disagreeable or obnoxious.) This is why personal love in this view is incomprehensible, even irrational. But in this view love's being a mystery is no strike against love or against any theory that conceives of love this way.[10]

An important issue regarding the first view of personal love is the relationship between y's having S as the cause of x's loving y (and thereby *y*'s having *S* being the explanation of *x*'s loving *y*) and *y*'s having *S* as *x*'s reason for loving *y*. We might appeal here to the notion that the distinction between causes and reasons is artificial: *x*'s reasons to do φ *are* the causes of *x*'s doing φ.[11] This move does not entirely work. Even if *x*'s reasons for loving *y* can be adequately conceived of as the cause of *x*'s loving *y* (in which case love's being reason-dependent is primary, while its being property-based is secondary), there is still room to think of nonreason-causes as the explanation of *x*'s loving *y* (in which case love's being property-based is primary and reason-dependence is secondary). Even if all reasons are causes (hence that *x*'s reason for loving *y* is the reason-cause explanation), not all causes are reasons (when *x*'s love is mostly explained by nonreason-causes). . . .

4. The Two Traditions

I am more concerned with the two views of personal love than I am with eros and agape themselves.[12] Plato's eros and God's agape are important because what is central to each of the two views I described above is a thesis extracted from these paradigms: one view claims that love is property-based and reason-dependent, while the other view denies that love can be adequately understood if conceived that way. Plato's eros and Paul's agape serve as models in the sense that our major question might be formulated: Is personal love more like the love a person has for God (eros) or more like the love that God has for persons (agape)? (Compare this question with the variants proposed below.) In this section I discuss to what extent the loves I have assigned to the eros and agape traditions exemplify these central themes.

For loves within the agape tradition, the attractive and unattractive properties of the object, the object's value, are entirely irrelevant. This irrelevance of merit is clear in agape as God's (or Jesus's) love for humans: "God does not love that which is already in itself worthy of love, but on the contrary, that which in itself has no worth acquires worth just by becoming the object of God's love. Agape has nothing to do with the kind of love that depends on the recognition of a valuable quality in its object; Agape does not recognise value, but creates it."[13] Why, then, does God love humans? "One 'reason' why God loves men is that God is God, and this is reason enough."[14] As Nygren says, "There is only one right answer . . . Because it is His nature to Love . . . The only ground for it is to be found in God himself."[15] But some Christians were drawn to the rationality of property-based love. Richard of St Victor, for example, could not imagine that "the Divine person could . . . have the highest love towards a person who was not worthy of the highest love."[16] Humans, having no worth, could not therefore be the recipients of God's love; ergo the Trinity, a device that, for Richard, supplied God with objects worthy of His love. Should we ask: Is it God's nature to love erosically or agapically? Does God love humans agapically only because we have no worth—that is, is He forced to love us agapically if He is to love us at all?

Love's not being based on the merit of its object is also characteristic of agape as Christian love of one's neighbour, which demands that humans love the sinner, the stranger, the sick, the ugly, and the enemy, as well as the righteous and one's kin. Given this list of appropriate objects of love, individual attractiveness obviously plays no role in neighbour-love. Nevertheless, neighbour-love is interpretable not as agape but as an erosic love. For example, if humans are not worthless precisely because

God has bestowed objective value on them, then neighbour-love could be construed as a property-based response to this value.[17] Or perhaps neighbour-love is a response to the piece or spark of God that exists in all humans.[18] Here we should distinguish the claim (about the basis of love) that x's neighbour-love for y is property-based, in that x loves y because y possesses the valuable property "contains a piece of God," from the claim (about the object of love) that in neighbour-love what one loves is not the human per se but that piece of God in the human.[19] Even this latter claim, however, implies that neighbour-love is an erosic love, if the human love for God is itself based on God's attractive properties and therefore, the love of the piece of God in humans is based on the attractive properties of that piece. Perhaps we should ask: Is neighbour-love more like a love of humans for humans (a heavenly eros) or more like the agape of God for humans?

Erich Fromm has argued that mother love is an agapic love, whereas father love is an erosic love (or, better, that the idea of mother love, or mother love as a Weberian "ideal type," fits into the agape tradition).[20] In mother love the child is loved unconditionally, just because she exists; in father love, the child is loved when or because she fulfills the father's expectations, obeys his moral demands, and achieves worldly success in his eyes (that is, in mother love, the child's merit is irrelevant; in father love, merit is central). Fromm also claims that the Old Testament God is a projection of this idea of father love, and the New Testament God a projection of mother love.[21] Thus, the theory of human parental love is not derived from the idea of God's love, but the idea of God's love is modelled after recognizable features of human parental love. Irving Singer has claimed that Fromm's social psychology of religion is

"hardly defensible" because "the distinction between mother's love and father's love cannot be upheld": mother love can also be conditional (she needs her children, and an "actual mother" also "imposes demands and expectations"), while in some cases a father's love is unconditional (Singer mentions the parable of the prodigal son).[22] However, these points do not undermine Fromm's view. First, if mothers and fathers do not love in accordance with the "ideal types," that fact has no relevance to Fromm's social psychology of religion, since what people project onto God is their idea of the perfect mother or father, or the observed behaviour of rare, exemplary mothers and fathers. Second, to point out that some fathers love unconditionally is not to destroy the distinction between (ideal) mother love and father love but only to challenge the claim (which might not be Fromm's) that styles of parental love are gender-linked.

Nevertheless, Singer's suspicion that mother love, or a genderless parental love, is even in its ideal form more erosic than agapic deserves consideration. First, parental love might fall within the eros tradition if the parent loves the child not on the basis of the child's mere existence but because the child has the property "is a child of mine," which is, from the parent's subjective perspective, a meritorious property. Because the parent loves the child in virtue of this property, the parent might then (consistently with the first view) attribute all manner of other properties to the child (beauty, intelligence, and so on). This common phenomenon of "seeing" these valuable properties in one's child does not, then, have to be explained as a second-view process. Second, the parent's reason for loving the child is both general and selective; if this is why the parent loves child x, the parent has equal reason for loving child *y*, yet has no reason for loving someone else's child. That is, parental love is preferential in a way that God's agape and neighbour-love could never be. Further, parental love is erosic if parents do not love all their children equally: if a parent loves child *x* more than child *y*, even though both have the property "is a child of mine," then some other (probably meritorious) properties possessed by child *x* are involved. (An example might be loving child *x* more than child *y* because the former has the property "first-born.") Parental love, then, differs significantly from agape in structure: God loves all His children, but everyone is one of His children (God's love is general but not selective), and God loves all His children equally (other meritorious properties are irrelevant). But does this imply that God's love is erosic after all?—God loves humans in virtue of their possessing the property "is a child, or creation, of mine," and that property is an attractive property. Perhaps, however, "is a creation of mine" does not register in God's eyes as a meritorious property or is not a reason why God loves humans.

Finally, consider friendship-love. In one version it exhibits the main feature of eros, arising in virtue of the attractiveness of the friend. For example, *x* and *y* are friends because they have common interests or goals that both see as valuable or because they respond to each other's excellence and character (more broadly, for Aristotle, "we do not feel affection for everything, but only for the lovable, and that means what is good, pleasant, or useful").[23] But opposed to this is Montaigne's friendship with Étienne de La Boétie, whose properties Montaigne claimed were irrelevant to, and afforded no explanation for, their love. Montaigne wrote of his beloved:

It is not one special consideration, nor two, nor three, nor four, nor a thousand: it is I know not what quintessence of all this mixture . . . If you press me to tell why I loved him, I feel that this cannot be expressed, except by answering: Because it was he, because it was I.[24]

Whether Montaigne is describing friendship is not important; what he wrote, however, arguably does capture the spirit of the second view of personal love and is for that reason illuminating. The Puritan Daniel Rogers held a similar view about friendship, in which a "secret instinct" ties two friends together: "A reason cannot be given by either partie, why they should be so tender each to other."[25] Edmund Leites comments that for some Puritans, the same "mystery [was] at the heart of marital love. Its causes are largely hidden and unknown, and hence beyond our control."[26] The scorching reply to Montaigne, Rogers, and St Bernard (who said about charity, "I love because I love")[27] is "To say *you* Love, but you *know not why*, is more beseeming Children or mad folks" (than, for example, two people contemplating marriage).[28]

For the loves of the eros tradition, the attractive properties of the object account for the existence of love and determine its course. This is almost perfectly clear in Plato's eros itself, where the beauty or goodness of an object (body, soul, law, theorem) grounds the subject's love (although a case can be made that Plato considers beauty to be love's object, not merely its basis). In courtly love, the lover chooses "one woman as the exemplar of all significant virtues and [uses] that as the reason for loving her. . . . The inherent excellence of her total personality . . . elicits his love,"[29] rather than his love eliciting her excellence. In sexual love, the properties of the object obviously play an important role, even if sexual desirability is subjective and some lovers are less discriminating than others. (Note that my term "erosic" is very far from "erotic," even though the structures of both loves are the same.) And in the love of humans for God, the fine qualities of the object, or the belief that God manifests perfection, is the ground of love.

Romantic love is a special case. Because romantic love is often seen as a historical development of courtly love, it may fall within the eros tradition and have the main features of the first view of personal love: powerful passion for the object is generated by an accurate perception of its goodness or beauty, and the lover realizes that these properties are responsible for the passion. But romantic love may also exhibit features of the second view: it arises (and disappears) mysteriously, incomprehensibly; the lover is not always expected to have reasons for his or her passion; and the lover is only under an illusion that the beloved has attractive properties. Whether romantic love is to be classified with the eros or the agape tradition depends not on the mere fact that x has an illusion about y's having P, but on the relationship between the illusion and x's loving y. If x's loving y leads x to have the illusion that y has P, then romantic love is agapic; but if x has the illusion that y has P and, on the basis of this falsely attributed property, x loves y, then it is erosic. In the first view of personal love, there is no structural difference between x's loving y because x believes truly that y has P, and x's loving y because x believes falsely that y has P, whether the false belief is the result of deliberate deception by y or x's need or desire to believe that y has P.

It is not clear how Stendhalian romantic love in particular is to be understood. Peter Gay apparently would put Stendhalian love within the second view: "[For Stendhal] it is not that all

beautiful creatures are loved, but that all loved creatures are beautiful," by which Gay means that x sees y as beautiful because x loves y.[30] Stendhal's statement that "from the moment he falls in love even the wisest man no longer sees anything *as it really is*"[31] would confirm Gay's impression, except for the fact that the passage leaves open the possibility that the love was earlier secured in a property-based fashion and only later encouraged "overvaluation." When Stendhal wrote that the lover will discover *new* perfections,[32] he seems to mean that x, already loving y in a property-based way, will find additional value in y. Furthermore, he also claims that admiration and other positive appraisals (for example, "how delightful it would be to kiss her") precede love,[33] in which case love itself does not generate all positive appraisals of the beloved.[34] Admiration is a property-based emotion, and if it plays a role in the genesis of romantic love, then love, too, is property-based.[35] Another issue is whether, for Stendhal, the discovery of new perfections by the lover is psychologically unsound (the result of deluded imagination or of wish fulfillment). There is no denying his remark that once x loves y, x "no longer sees" y as she "really" is. Although Irving Singer recognizes that this statement suggests psychological infirmity in the lover,[36] he argues that Stendhal had something else in mind: "The lover experiences no illusion in the sense of mistaken judgment: he merely refuses to limit his appreciative responses to what the rest of the world declares beautiful. . . . The lover's act of imagination consists in bestowing value upon attributes of the beloved that he *knows* are not beautiful."[37] That x finds P in y to be valuable just because x loves y does not mean x is guilty of a cognitive mistake or psychological foul-up. As a result of loving y, x may merely imagine that y has attractive properties and be blind to y's defects (perhaps x rationalizes, seeking an ex post facto justification for loving y). But, more soberly, x may deliberately bestow value on y or on y's properties because x loves y without being driven by neurotic processes. After all, if God bestows value on otherwise unworthy creatures, in virtue of His love for them, God would not be accused of making a cognitive mistake or of being the victim of a vicious psychological mechanism. Hence, as Singer argues, a Stendhalian lover may confer value upon the beloved unsuspiciously. And this may happen whether the love is or is not property-based.

Notes

1   Capellanus, *The Art of Courtly Love*, p. 2. (Full information on works cited in the endnotes can be found in the Bibliography.)

2   Descartes, *The Passions of the Soul* (*Philosophical Writings*, vol. 1, p. 356).

3   *The Four Loves*, p. 63.

4   Weston, "Toward the Reconstruction of Subjectivism," p. 182.

5   See C.S. Lewis, *The Four Loves*, pp. 81–2, 124, 154, 160–6; Smedes, *Love Within Limits*, pp. 6, 92–3; and de Rougemont, *Love in the Western World*, p. 311ff.

6   See Martha Nussbaum on the distinction between the "basis" and the "object" of love (*The Fragility of Goodness*, p. 355).

7   Robert Musil, "Tonka," in *Five Women*, p. 113. He continues: "But whereas in dreams there is still a hairs-breadth margin, a crack, separating the love from the beloved, in waking life: this split is not apparent; one is merely the victim of *doppelgänger*-trickery and cannot help seeing a human being as wonderful who is not so at all." See also George Eliot, *Daniel Deronda*, p. 658: "We may learn from the order of word-making, wherein *love* precedeth *lovable*." The view that x finds S in y valuable only because x loves y is also mildly suggested in Carson McCullers's *The Ballad of the Sad Café*, pp. 26–7.

8   Barry, *French Lovers*, p. 195.

9   One might read Pascal's remark (*Pensées* no. 423, p. 154)—the lover's "heart has its reasons of which reason knows nothing"—agapically. It is apparently a retraction of an earlier claim of his: "We have unaptly taken away the name of reason from love, and have opposed them to each other without good foundation. . . . Let us not . . . exclude reason from love, since they are inseparable. The poets were not right in painting Love blind" ("Discourse on the Passion of Love," pp. 522–3). A modern version of this "inseparability" thesis is defended by Nakhnikian, "Love in Human Reason."

10   Niklas Luhman claims that the second view of personal love historically postdates the first view. In the theory of courtly love, "A knowledge of the object's characteristics was essential." Later, "in the field of paradoxical codification" [romantic love], "love [was] justified . . . by means of imagination" (that is, x's perceiving S in y, even falsely imagining S, sufficed for love). But "once the autonomy of intimate relations had finally been established, it was possible to justify love simply by the inexplicable fact that one loved. . . . The beauty of the beloved . . . now no longer had to be in evidence, nor did it have to be imagined; this had ceased to be a reason for love, and rather was seen by the lovers as a consequence of their love" (*Love as Passion*, p. 44, italics deleted; see also p. 166: "The lover himself is the source of his love"). But also, of course, Plato preceded Paul.

11   See Davidson, "Reasons as Causes."

12 Comparisons of eros and agape have been enormously influential in my thinking; for example, Kierkegaard's *Works of Love*, Anders Nygren's *Agape and Eros*, and Gene Outka's *Agape: An Ethical Analysis*. Robert Solomon, in contrast, believes that this literature is dispensable: "Much of the history of Western love, written primarily by theological scholars and German philologists, has consisted in the mock battle between these two Greek words. . . . But all of this has nothing to do with love. . . . [I]t is rather a technique to indulge in scholarship and avoid looking at any actual experience. . . . Indeed, rather than clarify the issues, this scholarly piddling is itself another political move, a way of making an ordinary emotion sound impressively profound" (*Love: Emotion, Myth, and Metaphor*, p. 9).

13 Nygren, *Agape and Eros*, p. 78. See also Helmut Thielicke, *The Ethics of Sex*, p. 33.

14 Douglas Morgan, *Love: Plato, the Bible, and Freud*, p. 74.

15 Nygren, *Agape and Eros*, p. 75.

16 Quoted by Nygren, *Agape and Eros*, p. 654.

17 See Outka, *Agape*, pp. 158–60.

18 See Nygren, *Agape and Eros*, pp. 96–8, and Morgan, *Love*, p. 123, n. 74.

19 The similarity between Plato's eros and a neighbour-love that loves God-in-the-human is suggested by Shirley Letwin ("Romantic Love and Christianity," p. 133): "The object of Diotima's love is real, not an illusion. But this real object of love is neither a human being nor a human quality. It is the divine spark in all men." This spark is not a piece of the Christian God but the "participation" of a human in the Form of Beauty.

20 Fromm, *The Art of Loving*, pp. 33–7.

21 See Judith Van Herik, *Freud, Femininity, and Faith*, for a discussion of similar theses in Freud.

22 Singer, *The Nature of Love*, vol. 1, pp. 300–1.

23 Aristotle, *Nicomachean Ethics*, 1155b15–20. In this translation, Martin Ostwald reluctantly

uses "lovable"; see p. 217, n. 11. Both Gregory Vlastos ("The Individual as an Object of Love in Plato," p. 4, text and n. 4) and Nussbaum (*The Fragility of Goodness*, p. 354) think that *philin* is best translated as "love," not "friendship."

24 Montaigne, *Complete Essays*, book I, chap. 28, "Of Friendship," p. 139. Even though I am interpreting Montaigne as claiming that personal love has no reasons, other readings are possible: (1) Montaigne does have reasons, of which he was unconscious; or (2) Montaigne is claiming that all Boétie's properties, taken together, provided his reason for loving. "Because it was he," then, means "because he was the sum of his properties." See notes 69 and 71, below.

25 Rogers, *Matrimoniall Honour* (1642); quoted by Leites, *The Puritan Conscience and Modern Sexuality*, p. 101.

26 Leites, *The Puritan Conscience*, p. 101.

27 Quoted by Aldous Huxley, *The Perennial Philosophy*, p. 83.

28 Baxter, *A Christian Dictionary* (1678); quoted by Leites, *The Puritan Conscience*, p. 176, n. 82.

29 Singer, *The Nature of Love*, vol. 2, p. 49.

30 Gay, *The Tender Passion*, p. 65.

31 Stendhal, *Love*, p. 60.

32 Ibid., p. 59: "Why does one enjoy and delight in each new beauty discovered in the beloved?"

33 Ibid., pp. 45, 50.

34 See Russell Vannoy, *Sex Without Love*, p. 157, n. 3.

35 See my article, "The Unity of Romantic Love," pp. 388–95. George Eliot wrote that admiration was, fortunately, only a necessary condition for love: "Care has been taken not only that the trees should not sweep the stars down, but also that every man who admires a fair girl should not be enamoured of her. . . . [N]ature's order is certainly benignant in not obliging us one and all to be desperately in love with the most admirable mortal we have ever seen" (*Daniel Deronda*, p. 85). If we read this serious passage in a way

unintended by Eliot, it will sound like Woody
Allen's "Not only is there no God, but try getting
a plumber on weekends" (*Getting Even*, p. 25).

36 Singer, *The Nature of Love*, vol. 2, p. 361.
37 Ibid., p. 365.

HARRY G. FRANKFURT

In the Introduction to the Philosophy of Sex, I made reference to a *Euthyphro* problem that
Alan Soble raises for love: Do I love my beloved because she is loveable, or is she loveable
because I love her? Harry Frankfurt clearly thinks that the latter view is the right account
for the best kind of love. This means that Frankfurt's view of love is agapic in structure
since Frankfurt thinks that love, like Christian agape, issues from the lover without regard
for reasons or for the valuable properties of the beloved. But agape proper is the love that
is bestowed on humankind by God—a being that is perfect and self-sufficient. Presumably,
such a being has no need of antecedent reasons for love. Indeed, it is said to be in God's
nature to love and this love is unconditional. But is it possible for finite human beings to love
agapically? How might we love without such reasons? Frankfurt, without giving a detailed
account, suggests that natural selection might account for this kind of love. Frankfurt sets
up the love of a parent for her or his child as a kind of paradigm for real love, and indeed
parental love is often thought to be unconditional (or disinterested, to use Frankfurt's term).
Perhaps such love has served an evolutionary purpose by having the parent love the child
in this unconditional manner until she can attain her independence. Maybe there is some
survival advantage to the offspring when parents love in this unconditional manner. Such
love may address certain security needs in the child, giving him or her confidence to face the
world with all of its challenges. In a more indirect and complicated sense, maybe this need
accounts for agapic love in its religious form as well.

On Love and Its Reasons

Love is often understood as being, most basically, a response to the perceived worth of the
beloved. We are moved to love something, on
this account, by an appreciation of what we take
to be its exceptional inherent value. The appeal
of that value is what captivates us and turns us
into lovers. We begin loving the things that we
love because we are struck by their value, and
we continue to love them for the sake of their
value. If we did not find the beloved valuable,
we would not love it.

This may well fit certain cases of what
would commonly be identified as love. However, the sort of phenomenon that I have in
mind when referring here to love is essentially
something else. As I am construing it, love is
not necessarily a response grounded in awareness of the inherent value of its object. It may
sometimes arise like that, but it need not do
so. Love may be brought about—in ways that
are poorly understood—by a disparate variety
of natural causes. It is entirely possible for a
person to be caused to love something without noticing its value, or without being at all

impressed by its value, or despite recognizing that there really is nothing especially valuable about it. It is even possible for a person to come to love something despite recognizing that its inherent nature is actually and utterly bad. That sort of love is doubtless a misfortune. Still, such things happen.

It is true that the beloved invariably *is*, indeed, valuable to the lover. However, perceiving that value is not at all an indispensable *formative* or *grounding* condition of the love. It need not be a perception of value in what he loves that moves the lover to love it. The truly essential relationship between love and the value of the beloved goes in the opposite direction. It is not necessarily as a *result* of recognizing their value and of being captivated by it that we love things. Rather, what we love necessarily *acquires* value for us *because* we love it. The lover does invariably and necessarily perceive the beloved as valuable, but the value he sees it to possess is a value that derives from and that depends upon his love.

Consider the love of parents for their children. I can declare with unequivocal confidence that I do not love my children because I am aware of some value that inheres in them independent of my love for them. The fact is that I loved them even before they were born—before I had any especially relevant information about their personal characteristics or their particular merits and virtues. Furthermore, I do not believe that the valuable qualities they do happen to possess, strictly in their own rights, would really provide me with a very compelling basis for regarding them as having greater worth than many other possible objects of love that in fact I love much less. It is quite clear to me that I do not love them more than other children because I believe they are better.

At times, we speak of people or of other things as "unworthy" of our love. Perhaps this means that the cost of loving them would be greater than the benefit of doing so; or perhaps it means that to love those things would be in some way demeaning. In any case, if I ask myself whether my children are worthy of my love, my emphatic inclination is to reject the question as misguided. This is not because it goes so clearly without saying that my children *are* worthy. It is because my love for them is not at all a response to an evaluation either of them or of the consequences for me of loving them. If my children should turn out to be ferociously wicked, or if it should become apparent that loving them somehow threatened my hope of leading a decent life, I might perhaps recognize that my love for them was regrettable. But I suspect that after coming finally to acknowledge this, I would continue to love them anyhow.

It is not because I have noticed their value, then, that I love my children as I do. Of course, I do perceive them to have value; so far as I am concerned, indeed, their value is beyond measure. That, however, is not the basis of my love. It is really the other way around. The particular value that I attribute to my children is not inherent in them but depends upon my love for them. The reason they are so precious to me is simply that I love them so much. As for why it is that human beings do tend generally to love their children, the explanation presumably lies in the evolutionary pressures of natural selection. In any case, it is plainly *on account of* my love for them that they have acquired in my eyes a value that otherwise they would certainly not possess.

This relationship between love and the value of the beloved—namely, that love is not necessarily grounded in the value of the beloved but does necessarily make the beloved valuable to the lover—holds not only for parental love but quite generally.[1] Most profoundly, perhaps, it is love that accounts for the value to us of life itself. Our lives normally have for us a value that we accept as commandingly authoritative. Moreover, the value to us of living radiates pervasively. It radically conditions the value that we attribute to many other things. It is a powerful—indeed, a comprehensively foundational—generator of value. There are innumerable things that we care about a great deal, and that therefore are very important to us, just because of the ways in which they bear upon our interest in survival.

Why do we so naturally, and with such unquestioning assurance, take self-preservation to be an incomparably compelling and legitimate reason for pursuing certain courses of action? We certainly do not assign this overwhelming importance to staying alive because we believe that there is some great value inherent in our lives, or in what we are doing with them—a value that is independent of our own attitudes and dispositions. Even when we think rather well of ourselves, and suppose that our lives may actually be valuable in such a way, that is not normally why we are so determined to hang on to them. We take the fact that some course of action would contribute to our survival as a reason for pursuing it just because, presumably again thanks to natural selection, we are innately constituted to love living.

Let me now attempt to explain what I have in mind when I speak here of love.

The object of love is often a concrete individual: for instance, a person or a country. It may also be something more abstract: for instance, a tradition, or some moral or nonmoral ideal. There will frequently be greater

emotional colour and urgency in love when the beloved is an individual than when it is something like social justice, or scientific truth, or the way a certain family or a certain cultural group does things; but that is not always the case. In any event, it is not among the defining features of love that it must be hot rather than cool.

One distinctive feature of loving has to do with the particular status of the value that is accorded to its objects. Insofar as we care about something at all, we regard it as important to ourselves; but we may consider it to have that importance only because we regard it as a means to something else. When we love something, however, we go further. We care about it not as merely a means, but as an end. It is in the nature of loving that we consider its objects to be valuable in themselves and to be important to us for their own sakes.

Love is, most centrally, a *disinterested* concern for the existence of what is loved, and for what is good for it. The lover desires that his beloved flourish and not be harmed; and he does not desire this just for the sake of promoting some other goal. Someone might care about social justice only because it reduces the likelihood of rioting; and someone might care about the health of another person just because she cannot be useful to him unless she is in good shape. For the lover, the condition of his beloved is important in itself, apart from any bearing that it may have on other matters.

Love may involve strong feelings of attraction, which the lover supports and rationalizes with flattering descriptions of the beloved. Moreover, lovers often enjoy the company of their beloveds, cherish various types of intimate connection with them, and yearn for reciprocity. These enthusiasms are not essential. Nor is it essential that a person like what he loves. He may even find it distasteful. As in other modes of caring, the heart of the matter is neither affective nor cognitive. It is volitional. Loving something has less to do with what a person believes, or with how he feels, than with a configuration of the will that consists in a practical concern for what is good for the beloved. This volitional configuration shapes the dispositions and conduct of the lover with respect to what he loves, by guiding him in the design and ordering of his relevant purposes and priorities.

It is important to avoid confusing love—as circumscribed by the concept that I am defining—with infatuation, lust, obsession, possessiveness, and dependency in their various forms. In particular, relationships that are primarily romantic or sexual do not provide very authentic or illuminating paradigms of love as I am construing it. Relationships of those kinds typically include a number of vividly distracting elements, which do not belong to the essential nature of love as a mode of disinterested concern, but that are so confusing that they make it nearly impossible for anyone to be clear about just what is going on. Among relationships between humans, the love of parents for their infants or small children is the species of caring that comes closest to offering recognizably pure instances of love.

There is a certain variety of concern for others that may also be entirely disinterested, but that differs from love because it is impersonal. Someone who is devoted to helping the sick or the poor for their own sakes may be quite indifferent to the particularity of those whom he seeks to help. What qualifies people to be beneficiaries of his charitable concern is not that he loves them. His generosity is not a response to their identities as individuals; it is not aroused by their personal characteristics.

It is induced merely by the fact that he regards them as members of a relevant class. For someone who is eager to help the sick or the poor, any sick or poor person will do.

When it comes to what we love, on the other hand, that sort of indifference to the specificity of the object is out of the question. The significance to the lover of what he loves is not that his beloved is an instance or an exemplar. Its importance to him is not generic; it is ineluctably particular. For a person who wants simply to help the sick or the poor, it would make perfectly good sense to choose his beneficiaries randomly from among those who are sick or poor enough to qualify. It does not matter who in particular the needy persons are. Since he does not really care about any of them as such, they are entirely acceptable substitutes for each other. The situation of a lover is very different. There can be no equivalent substitute for his beloved. It might really be all the same to someone moved by charity whether he helps this needy person or that one. It cannot possibly be all the same to the lover whether he is devoting himself disinterestedly to what he actually does love or—no matter how similar it might be—to something else instead.

Finally, it is a necessary feature of love that it is not under our direct and immediate voluntary control. What a person cares about, and how much he cares about it, may under certain conditions be up to him. It may at times be possible for him to bring it about that he cares about something, or that he does not care about it, just by making up his mind one way or the other. Whether the requirements of protecting and supporting that thing provide him with acceptable reasons for acting, and how weighty those reasons are, depends in cases like that upon what he himself decides. With regard to certain things, however, a person may discover that he cannot affect whether or how much he cares about them merely by his own decision. The issue is not up to him at all.

For instance, under normal conditions people cannot help caring quite a bit about staying alive, about remaining physically intact, about not being radically isolated, about avoiding chronic frustration, and so on. They really have no choice. Canvassing reasons and making judgments and decisions will not change anything. Even if they should consider it a good idea to stop caring about whether they have any contact with other human beings, or about fulfilling their ambitions, or about their lives and their limbs, they would be unable to stop. They would find that, whatever they thought or decided, they were still disposed to protect themselves from extreme physical and psychic deprivation and harm. In matters like these, we are subject to a necessity that forcefully constrains the will and that we cannot elude merely by choosing or deciding to do so.[2]

The necessity by which a person is bound in cases like these is not a cognitive necessity, generated by the requirements of reason. The way in which it makes alternatives unavailable is not by limiting, as logical necessities do, the possibilities of coherent thought. When we understand that a proposition is self-contradictory, it is impossible for us to believe it; similarly, we cannot help accepting a proposition when we understand that to deny it would be to embrace a contradiction. What people cannot help caring about, on the other hand, is not mandated by logic. It is not primarily a constraint upon belief. It is a volitional necessity, which consists essentially in a limitation of the will.

There are certain things that people cannot do, despite possessing the relevant natural capacities or skills, because they cannot muster the will to do them. Loving is circumscribed by a necessity of that kind: what we love and what we fail to love is not up to us. Now the necessity that is characteristic of love does not constrain the movements of the will through an imperious surge of passion or compulsion by which the will is defeated and subdued. On the contrary, the constraint operates from within our own will itself. It is by our own will, and not by any external or alien force, that we are constrained. Someone who is bound by volitional necessity is unable to form a determined and effective intention— regardless of what motives and reasons he may have for doing so—to perform (or to refrain from performing) the action that is at issue. If he undertakes an attempt to perform it, he discovers that he simply cannot bring himself to carry the attempt all the way through.

Love comes in degrees. We love some things more than we love others. Accordingly, the necessity that love imposes on the will is rarely absolute. We may love something and yet be willing to harm it, in order to protect something else for which our love is greater. A person may well find it possible under certain conditions, then, to perform an act that under others he could not bring himself to perform. For instance, the fact that a person sacrifices his life when he believes that doing so will save his country from catastrophic harm does not reveal thereby that he does not love living; nor does his sacrifice show that he could also have brought himself to accept death willingly when he believed that there was less to be gained. Even of people who commit suicide because they are miserable, it is generally true that they love living. What they would really like, after all, would be to give up not their lives but their misery.

Notes

1   There are certain objects of love—certain ideals, for instance—that do appear in many instances to be loved on account of their value. However, it is not necessary that the love of an ideal originate or be grounded in that way. A person might come to love justice or truth or moral rectitude quite blindly, after all, merely as a result of having been brought up to do so. Moreover, it is generally not considerations of value that account for the fact that a person comes to be selflessly devoted to one ideal or value rather than to some other. What leads people to care more about truth than about justice, or more about beauty than about morality, or more about one religion than about another, is generally not some prior appreciation that what they love more has greater inherent value than what they care about less.

2   If someone under ordinary conditions cared nothing at all about dying or being mutilated, or about being deprived of all human contact, we would not regard him merely as atypical. We would consider him to be deranged. There is no strictly logical flaw in those attitudes, but they count nonetheless as irrational—i.e., as violating a defining condition of humanity. There is a sense of rationality that has very little to do with consistency or with other formal considerations. Thus suppose that a person deliberately causes death or deep suffering for no reason, or (Hume's example) seeks the destruction of a multitude in order to avoid a minor injury to one of his fingers. Anyone who could bring himself to do such things would naturally be regarded—despite his having made no logical error—as "crazy." He would be regarded, in other words, as lacking reason. We are accustomed to understanding rationality as precluding contradiction and incoherence—as limiting what it is possible for us to think. There is also a sense of rationality in which it limits what we can bring ourselves to do or to accept. In the one sense, the alternative to reason is what we recognize as inconceivable. In the other, it is what we find unthinkable.

Discussion

Frankfurt's naturalistic account of agapic love (without God) views parental love as love in its purest form. Love varies in degrees according to Frankfurt[1] but it is not clear in his account that it also differs in kinds. This means that other sorts of love, such as romantic love, either do not qualify as real love, or are lesser forms of love, or are love to a lesser degree. Does it make sense to talk of love in this way? Is love one phenomenon or emotion that differs in *degrees* (e.g., parental love being the highest, friendship being lower, and perhaps romantic love being even a lower form), or is love different in *kinds*? A pluralist would view love as essentially different in types. Parental love, which seems unavoidably hierarchical at least during the early part of a child's life, differs fundamentally in structure from friendship or romantic love, which aim at equality, even if it is not always achieved.

One of the challenges to Frankfurt's view has to do with the discriminant aspect of love. If love is not motivated by properties of the beloved, then how does one choose between loving John and loving Sam? Since love is aimed at a particular individual according to Frankfurt, then how does the lover choose this individual to begin with? Is there a way of accounting for the *choice* of a beloved through agapically structured love? Soble claims that agapic love is irrational and to see this clearly we should compare it to agapically structured hate. If we were to hate someone for no reason we would be accused of holding an irrational attitude. Soble thinks that we should apply the same standard to love, which is not an anomalous emotion, he argues.[2] Is there a way out of this problem for Frankfurt? Could love be a response to a person that is better characterized in affective terms rather than in terms of reasons? This might fit with Frankfurt's claim that the explanation is an evolutionary one.[3] Of course this would still mean love could be accounted for in terms of reasons, but the reasons may not be of the direct kind that Soble characterizes, having to do with the beloved's observable properties.

Is parental love a sufficient paradigm for love? Are romantic love and friendship, for instance, somehow inferior to parental love as forms of love? Both romantic love and friendship would seem to rely in part at least on an erosic structure. Both romantic love and friendship appear to be a response to something found in the beloved or the friend—whether that something be beauty, money, usefulness, or the person's good character. Philosophers such as Søren Kierkegaard and Max Scheler have thought that this feature of romantic love, erotic love, and friendship makes them selfish forms of love. Do you agree? Can the virtue of these forms of love be defended? Can they be defended against the charge of selfishness? Is there anything fundamentally unvirtuous or selfish (in a bad sense) in loving a person for his or her positive qualities?

Notes

1 H.G. Frankfurt, "On Love, and Its Reasons," in *The Reasons of Love* (Princeton: Princeton University Press, 2004), 46.
2 Alan Soble, *The Structure of Love* (New Haven, CT: Yale University Press, 1990), 112–28; Alan Soble, "Love and Value, Yet Again," *Essays in Philosophy: A Biannual Journal* 6, no. 1, (2005): 4–5.
3 Frankfurt himself rejects this option telling us, "As in other modes of caring, the heart of the matter is neither affective nor cognitive. It is volitional" (Frankfurt, "On Love, and Its Reasons," 42). But Robert Kraut offers an affective account of love in his article "Love *De Re*" (*Midwest Studies in Philosophy* 10, no. 1 [1987]: 413–30).

Suggestions for Further Reading

Gary Foster, "Bestowal without Appraisal: Problems in Frankfurt's Characterization of Love and Personal Identity," *Ethical Theory and Moral Practice* 12, no. 2 (2009): 153–68.

Søren Kierkegaard, *Works of Love*, edited and translated by H.V. Hong and E.H. Hong (Princeton: Princeton University Press, 1995).

Robert Kraut, "Love *De Re*," *Midwest Studies in Philosophy* 10, no. 1 (1987): 413–30.

Anders Nygren, *Agape and Eros: The Christian Idea of Love*, translated by Philip S. Watson (Chicago: University of Chicago Press, 1982).

Alan Soble, "Love and Value, Yet Again," *Essays in Philosophy: A Biannual Journal* 6, no. 1 (2005): 1–25.

Section V   Romantic Love

Chapter Twelve
Love and Identity

JEAN-PAUL SARTRE

In the first half of this book, I discussed Sartre's ontology of human existence and the role that sexual desire plays in the more general desire *to be*. In the following selection, which is also from Sartre's *Being and Nothingness*, we see a similar analysis of love. The desire to be (or to be complete) is expressed in love in one's desire to incorporate the subjectivity or freedom of the Other into one's own subjectivity so that one can experience the object side of one's own identity. Sartre describes this as the attempt to capture the freedom of the Other while wanting her or him to remain free. Capturing the freedom of the Other requires the lover to seduce the beloved. The lover does this by making himself a *fascinating object* for the beloved. Sartre sees in this making an object of oneself a *masochistic* attitude, for what is masochism but to make oneself into an object (of suffering) for the other person. But Sartre thinks that love fails in its objective. For either I make myself into an object for the Other (passive) and thus fail to subjectively experience my objectivity as the Other would, or I assume my subjectivity (active) and turn the Other into an object that cannot reveal to me my object side. Sartre's account of love assumes a romantic framework in the truest sense of the word since Romanticism was a philosophy of reconciliation whereby we as human beings reconciled ourselves with nature, with our fellow human beings, or with our selves. The Romantic idea held that as human beings we are alienated from our true being (our true being as both subjects and objects) and that love (as well as art, philosophy, politics) is a means for us to overcome our divided self. Even though Sartre accepts the Romantic framing of the problem, he rejects the solution, seeing it as offering an impossible ideal. But even though the ideal is impossible, the very striving towards it gives our lives meaning or a sense of purpose.

very early

First Attitude toward Others: Love, Language, Masochism

Everything which may be said of me in my relations with the Other applies to him as well. While I attempt to free myself from the hold of the Other, the Other is trying to free himself from mine; while I seek to enslave the Other, the Other seeks to enslave me. We are by no means dealing with unilateral relations with an object-in-itself, but with reciprocal and moving relations. The following descriptions of concrete behaviour must therefore be envisaged within the perspective of *conflict*. Conflict is the original meaning of being-for-others.

If we start with the first revelation of the Other as a *look*, we must recognize that we experience our inapprehensible being-for-others in the form of a *possession*. I am possessed by the Other; the Other's look fashions my body in its nakedness, causes it to be born, sculptures it, produces it as it is, sees it as I shall never see it. The Other holds a secret—the secret of what I am. He makes me be and thereby he possess me, and this possession is nothing other than the consciousness of possessing me. I in the recognition of my object-state have proof that he has this consciousness. By virtue of consciousness the Other is for me simultaneously the one who has stolen my being from me and the one who causes "there to be" a being which is my being. Thus I have a comprehension of this ontological structure: I am responsible for my being-for-others, but I am not the foundation of it. It appears to me therefore in the form of a contingent given for which I am nevertheless responsible; the Other founds my being in so far as this being is in the form of the "there is." But he is not responsible for my being although he founds it in complete freedom—in and by means of his free transcendence. Thus

to the extent that I am revealed to myself as responsible for my being, I *lay claim* to this being which I am; that is, I wish to recover it, or, more exactly, I am the project of the recovery of my being. I want to stretch out my hand and grab hold of this being which is presented to me as my being but at a distance—like the dinner of Tantalus; I want to found it by my very freedom. For if in one sense my being-as-object is an unbearable contingency and the pure "possession" of myself by another, still in another sense this being stands as the indication of what I should be obliged to recover and found in order to be the foundation of myself. But this is conceivable only if I assimilate the Other's freedom. Thus my project of recovering myself is fundamentally a project of absorbing the Other.

Nevertheless this project must leave the Other's nature intact. Two consequences result: (1) I do not thereby cease to assert the Other—that is, to deny concerning myself that I am the Other. Since the Other is the foundation of my being, he could not be dissolved in me without my being-for-others disappearing. Therefore if I project the realization of unity with the Other, this means that I project my assimilation of the Other's Otherness as my own possibility. In fact the problem for me is to make myself be by acquiring the possibility of taking the Other's point of view on myself. It is not a matter of acquiring a pure, abstract faculty of knowledge. It is not the pure category of the Other which I project appropriating to myself. This category is not conceived nor even conceivable. But on the occasion of concrete experience with the Other, an experience suffered and realized, it is this concrete Other as an absolute reality whom in his otherness I wish to incorporate into myself. (2) The Other whom I wish to assimilate is by no means the

Other-as-object. Or, if you prefer, my project of incorporating the Other in no way corresponds to a recapturing of my for-itself as myself and to a surpassing of the Other's transcendence toward my own possibilities. For me it is not a question of obliterating my object-state by making an object of the Other, which would amount to releasing myself from my being-for-others. Quite the contrary, I want to assimilate the Other as the Other-looking-at-me, and this project of assimilation includes an augmented recognition of my being-looked-at. In short, in order to maintain before me the Other's freedom which is looking at me, I identify myself totally with my being-looked-at. And since my being-as-object is the only possible relation between me and the Other, it is this being-as-object which alone can serve me as an instrument to effect my assimilation of the *other freedom*.

Thus as a reaction to the failure of the third ekstasis, the for-itself wishes to be identified with the Other's freedom as founding its own being-in-itself. To be other to oneself—the ideal always aimed at concretely in the form of being *this Other* to oneself—is the primary value of my relations with the Other. This means that my being-for-others is haunted by the indication of an absolute-being which would be itself as other and other as itself and which by freely giving to itself its being-itself as other and its being-other as itself, would be the very being of the ontological proof—that is, God. This ideal can not be realized without my surmounting the original contingency of my relations to the Other; that is, by overcoming the fact that there is no relation of internal negativity between the negation by which the Other is made other than I and the negation by which I am made other than the Other. We have seen that this contingency is insurmountable; it is the *fact* of my relations

with the Other, just as my body is the *fact* of my being-in-the-world. Unity with the Other is therefore *in fact* unrealizable. It is also unrealizable *in theory* for the assimilation of the for-itself and the Other in a single transcendence would necessarily involve the disappearance of the characteristic of otherness in the Other. Thus the condition on which I project the identification of myself with the Other is that I persist in denying that I am the Other. Finally this project of unification is the source of *conflict* since while I experience myself as an object for the Other and while I project assimilating him in and by means of this experience, the Other apprehends me as an object in the midst of the world and does not project identifying me with himself. It would therefore be necessary—since being for-others includes a double internal negation—to act upon the internal negation by which the Other transcends my transcendence and makes me exist for the Other; that is, *to act upon the Other's freedom.*

This unrealizable ideal which haunts my project of myself in the presence of the Other is not to be identified with love in so far as love is an enterprise; *i.e.,* an organic ensemble of projects toward my own possibilities. But it is the ideal of love, its motivation and its end, its unique value. Love as the primitive relation to the Other is the ensemble of the projects by which I aim at realizing this value.

These projects put me in direct connection with the Other's freedom. It is in this sense that love is a conflict. We have observed that the Other's freedom is the foundation of my being. But precisely because I exist by means of the Other's freedom, I have no security; I am in danger in this freedom. It moulds my being and *makes me be*, it confers values upon me and removes them from me; and my being receives from it a perpetual passive escape from self.

Irresponsible and beyond reach, this protean freedom in which I have engaged myself can in turn engage me in a thousand different ways of being. My project of recovering my being can be realized only if I get hold of this freedom and reduce it to being a freedom subject to my freedom. At the same time it is the only way in which I can act on the free negation of interiority by which the Other constitutes me as an Other; that is the only way in which I can prepare the way for a future identification of the Other with me. This will be clearer perhaps if we study the problem from a purely psychological aspect. Why does the lover want to be *loved*? If Love were in fact a pure desire for physical possession, it could in many cases be easily satisfied. Proust's hero, for example, who installs his mistress in his home, who can see her and possess her at any hour of the day, who has been able to make her completely dependent on him economically, ought to be free from worry. Yet we know that he is, on the contrary, continually gnawed by anxiety. Through her consciousness Albertine escapes Marcel even when he is at her side, and that is why he knows relief only when he gazes on her while she sleeps. It is certain then that the lover wishes to capture a "consciousness." But why does he wish it? And how?

The notion of "ownership," by which love is so often explained, is not actually primary. Why should I want to appropriate the Other if it were not precisely that the Other makes me be? But this implies precisely a certain mode of appropriation; it is the Other's freedom as such that we want to get hold of. Not because of a desire for power. The tyrant scorns love, he is content with fear. If he seeks to win the love of his subjects, it is for political reasons; and if he finds a more economical way to enslave them, he adopts it immediately. On the other hand,

the man who wants to be loved does not desire the enslavement of the beloved. He is not bent on becoming the object of passion which flows forth mechanically. He does not want to possess an automaton, and if we want to humiliate him, we need only try to persuade him that the beloved's passion is the result of a psychological determinism. The lover will then feel that both his love and his being are cheapened. If Tristan and Isolde fall madly in love because of a love potion, they are less interesting. The total enslavement of the beloved kills the love of the lover. The end is surpassed; if the beloved is transformed into an automaton, the lover finds himself alone. Thus the lover does not desire to possess the beloved as one possesses a thing; he demands a special type of appropriation. He wants to possess a freedom as freedom.

On the other hand, the lover can not be satisfied with that superior form of freedom which is a free and voluntary engagement. Who would be content with a love given as pure loyalty to a sworn oath? Who would be satisfied with the words, "I love you because I have freely engaged myself to love you and because I do not wish to go back on my word." Thus the lover demands a pledge, yet is irritated by a pledge. He wants to be loved by a freedom but demands that this freedom as freedom should no longer be free. He wishes that the Other's freedom should determine itself to become love—and this not only at the beginning of the affair but at each instant—and at the same time he wants this freedom to be captured *by itself*, to turn back upon itself, as in madness, as in a dream, so as to will its own captivity. This captivity must be a resignation that is both free and yet chained in our hands. In love it is not a determinism of the passions which we desire in the Other nor a freedom beyond reach; it is a freedom which *plays the role of* a determinism of the passions and which is caught in its own role. For himself the lover does not demand that he be the *cause* of this radical modification of freedom but that he be the unique and privileged occasion of it. In fact he could not want to be the cause of it without immediately submerging the beloved in the midst of the world as a tool which can be transcended. That is not the essence of love. On the contrary, in Love the Lover wants to be "the whole World" for the beloved. This means that he puts himself on the side of the world; he is the one who assumes and symbolizes the world; he is a *this* which includes all other *thises*. He is and consents to be an *object*. But on the other hand, he wants to be the object in which the Other's freedom consents to lose itself, the object in which the Other consents to find his being and his *raison d'être* as his second facticity—the object-limit of transcendence, that toward which the Other's transcendence transcends all other objects but which it can in no way transcend. And everywhere he desires the circle of the Other's freedom; that is, at each instant as the Other's freedom accepts this limit to his transcendence, this acceptance is *already* present as the motivation of the acceptance considered. It is in the capacity of an end already chosen that the lover wishes to be chosen as an end. This allows us to grasp what basically the lover demands of the beloved; he does not want to *act* on the Other's freedom but to exist *a priori* as the objective limit of this freedom; that is, to be given at one stroke along with it and in its very upsurge as the limit which the freedom must accept in order to be free. By this very fact, what he demands is a limiting, a gluing down of the Other's freedom by itself; this limit of structure is in fact a *given*, and the very appearance of the given as the limit of freedom means that the freedom *makes itself exist* within the given by being its own prohibition against surpassing it. This prohibition is envisaged by the lover *simultaneously* as something lived—that is, something suffered (in a word, as a facticity) and as something freely consented to. It must be freely consented to since it must be effected only with the upsurge of a freedom which chooses itself as freedom. But it must be only what is lived since it must be an impossibility always present, a facticity which surges back to the heart of the Other's freedom. This is expressed psychologically by the demand that the free decision to love me, which the beloved formerly has taken, must slip in as a magically determining motivation *within* his present free engagement. . . .

Thus my facticity is *saved*. It is no longer this unthinkable and insurmountable given which I am fleeing; it is that for which the Other freely makes himself exist; it is as an end which he has given to himself. I have infected him with my facticity, but as it is in the form of freedom that he has been infected with it, he refers it back to me as a facticity taken up and consented to. He is the foundation of it in order that it may be his end. By means of this love I then have a different apprehension of my alienation and of my own facticity. My facticity—as for-others—is no longer a fact but a right. My existence *is* because it is *given a name*. I am because I give myself away. These beloved veins on my hands exist—beneficently. How good I am to have eyes, hair, eyebrows and to lavish them away tirelessly in an overflow of generosity to this tireless desire which the Other freely makes himself be. Whereas before being loved we were uneasy about that unjustified, unjustifiable protuberance which was our existence, whereas we felt ourselves "*de trop,*" we now feel that our existence is taken up and willed even in its tiniest details by an absolute freedom which at the same time our existence conditions and which we ourselves will with our freedom. This is the basis for the joy of love when there is joy: we feel that our existence is justified.

By the same token if the beloved can love us, he is wholly ready to be assimilated by our freedom; for this being-loved which we desire is already the ontological proof applied to our being-for-others. Our objective essence implies the existence of the Other, and conversely it is the Other's freedom which founds our essence. If we could manage to interiorize the whole system, we should be our own foundation.

Such then is the real goal of the lover in so far as his love is an enterprise—*i.e.*, a project of himself. This project is going to provoke a conflict. The beloved in fact apprehends the lover as one Other-as-object among others; that is, he perceives the lover on the ground of the world, transcends him, and utilizes him. The beloved is a *look*. He can not therefore employ his transcendence to fix an ultimate limit to his surpassings, nor can he employ his freedom to captivate itself. The beloved can not will to love. Therefore the lover must seduce the beloved, and his love can in no way be distinguished from the enterprise of seduction. In seduction I do not try to reveal my subjectivity to the Other. Moreover I could do so only by *looking at* the other; but by this look I should cause the Other's subjectivity to disappear, and it is exactly this which I want to assimilate. To seduce is to risk assuming my object-state completely for the Other; it is to put myself beneath his look and to make him look at me; it is to risk the danger of *being-seen* in order to effect a new departure and to appropriate the Other in and by means of my object-ness. I refuse to leave the level on which I make proof of my object-ness; it is

on this level that I wish to engage in battle by making myself a *fascinating object*. In Part Two we defined fascination as a *state*. It is, we said, the non-thetic consciousness of being *nothing* in the presence of being. Seduction aims at producing in the Other the consciousness of his state of nothingness as he confronts the seductive object. By seduction I aim at constituting myself as a fullness of being and at making myself *recognized as such*. To accomplish this I constitute myself as a meaningful object. My acts must *point* in two directions: On the one hand, toward that which is wrongly called subjectivity and which is rather a depth of objective and hidden being; the act is not performed for itself only, but it points to an infinite, undifferentiated series of other real and possible acts which I give as constituting my objective, unperceived being. Thus I try to guide the transcendence which transcends me and to refer it to the infinity of my dead-possibilities precisely in order to be the unsurpassable and to the exact extent to which the only unsurpassable is the infinite. On the other hand, each of my acts tries to point to the great density of possible-world and must present me as bound to the vastest regions of the world. At the same time I *present* the world to the beloved, and I try to constitute myself as the necessary intermediary between her and the world; I manifest by my acts infinitely varied examples of my power over the world (money, position, "connections," *etc.*). In the first case I try to constitute myself as an infinity of depth, in the second case to identify myself with the world. Through these different procedures I propose myself as unsurpassable. This proposal could not be sufficient in itself; it is only a besieging of the Other. It can not take on value as fact without the consent of the Other's freedom, which I must capture by making it recognize itself as nothingness in the face of my plenitude of absolute being.

Someone may observe that these various attempts at expression *presuppose* language. We shall not disagree with this. But we shall say rather that they *are* language or, if you prefer, a fundamental mode of language. For while psychological and historical problems exist with regard to the existence, the learning and the use of *a particular* language, there is no special problem concerning what is called the discovery or invention of language. Language is not a phenomenon added on to being-for-others. It *is* originally being-for-others; that is, it is the fact that a subjectivity experiences itself as an object for the Other. In a universe of pure objects language could under no circumstances have been "invented" since it presupposes an original relation to another subject. In the intersubjectivity of the for-others, it is not necessary to invent language because it is already given in the recognition of the Other. I *am* language. By the sole fact that whatever I may do, my acts freely conceived and executed, my projects launched toward my possibilities have outside of them a meaning which escapes me and which I experience. It is in this sense—and in this sense only—that Heidegger is right in declaring that *I am what I say.*[1] Language is not an instinct of the constituted human creature, nor is it an invention of our subjectivity. But neither does it need to be referred to the pure "being-outside-of-self" of the *Dasein*. It forms part of the *human condition*; it is originally the proof which a for-itself can make of its being-for-others, and finally it is the surpassing of this proof and the utilization of it toward possibilities which are my possibilities; that is, toward my possibilities of being this or that for the Other. Language is therefore not distinct from the recognition of the Other's

existence. The Other's upsurge confronting me as a look makes language arise as the condition of my being. This primitive language is not necessarily seduction; we shall see other forms of it. Moreover we have noted that there is another primitive attitude confronting the Other and that the two succeed each other in a circle, each implying the other. But conversely seduction does not presuppose any earlier form of language; it is the complete realization of language. This means that language can be revealed entirely and at one stroke by seduction as a primitive mode of being of expression. Of course by language we mean all the phenomena of expression and not the articulated word, which is a derived and secondary mode whose appearance can be made the object of an historical study. Especially in seduction language does not *aim at giving to be known* but at causing to experience.

But in this first attempt to find a fascinating language I proceed blindly since I am guided only by the abstract and empty form of my object-state for the Other. I can not even conceive what effect my gestures and attitudes will have since they will always be taken up and founded by a freedom which will surpass them and since they can have a meaning only if this freedom confers one on them. Thus the "meaning" of my expressions always escapes me. I never know exactly if I signify what I wish to signify nor even if I *am* signifying anything. It would be necessary that at the precise instant I should read in the Other what on principle is inconceivable. For lack of knowing what I actually express for the Other, I constitute my language as an incomplete phenomenon of flight outside myself. As soon as I express myself, I can only guess at the meaning of what I express—i.e., the meaning of what I am—since in this perspective to express and to be are one. The Other is always there, present and experienced as the one who gives to language its meaning. Each expression, each gesture, each word is on my side a concrete proof of the alienating reality of the Other. It is only the psychopath who can say, "someone has stolen my thought"—as in cases of psychoses of influence, for example.[2] The very fact of expression is a stealing of thought since thought needs the cooperation of an alienating freedom in order to be constituted as an object. That is why this first aspect of language—in so far as it is I who employ it for the Other—is *sacred*. The sacred object is an object which is in the world and which points to a transcendence beyond the world. Language reveals to me the freedom (the transcendence) of the one who listens to me in silence.

But at the same moment I remain for the Other a meaningful object—that which I have always been. There is no path which departing from my object-state can lead the Other to my transcendence. Attitudes, expressions, and words can only indicate to him other attitudes, other expressions, and other words. Thus language remains for him a simple property of a magical object—and this magical object itself. It is an action at a distance whose effect the Other exactly knows. Thus the word is *sacred* when I employ it and *magic* when the Other hears it. Thus I do not know my language any more than I know my body for the Other. I can not hear myself speak nor see myself smile. The problem of language is exactly parallel to the problem of bodies, and the description which is valid in one case is valid in the other.

Fascination, however, even if it were to produce a state of being fascinated in the Other could not by itself succeed in producing love. We can be fascinated by an orator, by an actor, by a tightrope-walker, but this does not mean that we love him. To be sure we can not take our eyes off him, but he is still raised on the ground of the world, and fascination does not posit the fascinating object as the ultimate term of the transcendence. Quite the contrary, fascination is transcendence. When then will the beloved become in turn the lover?

The answer is easy: when the beloved projects being loved. By himself the Other-as-object never has enough strength to produce love. If love has for its ideal the appropriation of the Other qua Other (i.e., as a subjectivity which is looking at an object) this ideal can be projected only in terms of my encounter with the Other-as-subject, not with the Other-as-object. If the Other tries to seduce me by means of his object-state, then seduction can bestow upon the Other only the character of a *precious* object "to be possessed." Seduction will perhaps determine me to risk much to conquer the Other-as-object, but this desire to appropriate an object in the midst of the world should not be confused with love. Love therefore can be born in the beloved only from the proof which he makes of his alienation and his flight toward the Other. Still the beloved, if such is the case, will be transformed into a lover only if he projects being loved; that is, if what he wishes to overcome is not a body but the Other's subjectivity as such. In fact the only way that he could conceive to realize this appropriation is to make himself be loved. Thus it seems that to love is in essence the project of making oneself be loved. Hence this new contradiction and this new conflict: each of the lovers is entirely the captive of the Other inasmuch as each wishes to make himself loved by the Other to the exclusion of anyone else; but at the same time each one demands from the other a love which is not reducible to the "project of being-loved." What he demands in fact is that the Other without originally seeking to make himself be loved should have at once a contemplative and affective intuition of his beloved as the objective limit of his freedom, as the ineluctable and chosen foundation of his transcendence, as the totality of being and the supreme value. Love thus exacted from the other could not *ask for* anything; it is a pure engagement without reciprocity. Yet this love can not exist except in the form of a demand on the part of the lover.

The lover is held captive in a wholly different way. He is the captive of his very demand since love is the demand to be loved; he is a freedom which wills itself a body and which demands an outside, hence a freedom which imitates the flight toward the Other, a freedom which qua freedom lays claim to its alienation. The lover's freedom, in his very effort to make himself be loved as an object by the Other, is alienated by slipping into the body-for-others; that is, it is brought into existence with a dimension of flight toward the Other. It is the perpetual refusal to posit itself as pure selfness, for this affirmation of self as itself would involve the collapse of the Other as a look and the upsurge of the Other-as-object—hence a state of affairs in which the very possibility of being loved disappears since the Other is reduced to the dimension of objectivity. This refusal therefore constitutes freedom as dependent on the Other; and the Other as subjectivity becomes indeed an unsurpassable limit of the freedom of the for-itself, the goal and supreme end of the for-itself since the Other holds the key to its being. Here in fact we encounter the true ideal of love's enterprise: alienated freedom. But it is the one who wants to be loved who by the mere fact of wanting someone to love him alienates his freedom.

My freedom is alienated in the presence of the Other's pure subjectivity which founds my objectivity. It can never be alienated before the Other-as-object. In this form in fact the beloved's alienation, of which the lover dreams, would be contradictory since the beloved can found the being of the lover only by transcending it on principle toward other objects of the world; therefore this transcendence can constitute the object which it surpasses both as a transcended object and as an object limit of all transcendence. Thus each one of the lovers wants to be the object for which the Other's freedom is alienated in an original intuition; but this intuition which would be love in the true sense is only a contradictory ideal of the for-itself. Each one is alienated only to the exact extent to which he demands the alienation of the other. Each one wants the other to love him but does not take into account the fact that to love is to want to be loved and that thus by wanting the other to love him, he only wants the other to want to be loved in turn. Thus love relations are a system of indefinite reference—analogous to the pure "reflection-reflected" of consciousness—under the ideal standard of the *value* "love"; that is, in a fusion of consciousnesses in which each of them would preserve his otherness in order to found the other. This state of affairs is due to the fact that consciousnesses are separated by an insurmountable nothingness, a nothingness which is both the internal negation of the one by the other and a factual nothingness between the two internal negations. Love is a contradictory effort to surmount the factual negation while preserving the internal negation. I demand that the Other love me and I do everything possible to realize my project; but if the Other loves me, he radically deceives me by his very love. I demanded of him that he should found my being as a privileged object by maintaining himself as pure subjectivity confronting me;

and as soon as he loves me he experiences me as subject and is swallowed up in his objectivity confronting my subjectivity.

The problem of my being-for-others remains therefore without solution. The lovers remain each one for himself in a total subjectivity; nothing comes to relieve them of their duty to make themselves exist each one for himself; nothing comes to relieve their contingency nor to save them from facticity. At least each one has succeeded in escaping danger from the Other's freedom—but altogether differently than he expected. He escapes not because the Other makes him be as the object-limit of his transcendence but because the Other experiences him as subjectivity and wishes to experience him only as such. Again the gain is perpetually compromised. At the start, each of the consciousnesses can at any moment free itself from its chains and suddenly contemplate the other as an object. Then the spell is broken; the Other becomes one mean among means. He is indeed an object for-others as the lover desires but an object-as-tool, a perpetually transcended *object*. The illusion, the game of mirrors which makes the concrete reality of love, suddenly ceases. Later in the experience of love each consciousness seeks to shelter its being-for-others in the Other's freedom. This supposes that the Other is beyond the world as pure subjectivity, as the absolute by which the world comes into being. But it suffices that the lovers should be *looked at* together by a third person in order for each one to experience not only his own objectivation but that of the other as well. Immediately the Other is no longer for me the absolute transcendence which founds me in my being; he is a transcendence-transcended, not by me but by another. My original relation to him—i.e., my relation of being the beloved for my lover, is fixed as a dead-possibility. It is no longer the experienced relation between a limiting object of all transcendence and the freedom which founds it; it is a love-as-object which is wholly alienated toward the third. Such is the true reason why lovers seek solitude. It is because the appearance of a third person, whoever he may be, is the destruction of their love. But factual solitude (*e.g.*, we are alone in my room) is by no means a theoretical solitude. Even if nobody sees us, we exist for all consciousnesses and we are conscious of existing for all. The result is that love as a fundamental mode of being-for-others holds in its being-for-others the seed of its own destruction.

We have just defined the triple destructibility of love: in the first place it is, in essence, a deception and a reference to infinity since to love is to wish to be loved, hence to wish that the Other wish that I love him. A pre-ontological comprehension of this deception is given in the very impulse of love—hence the lover's perpetual dissatisfaction. It does not come, as is so often said, from the unworthiness of being loved but from an implicit comprehension of the fact that the amorous intuition is, as a fundamental-intuition, an ideal out of reach. The more I am loved, the more I lose my *being*, the more I am thrown back on my own responsibilities, on my own power to be. In the second place the Other's awakening is always possible; at any moment he can make me appear as an object—hence the lover's perpetual insecurity. In the third place love is an absolute which is perpetually *made relative* by others. One would have to be alone in the world with the beloved in order for love to preserve its character as an absolute axis of reference—hence the lover's perpetual shame (or pride—which here amounts to the same thing).

Notes

1   This formulation of Heidegger's position is that of A. de Waehlens, *La philosophie de Martin Heidegger* Louvain, 1942, p. 99. *Cf.* also Heidegger's text, which he quotes: "Diese Bezeugung meint nicht hier einen nachträglichen und bei her laufenden Ausdruck des Menschseins, sonder sie macht das Dasein des Menschen mit usw" (*Hölderlin und das Wesen der Dichtung*, p. 6). ("This affirmation does not mean here an additional and supplementary expression of human existence, but *it* does in the process make plain the existence of man." Douglas Scott's translation, *Existence and Being*, Chicago: Henry Regnery, 1949, p. 297).

2   Furthermore the psychosis of influence, like the majority of psychoses, is a special experience translated by myths, of a great metaphysical fact—here the fact of alienation. Even a madman in his own way realizes the human condition.

ROBERT C. SOLOMON

Robert Solomon presents us with an account of romantic love that explicitly implies a view of identity. On this view, which calls to mind Aristophanes' speech in the *Symposium*, romantic love involves a desire to form a shared identity with the beloved. But what is the nature of this shared identity? Solomon himself rejects the notion that this implies a kind of *merging* with the beloved. Not only is such a merging of identities impossible, but the implied loss of autonomy would appear undesirable. So, in what sense do two separate individual selves form some kind of shared identity in love? "The answer is that selves are not in fact so individual after all."[1] The idea of a relational self or social self is one that we see in the writings of the nineteenth-century German philosopher G.W.F. Hegel and a number of other philosophers since his time. We saw a version of this view when we looked at Jean-Paul Sartre's account of love in this chapter. The basic idea is that who we are can only be understood and realized through our relations with others. Since our relationship with our romantic partner is one of the most significant relationships we have, then it seems reasonable that in this relationship we will learn a lot about ourselves. Our beloved (like other people in our lives) sees aspects of our identity that we *in principle* cannot see. They see our moods, anxieties, and attitudes not as we experience them from the *inside* as it were, but as these are manifested in the world. It is in this sense that our beloved helps complete us or helps us to be our *true* self. They help us to become aware of who or what we really are. Who we really are is not something that we have private knowledge of; rather, such knowledge is something that we come to realize with the help of others who see our personality and our character expressed in our words and actions.

Note

1   Robert C. Solomon, *About Love: Reinventing Romance for Our Time* (New York: Simon and Schuster, 1988), 197.

Romantic Love

"I do think," he said, "that the world is only held together by the mystic conjunction, the ultimate unison between people—a bond. And the immediate bond is between man and woman."

—D.H. Lawrence, *Women in Love*

We are getting closer to our goal of pinning love down, removing the "mystery" and in its place supplying some concrete understanding of what love is, how it works, and how it can last. We began, innocently enough, by removing two prevalent obstacles to understanding— the honourable but nevertheless misleading temptation to think of love as a general attitude of loving instead of a particular passion that focuses—necessarily—on an individual person, and the mistaken idea that love is some form of admiration or desire, which treats the lover as an object rather than as a subject who might return one's affection. But this much is true of all forms of personal love, mother for a child, a brother for a brother, a friend for a friend. Romantic love is a certain kind of love, inappropriate or perverse between mother and child or between brothers, and it is quite distinct from friendship too. Our traditional paradigm of romantic love is a young, single man and woman "falling in love." But it is certainly not essential that they be young, or single, or be a man and a woman, or for that matter "fall" into anything.

Romantic love, unlike any form of family love, is distinguished by three features: (1) It is sexual in origin and motivation, no matter how otherwise inhibited, chaste, or sublimated; (2) it is spontaneous and voluntary, a matter of will and not just circumstances; and (3) it is an emotion appropriate only between equals, Cinderella and Lady Chatterley notwithstanding.

The first essential structure of romantic emotions is sex. Romantic love isn't *about* sex (a common fallacy) but it depends upon sex, thrives upon sex, utilizes sex as its medium, its language and often its primary content. Whatever else it may be, romantic love begins with the inspiration and exhilaration of sexual attraction (sexual performance is secondary and in many cases actually a distraction). Sexual attraction is not "just physical," of course, and it is not to be confused with the bodily fetishism and Hollywood charms that we too often confuse with attractiveness. But whatever else it may be, sex is bodily and sexual desire engages us as embodied creatures for whom "looks" and the blessings of nature are at least as important as the egalitarian insistence that we are all, "deep down," essentially the same. This suggestion has often offended the Foggers, with their idealized notion of spiritual love, and throughout the history of the subject theologians have struggled for an idealized concept of love that dispenses with sex altogether. (In just the last century American philosopher Ralph Waldo Emerson speaks rhapsodically of "a love that knows no sex," a refrain to be found over and over again since the beginning of the last millennium.) But as we have degraded friendship in favour of love, so, too, have we degraded sexuality. Sex is a spiritual impulse as well as a physical one. Sex, too, is part of the self, *even* the soul. One's true self-identity is something more than the honours, success, and status that are conferred fully-clothed in society: it is rather to be found in our emotional nakedness. Nietzsche remarks, sarcastically, "The body has the audacity to act as if it's *real!*" and, indeed, that is where our reality is to be found. There can be romance without "consummation," of course, for a dozen moral and medical reasons. But the *fact* is that romantic emotion is as intrinsically sexual as gourmet sensibilities are tied to food. "Man ist was Man isst" writes Feuerbach ("We are what we eat"). So, too, what we are is revealed by desire.

The second essential feature is the centrality of personal *choice* in love. On the one hand this is obvious, but at the same time it is so remarkable that only with a bit of distance from ourselves can we fully appreciate how much it sets us off from most of the world. To understand romantic love is to appreciate that peculiar sense of time and spontaneity that makes "love at first sight" and love between strangers possible. In societies where marriages are arranged, or, less formally, marriage is dictated within an established framework of social, religious, and economic expectations, there is very limited room for choice and, consequently, very little room for romantic love. Most forms of love, we should note, are "prescribed," set by one's situation. One does not choose one's (literal) brother or sister; one finds oneself in a family and makes the emotional best of it. Brotherly and sisterly love take years to develop. Motherly love, on the other hand, may begin at the child's birth, but it, too, has been gestating for nine months or much more, and the mother in any case (except in adoption) does not *choose* the recipient of her motherly affection. But we *look for* romantic love, or it "finds us" in the most unexpected of places. Love in general takes time, but romantic love can begin all at once. And though romantic love may "deepen" and become enriched over time, it need not—as we all know too well—increase in either intensity or significance. It is sometimes most intense *before* it has had time to develop, and

some authors deny that old, established love can still *be* "romantic" at all, just because it is no longer a matter of choice. Social significance, knowledge, and the long habits of domesticity have their undisputed value, but it has been said that they are more antagonistic than compatible with romantic love just because they are not spontaneous, not exciting, *not new*. In our culture, the tie between romantic love and marriage is virtually sacred, but if love is to last it must remain a matter of choice, a continuous decision. Love is the justification of marriage, not the other way around. In other cultures, love between a married man and woman may be possible and even desirable, but it is not the sine qua non of the relationship. In such societies, romantic love holds a low priority—if it is permissible or intelligible at all. Where choice is not available, romantic love will appear only as an aberration, even as a crime, in certain circumstances and societies.

The third, often neglected (or rejected) structure of romantic love is a powerful form of egalitarianism, not as a social or a political concept but concerning equality between two individuals. It is often remarked that love is a great "levelling" device, bringing the powerful down to the ordinary and raising the otherwise down if not out up to acceptable if not exceptional status. Romantic love not only requires equals, it, as the French Romantic Stendhal tells us, "creates" them, whether it be the scullery maid Cinderella becoming Prince Charming's Princess or Lady Chatterley visiting the gardener's hut. Indeed, it is for this reason that romantic love, originally a distinctively aristocratic emotion, now finds its greatest popularity in self-consciously egalitarian societies, an antidote to, a conspiracy against, class stratifications. The heroes of

Harlequins may still be nobility, but romantic love itself is unabashedly bourgeois.

And yet it is often charged that romantic love is a structurally inegalitarian emotion, casting the woman in a subservient role. This has been asserted as a right by certain macho males (represented somewhat paradoxically by George Gilder in *Sexual Suicide*) and as an offence and an outrage by a good many feminists. This, I want to argue, is an abuse and a misunderstanding of the nature of romantic love. Equality is a complex business in most love relationships and, in Orwellian phraseology, we might well point out that at any given time "some lovers are more equal than others." To insist that romantic love requires equality is not to deny that there are still gross injustices and institutionalized inequalities between the sexes; it is rather to point out that love presupposes a radical conception of privacy in which the public dimension is suspended, in which personal choice is definitive, in which equality is determined by two individuals and not by a structure that encloses them. Love is a democratic emotion, despite its aristocratic origins. It is clearly to be distinguished, in any case, from those brands of love in which domination or authority of one partner is essential, as in parent over child, as in beloved country over dutiful citizen, as in lover of pâté over pâté. Love of God, no matter how personal, is certainly not love of equals. (The very suggestion is what the Greeks called "hubris.") Romance is the vehicle, not obstacle, for equality. Cinderella could not remain a scullery maid once she had met her prince.

These three features begin to account not only for the differences between romantic love and other forms of personal love; they also give us some preliminary explanation of why romantic love should be such a powerful and celebrated emotion in our society. The sexuality of romance is already explosive, especially when it is forbidden, abused, or denied. The egalitarianism of love assures a continuing struggle for equal shares and status, a constant tension between demands, expectations, and sacrifices, not to mention the creation of a fertile field for envy and resentment. But most of all, the drama of love, the drama *in* love, is the result of spontaneity. Love appears unannounced, suddenly, often inappropriately, even disastrously. It is an emotion that is curiously severed from and even antithetical to our ordinary civil routines. It is an emotion—coupled with our vanity, pride, and obstinacy—that thrives on opposition and implausibility. But spontaneity does not mean passivity, and suddenness does not mean unpreparedness. We are never mere victims of love. It is always our choice, our vanity, our achievement, our embarrassment, our tragedy, or our comedy. Romantic love is essentially a decision—or a series of decisions—no matter how hard and arbitrary it seems to "hit" us. What's more, it is an emotion that has been publicly cultivated and encouraged—obsessively so—for the entirety of our lives, just so that—suddenly—it may seem to come out of nowhere.

Do we now have a "definition" of love? We are not even close. We have not yet said anything about the caring that is so essential to love, or the companionship, the compassion, the good times together. We have not said anything about time—the time love demands, the time it takes to let love grow. But most of all, we have not truly addressed what makes love *love*, as opposed to sex and friendship and companionship and caring and living together and shared interests and all of the other things that are familiar in but wholly possible without love. That central, definitive characteristic,

I want to show, is a special conception of personal identity, a redefining of ourselves in terms of another. To make things more complicated, the terms of this redefinition vary enormously. Love is a historical emotion, a product of particular cultures, and a special set of cultural circumstances. It is not a phenomenon that can be defined as such but rather a process that gets redefined and reinvented in every culture. There is no cross-cultural definition of love. Rather love is defined by a narrative, a culturally defined story (or set of stories) that weave our culture's sense of individual choice and autonomy, our natural sexuality, and our political and personal sense of equality into the familiar process of "falling in love" and its consequences. What sets romance off from all other love is—as the very word tells us—the sense of drama and plot development, the way in which, no matter how unique our love, we are following in the footsteps of millions of lovers before us who also thought their passion utterly unique and individual. To understand love is to understand this narrative of shared selfhood and how peculiar as well as exciting it is.

Perhaps the very special and peculiar role of romantic love in our lives may be summarized in a recent response of the thirteen-year-old daughter of two of my friends. During a conversation concerning the possibility of her dating one of the boys in her class, she replied, shocked, "Not Jimmy! He's a *friend*!" That reply seemed to cut so deep into the fabric of emotions and judgments that define our ideas about love that I call it, after the young theorist in question, Becky's Theorem. It shows how naive we are when we cozily collapse love, friendship, familiarity, and even marriage into the same gentle stew. Becky's Theorem makes explicit our strange obsession with an emotion that conscientiously severs itself from

assurances, knowledge, and the comforts of established relationships and then proceeds to define much of what we think of ourselves. It is a kind of love dramatically different from all other affections.

The Identity Theory of Love

I *am* Heathcliff—he's always, always in my mind—not as a pleasure, any more than I am always a pleasure to myself—but as my own being.

—Cathy, in Emily Brontë's *Wuthering Heights*

The key to lasting love is the concept of the self. Nothing else provides the solid bond that makes love endure, that allows love to weather calamity and crisis, that carries it through frustrating or infuriating periods of sexual disinterest, self-obsession, mutual anger or disappointment, distance, and the wrenching pressures of separate, demanding careers. Nor will the much-touted emphasis on "commitment" provide such a bond; indeed, commitment enters in precisely when that bond will not hold, when some extra effort is needed to hold a relationship together and love is no longer sufficient. Love endures because love creates a conceptual bond that is something more steadfast than sexual exhilaration, mutual concern, companionship, admiration, intimacy, and dreams. The durable core of love is a set of ideas, a very specific and well-focused way of conceiving of the world, oneself, and one's lover. In love one views the world in terms of a single intimacy and sees one's self—no matter how successful and otherwise fulfilled—as something incomplete, in need of the lover who is similarly incomplete and needful. Love is, as Aristophanes tells us in the *Symposium*, an attempt to create for ourselves a sense of wholeness or completion through a union—of both body and soul—with another. That whole, unlike the fragmented halves, has a solid integrity, and the love is so powerful because it promises that durable wholeness. We can forget about Aristophanes' whimsical tale about double androgynous creatures with two heads, four arms, and four legs with twice our intelligence, arrogance, and hubris. It is enough that we take his metaphor to heart and think about the idea that "ever since" we have been running around in this frenzy, trying to recapture our other halves. Love, in other words, is the attempt to find another person who will give us a sense of our "true" selves and make us feel complete, once and for all.

What is philosophically profound about Aristophanes' story is the idea that love is not just companionship or desire but the desperate effort to recapture something that is already ours but yet not ours, something that already defines the self but nevertheless seems elusive. As opposed to Socrates' classic view, also developed in the *Symposium*, which takes total self-sufficiency as the ideal and the love of abstract universals as the true meaning of love, Aristophanes recognizes that no one can be self-sufficient or complete alone and that love must be the concrete and detailed love of a particular individual who is in some sense literally one's other half. Thus where Socrates seems to believe that sexual desire drops out of the picture with true love, Aristophanes recognizes that sexual love is inescapable. No matter how ethereal and ideal the love, sexual union has its essential place just because we are physical beings and no sense of union—no matter how spiritual—can be intelligible without it. Our sexuality is not a specific desire so much as it is part of our basic bodily being—the way

we comport ourselves, the way we move, and the way we feel as well as the way we sense ourselves with others. Sexuality, like the self, is too often conceived as self-contained, something private and personal that a person *has* instead of a constant, pervasive bodily reaching out toward others, a sense of physical incompleteness. This is part of that "infinite yearning" of love that includes the desire for physical union but always goes beyond it too. It is a familiar part of our most beautiful sexual experiences—not just the brief sense of complete union but also that raging sense of not being close enough, not yet being truly merged as one. What we really want—as Aristophanes suggests we would ask of Hephaestus, the blacksmith of the gods—is to be welded together forever, body and soul.

The "identity theory" of love insists that this is indeed the nature and the purpose of love: to seek and establish a shared identity with another person, which may involve a drastic revision of both one's sense of oneself and each other. Because our most basic concepts of ourselves are at issue, much of the expression and development of love takes place where we are most vulnerable, most naked, most self-concerned. Thus the tight and often dramatic linkage of romantic love with sex and self-esteem, not because love is nothing but sublimated sexual desire (as many have argued) and not because love makes us so vulnerable (it can also make one feel invulnerable) but because love essentially provides our most basic sense of self-identity. It is a sense that precedes and takes precedence over notions of public success and social status and all of those other grand goals that, at least occasionally, move us to ask whether or not "it is all worth the trouble." In moments of despair, such a question may be aimed at love, too, but the query never catches because we know that lasting love is clearly worth the trouble. It has come to define who we really are.

The images of "merging," "union," and "fusion" have been a part of the love literature ever since the *Symposium*. They played a central role in the descriptions of courtly love in the late Middle Ages and are still an important part of post-Freudian accounts of love, as in Erich Fromm and Willard Gaylin. The problem is that these images of unity remain metaphorical. They are perhaps an apt description of a certain vague experience we enjoy when in love, and they clearly point toward something that, if literally true, would be striking and important indeed. But as a metaphor, what does it mean to say that two people "merge"? Physical union, even if it were not transient, would surely not be sufficient. Two minds can merge, at least temporarily, in the sense that they can get locked together in intense conversation or, a very different interpretation, they can agree about so much that they are, in a familiar sense, "of one mind." But intense conversation as such is not love, nor is agreement. And in our normal way of thinking about things, each of us has his or her own mind and the idea of two minds being shared makes no more sense than the idea of 1 plus 1 equalling 1. One can talk metaphysically, perhaps, about the merging of two souls, but this is to explain the metaphorical in terms of the obscure, for it is by no means clear what constitutes a single soul and even less clear what it would be for souls to mingle much less merge. So what is it for two selves to merge that is something more than physical intercourse, intense conversation, shared interests and opinions, and some symbolic sense of two souls having come together? The answer is that selves (and, perhaps, souls) are not in fact so individual after

all. Our selves are underdetermined by the facts about us—our appearance, our physical and mental abilities, our past history of accomplishments—and they are mutually rather than individually defined, defined with and through others. So conceived, the idea of sharing selves is not so implausible. To this we should add that our selves are constituted mainly out of emotions rather than of what we *think* of ourselves, and that the roles *we* play are far more important to the identity of our selves than any fixed "inner" truth about the individual. It is a strange distortion of Western thinking that has made the private, reflective self primary instead of the active, passionate self, and the shared identity of love is often misunderstood just because of this overly rational, overly "inner" view of the self. Love is the concentration and the intensive focus of mutual definition on a single individual, subjecting virtually every personal aspect of one's self to this process.

Every aspect of this merging of selves must be balanced by the fact that we are, before we fall in love, different from one another—different individuals with different backgrounds, our own eccentricities, a history of other romances, catastrophes, crushes, and frustrations. We were not originally halves of some primordial creature. Our "edges" do not fit together so neatly as two torn halves of a stick of wood or a broken plate. The smoother the fit, in fact, the less the passion may be; while the most intense love affairs may well be those whose fit is most difficult, even impossible. Thus passion is often the enemy of lasting love, not because love and passion are antithetical as such but because passion often represents the degree of implausibility of love. And in virtually every case the fit is a matter of compromise and adjustment, always imperfect, and so it lacks the absolute integrity that Aristophanes promises us. In other words, the ideal of shared identity gives us only half of the story. Love desires nothing more passionately than union with one's lover, but the presupposition of this desire is precisely that concept of individual existence that makes such a complete union impossible. Thus Irving Singer, in his monumental three-volume study *The Nature of Love*, rejects the "idealistic" concept of merging that played such an enormous role in medieval theories and nineteenth-century conceptions of love. He argues, rightly I believe, that the notion is indeed idealistic and impossible and neglects the importance of individuality in the conceptualization of love. This dialectical tension between union and individuality is what we earlier (Chapter 1) called "the paradox of love," and it must be taken very seriously. Individuality is the presupposition of love, but love itself is the desire to overcome that same individuality. It is the merging of two selves that makes love last, but those two selves are always to a large extent preformed and consequently ill-fitting, and it is this individuality, the difficulty we have in fitting together, that threatens even the most passionate and devoted love. Love is the dialectical tension between individual independence and autonomy on the one hand and the ideal of shared identity on the other. But before we try to tackle this paradox we have to understand what is literally true about love as shared identity. "Merging" and "union" are not just metaphors but deep insights into the nature of the self and the transformation of the self in love.

Discussion

What is your conception of romantic love? How does your own conception differ from the views presented by Sartre and Solomon? What is the relationship between love (romantic love) and individual identity? How should love affect our identity? Does the idea of a *shared identity* make sense? In a romantic relationship, does one *I* plus another *I* equal *we*? What does *we* mean in this context? Is there a danger of losing one's identity in the context of love? If so, does this mean we should stick firmly to our individual identity? Is love possible if there is not some change in our identity so that it is shared at least in some sense?

Sartre characterizes love in terms of conflict. In a manner reminiscent of Hegel's famous master-slave story, it is a conflict between two people who both want to establish their identity through the Other. In Hegel's story, two beings come into conflict with one another driven by the desire for recognition. What they want to be recognized as is the *essential being*, according to Hegel. Both of them stake their lives in this battle for recognition. The winner allows the loser to live on the condition that he or she occupy the position of slave, giving the winner (the master) the recognition that he or she desired. Over time, however, the master comes to realize that the recognition that he has received on the basis of coercion from the slave is deficient. True recognition can only come from another free and equal human being. For Sartre, the same is true of love. Love aims at a kind of completion of our identity through another person, but our fundamental separation from each other and our inability to experience the freedom or consciousness of another brings us into conflict with the Other. This conflict is over the truth about who we are. "You are so selfish!" your partner might say. "What do you mean?" you respond. We each understand our attitudes and our actions in a certain way, and our relations with others can be seen as a struggle towards determining the truth of who we each are. We know, as Sartre tells us, that the "other holds the key" to who we are, but we are reluctant to give them this power over us. We want the other to freely reveal to us that side of ourselves that is in principle hidden from us. But, at the same time, we want the picture that they give us to line up in a fundamental way with our own sense of self. Of course, allowing them the power to help us find our *true self* (if we want to call it that) implies great risk. Do we want to see ourselves as they see us? Do we trust the view of our self that the other person gives to us? Love implies great risk, but it also offers great reward.

Do you recognize what Sartre is saying in some of your own relationships? Does it make sense to understand love in terms of conflict in the way that he describes it? Is his view of love too negative?

Suggestions for Further Reading

Neil Delaney, "Romantic Love and Loving Commitment: Articulating a Modern Ideal," *American Philosophical Quarterly* 33, no. 4 (1996): 339–56.

Ilham Dilman, *Love and Human Separateness* (Oxford: Basil Blackwell, 1987).

G.W.F. Hegel, *Phenomenology of Spirit*, translated by A.V. Miller (Oxford: Oxford University Press, 1977).

Robert Nozick, "Love's Bond," in *The Examined Life: Philosophical Meditations* (New York: Simon and Schuster, 1989), 68–86.

Chapter Thirteen
Love and Identity in Question

SIMONE DE BEAUVOIR

In the last chapter, we saw the *identity theory* of romantic love, which is explicit in Robert Solomon's account and which serves as a frustrated endeavour in Sartre's. Robert Nozick similarly put forth the idea that, in love, two people form a romantic *we* that, as in Solomon's account, creates a new identity in addition to the two individual identities.[1] But Simone de Beauvoir, who was Sartre's lifelong romantic partner, friend, and philosophical colleague, shows us that the experience of love has not been the same for women as it has been for men. Women have been the "second sex," as the title of her famous book suggests. Historically, women have found their identity in love or in the love relationship; whereas, for men, the love relationship has been only one part of that identity. Men's ambitions, projects, passions, or professions have constituted the main part of their identity. But the shared identity, or the *we*, has often implied a loss of identity for the woman in love. Where does this leave romantic love? Is this kind of love a source of inequality or oppression? Beauvoir does not blame love *per se* for the disadvantaged situation of women but rather the social and historical conditions of inequality in which romantic love has been experienced.

Note

1. Robert Nozick, "Love's Bond," in *The Examined Life: Philosophical Meditations* (New York: Simon and Schuster, 1989), 68–86.

The Woman in Love

The word *love* has by no means the same sense for both sexes, and this is one cause of the serious misunderstandings that divide them. Byron well said: "Man's Love is of man's life a thing apart; 'Tis woman's whole existence." Nietzsche expresses the same idea in *The Gay Science*:

> The single word love in fact signifies two different things for man and woman. What woman understands by love is clear enough: it is not only devotion, it is a total gift of body and soul, without reservation, without regard for anything whatever. This unconditional nature of her love is what makes it a *faith*,[1] the only one she has. As for man, if he loves a woman, what he *wants*[1] is that love from her; he is in consequence far from postulating the same sentiment for himself as for woman; if there should be men who also felt that desire for complete abandonment, upon my word, they would not be men.

Men have found it possible to be passionate lovers at certain times in their lives, but there is not one of them who could be called "a great lover";[2] in their most violent transports, they never abdicate completely; even on their knees before a mistress, what they still want is to take possession of her; at the very heart of their lives they remain sovereign subjects; the beloved woman is only one value among others; they wish to integrate her into their existence and not to squander it entirely on her. For woman, on the contrary, to love is to relinquish everything for the benefit of a master. As Cécile Sauvage puts it, "Woman must forget her own personality when she is in love. It is a law of nature. A woman is nonexistent

without a master. Without a master, she is a scattered bouquet."

The fact is that we have nothing to do here with laws of nature. It is the difference in their situations that is reflected in the difference men and women show in their conceptions of love. The individual who is a subject, who is himself, if he has the courageous inclination toward transcendence, endeavours to extend his grasp on the world: he is ambitious, he acts. But an inessential creature is incapable of sensing the absolute at the heart of her subjectivity; a being doomed to immanence cannot find self-realization in acts. Shut up in the sphere of the relative, destined to the male from childhood, habituated to seeing in him a superb being whom she cannot possibly equal, the woman who has not repressed her claim to humanity will dream of transcending her being toward one of these superior beings, of amalgamating herself with the sovereign subject. There is no other way out for her than to lose herself, body and soul, in him who is represented to her as the absolute, as the essential. Since she is anyway doomed to dependence, she will prefer to serve a god rather than obey tyrants—parents, husband, or protector. She chooses to desire her enslavement so ardently that it will seem to her the expression of her liberty; she will try to rise above her situation as inessential object by fully accepting it; through her flesh, her feelings, her behaviour, she will enthrone him as supreme value and reality: she will humble herself to nothingness before him. Love becomes for her a religion.

As we have seen, the adolescent girl wishes at first to identify herself with males; when she gives that up, she then seeks to share in their masculinity by having one of them in love with her; it is not the individuality of this one or that one which attracts her; she is in love with man in general.[3] "And you, the men I shall love, how I await you!" writes Irène Reweliotty. "How I rejoice to think I shall know you soon: especially You, the first." Of course the male is to belong to the same class and race as hers, for sexual privilege is in play only within this frame. If man is to be a demigod, he must first of all be a human being, and to the colonial officer's daughter the native is not a man. If the young girl gives herself to an "inferior," it is for the reason that she wishes to degrade herself because she believes she is unworthy of love; but normally she is looking for a man who represents male superiority. She is soon to ascertain that many individuals of the favoured sex are sadly contingent and earthbound, but at first her presumption is favourable to them; they are called on less to prove their worth than to avoid too gross a disproof of it—which accounts for many mistakes, some of them serious. A naive young girl is caught by the gleam of virility, and in her eyes male worth is shown, according to circumstances, by physical strength, distinction of manner, wealth, cultivation, intelligence, authority, social status, a military uniform; but what she always wants is for her lover to represent the essence of manhood.

Familiarity is often sufficient to destroy his prestige; it may collapse, at the first kiss, or in daily association, or during the wedding night. Love at a distance, however, is only a fantasy, not a real experience. The desire for love becomes a passionate love only when it is carnally realized. Inversely, love can arise as a result of physical intercourse; in this case the sexually dominated woman acquires an exalted view of a man who at first seemed to her quite insignificant.

But it often happens that a woman succeeds in deifying none of the men she knows.

Love has a smaller place in woman's life than has often been supposed. Husband, children, home, amusements, social duties, vanity, sexuality, career, are much more important. Most women dream of a *grand amour*, a soul-searing love. They have known substitutes, they have been close to it; it has come to them in partial, bruised, ridiculous, imperfect, mendacious forms; but very few have truly dedicated their lives to it. The *grandes amoureuses* are most often women who have not frittered themselves away in juvenile affairs; they have first accepted the traditional feminine destiny: husband, home, children; or they have known pitiless solitude; or they have banked on some enterprise that has been more or less of a failure. And when they glimpse the opportunity to salvage a disappointing life by dedicating it to some superior person, they desperately give themselves up to this hope. Mlle Aïssé, Juliette Drouet, and Mme d'Agoult were almost thirty when their love-life began, Julie de Lespinasse not far from forty. No other aim in life which seemed worthwhile was open to them, love was their only way out.

Even if they can choose independence, this road seems the most attractive to a majority of women: it is agonizing for a woman to assume responsibility for her life. Even the male, when adolescent, is quite willing to turn to older women for guidance, education, mothering; but customary attitudes, the boy's training, and his own inner imperatives forbid him to content himself in the end with the easy solution of abdication; to him such affairs with older women are only a stage through which he passes. It is man's good fortune—in adulthood as in early childhood—to be obliged to take the most arduous roads, but the surest; it is woman's misfortune to be surrounded by almost irresistible temptations; everything incites her to follow the easy slopes; instead of being invited to fight her own way up, she is told that she has only to let herself slide and she will attain paradises of enchantment. When she perceives that she has been duped by a mirage, it is too late; her strength has been exhausted in a losing venture.

The psychoanalysts are wont to assert that woman seeks the father image in her lover; but it is because he is a man, not because he is a father, that he dazzles the girl child, and every man shares in this magical power. Woman does not long to reincarnate one individual in another, but to reconstruct a situation: that which she experienced as a little girl, under adult protection. She was deeply integrated with home and family, she knew the peace of quasi-passivity. Love will give her back her mother as well as her father, it will give her back her childhood. What she wants to recover is a roof over her head, walls that prevent her from feeling her abandonment in the wide world, authority that protects her against her liberty. This childish drama haunts the love of many women; they are happy to be called "my little girl, my dear child"; men know that the words: "you're just like a little girl," are among those that most surely touch a woman's heart. We have seen that many women suffer in becoming adults; and so a great number remain obstinately "babyish," prolonging their childhood indefinitely in manner and dress. To become like a child again in a man's arms fills their cup with joy. The hackneyed theme: "To feel so little in your arms, my love," recurs again and again in amorous dialogue and in love letters. "Baby mine," croons the lover, the woman calls herself "your little one," and so on. A young woman will write: "When will he come, he who can dominate me?" And when he comes, she will love to sense his manly superiority. A neurotic studied by Janet illustrates this attitude quite clearly:

> All my foolish acts and all the good things I have done have the same cause: an aspiration for a perfect and ideal love in which I can give myself completely, entrust my being to another, God, man, or woman, so superior to me that I will no longer need to think what to do in life or to watch over myself. . . . Someone to obey blindly and with confidence . . . who will bear me up and lead me gently and lovingly toward perfection. How I envy the ideal love of Mary Magdalen and Jesus: to be the ardent disciple of an adored and worthy master; to live and die for him, my idol, to win at last the victory of the Angel over the beast, to rest in his protecting arms, so small, so lost in his loving care, so wholly his that I exist no longer.

Many examples have already shown us that this dream of annihilation is in fact an avid will to exist. In all religions the adoration of God is combined with the devotee's concern with personal salvation; when woman gives herself completely to her idol, she hopes that he will give her at once possession of herself and of the universe he represents. In most cases she asks her lover first of all for the justification, the exaltation, of her ego. Many women do not abandon themselves to love unless they are loved in return; and sometimes the love shown them is enough to arouse their love. The young girl dreamed of herself as seen through men's eyes, and it is in men's eyes that the woman believes she has finally found herself. Cécile Sauvage writes,

> To walk by your side, to step forward with my little feet that you love, to feel them so tiny in

their high-heeled shoes with felt tops, makes me love all the love you throw around me. The least movements of my hands in my muff, of my arms, of my face, the tones of my voice, fill me with happiness.

The woman in love feels endowed with a high and undeniable value; she is at last allowed to idolize herself through the love she inspires. She is overjoyed to find in her lover a witness. This is what Colette's *Vagabonde* declares:

I admit I yielded, in permitting this man to come back the next day, to the desire to keep in him not a lover, not a friend, but an eager spectator of my life and my person. . . . One must be terribly old, Margot said to me one day, to renounce the vanity of living under someone's gaze.

In one of her letters to Middleton Murry, Katherine Mansfield wrote that she had just bought a ravishing mauve corset; she at once added: "Too bad there is no one to *see* it!" There is nothing more bitter than to feel oneself but the flower, the perfume, the treasure, which is the object of no desire: what kind of wealth is it that does not enrich myself and the gift of which no one wants? Love is the developer that brings out in clear, positive detail the dim negative, otherwise as useless as a blank exposure. Through love, woman's face, the curves of her body, her childhood memories, her former tears, her gowns, her accustomed ways, her universe, everything she is, all that belongs to her, escape contingency and become essential: she is a wondrous offering at the foot of the altar of her god.

This transforming power of love explains why it is that men of prestige who know how to flatter feminine vanity will arouse passionate attachments even if they are quite lacking in physical charm. Because of their lofty positions they embody the Law and the Truth: their perceptive powers disclose an unquestionable reality. The woman who finds favour in their sight feels herself transformed into a priceless treasure. D'Annunzio's success was due to this, as Isadora Duncan explains in the introduction to *My Life*:

When D'Annunzio loves a woman, he lifts her spirit from this earth to the divine region where Beatrice moves and shines. In turn he transforms each woman to a part of the divine essence, he carries her aloft until she believes herself really with Beatrice. . . . He flung over each favourite in turn a shining veil. She rose above the heads of ordinary mortals and walked surrounded by a strange radiance. But when the caprice of the poet ended, this veil vanished, the radiance was eclipsed, and the woman turned again to common clay. . . . To hear oneself praised with that magic peculiar to D'Annunzio is, I imagine, something like the experience of Eve when she heard the voice of the serpent in Paradise. D'Annunzio can make any woman feel that she is the centre of the universe.

Only in love can woman harmoniously reconcile her eroticism and her narcissism; we have seen that these sentiments are opposed in such a manner that it is very difficult for a woman to adapt herself to her sexual destiny. To make herself a carnal object, the prey of another, is in contradiction to her self-worship: it seems to her that embraces blight and sully her body or degrade her soul. Thus it is that some women take refuge in frigidity, thinking that in this way they can preserve the integrity of the ego. Others dissociate animal pleasure and lofty sentiment. In one of Stekel's cases the patient was frigid with her respected and eminent husband and, after his death, with an equally superior man, a great musician, whom she sincerely loved. But in an almost casual encounter with a rough, brutal forester she found complete physical satisfaction, "a wild intoxication followed by indescribable disgust" when she thought of her lover. Stekel remarks that "for many women a descent into animality is the necessary condition for orgasm." Such women see in physical love a debasement incompatible with esteem and affection.

But for other women, on the contrary, only the esteem, affection, and admiration of the man can eliminate the sense of abasement. They will not yield to a man unless they believe they are deeply loved. A woman must have a considerable amount of cynicism, indifference, or pride to regard physical relations as an exchange of pleasure by which each partner benefits equally. As much as woman—and perhaps more—man revolts against anyone who attempts to exploit him sexually;[4] but it is woman who generally feels that her partner is using her as an instrument. Nothing but high admiration can compensate for the humiliation of an act that she considers a defeat.

We have seen that the act of love requires of woman profound self-abandonment; she bathes in a passive languor; with closed eyes, anonymous, lost, she feels as if borne by waves, swept away in a storm, shrouded in darkness: darkness of the flesh, of the womb, of the grave. Annihilated, she becomes one with the Whole, her ego is abolished. But when the man moves from her, she finds herself back on earth, on a bed, in the light; she again has a name, a face: she is one vanquished, prey, object.

This is the moment when love becomes a necessity. As when the child, after weaning, seeks the reassuring gaze of its parents, so must a woman feel, through the man's loving contemplation, that she is, after all, still at one with the Whole from which her flesh is now painfully detached. She is seldom wholly satisfied even if she has felt the orgasm, she is not set completely free from the spell of her flesh; her desire continues in the form of affection. In giving her pleasure, the man increases her attachment, he does not liberate her. As for him, he no longer desires her; but she will not pardon this momentary indifference unless he has dedicated to her a timeless and absolute emotion. Then the immanence of the moment is transcended; hot memories are no regret, but a treasured delight; ebbing pleasure becomes hope and promise; enjoyment is justified; woman can gloriously accept her sexuality because she transcends it; excitement, pleasure, desire are no longer a state, but a benefaction; her body is no longer an object: it is a hymn, a flame.

Then she can yield with passion to the magic of eroticism; darkness becomes light; the loving woman can open her eyes, can look upon the man who loves her and whose gaze glorifies her; through him nothingness becomes fullness of being, and being is transmuted into worth; she no longer sinks in a sea of shadows, but is borne up on wings, exalted to the skies. Abandon becomes sacred ecstasy. When she *receives* her beloved, woman is dwelt in, visited, as was the Virgin by the Holy Ghost, as is the believer by the Host. This is what explains the obscene resemblance between pious hymns and erotic songs; it is not that mystical love always has a sexual character, but that the sexuality of the woman in love is tinged with mysticism. "My God, my adored one, my lord and master"—the same words fall from the lips of the saint on her knees and the loving woman on her bed; the one offers her flesh to the thunderbolt of Christ, she stretches out her hands to receive the stigmata of the Cross, she calls for the burning presence of divine Love; the other, also, offers and awaits: thunderbolt, dart, arrow, are incarnated in the male sex organ. In both women there is the same dream, the childhood dream, the mystic dream, the dream of love: to attain supreme existence through losing oneself in the other.

It has sometimes been maintained that this desire for annihilation leads to masochism.[5] But as I have noted in connection with eroticism, it can be called masochism only when I essay "to be fascinated by my own status as object, through the agency of others";[6] that is to say, when the consciousness of the subject is directed back toward the ego to see it in a humiliating position. Now, the woman in love is not simply and solely a narcissist identified with her ego; she feels, more than this, a passionate desire to transcend the limitations of self and become infinite, thanks to the intervention of another who has access to infinite reality. She abandons herself to love first of all to *save herself*; but the paradox of idolatrous love is that in trying to save herself she *denies herself* utterly in the end. Her feeling gains a mystical dimension; she requires her God no longer to admire her and approve of her; she wants to merge with him, to forget herself in his arms. "I would wish to be a saint of love," writes Mme d'Agoult.[7] "I would long for martyrdom in such moments of exaltation and ascetic frenzy." What comes to light in these words is a desire for a complete destruction of the self, abolishing the boundaries that separate her from the beloved. There is no question here of masochism, but of a dream of ecstatic union.

In order to realize this dream, what woman wants in the first place is to serve; for in responding to her lover's demands, a woman will feel that she is necessary; she will be integrated with his existence, she will share his worth, she will be justified. Even mystics like to believe, according to Angelus Silesius, that God needs man; otherwise they would be giving themselves in vain. The more demands the man makes, the more gratified the woman feels. Although the seclusion imposed by Victor Hugo on Juliette Drouet weighed heavily on the young woman, one feels that she is happy in obeying him: to stay by the fireside is to do something for the master's pleasure. She tries also to be useful to him in a positive way. She cooks choice dishes for him and arranges a little nest where he can be at home; she looks after his clothes. "I want you to tear your clothes as much as possible," she writes to him, "and I want to mend and clean them all myself." She reads the papers, clips out articles, classifies letters and notes, copies manuscripts, for him. She is grieved when the poet entrusts a part of the work to his daughter Léopoldine.

Such traits are found in every woman in love. If need be, she herself tyrannizes over herself in her lover's name; all she is, all she has, every moment of her life, must be devoted to him and thus gain their *raison d'être*; she wishes to possess nothing save in him; what makes her unhappy is for him to require nothing of her, so much so that a sensitive lover will invent demands. She at first sought in love a confirmation of what she was, of her past, of her personality; but she also involves her future in it, and to justify her future she puts it in the hands of one who possesses all values. Thus she gives up her transcendence, subordinating it to that of the essential other, to whom she makes herself vassal and slave. It was to find herself, to save herself, that she lost herself in him in the first place; and the fact is that little by little she does lose herself in him wholly; for her the whole of reality is in the other. The love that at the start seemed a narcissistic apotheosis is fulfilled in the bitter joys of a devotion that often leads to self-mutilation.

In the early days of a *grande passion* the woman becomes prettier, more elegant than formerly: "When Adèle does my hair, I look at my forehead, because you love it," writes Mme d'Agoult. This face, this body, this room, this I—she has found a *raison d'être* for them all, she cherishes them through the mediation of this beloved man who loves her. But a little later, quite to the contrary, she gives up all coquetry; if her lover wishes it, she changes that image which at first was more precious than love itself; she loses interest in it; what she is, what she has, she makes the fief of her lord; what he does not care for, she repudiates. She would consecrate each heartbeat to him, each drop of her blood, the marrow of her bones; and it is this that is expressed in a dream of martyrdom: she would extend her gift of herself to the point of torture, of death, of being the ground under her lover's feet, being nothing but what responds to his call. Everything useless to him she madly destroys. If the present she has made of herself is wholeheartedly accepted, no masochism appears; few traces of it are seen in, for example, Juliette Drouet. In the excess of her adoration she sometimes knelt before the poet's portrait and asked forgiveness for any faults she might have committed; she did not turn in anger against herself.

Yet the descent from generous warmth of feeling to masochistic madness is an easy one. The woman in love who before her lover is in the position of the child before its parents is also liable to that sense of guilt she felt with them; she chooses not to revolt against him as long as she loves him, but she revolts against herself. If he loves her less than she

wants him to, if she fails to engross him, to make him happy, to satisfy him, all her narcissism is transformed into self-disgust, into humiliation, into hatred of herself, which drive her to self-punishment. During a more or less lengthy crisis, sometimes for life, she will make herself a voluntary victim, she will struggle furiously to hurt her ego that has been unable to gratify him to the full. At this point her attitude is genuinely masochistic. But we must not confuse this case, in which the woman in love seeks her own suffering in order to take vengeance upon herself, with those cases in which her aim is the affirmation of her man's liberty and power. It is a commonplace—and seemingly a truth—that the prostitute is proud to be beaten by her man; but what exalts her is not the idea of her beaten and enslaved person, it is rather the strength and authority, the supremacy of the male upon whom she is dependent: she also likes to see him maltreat another male; indeed, she often incites him to engage in dangerous fighting, for she wants her master to possess and display the values recognized in the environment to which she belongs.

The woman who finds pleasure in submitting to male caprices also admires the evident action of a sovereign free being in the tyranny practiced on her. It must be noted that if for some reason the lover's prestige is destroyed, his blows and demands become odious; they are precious only if they manifest the divinity of the loved one. But if they do, it is intoxicating joy to feel herself the prey of another's free action. An existent finds it a most amazing adventure to be justified through the varying and imperious will of another; one wearies of living always in the same skin, and blind obedience is the only chance for radical transformation known to a human being. Woman is thus slave, queen, flower, hind, stained-glass window, wanton, servant, courtesan, muse, companion, mother, sister, child, according to the fugitive dreams, the imperious commands, of her lover. She lends herself to these metamorphoses with ravishment as long as she does not realize that all the time her lips have retained the unvarying savour of submission. On the level of love, as on that of eroticism, it seems evident that masochism is one of the bypaths taken by the unsatisfied woman, disappointed in both the other and herself; but it is not the natural tendency of a happy resignation. Masochism perpetuates the presence of the ego in a bruised and degraded condition; love brings forgetfulness of self in favour of the essential subject.

The supreme goal of human love, as of mystical love, is identification with the loved one.[8] The measure of values, the truth of the world, are in his consciousness; hence it is not enough to serve him. The woman in love tries to see with his eyes; she reads the books he reads, prefers the pictures and the music he prefers; she is interested only in the landscapes she sees with him, in the ideas that come from him; she adopts his friendships, his enmities, his opinions; when she questions herself, it is his reply she tries to hear; she wants to have in her lungs the air he has already breathed; the fruits and flowers that do not come from his hands have no taste and no fragrance. Her idea of location in space, even, is upset: the centre of the world is no longer the place where she is, but that occupied by her lover; all roads lead to his home, and from it. She uses his words, mimics his gestures, acquires his eccentricities and his tics. "I am Heathcliffe," says Catherine in *Wuthering Heights*; that is the cry of every woman in love; she is another incarnation of her loved one, his reflection, his double: she is

he. She lets her own world collapse in contingence, for she really lives in his.

The supreme happiness of the woman in love is to be recognized by the loved man as a part of himself; when he says "we," she is associated and identified with him, she shares his prestige and reigns with him over the rest of the world; she never tires of repeating—even to excess—this delectable "we." As one necessary to a being who is absolute necessity, who stands forth in the world seeking necessary goals and who gives her back the world in necessary form, the woman in love acquires in her submission that magnificent possession, the absolute. It is this certitude that gives her lofty joys; she feels exalted to a place at the right hand of God. Small matter to her to have only second place if she has *her* place, forever, in a most wonderfully ordered world. So long as she is in love and is loved by and necessary to her loved one, she feels herself wholly justified: she knows peace and happiness. Such was perhaps the lot of Mlle Aïssé[9] with the Chevalier d'Aydie before religious scruples troubled his soul, or that of Juliette Drouet in the mighty shadow of Victor Hugo.

But this glorious felicity rarely lasts. No man really is God. The relations sustained by the mystic with the divine Absence depend on her fervour alone; but the deified man, who is not God, is present. And from this fact are to come the torments of the woman in love. Her most common fate is summed up in the famous words of Julie de Lespinasse:[10] "Always, my dear friend, I love you, I suffer and I await you." To be sure, suffering is linked with love for men also but their pangs are either of short duration or not overly severe. Benjamin Constant wanted to die on account of Mme Récamier: he was cured in a twelvemonth. Stendhal regretted Métilde for years, but it was a regret that perfumed his life without destroying it. Whereas woman, in assuming her role as the inessential, accepting a total dependence, creates a hell for herself. Every woman in love recognizes herself in Hans Andersen's little mermaid who exchanged her fishtail for feminine legs through love and then found herself walking on needles and live coals. It is not true that the loved man is absolutely necessary, above chance and circumstance, and the woman is not necessary to him; he is not really in a position to justify the feminine being who is consecrated to his worship, and he does not permit himself to be possessed by her.

An authentic love should assume the contingence of the other; that is to say, his lacks, his limitations, and his basic gratuitousness. It would not pretend to be a mode of salvation, but a human interrelation. Idolatrous love attributes an absolute value to the loved one, a first falsity that is brilliantly apparent to all outsiders. "He isn't worth all that love," is whispered around the woman in love, and posterity wears a pitying smile at the thought of certain pallid heroes, like Count Guibert. It is a searing disappointment to the woman to discover the faults, the mediocrity of her idol. Novelists, like Colette, have often depicted this bitter anguish. The disillusion is still more cruel than that of the child who sees the father's prestige crumble, because the woman has herself selected the one to whom she has given over her entire being.

Even if the chosen one is worthy of the profoundest affection, his truth is of the earth, earthy, and it is no longer this mere man whom the woman loves as she kneels before a supreme being; she is duped by that spirit of seriousness which declines to take values as incidental— that is to say, declines to recognize that they have their source in human existence. Her bad faith[11] raises barriers between her and the man she adores. She offers him incense, she bows down, but she is not a friend to him since she does not realize that he is in danger in the world, that his projects and his aims are as fragile as he is; regarding him as the Faith, the Truth, she misunderstands his freedom—his hesitancy and anguish of spirit. This refusal to apply a human measuring scale to the lover explains many feminine paradoxes. The woman asks a favour from her lover. Is it granted? Then he is generous, rich, magnificent; he is kingly, he is divine. Is it refused? Then he is avaricious, mean, cruel; he is a devilish or a bestial creature. One might be tempted to object: if a "yes" is such an astounding and superb extravagance, should one be surprised at a "no"? If the "no" discloses such abject selfishness, why wonder so much at the "yes"? Between the superhuman and the inhuman is there no place for the human?

A fallen god is not a man: he is a fraud; the lover has no other alternative than to prove that he really is this king accepting adulation—or to confess himself a usurper. If he is no longer adored, he must be trampled on. In virtue of that glory with which she has haloed the brow of her beloved, the woman in love forbids him any weakness; she is disappointed and vexed if he does not live up to the image she has put in his place. If he gets tired or careless, if he gets hungry or thirsty at the wrong time, if he makes a mistake or contradicts himself, she asserts that he is "not himself" and she makes a grievance of it. In this indirect way she will go so far as to take him to task for any of his ventures that she disapproves; she judges her judge, and she denies him his liberty so that he may deserve to remain her master. Her worship sometimes finds better satisfaction in his absence than in his presence; as we have seen, there are women who devote themselves to dead or otherwise inaccessible heroes, so that they may never have to face them in person, for beings of flesh and blood would be fatally contrary to their dreams. Hence such disillusioned sayings as: "One must not believe in Prince Charming. Men are only poor creatures," and the like. They would not seem to be dwarfs if they had not been asked to be giants.

Notes

1 Nietzsche's italics.

2 In the sense that a woman may sometimes be called "*une grande amoureuse*."–TR.

3 Haenigsen's newspaper comic strip "Penny" gives never sagging popular expression to this truth.–TR.

4 Lawrence, for example, in *Lady Chatterley's Lover*, expresses through Mellors his aversion for women who make a man an instrument of pleasure.

5 As by Helene Deutsch in her *Psychology of Women*.

6 Sartre in *L'Être et le néant*.

7 She eloped with Franz Liszt and became the mother of Cosima Wagner. Under the name of Daniel Stem she wrote historical and philosophical books.–TR.

8 See T. Reik's *Psychology of Sex Relations* (Farrar, Straus & Co., 1945).–TR.

9 An account of her life, with her letters, will be found in *Lettres du XVIIe et du XVIIIe Siècle*, by Eugène Asse (Paris, 1873).–TR.

10 Famous intellectual woman of the eighteenth century, noted for her salon and her fervid correspondence with the rather undistinguished military officer and writer Count Guibert, mentioned below.–TR.

11 In Sartre's existentialist terminology, "bad faith" means abdication of the human self with its hard duty of choice, the wish therefore to become a thing, the flight from the anguish of liberty.–TR.

NOËL MERINO

Noël Merino calls into question the notion of a *joint* or *shared* identity in romantic love. While she accepts that romantic relationships, like other close relationships, will influence our identity, she highlights some problems with calling this a joint identity. She looks at three different interpretations of Solomon's and Nozick's accounts of this concept and finds each of them problematic. The problem has to do with trying to make sense of a notion of identity that both claims to be a new identity and yet adds something to the individual identities while allowing those identities to remain intact and autonomous. Merino thinks that the effect that romantic love has on our identity need not be characterized in terms of a joint identity. To do so implies the risks that Beauvoir had warned about whereby women in particular tend to lose their identity in love.

The Problem with "We": Rethinking Joint Identity in Romantic Love

A common claim about romantic love is that it entails developing a joint identity (also called a *we*, union, fusion, and shared identity).[1] In this paper I argue that we ought to avoid thinking of love in terms of a joining of identities. Before I turn to consider the accounts of joint identity that have been developed by contemporary philosophers, I point to a few historical accounts of joint identity in ancient philosophy, literature, and psychology in order to shed some light on the more recent accounts of joint identity. I identify three ways to construe the joint identity that is posited by these philosophers and consider the tenability of each interpretation. With respect to each of these ways of understanding joint identity, I argue that there is reason to resist an understanding of romantic love as involving joint identity.

1. Joint Identity

The notion of a joint identity in romantic love has a long history, going back as far as the ancient Greeks, where Aristophanes, in his speech recounted by Plato, argues that love is essentially the process of seeking our missing half. Aristophanes tells the story of the birth of love. Originally, human beings had four legs, four arms, two sets of sexual organs, and two faces. There were three types of these quadrapeds: the male kind, with two sets of male sexual organs; the female kind, with two sets of female sexual organs; and the androgynous kind, with a set of each. These original humans angered the gods and so, as punishment, the gods cut the humans in half. It was as a result of this punishment of splitting the humans into two that love was born:

> This, then, is the source of our desire to love each other. Love is born into every human being; it calls back the halves or our original nature together; it tries to make one out of two and heal the wound of human nature.[2]

The telos of love, then, is to unite with our other half and become one again. Although we cannot fully unite to the point of physical fusion, in love we seek to become as united as possible in our present state.

Similar accounts of the nature of love can be found in literature, psychology, and contemporary philosophy. In *Wuthering Heights*, Catherine describes her love for Heathcliff: "I *am* Heathcliff—he's always, always in my mind—not as a pleasure, any more than I am always a pleasure to myself—but, as my own being."[3] Here Catherine claims that Heathcliff is to her as she is to herself: identical. The psychoanalyst Erich Fromm, sounding very much like Aristophanes, claims that erotic love "is the craving for complete fusion, for union with one other person."[4] In the recent philosophical literature, this notion that, in love, two individuals fuse can be found in the work of Robert Nozick. In romantic love, he says,

> it feels to the two people that they have united to form and constitute a new entity in the world, what might be called a *we*. . . . The desire to form a *we* with that other person is not simply something that goes along with romantic love, something that contingently happens when love does. That desire is intrinsic to the nature of love, I think; it is an important part of what love intends.[5]

According to this view, the practice of referring to one's romantic partner as "my other half" is to be taken quite seriously.

While, as Aristophanes noted, total fusion is frustrated by the lovers' physical separateness, several philosophers have identified the sense in which two individuals in love become fused as a fusion of identity. Nozick explains the development of a joint identity in the following way:

> To be part of a *we* involves having a new identity, an additional one. This does *not* mean that you no longer have any individual identity or that your sole identity is as part of the *we*. However, the individual identity you did have will become altered. To have this new identity is to enter a certain psychological stance; and each party in the *we* has this stance toward the other. Each becomes psychologically part of the other's identity.[6]

According to Nozick, in love, one retains an individual identity, but that identity is now bound up with the identity of the loved one, so that the boundaries between the two are no longer as distinct as they were before joining. He explains:

> If we picture the individual self as a closed figure whose boundaries are continuous and solid, dividing what is inside from what is outside, then we might diagram the *we* as two figures with the boundary line between them erased where they come together.[7]

Thus, he claims the two individual identities are joined so that the individual identities are different than they were before joining. He asserts, however, that although the original individual identities are present within the *we*, both

individuals share this one enlarged identity: "In a *we*, the people *share* an identity and do not simply each have identities that are enlarged."[8] Thus, both individuals in the love relationship share this joint identity, or the *we*.[9]

Robert Solomon develops a notion of shared identity similar to Nozick's. He, too, endorses the blurring of the boundaries between the two lovers:

> It is often said that to love is to give in to another person's needs, indeed, to make them more important than one's own. But to love is rather to take the other's desires and needs *as* one's own. This is much more than a merely grammatical point. It is a redefinition of the self itself, as a shared self, as a self in which my personal desires no longer command a distinctive voice.[10]

According to Solomon's account of shared identity, the desires that a lover formerly took as his or her own become, within the shared identity, desires that are not clearly distinct from the desires of the beloved.[11] On Solomon's account, it appears that the lovers pool all their desires into one new identity and, indeed, Solomon claims, "a shared self, like an individual self, might be inconsistent or schizoid."[12] But while we may worry that the new shared self may have conflicting desires, Solomon wants to claim that this is no more a problem than the conflicting desires within individual nonshared selves.

Mark Fisher develops the notion of a fused self along lines similar to Nozick and Solomon. He argues that the development of a "single fused individual"[13] is the ideal of love, although because of facts about our physicality and psychology, "the fusion is partial and precarious."[14] Fisher describes what becomes shared in the fusion of love: "I will tend to absorb not only your desires but your concepts, beliefs, attitudes, conceptions, emotions and sentiments."[15] In the process of fusion, the lover takes, as his or her own, not only the desires of the beloved, but also a whole host of other mental states. The degree to which the lovers become fused is determined by

> the number of ways in which, and the extent to which, we come to perceive, feel and act as a single person, so that the perception, feeling or act does not exist unless both persons participate in it, and neither can say which of the two has originated it.[16]

At the point at which perception, feeling, and action are all shared, and at which the origin of such perception, feeling, and action is no longer felt to have come from a distinct individual in the couple, the fullest kind of fusion has been reached.

2. Three Interpretations of Joint Identity

I see at least three interpretations of joint identity available that appear compatible with both Nozick's and Solomon's explanation of the concept. First, a joint identity could be taken in its most literal sense, to denote an identity that replaces the individual identities of each of the lovers. Second, a joint identity could be understood as a third entity that is an identity in addition to the individual identities of the lovers. Finally, a joint identity could be a part of each individual identity that becomes incorporated in the process of love. I will consider each of these interpretations and argue that, under each interpretation, there is reason to reject an understanding of romantic love as involving joint identity.

Identity Replacement

The first interpretation of joint identity is that in which the individual identities of the lovers are each replaced with a joint identity. Nozick claims that within a *we*, "the people *share* an identity and do not simply each have identities that are enlarged."[17] Here he comes the closest to endorsing what sounds like an understanding of joint identity as identity replacement. Because of the physical and mental separateness of two lovers, a joint identity cannot be a literal shared identity, where each lover has exactly the same identity as the other. Fisher seems to suggest that something like this is possible when he claims that two lovers may get to the point at which neither of them is sure where a certain perception, feeling, or act originated. Assuming it is possible that lovers may not always be aware of the origination of perceptions, feelings, or acts, this certainly does not entail that there is not actually a definite origin in one lover, or the other, or both simultaneously.[18] The most extreme account of a joint identity, in which lovers share perceptions, feelings, and acts, is untenable simply because of our physical and mental separateness.

While recognizing that a strictly literal joint identity in terms of Aristophanic fusion is not possible, all the proponents of the joint identity view emphasize the most striking feature of a joint identity as a sharing of ends and desires. Thus, a better account of this first interpretation of joint identity as identity replacement is one that posits the actual sharing of ends. On this view, we can make some sense of the claims by Nozick and Solomon that the lovers retain some distinctive identity—the one that necessarily we have as physically distinct beings—while claiming that they share an identity in this important sense of sharing goals and desires.

Lovers can share goals and desires if each lover takes on the ends of the other, so that their goals and desires come into line with one another. Solomon claims that love is not the compromising of one's own ends to accommodate the ends of the other, but "rather to take the other's desires and needs *as* one's own."[19] At some points he seems to mean this quite literally, in the sense that within a shared self "personal desires no longer command a distinctive voice."[20] However, for the same reason that complete physical union is frustrated by our physical separateness, so too is the unqualified joining of ends. Taking on the ends of another cannot mean that they literally become your own ends. On this view, if my lover adopts the end of viewing Kurosawa films, then it also becomes my end to watch Kurosawa films. Surely the understanding of shared ends cannot be this literal, or else lovers would have to end up pursuing exactly the same goals as each other instead of simply supporting one another's goals.[21] This kind of literal sharing of ends does not seem to be what Solomon has in mind when he claims that "in love one may come to identify oneself wholly in terms of the relationship, but it does not follow that individual roles and differences are submerged."[22] There must, in the sharing of ends, be reference to the fact that some shared ends in joint identity are ends that are indexed to only one of the lovers.

Perhaps the sharing of ends means that the lovers in a joint identity take on the ends of one another with reference to which individual wishes to achieve the goal. Thus, if my lover wants to see Kurosawa films, then I adopt the end that *he* sees Kurosawa films. And if I want to complete a doctorate in philosophy, then I take it as one of my ends that *I* complete a doctorate in philosophy. Within this interpretation of the sharing of ends, it is quite clear which of my ends are about what I hope to achieve and which of my ends are about what I hope my beloved achieves. However, under this interpretation, it is not clear how we share a qualitatively indistinguishable identity in the sense of sharing goals and desire. Even if both partners adopt all of each other's ends, their goals and desires are distinct in being referenced to one party or both.

However, if we take heed of Solomon's claim that personal desires lose a distinctive voice, then we can make sense of how we can reference individuals in explaining the achievement of ends, while at the same time ensuring that both individuals share the same ends. Both lovers will desire, for instance, that *A* view Kurosawa films, *B* plant a garden, *A* become a designer, *B* complete a doctorate, and *A* and *B* move to Tuscany, without attaching any personal priority among these ends based on whether one is *A* or *B*. Thus, the sharing of ends involves the placing of the beloved's ends right alongside one's own without prioritizing one's own ends.

This view of the sharing of ends, however, seems to have a serious problem. Alan Soble rightly recognizes that by sharing ends in this way, all possibility of self-sacrifice is eliminated:

> In love, I take it, *x* at least sometimes gives up some of his own good in order to preserve or enhance *y*'s good. The well-beings of the lovers *not* being joined together is logically necessary for *x* to exhibit this sacrificial concern for *y*. For *x* to sacrifice his good for the good of *y* requires that their interests are disjoint enough so that *x*'s good does not always fare as *y*'s fares, sometimes changing in the opposite direction.[23]

If all of the lover's desires and goals are adopted by the beloved, and vice versa, without privileged reference in the case of each individual, then pursuing an end of a partner is essentially pursuing an end of one's own. Without the difference in identity between the two lovers, ends and desires cannot be prioritized in reference to whom they originate in but must be pursued as desires of the same entity: the joint identity. Thus, selflessness or self-sacrifice on behalf of one's partner is impossible.[24] I cannot sacrifice my own desires in some situation in order to accommodate my partner's, since both of our desires are *mine*. But this is implausible. If there is to be a joint identity in love, it must leave room for genuine self-sacrifice.

A related problem is that this view of the joint identity as replacing individual identities seems to ignore incompatibility between desires once they are pooled. Nozick argues that the existence of the *we* will not be constantly conflicted by different desires. Nozick claims that once within a joint identity, the development of certain ends will no longer be decided individually:

> People who form a *we* pool not only their well-being but also their autonomy. They limit or curtail their own decision-making power and rights; some decisions can no longer be made alone. . . . Each transfers some previous right to make certain decisions unilaterally into a joint pool; somehow, decisions will be made together about how to be together.[25]

Such a process of giving up unilateral decision making must be equally shared or else the relationship would be one of domination. Similarly, Solomon insists that a shared self does not entail that "one person becomes like the other, but rather that they define their differences—as well as their significant similarities—together."[26]

This sort of compromise, by pooling autonomy, may sound like the sort of self-sacrifice I claimed was lacking from a joint identity. However, this sort of compromise in the collective decision making of what ends to pursue can take place within a joint identity *only if* there are distinctive voices given to each partner, that is, if they each retain an identity that, to some degree, is importantly distinct from the other. On this first interpretation of joint identity, Nozick's view of joint identity as a pooling of autonomy seems to make each person in a couple profoundly affected in his or her identity at the start of entering into a joint identity. However, this kind of compromise can never happen again, since each lover, from that point forward, takes all pooled ends of the joint identity to be equally his or her own. Without distinct voices, it appears that the partners must compromise at some beginning point and, after that, never again be able to see their own individual ends within an identity as being any more their own than their lover's ends. Thus, Nozick's account of pooling autonomy overlooks the compromise of individual ends that occurs throughout the life of a love relationship and not just at the beginning.

In a joint identity, there needs to be some room for recognizing that the two individuals do have different ends, while at the same time recognizing that love may alter our ends and our prioritizing of ends. It is false that what happens to lovers is that they pool their ends together without any distinction between what ends ultimately originated in the one and what ends ultimately originated in the other, as this claim denies the existence of real self-sacrifice that occurs within romantic love. Thus, under the identity replacement interpretation of joint identity, it is implausible to claim that love involves joint identity.

Third-Entity Identity

At various points, both Nozick and Solomon insist that the lovers do not cease to possess individual identities. A second way of understanding joint identity is one in which the lovers retain their individual identities but share a joint identity as a third entity. Thus, the two individual identities of the lovers might constitute a joint identity in much the same way that individual citizens constitute a political party, or individual trees constitute a forest.

Solomon explains a metaphor for such a model based on the way atoms form molecules: "The atoms retain their identity as atoms of a certain element but, at the same time, they together form a new substance with quite different properties."[27] Similarly, two individuals with their individual identities come to form something new—a joint identity—when they love.

While this second interpretation looks promising, ultimately it does not seem to do the work it needs to do to show how the joint identity alters the individuals within it. Not only does a tenable account of joint identity have to explain how ends become shared, it also needs to explain how the joint identity alters the lovers. Both Nozick and Solomon make a point of stressing that the individual identity is profoundly altered in love. This account of joint identity as a third entity, however, does nothing to explain why someone would be altered in love, except by becoming a member of a joint identity. Just as an individual tree is not obviously changed by becoming a member of a forest, or an individual

person obviously changed by becoming a member of a political party, becoming half of a joint identity does not explain, in itself, how this importantly alters the individual. Why not become half of another identity, another forest, or another political party? This account might explain the ontology of a shared identity, but not the way in which participation in joint identity is supposed to profoundly impact the lovers. On this interpretation of shared additional identity, there is no explanation for why the lovers would care about having an additional identity with any particular person, since their initial identity is meant to remain unchanged (except for being part of this additional identity). Thus, in order to explain how the person is changed by becoming a member of a joint identity, there needs to be further explanation of how the individual self is affected other than simply being part of a third entity.

Identity Alteration

The last interpretation of joint identity is, then, a retention of individual identities with the joint identity forming an important part of the lovers' individual identities.[28] Nozick claims that having a *we* "does *not* mean that you no longer have any individual identity or that your sole identity is as part of the *we*."[29] Solomon also notes, "Love is the dialectical tension between individual independence and autonomy on the one hand and the *ideal* of shared identity on the other."[30] Neil Delaney seems to capture these sentiments of Nozick and Solomon while avoiding an account of joint identity in which there is an "unqualified merging of interests."[31] Delaney thinks that a balance must be struck between taking on one's lovers ends and retaining the distinctness of one's own ends:

Insofar as you can rightly regard your lover as taking her well-being to be directly connected with yours, while at the same time appreciating the distinctively personal dimensions to your achievements, the relationship looks to be maximally fulfilling.[32]

Delaney believes that lovers must go beyond merely wanting each other to achieve certain ends to having their well-being affected by how the other fares with respect to his or her ends. However, unlike those whose view of joint identity posits the pooling of ends into one identity, Delaney believes that it is very important for each partner to recognize the difference between his or her own ends and his or her beloved's ends.

I think that Delaney's view captures a tenable understanding of what Nozick and Solomon had in mind when considering the concept of a joint identity. However, I am hesitant to call it such. Perhaps the most alarming consequence of positing the existence of a joint identity in romantic love is that such a view puts too much distance between individual identities and joint identities. Part of what Solomon seems to be getting at in positing a shared identity is that one's individual identity is not ultimately distinct from the joint identity. Love itself helps to shape and alter one's own identity: "love involves a mutual, as well as reciprocal, definition of selves."[33] Solomon's notion of a dialectical identity is apparent when he notes, "In fact love is a struggle, albeit sometimes a delightful and always essential struggle, for mutual self-identity and a sense of independence at the same time."[34] Within this dialectic, however, it is not the case that there is the stark difference between the individual identity and the joint identity. The relationship of love profoundly alters and helps to define

the individual identity in virtue of the participation in a joint identity, but not because there are two types of identities and they can affect each other. Rather, the change in individual identity that occurs in love as a result of the impact the lovers have on each other *is* what is meant by having a joint identity.

Having your well-being importantly affected by the way your loved one fares certainly creates a change in identity from what it was before the relationship, but it is not clear that it is worth denoting "joint identity." Calling the alteration in identity a joint identity makes it sound as if all romantically single people have identities that are somehow tightly shut off from others, in which their ends are formed completely autonomously with no other identities impinging on their own, whereas couples have identities that are shared. It seems to insinuate that such strong identity change is limited to romantic love. Yet it seems more likely that there is no strong individual identity left when all the "joint identities" from lovers, friends, family members, coworkers, and institutions are stripped away.[35]

The sort of alteration to ends and sharing of ends that occurs in romantic love is not different, in kind, than what happens in numerous other interpersonal and social relationships. Whether or not it is different in degree may depend on the individual relationship, but I think an intensity of degree here is still not sufficient to deem this a special kind of identity that differs from other identities. If all that is meant by "joint identity" is a difference in degree of the change to the self, then I have no problem with the particular locution. However, as I have shown, the notion of joint identity that has been suggested by philosophers like Nozick and Solomon seems to rely heavily on a distinction between individual identities (those not involved in love) and joint identities (those that result from love). It seems correct to notice that, in love, we retain a sense of our own ends, while having our well-being affected by how our beloved fares with respect to her ends. Additionally, there is a sense in which we come to alter our ends and share certain ends: I may care as much about my beloved's fulfilling his own ends as I care about the fulfillment of my own ends. Nonetheless, this kind of effect on identity is no different in kind than the effect on identity from numerous other personal relationships and social interactions, even if it usually tends to be greater in degree.

I think we can gain some insight from the discussion of joint identity expounded by Nozick, Solomon, and Fisher in the way that it points out the importance of identity change in romantic love. We are connected to our lovers in virtue of having our identities developed partially in relation to them. Nonetheless, we should not denote this change as a joining, uniting, fusing, or sharing of identities. The extent to which our identities are altered and the significance of this relative to identity alteration in other aspects of our lives ought not to be exaggerated by claiming this identity alteration is a unique joining of identities that, in the absence of love, remain solitary.

Notes

1   Robert Nozick, "Love's Bond," in *The Examined Life* (New York: Simon and Schuster, 1989), 68–86; Alan Soble, "Union, Autonomy, and Concern," in *Love Analyzed* (Boulder, CO: Westview, 1997), ed. Roger E. Lamb, 65–92; Mark Fisher, *Personal Love* (London, England: Duckworth, 1990), chap. 2; Robert C. Solomon, "Reasons for Love," *Journal for the Theory of Social Behaviour* 32 (2002): 1–28, esp. 22; and *Love: Emotion, Myth, and Metaphor* (New York: Prometheus Books, 1990), esp. chap. 12.

2   Plato, *Symposium* (Indianapolis, Indiana: Hackett Publishing, 1989), ed. Alexander Nehamas and Paul Woodruff, 27.

3   Emily Bronte, *Wuthering Heights* (New York: Penguin, 1995), 82.

4   Erich Fromm, *The Art of Loving* (New York: HarperCollins, 1956), 48.

5   Nozick, "Love's Bond," 70.

6   Ibid., 71–72.

7   Ibid., 73.

8   Ibid., 82.

9   There seems to be a contradiction here between Nozick's claim that the lovers have an individual identity and his claim that they both share an identity, unless the claim that they retain individual identities is a rather vacuous claim (in the sense that the individual identities are retained insofar as the entire joint identity comprised of both individual identities is now shared). This will become apparent in my discussion later in this section, when I identify three possible interpretations of his account of joint identity.

10 Solomon, *Love: Emotion, Myth, and Metaphor*, 150.

11 I will be using the terms "love" and "beloved" to denote "the one loving" and "the one loved," respectively. However, no asymmetry in the love relationship ought to be assumed by the use of these terms, as what I say about the lover and the beloved applies equally to both individuals in the love relationship.

12 Solomon, *Love: Emotion, Myth, and Metaphor*, 150.

13 Fisher, *Personal Love*, 27.

14 Ibid., 31.

15 Ibid., 27.

16 Ibid., 28.

17 Nozick, "Love's Bond," 82.

18 Alan Soble remarks that such lack of awareness of the origination of perceptions, acts, and feelings "could be explained better as the effect of aging, or merely inadequate, memory; or as a result of inattentiveness to detail; or perhaps such confusions reflect merely an indifference on the part of the lovers as to whose great idea it was" ("Union, Autonomy, and Concern," 72).

19 Solomon, *Love: Emotion, Myth, and Metaphor,* 150.

20 Ibid.

21 Neil Delaney makes a similar point in "Romantic Love and Loving Commitment: Articulating a Modern Ideal," *American Philosophical Quarterly* 33 (1996): 339–56, at 340.

22 Solomon, *Love: Emotion, Myth, and Metaphor,* 152.

23 Soble, "Union, Autonomy, and Concern," 83.

24 So too is selfishness towards one's partner. Pursuing only half of the ends of one's joint identity might indicate *akrasia*, but certainly would not count as selfishness.

25 Nozick, "Love's Bond," 71.

26 Solomon, *Love: Emotion, Myth, and Metaphor,* 152.

27 Robert C. Solomon, *About Love: Reinventing Romance for Our Times* (New York: Madison, 2001), 65.

28 This view need not be seen as ruling out a certain kind of third-entity view. What would be added under this third interpretation is further change in the individual beyond simply being part of a joint identity.

29 Nozick, "Love's Bond," 71.

30 Solomon, *About Love: Reinventing Romance for Our Times,* 198 (emphasis added).

31 Delaney, "Romantic Love and Loving Commitment," 341.

32 Ibid., 342.

33 Solomon, *Love: Emotion, Myth, and Metaphor,* 148.

34 Ibid., 150.

35 I do not need to claim here that there is no identity left without interpersonal and social interactions to make my point and make no claims about what is left behind if all external forces are lifted away (whatever that would mean). My main point here is that whatever an individual identity is without external forces, it certainly is not enough to be called what we usually refer to as an identity.

Discussion

In criticizing *union* views of romantic love, Alan Soble has noted, in a similar manner to de Beauvoir, that a shared or joint identity has historically favoured men. Women have typically lost much of their autonomy in the love relationship and this gives us some reason to be suspicious of such views.¹ Is there a way of making sense of the shared identity view of romantic love so that it involves both joint and individual identities? Does Solomon's suggestion that selves are not so individual after all help matters? What does he mean by this? Does the fact that we are already shaped by other people who have been part of our lives (parents, friends, teachers, coaches, etc.) mean that in some sense our identities are already *shared* with others? Or, even if selves are not so individual (i.e., they are influenced by others), is union identity a problematic way of thinking about love? Does a union or shared notion of identity always imply a loss of identity by one of the participants? Does love require some form of identification with the person one loves, or can a relationship that exists between two independent, autonomous individuals be called love? Is there something about love that requires (or at least is made better by) a type of union of individuals?

Think about your own romantic attachments. How would you characterize your relationship with your boyfriend or girlfriend? Do you think that he or she characterizes the relationship differently than you do? When you talk about your romantic relationship with other people do you tend to use "we" or are you more likely to say "my partner and I"? Our close relationships cannot help but affect our identity in some way, but the question is *how should they affect our identity*? At one extreme we have the person who totally loses his or her identity in a love relationship, while at the other extreme we have people who live almost entirely separate lives. Can either kind of relationship be said to be a truly loving relationship? How do couples avoid both of these extremes? Or are these extremes simply different kinds of expressions of love? Can you think of a way of characterizing romantic relationships that strengthen rather than diminish the autonomy or well-being of both individuals?

Much of this discussion applies to friendships as well. Close friends, like romantic partners, sometimes take on a kind of identity in addition to their individual identities. This additional identity (if we want to call it that) is often seen most clearly by others who experience the friends as sharing a bond. Is the situation different for friendships than it is for romantic love? Is there something about the nature of romantic love itself that poses a greater threat to one's autonomy or individual identity? Or is this threat equally present in the case of close friendships? We have probably all witnessed friendships where one of the friends is more domineering than the other. Do you think the reason for this is essentially different from the reasons for one-sided dominance in a romantic context?

Note

1   Alan Soble, "Union, Autonomy, and Concern," in *Love Analyzed*, edited by Roger Lamb (Boulder, CO: Westview Press, 1997), 73.

Suggestions for Further Reading

Deborah Bergoffen, "Simone de Beauvoir and Jean-Paul Sartre: Woman, Man, and the Desire to be God," *Constellations* 9, no. 3 (2002): 409–18.

Shulamith Firestone, "Love," in *The Dialectic of Sex* (New York: Bantam Books, 1970), 126–45.

Caroline J. Simon, "Just Friends, Friends and Lovers, or?" in *Sex, Love, and Friendship: Studies of the Society for the Philosophy of Sex and Love: 1993–2003*, edited by Adrianne Leigh McEvoy (Amsterdam: Rodopi Press, 2011), 27–38.

Alan Soble, "Union, Autonomy, and Concern," in *Love Analyzed*, edited by Roger Lamb (Boulder, CO: Westview Press, 1997), 65–92.

Section VI Relationships and Marriage

Chapter Fourteen
Ethical Relationships

ALEXIS SHOTWELL

Are human beings *naturally* monogamous? Does the frequency of divorce, adultery, or cheating shed any light on this question? Does morality require us to be monogamous, or can we be polyamorous and still be ethical? Does polyamory increase the ethical problems by multiplying one's responsibilities to others, or does it give one a chance to be more honest about one's non-monogamous lifestyle preference? Alexis Shotwell claims that monogamy is a "failing norm" in our society and this fact provides some people with reasons for looking for relationship alternatives. She argues that it is possible to engage in multiple relationships in ethical and responsible ways. In fact, she turns the tables on those who would judge polyamory to be immoral by suggesting that it can constitute a more ethical practice than the many cases of monogamy that are in bad faith. If adherence to monogamy forces one to cheat or be dishonest with one's partner, then perhaps we need to rethink the high moral status it has been given in Western society. Shotwell's argument invokes a conception of self-hood or identity that is relational in nature, which finds its articulation not in the writings of Sartre or Solomon but rather in the work of Sue Campbell and Donna Haraway. Campbell's account of relational self-formation, combined with Haraway's notion of "significant otherness," provides Shotwell with an alternative ethical picture of intimate relationships.

Ethical Polyamory, Responsibility, and Significant Otherness[1]

The point of marriage is not to create a quick commonality by tearing down all boundaries; on the contrary, a good marriage is one in which each partner appoints the other to be the guardian of his solitude, and thus they show each other the greatest possible trust. A merging of two people is an impossibility, and where it seems to exist, it is a hemming-in, a mutual consent that robs one party or both parties of their fullest freedom and development. But once the realization is accepted that even between the closest people infinite distances exist, a marvelous living side-by-side can grow up for them, if they succeed in loving the expanse between them, which gives them the possibility of always seeing each other as a whole and before an immense sky.

—Rainer Maria Rilke, *Letters to a Young Poet*

Chances are good that, if you've been in a sexual or romantic relationship, you have had the experience of holding implicit or explicit trust, where you and the people you're involved with respect certain boundaries. Chances are also quite good that you've been in the position of betraying that trust or having your trust betrayed. Usually we call that "cheating," and this essay assumes that fooling around on people is unethical and possibly evil, in the sense that it is almost certain to produce harm. Even though monogamy is a norm in our society, it is also certainly a failing norm, at least in the sense that it is enormously common for people to fail to respect it. The fact that monogamy seems to so often not work, in one way or another, is one reason that many people think about alternatives.

If you were interested in having *ethical*, *consensual*, multiple, sexual, emotional, or romantic relationships, you would find available to you (at least on the Internet) a number of self-identified polyamants, swingers, non-monogamists, support groups, close to forty books on non-monogamy, weekend workshops, and more. Depending on where you lived, the people you ran into might not

gape in horror if they discovered that you were both involved with someone and available to become involved with them. You might even be able to keep your job, your kids, and your apartment without conforming to monogamous models of romantic relationships. So many ifs. But the most important question would be: "If I want to have the possibility of multiple relationships, is there a non-evil way to do them?"

This short essay will answer this question: Yes.

I examine the philosophical stakes behind core narratives of current polyamory. I begin with some provisional and contested (but common) definitions, and go on to situate these definitions in relation to accounts of how to meaningfully make and keep promises and to respect interpersonal boundaries. I supplement these approaches by drawing on Sue Campbell's account of relational self-formation and Donna Haraway's call for an ethics of alterity and "significant otherness"; both Campbell and Haraway offer us useful frameworks for understanding responsibility as a way of being in poly-relation.

Defining Our Terms

There's a t-shirt that says:

POLYAMORY IS WRONG!
It is either Multiamory
or Polyphilia
but mixing Greek and
Latin Roots? WRONG!

Some people love the term "polyamory," because it names the idea of having multiple loves, while others prefer "non-monogamy," because it says what it's against. I understand both of these terms, which are the most common, to name the practice of *consensually and mutually negotiating desire for more than one relationship*. Sometimes, polyamory names the fact of having multiple simultaneous relationships, but not always. This nuance is important: I don't think people stop being polyamorous just because they are not themselves involved at the moment in more than one relationship—or any relationship, for that matter. An important bit here is the "consensual" part of that definition, about which I will say only that consent is going to be complex and negotiated in the context of overlapping power relations. A poly relationship that people are in just because they're afraid their partner will leave them isn't going to count as consensual and mutual.

You might, if you got into non-monogamy explicitly, eventually need to decide how to characterize your poly relationship(s), and you would need a little more negotiation, consent, and perhaps definition. The labels on offer include: "primary relationship," "secondary relationships," "polyfidelitous," "closed group married," "triad," "quad," "puppy pile poly," and many, many more. These terms, and the clusters of concepts out of which they precipitate, are simultaneously ways to navigate the charges of irresponsible relationality attending non-monogamous practice and efforts to concretize in language heterodox relational practices. Extended, they map presumed practices for responsible polyamory and by extension give an account of the responsibilities involved in intimate relationships altogether.

The relationships these terms describe conform to and, at the same time, exceed their own bounds. This involves questions of power—who has it, who's experiencing it, and what it's doing. These terms are relevant not

only to people who identify as polyamorous or non-monogamous. Intimate relationships matter to all of us: too often, it is through our most closely interwoven connections with others, at our moments of deepest vulnerability, that the racist, sexist, beauty-normative, ablest patriarchy hits us hardest. When we are naked and vulnerable with someone who says we are too hairy or too fat, or not hairy enough, or too skinny, precisely because we are naked and vulnerable we might feel that judgment more harshly than in everyday life. Even people who move through straight monogamous relationships with relative ease are shaped by the standards that cause friction to others. Feminist philosophical accounts of the importance of relationality to self-formation call for fuller accounts of the everyday language of polyamory. The terms matter for what and how we imagine the world of intimate relationships, of intimacy, connection, and care in our lives.

What Is Monogamy, Then?

On the way toward my main argument here, let me start with what I think is an uncontentious claim: monogamy is a form of polyamory. It is "boilerplate," or like a pre-printed lease agreement, and it seems ubiquitous. We usually think of monogamy as sexual fidelity to one romantic partner, often codified in legal recognition by the state and socially sanctioned, and most people assume that people who identify as married or stably dating someone are this thing called monogamous. But scratch at that assumption a little, and most monogamous relations are themselves built on a set of tacit and explicit agreements that express a more-or-less consensual navigation of possible or actual desire for multiple relationships. Does what happens in Vegas stay in Vegas? Can you gaze with delight on a non-partner's luscious lips? Is watching porn and masturbating cheating? If you're thinking about a friend who is not your sexual partner during sex, is that cheating? What if you're thinking of a popular actor? An anime character? A dog? What about looking up a high school flame and re-starting an exciting correspondence? Can you go to a strip club and feel turned on? Is it possible to be monogamously attracted to many people at the same time, so long as you never act on that attraction? Some people in monogamous relationships will answer "yes" to at least one of these questions, others would answer "no" to all of them. Sometimes people in monogamous couples talk about these things explicitly, but most don't—and different expectations about what "counts" as cheating often produce friction.

Monogamous people frequently experience quite profound jealousy, betrayal, neglect, anger, pain, and other difficult feelings when they feel that their partners have not respected their implicit or explicit agreements around these kinds of questions. Sometimes jealousy is sparked not even by one's partner having desire for others, but simply for being desired or desirable. Sometimes people feel jealous of their partner's regard and attention toward close friends, pets, work, golf, and many other things. And it's significant that monogamy arises out of quite troubling histories of the assumed need to control women's bodies for the purposes of patrilineal (descent through the male line) property relations; the history of monogamy is a history of ownership, and so it shouldn't surprise us that so many discussions of relational boundaries return to practices of property and control. Marriage and monogamy as we currently know them are not as ancient

as many people think, and they're certainly not as necessary as they're made out to be.

A key thing to understand here is that monogamous and poly relationships alike meet the challenges that accompany being interested in people. People in all sorts of relationships work with the implications of making commitments to one another despite the potential for wanting something more or other than the commitment implies. All sorts of intimate relationships grapple with the question of how to respect loved others, and, in romantic or sexual relationships, how to be responsible in the face of a crush. Poly relationships frequently grapple more explicitly and with a less boilerplate approach, and because of that potentially more expansive mode they have something to teach us about responsibility and respect in relationships more generally.

Three Common Poly Frameworks

There are three very common ways that poly people talk about and practice ethical non-monogamy: (1) dyadic polyamory, (2) clear multiple roles, and (3) unbounded openness. Right off, it is important to stress this typification flattens the lived experience of poly negotiation; people's practices overlap and exceed how I typify these styles of poly practice. However, all of us—poly and non—could fruitfully use a fourth, alternative ethical frame in understanding how to have multiple relationships, which I am calling "relational significant otherness."

Dyadic poly practices often use a language of hierarchy and centrality: there are primary partners, who act more or less like monogamous partners on monogamy steroids—the primary relationship is so steady, so flexible, so strong that it can accommodate each partner having relationships with people beyond the dyad. But that dyad is, well, primary. It comes first, it's most important, it trumps all other connections. Then there are secondary relationships, which might open up spaces the primary partnership doesn't treat. In strong versions of this style, even the spaces opened by the secondary lovers are encompassed and claimed by the primary dyad, because it is the main reference point in terms of which the secondary relationship takes place. Hapless others who enter the matrix of the primary dyad take warning: you are secondary. Your desires are subordinate to the needs and desires of the authentic pair—even if that pair is something less than exactly a "normal" couple.

Non-dyadic practices that maintain clear roles and boundaries use language of practical accommodation to the realities of carving out a new practice of relationality in the context of a hostile, heteronormative imperative to monogamy: everyone has people who, for contingent/natural reasons, are closer and more central to their lives. They are long-term partners, co-parents, people living together and otherwise in intentional close proximity. It is responsible and necessary to name these relationships what they are, however that naming is negotiated. Clear boundaries and ethically adhered to agreements are only practical. People new to a given poly configuration must both understand and respect the boundaries and agreements necessary to healthy multiple relationships operating among sometimes many different webs of relationship. When new loves and lovers enter the picture of already existing relationships, they can enter with maximal autonomy when the terms and habits are obvious. By extension, people in ongoing relationships must take responsibility for communicating the terms and conditions on which they might become involved with others—it is deceptive, too utopian, and disingenuous to act as though the power involved in committed relationships, however defined, is not in play. Trying to resist naming something a primary relationship, for example, is politically and ethically irresponsible and sets everyone up—particularly potential new lovers—for painful disillusion.

A final important—though contested—discourse in today's polyamorous circles unfurls in a language of limitless possibility, opening a radical space for respectful and ethical relationship, unbound by the strictures of orthodox relationships. On this account, in their very being, poly relationships undermine the oppressive framework of normative monogamy. This means that even when poly people appear to function in relationships legible to the straight norm—passing as monogamous—the facts of how they live and love utterly destabilizes that norm. It is more than possible to have responsible multiple relationships without rendering them in terms of rigid hierarchies. People who advocate this kind of understanding of poly relationships might argue that to call these relationships "primary" or "secondary" or many other labels based on rigid agreements degrades and disrespects them. Just as we have multiple friendships, they say, we can have multiple loving or sexual relationships—without labels, fluid, flexible, moving like a flock of birds or a school of dolphins. Axes of responsibility fall organically along lines delineated by contingent circumstance. The main thing standing in our way is habits of naming that recreate hierarchies.

Each of these ways of talking about poly relationships, of contesting or accepting the language of bounded agreements ("primary," etc.) attempts to settle the messy, thick, tangled weave of the actual practice of being in relationship with others. Monogamous couples smooth out this weave by deciding not to act on whatever desires they might have for people outside their relationship, by sublimating sexual energy into heightened friend-crushes, or by cheating on their partner (in which case they're non-monogamous, but profoundly unethical, and so I think we should be profoundly uninterested in them). Polyamorous people do different versions of these things, but I would suggest that in many cases they are still constrained by a troubling relational continuum.

On one end of this continuum are boundaries so constraining that the agreements made in the context of primary or central relationships take priority over other connections to the extent that secondary or other lovers are categorically shut out—their desires and needs have no weight in decision making, and people within a relationship might have power to end their partner's or lover's relationship with someone else. On the other end, any and all desires and relationships are on the table, and no one in a given configuration has ethical standing to make demands or set limits on the timing or type of relationships their lovers take up.

Consider the end of the continuum we might think of as monogamy on steroids. It seems to me that to call something non-monogamous, or polyamorous, while agreeing to end other relationships at a partner's whim is to pretend to the throne of liberatory relationality while retaining the forms of monogamy in holographic colour. Granted, there are whims and then there are reasons, and the latter can be ethical. But it is crucial for many poly relationships that take the label "primary" that the central pair has ethical priority in any relational

matrix. When something is threatening the dyad, especially if it's a newer relationship, the primary partnership gets priority. Often this manifests in already set agreements, to which any third or fourth person has to accede. There is also the question of labelling: the primary partnership comes first—usually temporally, but ostensibly also in one's consideration. The objects of secondary relationships—sometimes happy to evade the responsibility implied by primariness—are expected to accept their lot, to not demand too much, to understand when they can't sleep over or shower with their lover, or be called a particular endearment, if those things are off limits within the primary relationship. Other considerations are, well, secondary. As are the people who might hold them. And even when the person in question is happy with that status, it troubles me to relate with people as something less than full constituents, with ethical rights, in decisions that involve them.

In contrast to the highly bounded and negotiated agreements that delimit some poly relationships, there are models that reject boundaries and agreements because they are seen to endorse ownership models of relationality. Many proponents of these approaches imply or take it that proper polyamory admits of no boundaries at all, that negotiated agreements are concessions to an oppressive and hierarchical model that poly relationships ought to categorically reject. Practitioners of polyamory on this end of the continuum might or might not tell their lovers about new partners, and might have agreements about safer sex, for example, but current connections are given no first pass priority over new relationships. While it might resist certain forms of oppression associated with ownership models of relationships, particularly as such models are predicated on men's sexual access and dominion over women's bodies, labour, and affective availability, this form of poly relationship—call it "no holds barred"—is troubling for different reasons than the "all holds negotiated" form above. Its refusal to consider ethical claims arising from relationality puts commitments to treat others with dignity and respect on the butcher's block of self-righteous political purity.

As I mentioned above, and as many feminist/anarchist theorists have pointed out (think of Emma Goldman and Voltairine de Cleyre, or Simone de Beauvoir), the Western system of coupledom and marriage is rooted in patriarchal ownership models, in which women moved from one man's house (her father's) to another's (her husband's), holding the status of property. In North America, female monogamy also references purity of parentage—knowing who the father of children is—and since race is always involved in parentage monogamy has also been intertwined with a racist imperative to keep the white race pure. Perhaps surprisingly, anxieties about polyamory are not only racialized: they also relate to keeping structures of capitalism stable. This is because current economic arrangements are based on a model of a two-parent family; taxes, health insurance, mortgage and rental agreements, and much more assume a monogamous couple as their base unit. These things combine to make many poly people feel that simply not being monogamous is enough to make a person a revolutionary. However, if polyamory ends up replicating other unethical tendencies along the continuum I outlined above (ranging from too much control to too little respect), it cannot be genuinely interesting as a relational practice. I aspire for a revolutionary,

loving practice of relationships that is about rebellion against bad norms and also accountability to others; about violating boundaries that support a racist capitalist patriarchy and also being kind to others and respecting their boundaries; about challenging our deepest fears and also keeping ourselves and others safe enough to flourish.

Relational Selves and Significant Otherness

And so I turn to Donna Haraway's conception of significant otherness and Sue Campbell's conception of relational co-constitution. Together, I think of these theorists as offering us the idea of relational significant otherness. Haraway might herself resist the torquing back toward the human I am about to do. She is attempting to think seriously about contingent, non-reductive, co-constitutive relations between humans and other species. She riffs on the term "significant other," writing, "Except in a party invitation or a philosophical discussion, 'significant other' won't do for human sexual partners; and the term performs little better to house the daily meanings of cobbled together kin relations in dogland" (Haraway 2003, 96). In contrast, she suggests the idea of "significant otherness" as a way to talk about valuing difference. This term points us beyond one single significant other, into an envisioning of what an "ethics and politics committed to the flourishing of significant otherness might look like" (Haraway 2003, 3). Polyamory might, very imperfectly, be one move toward this kind of flourishing.

"Significant otherness" points toward partial connections, in which the players involved are relationally constituted but do not entirely constitute each other. This is "vulnerable, on-the-ground work that cobbles together non-harmonious agencies and ways of living that are accountable both to their disparate inherited histories and to their barely possible but absolutely necessary joint futures" (Haraway 2003, 7). The significant otherness I imagine as a guiding aspiration for responsible polyamory is both a dilution and an ardent affirmation of this statement. Clearly, the success or failure of people *cobbling together non-harmonious agencies and ways of living*—something we do with everyone we are committed to working with—is not productive of *absolutely necessary* futures between those two or more folks. There are forms of significant otherness, which might involve seeing the *disparate histories* we bring and the futures we might cobble together with them. When we perceive the on-the-ground work involved in attempting polyamory, it frequently looks like this revolution is too messy, tiring, grinding, and boring to be worth it. *Disparate inherited histories* are individual—our stories written deep in us, the relationships we come along with—but they are also much broader. There is indubitably something wrong with a politics tied to heteronormative monogamy. And there seems to be something also wrong with a polyamory tied to rigid classifications of "primary" and "secondary" relationships; in the context of thinking significant otherness, these classificatory schemas show up as ways to tame non-harmonious agencies into something smaller.

Sue Campbell's understanding of relational self-construction is useful here. Campbell argues that it is profoundly inaccurate to imagine that we as selves are separable, stably-bounded individuals. Rather, she attends to the many ways we are formed in and through mattering relations with others—from the earliest childhood throughout our lives. I am interested here in her account of how our practices of being responsive to others shape the kinds of selves we are. For Campbell, being relationally shaped means that we are dynamic and contingent beings shaped in part by what commitments or responsibilities we take up. Campbell writes, "Taking responsibility is part of the expressive behavior that constitutes our emotional attachments to others . . . One does not form emotional attachments with others and then find oneself assigned responsibility on this basis. Taking responsibility brings us into relation with others" (2014, 123). I am thinking of "taking responsibility" in this sense as connected in lively ways to Haraway's claim that "entities with fully secured boundaries called possessive individuals (imagined as human or otherwise) are the wrong units for considering what is going on. That means not that a particular animal does not matter but that mattering is always inside connections that demand and enable response, not bare calculation or ranking. Response, of course, grows with the capacity to respond, that is, responsibility" (Haraway 2008, 70–71). Campbell's conception of responsibility also refused any idea of a bounded self, which she argues "obscures the generative role of taking responsibility in commitments and relationships" (2014, 125). The *generative role* Campbell envisages here, one I endorse, is the idea that through practices of open-ended being-in-response, holding response-ability, we become different kinds of beings. Understanding this in the context of work on memory and relationality, she writes, "requires a shift in focus from a self-sovereign individual who is secure in her or his identity to a self who lives with the tensions, instabilities, and possibilities of time consciousness and a concomitant uncertainty about boundaries and responsibilities" (2014, 126). Perhaps one reason that people aim for monogamy, or—equally—take up any of the pre-set forms of non-monogamy on offer, is to try to manage the felt threat of their lovers being in relation to others. Perhaps it is most frightening to us to think of ourselves as constituted in unbounded and uncertain relations of significant otherness toward which we have relations of responsibility-in-the-making.

Starting from a view that we are selves shaped in relations of responsibility toward non-reductive otherness, I want something far more nuanced and far more risky than the labels "primary" and "secondary" touch. I want everyone—monogamous and polyamorous and other—to understand relationality itself as a deep, life-changing risk. What poly relationships have revealed to me is the utter contingency of relationships *altogether.* The fact that we will all lose people we love is really, really obvious and really, really hard to hold in our mind. We are going to die, or they are, or they'll split up with us, or we'll split up with them. In the everyday course of life, when our lovers fall for other people we suddenly see the ways they are strange to us: they have whole realms of experience we cannot access, and ways of flourishing we can't encompass. Understanding every relationship in terms of significant otherness brings these facts into nervous light. In addition to refusing the shorthand of "primariness," we

might explode the categories of monogamy and polyamory themselves. Beyond the dichotomy of "being poly" only when you're actually having multiple simultaneous sexual relationships, we could begin to see relationality altogether as a commitment to the flourishing of significant others and significant otherness.

Significant otherness, always relational, in ardent affirmative mode, signals the possibility of joint futures that extend beyond the framework of the two or three or several relationships any one of us can reasonably maintain. This significant otherness yearns to flourish, it delights when others toward whom we are in relations of response-ability flourish, and it may recognize that humans are not the most significant actors in that flourishing. The kind of absolutely necessary futures I find here relate to liberatory politics broadly construed, in which human and non-human actors might seriously and playfully act with respect toward mutual flourishing. Power is here, of course, but it's complicated. There are, then, bonsai versions of relational significant otherness that we manage to carve out of serious flourishing—sites of respect for our lovers and partners where we can take seriously their disparate histories, our partial connections, the ways that overlapping networks of relationality tug at us and free us, alternately and simultaneously. These small, halting, often-failing attempts might prefigure a pattern we hope will ripple out, roots and branches untrimmed and tangled.

Note

1 I thank Kelly Ball, Ami Harbin, Ada Jaarsma, Carrie Ichikawa Jenkins, Sarah LaChance Adams, Natalie Loveless, and Sarah Clark Miller for welcome feedback on this piece.

Bibliography

Campbell, Sue. 2014. *Our Faithfulness to the Past: The Ethics and Politics of Memory*. New York: Oxford University Press.

Haraway, Donna J. 2003. *The Companion Species*

Manifesto: Dogs, People, and Significant Otherness. Chicago: Prickly Paradigm.

———. 2008. *When Species Meet*. Minneapolis: University of Minnesota Press.

LAUREN BIALYSTOK

Many of us take it for granted that equality in romantic or marriage relationships is important—necessary even—in order for a relationship to be ethical, just or even simply to be good. But what does equality amount to in the context of such relationships? Does equality in relationships require equality in income? Equality of responsibilities? Equality in decision making? Does it require all of these and perhaps more? How do emotional factors affect equality? If one person loves or desires the other person more, can the relationship be said to be truly equal? Isn't the person who loves more in a potentially vulnerable position in relation to her beloved? Lauren Bialystok argues that the traditional view of justice as implying equality, which has been adopted from the political realm, provides an inadequate model for relationships due to unavoidable inequalities (not necessarily hierarchical ones) between people. While she argues that equality is important to many areas of a relationship, there are some aspects of romantic partnerships that don't admit of this in a strict manner. Furthermore, Bialystok argues that attempts to produce equality in certain areas of intimate relationships are misguided. She offers an alternative way of thinking about relationship equality.

Different and Unequal: Rethinking Justice in Intimate Relationships

For decades, feminists have been urging the basic principle that women and men are equal. This notion has been the basis of major legal and social reforms. And as feminism has stressed that "the personal is political," it is not surprising that equality in personal relationships, and especially love relationships between men and women, has become an accepted norm. This is expressed not only in mainstream culture but also in psychological and medical literature referring to healthy relationships. Recent empirical work finds that perceived equality is associated with well-being, health, and happiness, while inequality is associated with psychological distress and marital dissatisfaction. Some of the most popular relationship guides available are based on the concept of intimate partners as "peers" or equals (Schwartz, 1994).

It is clear why equality in relationships has tremendous intuitive appeal and constitutes a vast improvement over the historical assumption that women were inferior to men. But what does it mean to say that people are "equal"? Feminist philosopher Eva Feder Kittay notes that "an overemphasis on equality, however formulated, misses the importance of the asymmetries and differences that are unavoidable and even desirable in human intercourse," yet "it is barely conceivable that a progressive agenda can do without some suitable conception of equality" (Kittay 1999, 17). She is right that equality is a brute instrument for sorting human characteristics. In the public sphere, we use the concept to prevent discrimination; equality before the law is a paradigm example. In the intimate realm of relationships, however, I will argue that equality is a misguided standard. Only superficial types of equality can be properly measured and accounted for in relationships, and these characteristics are unavoidably dependent on deeper characteristics that are inherently unequal.

I will begin by briefly reviewing the main arguments for and against using general standards of justice, and equality in particular, in the domestic or intimate sphere. I will then examine what we can mean concretely by "equality" in relationships and distinguish between three levels that seem to influence the quality of relationships. Finally, I will consider where we are left if equality is not able to perform the ethical gatekeeping function that it has been ascribed, and advance a notion of partners in an intimate relationship as different and unequal, but not hierarchical.

Both "equality" and "intimate relationships" are contested terms, so it will be useful to start with some parameters. Equality is always in some sense about difference and sameness.

The claim that men and women are, or ought to be, equal depends necessarily on some claim about sameness, as it does for claims of equality between any individuals or groups of people. People are equal if they are the same in relevant respects. They need not be the same in every respect. It is possible to be different but equal, as long as they are the same in the ways that matter for a given type of assessment. For example, players on a soccer team may be different ages, but play at the same skill level. We may then say that the players are equal for the purposes of competition.

By "intimate relationship" I mean a two-person relationship that is long-term, committed,[1] and romantic or sexual in nature. Questions of equality are less germane outside this context. Only long-term and romantic relationships necessarily feature the complicated dynamics and emotions that I will be examining in what follows. I will consider both heterosexual and same-sex relationships, although research shows differences between them, with lesbian relationships being the most materially equal. As we will see, some types of inequality are fundamentally related to gender—and thus may be resolved through a feminist revolution—and some are simply endemic to human interaction and personal identity. Distinguishing between these types of inequality is critical if we are to move toward more sensitive assessments of justice in relationships.

The question I wish to ask, then, is this: Are two people in a long-term, committed romantic relationship *the same in relevant respects*? I will develop the argument that, when it comes to the quality of the relationship, virtually everything about the partners is relevant, and no two people are the same, making equality an elusive, and inappropriate, goal.

1. Justice and Equality in the Domestic Sphere: Pro and Con

There is a history of both anti-equality and pro-equality theories of intimate relationships in the philosophical literature. Despite my suspicion about the prospect of true equality, I am actually more sympathetic to the pro theories, but will explain why we ought to think beyond these options.

The anti-equality argument is what I call the "justice is separate from family life" or "love cancels out equality" argument. Historically, philosophers have had no qualms about drawing sharp lines between public and private, or, to use Susan Moller Okin's more correct terms, public and domestic, spheres. Philosophers as canonical as Hume and Rousseau have argued that justice is a feature of governments and social collectivities, not a virtue for families. Even recent philosophers like Michael Sandel and Hugh LaFollette have made this argument, claiming that justice is supposed to compensate for lack of natural affection. Since the family is presumptively ruled by love, and everyone in a family unit ostensibly has each other's interests in mind, justice is a misplaced requirement. This would mean that we do not need equality between intimate partners for the relationship to be ethical.

These views fail to take into consideration the impact of gender roles on individual identity and behaviour, which have been the most prominent source of inequality and mistreatment in relationships—even loving relationships. On this view, for example, women can be completely financially dependent on men as long as they love each other. Since justice is only supposed to apply to public life, there is no reason to worry about partners having even basic equality.

While it makes sense to preserve some distinction between public and domestic spheres, it is dangerous to take a simple "love will see us through" attitude toward justice in families. Even if this is usually the case, there are many kinds and degrees of love and affection, not all of which necessarily guarantee the organic justice that Sandel and LaFollette presume; worse, there are relationships that are not, or not primarily, characterized by love and care, and parties in such relationships seem to deserve ethical tools at least as much as the rest of us. It is simply wishful thinking to declare that intimate relationships are immune to injustice.

The pro-equality argument takes the threat of injustice in the family seriously, and articulates the need for equality in different ways. One version of the argument can be situated in a liberal tradition of procedural justice. For example, John Wilson models justice in intimate relationships on the way contracts should be constructed in the public sphere: "*Everything . . . has to be up for negotiation. We have to start from scratch, to work out a deal with another equal person with nothing taken for granted*" (1995, 107).

While arguably unromantic, the notion that everything ought to be negotiable in intimate relationships is appealing because it recognizes that love is not a substitute for respect and communication. But as I will argue later, it is naive to think that intimate partners are equally capable of negotiating what they need for the relationship to be just. Wilson's argument is steeped in a formal liberal tradition that depends on a conception of individuals as rational choosers, an assumption that feminists in particular have criticized.

Feminist philosophers have stressed the importance of justice (sometimes in the form of equality) in the domestic sphere—just consider the need to protect women from domestic assault and spousal rape—while also questioning the applicability of familiar theories of justice to this domain. Okin powerfully argues that "major contemporary Anglo-American theories of justice are to a great extent about men with wives at home" (1989, 110). These theories cannot be seamlessly imported into the private realm because they take the family for granted in their very articulation of justice. Hence feminists tend to be suspicious of "sphere-bracketing" when it comes to justice, whether justice is also advocated within the home (à la Wilson) or not (à la Sandel and LaFollette).

As an example of how justice transcends settings, Kittay points out that dependency work—the care of children, the elderly, the disabled, and so on—is usually women's work, and the majority of it continues to be unpaid and even unrecognized as work. Women's inequality in larger society is thus preserved behind closed doors. The upshot is that, even if a couple is aiming at equality, as long as they are influenced by gendered notions of value, women are usually at a disadvantage. Psychologist Janice Steil has found that "for mothers, no matter how much they earned, either in absolute terms or in relation to their spouses' earnings, and no matter how important they perceived their own job to be relative to their husbands' job, they still retained the major responsibility for the children" (1997, 30). Feminism would have to make significant strides in society as a whole for the prospect of equality in relationships to become attainable. Okin concurs that "the unequal distribution of rights, benefits, responsibilities and power within the family is closely associated with inequalities in many other spheres of social and political life" (1989, 113).

Many forms of inequality in relationships, then, are inescapably gendered, and tend to disempower women. These forms—such as the assumption that women are more responsible for housework and child care, and deserve less income—should be tackled in coordinated ways, not just between individual partners. Yet, while I look forward to a grand revaluation of gender-related values, it is not clear that equality in a profound sense is the remedy we are seeking. Moreover, there are inequalities between partners that have nothing to do with gender, and may not be in any way vicious. To see this, we need to examine equality more closely.

2. Equality of What?

Equality is a formal notion, meaning that it picks out general features of human beings rather than individual characteristics. In much ethics literature about the importance of equality, philosophers ask, "equality of *what*?" What are the relevant ways in which people are, or ought to be, the same? For the most part, we are different, but the differences are considered irrelevant. In deciding how I am to be treated by a court of law, for instance, it is not supposed to matter what colour my skin is, how I am dressed, what I dreamed about last night, or whether I am having a fight with my mother. What matters is that I am held to the same law as everyone else in society. Intimate relationships, however, are concerned with the very things that are supposed to be bracketed in the public sphere. So what are the relevant ways in which partners are, or ought to be, the same?

I will consider three layers of putative equality in relationships: division of labour, procedural equality, and emotional equality.

We will see that everything that can apparently be equalized is really dependent on things that cannot be.

Studies show that a great degree of marital conflict and dissatisfaction revolves around the unequal distribution of labour. (Feminism has made it acceptable for women to point this out.) If one partner is doing significantly more uncompensated housework and unpleasant chores than the other, it is not surprising that this should lead to conflict. In principle, the quantity of labour performed by each partner is equalizable, or at least measurable. The partner who performs more of this work may understandably complain to the other that he or she ought to do more as a matter of justice.

Economic equality is very closely related to the division of labour. The partner who performs more unpaid housework typically has less economic autonomy and authority in the family than the one who performs less. Work and money are both highly gendered. A recent study found that "among [heterosexual] couples with children, when both spouses work full-time, women do 32 hours a week of housework, child care, shopping, and other family-related services, compared with the 21 hours men put in" (Mundy 2013).[2]

That this situation is unjust seems obvious, but rectifying it through equalization may not be as simple as it sounds. Certainly, some couples find ways of equalizing housework. Philip Blumstein and Pepper Schwartz (1983) found that gay and (especially) lesbian couples are much more likely to do equal amounts of domestic work. But keeping a ledger of each partner's housework may seem clinical and a misrepresentation of intimacy, which, as LaFollette correctly argues, is precisely characterized by the absence of the "tit-for-tat" accounting found in exchange relationships (1996, 140–41). Although love may not conquer all, we still do not want to treat our significant others in the same way we would treat a business partner—at least, not all the time.

More importantly, researchers repeatedly find that partners say that an exact 50–50 division of labour, or even an equitable alternative, is not the solution to relationship dissatisfaction. Partners are inclined to say "I just need to have *equal say* in how it's decided" rather than "I need my partner to do an exactly equal amount of work." As Wilson correctly points out, the procedure by which things are negotiated in relationships is more central to equality than what is ultimately negotiated.

In moving beyond strict equality, we should not lose the importance of this component of relationships. Some material equality is possible and important, and we risk perpetuating entrenched forms of sexism by overlooking who does what. Nevertheless, it is the unquantifiable factors affecting division of labour that are really at the heart of labour inequality. Do partners really have an equal say in decision making?

Procedural Equality

In order for negotiation between individuals to be just, each partner would need to begin with more or less equal power. This is the condition that Wilson entirely overlooks. If one partner has significantly more power, the resulting "agreement" ought to be regarded with suspicion—just as when a state with enormous economic and military strength enters "negotiations" with a weak and vulnerable state. Some types of relationships that used to be common in the West, such as the marriage of a middle-aged man to a teenaged virgin, are regarded as de facto wrong because the partners could not possibly be equally powerful. When it comes to two individuals who are not vastly different in age, social rank, or ability, however, power is notoriously elusive and hard to measure. Certainly it is insufficient to declare that two partners have equal power simply because there are no major systematic differences between them.

Psychologists have attempted to define the various types of power that individuals enjoy and exert over each other in relationships. Steil talks about "reward power" vs. "coercive power," where the former is the ability to entice behaviours from the partner by providing outcomes that the partner desires and the latter is the ability to coerce behaviours from the partner by providing undesired outcomes (1997, 46). But even these more finely labelled types of power are still intangible. For example, even assuming that partner A has the ability to withhold sex from partner B, the value of this power is highly indeterminate, depending, among other things, on B's desire for sex and the asymmetrical powers that B has over A. It would be simplistic to conclude that A has an advantage in negotiating the housework (or other matters) with B simply on the basis of this power.

Sometimes it is argued that what ought to be equalized in relationships is access to or control over resources, whether this is taken to be a measure of power itself or a separate category. Once more, it is hard to see how this important aspect of relationships can be equalized in any systematic way. Resources can be almost anything, and whether they are valuable or not just depends on how much they are wanted. As Steil explains, "because a resource must be valued by the person whom one wishes to influence, the amount of power associated with any given resource is to some

extent subjective" (1997, 45). There is no question that access to resources in relationships is related to justice, as it is in the public sphere. However, the public notion of access to resources, which is moderated by such institutions as welfare and public education, is not transferable to the domestic realm. Relationships are about complex patterns of sharing and influencing, with no impartial state apparatus to solve disputes.

There are other ways of conceiving of equality in intimate relationships, such as the consideration of interests (whose interests get more weight) and exit potential (the ability to threaten to leave the relationship). All of these candidates for procedural equality are relevant to how relationships function and ought to be viewed to some extent as measures of justice. However, the idea that justice depends on these factors being *equal* between partners is flawed, if not outright incoherent. To the extent that such powers are systematizable in the public sphere—which is highly doubtful—they are manifestly less so in intimate relationships. This is not only because they are abstract concepts that resist translation into empirically measurable outcomes (for example, how do you measure the weight of someone's interests?), but also because they perpetually appeal to the idiosyncrasies of the particular individuals and situations involved. Your ability to coerce your partner into doing something might well depend on whether you are having a fight with your mother. The anonymity presupposed in the public sphere is unthinkable in the context of intimacy. Equality of power, in other words, which is supposed to guarantee or absolve the need for strict material equality in relationships, depends on equality of a very non-procedural sort: what I will term for short, "emotional equality."

Emotional Equality

Emotional factors are not incidental to relationships. They *are* relationships. The assumption that we can distill an impersonal mechanism for achieving equality in relationships without reference to these things indeed misses the whole point of intimate relationships.

Is it possible for two people in an intimate relationship to be emotionally equal—that is, emotionally the same in relevant respects? This question is practically absurd. Emotions and personality traits are unique almost by definition, and always relevant to how individuals communicate with their intimates. A sampling of the factors that can affect how partners approach negotiation about concrete matters includes feelings of affection, frustration, jealousy, generosity, and vulnerability; erotic attraction; self-esteem and self-confidence; anxiety or depression; unconscious influences (dreams, latent memories, etc.); communication style; reasoning style; other intimate relationships in one's life; physical abilities and limitations; and perceived roles and responsibility in the wider society. These facts can have enormous influence on the way things are decoded and negotiated in relationships, and may imperceptibly skew even the most regimented procedures of equality.

In short, the very things that attract people to each other, which can be explored and actualized in intimate relationships, and which are at bottom about who we are and what makes us lovable as individuals, are the very things that are never equalizable. Even if we can strive to equalize other things—and perhaps ought to—those other things are only truly equalizable if partners start from the same emotional, social, psychological, and physical starting points. And this is impossible.

Consider one example of a common question faced by couples: Who makes dinner? On the first level, equality is a question of labour: we can measure who makes dinner (if not how well, or at what cost to herself or another) and may endorse a policy of alternating cooking days. But this strict equality is too simple: the point is not that A and B each make dinner 50 percent of the time, but that the determination of who makes dinner is achieved through some procedure in which A and B are equal. Hence we move to the second layer, procedural equality. But the very establishment of a decision-making procedure and the partners' respective abilities to negotiate and enact it depend on the third layer: their interests, abilities, feelings, and needs. These are not equal. If the third level fails, which it does by definition, the other levels fail too.

3. Beyond Equality: Where Do We Go from Here?

I said earlier that equality is a question of whether individuals or groups of people are the same in relevant respects. Are two people in an intimate relationship the same in relevant respects? I have been arguing that when we take this question seriously, we see that they are irreducibly different. This is not to say that they are not the same at all. Intimate partners are usually of the same socio-economic class, the same age bracket, the same broad political orientations, and may enjoy the same activities, belong to the same religion, and so on. But while they may start with such Internet-dating-checklist similarities, relationships do not sink or sail on the basis of these alone; otherwise any number of other partners would do just as well. All of one's eccentricities and peculiarities come to bear on relationships, and these are never all the same.

This means that partners are therefore never equal in a profound sense.

It is fashionable to argue that equality admits of difference, that we are all "different but equal." I have tried to show why this notion of equality is hollow when the differences between people play out in intimate relationships. When our whole self is at issue, we are all different and unequal. This phrase has worrying connotations for many ethicists, and is perhaps provocative coming from a feminist. Where does this diagnosis leave the concern for justice in relationships, as well as all of the socially structured inequalities that we ought to resist?

To be sure, if women and men truly had equal power and opportunity in our society, this would have transformative and mostly positive spillover effects on intimate relationships. Just look at same-sex relationships, in which the absence of default gender roles was found to be liberating: "The partners were found to interact more as unique individuals, rather than as pre-determined role-bearers, and there was much more discussion about how to organize their lives" (Mundy 2013).

But even if we could overcome gender stereotypes, close the wage gap, and put more women in positions of real power, we would not resolve every form of inequality between two individuals. This is further confirmed by looking at dynamics between same-sex partners, who were ostensibly socialized into the same gender norms. While studies show that same-sex couples share household duties more equally and negotiate more openly than their heterosexual counterparts, their emotional inequalities and non-gendered power differences obviously persist. For example, one study found that among gay men, frequently "one . . . partner would prefer to be monogamous, but gives in to the other partner" (Mundy 2013).

While systematic gender inequality is unjust, however, the unequal influence of one partner over another is not necessarily so. Inequality can be non-hierarchical.[3] Hierarchy implies a kind of standing priority of one over another, an all-things-considered superiority in virtue of age, rank, or some such quality. Inequalities of the type I have been considering, by contrast, may be subtle, ephemeral, accidental, and contextual. They are neither necessarily vicious nor even avoidable. For example, professional collaborators, such as co-authors on a scholarly article, may bring unequal skills and insights to a particular project without the relationship being hierarchical. Likewise, I see no reason why perfectly happy and healthy intimate relationships cannot flourish between people who are different and unequal.

Justice without Equality?

It may be thought that giving up on real equality in relationships threatens to leave us in an ethical vacuum. Equality is supposed to act as a moral safeguard against oppressive relationships such as the traditional institution of patriarchal marriage.[4] If, as Wilson, Okin, and Kittay have argued, justice is necessary in the domestic sphere, how is it to be adjudicated? What kind of principle separates the just relationships from the unjust ones, if they are all characterized by inequality?

The most egregious forms of injustice in relationships are such things as physical violence, emotional abuse, pathological deception, non-consensual sex, and other misuses of the vulnerability that comes with intimacy. We do not need equality per se to identify what is wrong with these things. Other ethical principles will do, such as non-maleficence or respect for autonomy. However, I am reluctant to offer up any of these alternatives as the single or correct principle for ensuring justice in relationships. Like equality, they fail to capture the full range of relevant factors in relationships and to make appropriate distinctions.[5] The point is that we can say that some dynamics between intimates are bad without relying on inequality to explain their badness.

In fact, even where conspicuous inequality is a factor, there can be injustice in relationships that is not at all explained by inequality. For example, one partner in a relationship may be significantly physically larger and stronger than the other. This is clearly an inequality. But if the larger and stronger partner uses her physique to hurt or intimidate the partner, it is not the inequality that makes this wrong. It is rather the use of force to obtain power. The inequality, considered alone, can be considered benign.

The successful mainstreaming of equality may be one of the most influential victories of the feminist and civil rights movements. In the public sphere, injustice very often is just about inequality, and it is necessary to adopt formal commitments to equality if we wish to overcome it. It is not surprising that gender

inequality is such a salient source of conflict in relationships because most people are heterosexual and were raised in a gender-polarized culture where men have more power than women. In relationships between individuals from other discrepant social groups, such as mixed-race relationships, similar dynamics are likely to occur. There is no question that dismantling the gender expectations around such things as the division of domestic labour would go a long way in addressing many of the most potent inequalities that we worry about in relationships. But inequality is not the only way of describing what is wrong in these situations, and demanding strict equality as a remedy is unrealistic. Kittay suggests that the requirement of equality in relationships is problematic, but it has been such an important political rallying cry for feminists and other marginalized groups that we are loath to give it up. I have argued that equality is cogent only at the most superficial levels of relationships. Once we understand its inherent limits, we can prepare, philosophically and politically, to move beyond it.

Notes

1   "Committed" here does not necessarily mean monogamous but does mean that the long-term nature of the relationship is intentional, and that the partners plan their futures together.

2   The study also found that "men do more paid work—45 hours, compared with 39 for women—but still have more free time: 31 hours, compared with 25 for women" (Mundy 2013).

3   Iddo Landau has argued against what he calls the "Marital Non-Hierarchy Standard" (2012), saying that it is irrational for marriage to be the only type of human relationship that is

categorically protected from hierarchy. He does not defend this assertion, however, so much as leave it in a rhetorical position. I reject the argument that hierarchy would be acceptable in a marriage, but it is not the case that all inequality is tantamount to hierarchy.

4   It is worth noting that even in very traditional marriages, the man does not automatically have more power than the woman in every domain. For example, the woman may well be less attracted to the man than vice versa, and therefore wield emotional and sexual power over him (of course, this power is merely theoretical if the

man has sex with her without her consent). Additionally, the fact that paternity could not be confirmed until very recently at least gave women control over something of great significance to their husbands.

5 For example, non-maleficence (not causing harm) is a brute measure of relationship ethics. Relationships always involve some harm, albeit usually unintentional: feelings get hurt, egos get bruised. Sex can cause harm: it can cause bodily pain or result in serious infections. Even breaking up with someone is a form of harm resulting from a relationship. It can be extremely painful without being morally vicious. So harm itself cannot be the relevant distinction between unjust relationships and just relationships.

Bibliography

Blumstein, Philip, and Pepper Schwartz. 1983. *American Couples: Money, Work, Sex.* New York: Morrow.

Kittay, Eva Feder. 1999. *Love's Labor: Essays on Women, Equality and Dependency.* New York: Routledge.

LaFollette, Hugh. 1996. *Personal Relationships: Love, Identity and Morality.* Oxford: Blackwell.

Landau, Iddo. 2012. "Should Marital Relations Be Non-Hierarchical?" *Ratio* 25 (1): 51-67.

Mundy, Liza. 2013. "The Gay Guide to Wedded Bliss." *The Atlantic,* June. http://www.theatlantic.com/magazine/archive/2013/06/the-gay-guide-to-wedded-bliss/309317/.

Okin, Susan Moller. 1989. *Justice, Gender, and the Family.* New York: Basic Books.

Sandel, Michael. 1982. *Liberalism and the Limits of Justice.* Cambridge: Cambridge University Press.

Schwartz, Pepper. 1994. *Peer Marriage: How Love Between Equals Really Works.* Toronto: Maxwell MacMillan.

Steil, Janice. 1997. *Marital Equality: Its Relationship to the Well-Being of Husbands and Wives.* Thousand Oaks, CA: Sage.

Wilson, John. 1995. *Love between Equals: A Philosophical Study of Love and Sexual Relationships.* Houndmills, UK: Macmillan.

Discussion

Alexis Shotwell makes the seemingly contradictory "uncontentious claim" that "monogamy is a form of polyamory." What does she mean by this? Shotwell calls into question the idea that monogamy, in practice at least, adheres to the ideal of full fidelity to one romantic partner whether this be in marriage or in a dating relationship. Within contemporary monogamous relationships there is often an implicit recognition that one's partner will be interested in or attracted to other people at some point in the relationship. This may take the form of flirting with a co-worker, fantasizing about someone other than your partner, viewing pornography, or, in more serious cases, an extramarital fling or affair (which could take the form of a cyber affair or could be a real-life physical one). If it is true that most relationships involve at least one of these occurrences, then Shotwell's claim seems to be, as she suggests, uncontentious. But do all of these things count equally as instances of non-monogamy? Does simply being attracted to another person or perhaps even being flirtatious on occasion constitute non-monogamy? Isn't this quite different from the clearly non-monogamous situation of having an affair? If we agree that these cases are different, then what sort of difference are we talking about? Are these differences in *kinds*, as philosophers say? Is flirting or fantasizing a different *kind* of act such that it does not constitute non-monogamy whereas having an affair—whether real or virtual—is indeed non-monogamous? Or should we say that these actions are different in *degree*? Characterizing the differences here as differences of degree, allows us to accept flirting or fantasizing as departures from monogamous practice—albeit less serious deviations. This latter characterization would seem to accord with Shotwell's view.

Are polyamorous relationships morally preferable to monogamous relationships in which one ends up cheating on one's partner? Is this a more honest approach? Can one be emotionally faithful and responsible to the needs of one's primary partner in a poly relationship? Can one treat other people who are not one's primary partner fairly since their status is secondary in relationship terms by definition? Are the factors involved in maintaining multiple romantic or sexual relationships akin to those that are expected when maintaining multiple friendships? Does the romantic or sexual dimension make a difference here?

Generally speaking, what role does morality play in love relationships? What are one's ethical responsibilities to one's beloved? Are the demands of love the same as the demands of morality or of justice? Are there times when doing what love demands causes us to violate what morality requires? In her article, Lauren Bialystok approaches the question of equality in romantic and marriage relationships in a nuanced way.

Think of the dynamics of human relationships. We rarely seem to find situations where two people love or desire each other equally for an extended period of time. Sometimes one person wants, needs, or loves the other person more and at other times the situation is reversed. In cases of emotional inequality, other factors such as inequality in wealth, physical strength, or the esteem of others may or may not help mitigate the differences. In his *Nicomachean Ethics*, Aristotle suggests that equality in friendship is not the same as equality in justice. Perhaps the same is true of romantic or marital relationships. Maybe love or friendship can compensate in some way for other inequalities (inequalities of wealth, physical strength, etc.). Of course, this kind of suggestion may open the door to inequalities of the wrong kind. But as Bialystok tells us in her article, many of the most serious injustices in relationships—physical violence, emotional abuse, non-consensual sex, and so on—are ones whose wrongness is addressed by ethical principles other than that of equality. Her main concern is with those inequalities that cannot or should not be eliminated from a relationship, the inequalities that are not based on oppression or political injustice and that might even be valued by the lovers in question.

Think of your own relationship or perhaps past relationships that you have been in. How would you characterize these relationships in terms of equality? Did your relationship work on more or less equal terms? Were you more or less equal in economic terms? How did you make decisions as a couple? Did you have a fair way of making decisions, or did one person tend to get his or her way more often than the other? Were you dependent on your partner in a way that decreased your "exit potential" for leaving the relationship? Was your partner dependent on you in this way? What aspects of a relationship do you think must be equal? Which areas do you think allow for inequalities that are not unjust or unethical?

Suggestions for Further Reading

Donna J. Haraway, *The Companion Species Manifesto: Dogs, People, and Significant Otherness* (Chicago: Prickly Paradigm, 2003).

Eva Feder Kittay, *Love's Labor: Essays on Women, Equality and Dependency* (New York: Routledge, 1999).

Hugh LaFollette, *Personal Relationships: Love, Identity and Morality* (Oxford: Blackwell, 1996).

Ann Tweedy, "Polyamory As a Sexual Orientation," *University of Cincinnati Law Review* 79 (2011): 1461–515.

John Wilson, *Love between Equals: A Philosophical Study of Love and Sexual Relationships* (Houndmills, UK: MacMillan, 1995).

Chapter Fifteen
Marriage

Introduction

The prospect of getting married, having a family, and "settling down" is an attractive one for many people. The institution of marriage continues to persist and remain popular in spite of its critics and in spite of the high divorce rate. Some cite the high divorce rate as evidence either that we are not naturally monogamous or that the institution of marriage is itself problematic. Whatever the case may be, marriage still holds an attraction for many people whether they are heterosexual or homosexual. The eighteenth-century philosopher Immanuel Kant claimed that marriage had its basis in nature. The view that he defends sees marriage as an institution that has as its goal the production and education of children. Kant, in keeping with the thinking of his time, seemed to take for granted that the upbringing of children could only take place in the context of a heterosexual union. In addition to this, marriage according to Kant implies both monogamy and equality.

IMMANUEL KANT

What exactly is meant by the term *marriage*? Is marriage an institution whose meaning and administration is determined by the state, or is marriage something whose origin and definition derive from religion? Settling this issue might help us make some headway in answering further questions such as: Is marriage by definition something that is limited to the union of a man and a woman? Are same-sex marriages genuine instances of marriage? Can unions involving more than two people be called marriage? Is marriage in some sense *natural*?

Marriage and Monogamy

The Natural Basis of Marriage

The domestic Relations are founded on Marriage, and Marriage is founded upon the natural Reciprocity or intercommunity (*commercium*) of the Sexes.[1] This natural union of the sexes proceeds either according to the mere animal Nature (*vaga libido, venus vulgivaga, fornicatio*), or according to Law. The latter is MARRIAGE (*matrimonium*), which is the Union of two Persons of different sex for life-long reciprocal possession of their sexual faculties.—The End of producing and educating children may be regarded as always the End of Nature in implanting mutual desire and inclination in the sexes; but it is not necessary for the rightfulness of marriage that those who marry should set this before themselves as the End of their Union, otherwise the Marriage would be dissolved of itself when the production of children ceased.

And even assuming that enjoyment in the reciprocal use of the sexual endowments is an end of marriage, yet the Contract of Marriage is not on that account a matter of arbitrary will, but is a Contract necessary in its nature by the Law of Humanity. In other words, if a man and a woman have the will to enter on reciprocal enjoyment in accordance with their sexual nature, they *must* necessarily marry each other; and this necessity is in accordance with the juridical Laws of Pure Reason.

The Rational Right of Marriage

For, this natural "*Commercium*"—as a "*usus membrorum sexualium alterius*"—is an enjoyment for which the one person is given up to the other. In this relation the human individual makes himself a "*res*" which is contrary to the Right of Humanity in his own Person. This, however, is only possible under the one condition, that as the one Person is acquired by the other as a *res*, that same Person also equally acquires the other reciprocally, and thus regains and re-establishes the rational Personality. The Acquisition of a part of the human organism being, on account of its unity, at the same time the acquisition of the whole Person, it follows that the surrender and acceptation of, or by, one sex in relation to the other, is not only *permissible* under the condition of Marriage, but is further *only* really possible under that condition. But the Personal Right thus acquired is at the same time, *real in kind*; and this characteristic of it is established by the fact that if one of the married Persons run away or enter into the possession of another, the other is entitled, at any time, and incontestably, to bring such a one back to the former relation, as if that Person were a Thing.

Monogamy and Equality in Marriage

For the same reasons, the relation of the Married Persons to each other is a relation of EQUALITY as regards the mutual possession of their Persons, as well as of their Goods. Consequently Marriage is only truly realized in MONOGAMY; for in the relation of Polygamy the Person who is given away on the one side, gains only a part of the one to whom that Person is given up, and therefore becomes a mere *res*. But in respect of their Goods, they have severally the Right to renounce the use of any part of them, although only by a special Contract.

From the Principle thus stated, it also follows that Concubinage is as little capable of being brought under a Contract of Right, as the hiring of a person on any one occasion, in the way of a *pactum fornicationis*. For, as regards such a Contract as this latter relation would imply, it must be admitted by all that any one who might enter into it could not be legally held to the fulfilment of their promise if they wished *to* resile from it. And as regards the former, a Contract of Concubinage would also fall as a *pactum turpe*; because as a Contract of the *hire (locatio, conductio)*, of a part for the use of another, on account of the inseparable unity of the members of a Person, any one entering into such a Contract would be actually surrendering as a *res* to the arbitrary Will of another. Hence any party may annul a Contract like this if entered into with any other, at any time and at pleasure; and that other would have no ground, in the circumstances, to complain of a lesion of his Right. The same holds likewise of a morganatic or "left-hand" Marriage contracted in order to turn the inequality in the social status of the two parties to advantage in the way of establishing the social supremacy of the one over the other; for, in fact, such a relation is not really different from Concubinage, according to the principles of Natural Right, and therefore does not constitute a real Marriage. Hence the question may be raised as to whether it is not contrary to the Equality of married Persons when the Law says in any way of the Husband in relation to the Wife, "he shall be thy master," so that he is represented as the one who commands, and she as the one who obeys. This, however, cannot be regarded as contrary to the natural Equality of a human pair, if such legal Supremacy is based only upon the natural superiority of the faculties of the Husband compared with the Wife, in the effectuation of the common interest of the household; and if the Right to command, is based merely upon this fact. For this Right may thus be deduced from the very duty of Unity and Equality in relation to the *End* involved.

Note

1 *Commercium sexuale est usus, membrorum et facultatum alterius.* This *"usus"* is either natural, by which human beings may reproduce their own kind, or unnatural, which, again, refers either to a person of the same sex or to an animal of another species than man. These transgressions of all Law, as *"crimina carnis contra naturam,"* are even "not to be named"; and as wrongs against all Humanity in the Person they cannot be saved, by any limitation or exception whatever, from entire reprobation.

JILL RUSIN

The *naturalness* of marriage that Kant defended has been called into question by many modern thinkers who argue that marriage is a *conventional* rather than *natural* institution or practice. But a form of the naturalness argument still remains. The form that it has taken more recently suggests that marriage, in addition to having elements of convention or social construction, is still a *natural kind* and therefore the term cannot be applied to just any kind of union. Arguments of this sort suggest that marriage, understood as a natural kind, is only meant to apply to unions of the opposite sex, just as the term *tree* is only meant to apply to a certain natural class of plants. In her article, Jill Rusin examines such arguments in light of contemporary claims for the legitimacy of same-sex marriage or other types of unions such as those argued for by Elizabeth Brake (for instance, involving friends or in some cases more than two people). In order to understand the meaning of marriage according to Rusin, we have to first understand what kind of concept it is.

The Meaning of Marriage

My two children, born in Canada and of elementary school age, know that adult couples can get married. And they know this is true of both same- and different-sex couples, though undoubtedly they've experienced countless more images, stories, and celebration of heterosex union (for every *King and King* there are a thousand retellings of *Cinderella* and *Sleeping Beauty*). Having been born after the federal government legalized same-sex marriage with the 2005 Civil Marriage Act, my children have never lived in a Canada without same-sex marriage. They might be surprised to learn that this hasn't always been the case, and that it isn't the case worldwide.

In the United States, where I was born, the matter of marriage has more recently been in flux. The current US president, Barack Obama, was once avowedly against legalizing same-sex marriage but is now in support of its legalization. The recent Supreme Court ruling *Obergefell v. Hodges* has vacated state laws banning same-sex marriage. States that until June 2015 considered marriage to be exclusive to a man and woman must now reconsider their understanding of marriage. Some of these states are reluctant to embrace a concept of marriage that includes same-sex couples. This resistance stems in part from the idea that accepting such a change is tantamount to "changing the meaning of marriage."

Are US conservatives, like Canadian conservatives before them, right to fear that their federal government is "changing the meaning of marriage"? Has the meaning of marriage been different between Canada and the United States over the past decade? Do we have one concept, misapplied in some states and countries, correctly applied in others, or two (or more) competing concepts? Do my children misunderstand what marriage is, or was, if they mistakenly assume two men could get married in Alberta in 2005 or in Texas in 2015? Elizabeth Brake, in this volume, argues in favour of an understanding of marriage, 'minimal marriage,' that would allow three people to be married or non-romantic friends to be married. Is Brake's 'minimal marriage' a form of marriage? Most generally, what does the meaning of 'marriage' have to do with the same-sex marriage debate, or more broadly, our understanding of a just institution of marriage?

In what follows I address such questions. There is undoubtedly much more to be said on the subject. My aim is modest: to dispel some confusion about whether changes to marriage law entail the loss of marriage as we know it. This is worth attention because fear of such loss can shut down consideration of change. It is not only worries about bad consequences that hamper conversation about marriage reform;[1] fear of loss of what we do value can have a similar result. A better understanding of the kind of concept marriage is can clear the way forward.

1. Humpty Dumpty and square circles

In Lewis Carroll's *Through the Looking Glass*, Alice argues with Humpty Dumpty about the meaning of the word 'glory' and about word meanings, quite generally. Humpty Dumpty wants to be master over his words. But Humpty's understanding of word mastery is not an ordinary understanding of what it would be to 'master' English—to have a broad vocabulary and show keen awareness of the nuances of word meaning. In Humpty's eyes this sort of mastery is entirely too submissive, involving as it does one be a conscientious student of words. Rather, Humpty wants to be the master of words the way one is master to a servant: the master's desires and intentions reign supreme.

> "When *I* use a word," Humpty Dumpty said, in rather a scornful tone, "it means just what I choose it to mean—neither more nor less."
>
> "The question is," said Alice, "whether you *can* make words mean so many different things."
>
> "The question is," said Humpty Dumpty, "which is to be master—that's all."
>
> Alice was too much puzzled to say anything; so after a minute Humpty Dumpty began again. "They've a temper some of them—particularly verbs: they're the proudest—adjectives you can do anything with, but not verbs—however, *I* can manage the whole lot of them!" (Carroll 1971, 190–91)

Clearly, Humpty doesn't want conventional meaning to dictate what *his* words mean. He wants to be boss over his words, so he believes his speaker's intention must determine meaning. Alice has noticed that this makes communication with Humpty quite confusing:

> "I don't know what you mean by 'glory,'" Alice said. Humpty Dumpty smiled contemptuously. "Of course you don't—till I tell you. I meant 'there's a nice knock-down argument for you!'" (Carroll 1971, 190)

Alice, who has a rather more public and conventional theory of the grounding of word meaning, demurs: "But 'glory' doesn't mean 'a nice knock-down argument'" (Carroll 1971, 190). Humpty and Alice disagree both about the meaning of 'glory' and the relationship conventional meaning bears to the meaning of a speaker's utterances. Humpty takes "meaning is use" quite literally, liberally, and individualistically: he considers conventional usage no constraint on how he could mean his words. Alice doesn't think it possible that speaker intent simply dictates meaning.

Conservative critics of same-sex marriage have argued that their opponents misuse the word 'marriage' akin to the way Humpty Dumpty misuses 'glory.' They disagree that marriage can mean just whatever we as a society decide for it to mean, but instead argue that marriage is "the union of a man and a woman who make a permanent and exclusive commitment to each other of the type that is naturally (inherently) fulfilled by bearing and rearing children together" (Girgis, George, and Anderson 2010, 246). In this view, since marriage *means* a union between a man and a woman, we cannot (even collectively) just decide to use the word 'marriage' to also refer to same-sex unions, much less the broader collection of care-based relationships Brake canvasses. Alliance Defense Fund's Jeffrey Ventrella explains, "To advocate same-sex marriage is logically equivalent to seeking to draw a 'square circle.'" Ventrella argues, "The public square has no room for square circles, because like the Tooth Fairy, they do not really exist" (qtd in Corvino 2012, 28).

These objections go beyond Alice's complaint against Humpty. Alice's complaint was primarily that an individual speaker cannot idiosyncratically depart from established usage and, by dint of will, have his words mean whatsoever he desires. Language is more public than Humpty imagines, and the meanings of our words depend on how others use them, not merely how an individual speaker understands or uses them. So, for example, my son at age two would say, "Kitty is in the chicken!" when meaning to convey that the cat was in the kitchen. The family understood that he used the word 'chicken' to mean kitchen and thus we could follow what he meant us to understand. But in so far as it is English he was speaking, still my son's claim that "kitty is in the chicken" would have been literally false, whatever room the cat was in, for we do not keep any kitten-eating chickens on our premises.[2]

This example illustrates the socially externalist character of meaning. But even if we depart from Humpty Dumpty and grant that the content of our utterances is in part determined by the practices of our linguistic community, Ventrella, Girgis, George, and Anderson want to argue for further constraints on what could be meant by 'marriage.' Not any communally shared usage and understanding of 'marriage' would be legitimate according to these thinkers. If all American English speakers decide to use 'marriage' to refer to a status that picks out the broader spectrum of care relationships Brake describes as "minimal marriage," or if

Canadians simply use 'marriage' to refer to their government's legal definition, this is not in fact the true meaning of 'marriage' according to these thinkers. This is because they believe that 'marriage' is grounded by natural meaning. If marriage is a social kind, it is not a social kind that is at bottom merely conventional, or only a social construction.

Maggie Gallagher, endorsing this view of Girgis et al., compares the type of word 'marriage' is to 'dog':[3]

> A law that insists the word 'dog' will now mean 'either dogs or cats' (in order to point out their deep similarities) may not in fact do any harm. We could say 'dogs that bark' if we want someone to buy us a dog and not a cat. (Just as Corvino proposes we say 'heterosexual marriage' when we mean a husband and wife).
>
> Nevertheless, to require people to call cats 'dogs' would be unjust because the statement is untrue.
>
> A law that insists we call all cohabitations 'marriage' might do no harm. Still, the law would be unjust because it required us to say something untrue. (Gallagher 2012, 102)

Just what is Gallagher arguing here? Does she imply, with this argument, that all contemporary Canadians who talk about marriage "say something untrue"? To discern her argument, it will help to make a few distinctions. Words that refer to kinds can pick out natural or social kinds. Social kinds themselves vary in type. Below, I elaborate on such distinctions so that we are better placed to understand and assess this argument from the 'natural meaning' of marriage. Once this argument is dispatched, we can assess any remaining confusions about the limits set on marriage by the meaning of 'marriage.'

2. Natural kind terms and externalist constraints on meaning

Gallagher claims that to require people to call cats 'dogs' would be untrue. What does she mean? We can imagine a language where 'dog' means cat and 'cat' means dog. In this language, to say "cats bark" would be true. There would be nothing untoward about saying this, or in using 'dog' to talk about cats. After all, 'chat' or 'katze' or 'gato' are all equally serviceable to refer to cats, so there is nothing about the word 'cat' itself that is necessary to refer to felines. Of course, the case Gallagher discusses above is slightly different: it is one where 'dog' refers to *both* cats and dogs. It is in this context that Gallagher complains using 'dog' to refer to cats would be "unjust" and "untrue." What Gallagher has in mind is that cats are a *natural kind*.

Gallagher's complaint is that to use the word 'dog' to pick out both cats and dogs would be to falsely assimilate two naturally distinct kinds. To do so would be like referring to both iron pyrites ("fool's gold") and gold as 'gold'; this kind of assimilation combines substances that have different density, atomic structure, reactivity, and natural frequency as if they were really a single type of substance. The fact is that FeS2 and Au are chemically distinct, with significantly different physical properties, whether we humans ever recognized this or not.

When we refer to a natural kind we refer to things that have a relevantly similar essence; it is the microstructure or other essential properties that determine the kind. Again, this is so whether or not these properties are identified and recognized by human beings. This is what Gallagher has in mind when she says it would be "untrue" to require people to say 'dog' to refer to both cats and dogs jointly.

But while dogs or gold are good candidates for being natural kinds (if anything is), surely marriage is not. After all, while gold and dogs could well exist in a world where humans never existed, we could not say the same of marriage. Marriage is a social kind, a human kind.[4]

'Natural meaning' advocates such as Gallagher obviously realize that marriage could not exist without humans, and is therefore ontologically subjective in this sense. And they recognize that civil marriage is a contractual legal status defined in a state's laws. But they also hold that this legal status should reflect what they believe is essentially a natural kind:

> Marriage is not a legal construct with totally malleable contours—not 'just a contract.' Otherwise, how could the law get marriage wrong? Rather, some sexual relationships are instances of a distinctive kind of relationship—call it real marriage—that has its own value and structure, whether the state recognizes it or not, and is not changed by laws based on a false conception of it. Like the relationship between parents and their children, or between the parties to an ordinary promise, real marriages are moral realities that create moral privileges and obligations between people, independently of legal enforcement. . . .
>
> If the state conferred the same status on a man and his two best friends or on a woman and an inanimate object, it would not thereby make them really married. It would merely give the title and (where possible) the benefits of legal marriages to what are not actually marriages at all. . . .
>
> The state is justified in recognizing only real marriages as marriages. (Girgis, George, and Anderson 2010, 250–51)

To Girgis et al., marriage is a social kind routed in a natural order, which marriage law can correctly or incorrectly reflect. In their view, the law could "get marriage wrong." So although marriage could not exist without humans, they clearly find it to nonetheless be a social kind with a reality that does not depend on human recognition for its existence. For such thinkers, marriage has a natural ontological objectivity insofar as it has an essence that is independent of its legal definition by a state. For Girgis et al., to recognize same-sex or minimal marriage arrangements as marriages in law would be like classifying iron pyrites as gold or whales as fish. We could call a whale a 'fish,' but this would obscure its mammalian characteristics—that it breathes air, has lungs, is warm-blooded, gives birth to live young. This is why Girgis et al. say that "real marriage . . . has its own value and structure, whether the state recognizes it or not." They believe that what they call real marriage[5] is the kind we refer to with the word 'marriage.' Changing the law would not change what marriage is or what 'marriage' truly means, for these thinkers. The natural order of things puts constraints on the real meaning of 'marriage,' just as the microstructure of water or gold puts constraints on what we mean by 'water' or 'gold."[6]

Does it make sense to say that a social kind could also be a natural kind, as is required by these arguments? To see whether this is the case, we ought to distinguish different sorts of social kinds. Then we can assess the natural meaning argument and address remaining issues regarding the alleged limits on marriage set by the meaning of 'marriage.'

3. Social kinds

Perhaps the most obvious examples of social kinds are those that are clearly conventional and institutional in nature. John Searle (1995) describes entities whose status as particular kinds depends on collective intentionality to regard them as such: *money, the presidency, driver's licences*. Money, for example, only exists because people regard certain pieces of paper and bits of metal as money. A given bit of metal or paper could of course exist without being regarded by humans at all, and so it could exist without being regarded as money. But for paper or metal to be money, people must collectively conceive of them *as* money. Searle says that such things exist "only because we believe them to exist" (1995, 1). These kinds are "what they are because that is what we believe that they are" (Searle 2007, 4).

Amie Thomasson argues that not all social kinds are of this sort; unlike money or driver's licences, *racism, superstition, recession* are kinds that can have instances without anyone conceiving of them as kinds at all (2003, 606). In response, Khalidi (2013) suggests that we disambiguate three types of social kinds: (1) those social kinds that, like Thomasson's examples of racism, superstition, or recession, may exist without any beliefs about that kind at all; (2) those social kinds, like money, that do not exist but for human attitudes, although, given the kind, particular instances might count as such without any corresponding attitudes; (3) social kinds, like permanent resident, that in type and all particular instances only exist as such due to human attitudes so conceiving of them.[7]

All three categories of social kind are mind-dependent. None of these social kinds would exist without the existence of humans.[8] Categories (2) and (3) show constitutive, not just material, dependence on human attitudes. But this does not mean that we cannot make objective claims about these phenomena:

"There was a recession in 2008," or "That is a counterfeit bill." Nor does it mean that these social kinds might not also be natural kinds, or based in natural kinds. Whether they are will depend on whether their properties are causal and sufficiently independent of convention.[9] Our third category of social kind (social kinds each of whose instances counts as exemplar of the kind only insofar as some humans have the associated attitude—e.g., *this person counts as a permanent resident*) is the least likely candidate for being natural. It is conventionally constituted both in category and in instances. The first category, which could have instances without having ever been conceived of as a kind by any humans ever, seems the most likely candidate for a social kind which is also natural, if indeed any are.

We can now properly see how it is that the proponents of a natural meaning of marriage diverge from opponents. Searle repeatedly used marriage as an example of the kind of status one has only if and only because other humans believe one to have that status. That one is or is not married is an institutional fact; it is a conventional, not a natural status. While Girgis et al. must recognize there is a legal status in Canada that a woman can contractually attain in virtue of marrying another woman, they do not regard this legal status as *real* marriage. For these theorists, marriage cannot be a social kind of type (2) or (3); it must be a type (1) social kind. When we speak about marriage, they think the idea we intend is at bottom natural.[10] They argue that to think otherwise is a misunderstanding, a confusion about our own concept. For such theorists, the true meaning of 'marriage' cannot be as the majority of Canadians and Americans believe, and certainly not as Brake proposes. At bottom, their argument is that we should

not legalize same-sex or minimal marriage, because this is not what marriage *can* mean, grounded as it is in a natural kind that prevents such interpretation.

4. Further questions about the limits of meaning and marriage

If we disagree with these natural meaning theorists about the meaning of marriage, and reject their suggestion that Canadians must misunderstand our own concept, is there anything left to worry or wonder about in regard to what 'marriage' means? What of the conservative worry that legalizing same-sex marriage "changes the meaning of marriage"? Insofar as our society celebrates marriage, conservatives here tap into a worry that we might lose something many in our society value. If marriage law is changed in a country, is marriage changed? Do we now mean something different?

John Corvino cites conservative thinker Robert H. Knight's illustration of the worry:

> When the meaning of a word becomes more inclusive, the exclusivity that it previously defined is lost. For instance, if the state of Hawaii decided to extend the famous—and exclusive—'Maui onion' appellation to all onions grown in Hawaii, the term 'Maui onion' would lose its original meaning as a specific thing. Consumers would lack confidence in buying a bag of 'Maui onions' if all onions could be labeled as such. (Knight, qtd in Corvino 2012, 28–29)

Knight is worried about the loss of 'exclusivity' of marriage to heterosexuals. He suggests there would be an important loss of marriage's "original meaning as a specific thing." In response to the 'Maui onion' comparison, Corvino humorously points out that it is not as if, once same-sex marriage is legalized, "grooms will meet brides at the altar, lift their veils, and exclaim in shock, 'Damn, you're a dude!'" (2012, 29). So why does Knight describe the change as a 'loss'? Characterizing a move away from 'exclusivity' as a 'loss' depends on whose interests are served by exclusivity. When the famous Augusta National Golf Club was finally opened to female members in 2012, membership was thereby more inclusive, less exclusive; this move towards inclusiveness would only be viewed as a loss from a very particular perspective, however. Why, in either of these cases, think of the change to eligibility for membership in a golf club or participation in marriage as a change in meaning at all? When women become eligible for membership at Augusta National, has the meaning of 'member' changed, or merely its permissible range of application? Of course the passage of C-38 in Canada changed the legal definition of marriage to describe a status pertaining to "two persons" rather than a man and a woman, but is the meaning of marriage thereby changed, or just access to the institution?

The answer here depends on how we conceive of the *social meaning* of marriage. While the natural meaning theorists are wrong to think that our concept of marriage is in fact that of a natural kind, they are right to notice that there is an extra-legal meaning to our concept. Our concept of marriage is that of a contractual legal status with attendant responsibilities and benefits, but it [is] also a contract and status with attendant social meaning. Ralph Wedgwood, who has argued that the social meaning of marriage is essential to its core meaning and function, describes it thusly:

> Social meaning consists of certain *generally shared expectations* about the sort of relationship that married couples typically have; these expectations are 'generally shared' in the sense that it is common knowledge that practically everyone expects married couples typically to have a relationship of this sort. These shared understandings and expectations have changed over time. (1999, 229)

Wedgwood expects that the contours of marriage's social meaning can change over time, and he also argues that not every general expectation is essential:

> It is certainly part of the *current* social meaning of the institution that a marriage is assumed to be the union of one man and one woman: if you say 'I'm married,' everyone assumes that you are married to someone of the opposite sex. But, I claim, this assumption is not part of marriage's *essential* social meaning. The fact that marriage is known to be reserved for opposite-sex couples seems much less important for explaining why marriage is so central in people's lives than the fact that marriage is generally expected to involve domestic and economic cooperation, sexual intimacy and a mutual commitment to maintaining the relationship. (1999, 230)

Wedgwood's explication of what is more essential and what is peripheral to our concept of marriage and its social meaning can help explain our conflicting intuitions about how and whether marriage is changed by a change in law like C-38. On Wedgwood's view, our social understanding is updated but the essential meaning is intact.

On the other hand, feminists and race theorists have taught us that it is not only our idealized concepts but their actual shape in practice that is important to what we should call their meaning. Philosopher Charles Mills provocatively argues that a look at American history reveals a history where "all persons are equal, but only white males are persons" (1998, 70). What Mills emphasizes is how the concept of person has actually operated in US history, and that this operative understanding has a claim to characterize our concepts as much as some idealized but non-instantiated version.[11]

Finally, in thinking through questions of what limits, if any, our concept of marriage might set for us as to the shape the institution might take, we should attend to what Sally Haslanger has called the *ameliorative* concept. I've argued that the natural meaning theorists draw on a faulty conception of what marriage already is to tell us what it could be. The fact that marriage does nonetheless have extra-legal meaning shows how there can be continuity in our concept through legal redefinition. But our concept of marriage could survive even through change to what Wedgwood calls the essential social meaning of marriage. How? Haslanger explains the idea of an ameliorative concept as follows: "Ameliorative projects, in contrast, begin by asking: What is the point of having the concept in question; for example, why do we have a concept of knowledge or a concept of belief? What concept (if any) would do the work best?" (2006, 95). These normative questions—what we want and think a particular concept (institution) good for, what does and should justify it—have an important claim to being an essential part of our concepts as well. And they invite the sort of far-reaching questions Elizabeth Brake asks in her essay in this volume. The normative commitments implicit in our concepts, drawn out by ameliorative conceptions, can explain how radically our understanding of marriage might legitimately change, yet still be recognizably our own.

Notes

1   See Brake, this volume, for a discussion of how fear of the alleged 'slippery slope' to bestiality or pedophilia, for example, can hamper discussion and consideration of marriage reform.

2   This anti-Humpty, pro-Alice observation of the socially externalist nature of language is the point of Tyler Burge's well-known 'arthritis' example. Bob has a pain in his thigh and, not understanding that arthritis is a disease of the joints, thinks it could be arthritis. He complains to the doctor, "I have arthritis in my thigh," and thereby makes a false claim about arthritis. The meaning of 'arthritis' in Bob's utterance is not determined solely by his own (mis)understanding of the term; it does not in Bob's utterance mean a disease one could have in one's thigh. Bob means arthritis by 'arthritis' even if he doesn't fully understand the term correctly, even if he has false beliefs about arthritis. See Burge 1979.

3   Here one can't help but think that Claudia Card, a feminist who has argued for abolitionism in regard to marriage in her article "Against Marriage and Motherhood," might have howled with laughter to read the terms Gallagher has picked as comparators: marriage, mother, dog. I wonder whether Gallagher, a champion of traditional heterosexual marriage, notices that these particular terms make for an unfortunate triad?

4   As Khalidi points out, these terms are not necessarily coextensive: "There may be human kinds that are not social (e.g., sickle cell anemia) or social kinds that are not human (e.g.,

dominant male, as applied to macaque monkeys; cf. Ereshefsky 2004)" (2013, 2). But for our purposes this potential divergence is of little consequence.

5   See Girgis, George, and Anderson (2010, 246) for their full definition of what they call 'conjugal marriage,' their understanding of the correct and real conception of marriage. See also George 2000.

6   For the *loci classici* of such arguments concerning the semantics of natural kind terms, see Kripke 1972 and Putnam 1975.

7   To illustrate category (2), Khalidi gives the following example: suppose a ten-dollar bill was printed but then immediately fell unnoticed between some floorboards. This ten-dollar bill would count as money even though no person ever conceived of it as such, no one ever had the appropriate classificatory attitude toward it.

8   Again, note this may be an oversimplification for the reasons alluded to in note 4 above; there may be social kinds that are not human.

9   The existence and understanding of the natural kinds is a matter of considerable philosophical dispute. Contrasting views can be found, for instance in LaPorte 2004 and Dupre 1993. For a helpful overview, see Bird and Tobin 2015.

10 "The demands of our common human nature have shaped (however imperfectly) all of our religious traditions to recognize this natural institution" (Girgis, George, and Anderson 2010, 247).

11 The terminology of *operative* concept is Sally Haslanger's, as is the use of Mills to illustrate the difference between what she calls *operative* versus *manifest* concepts. These both contrast with the *ameliorative* concept, which I discuss in the body of text just following. See Haslanger 2006 for further discussion.

Bibliography

Bill C-38: *An Act Respecting Certain Aspects of Legal Capacity for Marriage for Civil Purposes.* Assented July 20, 2005, 38th Parliament, 1st Session. In *Statutes of Canada.* www.parl.gc.ca/HousePublications/Publication.aspx?Docid=3293341&file=4.

Bird, Alexander, and Emma Tobin. 2015. "Natural Kinds." In *The Stanford Encyclopedia of Philosophy*, Spring 2015 Edition, edited by Edward N. Zalta. Substantive revision published January 27, 2015. http://plato.stanford.edu/archives/spr2015/entries/natural-kinds/.

Burge, Tyler. 1979. "Individualism and the Mental." In *Midwest Studies in Philosophy*, vol. 4, edited by Peter A. French, Theodore E. Uehling Jr., and Howard K. Wettstein, 73–121. Minneapolis: University of Minnesota Press.

Brake, Elizabeth. 2012. *Minimizing Marriage: Marriage, Morality, and the Law.* New York: Oxford University Press.

———. "Marriage for Everybody: What Is Marriage Equality? This volume.

Card, Claudia. 1996. "Against Marriage and Motherhood." *Hypatia* 11 (3): 1–23.

Carroll, Lewis. 1971. *Alice's Adventures in Wonderland and Through the Looking Glass and What Alice Found There*, ed. Roger L. Green. New York: Oxford English Novels.

Corvino, John. 2012. "The Case for Same-Sex Marriage." *Debating Same-Sex Marriage*, by John Corvino and Maggie Gallagher, 4–90. New York: Oxford University Press.

Dupre, J. 1993. *The Disorder of Things: Metaphysical Foundations of the Disunity of Science.* Cambridge, MA: Harvard University Press.

Ereshefsky, M. 2004. "Bridging the Gap between Human Kinds and Biological Kinds." *Philosophy of Science* 71:912–21.

Gallagher, Maggie. 2012. "The Case against Same-Sex Marriage." *Debating Same-Sex Marriage*, by John Corvino and Maggie Gallagher, 91–178. New York: Oxford University Press.

George, Robert P. 2000. "'Same-Sex Marriage' and 'Moral Neutrality.'" In *Homosexuality and American Public Life*, edited by Christopher Wolfe, 141–53. Dallas: Spence Publishing.

Girgis, Sherif, Robert George, and Ryan T. Anderson. 2010. "What Is Marriage?" *Harvard Journal of Law & Public Policy* 34 (1): 245–87.

Haslanger, Sally. 2006. "What Good Are Our Intuitions? Philosophical Analysis and Social Kinds." *Aristotelian Society* Supplementary volume 80 (1): 89–118.

Khalidi, Muhammad Ali. 2013. "Three Kinds of Social Kinds." *Philosophy and Phenomenological Research* 90 (1): 96–112.

Knight, Robert H. 1997. "How Domestic Partnerships and 'Gay Marriage' Threaten the Family." In *Same Sex: Debating the Ethics, Science, and Culture of Homosexuality*, edited by John Covino, 288–302. Lanham, MD: Rowman and Littlefield.

Kripke, Saul. 1972. "Naming and Necessity." In *Semantics of Natural Language*, edited by G. Harman & D. Davidson, 253–355. Dordrecht: Reidel.

LaPorte, Joseph. 2004. *Natural Kinds and Conceptual Change*. Cambridge: Cambridge University Press.

Mills, Charles. 1998. *Blackness Visible: Essays on Philosophy and Race*. Ithaca, NY: Cornell University Press.

Putnam, Hilary. 1975. "The Meaning of 'Meaning.'" *Minnesota Studies in the Philosophy of Science* 7:215–71.

Searle, John. 1995. *The Construction of Social Reality*. New York: Free Press.

———. 2007. "Social Ontology and the Philosophy of Society." In *Creations of the Mind*, edited by Eric Margolis and Stephen Laurence, 3–17. New York: Oxford University Press.

Thomasson, Amie. 2003. "Realism and Human Kinds." *Philosophy and Phenomenological Research* 67:580–609.

Ventrella, Jeffrey. 2005. "Square Circles?!! Restoring Rationality to the Same-Sex 'Marriage' Debate." *Hastings Constitutional Law Quarterly* 32:681–724.

Wedgwood, Ralph. 1999. "The Fundamental Argument for Same-Sex Marriage." *Journal of Political Philosophy* 7 (3): 225–42.

ELIZABETH BRAKE

As Elizabeth Brake tells us in her article, many people have called for the abolition of marriage or at least the abolition of state-sanctioned marriage, arguing that it has been oppressive to women as well as sexual minorities. Since the institution of marriage has strong historical ties with religion, the disestablishment of marriage would seem consistent with the idea of a liberal state. The aim of a liberal state is to be neutral on matters such as religion and to allow citizens to pursue their own conception of the good in a context of freedom and tolerance. But Brake's own proposal aims at social and political equality not by getting rid of state-sponsored marriage but rather by making it and its benefits available to everyone. The idea here is that everyone should have access to the state-sanctioned benefits of marriage by way of their closest relationships (even if we do not call the union marriage).

More specifically, since marriage is meant to establish a legal foundation for caregiving, then any primary relationship that serves this function should be considered (potentially, at least) eligible for the state benefits associated with marriage. Her concept of "minimal marriage" covers relationships such as those between close friends, groups of friends, polyamorous lovers, and more.

Marriage for Everybody: What Is Marriage Equality?

Debates over same-sex marriage often ignore an underlying question. Before we can answer questions such as same-sex marriage—or not?, polygamy—or not?, temporary marriage—or not?, we must first answer a more fundamental question: marriage—or not? That is, should there be a law of marriage at all?

A number of philosophers, law professors, and political theorists have argued that the state should simply leave marriage to the churches, or Las Vegas chapels, or backyard ceremonies. Marriage, they argue, is essentially a social and religious institution in which the state should not be involved any more than it should be involved in baptisms or bar mitzvahs (see Garrett 2009; Metz 2010). Like religion, it should be *disestablished* in a liberal society. (Some also argue that disestablishment would be a good strategy for disarming debate over same-sex marriage (see Sunstein and Thaler 2008); they suggest, as a compromise position, that legal marriage be replaced with a civil union status for everyone.)

Some go further and argue that marriage is oppressive—a heterosexual and sexist norm that harms women and sexual minorities (see Card 1996; Chambers 2013). They point to harms such as domestic violence and economic dependency within marriage, as well as invidious stereotypes targeting the unmarried and their children. And they argue that marriage

law recognizes only one type of the plethora of human relationships, forcing the variety of possible sex and love relationships into a narrow monogamous model.

Against these marriage disestablishers and "abolitionists," I argue that the state should be involved in marriage, or marriage-like legal structures. Precisely because caring relationships are so important, the state should be involved in supporting them—all of them, on an equal basis. It should be involved in supporting the full range of caring relationships, including small polyamorous groups, friendships and networks of friends, and, within certain important constraints, polygamy or group marriage.

To be clear, this proposal concerns marriage law. As it exists now in Canada and the United States, for example, marriage law recognizes certain marriages with certain legal entitlements and obligations. The question I am addressing is what the law of marriage should be—not how different religions should understand it (religious freedom protects their rights to define it as they see fit) nor about what society should recognize as marriage and how it should treat it (again, this is often a matter for individual decisions). This is a proposal about what a state that values both liberty and equality should recognize as marriage.

I call this proposal, which I argue for in my book *Minimizing Marriage*, "minimal marriage." The arguments draw on the liberty and equality concerns of disestablishers and abolitionists. I argue that there is no valid basis for the liberal state to distinguish between different caring relationships: different-sex or same-sex, groups of two or three or four, friendships, or romantic love relationships. Polyamory and friendships deserve treatment on a par with dyadic monogamous romantic love relationships. But I also provided a reason why liberal states should recognize marriage (or something like it) in law. The central thought was that caring relationships are important political goods of the kind the state should support and protect, and that marriage-like legal frameworks provide such support and protection. This proposal raises many questions, theoretical and practical. First, let's consider two cases.

1. Case Studies

In 2012, the 73-year-old American companion of an 83-year-old Canadian woman was deported from Canada despite their longstanding relationship of 30 years: "She and her friend of three decades, Ms. Sanford, 83, are inseparable. In addition, Ms. Sanford suffers from a heart condition and dementia and Ms. Inferrera looks after her" (Taber 2012). The American woman had been refused permanent residency in Canada in spite of numerous appeals, even though she performs extensive caregiving for her friend. The two women are not romantically involved—in fact, if they were lesbians, they could have legally married in Canada. But they are "just friends." As such, their relationship, no matter how longterm or how caring, received no legal protection. (In a happy turn of events, the Canadian government relented once the women's plight was publicized.) This lack of legal recognition seems arbitrary in multiple ways: had they been

romantically involved or identified as lesbians, they would have been eligible for the extensive protections of marriage. Moreover, their 30-year, mutually caring relationship lasted longer than many marriages. If the purpose of marriage is to promote and protect caregiving, why should these women be excluded from its protections?

Arguments for same-sex marriage often invoke similar sad cases, where longstanding relationships are ignored in contexts such as immigration, hospital and prison visitation rights, inheritance, bereavement and caretaking leave, tax status, spousal relocation, and eligibility for third-party benefits such as health insurance or spousal preferential hiring. Defenders of same-sex marriage argue that same-sex relationships deserve these protections as much as different-sex relationships do. But, adopting the same reasoning, one can ask why a relationship should lack legal recognition because its members are "merely" friends—even friends, as in the Canadian case, who have cohabited for three decades and take care of one another. Such a friendship serves one of the primary purposes of marriage—mutual longterm caretaking and companionship. As such, it deserves legal protections similar to those in marriage.

Let's consider another case that I describe in my book. This case is imaginary, but many people live in similar arrangements. As recent U.S. Census data indicate, the percentage of married two-parent families has decreased steeply over the past few decades as other living arrangements have increased (Vespa, Lewis, and Kreider 2013; see Cagen 2006; Watters 2003). Extended family members or friends live together to lower costs, and some single mothers are opting to cohabit to share resources.

Imagine two people, Rose and Octavian, living together in a non-traditional way. They share household expenses, and, while they do not intend to have a permanent relationship, they have bought property together, share homeowner and car insurance, and a bank account for shared expenses. They foresee that a future work transfer will limit their relationship—one will move, the other will not—but they agree to cohabit until then, sharing the burdens and benefits of domesticity.

Notice that we have said nothing about the kind of relationship they have. Such a couple might be "mere" friends, with no romantic or sexual involvement. Both could be dating—or in long-term relationships with—other people, in same-sex or different-sex relationships. They might be polyamorous, involved in multiple love and sex relationships at the same time. Rose might be close to an ex-partner, with whom she is involved in co-parenting. Whatever their sexual and romantic relationships, they might also have other close friends or family members who are not part of their household.[1]

Many readers will recognize people they know in this imaginary case. Not everyone's lives conform to the dyadic, monogamous, amorous relationship that marriage law recognizes. Those living outside such relationships are not eligible for the many supports and protections which legal marriage provides. This, I argue, is an injustice.

My contention is that these relationships lack the important protections and supports that marriage provides. These include those listed above. One category of rights protects relationships by ensuring that people can spend time together—such as special immigration eligibility, caretaking leave, spousal relocation policies, visitation rights, and access to marital housing. A second category recognizes the relationship, allowing people to express its value socially: these would include bereavement leave and rights to burial together in a veterans' cemetery. A third category provides eligibility for financial and other benefits that recognize financial interdependence: these might include eligibility for health insurance (employers often subsidize spousal health insurance), pensions, untaxed transfers of property or special tax status, and even "family rates" at tourist attractions, clubs, and gyms.

Before proceeding, I should address the threat of the "slippery slope" argument. Opponents of same-sex marriage have famously commented that once same-sex marriage is recognized, we will be on a slippery slope to recognizing other, undesirable, relationships.[2] The invocation of bestiality, pedophilia, or oppressive polygyny, however, is absurd. There is no reason that recognizing same-sex marriage would lead to countenancing criminal acts (marriage with children), impossible contracts (with non-human animals), or oppressive communities. To repeat, marriage is a legal contract, one that children and animals could not enter into, and there is no reason that extending marriage law would force a change in criminal law or rethinking the weighty reasons for prohibiting adult–child sex. Furthermore, although I argue for extending rights to small groups, such rights can be conditional on spouses having free choice of entry and exit.[3]

The political pressure to pre-empt such absurd charges has too often prevented discussion of same-sex marriage from proceeding to examine why, exactly, equal rights for personal relationships should stop with amorous same-sex couples. Indeed, the same principles of equal treatment and non-discrimination that call for recognizing same-sex marriage also imply that some other non-traditional relationships deserve legal recognition and support as well. While it might be confusing to label such relationships "marriage"—after all, Ms. Sanford and Ms. Inferrera, who could have legally married in Canada, presumably do not consider themselves married—such relationships deserve equal access to the many rights, accessible exclusively in marriage or kinship, that protect relationships.

2. Equality and the Purpose of Marriage

Marriage law should be guided by the purpose or function of the institution. This purpose or function will affect equality arguments. For example, some have held that the unique good of marriage is biological procreation, and such a purpose would obviously circumscribe equality arguments: only those capable of biological procreation within marriage should be treated equally by marriage law (just as, for example, only those capable of driving should be treated equally by drivers licensing laws) (Finnis 2008). However, as has often been noted, a problem with this line of argument is that legal marriage actually serves many other functions. Marrying couples are not tested for fertility or precluded from marriage if they do not intend to have children. Marriage serves other goods, such as protecting loving relationships and signalling their importance socially and to third-party benefit providers (such as employers).

The argument for same-sex marriage draws on this function of protecting loving relationships. As same-sex relationships can be just as committed, loving, intimate, and so on as different-sex relationships, the state has no reason to treat them differently. If the function of marriage is to recognize such relationships, then all loving relationships should have access to

this recognition, regardless of the sex of the partners. Same-sex marriage is thus required as a matter of equal treatment.[4]

The question raised by abolitionists in the marriage debate is why the state should be involved in protecting such relationships at all. Insofar as marriage confers a privileged status, they argue, everyone would be treated equally only by eliminating legal marriage. So far as marriage is essentially a religious or ethical ideal, the state is favouring one particular ideal of the good life by favouring marriage-type relationships with its recognition. But a central tenet of contemporary political liberalism is that the state has no business arbitrating between different ideals of the good life, any more than it does between competing religions. State support for one established form of marriage is like state support for an established religion, on this view.[5] At its extreme, this view tends toward privatizing marriage, relegating arrangements between spouses to existing private contract law.

According to the contemporary ideal of a politically liberal state, in important matters law should be justifiable to citizens in terms they could endorse from their diverse religious, philosophical, and ethical backgrounds. The ideal requires not that everyone agree with every law and policy—an impossible standard—but that public political reasons, reasons that don't rely on a narrow and contested view of the good, can be given for law. On this standard, it is not acceptable to restrict marriage on the basis of a particular religious view, but more general political values can be appealed to, such as women's equality or child welfare (see Rawls 1997, esp. 765–807, 787–91).

However, children's welfare does not give strong enough reason to justify privileging marriage with exclusive and substantial entitlements. Child welfare—especially that of children outside marriage—can be promoted in other ways, and not all marriages involve children. Likewise, feminists have argued that marriage does not protect women's equality (see Brake 2012; Card 1996; Chambers 2013). If this is correct, what political value could justify marriage law?

I have argued that the good of caring relationships is what provides political reason for marriage law. The best reason for state support of marriage is that long-term caring relationships are themselves a widely shared good, one that transcends religious and ethical differences. Most plans of life involve such relationships as central goods. And caring relationships are good for us, psychologically and, when parties take care of one another, materially. (I distinguish material caregiving from caring relationships. The two can, of course, be combined. By "caring relationships," I mean only attitudinally caring relationships, defined by mutual concern with the other's welfare.) This good is so widespread, so normally a part of pursuing a life, that it is the kind of shared political value that can justify law and policy within political liberalism.

Whether or not the legal nomenclature of marriage is apt, there are reasons that intimate caring relationships should have legal supports. It might be thought that long-term caring relationships need no special support or recognition. But in an array of contexts, such as immigration, caring relationships need state protection to enable the parties to continue playing key roles in each other's lives. Some such entitlements are currently only available through marriage, and while others can be contracted independently, this involves lawyer's fees far in excess of the cost

of the marriage licence. Abolishing the conflicted term "marriage" as a legal status may be the best way to treat everyone equally, without drawing hierarchical distinctions between relationships. But abolishing marriage-like entitlements would leave caring relationships unprotected.

So how far do arguments for same-sex marriage lead down the slippery slope? They imply that friends and small groups should have equivalent legal benefits. What conservative critics have right is that the fundamental arguments for same-sex marriage do imply that other neglected constituencies also deserve some marriage-like entitlements. This would include seniors cohabiting for companionship and support, single mothers who co-parent, or close friends who build a life together. The central state interest in marriage is to support such long-term caring relationships; the fact that people are "merely" friends—and not sexually or romantically involved—does not diminish their ability to engage in mutual long-term care. All caring relationships equally deserve support, regardless of their romantic or sexual affiliation.

Like the argument for same-sex marriage, this is an equality argument. From the state's point of view, what can justify differential treatment of "mere" friends and romantic lovers? Friends, as the case of Ms. Inferrera and Ms. Sanford shows, can have longer and more committed and caring relationships than some romantic lovers or married people. While I argued that caring relationships are a widely shared good, such relationships are much broader than romantic love. Some percentage of the population is asexual; some people do not seek marriage-like relationships or simply do not end up in one. The good of caring relationships is far more widespread than the good of monogamous romantic love coupledom.

Furthermore—and less comfortably, for many—this same equality argument applies to small groups of friends, or adult care networks, whose members provide one another with long-term care and companionship. This also includes polyamorous groups characterized by mutual care (a requirement that sets limits on the size of the group). Once again, what is pertinent is the existence of a mutual long-term caring relationship. The goods of care that the state rightly promotes in marriage can be found equally in these other forms of relationship. Whether the relationships are platonic or romantic is beyond the remit of a liberal state's concern. Similarly, whether they are between two or three or four people should not make a difference from the state's point of view. (However, whether they respect the rights of all parties and have adequate exit options gives reason to rule out some forms of polygamy.) As I will explain in the next section, there may be practical reasons not to pursue recognizing these as group *marriages*, but they do deserve the same legal rights and protection as other caring relationships.

Marriage law, like the wider culture, privileges sexual, romantic partnerships far above the many other forms of relationship in which lives unfurl, such as long-term friendships and care networks. But significant caretaking can occur in platonic friendships, as much as in marriages; and mutual caretaking can occur between three as well as between two. The demographic shift away from marriage corresponds with a shift into other ways of arranging intimate life. The principles of equal treatment that require recognizing same-sex marriage also require extending marriage-like protections to other long-term caring relationships,

since the best rationale for state involvement in marriage is supporting such relationships.

3. Feasibility: How Would It Work in Practice?

Such a policy may seem wildly unlikely to be implemented, particularly in a country such as the United States where even same-sex marriage has sparked considerable controversy. Even if it were to be legally implemented, there are practical questions as to how minimal marriage could be legislated: marriage as a legal status runs through so many areas of law that revising and extending its entitlements and obligations, "minimizing" it, is unthinkable to many lawyers. Group marriage raises special problems with evidentiary privilege, tax status, and benefits.[6] For example, would a spouse's immunity from being compelled to testify against her spouse apply to all spouses in a group marriage?

However, law and public opinion can change relatively rapidly, as happened with same-sex marriage. In the conservative state of Utah, for instance, "between 2004 and 2012, the percentage of . . . voters who opposed any legal recognition of same-sex relationships had slid from 54 percent to 29 percent" (Saletan 2014). The first US state, Massachusetts, recognized same-sex marriage in 2004; it took only eleven years for the US Supreme Court to rule, in 2015's *Obergefell v. Hodges*, that all fifty states must recognize it.

It is true, nevertheless, that expecting public opinion to shift towards approving of polyamory and polygamy, or recognizing friendships as equivalent to marriages, is a stretch: the case for same-sex marriage relied heavily on the conservative analogy with "traditional" marriage. Still, the state can distribute the social bases of caring relationships more fairly than it does currently, while negotiating public opinion and feasibility.

For one thing, the state could implement adult interdependent partnership models, or civil unions, which do not require sexual consummation or expect a monogamous romantic relationship. The Canadian province of Alberta has such a law, permitting two people with any kind of interdependent relationship—"platonic" friends, extended family, caregiver and cared-for—to access many of the entitlements of marriage after three years of cohabitation. This legislation, in a conservative province, seems to have attracted no controversy or concerns about abuse. Why? Because it avoids the term "marriage" and broadens entitlements to non-sexual caregiving relationships, which does not provoke the same opposition as same-sex marriage. Such laws would protect friends like Ms. Inferrera and Ms. Sanford, or Rose and Octavian. Such laws, while less controversial than other reforms, would still limit entry to only two people.

Recognizing group marriage poses greater challenges for legislation than does recognizing dyads, and not just due to controversy. It raises thorny legal problems such as how to handle evidentiary privilege, tax status, or special immigration eligibility. But a first step would be decriminalizing bigamous cohabitation, in jurisdictions where it is prohibited. Polygyny in small communities poses special challenges of harms to women and children, although advocates for recognition argue that recognizing it would actually protect women (Goldfeder 2013). However, in the cases of consensual relationships between adults, criminalization is inappropriate. While literature on the polyamorous is scarce, a first study tracing 22 children in polyamorous families over 15 years finds no harms to children reared in such families (Sheff 2013).

Another small step with potentially huge effects would be non-discrimination protections on the basis of family, a high priority for polyamorists: "in one survey, polyamorists identified 'employment nondiscrimination as one of their three highest priority legal issues'" (Emens cited in Tweedy 2011, 1489–90). (Non-discrimination rules could also apply to singles, who also face employment discrimination [DePaulo 2006].) Indeed, polyamorists do not clamour for group marriage rights; in a survey, they preferred them only "if something more radical—like the abolition of marriage—is unavailable." Among those surveyed, their "three highest priority legal issues . . . were: medical rights for poly partners; nondiscrimination in employment, and zoning which allows for non-related people to live together'" (Emens 2004, n415).[7] Employment and zoning non-discrimination would allow people to live openly in the caring relationships they already have, and, again, would likely be less controversial and easier to implement than marriage rights. This also applies to child custody. Children should not be removed from otherwise adequate parents simply because the parents are polyamorous.[8]

These incremental measures towards greater inclusivity would sustain and protect existing caring relationships. Such measures could also increase social justice in other ways. By reshaping how we think about relationships, same-sex marriage and friendship or group "marriages" (legally recognized and protected statuses) could eventually reshape the gender-structured division of labour within marriage, bringing us closer to gender equality. In the near term, domestic partnership laws such as Alberta's could help broaden recognition that caregiving need not always be done by those related by blood or marriage, that "family" (understood as a structure to provide care) can take many forms.

Still, these measures do not help those without relationships. Those lacking care might simply be thought unlucky, and hence their plight might be thought not an issue of justice. However, insofar as care is a politically important good, the state's failure to ensure the fair distribution of access to it is a matter of justice (Brake 2015). This includes elderly citizens or those who cannot leave their homes without assistance. And, increasingly, it includes lower-income citizens. "The other marriage inequality" is the marriage gap between better- and worse-off members of society: wealthier and college-educated people tend to marry at higher rates, and to pass on their advantages to offspring (McClain 2013). Arguably, this gap in part reflects the difficulty of forging a relationship or starting a family for people unable to access adequate housing or job stability. A proposal to distribute care more fairly will address those who lack the means to access or engage in caring relationships.

Notes

1 This case is described in detail in Brake 2012, 166.
2 Rick Santorum, former US senator, is one example, according to news reports.
3 See Brake 2014 and Calhoun 2005 for more on this.
4 See Rajczi 2008 and Wedgwood 1999 for two versions of this argument.
5 See Metz 2010 and Brake 2012, part 2, for more detailed explanations of this view.
6 Thanks to Elizabeth Emens and Rebecca Tsosie, among others, for drawing my attention to these difficulties.
7 For more on polyamory, see Brake 2014.
8 See Emens 2004, 310, 312, for discussion of such a case.

Bibliography

Brake, Elizabeth. 2012. *Minimizing Marriage: Marriage, Morality, and the Law.* New York: Oxford University Press.

———. 2014. "Recognizing Care: The Case for Friendship and Polyamory." *Syracuse Law and Civic Engagement Journal* 1. http://slace.syr.edu/.

———. 2015. "Just Care: What Society Owes the Elderly." *Philosop-her* blog, January 16, 2015. http://politicalphilosopher.net/.

Cagen, Sasha. 2006. *Quirkyalone.* New York: Harper Collins.

Calhoun, Cheshire. 2005. "Who's Afraid of Polygamous Marriage? Lessons for Same-Sex Marriage Advocacy from the History of Polygamy." *San Diego Law Review* 42:1023–42.

Card, Claudia. 1996. "Against Marriage and Motherhood." *Hypatia* 11 (3): 1–23.

Chambers, Clare. 2013. "The Marriage-Free State." *Proceedings of the Aristotelian Society* 113 (2): 123–43.

DePaulo, Bella. 2006. *Singled Out: How Singles Are Stereotyped, Stigmatized, and Ignored, and Still Live Happily Ever After.* New York: St. Martin's Press.

Emens, Elizabeth F. 2004. "Monogamy's Law: Compulsory Monogamy and Polyamorous

Existence." *New York University Review of Law and Social Change* 29:277–376.

Finnis, John. 2008. "Marriage: A Basic and Exigent Good." *The Monist* 91:388–406.

Garrett, Jeremy. 2009. "Marriage Unhitched from the State: A Defense." *Public Affairs Quarterly* 23 (2): 161–80.

Goldfeder, Mark. 2013. "It's Time to Reconsider Polygamy." *CNN Opinion*, December 16. http://www.cnn.com/2013/12/16/opinion/goldfeder-polygamy-laws/index.html?hpt=op_t1.

Hartley, Christie, and Lori Watson. 2012. "Political Liberalism, Marriage and the Family." *Law and Philosophy* 31 (2): 185–212.

McClain, Linda C. 2013. "The Other Marriage Equality Problem." *Boston University Law Review* 93 (3): 921–70.

Metz, Tamara. 2010. *Untying the Knot: Marriage, the State, and the Case for their Divorce.* Princeton: Princeton University Press.

Rajczi, Alex. 2008. "A Populist Argument for Same-Sex Marriage." *The Monist* 91 (3/4): 475–505.

Rawls, John. 1997. "The Idea of Public Reason Revisited." *The University of Chicago Law Review* 64 (3): 765–807.

Saletan, William. 2014. "Utah and Gay Marriage: A Courtship." *Slate.com*, January 17. http://www. slate.com/blogs/saletan/2014/01/17/utah_gay_marriage_polls_are_civil_unions_the_path_to_same_sex_marriage.html.

Sheff, Elisabeth. 2013. *The Polyamorists Next Door: Inside Multiple-Partner Relationships and Families.* Lanham, MD: Rowman and Littlefield.

Sunstein, Cass, and Richard Thaler. 2008. "Privatizing Marriage." *The Monist* 91 (3/4): 377–87.

Taber, Jane. 2012. "Elderly American Caregiver Being Deported Has Been Granted Temporary Visa." *Globe and Mail*, November 15. http://www.theglobeandmail.com/news/national/elderly-american-caregiver-of-elderly-canadian-deported-to-us/article5328771/.

Tweedy, Ann. 2011. "Polyamory As a Sexual Orientation." *University of Cincinnati Law Review* 79:1461–1515.

Vespa, Jonathan, Jamie M. Lewis, and Rose M. Kreider. 2013. "America's Families and Living Arrangements: 2012." U.S. Census Bureau. http://www.census.gov/prod/2013pubs/p20-570.pdf.

Watters, Ethan. 2003. *Urban Tribes: Are Friends the New Family?* New York: Bloomsbury.

Wedgwood, Ralph. 1999. "The Fundamental Argument for Same-Sex Marriage." *Journal of Political Philosophy* 7 (3): 225–42.

Discussion

Is there something *natural* about marriage understood as a union between a man and a woman? Does the possibility of procreation make this a natural union? Does the fact that many people marry without having children give us reason to doubt the procreation argument for the naturalness of marriage? Jill Rusin distinguishes between *social* kinds and *natural* kinds. What is the difference between the two? Natural kinds, we are told, refer to things that share the kind of properties that make them the kind of thing that they are. In other words, certain things are defined according to their essential properties or their (similar at least) essence. A tree is an example of a natural kind since for a thing to qualify as being a tree it needs to possess certain *essential* properties such as roots, branches, a trunk, and so on. Social kinds, on the other hand, refer to things that are defined according to convention. A student ID card and its accompanying ID number for instance, only derives its meaning and function from the role it plays within the institution of a university. It has no meaning outside of that institution (except perhaps on student discount days at Shopper's Drug Mart). The question, then, is whether marriage is a natural kind due to its association with the natural act of procreation and child rearing, or a social kind, due to the fact that churches and states have created the rules, ceremonies, and limits of the institution.

What does Elizabeth Brake mean precisely by the term "minimal marriage"? Why does she defend such a concept? What would be some benefits of extending the concept of marriage in the way that she does? Is what she is talking about really *marriage* or does it warrant a different name? How feasible do you think it would be to implement her notion of marriage in our society? What would be some of the obstacles?

Think, for instance, of what it would mean to extend marriage along with its benefits to relationships between people who are simply friends or roommates but who rely on one another in different ways. Often people live together to make life more affordable. They share the cost of rent, utilities, and perhaps even food. They may even share a car, or perhaps one of them looks after the other's child or pet from time to time. These people may not choose to *marry* in the traditional sense of the term, but does that mean they should not be entitled to the kinds of benefits that other types of co-dependent relationships have a right to? If they support each other and provide some degree of care for each other, then are they not fulfilling one of the key functions of marriage? Do you think that the American woman Ms. Inferrera who looked after her Canadian friend Ms. Sanford should have been allowed to stay in Canada? Do you think that she should have received the same kind of benefits that a partner in a traditional marriage receives as a consequence of being in that relationship? As Brake tells us, if they had been in a lesbian relationship, they would have been able to marry and receive those benefits. Why must the relationship be of a romantic or sexual nature?

Suggestions for Further Reading

Elizabeth Brake, *Minimizing Marriage: Marriage, Morality, and the Law* (Toronto: Oxford University Press, 2012).

Elizabeth Brake, "Recognizing Care: The Case for Friendship and Polyamory," *Syracuse Law and Civic Engagement Journal* 1 (2014). http://slace.syr.edu/.

Cheshire Calhoun, "Who's Afraid of Polygamous Marriage? Lessons for Same-Sex Marriage Advocacy from the History of Polygamy," *San Diego Law Review* 42 (2005): 1023–42.

Claudia Card, "Against Marriage and Motherhood," *Hypatia* 11, no. 3 (1996): 1–23.

Cass Sunstein and Richard Thaler, "Privatizing Marriage," *The Monist* 91, nos. 3/4 (2008): 377–87.

Section VII Friendship

Chapter Sixteen
What Is Friendship?

Introduction

If you were asked *who* your real friends are you would probably be able to give a fairly confident answer. But if you were asked *what* constitutes real friendship, you might need to think about this for a while. Over two millenia ago, Aristotle contemplated this latter question and explored the role of friendships in our lives. Aristotle thought that there were friendships based on usefulness, friendships based on pleasure, and friendships based on the friend's good character. Only the third of these is friendship in the truest sense. Even today we might recognize something like his three types of friendship in some of the relationships we have with other people. There are those people who we call our *real* friends and with whom we spend a lot of time and are closely involved in their lives. On the other hand, there are people with whom we have good relations, but our interaction is more that of co-workers, teammates, classmates, or perhaps only Facebook friends. What is it that makes a person one's *true* friend?

ARISTOTLE

How do you know when someone is your friend? Friendship, as Aristotle tells us, seems to require that not only both people think well of each other but also that they know that the other person feels this way. How is friendship possible between people who are quite different from one another? Can or should friendships last if one of the friends has changed significantly? Is self-love compatible with friendship? What does this mean? Must one have friends to be happy? These are some of the questions that Aristotle raises in these readings from his *Nicomachean Ethics*, books VIII and IX.

Think about your current friendships. In what ways are you and your friends alike? In what ways are you different? Think about some of the friendships that you once had but that no longer exist. What changes took place in your life or in the life of your friend that caused the friendship to end? Sometimes, when one friend moves to a different city, province, or country, the friendship fades over time. At other times, what one finds important or interesting changes as a result of one's studies, life experiences, new friendships, and so on. When you meet the person who was once a close friend you no longer have much to talk about. Of course, there are also those cases where friendship ends due to a falling out. Two people get mad at each other based on a disagreement, a misunderstanding, a betrayal, or a build-up of annoying or hurtful incidents. Some friendships, the ones we regard as genuine, seem to survive distance, change, disagreements, and misunderstandings.

Friendship

Book VIII

1. After what we have said, a discussion of friendship would naturally follow, since it is an excellence or implies excellence, and is besides most necessary with a view to living. For without friends no one would choose to live, though he had all other goods; even rich men and those in possession of office and of dominating power are thought to need friends most of all; for what is the use of such prosperity without the opportunity of beneficence, which is exercised chiefly and in its most laudable form towards friends? Or how can prosperity be guarded and preserved without friends? The greater it is, the more exposed is it to risk. And in poverty and in other misfortunes men think friends are the only refuge. It helps the young, too, to keep from error; it aids older people by ministering to their needs and supplementing the activities that are failing from weakness; those in the prime of life it stimulates to noble actions—"two going together"—for with friends men are more able both to think and to act. Again, parent seems by nature to feel it for offspring and offspring for parent, not only among men but among birds and among most animals; it is felt mutually by members of the same race, and especially by men, whence we praise lovers of their fellow men. We may see even in our travels how near and dear every man is to every other. Friendship seems too to hold states together, and lawgivers to care more for it than for justice; for unanimity seems to be something like friendship, and this they aim at most of all, and expel faction as their worst enemy; and when men are friends they have no need of justice, while when they are just they need friendship as well, and the truest form of justice is thought to be a friendly quality.

But it is not only necessary but also noble; for we praise those who love their friends, and it is thought to be a fine thing to have many friends; and again we think it is the same people that are good men and are friends.

Not a few things about friendship are matters of debate. Some define it as a kind of likeness and say like people are friends, whence come the sayings "like to like," "birds of a feather flock together," and so on; others on the contrary say "two of a trade never agree." On this very question they inquire more deeply and in a more scientific fashion, Euripides saying that "parched earth loves the rain, and stately heaven when filled with rain loves to fall to earth," and Heraclitus that "it is what opposes that helps" and "from different tones comes the fairest tune" and "all things are produced through strife"; while Empedocles, as well as others, expresses the opposite view that like aims at like. The scientific problems we may leave alone (for they do not belong to the present inquiry); let us examine those which are human and involve character and feeling, e.g., whether friendship can arise between any two people or people cannot be friends if they are wicked, and whether there is one species of friendship or more than one. Those who think there is only one because it admits of degrees have relied on an inadequate indication; for even things different in species admit of degree. We have discussed this matter previously.

2. The kinds of friendship may perhaps be cleared up if we first come to know the object of love. For not everything seems to be loved but only the lovable, and this is good, pleasant, or useful; but it would seem to be that by which some good or pleasure is produced that is useful, so that it is the good and the pleasant that are lovable as ends. Do men love, then, *the* good, or what is good for *them*? These sometimes clash. So too with regard to the pleasant. Now it is thought that each loves what is good for himself, and that the good is without qualification lovable, and what is good for each man is lovable for him; but each man loves not what is good for him but what seems good. This however will make no difference; we shall just have to say that this is that which seems lovable. Now there are three grounds on which people love; of the love of lifeless objects we do not use the word "friendship"; for it is not mutual love, nor is there a wishing of good to the other (for it would surely be ridiculous to wish wine well; if one wishes anything for it, it is that it may keep, so that one may have it oneself);

but to a friend we say we ought to wish what is good for his sake. But to those who thus wish good we ascribe only goodwill, if the wish is not reciprocated; goodwill when it is reciprocal being friendship. Or must we add "when it is recognized"? For many people have goodwill to those whom they have not seen but judge to be good or useful; and one of these might return this feeling. These people seem to bear goodwill to each other; but how could one call them friends when they do not know their mutual feelings? To be friends, then, they must be mutually recognized as bearing goodwill and wishing well to each other for one of the aforesaid reasons.

3. Now these reasons differ from each other in kind; so therefore, do the corresponding forms of love and friendship. There are therefore three kinds of friendship, equal in number to the things that are lovable; for with respect to each there is a mutual and recognized love, and those who love each other wish well to each other in that respect in which they love one another. Now those who love each other for their utility do not love each other for themselves but in virtue of some good which they get from each other. So too with those who love for the sake of pleasure; it is not for their character that men love ready-witted people, but because they find them pleasant. Therefore those who love for the sake of utility love for the sake of what is good for *themselves*, and those who love for the sake of pleasure do so for the sake of what is pleasant to *themselves*, and not in so far as the other is the person loved but in so far as he is useful or pleasant. And thus these friendships are only incidental; for it is not as being the man he is that the loved person is loved, but as providing some good or pleasure. Such friendships, then, are easily dissolved, if the parties do not remain like themselves; for if the one party is no longer pleasant or useful the other ceases to love him.

Now the useful is not permanent but is always changing. Thus when the motive of the friendship is done away, the friendship is dissolved, inasmuch as it existed only for the ends in question. This kind of friendship seems to exist chiefly between old people (for at that age people pursue not the pleasant but the useful) and, of those who are in their prime or young, between those who pursue utility. And such people do not live much with each other either; for sometimes they do not even find each other pleasant; therefore they do not need such companionship unless they are useful to each other; for they are pleasant to each other only in so far as they rouse in each other hopes of something good to come. Among such friendships people also class the friendship of host and guest. On the other hand the friendship of young people seems to aim at pleasure; for they live under the guidance of emotion, and pursue above all what is pleasant to themselves and what is immediately before them; but with increasing age their pleasures become different. This is why they quickly become friends and quickly cease to be so; their friendship changes with the object that is found pleasant, and such pleasure alters quickly. Young people are amorous too; for the greater part of the friendship of love depends on emotion and aims at pleasure; this is why they fall in love and quickly fall out of love, changing often within a single day. But these people do wish to spend their days and lives together; for it is thus that they attain the purpose of their friendship.

Perfect friendship is the friendship of men who are good and alike in excellence; for these wish well alike to each other *qua* good, and they are good in themselves. Now those

who wish well to their friends for their sake are most truly friends; for they do this by reason of their own nature and not incidentally; therefore their friendship lasts as long as they are good—and excellence is an enduring thing. And each is good without qualification and to his friend, for the good are both good without qualification and useful to each other. So too they are pleasant; for the good are pleasant both without qualification and to each other, since to each his own activities and others like them are pleasurable, and the actions of the good *are* the same or like. And such a friendship is as might be expected lasting since there meet in it all the qualities that friends should have. For all friendship is for the sake of good or of pleasure—good or pleasure either in the abstract or such as will be enjoyed by him who has the friendly feeling—and is based on a certain resemblance; and to a friendship of good men all the qualities we have named belong in virtue of the nature of the friends themselves; for in the case of this kind of friendship the other qualities also are alike in both friends, and that which is good without qualification is also without qualification pleasant, and these are the most lovable qualities. Love and friendship therefore are found most and in their best form between such men.

But it is natural that such friendships should be infrequent; for such men are rare. Further, such friendship requires time and familiarity; as the proverb says, men cannot know each other till they have "eaten salt together"; nor can they admit each other to friendship or be friends till each has been found lovable and been trusted by each. Those who quickly show the marks of friendship to each other wish to be friends, but are not friends unless they both are lovable and know the fact; for a wish for friendship may arise quickly, but friendship does not.

4. This kind of friendship, then is complete both in respect of duration and in all other respects, and in it each gets from each in all respects the same as, or something like what, he gives; which is what ought to happen between friends. Friendship for the sake of pleasure bears a resemblance to this kind; for good people too are pleasant to each other. So too does friendship for the sake of utility; for the good are also useful to each other. Among men of these sorts too, friendships are most permanent when the friends get the same thing from each other (e.g., pleasure), and not only that but also from the same source, as happens between ready-witted people, not as happens between lover and beloved. For these do not take pleasure in the same things, but the one in seeing the beloved and the other in receiving attentions from his lover; and when the bloom of youth is passing the friendship sometimes passes too (for the one finds no pleasure in the sight of the other, and the other gets no attentions from the first); but many lovers on the other hand are constant, if familiarity has led them to love each other's characters, these being alike. But those who exchange not pleasure but utility in their love are both less truly friends and less constant. Those who are friends for the sake of utility part when the advantage is at an end; for they were lovers not of each other but of profit.

For the sake of pleasure or utility, then, even bad men may be friends of each other, or good men of bad, or one who is neither good nor bad may be a friend to any sort of person, but for their own sake clearly only good men can be friends; for bad men do not delight in each other unless some advantage come of the relation.

The friendship of the good too alone is proof against slander; for it is not easy to trust any one's talk about a man who has long been tested by oneself; and it is among good men that trust and the feeling that he would never wrong me and all the other things that are demanded in true friendship are found. In the other kinds of friendship, however, there is nothing to prevent these evils arising.

For men apply the name of friends even to those whose motive is utility, in which sense states are said to be friendly (for the alliances of states seem to aim at advantage), and to those who love each other for the sake of pleasure, in which sense children are called friends. Therefore we too ought perhaps to call such people friends, and say that there are several kinds of friendship—firstly and in the proper sense that of good men *qua* good, and by similarity the other kinds; for it is in virtue of something good and something similar that they are friends, since even the pleasant is good for the lovers of pleasure. But these two kinds of friendship are not often united, nor do the same people become friends for the sake of utility and of pleasure; for things that are only incidentally connected are not often coupled together.

Friendship being divided into these kinds; bad men will be friends for the sake of pleasure or of utility, being in this respect like each other, but good men will be friends for their own sake, i.e., in virtue of their goodness. These then, are friends without qualification; the others are friends incidentally and through a resemblance to these.

5. As in regard to the excellences some men are called good in respect of a state, others in respect of an activity, so too in the case of friendship; for those who live together delight in each other and confer benefits on each other, but those who are asleep or locally separated are not performing, but are disposed to perform, the activities of friendship; distance does not break off the friendship absolutely, but only the activity of it. But if the absence is lasting, it seems actually to make men forget their friendship; hence the saying "out of sight, out of mind." Neither old people nor sour people seem to make friends easily; for there is little that is pleasant in them, and no one can spend his days with one whose company is painful, or not pleasant, since nature seems above all to avoid the painful and to aim at the pleasant. Those, however, who approve of each other but do not live together seem to be well-disposed rather than actual friends. For there is nothing so characteristic of friends as living together (since while it is people who are in need that desire benefits, even those who are blessed desire to spend their days together; for solitude suits such people least of all); but people cannot live together if they are not pleasant and do not enjoy the same things, as friends who are companions seem to do.

The truest friendship, then, is that of the good, as we have frequently said; for that which is without qualification good or pleasant seems to be lovable and desirable, and for each person that which is good or pleasant to him; and the good man is lovable and desirable to the good man for both these reasons. Now it looks as if love were a passion, friendship a state; for love may be felt just as much towards lifeless things, but mutual love involves choice and choice springs from a state; and men wish well to those whom they love, for their sake, not as a result of passion but as a result of a state. And in loving a friend men love what is good for themselves; for the good man in becoming a friend becomes a good to his friend.

Each, then, both loves what is good for himself, and makes an equal return in goodwill and in pleasantness; for friendship is said to be equality, and both of these are found most in the friendship of the good.

Book IX

1. In all friendships between dissimilars it is, as we have said, proportion that equalizes the parties and preserves the friendship; e.g., in the political form of friendship the shoemaker gets a return for his shoes in proportion to his worth, and the weaver and the rest do the same. Now here a common measure has been provided in the form of money, and therefore everything is referred to this and measured by this; but in the friendship of lovers sometimes the lover complains that his excess of love is not met by love in return (though perhaps there is nothing lovable about him), while often the beloved complains that the lover who formerly promised everything now performs nothing. Such incidents happen when the lover loves the beloved for the sake of pleasure while the beloved loves the lover for the sake of utility, and they do not both possess the qualities expected of them. If these be the objects of the friendship it is dissolved when they do not get the things that formed the motives of their love; for each did not love the other person himself but the qualities he had, and these were not enduring; that is why the friendships also are transient. But the love of characters, as has been said, endures because it is self-dependent. Differences arise when what they get is something different and not what they desire; for it is like getting nothing at all when we do not get what we aim at; compare the story of the person who made promises to a lyre-player, promising him the more, the better he sang, but in the morning, when the other demanded the fulfilment of his promises, said that he had given pleasure for pleasure. Now if this had been what each wanted, all would have been well; but if the one wanted enjoyment but the other gain, and the one has what he wants while the other has not, the terms of the association will not have been properly fulfilled; for what each in fact wants is what he attends to, and it is for the sake of that that he will give what he has.

But who is to fix the worth of the service; he who makes the offer or he who has got the advantage? At any rate the one who offers seems to leave it to him. This is what they say Protagoras used to do; whenever he taught anything whatsoever, he bade the learner assess the value of the knowledge, and accepted the amount so fixed. But in such matters some men approve of the saying "let a man have his fixed reward."[1]

Those who get the money first and then do none of the things they said they would, owing to the extravagance of their promises, naturally find themselves the objects of complaint; for they do not fulfill what they agreed to. The sophists are perhaps compelled to do this because no one would give money for the things they *do* know. These people then, if they do not do what they have been paid for, are naturally made the objects of complaint.

But where there is *no* contract of service, those who offer something for the sake of the other party cannot (as we have said) be complained of (for that is the nature of the friendship of excellence), and the return to them must be made on the basis of their choice (for it is choice that is the characteristic thing in a friend and in excellence). And so too, it seems, should one make a return to those with whom one has studied philosophy; for their worth cannot be measured against money, and they

can get no honour which will balance their services, but still it is perhaps enough, as it is with the gods and with one's parents, to give them what one can.

If the gift was not of this sort, but was made on conditions, it is no doubt preferable that the return made should be one that seems fair to both parties, but if this cannot be achieved, it would seem not only necessary that the person who gets the first service should fix the reward, but also just; for if the other gets in return the equivalent of the advantage the beneficiary has received, or the price he would have paid for the pleasure, he will have got what is fair as from the other.

We see this happening too with things put up for sale, and in some places there are laws providing that no actions shall arise out of voluntary contracts, on the assumption that one should settle with a person whom one has trusted, in the spirit in which one bargained with him. The law holds that it is more just that the person to whom credit was given should fix the terms than that the person who gave credit should do so. For most things are not assessed at the same value by those who have them and those who want them; each class values highly what is its own and what it is offering; yet the return is made on the terms fixed by the receiver. But no doubt the receiver should assess a thing not at what it seems worth when he has it, but at what he assessed it at before he had it. . . .

3. Another question that arises is whether friendships should or should not be broken off when the other party does not remain the same. Perhaps we may say that there is nothing strange in breaking off a friendship based on utility or pleasure, when our friends no longer have these attributes. For it was of these attributes that we were the friends; and when these have failed it is reasonable to love no longer. But one might complain of another if, when he loved us for our usefulness or pleasantness, he pretended to love us for our character. For, as we said at the outset, most differences arise between friends when they are not friends in the spirit in which they think they are. So when a man has made a mistake and has thought he was being loved for his character, when the other person was doing nothing of the kind, he must blame himself; but when he has been deceived by the pretences of the other person, it is just that he should complain against his deceiver—and with more justice than one does against people who counterfeit the currency, inasmuch as the wrongdoing is concerned with something more valuable.

But if one accepts another man as good, and he becomes bad and is seen to do so, must one still love him? Surely it is impossible, since not everything can be loved, but only what is good. What is evil neither can nor should be loved; for one should not be a lover of evil, nor become like what is bad; and we have said that like is dear to like. Must the friendship, then, be forthwith broken off? Or is this not so in all cases, but only when one's friends are incurable in their wickedness? If they are capable of being reformed one should rather come to the assistance of their character or their property, inasmuch as this is better and more characteristic of friendship. But a man who breaks off such a friendship would seem to be doing nothing strange; for it was not to a man of this sort that he was a friend; when his friend has changed, therefore, and he is unable to save him, he gives him up.

But if one friend remained the same while the other became better and far outstripped him in excellence, should the latter treat the former as a friend? Surely he cannot. When the interval is great this becomes most plain, e.g., in the case of childish friendships; if one friend remained a child in intellect while the other became a fully developed man, how could they be friends when they neither approved of the same things nor delighted in and were pained by the same things? For not even with regard to each other will their tastes agree, and without this (as we saw) they cannot be friends; for they cannot live together. But we have discussed these matters.

Should he, then, behave no otherwise towards him than he would if he had never been his friend? Surely he should keep a remembrance of their former intimacy, and as we think we ought to oblige friends rather than strangers, so to those who have been our friends we ought to make some allowance for our former friendship, when the breach has not been due to excess of wickedness.

4. Friendly relations with one's neighbours, and the marks by which friendships are defined, seem to have proceeded from a man's relations to himself. For men think a friend is one who wishes and does what is good, or seems so, for the sake of his friend, or one who wishes his friend to exist and live, for his sake; which mothers do to their children, and friends do who have come into conflict. And others think a friend is one who lives with and has the same tastes as another, or one who grieves and rejoices with his friend; and this too is found in mothers most of all. It is by some one of these characteristics that friendship too is defined.

Now each of these is true of the good man's relation to himself (and of all other men in so far as they think themselves good; excellence and the good man seem, as has been said, to be the measure of every class of things). For his opinions are harmonious, and he desires the same things with all his soul; and therefore he wishes for himself what is good and what seems so, and does it (for it is characteristic of the good man to exert himself for the good), and does so for his own sake (for he does it for the sake of the intellectual element in him, which is thought to be the man himself); and he wishes himself to live and be preserved, and especially the element by virtue of which he thinks. For existence is good to the good man, and each man wishes himself what is good, while no one chooses to possess the whole world if he has first to become someone else (for that matter, even now God possesses the good); he wishes for this only on condition of being whatever he is; and the element that thinks would seem to be the individual man, or to be so more than any other element in him. And such a man wishes to live with himself; for he does so with pleasure, since the memories of his past acts are delightful and his hopes for the future are good, and therefore pleasant. His mind is well stored too with subjects of contemplation. And he grieves and rejoices, more than any other, with himself; for the same thing is always painful, and the same thing always pleasant, and not one thing at one time and another at another; he has, so to speak, nothing to regret.

Therefore, since each of these characteristics belongs to the good man in relation to himself, and he is related to his friend as to himself (for his friend is another self), friendship too is thought to be one of these attributes, and those who have these attributes to be friends. Whether there is or is not friendship between a man and himself is a question we may dismiss for the present; there would seem to be friendship in so far as he is two or more, to judge from what has been said, and from the fact that the extreme of friendship is likened to one's love for oneself.

But the attributes named seem to belong even to the majority of men, poor creatures though they may be. Are we to say then that in so far as they are satisfied with themselves and think they are good, they share in these attributes? Certainly no one who is thoroughly bad and impious has these attributes, or even seems to do so. They hardly belong even to inferior people; for they are at variance with themselves, and have appetites for some things and wishes for others. This is true, for instance, of incontinent people; for they choose, instead of the things they themselves think good, things that are pleasant but hurtful; while others again, through cowardice and laziness, shrink from doing what they think best for themselves. And those who have done many terrible deeds and are hated for their wickedness even shrink from life and destroy themselves. And wicked men seek for people with whom to spend their days, and shun themselves; for they remember many a grievous deed, and anticipate others like them, when they are by themselves, but when they are with others they forget. And having nothing lovable in them they have no feeling of love to themselves. Therefore also such men do not rejoice or grieve with themselves; for their soul is rent by faction, and one element in it by reason of its wickedness grieves when it abstains from certain acts, while the other part is pleased, and one draws them this way and the other that, as if they were pulling them in pieces. If a man cannot at the same time be pained and pleased, at all events after a short time he is pained *because* he was pleased, and he could have wished that these things had not been pleasant to him; for bad men are laden with regrets.

Therefore the bad man does not seem to be amicably disposed even to himself, because there is nothing in him to love; so that if to be thus is the height of wretchedness, we should strain every nerve to avoid wickedness and should endeavour to be good; for so one may be both friendly to oneself and a friend to another.

5. Goodwill is a friendly sort of relation, but is not *identical* with friendship; for one may have goodwill both towards people whom one does not know, and without their knowing it, but not friendship. This has indeed been said already. But goodwill is not even friendly feeling. For it does not involve intensity or desire, whereas these accompany friendly feeling; and friendly feeling implies intimacy while goodwill may arise of a sudden, as it does towards competitors in a contest; we come to feel goodwill for them and to share in their wishes, but we would not *do* anything with them; for, as we said, we feel goodwill suddenly and love them only superficially.

Goodwill seems, then, to be a beginning of friendship, as the pleasure of the eye is the beginning of love. For no one loves if he has not first been delighted by the form of the beloved, but he who delights in the form of another does not, for all that, love him, but only does so when he also longs for him when absent and craves for his presence; so too it is not possible for people to be friends if they have not come to feel goodwill for each other, but those who feel goodwill are not for all that friends; for they only *wish* well to those for whom they feel goodwill, and would not do anything with them nor take trouble for them. And so one might by an extension of the term say that goodwill is inactive friendship, though when it is prolonged and reaches the point of intimacy it becomes friendship—not the friendship based on utility nor that based on pleasure; for goodwill too does not arise on those terms. The man who has received a benefit bestows goodwill in return for what has been done to him, and in doing so is doing what is just; while he who wishes some one to prosper because he hopes for enrichment through him seems to have goodwill not to him but rather to himself, just as a man is not a friend to another if he cherishes him for the sake of some use to be made of him. In general, goodwill arises on account of some excellence and worth, when one man seems to another beautiful or brave or something of the sort, as we pointed out in the case of competitors in a contest. . . .

8. The question is also debated, whether a man should love himself most, or some one else. People criticize those who love themselves most, and call them self-lovers, using this as an epithet of disgrace, and a bad man seems to do everything for his own sake, and the more so the more wicked he is—and so men reproach him, for instance, with doing nothing of his own accord—while the good man acts for honour's sake, and the more so the better he is, and acts for his friend's sake, and sacrifices his own interest.

But the facts clash with these arguments, and this is not surprising. For men say that one ought to love best one's best friend, and a man's best friend is one who wishes well to the object of his wish for his sake, even if no one is to know of it; and these attributes are found most of all in a man's attitude towards himself, and so are all the other attributes by which a friend is defined; for, as we have said, it is from this relation that all the characteristics of friendship have extended to others. All the proverbs, too, agree with this, e.g., "a single soul," and "what friends have is common property," and "friendship is equality," and "charity begins at home"; for all these marks will be found most in a man's relation to himself; he is his own best friend and therefore ought to love himself best. It is therefore a reasonable question, which of the two views we should follow; for both are plausible.

Perhaps we ought to mark off such arguments from each other and determine how far and in what respects each view is right. Now if we grasp the sense in which each party uses the phrase "lover of self," the truth may become evident. Those who use the term as one of reproach ascribe self-love to people who assign to themselves the greater share of wealth, honours, and bodily pleasures; for these are what most people desire, and busy themselves about as though they were the best of all things, which is the reason, too, why they become objects of competition. So those who are grasping with regard to these things gratify their appetites and in general their feelings and the irrational element of the soul; and most men are of this nature thus the epithet has taken its meaning from the prevailing type of self-love, which is a bad one; it is just, therefore, that men who are lovers of self in this way are reproached for being so. That it is those who give themselves the preference in regard to objects of this sort that most people usually call lovers of self is plain; for if a man were always anxious that he himself, above all things, should act justly, temperately, or in accordance with any other of the excellences, and in general were always to try to secure for himself the honourable course, no one will call such a man a lover of self or blame him.

But such a man would seem more than the other a lover of self; at all events he assigns to himself the things that are noblest and best,

and gratifies the most authoritative element in himself and in all things obeys this; and just as a city or any other systematic whole is most properly identified with the most authoritative element in it, so is a man; and therefore the man who loves this and gratifies it is most of all a lover of self. Besides, a man is said to have or not to have self-control according as his intellect has or has not the control, on the assumption that this is the man himself; and the things men have done from reason are thought most properly their own acts and voluntary acts. That this is the man himself, then, or is so more than anything else, is plain, and also that the good man loves most this part of him. Whence it follows that he is most truly a lover of self, of another type than that which is a matter of reproach, and as different from that as living according to reason is from living as passion dictates, and desiring what is noble from desiring what seems advantageous. Those, then, who busy themselves in an exceptional degree with noble actions all men approve and praise; and if *all* were to strive towards what is noble and strain every nerve to do the noblest deeds everything would be as it should be for the common good, and every one would secure for himself the goods that are greatest, since excellence is the greatest of goods.

Therefore the good man should be a lover of self (for he will both himself profit by doing noble acts, and will benefit his fellows), but the wicked man should not; for he will hurt both himself and his neighbours, following as he does evil passions. For the wicked man, what he does clashes with what he ought to do, but what the good man ought to do he does; for the intellect always chooses what is best for itself, and the good man obeys his intellect. It is true of the good man too that he does many acts for the sake of his friends and his country, and if necessary dies for them; for he will throw away both wealth and honours and in general the goods that are objects of competition, gaining for himself nobility; since he would prefer a short period of intense pleasure to a long one of mild enjoyment, a twelvemonth of noble life to many years of humdrum existence, and one great and noble action to many trivial ones. Now those who die for others doubtless attain this result; it is therefore a great prize that they choose for themselves. They will throw away wealth too on condition that their friends will gain more; for while a man's friend gains wealth he himself achieves nobility; he is therefore assigning the greater good to himself. The same too is true of honour and office; all these things he will sacrifice to his friend; for this is noble and laudable for himself. Rightly then is he thought to be good, since he chooses nobility before all else. But he may even give up actions to his friend; it may be nobler to become the cause of his friend's acting than to act himself. In all the actions, therefore, that men are praised for, the good man is seen to assign to himself the greater share in what is noble. In this sense, then, as has been said, a man should be a lover of self; but in the sense in which most men are so, he ought not.

9. It is also disputed whether the happy man will need friends or not. It is said that those who are blessed and self-sufficient have no need of friends; for they have the things that are good, and therefore being self-sufficient they need nothing further while a friend, being another self, furnishes what a man cannot provide by his own effort; whence the saying "when fortune is kind, what need of friends?"[2] But it seems strange, when one assigns all

good things to the happy man, not to assign friends, who are thought the greatest of external goods. And if it is more characteristic of a friend to do well by another than to be well done by, and to confer benefits is characteristic of the good man and of excellence, and it is nobler to do well by friends than by strangers, the good man will need people to do well by. This is why the question is asked whether we need friends more in prosperity or in adversity, on the assumption that not only does a man in adversity need people to confer benefits on him, but also those who are prospering need people to do well by. Surely it is strange, too, to make the blessed man a solitary; for no one would choose to possess all good things on condition of being alone, since man is a political creature and one whose nature is to live with others. Therefore even the happy man lives with others; for he has the things that are by nature good. And plainly it is better to spend his days with friends and good men than with strangers or any chance persons. Therefore the happy man needs friends.

What then is it that the first party means, and in what respect is it right? Is it that most men identify friends with useful people? Of such friends indeed the blessed man will have no need, since he already has the things that are good; nor will he need those whom one makes one's friends because of their pleasantness, or he will need them only to a small extent (for his life, being pleasant, has no need of adventitious pleasure); and because he does not need *such* friends he is thought not to need friends.

But that is surely not true. For we have said at the outset that happiness is an activity; and activity plainly comes into being and is not present at the start like a piece of property. If happiness lies in living and being active, and the good man's activity is virtuous and pleasant in itself, as we have said at the outset, and if a thing's being one's own is one of the attributes that make it pleasant, and if we can contemplate our neighbours better than ourselves and their actions better than our own, and if the actions of virtuous men who are their friends are pleasant to good men (since these have both the attributes that are naturally pleasant)—if this be so, the blessed man will need friends of this sort, since he chooses to contemplate worthy actions and actions that are his own, and the actions of a good man who is his friend have both these qualities.

Further, men think that the happy man ought to live pleasantly. Now if he were a solitary, life would be hard for him; for by oneself it is not easy to be continuously active; but with others and towards others it is easier. With others therefore his activity will be more continuous, being in itself pleasant, as it ought to be for the man who is blessed; for a good man *qua* good delights in excellent actions and is vexed at vicious ones, as a musical man enjoys beautiful tunes but is pained at bad ones. A certain training in excellence arises also from the company of the good, as Theognis remarks.

If we look deeper into the nature of things, a virtuous friend seems to be naturally desirable for a virtuous man. For that which is good by nature, we have said, is for the virtuous man good and pleasant in itself. Now life is defined in the case of animals by the power of perception, in that of man by the power of perception or thought; and a power is referred to the corresponding activity, which is the essential thing; therefore life seems to be essentially perceiving or thinking. And life is among the things that are good and pleasant in themselves, since it is determinate and the determinate is of the nature of the good; and that which is good

by nature is also good for the virtuous man (which is the reason why life seems pleasant to all men); but we must not apply this to a wicked and corrupt life nor to a life spent in pain; for such a life is indeterminate, as are its attributes. The nature of pain will become plainer in what follows. But if life itself is good and pleasant (which it seems to be, from the very fact that all men desire it, and particularly those who are good and blessed; for to such men life is most desirable, and their existence is the most blessed; and if he who sees perceives that he sees, and he who hears, that he hears, and he who walks, that he walks, and in the case of all other activities similarly there is something which perceives that we are active, so that if we perceive, we perceive that we perceive, and if we think, that we think; and if to perceive that we perceive or think is to perceive that we exist (for existence was defined as perceiving or thinking); and if perceiving that one lives is one of the things that are pleasant in themselves (for life is by nature good, and to perceive what is good present in oneself is pleasant); and if life is desirable, and particularly so for good men, because to them existence is good and pleasant (for they are pleased at the consciousness of what is in itself good); and if as the virtuous man is to himself, he is to his friend also (for his friend is another self):—then as his own existence is desirable for each man, so, or almost so, is that of his friend. Now his existence was seen to be desirable because he perceived his own goodness, and such perception is pleasant in itself. He needs, therefore, to be conscious of the existence of his friend as well, and this will be realized in their living together and sharing in discussion and thought; for this is what living together would seem to mean in the case of man, and not, as in the case of cattle, feeding in the same place.

If, then, existence is in itself desirable for the blessed man (since it is by its nature good and pleasant), and that of his friend is very much the same, a friend will be one of the things that are desirable. Now that which is desirable for him he must have, or he will be deficient in this respect. The man who is to be happy will therefore need virtuous friends.

Notes

1   Hesiod, *Works and Days* 370.
2   Euripides, *Orestes* 667.

Discussion

What does true friendship consist of? Do you agree with Aristotle's classification of the three types of friendship or would you categorize them differently? What role do friends play in our lives? Can friendships exist between people who are very different in wealth, status, tastes, sense of humour, hobbies, interests, political views, religious beliefs, and so on? What kinds of differences do you think you can have with your friends and still be friends? What kinds of differences do you think would make friendship with someone impossible?

In chapter four of Book IX, Aristotle says something that at first may sound quite strange. He tells us, "Friendly relations with one's neighbours, and the marks by which friendships are defined, seem to have proceeded from a man's relation to himself." What does he mean by this? Aristotle thought that friendship required a form of self-love. He believed that there was a good and a bad form of self-love. The good form of self-love is much like his truest form of friendship, which he presented in the first reading. Just as that form of friendship depended on loving one's friend's good character, or loving her for her own sake, so the good form of self-love depends on one loving oneself for one's own sake, or for one's own good character. But for Aristotle it would seem that love for oneself must come first, and then one's love for his friends is modelled or based on that self-love. Does this sound right? You have probably heard the popular slogan "you must love yourself before you can love others." Aristotle is saying "yes, this is correct." We understand what it is to love ourselves for our own sake (and not for the sake of pleasure or usefulness), and this is the basis for how we can truly love others. Do you agree with Aristotle that this is necessary for friendship? Can we love others without loving ourselves? We do see cases where people seem to love others much more than they love themselves (the self-sacrifice of a parent for her child or the romantic lover who risks everything for his or her beloved). Do these examples contradict Aristotle's claims, or is (healthy) self-love still present in these cases? Is the claim that we must love ourselves in order to love others, whether it be made by Aristotle or by a contributor to *Psychology Today*, simply a slogan whose truth is unsubstantiated?

Aristotle continues the discussion of self-love in Book IX, chapter eight. Here he alludes to a bad form of self-love. He notes that the term "lover of self" is often used, as it is today, as a form of criticism for one's character. What people have in mind when they criticize a person for this form of self-love is "people who assign to themselves the greater share of wealth, honours, and bodily pleasures." They are what we call *selfish*. What Aristotle has in mind by self-love is not selfishness but rather a healthy love for one's own character or person. This healthy self-love requires that one possess or strive to attain a good or virtuous character. By doing so, one is loving the right thing in his own self (the good in his or her self), and, in truly loving one's friend, one is doing the same (loving the good in her or him). Is there a sense in which we still love like this today? When we love our friends is it their good character that we love? Or do we love something else? Do we, or can we, love someone with a bad character?

Suggestions for Further Reading

Neera Kapur Badhwar, ed. *Friendship: A Philosophical Reader* (Ithaca, NY: Cornell University Press, 1993).

Marilyn Friedman, *What Are Friends For? Feminist Perspectives on Personal Relationships and Moral Theory* (Ithaca, NY: Cornell University Press, 1993).

A.W. Price, *Love and Friendship in Plato and Aristotle* (Oxford, Clarendon Press, 1989).

Chapter Seventeen
Friendship and Value

Introduction

In the last chapter, we looked at Aristotle's discussion of friendship. Many of his observations continue to resonate today as we still tend to make similar distinctions between kinds of friendships and we still tend to think of friendship, like other forms of love, as a necessary part of a good or happy life. But can love or friendship play a role in political life? This possibility has been met with suspicion by philosophers since love is understood to be partial and politics is meant to be practised impartially. Tony Milligan explores this issue and puts forth the possibility of an Aristotelian-inspired *political* friendship. Modern states, he notes, tend to emphasize liberty and equality but not fraternity. Arguably, the neglect of this feature weakens the bonds of modern societies.

TONY MILLIGAN

Milligan acknowledges that this sort of political friendship will be based more or less on Aristotle's friendship of utility rather than his highest form of friendship. This would make sense since the kind of friendships that exist between states or between citizens within a particular state tend to be based more on mutual advantage rather than genuine concern. But he follows this up by noting that utility friendship can be seen as a stage in the desire for true friendship. How would this be possible in the context of a state? It seems to me that we see examples of this all the time, even if it is not easy to draw formalized principles from what these instances teach us. The recent willingness of citizens and leaders in Canada and in many European countries to accept Syrian refugees suggests that something more than a principle of fairness or equality is at stake. It seems that many citizens of the countries that have accepted refugees have been moved by their plight and suffering rather than by formal arguments about justice (of course the latter are important as well).

The Politics of Love

As a result of discrimination, prejudice, and gender inequality, sex and politics are deeply entwined. We have a clear idea of what sexual politics might involve. Love, by contrast, seems strictly personal, situated at some distance from the political domain and only brought together with the latter in ways that are forced and artificial. So, for example, it might be claimed that liberally minded person x should not love person y *because of* the latter's illiberal politics. This is a type of claim about which we may be suspicious. After all, the heart wants what the heart wants. We do not get to choose who we love, or, at least, we do not choose them in the way that we choose who to vote for in an election. Prominent liberal thinkers who have otherwise been persistently fascinated with love, such as Hannah Arendt (1996, 3) and Iris Murdoch (1993, 14), have also been insistent that we must distinguish between the individual as citizen and the individual as loving agent, or between what Jan Bransen calls a "loving attitude" and a "citizen attitude" (2014, 144).

Those who buy into such a separation typically do so for reasons that concern impartiality, love's distance from the rational, and the fact that love can be too powerful to control. In brief, we love partially, beyond reason, and sometimes rather dangerously. And so it seems that love, which is an inextricable part of private life, is not something that we ought to unleash upon the political domain. What follows will suggest that each of these reasons touches upon worries that cannot be entirely silenced but that can be constrained, trumped, or otherwise out-weighed.

1. Loving Partiality

Consider, first, the problem of impartiality. Love is, or at least paradigmatic forms of love *are*, all about special relationships that involve favouring one person over another. By contrast, liberal politics aims to place everyone on an equal footing. Equality and the partiality of love seem to conflict directly. This is one of the reasons why Arendt regarded love as politically suspect. When, as a result of her controversial claims about the role of Jewish community leaders in the Holocaust, she was charged with a lack of love for the Jewish people, Arendt's response was that she loved only her friends. Loving a people, or a nation, or one set of people in contrast to another paves the way for loving them *at the expense of* another. And that is a problem for democracy. As we are human, there must always be a place for love in our lives, but that place is safely (protectively) outside of the political domain (Arendt 2007, 466–67; Nixon 2015, 17).

If we accept this idea that love must always be partial, or that the kind of love that is in danger of spilling over into the political domain may well be partial, it is still open to us to point out that not every kind of loving partiality amounts to "prejudice" (Merrill 2014, 177). It would be odd to refer to the parent who prepares meals for their children rather than other children as someone engaged in unfair discrimination. There may be a defensible, loving partiality, although admittedly Arendt may have been right about the dangers that it carries. Yet it is not obvious that she was equally right about shunning such dangers. After all, who ever thought that politics was comprehensively safe? This may count as one of those contexts in which a certain kind of risk is a precondition of accomplishment.

Alternatively, we may reflect that not every kind of love *is* partial. The tradition of love that is associated with St Paul and Christianity (love as *agape*) praises it as an unconditional response that reaches out even to strangers, tax collectors, and enemies. But a familiar concern about such love is that it may be rather too inclusive, pathologically forgiving, or simply unavailable. Perhaps, if a creator God existed, then such a being might still love Hitler or Pol Pot or Jack the Ripper (in the way that a parent may continue to love errant children). But as political agents, our situation is rather different. We are not, with regard to the perpetrators of evil, *in loco parentis* and it may be hubris to think otherwise. It would certainly be very odd to suggest that Holocaust victims who did not love Hitler were guilty of a moral failure. There, are, in any case, other ways to acknowledge the humanity of those who have carried out great evil, without loving them. Something closer to *respect* may be enough. Respect can offer recognition without forgiveness and without the vulnerability that seems to be inseparable from love.

Such an example may, however, be something of an "outlier." We may wonder just what these extreme cases tell us about everyday ethical or political requirements. Most of our fellow citizens are not Hitler or Pol Pot. Yet most of them *are* strangers, and it is difficult to make sense of the practicality or intelligibility of love for those we do not know. We can be compassionate or civil towards them, but it is not obvious that this really amounts to a form of love that deserves the name. After all, we strongly associate love with intimacy or at least with familiarity and a shared history (Grau 2010, 249). And while we may, sometimes speak of "love at first sight," which suggests the possibility of love without history, what this

amounts to, under analysis, may be something else: the striking feeling that we are starting to fall for someone, the sense that here is someone with whom we could be open, caring, and content. Accepting the possibility for actual love for strangers would also come at a price. We would lose one of the most familiar features of love: its intimate connection with grief. We can feel sorrow at the death of those we do not know, but we cannot grieve over them. And without vulnerability to grief, talk of love seems misplaced (Milligan 2011, 127–32).

Even so, it is difficult to dismiss the idea of a universal love and all the more so given that it is not a theme that appears only in the Christian tradition. It is not a localized religious artifact. It has counterparts in other traditions (*metta* in Buddhism and *ahimsa* in Hinduism, where both are read in a particular way that reaches beyond the avoidance of harm). It may be an idea that we can send quickly into exile by means of a clever argument, but keeping it in exile could be more difficult. There is also a way to save the concept without doing violence to our ordinary understanding of what love involves. Perhaps the object of such love might be humanity, the moral community as a whole, and not particular individuals. Such an attitude might express itself in our ways of responding to individuals, but they would not be the true objects of the love. This does make at least some sense in terms of political motivation. Gandhi, for example, continuously appealed to humanity as both a suitable object of loving concern and as the claimed basis of his non-violent political tactics. Even so, such love, while not really focused upon individuals, may remain partial. Communities have an outside as well as an interior. However, it may be inclusive enough to address Arendt's concern.

2. Loving Beyond Reason

Arendt's suspicions about the partiality of love dovetail with a concern that is exemplified by Kant's frequently repeated claim that love is too pathological an emotion to fall within the domain of morality. It may function as a useful occasional ally, or as a force that conveniently joins in on the winning side, but love's allegiance is too fleeting and unstable to be relied upon by rational agents. This attitude, a qualified pessimism about the nature of love, continues to feature in contemporary discussions of the philosophy of love, primarily through the idea that love is not answerable to reasons (Smuts 2014, 99–101; Frankfurt, 2004, 39–40). On such a view, if my wife Suzanne does not love me, this may be heartbreaking, but it cannot involve a failure of her rationality. Nor can I persuade her to love me solely on the basis of the available facts and sound argumentation. Even if I were a better person, Saint Francis and the Dalai Llama rolled into one, I still could not do so. Conversely, if she does love me, this is not a triumph of her rationality over the darker angels of her nature. There may, of course, be prudential reasons why one person would want to love another, but *wanting to love* and *loving* are not the same, and so there seem to be no reasons at all for love itself. This disconnection from rational standards places love at odds with the need for a modern and liberal polity to sustain an open and, above all, rational public discourse.

Yet, although love involves various ways of feeling or at least *dispositions* to feel, love is not just a "feeling" and certainly not simply a feeling that can easily be set in contrast to rationality. When, for example, we are asked why we love one person rather than another, we are usually not stuck for an answer. I love Suzanne because she has cared for me in hard times and has not turned away when I have been foolish. I love her because we met at the end of our teens and sat out together under the stars. I have a shared history with her that I lack with all others. Moreover, this is a shared history of the right sort for love. We may also share history with sworn enemies, if we happen to have any of the latter, but it is not the kind of history that would ordinarily figure in a practice of explaining why someone is a suitable participant in a loving relationship.

A cautionary note here is that the words that we supply, when stating our reasons for love, are often placeholders for something else. The person who says, I love him because of the way he wears his hat and sips his tea, does not literally mean this (Velleman 1999). They would not, for example, trade up for a better hat wearer or sipper of tea. But they do mean something, and part of what they mean is that their beloved is irreplaceable and that their love is not arbitrary.

Yet, while we are usually able to offer considerations for why we love, no such reasons ever seem to be conclusive. It always remains intelligible that the relevant consideration could be in place without the love. And an agent who did not love because of the consideration would not thereby be guilty of irrationality. If, in spite of our having sat out under the stars, Suzanne did not love me, this would, again, not indicate that her rationality was compromised. But here, what is brought into play is a particular conception of reasons and not just a conception of love. When someone says that there really are reasons for love, what they mean (or what they *ought* to mean) is not that there are "necessary and sufficient conditions for loving rationally." Rather, the reasons for love are characteristically, "contributory reasons," and these are precisely the reasons that seem to do much of the work in explaining our responsiveness to others more generally. The reasons explain but they do not necessitate. They may weigh more or less heavily. They may be outweighed by other considerations. So, for example, if it turns out that I am guilty of some great crime, or even persistent neglect, this may be more important than our having shared our lives together and Suzanne may begin (with good reason) to fall out of love with me.

If this picture is largely correct, it still remains possible to love because of a shared prejudice, to love because of delusions (as the crowds loved Hitler), or to love in ways that *are* allied to irrationality. But the same is true of belief and this does not make either love or belief into a natural ally of the non-rational or (more worryingly) of the irrational. To guard the political domain against a slide into unreason is not necessarily to guard it against the intrusion of love but only to guard it against those forms and instances of love that involve special kinds of failure such as a failure to be just or to be truthful.

3. Loving Dangerously

Finally, from Iris Murdoch, we have a different sort of concern, one that is framed in the language of Plato rather than (as with Arendt) the language of Kant: love may not be the *intrinsically* non-rational or irrational force that is sometimes claimed but it is simply too powerful and ambivalent to be controlled. Love, as *eros*, is akin to a self-constituting desire that makes us what we are; it is a power that can be directed towards *this* object or *that* object. But what if it is directed, channelled ("cathected," in more Freudian terms) the wrong way? Love may ultimately seek out the Good, but what if

we are wrong about what is good? Fanaticism can ensue: love for the fatherland, or for the leader, or for some imagined political fantasy. For Murdoch, love is too dangerous, the risk is too high. Love shapes our personal lives and we must work with and through it. But in the public domain it should be held in check. Within the latter, axioms and above all happiness (crudely understood) rather than a loving, perfectionist moral struggle by loving agents holds sway (Murdoch 1993, 362). This distinction here is not absolute but it is strong enough to support a central claim that love primarily belongs to the private sphere while axiomatic happiness belongs to the public sphere.

But here we may wonder whether even a qualified distinction of this sort can make sense of what it is to be politically engaged in a suitable manner. Simone Weil (2001), who influenced Murdoch in many respects, thought not. For Weil, if we do not love the right thing, then we will love the wrong thing or else remain demotivated. A similar claim has been a persistent feature of the politics of dissent since the late nineteenth century, particularly within the civil disobedience tradition. From Leo Tolstoy, through Gandhi and Martin Luther King, accounts of *protest beyond the law* have been presented as a politicized theory of love, where again love is channelled towards some political good (Milligan 2013, 93–96). The channelling metaphor, which draws from Plato and Freud, occurs especially in Gandhi and King who were not naive enough to ignore or set aside the anger that mass political movements must tap into. The idea was not to *eliminate* popular emotional engagement, but to *transform* it from anger into something more constructive.

Yet here we may worry about the possibility that such high idealism may be too demanding for ordinary political agents, in which case it must collapse into pretence or into some manner of elitism where agents who remain angry are part of a loving movement only because of the loving attitude of their leaders. Closer familiarity with the great civil disobedience movements of the twentieth century may provide some support for skepticism. In practice, Gandhi supplemented demanding talk about love with more practical appeals to civility. And King may have retained his earlier rhetorical commitment to a politics of love and the winning over of the hearts of the enemy, but in practice this reduced down to using non-violence as a means of embarrassing the federal government into action against publicly violent racists whose hearts were rarely won over. The underlying Platonic and quasi-Freudian moral psychology of channelling emotional upheaval into love may also be challenged.

Even so, these ideas are not easy to set aside. As an example of their resilience, we may think of the pro-democracy campaigners in Hong Kong in 2014 operating under the banner of an "Occupy Central with Love and Peace" movement. There are moments in politics when such movements may at least *seem* capable of averting great bloodshed and when their absence promises confrontation of the most destructive sort. However, this is a modification of the strict Platonic position in which the *regular* practice of politics is governed by the channelling of love as *eros*. The intermittent channelling of anger into love represents politics in a rather different way.

4. Politicizing Love

These objections, although in each instance inconclusive, can help us to make sense of why modern liberalism has been concerned to keep love and politics apart. Love can be partial, irrational, and dangerous, even if these are only some of love's possibilities. But what may always seem a little problematic about any overly sharp contrast of the "citizen attitude" and a "loving attitude" is, on the one hand, its artificiality (we are, after all, unitary beings) and, on the other, the recognition that a loving attitude (of the right sort) is better placed to recognize us as we truly are. Symptomatically, Jan Bransen makes the "loving attitude"/"citizen attitude" distinction but then favours the latter (2014, 156–57). Iris Murdoch too; while holding that "liberal political thought posits a certain fundamental distinction between the person as citizen and the person as moral-spiritual individual," accepts that the former, when thought of apart from the latter, is something of a fiction (Murdoch 1993, 356–57). As citizens, others are uniform bearers of rational political agency; or, more simply, they are indistinguishable parts of an electorate; or, in more neoliberal terms, they are taxpayers. They are not the unique, particular, individuals known through love. Or rather, their particularity is set aside in the interests of an imagined uniformity.

But if the Arendt-Murdoch criticisms of a politicization of love give us only reasons for caution, defeasible considerations that might lead us only into suspicion about particular instances of a politicized love, the prospect of some other manner of cautious politicization remains intact. But just how do we, cautiously, politicize love? Two broad pathways seem open. One pathway involves the adoption of a modified version of the Platonic theory with its metaphors of channelling, and something of this sort may be an ineradicable aspect of certain kinds of principled political dissent. However, as suggested above, this would establish only an intermittent connection between love and politics as, from time to time, political movements attempted to channel popular anger in a productive, constructive, and loving way.

The other pathway involves making the connection between love and politics in a more ongoing manner by appeal to resources from Aristotle and to the idea that the political community is held together, in some way, by bonds of friendship. Without friendships, there is no community. "Democracy has seldom represented itself without the possibility of at least that which always resembles—if one is willing to nudge the accent of this word—the possibility of a *fraternization*" (Derrida 2005, viii). Jacques Derrida (2005) has suggested that a neglect of this somewhat obvious fact is an important and worrying aspect of contemporary liberal thought, exemplified by free-market neoliberalism. Liberty and Equality have been emphasized while Fraternity (understood as various, shifting forms of social solidarity) has been downgraded. The perceived need for a fraternal connection between citizens, for a form of politicized mutual-concern, has been displaced by a (usually negative) liberal equality before the law and the liberty to do as one wishes so long as one has the required funds and others are harmed only indirectly, through commerce and the market, rather than by direct physical assault. This is a stark but familiar picture in which care for the other, or any political conception of interpersonal concern, finds no secure foothold. Martha Nussbaum too has stressed the way in which love operates on the ground floor of the political community by undermining barriers to justice such as hostility and disgust and by binding citizens to the common ground of freedoms and ideals. With regard to this task, respect is

not enough (Nussbaum 2013, 380). "We might say that a liberal state asks citizens who have different overall conceptions of the meaning and purpose of life to overlap and agree in a shared political space, the space of fundamental principles and constitutional ideals. But if those principles are to be efficacious, the state must also encourage love and devotion to those ideals" (Nussbaum 2013, 7).

I want to close by suggesting a further connection in a similarly Aristotelian vein, an extension of the intuition shared by Derrida and Nussbaum. Like Derrida, I want to draw attention directly to what Aristotle called political friendship—that is, *phila politike* and its relation to a primary kind of trust (without which any thought of community breaks down). This is a subject matter on which a great deal of ink has been spilt over questions of interpretation and over the legitimacy of claiming that it is truly a form of friendship. To say that the citizens of a good polity are bound together by a form of friendship is, after all, to appeal to a friendship of utility rather than a meeting of hearts. Yet, for Aristotle, utility friendships aspire towards and express a desire for friendship of a fuller sort. And it is this idea, the idea of fellow citizens as, or akin to friends, that inspires Derrida's suggestion that something important has been left out of modern liberalism's more restricted, liberty and equality, approach.

However, an account of *philia politike* does not require us to buy into any impossibly demanding requirement to love everyone individually. Rather, it depends upon the sensible point that political societies are not made up of the isolated individuals of a pared-back liberal discourse. They are composed of social beings, connected in clusters to one another by all manner of personal ties, one of the most important of which is friendship *in the fullest sense.* (Not utility friendship, but the genuine, matured, item.) From an Aristotelian point of view, without a complex overlapping network of agents who are bound together through friendships, of all sorts and degrees, and through other loving connections as well, we simply do not have the kind of solidarity that a functional political system requires. So far, I restate what I take to be a Derrida/Nussbaum point.

However, this also means that we simply cannot regard anyone as a potential fellow citizen unless we also regard them as *at least capable of* fitting appropriately into such interpersonal relations. The obvious candidates for those who fail to do so are precisely those who have been guilty of evil beyond vice. We may recognize their continuing humanity, and so the idea that they are "moral monsters" may be out of place. But their relation to the political community is, properly, one of containment by the latter rather than a pursuit of mutual flourishing as part of the common good. Drawing upon a visual metaphor shared by both Plato and Aristotle, one that is at the heart of a good deal of the literature on love, we can only *see* someone as having the potential to *be* a fellow citizen if we can also view them as a potential recipient of a legitimate love by at least some other fellow citizen or citizens. In at least this limited sense, a loving attitude and a citizen attitude seem inextricably entwined.

Acknowledgements

Previous versions of this paper were delivered as a lecture hosted by the UK Love Research Network, hosted by the Open University, London, in September 2014 and at the Human Sciences Symposium at the Magdalen Auditorium, Oxford, in February 2015. Special thanks for improving comments and suggestions go to Tomas Hejduk and Simon May.

Bibliography

Arendt, Hannah. 1996. *Love and Saint Augustine.* Chicago: Chicago University Press.

———. 2007. *The Jewish Writings.* New York: Schocken Books.

Bransen, Jan. 2014. "Loving a Stranger." In *Love and Its Objects: What Can We Care For?*, edited by Christian Maurer, Tony Milligan, and Kamila Pacovská, 143–59. Basingstoke, UK: Palgrave Macmillan.

Derrida, Jacques. 2005. *The Politics of Friendship.* London: Verso.

Frankfurt, Harry G. 2004. *Reasons of Love.* Princeton: Princeton University Press.

Grau, Christopher. 2010. "Love and History." *The Southern Journal of Philosophy* 48 (3): 246–71.

Maurer, Christian, Tony Milligan, and Kamila Pacovská, eds. 2014. *Love and Its Objects: What Can We Care For?* Basingstoke, UK: Palgrave Macmillan.

Merrill, Roberto. 2014. "L'amour comme émotion morale? Partialité parentale et égalité des chances." *Raison publique* 19:177–96.

Milligan, Tony. 2011. *Love.* London: Routledge.

———. 2013. *Civil Disobedience: Protest, Justification and the Law.* New York: Bloomsbury.

Murdoch, Iris. 1993. *Metaphysics as a Guide to Morals.* London: Penguin.

Nixon, Jon. 2015. *Hannah Arendt and the Politics of Friendship.* New York: Bloomsbury.

Nussbaum, Martha. 2013. *Political Emotions: Why Love Matters for Justice*. Cambridge, MA: Harvard University Press.

Smuts, Aaron. 2014. "Is It Better to Love Better Things?" In *Love and Its Objects: What Can We Care For?*, edited by Christian Maurer, Tony Milligan, and Kamila Pacovská, 91–107. Basingstoke, UK: Palgrave Macmillan.

Velleman, David. 1999. "Love as a Moral Emotion." *Ethics* 109 (2): 338–74.

Weil, Simone. 2001. *The Need for Roots: Prelude to a Declaration of Duties Towards Mankind*. London: Routledge.

ANNETTE C. BAIER

We tend to think more about how to make friends or keep friends than we do about how to lose friends. In her provocatively titled essay, Annette Baier explores the latter. As she suggests, most of us have lost friends through distance or time apart. As children we probably made and lost the same friends over the course of summer holidays (or perhaps over the course of one day). Baier notes that it is not only loss of contact due to distance or time apart that can dissolve friendships but also too much closeness or time together, as those who have had roommates can attest. Ultimately, though, she thinks that losing friends is natural in a certain sense. As we grow older, some friends move away, some die, and some change in ways that are no longer compatible with our interests, values, or lifestyle. Also, as Aristotle noted long ago, as we grow older it becomes harder to make new friends. We establish many of our friends during university or in the years shortly after. As time goes on, people get settled in their routines with family, work, and so on, which makes it harder to meet new people. Baier entertains the thought that maybe for some people a solitary life is more suitable in any case.

How to Lose Friends
Some Simple Ways

In order to lose friends, we must first have made them. Making friends is something children usually do readily and frequently, but the older we grow the less easy it seems to become to make new friends. As Aristotle points out, "Older people and sour people do not appear to be prone to friendship. For there is little pleasure to be found in them, and no one can spend his days with what is painful or not pleasant."[1] Even if the older person avoids becoming "sour," her company will often not be as agreeable as that of the younger person, so she will not make new friends easily. This would not leave her friendless, if the friends of her youth remained her friends as she aged, but typically only a few of them do.

We lose friends through death, through physical distance and neglecting to keep in touch across that distance, through change and the falling away of common interests, through increasing sourness, and occasionally through quarrel. Of course, children often punctuate their friendships with quarrels, either soon dramatically made up, or ending the friendship. They lose friends as easily as they make them, so that a turnover of friends is fairly normal. "I don't want to play in your yard. I don't like you anymore. You'll be sorry when you see me, swinging on our garden door." It takes experimentation with a range of close companions for a child to find those she can continue to want as companions, and for her to develop the skills of friendship. By adolescence these skills are usually in place, and tastes in companions more confident and stable, so that this is the time when close, resilient, and fairly lasting friendships tend to be made. The young adult knows whom she does and does not want as a friend, and knows the demands of friendship, so, unlike the child, knows that these demands limit the number of friendships she can nurture. But the friendships of our youth do not always last, nor is it only death and distance that end them. My interest in this essay is with losing friends for other less inevitable reasons, losing them through some failure to maintain the friendship. Such failure is common. The ability to keep friends through thick and thin is as difficult as it is rare.

Friendship usually begins in shared beliefs, interests, and tastes, but, if it is to last, it requires some sympathetic sharing of the friend's interests when these are not, or are not at first, one's own. Nicholas Blake, in his novel *Room Temperature*,[2] has a great description of the difficulties of this project of keeping up with the other's changing tastes, when one reason for the change is the other's very success in coming to share what were one's own tastes. His pair are husband and wife, but the same situation can face any close friends:

> And she too was at work on learning why the things that pleased me did please me, testing her progress against my reactions. This reciprocally

crossed effort to master the other's interests meant a temporary subjugation of one's own, so that, for example, when Patty pointed out a beautiful book of photographs and engineering drawings of gears (sepia, gray, black) in a Rizzoli bookstore, not saying "Hey, here's something you'll like . . . " but rather "Oh, how beautiful these gears are!" as if an enthusiasm for mechanical engineering had been innate in her, I had to force myself back into my old technologically appreciative self and go "Oh Momma! Cycloids! . . . " when I myself had been scanning the same table of books to predict which one (*Blue and White China? Long Island Landscape?*) she might have exclaimed about had she not been trying to second guess my exclamation. And there we both reinforced a fixed earlier self with its simpler enthusiasms in order to reward each other for having seen and understood them, even when our more fluid present selves began adjusting to new admixtures, and we became proud of how far we had left those primitively in-character tastes behind.[3]

Mutual understanding becomes extraordinarily difficult, and full sincerity of response virtually impossible, when there is this never quite up-to-date effort to share the other's tastes. It begins to look miraculous that close friendships ever survive for long.[4] But few friends (and almost as few lovers) are quite as ambitious as Blake's pair about sharing each other's enthusiasms. Most friends are content to have some, but not all, their interests in common, and to show no more than some understanding of, and friendly tolerance for, the unshared interests. It is enough if one can correctly say, "Here's something you'll like"; not necessary that one like it as much oneself. Some friendships may fail through the impossible demand that all the friends' interests and tastes coincide, and the failed attempt to achieve this mutual mirroring, but more fail through too small rather than too great an effort to share, to some degree, the other's tastes and interests.

What friends do often expect each other to share are their enmities. "Love me, love my dog" is not as important as "Love me, hate my enemies." So one sure way to lose friends is to have made friends with those who become each other's enemies. Even if it is not necessary that "Your friends are my friends and my friends are your friends," one's several friends had better not become outright enemies if any of these friendships are to survive. For if one is caught between hostile parties, each expecting one's "loyalty" and support, either one chooses sides and makes an enemy of a former friend, or one plays the thankless role of would-be peacemaker, and likely offends both parties by one's incomplete identification with each's cause, or one tries to keep right out of the quarrel and so weakens or kills both friendships. As one chooses one's friends, one needs to be blessed with some prophetic powers as to who is likely to fall out with whom, if the friendships are to prove mutually compatible over the long haul. Maybe this is one reason why Aristotle advises that our friendships be "character-friendships."[5] Those of good character are less likely than others to get into quarrels, but it is surely not a sign of a bad character to have acquired any enemies. Ex-friends do not normally become enemies, but when the end of the friendship is due, directly or indirectly, to quarrel, there is the danger that in losing a friend one is gaining an enemy. At any rate, the peaceable will be ill-advised to make friends with the less peaceable.

A friendship can have a dramatic ending in a charge of treachery. The self-disclosure that is typical of friendship makes friends vulnerable to each's special knowledge of the other, and this, as Kant warned, can lead to charges of perfidy when this knowledge is perceived to have been misused, or shared with unsuitable others. Friends can be lost through the perception of perfidy, on the part of one of the friends, and that loss may be good riddance, if the perception is correct, or even if it is not, if it reveals undue suspiciousness in the perceiver. Aristotle links the mutual self-disclosure of friends to their assistance to each other in the worthy aim of self-knowledge, and another less dramatic way that a friendship can die is through the fading of interest, on the part of one of the friends, in this Socratic project. To be reluctant to receive, or to fail to show sufficient interest in, what the other is disclosing to one, or to fail to offer any return disclosures, can put the friendship at risk. Aristotle advises us to end friendships with those whose character has changed for the worse, and Aristotelians will perceive a developing boredom with self-knowledge, one's own or one's friend's, as such a change. But, like increasing sourness, it may be a change that comes quite normally with aging. After all, if one does not know oneself by, say, age 60, one is unlikely ever to, and it is also possible that one has, by then, found more interesting things to get to know. But such developments, if not occurring in a coordinated way in both friends, are not conducive to the health of the friendship.

Fortunately not all friendships are based on this shared narcissistic concern to know oneself, and see oneself mirrored in one's second self. Youthful friendships may have such a basis, but mature friendships can merit C.S. Lewis's characterization: "We picture lovers face to face, but friends side by side."[6] Some friendships that are quite casual have an amazing resiliency, and can withstand lack of contact over years, or even decades, when this lack is due to physical separation, and even to the failure to keep track of the whereabouts of the friend. I have had friends of this sort, who reappear unexpectedly in my path, and the easy companionship resumes as if never interrupted. Had such friendships been of the intimate, intense sort, with confidences exchanged, they very likely would not have proved so immune to death through neglect. Is it that the less demanding the friendship, the hardier it is? We could call such reappearing friends "prodigal friends," and they have the special value the New Testament ascribes to returning prodigal sons.

It is not only loss of contact over long periods that some friendships can survive, against all reasonable expectations. They can also survive too close contact with the friend's spouse, that is to say love affairs known to the "betrayed" spouse and friend. This may show as much about the amazing generosity of spirit of some friends as it shows about the tenacity of some friendships. There is as much to wonder at in the survival of some friendships as there is to interest the anthropologically inclined philosopher in other friendships' endings. And in both cases, the wisdom of the great philosophers fails dismally in helping us to understand which friendships survive, and why.

Kant writes that friends flatter themselves that, in case of need (and he is thinking of more vital needs than self-knowledge), they can count on each other's help, but that they will hesitate to ask for such help, since to receive it would put the recipient "a step lower, inasmuch as he is obligated and yet not reciprocally able to obligate," thus spoiling the equality of respect there should be between friends, and contaminating the mutual ties of friendship with one-sided gratitude.[7] Kantian friends are reluctant to have to feel gratitude, and preserve their friendship through carefully avoiding any threat to their equality of moral status. Each friend "is magnanimously concerned with sparing the other any burden, bearing any such burden himself, and, yes, even completely concealing it from the other."[8] Not everyone is content with merely Kantian kid-glove friendships; many of us expect friends indeed to be friends in need. I once endangered a close friendship by not phoning my friend, who was also my neighbour, at 3 a.m. when I was alone in my home, taken ill, and needing to be driven to the emergency ward of a hospital. Given the ungodly hour, I called a taxi. But there was no question of "concealing my burden" for long, and when the friend visited me in hospital I had to meet the reproach, "Why did you not phone me for help? Am I not your friend?" I did not lose this friend by my unwillingness to be a burden, but there was something to be forgiven, and something learned. I had never been much of a Kantian in my ethics, but I was even less a one after this inadvertent and unwise obedience to Kantian rules of friendship. These are more recipes for killing friendships than analyses of "true" friendships.

Another thing that Kant, repeating Aristotle, says that true friends expect of one another is frank criticism, when criticism is due. But mutual correction is not always a reliable sustainer of friendship, and one-sided correction is, for adult–adult friendship, often fatal. Should one's friend be the one to teach one to drive? Only if the friend is a superb driving instructor, and if becoming a driver matters more to one than the friendship. And experience has shown me that, unless one intends to write a rave notice, a blurb rather than a critical review, it is very unwise to agree to review a friend's publications, even if one thinks that one would oneself have been able to take a critical review from that friend, or former friend. (One is likely to be self-deceived about that.) Nor need the review be sour in order to offend. Indeed, a witty review, if the wit is at the author's expense, is particularly unforgivable. A return unkind review from a friend earlier lost by a too frank or, heaven forbid, a sarcastic review from one's unruly pen can be, however, quite easily accepted as a sort of requiem for the friendship. Correction of judgment may be the end of life, as Kant would have it, but it can also be the end of a friendship. Friends respect each other's vulnerabilities, and it is difficult to overestimate the sensibilities of most authors to reviewers, especially when they know those reviewers.

One qualification to this gloomy estimate of the advisability of mutual criticism between friends, especially publishing friends, is in order. Publishing friends can be not just tolerant of, but grateful for, privately given criticism of drafts of what will later be submitted for publication, especially when they have solicited such criticism. What offends in an unfavourable book review from a friend, or even a friendly acquaintance, is the public airing of what it is felt, perhaps optimistically, would have been quite acceptable if communicated in private. It is even as if the offended author is charging the unkind reviewer with failing to make the criticism at the proper time and in the appropriate way, namely before publication, and tactfully. But if the critic has not been asked for private comments on the pre-publication manuscript, this charge is, of course, unreasonable. In theory, in publishing one is submitting one's writing to the critical scrutiny of anyone and everyone, and to the published judgment of whatever reviewer a journal chooses. But in practice, writers do not expect their friends to be frank about their writing's perceived faults, especially not in public. (I have lost at least three friends by too frank reviews of their books.)

Even when criticism is private, if unsolicited it seems bound to offend the touchy pride of writers. Recently I read a book about a long-ago acquaintance of mine, written by his son, who was an infant when his father died. I had never met the son, but I took the liberty of writing to him, expressing my appreciation for his book, but noting that his treatment of some of his father's deceased relatives and colleagues, all of them known to me, did not show that generosity of spirit that he had rightly attributed to his father. In reply, I received a letter from the author which, after thanking me for some factual details about his father that he had not known, went on to reprove me for passing any judgment on the generosity of spirit shown by the son, compared to the father, when I knew nothing, except his book, of the son. In this case, it seems, only a friend or close acquaintance was allowed to express a judgment, even in a private letter, about the personal attributes of the author, as expressed in his published comments about other people. (Not only am I prone to risk losing friends by published criticisms of their books, I also preclude new friendships by unsolicited unpublished criticisms of those I know only through their books.)

Writing memoirs of any kind is in any case a very dangerous business, as far as relations with those mentioned in the memoirs, or their friends, is concerned. Memories of the events related by the memoirist often diverge, or have been differently edited by different persons' selective and usually self-protective memories. Friendships can be put at risk when one of the friends puts on paper the way the shared past appears to her. It is nearly impossible to write non-self-serving memoirs, and almost as difficult to read non-defensively memoirs in which one figures. If one is asked for comments on such memoirs before publication, the temptation is very great to say "Not true!" whenever one remembers differently.

The fact that private criticism of a piece of writing has been requested is not always enough to make the criticism acceptable to a proud author. A German academic associate of mine, whose English was a lot better than my German, had an article he had written in English accepted by a journal on condition that he have some native English speaker go through it with him to eliminate some stiff and uncolloquial turns of phrase. He asked me to do this, and I was pleased, perhaps too pleased, to oblige, since he had been generous with his criticism of my German conversation. But it was no easy task to persuade him to alter any of his carefully composed, grammatically correct, but sometimes pedantic, sentences. Our tentative friendship was slightly strained by this requested but unwelcome reciprocity of assistance in use of a foreign language. Writers are naturally more sensitive than mere talkers to criticism of the words they choose, since the spoken word, or at least the word spoken in conversation, is not expected to last. Writers tend to have an unreasoning parental love of their written offspring. (This author graciously forgave me for correcting his English, and when we parted gave me a pretty little gift inscribed with congratulations on my progress in the German language, thereby, by Kantian rules, regaining the upper linguistic hand. Clearly the asked-for assistance had destabilized the delicate balance of the relationship. But then only someone with a proven track record of losing friends, and risking that loss, can speak knowledgeably about the topic that the editors of this volume on friendship[9] have agreed should be mine.)

A tendency to wit, sarcasm, and critical remarks can be something one values in one's friend, that makes her good company, even if one is sometimes the butt of her humour. But there is a time and a place, it seems, for cutting remarks. I was told recently of the distress caused in a group of old and close friends, when one of them, known for her sharp tongue, was dying, and kept up the habit of uncensored critical comments as long as she had breath. Her old friends were rallying around to help care for her in her final weeks, but were hurt by her apparent lack of appreciation, and by her acerbic words about their efforts to be helpful. One of them remarked that she would be lucky if she had any friends left by the end, to attend her funeral. Is one expected to change character when suffering and dying, so that one's sad and solemn friends not be offended by the tenor of one's remarks, even when that tenor is typical of one, and is what those friends once valued in one?

Does it matter, in any case, if one has no friends left to attend one's funeral? (The woman discussed in the previous paragraph in fact had a good turnout at hers, including all the offended deathbed helpers.) It is said that we die alone, so some last-minute shedding of friends, or apparent turning away from them, may be a sort of preparation for that, a turning of one's face to the wall. And some may begin doing this earlier than others.

So far in this essay I have been assuming that to live without friends is to be pitiable. But is it really true that, even if some choose to die without friends, no one would choose to live without them, as Aristotle, Hume, and a host of others have claimed? As Sebastian Barry's exiled, itinerant, and friend-pursued character Eneas McNulty reflects, "it is a mighty thing to enjoy the fact of a friend in the world. A mighty thing."[10] But this mighty thing is what in the end kills Eneas. Doubtless an entire life without friends is a poor life, but the one who has lost all her friends has of necessity once had friends. Should the loss of her friends have occurred through normal processes of attrition, that is to say through death, change, distance, and some failure to keep in touch across that distance, along with her not making new friends in her declining years, or even if some losses have occurred through her getting involved, directly or indirectly, in quarrels, or through too sharp a tongue or too little tolerance of a friend's sharp tongue, the friendless life need not be a bad life, for the friendless person. (I do not think it is necessarily worse for one's fellow persons, so worse morally, either. Even if there is a duty to associate, is there a duty of voluntary close association? Kant complained of the sentimentalists' overpraise of friendship, but contemporary moralists and virtue theorists too are in danger of overvaluing its moral status.[11] My main interest in this essay is in losing friends, as a natural rather than a moral phenomenon, and in the hedonic significance of such losses.) Friends are or were welcome companions. If they are physically absent, they can no longer be companions, and the pleasures of email are a poor substitute for talk, eye contact, body language, companionable silences, doing things together. Letters are better, but the art of letter-writing seems to be a dying one. So if one is without friends-as-companions, even if some old friendships are still intact, would it be so much worse to become friendless? At this point we are in the danger Socrates purported to find himself in, towards the end of Plato's *Lysis*, of associating friendship too closely with the useless. And that, as Socrates says, would strike a sour note. But memories of friendship are never useless. As long as one has the memories of good times with one's then friends, and is at peace

with oneself, one's own company can be not so bad. (I have found that I notice and so enjoy the beauties of nature more on solitary than on accompanied walks, when attention to conversation can distract from looking and seeing. As John Updike writes, "Aging calls us outdoors . . . in truth all views have something glorious about them. The act of seeing is itself glorious . . ."[12] The pleasures of solitude are not to be despised. Nor need one resort to the inner eye to discover the bliss of solitude: the outer eye too can have its vision improved. As Updike wisely remarks, "People are fun, but not quite serious or trustworthy in the way that nature is."[13])

Reading, and for that matter writing, are for most people solitary activities, so their pleasures are little affected by friendlessness. (This is not to deny that one needs critics for one's writing, but friends are not necessarily the best such critics. Nor is it to deny the special, but these days rare, pleasures of being a member of a group who listen to and perhaps discuss what one of them reads aloud.) Listening to music is another pleasure that survives well in solitude. Even if some of one's best memories of times with friends are of attending concerts together, one does not need a fellow listener to enjoy the music itself, as distinct from the talk before and after it. (This is especially true of recorded music, but even live music can be enjoyed as much by single as by accompanied concert or recital goers, and some people, even if accompanied, shut their eyes during the performance to block out distracting stimuli.)

Some philosophers, Kierkegaard for example,[14] have suggested that close friendships might interfere with one's less exclusive ties, those of neighbourliness, and humanitarianism. And, as E.M. Forster famously pointed out, one may have to betray one's country to avoid betraying one's friend. It seems to me unlikely that the friendless person will be a better neighbour, or better citizen, or better humanitarian, than the person with a circle of close friends. If a person has come to value the pleasures of solitude, she is in some danger of becoming antisocial, so is not very likely to be joining all those community associations that do good to her fellow persons. She may still support them financially, but if she seeks out the company of her neighbours and fellow do-gooders, she is likely to acquire friends from among them. As Emerson and C.S. Lewis say, friends see the same truth, engage in some valued joint activity.[15] So even if one is not, at first, close friends with the other members of one's community improvement group, or the local Save-the-Little-Blue-Penguin or Hands-Off-the-Greenstone-Valley group, if one meets regularly with them, one is choosing companions who see the same truth, and so, unless one is very prickly company, one acquires at least potential friends.

The person who has lost her old friends and not made new ones does not, however, inevitably become antisocial, let alone a recluse, simply because she enjoys the admittedly insidious pleasures of solitude. She need not become a glutton for such pleasures. She can still enjoy passing encounters, and conversations with those she meets as part of a normal life, with her family (who are closer than friends, and do not cease to be her family when they or she become sour and bad company), with shopkeepers, with the plumbers who unclog her drains, with those who sit beside her on public transport, with those who attend the lectures that she attends, and with strangers who, during the interval at concerts, engage her in conversation about the quality of the performance. (The upper balcony at Carnegie Hall is a particularly good place for such brief musical encounters.) She can still have a host of friendly relationships, one-shot or recurrent, when she has lost her close friends. And she can still enjoy the company of, and even conversations of a sort with, her intelligent, charming, understanding, and communicative cat, Clara, who, though wonderfully responsive, and not without ideas of her own, is blessedly unverbose. (Indeed she has a Luddite tendency when it comes to word processors.) Is this what Solon meant when he advocated that the friends we need to keep are our children, our trusty steed, and a host abroad?

Friendship may indeed be a mighty thing, a crown of life and a school of virtue, but there are other fine things, other crowns and other schools.

I seem to have turned from my topic of how to lose friends to the related topic of where one is left, in terms of quality of life, if one loses all or most of them, as if my title had been "The Consolations of Friendlessness." I now return very briefly to my official topic to add an irresistible postscript: one final way to lose any remaining friends may be to write an anecdotal essay about losing them.

Notes

1 Aristotle, *Nicomachean Ethics* 1157[b]14–17.
2 Nicholas Blake, *Room Temperature* (New York: Grove Weidenfeld, 1986).
3 Ibid., 26.
4 For more on this, see A. Rorty, "The Historicity of Psychological Attitudes: Love Is Not Love Which Alters Not When It Alteration Finds," in Neera Kapur Badhwar (ed.), *Friendship: A Philosophical Reader* (Ithaca, NY: Cornell University Press, 1993), 71–88; first pub. in *Midwest Studies in Philosophy*, 10 (University of Minnesota Press, 1986).

5 See John M. Cooper, "Aristotle on the Forms of Friendship," in Cooper, *Reason and Emotion: Essays on Ancient Moral Psychology and Ethical Theory* (Princeton: Princeton University Press, 1998).

6 C.S. Lewis, *The Four Loves* (London: Geoffrey Bles, 1960), quoted in Badhwar (ed.), *Friendship*, 42.

7 Kant, *The Metaphysics of Morals*, pt. II, sect. 46.

8 Ibid.

9 This essay was first published in French in Jean-Christophe Merle and Bernard N. Schumacher (eds.), *L'Amitié* (Paris: Presses Universitaires de France, 2005).

10 Sebastian Barry, *The Whereabouts of Eneas McNulty* (London: Picador, 1998), 77.

11 See Lawrence Blum, "Friendship as a Moral Phenomenon," taken from his *Friendship, Altruism and Morality* (London: Routledge and Kegan Paul, 1980), in Badhwar (ed.), *Friendship*.

12 John Updike, *Self-Consciousness: Memoirs* (London: André Deutsch, 1989), 235.

13 Ibid., 245.

14 Kierkegaard, *Works of Love*, pt. 1, ch. 2B.

15 Ralph Waldo Emerson, *Friendship*, vol. ii of *The Complete Works of Ralph Waldo Emerson* (Cambridge, MA: Riverside Press, 1883); Lewis, *The Four Loves*.

Discussion

Can love or friendship play a part in politics? Can it play a role in keeping a country together? What are some of the dangers involved in applying principles of love or friendship to the political realm? Would impartiality or fairness need to be sacrificed in order to include such considerations? Is there a sense in which, as Milligan suggests, our political associations are weakened by a lack of fraternity and community? If he is right, how might we develop a form of *citizen friendship*?

Generally in countries whose political orientation is broadly liberal, our relation to our fellow citizens is strictly "political" in the neutral sense of the term for which liberalism is famous. This means that what we owe each other at a minimum is respect for rights. The most minimal of liberal states limits these rights to negative ones that imply a duty on the part of all citizens not to interfere with each other (to respect their property, freedom, etc.). Other liberal states allow for some positive rights, such as the right to education or health care. But can a state make allowance for something that goes beyond rights? Friendship, as we normally understand it, is not defined in terms of rights and duties. Can there exist something like an attitude of friendship towards our fellow citizens that would strengthen the political life of a nation rather than creating an unhealthy form of nationalism?

In her article "How to Lose Friends," Annette Baier tells us that throughout one's life the ending of friendships is a somewhat natural occurrence. Not only is it natural, but the loss of friendships, according to Baier, is not always a bad thing. An analogy with death might illustrate her point. Just as death is not always considered a bad thing when the deceased has lived a good and long life and no longer wishes to suffer, so certain friendships that have once brought joy or meaning to one's life may be better off ending rather than degenerating into something unpleasant based solely on nostalgia or a sense of duty. Do you agree with this? Of course, some friendships end due to the death of one of the friends. Other friendships end due to distance and time apart. As I mentioned in the previous chapter, many friendships end due to changes that take place in the lives of the two friends. Our interests, knowledge, point of view, and so on change over the course of our lives. Baier makes a couple of interesting points in this regard. As we get to know someone else—a friend—we are quite up-to-date with his or her tastes or interests. Just when we have come to appreciate or understand why our friend or lover likes a certain thing and have become competent in discussing it, we may find that it no longer holds such an important place in our friend's life (or he or she may pretend it still does so as not to disappoint us after all that effort). Not only is this true, but Baier suggests that perhaps casual friendships can be more enduring than these deeper friendships where two people share mutual interests. Sometimes "less demanding friendships" are more durable because the two people enjoy each other's company even when they haven't seen each other in years. They do not have to negotiate all of the subtle intimacies, mood swings, secrets, and so on that accompany day-to-day friendships. How important is it for friends to know and appreciate the interests or passions of each other? Can casual friendships be *true* friendships when the *friends* spend most of their time apart? Are such friendships a bit illusory since they do not demand the kind of sacrifice and attention that more intimate friendships require? Does real friendship require that friends spend a lot of time together? Or is it better if friends spend a significant amount of time apart?

If it is true that we have established most of our lasting friendships by the time we reach middle age, then it would seem quite important to try to hold on to those friendships. But even at this time of life friendships break up. People change, get fed up with the other person's stubbornness or annoying habits, or simply drift apart due to distance or busy lifestyles. It is sometimes interesting to observe friendships among people who are older. They are so used to each other that their interactions, disagreements, arguments, and so on are almost predictable. (I am already seeing this in my own friendships.) At times, it looks as if they hate each other or at least drive each other crazy. But many of these friendships endure and when one of the friends dies, the other really feels the loss. It is probably true that we *should* lose certain friends (friendships that affect us negatively), but when do we know when a friendship should be terminated? Are certain types of people better suited to being on their own—enjoying nature or non-human companions? Are our pets truly friends in the relevant sense?

Suggestions for Further Reading

Jan Bransen, "Loving a Stranger," in *Love and Its Objects: What Can We Care For?*, edited by Christian Maurer, Tony Milligan, and Kamila Pacovská, 143–59 (Basingstoke, UK: Palgrave Macmillan, 2014).

Jacques Derrida. *The Politics of Friendship* (London: Verso, 2005).

Troy Jollimore, *Love's Vision* (Princeton: Princeton University Press, 2011).

Martha Nussbaum, *Political Emotions: Why Love Matters for Justice* (Cambridge, MA: Harvard University Press, 2013).

A.O. Rorty, "The Historicity of Psychological Attitudes: Love Is Not Love Which Alters Not When It Alteration Finds." *Midwest Studies in Philosophy* 10 (1986): 399–412.

Chapter Eighteen
Friendship and Love Online

Introduction

Today we spend a lot of time communicating with friends and family in one form or another online. Texting has surpassed email, of course, but we still use the latter for certain types of longer or more in-depth kinds of communications. But how effectively or deeply can we communicate online? Can we ever replicate or surpass the kind of communication or interaction that we have in person? Will online interaction only ever be a supplemental form of communication between people? Or can people truly develop friendships or perhaps even love relationships online? Robert Sharp examines this question in light of Aristotle's concept of friendship. Even though Aristotle's first two types of friendship might be achieved online, Sharp thinks it will be difficult, if not impossible, to achieve his highest type of friendship.

ROBERT SHARP

The Obstacles against Reaching the Highest Level of Aristotelian Friendship Online

Friendships today appear remarkably different than they did just a decade ago. With the proliferation of various social networks, from Facebook to Twitter, as well as the ubiquity of instant connectivity, we are rarely removed from an opportunity to communicate with our friends. In many ways, this has made friendship easier, and one might argue that friends today are closer to each other than at any other point in history. We are also able to befriend more people at once, since the barriers of physical proximity have been dissolved. In fact, many people consider online acquaintances to be friends, despite never having met in person. Past friendships are also easily renewed, allowing us to reconnect with people we have not seen in years. This friendship explosion is not without its critics, many of whom see online friendships as too shallow to carry any significance. While this debate interests me, I would like to focus on a different kind of problem with online friendships, one specifically related to the work of Aristotle. My concern is that the types of friendships we cultivate online are incapable of reaching the highest level of friendship as given by Aristotle's taxonomy. This creates a problem because it eliminates a viable and valuable tool in the path to the virtuous life. Our friendships influence our character, and certain types of friendships appear to be deeper than others. If, as I believe, online friendships face significant obstacles in reaching the kind of consummate friendship that Aristotle discusses, and if the possibility of such a level of friendship is an important tool for realizing virtues, then our propensity to develop our friendships largely or solely online could be damaging our ability to develop as fully virtuous members of society.

Before detailing this problem, I must explain why we should care about the concept of friendship adopted by an ancient Greek philosopher who lived in a very different society from our own. The short answer is that most of what Aristotle says about ethics and friendship still rings true today. Aristotle is among the earliest proponents of a view now labelled Virtue Ethics, which states that our actions are only part of the moral picture. Equally important are the character traits that led to those actions. For example, a person who refrains from lying solely because he or she is afraid of being caught would be seen as less virtuous than a person who has the character trait of being honest. The latter is more likely to act ethically in all situations, including those where there is no chance of being caught (a situation that the anonymity of the Internet often readily provides). While Aristotle's list of virtues include many traits that are still valued today, such as bravery, generosity, and honesty (Aristotle 1991, 1107b–1108b), what is important for my argument is not the specific virtues but rather the overall tendency to praise certain character traits over others.

One of the ways we cultivate such traits is through friendship, since our friends influence our habits and thus our virtues (or vices). Aristotle writes that "friendship is a virtue or something with virtue, and, besides, it is most necessary to life; for no one would choose to live without friends, though he were to have all the other goods" (Aristotle 1991, 1155a, 3–6). Obviously, humans are capable of living without friends. What Aristotle likely means is that we cannot live a good life, unless we have some sort of friendship in it. In this context 'good' refers to fullness or completeness, a state of contentment in which a person would change little or nothing about his or her life. Within a social context, those who have friends tend to lead better lives than those who do not.

Having friends makes us feel more secure and aids us in realizing other goals. Not all of these goals are necessarily good, which is why Aristotle might appear a bit naive when he writes that "friendship is not only necessary, but also noble" (1155a, 29). Surely, there are friendships that are ignoble, leading not to virtue but to vice. If a young man joins a gang because of his friends, and that association leads him to become a thief or a murderer, then we would hardly call this "not only necessary, but also noble." There are good friends and bad friends, in the sense that there are friends that elevate and support us and friends that corrupt and ruin us.

Elsewhere, however, Aristotle seems to be aware of this, at least indirectly, and is likely focusing on the good aspects in order to support his point that friendship is a critical part of the virtuous life. Our friends contribute to the types of persons that we become. If we befriend virtuous people, they will likely influence us in positive ways, pushing us to become better human beings. If our friends carry vices, our own personalities risk corruption. This explains why Aristotle ultimately proposes that we should strive for perfect friendship, where friends share a common pursuit of virtue.

As an empiricist, Aristotle cannot deny that most friendships fall short of this ideal. In fact, he recognizes three different levels of friendship. The first is a relationship based on utility, which means that two people are friends because "some good may be obtained from each other" (Aristotle 1991, 1156a, 11–12). Business relationships fall into this category, since both persons are attempting to gain from each other. Today, we might not consider this friendship at all, but rather an association. Still, very close associations can be formed on the basis of reciprocal utility, as long as the benefits to each person can be maintained for any length of time.

More often, we save 'friend' for Aristotle's second category, where people "like each other for the sake of pleasure" (1156a, 13). In these cases, a general feeling of well-being is experienced by both parties when they are near each other. People who simply enjoy each other's company fall into this category of friendship, and it encompasses most of what we mean by friendship today. People with shared interests are often bonded by those interests. For example, fans of a sports team might become friends through their shared passion. This

level of friendship also includes familial and spousal bonds, though Aristotle admits that the friendship between a father and son will carry different pleasures than that between brothers, since the power structures differ as do the benefits received (1162a). Also, in Aristotle's time, many marriages would be based on utility (e.g., political expediency), rather than pleasure. Today we tend to emphasize the latter, where marriage is concerned, though this still varies somewhat by culture.

Almost anyone can reach one of these first two levels of friendship, but Aristotle adds a third category, one that is reserved for those few people who truly seek a life of virtue. Such perfect friendship "exists between men who are good and are alike with respect to virtue" (1156b, 8–9). Friends that have reached this level wish only good things for each other, and "such men are good in themselves." In other words, perfect friendship can only happen between people who are virtuous, or at least sincerely pursue virtue. The relationship formed "is perfect both in duration and in the other respects" (1156b, 34). In his commentary, Hippocrates Apostle points out that both utility and pleasure would still be present amongst such friends, but they would be part of a larger commitment to the other person's good (Apostle 1991, 322). The lesser forms of friendship are more selfish, orienting toward one's own utility or pleasure, while perfect friendship would pursue utility or pleasure only through virtue.

One of the most critical aspects of Aristotelian friendship is its reciprocity, which manifests as a genuine desire to see a friend become a better person. According to Aristotle, "good men as such neither err nor allow their friends to fall into error" (1159b 6–8). The suggestion that good men do not err would be a product of equating the good with the right and thus the true. A good person does not make mistakes because mistakes are bad. However, he or she also strives to keep friends from falling into error. The two friends reinforce each other's virtues in the same way (and for the same reasons) as their own. As Dale Jacquette explains, "virtuous friends in the true or highest sense can help each other through periods when weakness of moral will threatens an otherwise good person with the temptation to act immorally" (Jacquette 2001, 383). Since virtue is a constant process, requiring the maintenance of rigorous habits of good behaviour and motives, slipping would be quite easy, especially in times of duress or change, times when our good habits are most threatened. A true friend helps us through these times, both directly and indirectly. Directly, the friend might stay our hand or simply talk us out of a rash choice. Indirectly, the friend continues to serve as an example, a sort of reflection of ourselves as we should be. Such reinforcement is invaluable because our friends play a major role in the type of person that we become. This is the most important reason why such friendship matters, whether in today's world or Aristotle's time. People who pursue a life of virtue are greatly aided by having friends with the same goals, but these friends must be available in a way that allows for reciprocal influences.

Some of these reciprocal influences among friends can still be provided through an online medium. A person might post about her charitable activities, which in turn reminds her friends of their duties toward others. An online friend might tell an anecdote of some temptation that he overcame recently, renewing our own ability to resist such situations. More directly, online discussions with friends might reveal moral flaws or slips, thus providing an opportunity to correct those mistakes.

A hypothetical example can help clarify these points. Suppose that during an online chat a man named David gives subtle indications to his friend Keith that he is tempted to start an affair with a co-worker. Keith now has a chance to remind David of his commitment to his wife and children as well as the vices that might arise from too much lustful thinking. This could be enough to help David realize his mistake and avoid a moral collapse. At first glance, this kind of exchange would not seem to require friendship, but that would be misleading. First, David is more likely to listen to a friend than to a stranger, and second, the friendship between the two men may be what allows Keith to pick up on the signals in the conversation and read them correctly. Finally, some level of care for David is likely necessary before Keith would bother to give such advice, much less follow through to make sure it is followed. However, the specific advice that Keith offers could be good or bad, depending on his character, and this is where the possibility of Aristotle's highest level of friendship becomes important. If Keith is an adulterer himself, he may be less likely to condemn it in others. So friendship alone is not enough. We need virtuous friends, who will help us make good decisions and act as positive reinforcement for those decisions. Overall, those who have the highest level of Aristotelian friendship will be more likely to be virtuous and maintain that virtue over time. We do not need to agree with Aristotle's apparent belief that such friendships are a necessary part of the virtuous life in order to acknowledge that they are incredibly useful and fulfilling. If online friendships cannot reach this level of friendship, then we need to be aware of this, so that we can look for them elsewhere and not fool ourselves into believing that we either have or could have such friends online. If it is possible to reach such a level in online friendship, then we still need to be aware of the obstacles that the online medium might place before us in this regard.

Perception of the Other

One of those obstacles comes from the relative lack of feedback that we receive when talking to people online. The reciprocal influence that forms the essential foundation of Aristotelian friendship is only possible if both participants are able to experience each other fully. In theory, such friends should be completely open with each other, since they are both virtuous. In practice, such openness may be stifled by the medium itself, which tends to make full disclosure unlikely, if not impossible. The central problem is one of perception. We cannot fully see or experience the other person online, since we are only privy to the information he or she provides us, information that is self selected and edited in ways that are not as achievable when people meet in person.

This problem occurs in two related but distinct ways: intentional non-disclosure and unintentional obfuscation. The first includes anything from outright lying to simply omitting information. Lying does not interest me here, because a person who wilfully deceives another is not pursuing Aristotelian friendship. Omitting information is, however, made easier by the Internet. If Keith only gets information about David from status updates, emails, and similar forms of disclosure, David could easily leave out important information. But why would he do this to a friend? One simple explanation is that many people keep difficult moral decisions private. After all, David cannot

post a status update about his extramarital temptations without his wife seeing it. He could, of course, simply email or message his friend directly, but again he will only do so if he is actively soliciting the friend's advice. This requires him to admit a potential moral failing, something most of us hesitate to do. In theory, a virtuous person will be honest about his or her failings, but David is on the verge of moral failure, which means we can no longer count on him to do what the theoretically virtuous person would do. With no other access to David's thoughts, Keith will have a difficult time determining that anything is amiss.

Such intentional non-disclosure may be lessening, however, or at least changing. As online social networks become more prolific, the amount of online disclosure appears to be growing. In *Socialnomics*, Erik Qualman notes that those who have grown up with the Internet care far less about privacy than those who came before them (Qualman 2009, 119–23). We may be seeing a new age of transparency, where people cannot easily distinguish between what should or should not be publically exposed. Perhaps there will be no such distinction. If so, people online may speak to each other about the same way they would in person. There may even be more openness online, since we cannot see the potentially judgmental face of the other person.[1] Certainly, the anonymity of online communication allows for some extraordinary disclosures that rarely happen offline. But even where real names are used, the medium presents a sort of judgment buffer zone that may allow us to confide in our friends more than we would otherwise.

Whether such openness will prove good or bad remains unclear, but this sociological change will not, in itself, overcome the problems of perceiving others online. Posting more intimate details about one's life does not necessitate that those details tell the whole story. Some intentional non-disclosure is likely to remain.

Even with complete (or relatively high) openness, there still remains the issue of unintentional obfuscation. Whatever our good intentions, we all lack at least some self-awareness. We may self-report that all is well, honestly believing this to be true, even though something is wrong. There is no intent to deceive, but there is also no way for others to see through this unintentional obfuscation if they only interact with us online. One of the vital roles that a friend provides is that of an outside observer, who can detect our faults (or praise our virtues) and give perspective that we lack. However, this role becomes difficult to follow online, without the cues that are available in physical interaction.

I certainly do not mean to suggest that offline friendships are perfectly transparent and thus free of unintentional obfuscation. The same perceptual problems can exist in face-to-face encounters. If David and Keith worked together, David might still keep his thoughts to himself, effectively preventing Keith from helping him. The key difference, though, is that Keith could find out in some other way. Physical proximity could allow him to see changes in David's behaviour. He might even catch him flirting with the other co-worker, which would allow Keith to gently remind his friend of the dangers of going too far, perhaps even before David entertains the idea of an affair. All of this is hypothetical, but the point is that physical proximity allows us to perceive signals that are simply not present online.

Without the ability to physically see and assess what our friends are doing, we can never be sure that what they post online matches their offline realities. I do not mean that they may be lying (though this is possible), but that there is insufficient information for determining the state of the other person. This is especially problematic at the beginning of a relationship, where there is no baseline for determining character. But the problem remains once friendship is formed, even if the other person intends to be completely honest. Text only conveys so much, which is why emoticons have become such a common way to avoid online misunderstandings. The lack of tone, gesture, cadence, and similar linguistic features robs online language of depth.

Such problems are somewhat ameliorated if we know the person offline as well. We might then be able to detect changes in attitude and comments that seem out of character. But such relationships are not really online friendships, at least not in the fullest sense. They are friendships that happen to have an online component. When dealing with someone that we *only* know online, our lack of ability to fully perceive the other person presents us with potentially insurmountable difficulties in assessing their character.

For those who do know each other offline, however, the Internet can provide a great source for enhancing friendship, though it cannot serve as a complete substitute for social skills. Research shows that most people display the same skills when making friends online as they do offline.[2] In a fascinating summation of several psychology and sociology studies, David Disalvo finds that people who are already lonely cannot ease that loneliness simply by joining social networks (Disalvo 2010). The skills that we need for good friendships must be brought with us into the online world. Certainly, as Disalvo discovers, having access to a wide range of people can help those who are young and just learning how to develop social skills (50–52). Ultimately, however, "the social networkers who fare the best are ones who use the technology to support their existing friendships" (55). Disalvo's article concludes with the point that the success of online friendships directly correlates with whether people know each other offline as well (55). Such friendships tend to be enriched by the extra access to others that the Internet provides.

Given this research, perhaps finding like-minded people capable of the same levels of friendship is more likely than I have suggested. In the long run, the true character of a person may manifest online just as it does offline. It might take longer, but the possibility that people can be basically the same when online could mean that Aristotelian friendship is also achievable, at least in theory. We might lose some of the advantages of that friendship, especially where reciprocity is concerned, because of the communication issues discussed above. Still, certain character traits may show through, allowing some of the benefits of such friendship. I remain unconvinced that enough would remain to reach the highest levels that Aristotle has in mind, but perhaps as online communication evolves, so will our ability to perceive each other in this medium, which in turn would enable us to influence each other in more direct and positive ways.

Perception through the Other (Apperception)

While perceiving the other person is an important part of friendship, the true power of friendship comes from how it helps us perceive ourselves. When a friend does something hurtful, we might realize that we often do the same thing. This can lead to new awareness of the effects our actions have on others. Of course, we can and do learn such lessons from strangers, but since we pay more attention to our friends, we are more likely to notice the consequences of our actions upon them. More importantly, because we care about what our friends think of us, we are likely to consider what they think of those actions. In other words, friendship can make us more self-aware by leading us to imagine how we must appear to others. This external standard pushes us outside of our egocentric thoughts, though the degree to which we do this, and the insights gained, vary by the depth of the friendship involved.

Before viewing those differences, a quick point on terminology is necessary. I shall label the process of understanding ourselves through how we perceive that others perceive us 'apperception,' borrowing a term that has multiple possible meanings. Kant used it to represent a sort of "necessary unity" of "self-consciousness" (Ameriks 1995, 401), which I take to mean that it elevates our self-awareness as moral agents. While that usage is part of what I mean, my use of the term shall refer more specifically to our ability to perceive our own selves in new ways by considering how we are (or might be) perceived by others. This usage derives from Edmund Husserl's "Fifth Meditation" in the *Cartesian Meditations* (Husserl 1929). 'Apperception' will stand as a shorthand for the process by which we come to understand ourselves through the actions and judgments of other people, which is a key part of our personal identity. The process of developing self-perception is beyond the scope of this paper, but for the present discussion all that needs to be acknowledged is that our personal identities are largely reflections of how we think others view us. This explains why most people act differently around their parents when compared to their friends. To some degree, we try to live up to the roles that we think others expect from us. This concern for what others think (through our apperception of ourselves through them) forms a critical part of the positive and negative influences that friends provide.

In the first level of Aristotelian friendship (utility), apperception could lead us to temporarily change ourselves to accommodate another in order to gain what we want. A sales person might pretend to be a football fan in order to sell a car to someone wearing a football jersey. In such cases, the influence is likely to be temporary, since it leads to a pretense rather than a real change. However, changing our stated values in order to reach some goal could lead to a diminished commitment to those values, especially in cases where our original values were not strongly held. In general, though, such temporary shifts into a useful role are unlikely to create dramatic changes in values.

A good example of how apperception could work in Aristotle's second level of friendship (pleasure) is the case of peer pressure. In order to maintain a pleasurable relationship, we might find ourselves adjusting to fit what we conceive the other person to want. For example, if I enjoy discussing religion with someone, I might feign interest in a doctrine that my friend finds interesting, even if I do not. This might begin as a way of avoiding unnecessary confrontation, but in some cases it can end with my judgments actually changing to fit the desires (real or imagined) of the other person. In either case, the change is made in order to maintain the pleasurable connection to the other person, rather than out of some

noble attempt to become a better person. Such changes could be good or bad, depending on our associates, but in either case they are more likely to stick than those discussed in utility friendships, in part because pleasure friendships involve more time spent with the other person. The more time we spend playing a role, the more likely that role will become part of who we are.

Such influences are very common, but we are here concerned with Aristotle's highest level of friendship, where two virtuous individuals see themselves in each other. At this level, apperception should lead only to positive influences, since the other person is not only virtuous but expects the same from his or her friend. In fact, Aristotle appears to recognize the apperception inherent in this kind of friendship (though the word itself had not yet been coined). Such friendship requires some sort of recognition of one's self in the other person: "good men wish what is good for those whom they like for the latter's sake, not by feeling but by disposition. And in liking a friend, they like what is good for themselves" (Aristotle 1991, 1157b, 32–34). Essentially, there is no difference between two virtuous friends. Their needs and desires are practically the same. As H.G. Gadamer explains, this means more than just a "sense of 'he is too.' Far more in the sense that we grant to one another our being as Other" (Gadamer 1999, 9). The other person must be both our recognition of ourselves expanded outward and an allowance that we be expanded in such a way. It is an absence of narcissism, a sort of anti-narcissism. We must transpose what is good for us onto the other person and vice versa. The interest in the other person that emerges from this is virtually the same as an interest in one's self. Such friendship is a tiny community of two, but a community with full solidarity, one that strives for virtue and perfection.

Gadamer worries that such solidarity is becoming increasingly implausible as our society becomes more anonymous. At the time of his writing (in 1999), his main concern was not so much the Internet itself as the tendency to reduce everyone to numbers and statistics, removing personal identity as much as possible. "When one declares oneself as in solidarity," Gadamer explains, "in every case there lies a renunciation of one's own interests and preferences" (11). Moreover, this renunciation "must be conscious, only then does it work." For full friendship, we must intentionally join with the other in such a way that we both renounce our own personal interests and receive that interest back under the umbrage of solidarity. In order to do this, we must have personal interests and a sense of self, even a kind of self-love (Gadamer 1999, 8). This should not be confused with selfishness. Virtuous self-love is really just love of virtue, the virtue that is present in one's self. Similarly, the love of a friend (at the highest level) results from the love of the virtue of the other person and a true desire to see that virtue remain. In this way, self-love and the love of the other are the same in Aristotle.

Such a friendship requires a certain level of intimacy. We must see and be seen in some way, and the influential effects of the friendship must be exercised on both parties. Aristotle suggests we must even live together in order to be friends of this caliber (1157b, 19–20). I doubt this is meant literally, but it does show that he believes friendship must be exercised and somehow continuous. The beneficial aspects of the friendship cannot occur otherwise. There must be a constant and deep conversation that takes place between friends

of this sort, and this is where the Internet and social media seem to fail us.

At the time of this writing, the average Facebook user has around 130 friends (www.facebook.com/press/info.php?statistics). We can probably assume that a few of these are celebrities or interest groups. Still, that leaves a sizable group of friends for most users. While the majority of Facebook users would admit that 'friend' is used very loosely, the tendency to use that term at all may diminish its force. In a recent lecture on Aristotle's friendship, I asked my students to raise their hands if they believed they had friends of the sort that Aristotle described. Nearly all of them did so. Perhaps my explanation was poor, since the chances of any of my students having such a friend should be very low, according to Aristotle. Nevertheless, many of us believe we have such friends, often because we conflate closeness with the sort of connection Aristotle has in mind. They are not the same, but even if they were, how would we find the time to get so close to one individual when we are monitoring the statuses and updates of so many people?

As Aristotle explains, perfect friendship is not only rare but time consuming. He writes:

> It is impossible to be a friend to many men in a perfect friendship, just as it is impossible to be in love with many persons at the same time; for love is like an excess, and such excess is by its nature felt towards one person only, and it is not easy for many people to satisfy very much the same person at the same time, or perhaps for many persons to be good at the same time. Besides, one must also acquire experience and become familiar with many persons, and this is extremely difficult. (Aristotle 1991, 1158a, 11–15).

Perfect friendships "require time and familiarity" in order to gain the level of trust and understanding necessary (1156b, 25). Even extended online chats do not reach this level. Such interactions are self-chosen and easily edited. They also fail to convey the tone and gestures that we use in order to discern another's state of mind. Through physical proximity, we can see how a person reacts to different situations while under various levels of duress. Aspects of personality are exposed more quickly, while being harder to hide. We also get the instant facial reactions to our words and actions that are a key part of apperception. In order to grasp how our actions affect others, we must see those effects immediately.

The depth to which computer-mediated interaction modifies our ability to both perceive and apperceive can be illustrated by how easily humans are fooled into believing computer programs have human qualities. In his book about how the Internet is changing the way we think, Nicholas Carr explains how the computer scientist Joseph Weizenbaum's ELIZA program can fool people into believing it is having a conversation with them. As Carr explains, "Weizenbaum's program, following a set of simple rules about English grammar, would identify a salient word or phrase in the sentence and analyze the syntactical context in which it was used" (201). It would then respond based on these same rules, "giving the illusion of a conversation." Weizenbaum himself was troubled by how easily users were fooled into believing they were having a real conversation, including "his secretary, who had watched him write the code for ELIZA" (205).

Such programs can trick us into thinking we are having a moment of apperception when in fact we are simply self-reflecting (at best). Most of ELIZA's conversations consist of the program rearranging what we input as a question, mimicking the way a psychologist might push us to probe our own thoughts. More recent programs of this sort have gotten even more realistic.[3] The feedback we receive is a self-reflection, and that is a valid part of apperception. In theory, a virtuous person might gain from this, in the same way that person gains from any self-reflective therapy. What will not be gained is insights from another person. This is especially problematic in the case of Aristotelian friendship, because the extra moral force of the other person is lost and the individual is essentially left to self-develop without any external aid. This might be possible, but it is not friendship.

Imagine a program like ELIZA as a Facebook application. Since people cannot easily judge who is behind a text-based message, they could have conversations with this program, even friend it, without ever knowing it was just a series of programmed responses. ELIZA might even become a person's best online friend, since she is a great listener. She does not judge or condemn, but simply repeats what she hears. All of the semblance of a profound conversation and relationship might appear to exist here, but in fact every thought ELIZA offers is but an echo of our own. Any feelings of empathy that we experience would really be our own self-interest reflected back at us. Apperception would be happening, but solely from our own imaginations, which means that ELIZA would only be able to confirm what we already believe about ourselves. This is the opposite of personal progress.

If apperception in friendship is to work, there must be actual empathy between two friends, each capable not only of understanding his or her own thoughts but also those of another. Understanding a friend's feelings allows us to correctly assess their moral state and how we might help them achieve a better one. It is also critical to our apperception of ourselves, since empathy enables us to perceive and understand the effects we have on others.

Unfortunately, our ability to empathize with other people may already be diminishing from our increased tendency to communicate with other people more indirectly. Psychologist Sara Konrath and her research team recently engaged the question of whether empathy among college students has declined since the increase of online and text-based communication. According to the study, their "meta-analysis of 72 samples of American college students found a decrease in Empathic Concern and Perspective Taking, especially in the past decade" (Konrath 2010, 22). When compared to previous generations, students today report less empathic behaviour toward their fellow humans. There are many factors that could account for this, and blaming the Internet alone would be fallacy of haste. Still, according to a *New York Times* article, "the authors speculate a millennial mixture of video games, social media, reality TV and hyper-competition have left young people self-involved, shallow and unfettered in their individualism and ambition" (Paul 2010). In an email correspondence, Konrath herself reminded me that such speculation is premature, but also noted that Jean Twenge's recent studies that show a rise of narcissism associated with using MySpace give reason to believe that the Internet is capable of changing our personality traits.

At the very least, these correlations should lead us to ask serious questions about what friendship, and relationships more generally, will mean in a world based around so much online communication. Face-to-face interaction

is a key part of how we learn to understand the feelings of others. Social skills develop as we experience visual cues and feedback from personal exchanges. These exchanges are especially important for younger people, who are still learning how to interact with others.

This is why Aristotle dismisses the notion that young people can have perfect friendships. According to him, "friendship between young men is thought to exist for the sake of receiving pleasure, for they live by their passions and pursue mostly what is pleasurable to themselves and what exists at the moment" (1156a 31–33). Since their passions and pleasures change quickly, their friendships seldom last very long. Those of us who barely (if ever) communicate with our best friends from high school can understand Aristotle's meaning here. In order to have lifelong commitments, we must have some core quality in common with the other person. Young people are still developing their identities and are thus unlikely to have that stable core.

In order to see yourself in someone else, you must first have some sense of who you are, and in Aristotelian terms this would require a developed character of some sort. Then you must be able to see that character in the other person, as a kind of reflection. For such a reflection to have any depth, our perception of the other person must also be fairly complete. Seeing that the other person likes the same music or books would be too superficial for this level of apperception. Friendships of utility or pleasure could find a basis in these commonalities, but the highest friendship needs more than this. We must be able to perceive the virtue in the other person and through that perception, see the virtues in ourselves.

We simply cannot discover enough about another person through Facebook updates and text messages. We can determine hobbies and interests, but there is no way to discern the passion behind them. The self-report that people provide on the Internet often misrepresents the reality. One woman I know only through an online forum recently bemoaned that a friend of hers created an online dating profile in which he represented himself as a "bad boy" when he is "very, very far from it!" A potential match will have no way of discovering this until she meets him in person. Here we see the problems of perception and apperception converging. Since we cannot tell whether the person behind the words is sincere or self-aware, we can never know for certain whether he or she really embodies a kindred spirit until we face that person in real life.

Studies suggest that the more time we spend with a friend in different spaces (e.g., online, offline, working, social, etc.), the closer and more intimate our bonds become (see Lijun 2010 for a case study). This makes intuitive sense and matches our experiences. One recent study found that even among those who experience secure attachments to others (the only group that would really matter for Aristotelian friendship), the quality and intimacy of friendships was greater offline (Boute et al. 2009, 564–66). Since this study was conducted among college-aged people, the participants are likely familiar with online interaction and social media. Nevertheless, their friendships are more secure when achieved and maintained offline rather than solely online.

These studies are inconclusive to our purpose in some ways, but they do indicate a greater ease and satisfaction in offline friendships. This is somewhat surprising, since disclosure of personal details might be seen as easier online, where we cannot experience immediacy

of judgment. But it also fits with our need for support in our friendships. The actual presence of a friend carries more emotional weight. Encouraging messages can only take us so far. Also, many of our problems require physical aid, which is something an online friend cannot provide.

Without the ability to see and be seen in direct ways, complex friendships will be at best very difficult to achieve, and perhaps impossible. Perhaps perception and apperception online will be facilitated by advances in technology, but at present, many of our online communications are becoming *more* shallow rather than less. The advent of Twitter and the desire for smaller, tighter status updates have led us to peruse the lives of others in brief snippets rather than seeking a deeper connection. We can track more of our acquaintances this way, staying in touch with a hundred people or more, as we get continuous updates on their lives. But these updates are superficial by necessity, obstructing the possibility of really getting to know the other person. Current Internet trends are thus making perfect friendship less likely every day.

One Last Attempt at Perfect Online Friendships

At this point, I would expect an observant reader to note that many of the problems I have suggested deal less with whether perfect friendships are possible at all online and more with how difficult they would be to achieve. This is a fair point and worth a response. The problems of perceiving, being perceived, and perceiving oneself through a connection to another are all inherent in the medium of online communication. These are difficulties that result from distance between the two communicants, a distance that is not lessened by the Internet as much as we might think.

However, there may still be cases where two virtuous people find each other online. Because they are virtuous (or try to be), they will not be intentionally duplicitous. They will have some degree of self-awareness and will strive to be open and honest, even about their shortcomings. When they struggle with moral temptation, they will actively seek the aid of a friend, and that friend, being virtuous, will fill his or her role as well as possible. Under these circumstances, might two people find perfect friendship online?

In theory, such a connection seems possible. It would require extraordinary openness from both parties and a willingness to communicate as often as possible. The lack of shared physical activities might still prove a barrier to perfect friendship, but perhaps certain experiences could still be close enough to each other to seem shared. I am hesitant to say that the virtues formed would be similar enough, however, since Aristotle admits that virtue will vary a bit depending on the nature of the person and the situations within which we find ourselves (Aristotle 1991, 1106a 25–1106b 7).

In any case, I think we must admit that the Internet is an invaluable supplement to a good friendship. It allows us to communicate with each other even when we are not together. A friendship that begins with face-to-face interaction could be strengthened by the increased connection that the Internet provides.

The Internet can be a wonderful tool for staying in touch in situations that would previously have made communication inconvenient, if not impossible. We sometimes cannot avoid travelling or otherwise disconnecting from our friends. In Aristotle's time, this could mean the loss of a friend, especially if a move was permanent. Writing letters was insufficient substitute for personal contact and took so much time to deliver that any help offered could easily be too late. Today, contact is immediate, and while it may still be insufficient in many ways, it is better than nothing, especially in cases where the friend will return. An actual move might create other problems, because the distance would lead to the issues above. But as a tool for staying in touch during necessary travel, friendship can benefit from the Internet.

My concerns focus on friendships developed either solely or largely online. The Internet cannot act as a substitute for true proximity, for those times when we experience another person in person. We must be able to perceive the other person in a full, rich way, and he or she must be able to perceive us as well. This creates the necessary bond, one that will allow the fullest communication of feelings and goals, with the least ability to fool the other person or hide our vices. Unless something dramatically changes, I do not believe that friendships formed largely or wholly online can ever reach the level of perfect, Aristotelian friendship.

Notes

1   I will address this notion of being judged below, in the section on apperception.
2   The most obvious exception to this rule is the case of a handicapped person who is able to overcome the stigma barrier through the anonymity that internet communication provides. In such cases, making friends online may be easier, at least in the initial stages. This has

little bearing on the possibility of full Aristotelian friendship.

3 Many of these programs use video of actual actors, in order to complete the illusion. At some point, discerning the difference between speaking to an actual human and speaking to a computer program will be difficult at best. ELIZA was written in the 1960s and was already fooling users!

GARY FOSTER

If friendship in its truest form cannot be achieved online, then what does this imply for love? Are we any more likely to experience love in this way? In my own article, I discuss the philosophical issue of personal identity in the context of searching for love online. Personal identity has been a topic of interest to philosophers at least since Plato. What does it mean to be a person? Are persons simply the sum of their properties, or is there a soul or a self that exists independent of our normal physical properties? I propose a different view. I look at the presentation of *persons* through online dating profiles to try to show how a person's properties or characteristics are revealed online, as opposed to offline. I argue that some philosophers have understood properties of persons in a way that abstracts those properties from the persons themselves. In this sense, their approach mirrors online dating profiles, which separate the properties of persons according to various categories.

Internet Dating: Challenges to Love and Personal Identity

Internet dating has changed the way many people engage in romantic relationships or seek marriage partners. A new space for meeting people has evolved via the cyberworld and given rise to a new culture for dating that involves changes in etiquette, expectations, ways of flirting, as well as ritual meanings. From a philosophical perspective, one of the potentially most significant changes that Internet dating has effected is in our experience of persons or our perception of personal identity. When we check out someone's profile on Match.com or Plenty of Fish, or scroll through OkCupid or Tinder, we see a person's identity as structured by the specific dating site or app. We see a picture, read a list of facts (age, height, body type, smoker/non-smoker, wants children/does not want children, likes movies, likes baseball, etc.) as well as a more personal account wherein the *candidate* is meant to express a bit of who they are beyond merely the aforementioned facts. This piece-by-piece introduction to a person is surely different from the subtle kinds of courting and flirtation that we perform in a public space (a bar, coffee shop, volunteer organization), but how significant are those differences? Of course, I can send a "wink" on Match.com or a "flirt" on Plenty of Fish, but these online gestures are only remotely related to the subtle (and not so subtle) interactions we experience in the flesh. Do interactions through online dating sites change the way that we experience another *person*? In this essay, I want to explore two questions: Do online sites and apps, which present the person as a collection of separate properties (e.g., tall, athletic, artsy, fun, etc.), give us an inadequate experience of persons? Does the properties view of personal identity, with its tendency to abstract properties from their embodied state, provide an inadequate understanding of persons?

Personal Identity: Conflicting Views

The discussion of personal identity has long been part of the history of philosophy. A central theme of this discussion can be characterized as the relation or dialectic between constancy and change or between identity and diversity. We see the tension that these opposing notions give rise to already in Plato's characterization of identity. In his *Symposium*, Plato presents the view of Diotima as follows:

> We . . . assume that a man is the same person in his old age as in his infancy, yet although we call him the same, every bit of him is different, and every day he is becoming a new man, while the old man is ceasing to exist, as you can see from his hair, his flesh, his bones, his blood, and all the rest of his body. And not only his body, for the same thing happens to his soul. And neither his manners, nor his dispositions, nor his thoughts, nor his desires, nor his pleasures, nor his sufferings, nor his fears are the same throughout his life. . . . Thus, unlike the gods, a mortal creature cannot remain the same throughout eternity; it can only leave behind a new life to fill the vacancy that is left as it passes away. (1989, 351)

This view characterizes personal identity as being in constant flux and suggests that there is no enduring self. In his dialogue *Phaedo*, however, Plato describes the soul as that which endures and is more real than the perishing body: "The soul is the very likeness of the divine,

and immortal, and intellectual, and uniform, and indissoluble, and unchangeable; and the body is in the very likeness of the human, and mortal, and unintellectual, and multiform, and dissoluble, and changeable" (513–14). The idea of the soul would evolve into the notion of the self in modern times, but the idea that this self is something constant or enduring has not disappeared quietly.

John Locke tried to reconcile the notions of constancy and change in his own unique view of personal identity. Locke recognized that people and things change and yet there is a sense in which they remain the same *thing* or the same *person*. For instance, a tree changes its matter entirely over the course of its life and yet we regard the large old oak that our grandfather planted as the same tree that was tiny and delicate after he first planted it. If the material that constitutes the tree has changed entirely over the course of its existence, then why do we call it the *same* tree? Locke writes,

> We must therefore consider wherein an oak differs from a mass of matter, and that seems to me to be in this, that the one is only the cohesion of particles of matter any how united, the other such a disposition of them as constitutes the parts of an oak; and such an organization of those parts as is fit to receive and distribute nourishment, so as to continue and frame the wood, bark, and leaves, &c., of an oak, in which consists the vegetable life. That being then one plant which has such an organization of parts in one coherent body, partaking of one common life, it continues to be the same plant as long as it partakes of the same life. (1924, 185)

For Locke, it is the continued organization of the tree or the continuous life of the tree that makes it the same tree, not the material itself, which changes over the life of the tree. Locke applies essentially the same criterion to our identity as a human being. Even though the cells that make up our bodies change over time, we can be identified as the same human being by the continued organization of our body over the course of our life (having the same DNA, for instance). But Locke makes a distinction between human identity and personal identity. To be the same human being is not the same as being the same person. To be a person involves being conscious of our self or having a relation to our self.

> To find wherein personal identity consists, we must consider what person stands for;– which, I think, is a thinking intelligent being, that has reason and reflection, and can consider itself as itself, the same thinking thing, in different times and places; which it does only by that consciousness which is inseparable from thinking, and, as it seems to me, essential to it . . . For, since consciousness always accompanies thinking, and it is that which makes every one to be what he calls self . . . in this alone consists personal identity, i.e., the sameness of a rational being: and as far as this consciousness can be extended backwards to any past action or thought, so far reaches the identity of that person. (Locke, 188)

We can consider ourselves to be the same person over time, according to Locke, to the extent that we can extend consciousness into the past and take ownership for certain actions or experiences.[1]

Other philosophers have had a different take on personal identity. David Hume, for instance, argued that personal identity, or what we call the self, was simply a bundle of our perceptions. There is no constant, unchanging self, but our memory and imagination unites our perceptions and experiences and makes us think that we possess a unified and enduring self. In opposition to Hume, Immanuel Kant thought there must be some basis for unity within us. In order for experience to be human experience and more specifically to be "my" experience, there had to be something in that experience that is constant and unified. Kant thought that the mind and our consciousness was structured in a unifying way so that our experiences were not just random noises, sounds, colours, and so on.

More recently the debate about personal identity has been characterized in terms of *persons* versus *properties*. Are persons simply reducible to their properties or is there something beyond properties that constitutes or defines personhood? Derek Parfit, in a manner similar to Hume, has argued that there is nothing more to personhood than the experiences and memories one possesses. There is no "further fact" of personal identity, as Parfit puts it (1986, 242), which means that there is no soul or Cartesian ego in addition to one's experiences and memories. Similarly, Alan Soble, while writing about love, tells us that the object of love is a person, but what he means by this is the collection of properties that grounds one's love (1990, 307–8). But others, such as David Velleman, have followed Kant in thinking that there may be something that we can call our true self that is not reducible to our normal empirical properties. He does not regard this *something* as a separate substance or a soul in the Platonic sense, but rather as our capacity for valuation. It is this capacity that he sees as distinct from our empirical properties. For Velleman, our empirical properties, including our smile, our sense of style, and so on, reveal our true self or our capacity for valuation (what

Kant calls our rational nature) to others (1999, 371–72). It is this *true self* that is the proper object of love.

In the next section, I want to examine how we experience persons or the identity of persons in the context of online dating. Profiles on sites such as Match.com or Plenty of Fish present the properties of a person in a somewhat systematic manner based on a common template, while allowing space for the participants to express something of their personality or what we have traditionally regarded as their *real* self.

Online Identity

It would be quite natural to think that online dating sites reinforce a *properties* view of persons—that is, that persons are collections of properties and nothing more—given that dating profiles on these sites are not only set up to present various properties (age, height, body type, hobbies, etc.) but many of these sites also send members matches based on properties (either on matching properties or on the properties that the member desires in a partner). Indeed, I think that there is a sense in which such sites do reinforce this type of view of identity. As one looks at numerous profiles and eliminates various dating or relationship candidates based on undesirable or incompatible properties, it seems somewhat inevitable that the person will come to think of other people in these terms. On the other hand, the profiles are also designed to allow members to express something of their personalities. Most sites have a section of the profile where people are encouraged to write something more personal about themselves. In these sections, people attempt to distinguish themselves with humour, a story of a unique experience, or a

description of how friends characterize them, for example.

An interesting difference between online and offline interaction is the way that the various features of a person, their properties and personality, are experienced. These features are separated into different categories online. We are given a description of the person's physical characteristics and, in many cases, a picture or pictures. We are also given other information pertaining to their likes and dislikes, activities, and so on, as well as the aforementioned self-description. Our imagination then creates a picture of the person that combines these qualities. We get a *composite*, as it were. Of course, continued interaction online with a person may allow us to get a better sense of *who* he or she is, but we often think that there is still something missing in this picture. Offline, we experience people's properties as embodied and partly as an expression of who they are (through a smile, a glance,[2] etc.). We are able to see the person's properties not as abstract details on an itemized profile but as part of their whole being. There is less room for the imagination. Of course, our imagination still plays a role in uniting the identity of the other person in offline situations.[3] We project and create an image of the person that reflects our own desires, interests, perspective, and so on. But, in our offline encounters, our imagination is kept partly in check by the physical existence of the other person, which in many cases defies the picture we have created.

It is this embodied identity that I think is the key to understanding the difference between online and offline romance. We are embodied beings. What does this mean? Well, it suggests that as persons our properties are not things that exist independent of us, like our car or our TV. There is an important sense in which we *are* our properties or, more accurately, we are our body. Tall, funny, athletic, blond, and so on are not simply properties that we *possess*; they are descriptions of our self or our identity. When we list these things in an online dating profile, we separate these various properties and, in a sense, disassemble our personhood. Now this is not to say that online dating is a bad thing. It is typically used as a bridge or a connection point for later offline relationships. But it does point out an important difference between the two types of romantic interactions, which I believe has further implications.

Persons and Profiles: Getting to Know a Person Online

Writers on this topic have argued that the development of online relationships differs from those offline. For instance, Monica Whitty and Adrian Carr suggest that online dating profiles accelerate certain normal aspects of getting to know another person because of how personal information is provided in profiles (2006, 129). Rather than getting to know a person gradually, profiles are set up to reveal a breadth and depth of information all at once. As I mentioned in the last section, a profile reveals numerous details about a person (breadth) and encourages the member to discuss his or her personality and character (depth). Offline, these kinds of details are typically revealed to us gradually, but online we receive this information as a package. Possessing this relatively large amount of information may give us the mistaken impression that we know the person better than we actually do. Similarly, John Bridges refers to the "illusion of intimacy" as that phenomenon common to both online and offline romantic interactions whereby one feels a connection with another person and comes to believe that

he or she knows him or her much better than is possible in a short amount of time (2012, 43–44). Bridges's discussion of the illusion of intimacy focuses on the online context, which he thinks helps create the illusion more frequently than in offline situations. The self-description that accompanies an online profile is highly selective and aims primarily to gain a response from the reader rather than reveal who he or she really is (Bridges 2012, 47–48). Likewise, Whitty tells us that self-presentations online can be a quite strategic affair (Whitty 2007, 58–59). It is important to note that *strategic* in this case need not mean intentionally deceptive. The Internet gives us room to play or experiment with our identities and to try out different selves or different aspects of our identity (Turkle 2011, 212–15; Albright 2007, 81–93). We may actually believe these aspects of our identity or these personae to be true in some sense. This identity exploration may be healthy. But it may also serve to create the problems suggested by Bridges and others. We may either gain a false picture of the person in question or we may gain a false sense of intimacy in relation to him or her. Once again, deception of this sort can take place offline as well, and people can experience the illusion of intimacy in that context, but it is the structure of online dating that seems to make this problem more unavoidable.

During offline dates, especially at the beginning, people tend to put their best foot forward or present a side of themselves that they think is more attractive to others. But, in this context, one arguably has more to work with in making judgments about who or what the other person is. Rather than reading a list of properties or a self-description, one can see for oneself both the acknowledged and unacknowledged characteristics of the other person as they are expressed or revealed in an embodied encounter. One also experiences the other as a living presence who is unable to delete or correct the words he or she speaks and is unable to give a perfect self-presentation. Arguably, one can gain a better sense of who the other is in such a context as well as gain an impression of his or her character. A glance, a smile, a spontaneous joke or funny remark, or even an act that ignores etiquette tells us something that a strategic profile, which has been long thought out, does not.

Alternatively, one might see more of the person's properties or characteristics through reading a profile, assuming that the person writing the profile is honest and self-revealing. She or he may disclose things that one would not normally discover for a long time, if at all. But this form of self-revelation, detached as it is from the embodied person, seems significantly different from the experience we have of the characteristics of a person whom we experience in the flesh.

Persons, Properties, and Personality

The difference that I have been discussing between the online and offline encounter with another person reveals an important insight into the nature of personal identity. Persons, I want to argue, are more than a collection of properties. This claim does not necessarily imply that to be a person requires that one possess a soul or that there is some "further fact" in addition to properties or characteristics that constitutes persons, but it has rather to do with the way we experience our properties and characteristics as embodied beings. Our properties or characteristics are not entities that can be *abstracted* away from our lived body. Philosophers discussing this issue sometimes speak as if they can.

Alan Soble's book *The Structure of Love* has long been one of the most important works in the philosophy of love. In it, Soble addresses almost every important aspect of the structure of personal love. Most relevant to the current discussion is the final chapter, "The Object of Love." Soble tells us that the object of love is a *person* and not a person's properties. But what does he mean by the word *person* here? He tells us, "If x loves y and y is her properties, it does not follow that x loves properties . . . it does not follow that x loves individually any or each of y's properties, but only that x loves the collection of properties that y is" (1990, 307–8). Soble's view resembles Hume's "bundle" conception of selfhood. As mentioned in Section I of this volume, Hume viewed the self as a bundle of perceptions. Soble, although not explicitly giving an account of personal identity, tells us that the object of love is a person and suggests that what he means by *person* is the collection of properties that constitute her. Such a view of a person would seem to fit well with online romance. Perhaps a better way of putting it is that online dating sites reinforce such a view of personhood by presenting the person by way of a list of properties. Conceiving of persons in this manner gives rise to the suggestion that persons are replaceable when it comes to loving them since properties are replaceable or are fungible (Soble 1990, 45–47; Parfit 1986, 293–98). But this view of persons and their properties abstracts properties from persons, much like dating profiles do. As a result, I would argue, we get a false picture of the relation between a person and her properties, which has lead philosophers to draw questionable conclusions about their role in love (such as the conclusion that persons are fungible). There is a sense in which persons are fungible in the world of online dating. We can sort them according to properties, personality type, and so on. We can decide to make contact with I♥*summer21* if it turns out that *beachgirl22* with similar properties is no longer available for dating. But this kind of fungibility based on properties is not quite what we have in mind when we are considering a life spent with a future love.

I propose instead a view of persons in which their properties and characteristics, including their height, hair colour, smile, sense of humour, and so on, are embodied expressions of their personhood. Just as one person may be faster or stronger than another, or better at math or auto mechanics, so our embodied properties may express differences in our personhood. Of course, for the sake of clarity, we can divide properties such as height, weight, eye colour, hair colour, and so on, which people share in common with objects (objects can be tall or short, green or blue) from those that distinctly express *personality*, such as sense of humour or taste, but each of these properties or characteristics are still *embodied* features of persons that can only be viewed apart from them in the abstract. When we meet someone in an offline date, for instance, at a bar or café, we see their characteristics expressed in a unified way. When I say unified, I mean as part of their bodily being, not as characteristics that can be separated from the person. A person's sense of humour is expressed not only in her words but in her mischievous smile, the timing of her delivery, and the tone of her voice. Likewise, a person's warmth gets expressed in his voice, his smile, his look of concern, and so on. Written words via emails or IMs can express these things to a certain extent, but not in the same immediate way as spoken expressions of one's thoughts

and the embodied reality of those thoughts. Even though misunderstandings do take place between people who are communicating in the flesh, misunderstandings on email or texting often seem due to the lack of ability to discern the tone of the other person.

The view that I am defending shares Kant's and Velleman's dissatisfaction with the bundle theory (and the related properties view of personhood) put forth by Hume. On the Humean view, the unity of the person is a fictitious one that unites properties through memory and imagination. I believe that selves or personhood must be more than a bundle of perceptions or a collection of properties. Unlike Velleman, however, I do not characterize the human capacity for valuation as the true self or as that which can be separated from our empirical properties. In this regard, my view more closely resembles the view of Jean-Paul Sartre. According to Sartre, our capacity for valuation expresses itself in a fundamental choice or a fundamental attitude that we take towards life. This attitude expresses its nature in the life *project* that we engage in, which is really the project of becoming a self. So, our true self, if we want to call it that, will be found in our characteristics or, in that unified version of our characteristics that we call character. It is our fundamental project that gives unity to our personhood or our character, and it is our fundamental attitude (or choice as Sartre calls it) that personalizes our characteristics and in doing so, expresses our personality. Personality, and the fundamental attitude that it expresses, is not a loose or accidental collection of properties, characteristics, or impressions.

I believe that this fundamental attitude is an expression of our capacity for valuation but, as I mentioned above, it is not to be solely equated with our true self. Our true self, if there is such a thing, will be found not only in that fundamental attitude but also in our empirical properties and characteristics. Our self is not something hidden behind these properties, but, in an important sense, the self is these properties. But of course when I say this, it is important to remember that these properties are not to be thought of as isolated from or abstracted from our person. Who we are as a person is to be understood as an embodied whole whose personality or character is expressed in a bodily manner. It is this embodied self that does not get communicated or represented in online interaction. Online dating profiles, like various properties views of persons, separate persons from properties and, in so doing, present an inadequate picture of the prospective romantic partner.

Notes

1 The structure of the discussion of personal identity in terms of constancy and change follows Rockney Jacobsen's very useful presentation (2016, 45–53).

2 Arthur Schopenhauer claimed that one's personal identity is revealed through the expression of the glance (and not through memory, physical continuity, psychological continuity, etc.), Schopenhauer, 1966, 238.

3 David Hume in the eighteenth century and Jean-Paul Sartre in the twentieth century have highlighted the role of the imagination in the construction of personal identity.

Bibliography

Albright, Julie M. 2007. "How Do I Love Thee and Thee and Thee: Self-Presentation, Deception, and Multiple Relationships Online." In *Online Matchmaking*, edited by Monica T. Whitty, Andrea J. Baker, and James A. Inman, 81–93. Houndmills, UK: Palgrave Macmillan.

Bridges, John C. 2012. *The Illusion of Intimacy: Problems in the World of Online Dating*. Santa Barbara, CA: Praeger.

Hume, David. 1978. *A Treatise of Human Nature*. 2nd ed. Oxford: Clarendon Press.

Jacobsen, Rockney. 2016. *An Introduction to Philosophy: Knowledge and Reality*. Toronto: Pearson.

Locke, John. 1924. *An Essay Concerning Human Understanding*. Oxford: Clarendon Press.

Parfit, Derek. 1986. *Reasons and Persons*. Oxford: Oxford University Press.

Plato. 1989. Symposium and Phaedo. In *Plato: The Republic and Other Works*, translated by B. Jowett, 315–65 and 487–552. New York: Anchor Books.

Sartre, Jean-Paul. 1956. *Being and Nothingness: An Essay on Phenomenological Ontology*. Translated by Hazel E. Barnes. New York: Philosophical Library.

Schopenhauer, Arthur. 1966. *The World as Will and Representation*, vol. 2, translated by E.F. Payne. New York: Dover Publications.

Soble, Alan. 1990. *The Structure of Love*. New Haven, CT: Yale University Press.

Turkle, Sherry. 2011. *Alone Together: Why We Expect More from Technology and Less from Each Other.* New York: Basic Books.

Velleman, David. 1999. "Love as a Moral Emotion." *Ethics* 109 (2): 338–74.

Whitty, Monica, and Adrian Carr. 2006. *Cyberspace Romance: The Psychology of Online Relationships.* Houndmills, UK: Palgrave Macmillan.

Whitty, Monica T. 2007. "The Art of Selling One's Self on an Online Dating Site: The BAR Approach." In *Online Matchmaking*, edited by Monica T. Whitty, Andrea J. Baker, and James A. Inman, 57–69. Houndmills, UK: Palgrave Macmillan.

Discussion

How well can we get to know someone through online interaction? Some people argue that we can get to know a person *better* online since irrelevant (or less relevant) features such as appearance or physical attraction do not get in the way. But is this really getting to know a person? Are appearance and other physical features unimportant? Even if we value a person's intellect more than his or her physical strength or beauty, for instance, does that mean that these other properties are not part of who that person is? Can we really be friends with a person online? Can we be friends in the truest sense of being friends? Can we really love someone with whom we only interact online? Is there something crucial to love or friendship that is missing in online relationships? What role might online interaction play in helping us start friendships or romance? What role might it play in helping us maintain relationships with friends or lovers?

In his article, Robert Sharp thinks that an important aspect of human interaction is absent in online friendships. In the context of online communication, one cannot see the expressions, reactions, or the various subtle signs of the other person's state of being. These reactions and expressions, which are often somewhat involuntary, are crucial to the knowledge someone has of her friend. If a person is virtuous and is concerned with her friend's virtue as well, then the Internet may prevent her from perceiving her friend's situation correctly. It is easier to hide certain aspects of one's life—intentionally or unintentionally—in an online context. But it is not only our perception of our friend that is limited through online interaction; our perception of our self through our friend—what Sharp calls *apperception*—is also limited. Friends help us to become more virtuous by helping us to become more self-aware. Our closeness with our friends allows us to see in their behaviour a reflection of ourselves. When they do something hurtful or insensitive to someone else (or to us), we can imagine ourselves doing the same, or we can see that we have done such things in the past. When they do something good or helpful, we can likewise see our own positive actions. In both cases, by observing our friends' actions, we realize that our actions are observed and are judged as good or bad. In this sense, friends help us to know ourselves better. They provide a kind of mirror to our self. Sharp does not think that we can truly experience this apperception online. Do you agree with him? If you disagree, then how might this apperception be possible? If you agree with him, then what crucial element or elements are missing from online interaction?

What do you think constitutes the *identity* of a person? To what extent do online dating profiles reveal this identity? What kind of picture do we get of a person through these profiles? How does this approach, which divides the person's properties into categories (height, body type, ethnicity, interests, etc.), differ from our experience of the embodied properties of someone whom we meet in person at a bar, café, a university classroom, or a student group? Do you think that a person is something *more* than his or her properties? Why or why not? When we decide to contact a person based on the details of her or his online profile, does the subsequent online interaction adequately fill in the missing details of her or his identity, or is there still something significant absent from that picture? If there is something missing, what would that be? Should we consider interaction with people through online dating sites to be simply a kind of screening process for potential dating candidates? If so, does that mean that such interaction actually gives us what we need in order to make a decision on whether or not to pursue the interaction further? Or are online relationships capable of being much more than merely an introductory step? Can a genuine romantic relationship take place *online* with someone whom one has never met offline?

Suggestions for Further Reading

John C. Bridges, *The Illusion of Intimacy: Problems in the World of Online Dating* (Santa Barbara, CA: Praeger, 2012).

Troy Jollimore, "The Endless Space Between the Words: The Limits of Love in Spike Jonze's *Her. Midwest Studies in Philosophy, Special Issue: Philosophy and Science Fiction.* Volume 39, Issue 1, 120–43, September 2015.

Sherry Turkle, *Life on the Screen: Identity in the Age of the Internet* (New York: Simon and Schuster, 1997).

Sherry Turkle, *The Second Self: Computers and the Human Spirit.* Twentieth Anniversary Edition (Cambridge, MA: MIT Press, 2005).

Monica Whitty and Adrian Carr, *Cyberspace Romance: The Psychology of Online Relationships.* Houndmills, UK: Palgrave Macmillan, 2006.

Bibliography

Aristotle. 1984. "Nicomachean Ethics." *The Complete Works of Aristotle: The Revised Oxford Translation, Volume 2*, edited by Jonathan Barnes. Princeton, NJ: Princeton University Press.

Baier, Annette C. 2010. "How to Lose Friends: Some Simple Ways." *Reflections on How We Live*. Oxford, UK: Oxford University Press.

Beauvoir, Simone de. 1989. *The Second Sex*. New York: Vintage Books.

Collins, Louise. 2008. "Is Cybersex Sex?" *The Philosophy of Sex: Contemporary Readings*, edited by Alan Soble and Nicholas Power. Lanham, Maryland: Rowman and Littlefield: 117–131.

Foucault, Michel. 1980. *The History of Sexuality (Volume 1: An Introduction)*. New York: Vintage Books.

Frankfurt, H.G. 2004. "On Love, and Its Reasons." *The Reasons of Love*. Princeton, NJ: Princeton University Press.

Goldman, Alan. 1977. "Plain Sex" in *Philosophy and Public Affairs*, Vol. 6, No. 3: 267–287.

Kant, Immanuel. 1887. *The Philosophy of Law: An Exposition of the Fundamental Principles of Jurisprudence as The Science of Right*. Translated by W. Hastie. Edinburgh: T. & T. Clarke.

Kant, Immanuel. 1997. *Lectures on Ethics (The Cambridge Edition of the Works of Immanuel Kant)*. Edited and translated by Peter Heath; edited by J.B. Schneewind. Cambridge, UK: Cambridge University Press.

Kierkegaard, Søren. 1995. *Works of Love*. Edited and translated by Howard V. Hong and Edna H. Hong. Princeton, NJ: Princeton University Press.

Marino, Patricia. 2008. "The Ethics of Sexual Objectification: Autonomy and Consent." *Inquiry: An Interdisciplinary Journal of Philosophy*, Vol. 51, no. 4: 345–364.

Merino, Noël. 2004. "The Problem with 'We': Rethinking Joint Identity in Romantic Love." *Journal of Social Philosophy*, Vol. 35, No. 1: 123–132.

Moulton, Janice. 1976. "Sexual Behaviour: Another Position." *The Journal of Philosophy*, Vol. 73, No. 16: 537–546.

Nagel, Thomas. 1969. "Sexual Perversion." *The Journal of Philosophy*, Vol. 66, No. 1: 5–17.

Nozick, Robert. 1989. "Love's Bond." *The Examined Life*. New York: Simon and Schuster: 68–86.

Nussbaum, Martha C. 1995. "Objectification." *Philosophy and Public Affairs* Vol. 24, No. 4: 249–291.

Nygren, Anders. *Eros and Agape*. Chicago: The University of Chicago Press.

Plato. 1997. "Symposium." *Plato: Complete Works*, edited by John M. Cooper and D.S. Hutchinson. Indianapolis, IN: Hacket.

Ruddick, Sara. 1998. "Better Sex." *Philosophy and Sex* (3rd ed.), edited by Robert Baker, Frederick Elliston, and Kathleen Wininger. Amherst, NY: Prometheus Books: 280–299.

Sartre, Jean-Paul. 1956. *Being and Nothingness: An Essay on Phenomenological Ontology*. Translated by Hazel E. Barnes. New York: Philosophical Library.

Sartre, Jean-Paul. 1992. *Notebooks for an Ethics*. Translated by David Pellauer. Chicago: University of Chicago Press.

Schopenhauer, Arthur. 1966. *The World as Will and Representation* (Vol. 2). Translated by E.F.J. Payne. Mineola, NY: Dover Press.

Sharp, Robert. 2012. "The Obstacles against Reaching the Highest Level of Aristotelian Friendship Online." *Ethics and Information Technology*, Vol. 14: 231–239.

Singer, Irving. 1984. *The Nature of Love 1: Plato to Luther* (2nd ed.). Chicago: University of Chicago Press.

Soble, Alan. 1990. *The Structure of Love*. New Haven, CT: Yale University Press.

Soble, Alan. 1994. "Union, Autonomy, and Concern." *Love Analyzed*, edited by Roger Lamb. Boulder, Colorado: Westview Press.

Soble, Alan. 2005. "Love and Value, Yet Again." *Essays in Philosophy: A Biannual Journal*, Vol. 6, No. 1.

Solomon, Robert C. 1974. "Sexual Paradigms." *The Journal of Philosophy*, Vol. 71, No. 11: 336–345.

Solomon, Robert C. 1988. *About Love: Reinventing Romance for Our Time*. New York: Simon and Schuster.

Solomon, Robert C. 1990. *Love: Emotion, Myth, and Metaphor*. Amherst, NY: Prometheus Books.

Credits